Pharmacy Management, Leadership, Marketing, and Finance

EDITED BY

Marie A. Chisholm-Burns, PharmD, MPH, FCCP, FASHP

Professor and Head of the Department of Pharmacy Practice and Science
The University of Arizona College of Pharmacy
Professor, Department of Surgery
The University of Arizona College of Medicine
Tucson, Arizona

Allison M. Vaillancourt, PhD, SPHR

Vice President for Human Resources
The University of Arizona
Faculty
The University of Arizona
School of Government and Public Policy
Tucson, Arizona

Marv Shepherd, PhD, MS, RPh

Director of the Center for Pharmacoeconomic Studies and Chairman of the
Pharmacy Administration Division
The University of Texas at Austin
College of Pharmacy
Austin, Texas

JONES AND BARTLETT PUBLISHERS

Sudbury, Massachusetts

BOSTON   TORONTO   LONDON   SINGAPORE

World Headquarters

Jones and Bartlett Publishers
40 Tall Pine Drive
Sudbury, MA 01776
978-443-5000
info@jbpub.com
www.jbpub.com

Jones and Bartlett Publishers
 Canada
6339 Ormindale Way
Mississauga, Ontario L5V 1J2
Canada

Jones and Bartlett Publishers
 International
Barb House, Barb Mews
London W6 7PA
United Kingdom

Jones and Bartlett's books and products are available through most bookstores and online booksellers. To contact Jones and Bartlett Publishers directly, call 800-832-0034, fax 978-443-8000, or visit our website, www.jbpub.com.

Substantial discounts on bulk quantities of Jones and Bartlett's publications are available to corporations, professional associations, and other qualified organizations. For details and specific discount information, contact the special sales department at Jones and Bartlett via the above contact information or send an email to specialsales@jbpub.com.

This publication is designed to provide accurate and authoritative information in regard to the subject matter covered. It is sold with the understanding that the publisher is not engaged in rendering legal, accounting, or other professional service. If legal advice or other expert assistance is required, the service of a competent professional person should be sought.

Production Credits
Publisher: David Cella
Associate Editor: Maro Gartside
Senior Production Editor: Renée Sekerak
Production Assistant: Jill Morton
Marketing Manager: Grace Richards
Manufacturing and Inventory Control Supervisor: Amy Bacus
Composition: Toppan Best-set Premedia Limited
Cover and Title Page Design: Kristin E. Parker
Associate Photo Researcher: Sarah Cebulski
Cover and Title Page Images: Medical sign of Hygieia, © axyse/ShutterStock, Inc.; Detail of paint strokes on canvas, © Joanne Zh/Dreamstime.com; Abstract sound waves in blue, © Clearviewstock/Dreamstime.com; Abstract of cream paper, © Ben Crochet/Dreamstime.com; Text and signature on paper, © Janaka Dharmasena/Dreamstime.com
Printing and Binding: Malloy Incorporated
Cover Printing: Malloy Incorporated

To order this product, use ISBN: 978-1-4496-1343-3

Library of Congress Cataloging-in-Publication Data
Pharmacy management, leadership, marketing, and finance /
[edited] by Marie A. Chisholm-Burns, Allison M. Vaillancourt,
and Marv Shepherd.
    p. ; cm.
Includes bibliographical references and index.
ISBN-13: 978-0-7637-6326-8
ISBN-10: 0-7637-6326-8
  1. Pharmacy management. I. Chisholm-Burns, Marie A.
II. Vaillancourt, Allison M.   III. Shepherd, Marv.
  [DNLM: 1. Pharmacy Administration. 2. Financial
Management. 3. Leadership. 4. Marketing. 5. Pharmacies—
economics. QV 737 P5359 2011]
  RS100.P483 2011
  615'.1068—dc22
                                        2010000372
6048

Printed in the United States of America
15 14 13 12 11 10 9 8 7 6 5 4 3

BRIEF CONTENTS

CONTENTS

Grant H. Skrepnek, PhD, MSc, RPh
Jesse C. Fishman, PharmD
Kenneth M. Duke, MBA, RPh
Elizabeth Hall-Lipsy, JD, MPH
Amy Marie Haddad, PhD
Kathryn R. Matthias, PharmD, BCPS

PREFACE

There are countless volumes about leadership and management, with many such works written specifically for the business professional and applied to other industries or professions. We, as pharmacists and student pharmacists, have limited profession-specific works on these subjects. Only in recent years have the enduring topics of management and leadership been a focus in our profession, due in large part to pharmacy's impending "leadership crisis." Responding to leadership demands in today's environment makes it ever more important to prepare pharmacy professionals for management and leadership roles. This preparation requires an integration of knowledge, skills, attitudes, and values that can be acquired and considered through multiple methods, including a structured learning process that includes classroom work, independent study, and hands-on experience.

Pharmacy Management, Leadership, Marketing, and Finance is designed to meet the classroom and independent study needs of today's learners. In addition to topics such as operations management, reimbursement, and marketing, this book features sections on communication, conflict management, and human resource strategies—vital competencies for pharmacy leaders and managers. Our goal as editors was to produce a highly practical text that addresses the range of issues pharmacy professionals will face in their day-to-day work regardless of whether they hold formal or informal leadership roles—thus making this book *essential* for pharmacy students and practitioners.

Each chapter is written in a concise and reader-friendly style that facilitates an in-depth level of understanding of essential leadership and management concepts. While this book is intended to be read in its entirety, as many chapters build on one another, pharmacy professionals may find the text useful as a reference tool as they encounter challenges within their pharmacy practices. Chapters were written and reviewed by academic pharmacy faculty, practicing pharmacy managers and leaders, human resources professionals, and practicing attorneys to incorporate both theory and real-world experiences.

The learning features used in *Pharmacy Management, Leadership, Marketing, and Finance* were designed in collaboration with educational design specialists to enhance learning and retention. These features include:

- *Structured learning objectives.* These are listed at the beginning of each chapter and help guide learning.
- *Key concepts.* Designed to help focus learning, these key concepts are listed at the beginning of each chapter. Textual material that develops these concepts is easily identified by diamond-shaped numbered icons (◆) throughout the chapter.
- *Case scenarios.* Found at the end of each chapter, case scenarios facilitate critical thinking skills and lend relevance to the principles provided.
- *Up-to-date literature citations.* A comprehensive reference list for each chapter is provided to substantiate materials.

- *Economic principles discussed.* The textbook includes explanations of economic principles, such as cost minimization analysis, cost-effectiveness analysis, cost-benefit analysis, cost-utility analysis, and sensitivity analysis.
- *Generous use of tables and figures.* These visual features enhance understanding of leadership and management principles.
- *Glossary terms.* The glossary is located at the end of the book; the first use of each glossary term in a chapter appears in bold font.
- *Self-assessment questions and answers for each chapter.* Visit the Student Companion Web site at http://healthprofessions.jbpub.com/pharmacymanagement for interactive study tools and other resources. These questions are not only designed to evaluate student learning but to actively engage students in the learning process.
- *Continuing Education Credit for Pharmacists.* Thirty hours (3.0 CEU) of continuing pharmacy education credit is offered through this textbook. For details and registration information, visit http://www.rxugace.com. Click on Books/Series and then select *Pharmacy Management, Leadership, Marketing, and Finance.*

The Student Companion Web site provides self-assessment questions with the ability to grade and provide immediate feedback, as well as reporting capabilities, interactive glossary, crossword puzzles, flashcards, links to supplementary Web-based materials including videos and links featuring world-renowned experts on various topics addressed in the textbook, and other features and activities designed to support learning. There are also Lesson Plans, PowerPoint Slides, a Sample Syllabus, and other downloadable materials exclusively for instructors.

This book and the companion Web site should be used as tools to facilitate your management and leadership training. The first two chapters, "Leadership Essentials for Pharmacists" and "Management Essentials for Pharmacists," are designed to provide a basic overview of leadership and management and serve as the introduction for this textbook. The chapters that follow build on the conceptual foundation provided by these two introductory chapters and focus on real-world application of management and leadership principles, concepts, and practices in pharmacy-related environments. Collectively, the chapters in this textbook and companion Web site for instructors and students provide a complete and enriched learning experience.

We thank the chapter authors and reviewers who represent more than 80 colleges or schools of pharmacy and national and international institutions, as well as other support received for this work. Finally, we, the editors, wish you all the best in your career and future goals.

Continuing Pharmacy Education Credit

 The University of Georgia College of Pharmacy offers 30 hours (3.0 CEU) of continuing pharmacy education for this textbook.

Information and Registration

For details and registration information, visit www.rxugace.com. Click on Books/Series and then select *Pharmacy Management, Leadership, Marketing, and Finance.*

Accreditation

 The University of Georgia College of Pharmacy is accredited by the Accreditation Council for Pharmacy Education as a provider of continuing pharmacy education.

Acknowledgments

We would like to acknowledge the commitment and dedication of over 50 contributing authors and over 70 reviewers of the chapters who dedicated their talents to make this text a high-quality learning tool (lists of contributors and reviewers are included in the following pages). We also extend our thanks to Dr. Christina Spivey for all her insights and dedication and to Jones and Bartlett Publishers, especially Maro Gartside, Jill Morton, and David Cella, for their dedication to and guidance on this project. Finally, we thank our families for their patience and support of our goal to facilitate leadership and management skills in the pharmacy profession.

Marie A. Chisholm-Burns, PharmD, MPH, FCCP, FASHP, is professor and head of the Department of Pharmacy Practice and Science at The University of Arizona College of Pharmacy. She received her BS in psychology and biology from Georgia College, BS in pharmacy and Doctor of Pharmacy degrees from The University of Georgia, and Master of Public Health degree from Emory University. She completed her residency at Mercer University Southern School of Pharmacy and at Piedmont Hospital in Atlanta, Georgia. Dr. Chisholm-Burns is founder and executive director of the Medication Access Program, which increases medication access to transplant patients. She has also served in numerous elected leadership positions in several different professional organizations and has worked in multiple pharmacy settings. She is a prolific scholar, with more than 200 publications and greater than $8 million in external funding as principal investigator from organizations such as the National Institutes of Health and several foundations. She has received numerous awards and honors, including the Robert K. Chalmers Distinguished Pharmacy Educator Award from the American Association of Colleges of Pharmacy, the Clinical Pharmacy Education Award from the American College of Clinical Pharmacy, the Clinical Practice Award from the American College of Clinical Pharmacy, the Daniel B. Smith Practice Excellence Award from the American Pharmacists Association, and the Rufus A. Lyman Award for the most outstanding publication in the *American Journal of Pharmaceutical Education* (in both 1996 and 2007). Dr. Chisholm-Burns is also a Fulbright Scholar. She lives in Tucson, Arizona, with her husband and son and enjoys writing, cycling, and playing chess.

Allison M. Vaillancourt, PhD, SPHR, is vice president for human resources at The University of Arizona and teaches in the university's School of Government and Public Policy. She received a BA in political science and an MA in public policy and administration from the University of Wisconsin–Madison, and earned a PhD in public policy and administration from the University of Colorado Denver's School of Public Affairs. Before beginning her career in human resources in the early 1990s, Dr. Vaillancourt held positions as a journalist, nonprofit executive, and research administrator. She has held several leadership roles in national human resources organizations and consults and presents nationally on issues related to strategic planning, business analytics, management, human resources, organizational culture, and communication. Dr. Vaillancourt is a co-principal investigator of a National Science Foundation ADVANCE grant designed to increase the number of women in the fields of science, technology, engineering, and math. A marathon runner and long-distance cyclist, she lives in Tucson, Arizona, with her husband and two daughters.

Marv Shepherd, PhD, MS, RPh, is the director of the Center for Pharmacoeconomic Studies and chairman of the Pharmacy Administration Division at The University of Texas at Austin, College of Pharmacy. He earned his BS in biology from Michigan Technological

University, a BS in pharmacy from Ferris State University, an MS from the University of Rhode Island (1978), and a PhD from Purdue University. Dr. Shepherd received a commission in the U.S. Army and was a Special Forces (Green Beret) officer. He is president of the Partnership for Safe Medicines, a group dedicated to protecting the public from counterfeit, diverted, and substandard medications. Since 1994, Dr. Shepherd has studied drug importation and distribution of counterfeit medications. He has testified before congressional committees four times, and his expertise on drug counterfeiting has been featured in such media as *CNN News, NPR Radio: First Edition, Newsweek, The Wall Street Journal, Money Magazine, Prevention Magazine, US News and World Report, The New York Times, USA Today,* and *The Washington Post.* Dr. Shepherd has more than 100 publications, including six book chapters. He is a past president and fellow of the Academy of Pharmaceutical Research and Science of the American Pharmaceutical Association. He is the chairman of the Editorial Advisory Board for the *Journal of Managed Care Pharmacy.* He received the Award of Excellence from the American Society of Health-System Pharmacists in 2006. Dr. Shepherd is married, has two children, and lives in Austin, Texas.

CONTRIBUTORS

Steven R. Abel, PharmD, FASHP
Assistant Dean for Clinical Programs
Bucke Professor and Head,
  Department of Pharmacy Practice
Purdue University School of
  Pharmacy and Pharmacy Practice

Candace W. Barnett, PhD, RPh
Senior Associate Dean and Professor
Mercer University College of
  Pharmacy and Health Sciences

Robert S. Beardsley, PhD, RPh
Professor
University of Maryland School of
  Pharmacy

Prachi D. Bhatt
University of the Sciences in
  Philadelphia
Mayes College of Healthcare
  Business and Policy

Mark D. Boesen, PharmD
Clinical Instructor
The University of Arizona College of
  Pharmacy

Director of Pharmacy Operations
The Apothecary Shops

Alicia S. Bouldin, PhD, RPh
Associate Professor of Pharmacy
  Administration
Research Associate Professor for
  Instructional Assessment and
  Advancement
The University of Mississippi School
  of Pharmacy

Lynette R. Bradley-Baker, PhD, RPh
Assistant Professor, Department of
  Pharmaceutical Health Services Research
University of Maryland School of Pharmacy

Diana I. Brixner, PhD, RPh
Associate Professor and Chair, Department of
  Pharmacotherapy
University of Utah College of Pharmacy

**Marie A. Chisholm-Burns, PharmD, MPH,
  FCCP, FASHP**
Professor and Head, Department of Pharmacy
  Practice & Science
The University of Arizona College of Pharmacy

Professor, Department of Surgery
The University of Arizona College of Medicine

John A. Daly, PhD
Lidell Professor of Communication and
  Management
The University of Texas at Austin

Ann Hein DeVoe, RPh
Registered Pharmacist
The University of Mississippi School of Pharmacy
Community Pharmacist

Joseph T. DiPiro, PharmD, FCCP
Executive Dean and Professor
South Carolina College of Pharmacy
University of South Carolina and the Medical
  University of South Carolina

Kenneth M. Duke, MBA, RPh
Clinical Assistant Professor
Assistant to the Dean
The University of Georgia College of Pharmacy

Sharon Murphy Enright, MBA, RPh
Senior Manager
Ernst & Young Health Science Advisory Series

Jesse C. Fishman, PharmD
Senior Medical Information Associate
Sciele Pharma, Inc.

Critical Care Pharmacist
Children's Healthcare of Atlanta

Dewey D. Garner, PhD, RPh
Professor of Pharmacy Administration
The University of Mississippi School of Pharmacy

Tad A. Gomez, MS, RPh
Director of Pharmacy and Pharmacy Residency
    Programs
Medical College of Georgia

Vicki Gotkin, JD
University Attorney
The University of Arizona Office of General
    Counsel

Amy Marie Haddad, PhD
Director, Center for Health Policy and Ethics
Dr. C. C. and Mabel L. Criss Endowed Chair in
    Health Sciences
Creighton University

Elizabeth Hall-Lipsy, JD, MPH
Program Manager, Health Disparities Initiatives,
    Community Outreach
The University of Arizona College of Pharmacy

**Dana Lynn Purkerson Hammer, PhD, MS,
RPh**
Senior Lecturer
Director of Bracken Pharmaceutical Care
    Learning Center
University of Washington School of Pharmacy

Jan K. Hastings, PharmD, FAPhA
Associate Professor, Pharmacy Practice
University of Arkansas for Medical Sciences
    College of Pharmacy

Keith Nicolas Herist, PharmD, CPA
Clinical Associate Professor
Department of Clinical and Administrative
    Pharmacy
The University of Georgia College of Pharmacy

Erin Renee Holmes, PharmD, PhD
Assistant Professor of Pharmacy Administration
Research Assistant Professor
Research Institute of Pharmaceutical Sciences
The University of Mississippi School of Pharmacy

Rebekah M. Jackowski, PharmD
Clinical Assistant Professor
The University of Arizona College of Pharmacy

Tara L. Jenkins, PhD, RPh
Assistant Professor
Department of Pharmacy Practice
University of Kansas Medical Center

Mary Ann Kliethermes, PharmD
Associate Professor
Vice-Chair, Ambulatory Care
Midwestern University
Chiro College of Pharmacy

Lesa Waggoner Lawrence, PhD, MBA
Associate Dean, Assessment and Outcome
    Research
Associate Professor, Pharmacy Administration
University of Louisiana, Monroe, College of
    Pharmacy

Kenneth A. Lawson, PhD, RPh
Associate Professor, Pharmacy Administration
    Division
The University of Texas at Austin, College of
    Pharmacy

Christopher D. Lee, PhD, SPHR
Associate Vice Chancellor for Human Resource
    Services
Virginia Community College System

Mary L. Maher, MA
Vice President of Human Resources
The University of Texas Health Science Center at
    San Antonio

Scott M. Mark, PharmD, MS, MEd, MBA, FASHP, FACHE, FABC
Director of Pharmacy
Director, Pharmacy Practice Management Residency Program
University of Pittsburgh Medical Center

Assistant Professor and Vice Chair of Pharmacy Systems
University of Pittsburgh School of Pharmacy

Kathryn R. Matthias, PharmD, BCPS
Clinical Assistant Professor
The University of Arizona College of Pharmacy

James C. McAllister IV, PharmD, MS
Pharmacy Manager
Medical College of Georgia

Kavita V. Nair, PhD
Associate Professor
University of Colorado School of Pharmacy

Brenna Neumann, PharmD
Adjunct Clinical Assistant Professor
University of Missouri–Kansas City

Pharmacist in Charge
Advantage Healthcare

Christy Monique Norman, PharmD, MS
Pharmacy Manager
Medical College of Georgia

Melanie B. Oates, PhD, MBA, RN
Assistant Professor
Director, Undergraduate Business Programs
University of the Sciences in Philadelphia
Mayes College of Healthcare Business and Policy

Nathan D. Pope, PharmD
Clinical Assistant Professor, Community Practice
The University of Texas at Austin, College of Pharmacy

Dana Reed-Kane, PharmD, FIACP, FACA, NFPPhC, FCP
Co-owner, Compounding Pharmacist
Reed's Compounding Pharmacy

Clinical Instructor, Department of Pharmacy Practice and Science
The University of Arizona College of Pharmacy

Glenn Rosenthal, EdD, MA, MBA
Associate Professor
University of New England

Leigh Ann Ross, PharmD, BCPS
Associate Dean for Clinical Affairs
Associate Professor and Chair
Department of Pharmacy Practice
The University of Mississippi School of Pharmacy

Rafael Saenz, PharmD, MS
Instructor
University of Pittsburgh School of Pharmacy

Grant H. Skrepnek, PhD, MSc, RPh
Associate Professor
The University of Arizona College of Pharmacy

Christina A. Spivey, PhD
Coordinator of Research and Administration
The University of Arizona College of Pharmacy

JoAnn Stubbings, MHCA, RPh
Clinical Assistant Professor
Department of Pharmacy Practice and Center for Pharmacoeconomic Research
Manager, Research and Public Policy, Clinical Staff Pharmacist
Ambulatory Care Pharmacy Department
University of Illinois at Chicago College of Pharmacy

Allison M. Vaillancourt, PhD, SPHR
Vice President for Human Resources
Faculty, School of Government and Public Policy
The University of Arizona

Lee C. Vermeulen, MS, FCCP, RPh
Clinical Associate Professor
University of Wisconsin–Madison School of Pharmacy

Director, Center for Drug Policy
University of Wisconsin Hospital and Clinics

Trina J. von Waldner, PharmD
Director of Postgraduate Continuing Education
The University of Georgia College of Pharmacy

William E. Wade, PharmD, FASHP, FCCP
Kroger Professor in Community Pharmacy
Department of Clinical and Administrative
   Pharmacy
The University of Georgia College of Pharmacy

Donna S. West-Strum, PhD, MS, RPh
Chair and Associate Professor of Pharmacy
   Administration
Research Associate Professor
Research Institute of Pharmaceutical Sciences
The University of Mississippi School of Pharmacy

**Glenn Y. Yokoyama, PharmD, FCSHP,
   FAPhA**
Assistant Clinical Professor, South Bay Program
   Director
Department of Clinical Pharmacy
University of California San Francisco

REVIEWERS

Richard R. Abood, BSPharm, JD
Professor, Pharmacy Practice
University of the Pacific

Erin Albert, PharmD, MBA
Assistant Professor and Director
Ribordy Center for Community
  Practice
Butler University

Fadi M. Alkhateeb, BSPharm, PhD
Assistant Professor of Pharmaceutical
  Marketing
University of Charleston School of
  Pharmacy

Gregory L. Alston, PharmD
Assistant Dean for Assessment,
  Associate Professor
Wingate University School of
  Pharmacy
Community Practice Pharmacist

Keith Bailey, BScPharm, MBA
Guest Lecturer
Memorial University

Ann R. Barbre, PhD, MS, BS
Professor of Pharmacy
  Administration
Xavier University of Louisiana
College of Pharmacy

Donna G. Beall, PharmD, BCPS, FCCP
Professor
Department of Pharmacy Practice
University of Montana

J. Lyle Bootman, PhD, ScD
Dean and Professor
The University of Arizona College of Pharmacy

Jack Brown, PharmD, MS, BCPS
Assistant Professor of Pharmacy
Pharmaceutical Science and Public Health
State University of New York at Buffalo

Infectious Disease Specialist
University of Rochester Medical Center

Keysha L. Bryant, PharmD
Assistant Professor of Pharmacy Administration
Palm Atlantic University

Paul S. Cady, PhD, RPh
Interim Dean and Professor
Idaho State University College of Pharmacy

Jeffrey John Cain, EdD, MS
University of Kentucky College of Pharmacy

Ina Lee Calligaro, PharmD
Assistant Dean for Education
Associate Professor of Pharmacy Practice
Temple University

Nicholas A. Campagna, Jr., MBA
Assistant Professor
Director of the Pharmaceutical Marketing and
  Management Program
Massachusetts College of Pharmacy and Health
  Sciences

Norman V. Carroll, PhD, RPh
Professor of Pharmacy Administration
School of Pharmacy
Virginia Commonwealth University

Chia-Hung Chou, PhD
Assistant Professor
Northeastern University School of Pharmacy

Robert M. Cisneros, BSPharm, PhD, MS, MBA
Assistant Professor
Campbell University School of Pharmacy

John S. Clark, PharmD, MS, BCPS
Clinical Assistant Professor
University of Michigan College of Pharmacy
Associate Director of Pharmacy
University of Michigan Hospitals and Health Centers

Joseph E. Crea, DO, MHA
Assistant Professor
University of Findlay College of Pharmacy

Nancy L. DeGuire, PharmD
Assistant Dean, External Relations
Assistant Clinical Professor, Pharmacy Practice
Thomas J. Long School of Pharmacy and Health Sciences
University of the Pacific

Natalie A. DiPietro, PharmD, MPH
Assistant Professor of Pharmacy Practice
Raabe College of Pharmacy
Ohio Northern University

Arjun P. Dutta, BSPharm, PhD
Associate Professor and Associate Dean
Touro College of Pharmacy

Lea S. Eiland, PharmD, BCPS
Associate Clinical Professor of Pharmacy Practice
Auburn University
Harrison School of Pharmacy

Scott Evans, PharmD
Assistant Professor of Pharmacy Practice
Director, Acute Care Pharmacy Residencies
University of Southern California School of Pharmacy

Chief Operating Officer
USC University Hospital

Daniel Friesner, PhD
Associate Professor of Social and Administrative Sciences
North Dakota State University

Lois A. Garland-Patterson, BSPharm, PhD, MBA
Associate Professor and Assistant Dean for Assessment and Student Affairs
Touro College of Pharmacy

Dennis W. Grauer, PhD, MS, BS
Associate Professor
University of Kansas School of Pharmacy

Gireesh V. Gupchup, BSPharm, PhD
Professor and Associate Dean
Southern Illinois University Edwardsville School of Pharmacy

Clinical Associate Professor
University of New Mexico Health Sciences Center

Ronald S. Hadsall, PhD
Professor
University of Minnesota College of Pharmacy

Richard A. Hansen, PhD
Associate Professor of Pharmacy
Division of Pharmaceutical Outcomes and Policy
University of North Carolina at Chapel Hill
Eshelman School of Pharmacy

David L. Helgeland, BSPharm, EdD, MBA
Professor, Pharmacy Practice
South Dakota State University College of Pharmacy

Carol J. Hermansen-Kobulnicky, BSPharm, PhD, MS
Associate Professor
University of Wyoming School of Pharmacy

Jan D. Hirsch, PhD
Assistant Professor of Clinical Pharmacy
Skaggs School of Pharmacy and Pharmaceutical Sciences
University of California San Diego

Samuel A. Hoagland, JD, RPh
Attorney and Counselor at Law

James M. Hoffman, PharmD, MS, BCPS
Assistant Professor of Clinical Pharmacy
University of Tennessee Health Science Center

Medication Outcomes and Safety Officer
St. Jude Children's Research Hospital

Jan Kavookjian, PhD, MBA
Associate Professor
Auburn University
Harrison School of Pharmacy

Edward T. Kelly III, PhD
Professor of Pharmacy Administration
Massachusetts College of Pharmacy and Health
  Sciences

Laurence Kennedy, PhD, MS, BS
Associate Professor of Social and Administrative
  Pharmacy
Butler University College of Pharmacy and Health
  Sciences

Nasreen Khan, PhD
Assistant Professor
University of New Mexico College of Pharmacy

Kem P. Krueger, PharmD, PhD
Associate Professor
University of Wyoming School of Pharmacy

Anandi V. Law, PhD, BPharm
Associate Professor and Chair
Department of Pharmacy Practice and
  Administration
Western University of Health Sciences, College of
  Pharmacy

Alex C. Lin, PhD
Assistant Professor of Pharmacy Systems and
  Administration
Division of Pharmacy Practice and Administrative
  Sciences
University of Cincinnati
James L. Winkle College of Pharmacy

Earlene E. Lipowski, PhD
Professor
Department of Pharmaceutical Outcomes and
  Policy
University of Florida College of Pharmacy

John M. Lonie, EdD, RPh
Associate Professor, Social and Administrative
  Sciences
Long Island University
Arnold and Marie Schwartz College of Pharmacy
  and Health Sciences

Wallace Marsh, PhD, MBA
Associate Professor
Shenandoah University School of Pharmacy

Leisa L. Marshall, PharmD, FASCP
Clinical Associate Professor
Mercer University College of Pharmacy and
  Health Sciences

J. Russell May, PharmD, FASHP
Clinical Professor
The University of Georgia College of Pharmacy
Clinical Pharmacy Specialist
Medical College of Georgia

Andrea L. McKeever, PharmD, BCPS
Associate Professor
Department of Pharmacy Practice
Director, Drug Information Service
South University School of Pharmacy

Mary R. Monk-Tutor, PhD, MS, RPh, FASHP
Professor of Pharmacy Administration
Director of Assessment
Samford University
McWhorter School of Pharmacy

Homero A. Monsanto, PhD, RPh
Professor (Ad Honorem)
University of Puerto Rico School of Pharmacy

Outcomes Research Manager
Merck Sharp & Dohme

Rashid Mosavin, PhD, MBA
Associate Professor and Department Chair
Department of Pharmaceutical Science
Loma Linda University School of Pharmacy

Aisha Morris Moultry, PharmD, MS
Assistant Professor of Pharmacy Practice
Texas Southern University
Clinical Adjunct Faculty
Harris County Hospital District

John E. Murphy, PharmD
Professor of Pharmacy Practice and Science
Associate Dean
The University of Arizona College of Pharmacy

Gloria J. Nichols-English, BSPharm, PhD, MED, RPh
Associate Professor and Senior Research Fellow
Center for Minority Health Services Research
Howard University College of Pharmacy, Nursing, and Allied Health Sciences

Roland A. Patry, DrPH, FASHP
Professor and Chair
Department of Pharmacy Practice
Texas Tech University Health Sciences Center, School of Pharmacy

Therese I. Poirier, PharmD, MPH
Professor of Pharmacy Practice
Associate Dean, Academic Affairs
Southern Illinois University Edwardsville
School of Pharmacy

Anne Policastri, PharmD, MBA
Assistant Director of Experiential Education
Clinical Assistant Professor
University of Kentucky College of Pharmacy

Stacy J. Ramirez, PharmD
Clinical Assistant Professor
Oregon State University College of Pharmacy
Clinical Pharmacist
Community Health Center of Benton and Linn Counties and Medicap Pharmacy

Warren Richards, PhD
Associate Dean, Associate Professor
Department of Pharmacy Practice and Administration
Wegmans School of Pharmacy
St. John Fisher University

Nathaniel M. Rickles, PharmD, PhD, BCPP
Assistant Professor of Pharmacy Practice and Administration
Northeastern University

Michael T. Rupp, BPharm, PhD
Professor of Pharmacy Administration
Midwestern University–Glendale

Nisaratana Sangasubana, PhD
Assistant Professor
Sociobehavioral and Administrative Pharmacy Department
Nova Southeastern University College of Pharmacy

Sujit S. Sansgiry, PhD
Associate Professor and Director
University of Houston College of Pharmacy

Lauren S. Schlesselman, PharmD
Director, Office of Assessment and Accreditation
Assistant Clinical Professor
University of Connecticut School of Pharmacy

Jon C. Schommer, PhD
Professor
University of Minnesota College of Pharmacy

Kelly M. Smith, PharmD, BCPS, FASHP, FCCP
Assistant Dean, Academic and Student Affairs
Associate Professor, Pharmacy Practice and Science
University of Kentucky College of Pharmacy

Marie A. Smith, PharmD
Clinical Professor and Department Head
Pharmacy Practice
University of Connecticut School of Pharmacy

Alan R. Spies, JD, PhD, MBA, RPh
Assistant Professor of Pharmaceutical Sciences
Southwestern Oklahoma State University
College of Pharmacy

Salisa C. Westrick, PhD
Assistant Professor, Pharmacy Care Systems
Auburn University
Harrison School of Pharmacy

Angela Lowe Winegar, MS
Doctoral Candidate
The University of Texas at Austin, College of
  Pharmacy

Keith Yoshizukam, PharmD, MBA, ND
Assistant Professor
Touro University College of Pharmacy

Darla A. Zarley, PharmD
Assistant Professor of Pharmacy Practice
University of Southern Nevada College of
  Pharmacy

LEADING AND MANAGING

CHAPTER 1

LEADERSHIP ESSENTIALS FOR PHARMACISTS

SCOTT M. MARK, PharmD, MS, MEd, MBA, FASHP, FACHE, FABC

RAFAEL SAENZ, PharmD, MS

LEARNING OBJECTIVES

After completing the chapter, the reader will be able to

1. Describe the current state of the pharmacy profession's leadership shortage.
2. Explain possible paths to a leadership role.
3. Explain the difference between formal and informal leadership.
4. Cite common traits of an effective leader.
5. Differentiate between leadership and management.
6. Describe different leadership types and styles.
7. Suggest leadership development strategies.

KEY CONCEPTS

❶ The shortage of pharmacist leaders is more than four times greater than it is for pharmacists. With 70–80% of pharmacist leaders expected to retire within the next decade, the number of leadership positions available in pharmacy is growing.

❷ In the pharmacy profession, transition into a leadership role often happens serendipitously, resulting in what is sometimes called "accidental leadership."

❸ Leadership is the process of influence in which one person is able to enlist the aid and support of others in accomplishing a common task, and the effectiveness of leaders is determined by both their level of influence and the outcomes of their decisions.

❹ There is a difference between holding a leadership position and being a leader. Likewise, there is a difference between having power or authority that is earned and having power or authority that is bestowed.

❺ Despite your title, role, or position on an organizational chart, you have the power to be a leader. Leadership is something acknowledged by others as a result of demonstrated vision, self-motivation, performance, determination, communication skills, credibility, ethical behavior, and ability to mobilize, motivate, and achieve desired results through others. A high-level position or formal leadership role is not required for you to be perceived as a leader.

⑥ Pharmacist leaders must fuse the traits of leadership with the professionalism expected within the pharmacy profession. Professionalism is defined as the standards, behaviors, and character of an individual engaged in tasks related to his or her work or profession.

⑦ Although management is similar to leadership in many ways, as management and leadership skills often overlap, management generally focuses on more operational aspects of an organization to achieve goals. Leadership is about "doing the right things," whereas management involves "doing things right."

⑧ Leadership theorists have characterized a variety of leadership styles, and each style has both pros and cons.

⑨ Although several leadership styles may work, leaders will be most effective when they select a style consistent with their personality, their brand, the environment in which they exist, and the people with whom they interact. Optimally, leaders will be able to find environments in which they are able to demonstrate their preferred approach to leading others.

⑩ Growing your leadership capacity requires sustained and deliberate effort.

INTRODUCTION

Unless pharmacy students have considered the possibility of being called on to lead, they may not seek to develop the necessary skills to be successful in a **leadership** role; however, given the current state of our profession, learning about leadership is more important than ever. ❶ *The shortage of pharmacist leaders is more than four times greater than it is for pharmacists. With 70–80% of pharmacist leaders expected to retire within the next decade, the number of leadership positions* available in pharmacy is growing.[1] Given these trends, it is not surprising that highly trained pharmacists are targets for roles in which they will provide guidance on professional and patient care decisions. If you are a pharmacist who is good at what you do, you will likely be asked to assume leadership responsibilities. Thus, a better understanding of the concept of leadership is vital.[2]

Advancement to a leadership position could be part of a formal organizational succession plan or a next step in an individual pharmacist's **career map**.[3] ❷ *In the pharmacy profession, transition into a leadership role often happens serendipitously, resulting in what is sometimes called "accidental leadership."*[3] Situations that may result in leadership opportunities can range from an unexpected vacancy on an executive team to recognition for a novel idea. Additional opportunities are presented in **Table 1–1**.[4,5] Several leadership topics are addressed in this chapter, including the definition of leadership, what it means to be a leader, leadership characteristics, the differences between leadership and **management**, styles of leadership, and strategies for developing leadership competencies. This chapter and Chapter 2, "Management Essentials for Pharmacists," serve as the introduction for this textbook, as concepts presented in these chapters will be built on in later chapters.

LEADERSHIP DEFINED

True leadership is the ability to mobilize and inspire others; it is not solely about a title or a position. As leadership authority John C. Maxwell noted, "The true measure of leadership is influence —nothing more, nothing less."[6(p11)] ❸ *Leadership is the process of influence in which one person is able to enlist the aid and support of others in accomplishing a common task, and the effectiveness of leaders is determined by both their level of influence and the outcomes of their decisions.*[7,8] In *Leading Minds: An Anatomy of Leadership*, psychologist and scholar Howard Gardner states, "A leader is an individual . . . who significantly affects the thoughts, feelings, and/or behaviors of a significant number of individuals."[9(pix)] This is perhaps the most appealing aspect of leadership—the ability to inspire and influence others in profound and compelling ways.

TABLE **1—1**	**Examples of Opportunities Resulting in Leadership Positions**

Lead pharmacist who is asked to assume some leadership responsibilities after his or her manager or director leaves the organization suddenly.

Pharmacist who is seen as an advocate for patient care and is subsequently asked to lead a new clinical expansion.

Pharmacist who shared an innovative idea with a colleague and is then asked to present this idea to others.

Pharmacist who is known for managing and completing complex problems.

Pharmacist who is frequently asked to present at Pharmacy and Therapeutics (P&T) and other high-profile medical staff meetings.

Pharmacist team member whom other team members admire.

Pharmacist whose knowledge and intelligence impress many and who is often asked to present his or her work or ideas.

Source: Data from Mark SM. Succession planning: the forgotten art. *Hosp Pharm* 2008;43:593–600. Betof E, Harwood F. *Just Promoted: How to Survive and Thrive in Your First 12 Months as a Manager.* New York, NY: McGraw-Hill; 1992.

Leadership can be found both formally and informally at any organizational level.[10] **Formal leaders** have formal power—the right (authority) to hire and fire, transfer, demote or promote, and reward. Formal power is bestowed through organizational authority, and it is often the result of a position held within the organization (such as chief executive officer) or a specific assigned role affecting key outcomes (such as a designated project team leader). Informal power, however, is earned through relationships and experience. **Informal leaders**, like so many social, political, cultural, and scientific trailblazers who have transformed their nations, communities, industries, and professions, rely on the creation and articulation of a compelling **vision** of the future in order to achieve success but do so without the power and authority granted to formal leaders. They often have personal magnetism or charisma, expertise in their fields, a recognized history with the organization, or the ability to inspire others. In many cases, informal leaders have more influence on their fellow employees than formal leaders.[11]

Issues pertaining to informal power and allegiance are part of a formal leader's responsibility. Savvy formal leaders determine which individuals possess informal power and assess how they choose to use it. They then use this information to mobilize their support or work to ensure that they do not create unnecessary obstacles. Seasoned formal leaders appreciate the value of recognizing, engaging, and involving informal leaders in decision making and other key organizational tasks.[12,13]

In the event you are called on to serve as a leader, whether formally or informally, you will face a choice. You can accept the role and hope to rely on the power of your title and responsibilities to accomplish organizational goals, or you can cultivate leadership competencies and compel people to action by the way you think, behave, and interact with others. Given the increasingly dynamic nature of organizations, it is possible to hold a position today and lose it tomorrow. Building competencies to be both an informal and a formal leader will provide you with an expanded array of opportunities.

Transitioning into the Leadership Position

For some, the transition into leadership is exciting, as many view leadership as a chance to make a difference, grow professionally, and advance their career.[14] For others, the transition may be more daunting. From either perspective, making the transition to leadership is a big step. People who say otherwise have either never done it, are too far removed from their own transition to remember accurately how challenging it was, or experienced that rare occurrence—an easy transition. This adjustment or "speed bump" is felt with most transitions; however, people grow from challenges.[15] Moreover, leadership positions are not bestowed by luck; pharmacist leaders are selected because organizational administration believes they are qualified to handle the role and assume greater responsibility.[16] Thus, new leaders should trust their abilities and potential and embrace the challenges of leadership, as the reward—the opportunity to inspire and affect the lives of others—is immense.

WHAT DOES IT MEAN TO BE A LEADER?

❹ *As implied in the previous discussion of formal and informal leadership, there is a difference between holding a leadership position and being a leader. Likewise, there is a difference between having power or authority that is earned and having power or authority that is bestowed.* Sociologist Max Weber contributed greatly to the literature on leadership, noting that people are perceived to be leaders or to have authority for several reasons. According to Weber, there are three origins of authority:[17]

- *Traditional authority* is associated with custom or tradition, such as lines of royal succession in the case of kings, queens, etc. In a more modern setting, traditional authority is based on one's position or rank. For example, the titles of director, chief, and department head represent traditional authority titles in various areas of pharmacy.
- *Bureaucratic authority* is based on rules or established laws. Bureaucratic leaders demonstrate their power by such tactics as enforc-

ing rules, managing information, and requiring strict codes of organizational behavior. Military pharmacies are an example of a system in which a more established, stricter code of organizational behavior may be found, largely because of the value placed on discipline and rank.
- *Charismatic authority* is based on how leaders use their powers of persuasion and sense of personal magnetism to acquire followers and, often, devotees. Charismatic leaders tend to focus on transformation and use their personalities to make change. They often possess no formal power or authority but rely on their magnetism and vision to get things done. For instance, a staff pharmacist with extraordinary public speaking skills, a strong network, and commitment to serving low-income populations could positively transform a community pharmacy's image by serving underserved individuals.

In their 1959 work, "The Bases of Social Power," John French and Bertram Raven took a slightly different approach and suggested five sources of power:[18]

- *Reward power*: Based on a person's ability to provide material or nonmaterial inducements
- *Legitimate power*: Derived from the follower's perception that a leader has a right to lead, make demands, and expect obedience from others
- *Expert power*: Based on an individual's knowledge and expertise
- *Referent power*: Stemmed from a person's charm or appeal and a follower's desire to identify or emulate these characteristics
- *Coercive power*: Based on an individual's ability to threaten or punish

Weber's research, as well as French and Raven's, underpins the notion that leadership is not reserved for people in formal leadership roles, a concept critical for those entering the profession of pharmacy. ❺ *Despite your title, role, or position on an organizational chart, you have the power to be a leader. Leadership is something that is acknowledged by others as a result of demonstrated* *vision, self-**motivation**, performance, determination, communication skills, credibility, ethical behavior, and ability to mobilize, motivate, and achieve desired results through others. A high-level position or formal leadership role is not required for you to be perceived as a leader.*

CHARACTERISTICS OF TRUE LEADERS

What do true leaders do and how do they behave? As discussed earlier, true leaders have a unique ability to move others to action. They do this because they tend to possess several common characteristics (**Table 1–2** lists common behaviors and traits of effective leaders):[19-24]

- *The ability to articulate a compelling vision for the future*: A compelling vision can attract and inspire others, increase commitment to organizational goals, provide purpose and meaning to work activities, link current work activities to future accomplishments, and promote change.[25] The ability to create a compelling vision and garner widespread support to realize it is a critical leadership

TABLE **1–2**	**Common Behaviors and Traits of Effective Pharmacist Leaders**
Behaviors	**Traits**
• Communicates well	• Decisive
• Listens	• Passionate
• Encourages	• Competent
• Acts assertively	• Innovative
• Innovates	• Visionary
• Delegates, entrusts, and empowers	• Persuasive
• Resolves conflict	• Optimistic
• Provides good direction	• Credible
• Makes others feel important	• Responsible
• Admits mistakes	• Emotionally stable
• Stays involved	• Diplomatic
• Negotiates successfully	• Cooperative
• Challenges the status quo	• Intelligent
• Demonstrates integrity	• Systems thinker

Sources: Data from Hogan R, Curphy GJ, Hogan J. What we know about leadership: effectiveness and personality. *Am Psychol* 1994;49:493–504. Straub JT. *The Rookie Manager*. New York, NY: AMACOM; 2000. Broadwell MM, Dietrich, CB. *The New Supervisor: How to Thrive in Your First Year as a Manager*. Cambridge, MA: Perseus Books; 1998. Rowitz L. *Public Health Leadership: Putting Principles into Practice*. Sudbury, MA: Jones and Bartlett Publishers; 2003. Bennis W. *On Becoming a Leader*. Cambridge, MA: Perseus Books; 1989. Kouzes J, Posner B. *The Leadership Challenge*. San Francisco, CA: Jossey Bass; 2002.

competency.[23,24] For example, a meticulous staff pharmacist who strives to provide the safest and most efficacious care possible develops a vision in which medication errors would be reduced to nearly 0% over the next three years. To this end, she proposes the implementation of a new automation system to promote medication safety. The articulation of her vision regarding the use of automated technology and its positive effect on patient care inspires support for her proposal among her colleagues, which is instrumental in convincing the pharmacy's administration not only to purchase the equipment but also to implement its use, thus promoting goal attainment.

- *Passion*: True leaders are absolutely committed to their vision and enjoy working toward it.[23] This passion gives them the energy to persist even during setbacks. The pharmacist's passion for promoting medication safety, described in the previous example, contributed greatly to her persistence in recruiting her colleagues in efforts to compel the administration to act on her automation proposal.
- *Integrity*: Leaders know their strengths, are honest about their limitations, establish high standards (such as those set by our medication safety-promoting staff pharmacist), and are consistent in their approach. They also honor their commitments, treat others with respect, and serve as role models.[23]
- *Encouragement of others*: The tombstone of Andrew Carnegie, one of the twentieth century's notable leaders, reads: "Here lies a man who knew how to enlist the service of better men than himself."[26] Carnegie believed that great things required the support of others and that effective leaders harnessed the power and ideas of others.[27] Indeed, it has been said that leadership is about "creating a way for people to contribute to making something extraordinary happen."[14,28] Leaders understand the importance of engaging the collective talents of many people and facilitating teamwork and collaboration by creating an atmosphere of mutual trust and respect. They make it possible for people to be successful

and recognize them for their accomplishments and contributions.[23,24] As a pharmacist leader, your success depends, to some degree, on your own technical and pharmaceutical knowledge but, more significantly, on your ability to mobilize others.[29] Returning to our example, the pharmacist understood that without the support of her colleagues, her proposal would not have the power or momentum to gain the attention of decision makers within the organization. This reliance on the mobilization of others may represent a whole new way of thinking for those who moved to leadership roles after establishing themselves as take-charge pharmacists who solve their challenges independently.[30]

- *Curiosity and daring*: Leaders are not afraid to challenge the status quo and are willing to take risks to effect important change. They are not afraid to make mistakes in pursuing their goals and use adversity to prepare for future opportunities.[23,24] Because of the expense involved in purchasing automation, the training required, and the widespread belief that such technology would result in job cuts, the pharmacist faced an uphill battle among colleagues and administrators. Yet she continued to challenge the embedded belief systems about automation to facilitate a better understanding of its cost, benefits, and impact.

❻ *Pharmacist leaders must fuse the traits of leadership with the* **professionalism** *expected within the pharmacy profession. Professionalism is defined as the standards, behaviors, and character of an individual engaged in tasks related to his or her work or profession.* Moreover, pharmacist leaders always consider the ethical and legal ramifications of their decisions and actions. Professionalism requires that pharmacists and pharmacist leaders commit to (1) promoting the highest standards of excellence in pharmacy practice, (2) advocating and serving the interests and welfare of patients, and (3) addressing health needs on a societal level.[31] **Table 1–3** details the traits of pharmacy professionalism.[32] For further details, refer to Chapter 5 ("Significant Laws Affecting Pharmacy Practice Management"), Chapter 6 ("Ethical Decision Making"), Chapter 17 ("Employ-

TABLE **1–3**	Traits of Pharmacy Professionalism

- Accountability for actions, decisions, and work efforts
- Knowledge and skills of pharmacy profession
- Commitment to improving the skills/knowledge of self and others
- Trustworthiness
- Creativity and innovative thinking
- Ethically sound decision making
- Pride in pharmacy profession
- Service orientation
- Covenantal relationship with patients

Source: Data adapted from American Pharmacist Association Academy of Students of Pharmacy–American Association of Colleges of Pharmacy Council of Deans Task Force on Professionalism. White paper on pharmacy student professionalism. *J Am Pharm Assoc* 2000;40:96–102.

ment Law Essentials"), and Chapter 25 ("Developing Professionalism").

DISTINGUISHING BETWEEN MANAGEMENT AND LEADERSHIP

There are some key differences between leadership and management.[22] ◆ *Although management is similar to leadership in many ways, as management and leadership skills often overlap, management generally focuses on more operational aspects of an organization to achieve goals.*[33] *It is sometimes said that leadership is about "doing the right things," whereas management involves "doing things right."*[34(p7)] In other words, leaders are concerned with the broad, general mission, or vision, of an organization, while managers are concerned with more operational details, such as budgeting, planning, hiring, and developing employees to accomplish that mission or vision. Although this is a somewhat simplistic overgeneralization, it speaks to the essential difference between management and leadership. It is one thing to be a good planner and an effective manager of human, financial, and

physical resources, but it is something quite different to inspire others to action. Managers do the former, and leaders do the latter. In a pharmacy setting, managers ensure that the work gets done, and leaders get people excited about doing it. Managers plan, and leaders envision an exciting future. Managers think critically, and leaders think creatively and strategically. Managers ensure that employees are prepared to fulfill their roles, and leaders facilitate collective and continual learning among employees to expand the ways they think and achieve results.[35] For further details, refer to Chapter 2 ("Management Essentials for Pharmacists"), Chapter 13 ("Achieving Results Through Others and Strategic Planning"), and Chapter 19 ("Effective Performance Management"). Although there are distinct differences between leaders and managers, many leaders possess outstanding management skills and many managers have excellent leadership qualities. **Table 1–4** provides a list of competencies for pharmacist leaders and managers, key actions used to achieve these competencies, and textbook chapters that address these competencies and key actions.[36] Several of

TABLE 1–4	Competencies for Pharmacist Leaders and Managers		
Competency	**Key Actions**		**Textbook Chapters Related to Competency**
Accurate self-insight: demonstrating an awareness of your own strengths and development needs, as well as the affect of your own behavior on others	Inviting feedback, performing self-assessment, understanding impact		Chapter 1. *Leadership Essentials for Pharmacists* Chapter 2. *Management Essentials for Pharmacists* Chapter 24. *Managing Your Time* Chapter 25. *Developing Professionalism* Chapter 26. *Creating Your Personal Brand and Influencing Others* Chapter 27. *Personal Finance*
Building business relationships: using appropriate interpersonal styles and communication methods to work effectively with business partners, such as peers and external vendors, to meet mutual goals; building networks to obtain cooperation without relying on authority	Establishing shared goals, collaboratively developing solutions, influencing action, confirming agreement, facilitating, acknowledging contributions, establishing communication systems		Chapter 1. *Leadership Essentials for Pharmacists* Chapter 2. *Management Essentials for Pharmacists* Chapter 13. *Achieving Results Through Others and Strategic Planning* Chapter 21. *Communicating Effectively with Others* Chapter 22. *Negotiation Techniques* Chapter 23. *Managing Conflict and Building Consensus* Chapter 25. *Developing Professionalism*
Building organizational talent: attracting, developing, and retaining talented individuals; creating a learning environment that ensures associates realize their highest potential, allowing the organization as a whole to meet future challenges; creating and maintaining an environment that naturally enables all participants to contribute to their full potential in the pursuit of organizational objectives	Diagnosing capability and developmental needs, scanning environment for developmental assignments, demonstrating advocacy for talent, creating a learning culture, ensuring differential reward systems and processes, emphasizing retention, demonstrating inclusive behavior, demonstrating advocacy for diversity		Chapter 2. *Management Essentials for Pharmacists* Chapter 13. *Achieving Results Through Others and Strategic Planning* Chapter 18. *Successful Recruitment and Hiring Strategies* Chapter 19. *Effective Performance Management* Chapter 20. *Creating and Identifying Desirable Workplaces*

Change leadership: continuously seeking (or encouraging others to seek) opportunities for innovative approaches to organizational problems and opportunities	Recognizing opportunities; valuing sound approaches; encouraging boundary breaking; addressing resistance to change; managing complexity, contradictions, and paradoxes; driving toward improvement	Chapter 3. *Leading and Managing Change* Chapter 4. *Innovation and Entrepreneurship*
Communicating with impact: expressing thoughts, feelings, and ideas in a clear, succinct, and compelling manner in both individual and group situations; adjusting language to capture the attention of the audience	Delivering clear messages, presenting with impact, creating clear written communications, adjusting to the audience, ensuring understanding	Chapter 15. *Understanding and Applying Marketing Strategies* Chapter 16. *Advertising and Promotion* Chapter 21. *Communicating Effectively with Others* Chapter 22. *Negotiation Techniques* Chapter 23. *Managing Conflict and Building Consensus*
Customer focus: cultivating strategic customer relationships and ensuring that the customer perspective is the driving force behind all value-added business activities	Seeking to understand customers, educating customers, maintaining trust, acting to meet customer needs and concerns, developing partnerships, recognizing customer service issues, creating win–win solutions	Chapter 11. *Justifying and Planning Patient Care Services* Chapter 12. *Achieving and Measuring Patient Satisfaction* Chapter 25. *Developing Professionalism*
Driving for results: setting high goals for personal and group accomplishments, measuring progress toward goals, working tenaciously to meet or exceed goals while deriving satisfaction from goal achievement and continuous improvement	Targeting opportunities, establishing and reaching for goals, staying focused, evaluating performance	Chapter 13. *Achieving Results Through Others and Strategic Planning* Chapter 19. *Effective Performance Management*

(continues)

TABLE 1–4 (continued)

Competency	Key Actions	Textbook Chapters Related to Competency
Establishing strategic direction: establishing and committing to a long-range course of action to achieve a strategic goal or vision after analyzing factual information and assumptions and considering resources, constraints, and organizational values	Gathering and organizing information, analyzing data, evaluating and selecting strategies, developing timelines, executing plans	Chapter 13. *Achieving Results Through Others and Strategic Planning* Chapter 14. *Pharmacy Business and Staff Planning*
Executive presence: conveying an image that is consistent with the organization's values; demonstrating the qualities, traits, and demeanor (excluding intelligence, competency, or special talents) that command leadership respect	Advocating for the organization, managing stress, creating an impact, exhibiting flexibility and adaptability	Chapter 1. *Leadership Essentials for Pharmacists* Chapter 13. *Achieving Results Through Others and Strategic Planning* Chapter 25. *Developing Professionalism*
Leading through vision and values: Keeping the organization's vision at the forefront of decision making and action	Communicating the importance of vision and values, moving others to action, modeling vision and values, rewarding others who display vision and values	Chapter 1. *Leadership Essentials for Pharmacists* Chapter 3. *Leading and Managing Change* Chapter 13. *Achieving Results Through Others and Strategic Planning*
Managing diversity: creating and maintaining an environment that naturally enables all participants to contribute to their full potential in pursuit of organizational objectives	Creating an equitable work environment, ensuring inclusivity of policies, recognizing diversity as an organizational asset, promoting the use of diverse resources, promoting increased diversity among the staff, setting standards of behavior based on respect and dignity	Chapter 17. *Employment Law Essentials* Chapter 18. *Successful Recruitment and Hiring Strategies* Chapter 20. *Creating and Identifying Desirable Workplaces*

Competency	Description	Chapters
Operational decision making: relating and comparing data on operational effectiveness from different sources; establishing goals and requirements that reflect organizational objectives and values, including the importance of continuous improvement; securing relevant information and identifying key issues, key people, and cause-and-effect relationships from a base of information; committing to an action after exploring alternative courses of action	Seeking and organizing information, analyzing data, developing and considering alternatives, gaining commitments, demonstrating decisiveness and action	Chapter 5. *Significant Laws Affecting Pharmacy Practice Management* Chapter 6. *Ethical Decision Making* Chapter 7. *Pharmacy Operations: Workflow, Practice Activities, Medication Safety, Technology, and Quality* Chapter 10. *Cents and Sensibility: Understanding the Numbers* Chapter 13. *Achieving Results Through Others and Strategic Planning* Chapter 14. *Pharmacy Business and Staff Planning*
Organizational acumen: understanding and using economic, financial, and industry data accurately to diagnose business strengths and weaknesses; identifying key issues; and developing strategies and plans	Analyzing, integrating, and understanding the application of financial strategies and systems	Chapter 3. *Leading and Managing Change* Chapter 8. *Purchasing and Managing Inventory* Chapter 9. *Third-Party Payment for Prescription Medications in the Retail Sector* Chapter 10. *Cents and Sensibility: Understanding the Numbers* Chapter 11. *Justifying and Planning Patient Care Services* Chapter 13. *Achieving Results Through Others and Strategic Planning* Chapter 14. *Pharmacy Business and Staff Planning*
Process improvement: acting to improve existing conditions and processes	Assessing opportunities, determining causes, targeting and implementing improvements	Chapter 7. *Pharmacy Operations: Workflow, Practice Activities, Medication Safety, Technology, and Quality*
Professional or industry knowledge: having a satisfactory level of technical and professional skill or knowledge in position-related areas, keeping up with current developments and trends in areas of expertise	Engaging in continuous learning, applying state-of-the-art technology and concepts, developing and maintaining industry awareness	Chapter 1. *Leadership Essentials for Pharmacists* Chapter 2. *Management Essentials for Pharmacists* Chapter 14. *Pharmacy Business and Staff Planning* Chapter 18. *Successful Recruitment and Hiring Strategies* Chapter 25. *Developing Professionalism*

Source: Originally published in Zilz DA, Woodward BW, Thilke TS, Shane RR, Scott B. Leadership skills for a high-performance pharmacy practice. *Am J Health-Syst Pharm* 2004;61:2562–2574. © 2004, American Society of Health-System Pharmacists, Inc. Adapted with permission. (R0914)

these competencies and key actions are discussed in Chapter 2 ("Management Essentials for Pharmacists").

DEFINING YOUR LEADERSHIP STYLE

In the management classic *Good to Great*, author Jim Collins asserts that there is a hierarchy of executive behaviors.[37] Level 1 includes individuals who make their contributions independently. Level 2 comprises people who work well in team settings. Level 3 is composed of what Collins calls "competent managers," individuals who are proficient at managing people and resources. Level 4 includes the classic definition of a leader, someone who "catalyzes commitment to and vigorous pursuit of a clear and compelling vision, stimulating higher performance standards."[37(p20)] According to Collins, a smaller cadre of individuals achieve extraordinary success through "a paradoxical blend of personal humility and professional will."[37(p20)] Collins calls these individuals "Level 5 Executives."[37]

Unlike their often charismatic counterparts, Level 5 executives move quietly, modestly, and resolutely toward their goals. Collins uses Abraham Lincoln to illustrate the characteristics of a Level 5 executive—someone who is more focused on the organization or cause than on him- or herself and who is more driven by goals than recognition, fortune, or power.[37] In the pharmacy profession, an excellent example of a Level 5 leader is Gloria Niemeyer Francke. Dr. Francke graduated from pharmacy school in the early 1940s, a time when few women entered the profession. She held multiple leadership positions, including assistant director of a hospital pharmacy, first executive secretary of the American Society of Hospital Pharmacists (later renamed the American Society of Health-System Pharmacists), and chairperson of the American Pharmacists Association Advisory Group to the Office of Women's Affairs. During her more than 60-year career, Dr. Francke actively advocated and advanced gender equality and the roles of women in pharmacy and pharmacy leadership. She was also the first female recipient of the American Pharmacists Association's Remington Medal, considered by many as the pharmacy profession's highest honor.[38]

Level 5 leaders, as described by Collins, exhibit one of many possible leadership styles. You will need to find a style that comports with your talents and values. Leadership approaches vary markedly, and your relationship skills, comfort with people, decision-making style, ability to handle ambiguity, and communication abilities will all influence the approach you develop and cultivate. ❽ *Leadership theorists have characterized a variety of leadership styles, and each style has both pros and cons.* These styles include

- *Affiliative*: Affiliative leaders are masters at forging relationships with others and can be especially effective at building productive teams. Although they are effective at using the power of networks and connections to accomplish goals, they sometimes find it difficult to deliver bad news that may disappoint others, including feedback about underperformance.[16]
- *Autocratic*: Autocratic leaders make decisions independently, without engaging or consulting others.[39] Although this style works well in crisis situations, it does not typically engage the thinking or talents of others.
- *Democratic*: Democratic leaders value fair process and tend to give all members of the organization an opportunity to weigh in with their preferences and recommendations.[16,39] Democratic leaders excel in engaging others, but their commitment to collecting input and establishing buy-in can sometimes be inefficient.
- *Laissez-faire*: Laissez-faire leaders provide critical resources and information, but tend to provide little direction. This form of leadership works well with highly competent and independent individuals but may lead some people to feel abandoned or ignored.[39]
- *Transformational*: Transformational leaders believe that social and spiritual values can be employed to raise employees to even higher levels of performance and motivation.[40] According to James Burns, who coined this term, transformational leaders include intellectual leaders who transform organizations or society by thinking in new ways, charismatic leaders who use charm and personality to promote change, revolutionary leaders who promote change by using effective methodologies, and reform leaders who focus on a

single moral issue.[40] Transformational leaders tend to be "idea" people and may need help attending to the details of their plans. In some cases, their passion can exhaust others.

- *Servant*: Servant leaders view their role as being in service to others, meeting the needs of those they lead, and helping them to grow by building individual capacity and a sense of community. Servant leaders believe that attending to the needs of employees or followers will enable them to achieve their full potential—and when potential is fully realized, the organization will benefit.[41] Although the people within organizations led by servant leaders tend to feel valued and supported, some criticize the approach, suggesting that it focuses too much on developing others and not enough on setting direction to get things done.[42]

Regardless of the leadership style you adopt, it is important to understand that styles can be situational. According to Vroom and Jago, developers of contingency leadership theory, or situational leadership theory, "a leadership style that is effective in one situation may prove completely ineffective in a different situation."[43(p23)] Thus, most leaders will likely encounter situations in which their default leadership style is ineffective or at least not optimal.[44] For example, a pharmacist leader who typically uses a laissez-faire approach to leadership will not find this style effective if the leader is asked to take over a hospital pharmacy staffed by several newly graduated pharmacists. Likewise, a transformational leader who thrives on change will probably not be successful (and likely will not be happy) in a family-owned community pharmacy with no need or interest in reorganizing or significantly revamping its products or services. There are clearly times when uncomfortable approaches are required to move through difficult situations or to be successful in an organization that does not value your preferred approach.[29,45]

❾ *Although several leadership styles may work, leaders will be most effective when they select a style consistent with their personality, their brand, the environment in which they exist, and the people with whom they interact.[46] Optimally, leaders will be able to find environments in which they are able to demonstrate their preferred approach to leading others.*

Leadership requires authenticity, and we can only be authentic when we are acting in accordance with our personal and professional values.

DEVELOPING YOUR LEADERSHIP POTENTIAL

❿ *Growing your leadership capacity requires sustained and deliberate effort.* Expanding your base of experience is an essential development strategy, and there are many strategies to do this. You may decide to

- *Pursue leadership roles within community organizations:*[24] The varied and often underfunded needs of community organizations provide volunteers with opportunities to pursue and build skills that would not normally be possible with one's employer. Volunteering to work on a campaign to promote literacy, managing contributions for a fund-raising event, or soliciting contributions for a local marathon are strategies to build marketing, financial, and persuasive competencies.
- *Volunteer for leadership roles within your professional associations:*[24] Recruiting corporate partners for a pharmacy conference or leading program planning for a local, state, regional, national, or international pharmacy association will give you an opportunity to meet new people and network, acquire new skills, and learn about how professional pharmacy organizations work. These kinds of assignments also tend to hone communication, persuasion, and negotiation skills.
- *Find one or more mentors*: The best mentors may be individuals outside of your management chain. For example, a staff pharmacist in a hospital setting may look to the director of nursing or medical director for mentorship. Mentors can support leadership development by opening doors and expanding networks and by providing feedback about issues ranging from style and presence to approaches to managing conflict. Mentors can steer you to high-profile assignments that increase your visibility, encourage you to think in new ways, model successful behaviors and attitudes, and support you through difficult situations. **Table 1–5** describes the many roles of a mentor.

TABLE 1–5	Mentoring Roles

Elements	Description of Mentor's Activities/Responsibilities
Sponsorship	Opens doors that would otherwise be closed
Coaching	Teaches and provides feedback
Protection	Supports the protégé and/or acts as a buffer
Challenge	Encourages new ways of thinking and acting, and pushes the protégé to stretch his or her abilities
Exposure and visibility	Steers the protégé into assignments that make him or her known to top management
Role modeling	Demonstrates the kind of behaviors, attitudes, and values that lead to success
Counseling	Helps the protégé with difficult professional dilemmas
Acceptance and confirmation	Supports the protégé and shows respect
Friendship	Demonstrates personal caring that goes beyond business requirements

- *Ask for difficult assignments*:[24] Challenging assignments encourage growth and can result in organizational recognition. Once you have been successful with one project, you will likely be called on to work on another. This trend will expand your knowledge and experience base, provide you with opportunities to try new things, and increase your connections with others. For example, a pharmacist may request to be included on a team assigned to develop new practice guidelines for chronic disease management.

- *Stay informed*: A solid grasp of the context in which one works is required for strategic thinking. Learning about your pharmacy's expansion plans, reading journals to stay abreast of current therapy, using a professional organization Listserv to converse about the effect of a medication, reviewing financial statements to learn more about your organization's financial stability, and introducing yourself to colleagues at professional meetings are just some of the ways to learn more about your profession and the trends affecting it.

- *Observe others*: Pay attention to the traits and behaviors of leaders you admire. How do they handle opposition? What words do they use to move others to action? Where do they invest their time and energy? We can learn a great deal by studying role models.

- *Read about leaders*: Politicians, revolutionaries, inventors, groundbreaking scientists, sports figures, corporate leaders—all have lessons from which we can learn. Read their stories to learn about the techniques they employ, the words they use, and the behaviors they exhibit.

- *Take leadership tests and inventories*: A number of leadership style assessment tools can be illuminating.[47,48] Online tools, career offices within universities, and career coaches within the community are among the resources available to suggest useful resources. The more you understand your personal strengths and interests, the better you will be positioned to develop a leadership style that feels right for you.

- *Do not wait to be ready*: We all need stretch assignments, so do not wait to be fully proficient before tackling assignments. Act with confidence and be ready to ask others for support in the event you need it.

SUMMARY

Leaders can conceive and articulate goals that lift people out of their petty preoccupations . . . and unite them in pursuit of objectives worthy of their best efforts.[49]

—*John W. Gardner*

As a pharmacist, it is likely that you will be called upon to lead. Effective leadership, like any other skill, requires practice and patience. This chapter provides an introduction to leadership and the need for leaders within the pharmacy profession. This chapter also discusses the differences between leadership and management and addresses critical aspects of the leadership role, including (1) formal and informal power, (2) leadership types and styles, and (3) strategies to build leadership competencies. The future of pharmacy is highly dependent on future pharmacist leaders. Thus, the development of successful leaders is imperative to the profession of pharmacy. This textbook, which is written and reviewed by pharmacist leaders, managers, and human resource experts, will elaborate on this cultivation in the following chapters.

References

1. White SJ. Will there be a pharmacy leadership crisis? An ASHP Foundation Scholar-in-Residence report. *Am J Health-Syst Pharm* 2005;62:845–855.

2. Raiffa H. *The Art and Science of Negotiation*. Boston, MA: Belknap Press; 2005.

3. Robbins H, Finley M. *The Accidental Leader: What to Do When You Are Suddenly in Charge*. San Francisco, CA: Jossey-Bass; 2004.

4. Mark SM. Succession planning: the forgotten art. *Hosp Pharm* 2008;43:593–600.

5. Betof E, Harwood F. *Just Promoted: How to Survive and Thrive in Your First 12 Months as a Manager*. New York, NY: McGraw-Hill; 1992.

6. Maxwell JC. *The 21 Irrefutable Laws of Leadership*. Nashville, TN: Thomas Nelson; 2007.

7. Brousseau KR, Driver MJ, Hourihan G, Larsson R. The seasoned executive's decision-making style. *Harv Bus Rev* 2006;84(2):110–121.

8. Michelman P, Kleiner A. Debriefing Art Kleiner: how to lead when your influence goes off the (org) chart. *Harv Manag* 2004;9(5).

9. Gardner H. *Leading Minds: An Anatomy of Leadership*. New York, NY: Basic Books; 1996.

10. Hill LA. *Building Effective One-on-One Work Relationships*. Boston, MA: Harvard Business Publishing; 1996.

11. Mintzberg H, Van der Heyden L. Organigraphs: drawing how companies really work. *Harv Bus Rev* 1999;77(5):87–94.

12. Garvin DA, Roberto MA. What you don't know about making decisions. *Harv Bus Rev* 2001;79(8):108–116.

13. Collins JC. Turning goals into results: the power of catalytic mechanisms. *Harv Bus Rev* 1999;77(4):70–82.

14. Stettner M. *Skills for New Managers*. New York, NY: McGraw-Hill; 2000.

15. Bunker KA, Wakefield M. Leading in times of change. *Harv Manag Update* 2006;11(5):3–6.

16. Goleman D. What makes a leader? *Harv Bus Rev* 2004;82(1):82–91.

17. Weber M. *The Theory of Social and Economic Organization*. Henderson AM, Parsons T, trans. New York, NY: Free Press; 1947.

18. French JR, Raven B. The bases of social power. In: Cartwright D, ed. *Studies in Social Power*. Ann Arbor, MI: University of Michigan; 1959.

19. Hogan R, Curphy GJ, Hogan J. What we know about leadership: effectiveness and personality. *Am Psychol* 1994;49:493–504.

20. Straub JT. *The Rookie Manager*. New York, NY: AMACOM; 2000.

21. Broadwell MM, Dietrich CB. *The New Supervisor: How to Thrive in Your First Year as a Manager*. Cambridge, MA: Perseus Books; 1998.

22. Rowitz L. *Public Health Leadership: Putting Principles into Practice*. Sudbury, MA: Jones and Bartlett Publishers; 2003.

23. Bennis W. *On Becoming a Leader*. Cambridge, MA: Perseus Books; 1989.

24. Kouzes J, Posner B. *The Leadership Challenge*. San Francisco, CA: Jossey Bass; 2002.

25. Lashway L. *Leading with Vision*. Eugene, OR: ERIC Clearinghouse on Organizational Management; 1997.

26. Lifeorganizaers.com. Tombstone of Andrew Carnegie's. Available at: http://www.lifeorganizers.com/Business-Solutions/Daily-Business-Quote/Tombstone-of-Andrew-Carnegie-s.html. Accessed August 13, 2009.

27. Johnson LK. Are you delegating so it sticks? *Harv Manag Update* 2007;12(9):3–5.

28. Brady C, Woodward O. *Launching a Leadership Revolution—Mastering the Five Levels of Influence*. Lebanon, IN: Business Plus; 2007.

29. Cohn JM, Khurana R, Reeves L. Growing talent as if your business depended on it. *Harv Bus Rev* 2005; 83(10):62–70.

30. Walker CA. Saving your rookie managers from themselves. *Harv Bus Rev* 2002;80(4):97–102.

31. American Board of Internal Medicine Committees on Evaluation of Clinical Competence and Clinical Competence and Communication Programs. Project professionalism; Philadelphia, PA; 2001:5–6.

32. American Pharmacist Association Academy of Students of Pharmacy–American Association of Colleges of Pharmacy Council of Deans Task Force on Professionalism. White paper on pharmacy student professionalism. *J Am Pharm Assoc* 2000;40:96–102.

33. Zaleznik A. Managers and leaders: are they different? *Harv Bus Rev* 2004;82(1):74–81.

34. Bennis W, Goldsmith J. *Learning to Lead: A Workbook on Becoming a Leader*. New York, NY: Basic Books; 2003.

35. Senge P. *The Fifth Discipline: The Art and Practice of the Learning Organization*. London: Random House; 1990.

36. Zilz DA, Woodward BW, Thilke TS, Shane RR, Scott B. Leadership skills for a high-performance pharmacy practice. *Am J Health-Syst Pharm* 2004;61: 2562–2574.

37. Collins J. *Good to Great*. New York, NY: HarperCollins Publishers Inc; 2001.

38. Maine LL, O'Brien JM. Lessons learned from an unsung hero: Gloria Niemeyer Francke. *Am J Pharm Educ* 2008;72:115.

39. Lewin K, Lippitt R, White RK. Patterns of aggressive behavior in experimentally created social climates. *J Soc Psychol* 1939;10:271–299.

40. Burns JM. Leadership. New York: Harper & Row; 1978.

41. Greenleaf R. *Servant Leadership*. Mahwah, NJ: Paulist Press; 2002.

42. Manfelow J. Servant Leadership: Opinion. Available at: http://www.mindtools.com/pages/article/new LDR_93.htm. Accessed July 30, 2009.

43. Vroom VH, Jago AG. The role of the situation in leadership. *Am Psychol* 2007;62:17–24.

44. Jackson J, Bosse-Smith L. *Leveraging Your Leadership Style Workbook: Maximize Your Influence by Discovering the Leader Within*. Nashville, TN: Abingdon Press; 2008.

45. Schein EH. Three cultures of management: the key to organizational learning. *Sloan Manag Rev* 1996;38(1): 9–20.

46. Schaeffer LD. The leadership journey. *Harv Bus Rev* 2002;80(10):42–47.

47. Kippenberger T. *Leadership Styles*. Oxford: Wiley; 2002.

48. Miller RF, Mark SM, Powell M. Assessing your aptitude for pharmacy leadership. *Am J Health-Syst Pharm* 2008;65:1–4.

49. Thinkexist.com. John W. Gardner quotes. Available at: http://thinkexist.com/quotes/john_w._gardner/3.html. Accessed August 14, 2009.

Abbreviations

P&T: Pharmacy and Therapeutics

Case Scenarios

CASE ONE: Your colleague, Juno Cerrone, was recently appointed the pharmacist manager for a retail setting that, according to corporate officials, needs "a serious makeover." Juno has several ideas and plenty of energy, but his newly acquired staff seems almost hostile to the idea of changing established approaches. "They all know that I'm the boss," he explains to you, "but they refuse to give me the respect I deserve." What can he do to turn things around?

CASE TWO: Lucy Spiegel is a pharmacist at a small hospital pharmacy experiencing regular medication errors. Despite frequent expressions of concern to her pharmacy colleagues, there is a general sense of apathy toward solving the problem, and the pharmacist manager seems unconcerned. Each error seems to have a unique set of circumstances, and there does not seem to be a clear pattern. Dr. Spiegel is frustrated by this, but because she is not in a formal leadership role, she is unsure about what can evoke real change. What strategies might she employ?

CASE THREE: As a pharmacist manager, you are committed to cultivating your employees' talents. You are increasingly impressed by Dr. Daniels, a newly graduated pharmacist who is passionate about his profession. His ideas are creative, salient, and on point. On the down side, he can be overly direct and even condescending in his communication with others. You see tremendous leadership potential in Dr. Daniels if he can conquer some of his interpersonal communication challenges. What can you do to help him reach his potential?

CASE FOUR: After years of financial success and community recognition for being "the only 24/7 pharmacy in the county," changing demographics and a poor economy have made it necessary to move to a more traditional service model. Your staff has traditionally taken pride in being part of an organization perceived as responsive and has asked you to reconsider your decision. Leaders within the community have made the same request. How should you respond?

Additional Resources Available Online!

Visit the Student Companion Web site at http://healthprofessions.jbpub.com/pharmacymanagement for interactive study tools and additional resources.

See www.rxugace.com to learn how you can obtain continuing pharmacy education for this content.

CHAPTER 2

MANAGEMENT ESSENTIALS FOR PHARMACISTS

SCOTT M. MARK, PharmD, MS, MEd, MBA, FASHP, FACHE, FABC

RAFAEL SAENZ, PharmD, MS

LEARNING OBJECTIVES

After completing the chapter, the reader will be able to

1. Evaluate the evolution of various theories that influence management.
2. Explain key tasks involved in hiring.
3. Cite factors that motivate pharmacy employees.
4. Discern the importance of feedback.
5. Define coaching, its essential components, and its benefits.
6. Differentiate the four basic elements of communication and how each relates to effective communication.
7. Assess strategies for managers to demonstrate support for the success of employees/teams.
8. Discuss the importance of delegation and strategies for delegating effectively.
9. Define "managing up" and describe strategies to facilitate this process.
10. Identify ways to solicit employee input.

KEY CONCEPTS

❶ Management is the art of maximizing productivity by using and developing people's talent, while providing them with self-enrichment and opportunities for growth. Management is also concerned with the allocation and use of resources to accomplish tasks and achieve objectives.

❷ Knowledge about the origins of various management approaches and insights concerning conceptual frameworks that have been most effective can help pharmacist managers focus on management approaches that work and avoid those that do not.

❸ Although management fundamentals may be similar from organization to organization, the most effective managers are those who understand the context in which their organizations exist, the organization's unique culture, and the industry- and organization-specific knowledge required to get things done.

4 Strong managers surround themselves with talented people and develop these individuals into high-performing team members who can translate vision into reality.

5 Although competitive and equitable pay matters, decades of research and hundreds of studies have demonstrated that, while money can be a demotivator, it rarely matters most to employees. Many pharmacists enter the profession because they are interested in providing patient care; however, other motivation factors are in play, among them, interesting, challenging, and purposeful work; recognition and appreciation; a sense of accomplishment; and growth opportunities, including the opportunity to acquire new knowledge and build connections with others.

6 Feedback serves as both a preventive and a corrective measure; it is a mechanism not only to help identify and develop solutions to potential work-related barriers or problems but also to get assignments back on track when problems arise or when mistakes are made. Therefore, feedback is a critical aspect of managing employees and accomplishing desired results. Failing to provide feedback is a failure to manage.

7 Communication is one of the most important management competencies and includes sharing information through verbal means, body language, written documents, and compelling presentations. Pharmacist managers who master communication have a unique ability to connect with people to achieve organizational results.

8 Effective managers are good planners who manage their time well, establish reasonable budgets, deploy people appropriately, and prepare for contingencies. Managers cannot possibly prevent all emergencies, but they can take steps to minimize surprises. Although crisis-level events are generally considered negative, they *can* open doors to more positive opportunities and possibilities.

9 Delegation is most effective when managers (1) entrust employees with a job; (2) give employees adequate freedom to get a job done (the act of empowering employees); (3) provide employees with the appropriate level of support to get the job done well, including information, training, and resources; and (4) hold employees accountable to produce desirable outcomes. Thus, managers do not have to be hands-on for the right outcomes to occur, but neither do they have to be uninvolved and unaware of what is occurring.

10 "Managing up" is the process of consciously working with your boss to obtain the best possible results for you, your boss, and your organization. "Managing" in this context is not the result of formal authority over one's supervisor but is rather a method for developing a positive and effective working relationship with him or her.

INTRODUCTION

Whether or not they have formal authority, most pharmacists are managers. Some pharmacists manage people, some manage processes, and some manage entire organizations. As a pharmacist, you may supervise technicians or oversee a department. You may be asked to develop project plans and budgets, create work schedules, or provide an orientation to others. Given the range of possible formal and informal **management** responsibilities in a pharmacy setting, it is imperative for pharmacists to understand fundamental management principles. This chapter provides an overview of the evolution of management theory and the competencies managers use each day, including (but not limited to) managing personnel, communicating effectively, organizing meetings, and managing one's boss ("**managing up**"). This chapter, along with Chapter 1 ("Leadership Essentials for Pharmacists"), provides the foundational concepts discussed throughout this textbook.

THE EVOLUTION OF MANAGEMENT THEORY

❶*Management is the art of maximizing productivity by using and developing people's talent, while providing them with self-enrichment and opportunities for growth.*[1] *Management is also concerned with the allocation and use of resources to accomplish tasks and achieve objectives.* The definition of management has been the subject of much debate for more than 100 years, as management theorists have argued about its essential components and how it should be practiced. A review of the management theories that have advanced during the past century or so reveals an evolution in how people think about the best way to maximize performance and productivity. Although examining trends in management theory may seem like an unnecessary exercise, understanding the evolution of management theory can actually make pharmacist managers more effective. ❷*Knowledge about the origins of various management approaches and insights concerning conceptual frameworks that have been most effective can help pharmacist managers focus on management approaches that work and avoid those that do not.* This section will review some of the classic theories about management.

Scientific Management (Beginning in the 1880s)

As the United States moved from an agrarian to an increasingly industrialized nation around the turn of the twentieth century, the nature of work and work relationships changed profoundly. Until this period, most people worked as independent producers (e.g., cobblers, farmers, craftspeople), but industrialization brought both people and machines together and, more important, prompted new ways of thinking about how best to organize labor. Believing that productivity could be enhanced by tightly organizing the way work was performed, many sought to create a science of management. Scientific management theorists Frederick Taylor, Frank and Lillian Gilbreth, and Henry Gantt were among those who conducted research that led to recommendations for efficiency through techniques such as work design, specialization, standardization, and time and motion studies.[2-4] Although elements of scientific management principles are still in evidence today, several components of this approach have fallen out of favor in certain work environments or in accomplishing certain tasks, especially the focus on breaking down each job into its component parts and having employees work in a specialized manner. For example, in a pharmacy environment, rather than allowing a technician to take an order, review insurance information, and then fill a prescription, a scientific management approach would argue that the greatest efficiencies can be achieved by having one person perform the same task all day. For example, one person would receive prescriptions, one person would count pills, and one person would label vials. While robots may be able to do the same task repeatedly, most humans are not inclined to work that way, and overspecialization of tasks (especially technical tasks) can lead to boredom and disconnection between one's work and the overall purpose of the organization.[5]

Bureaucratic and Administrative Management (Beginning in the 1910s)

The scientific management approach was followed by management theories that attempted to define management and appropriate organizational structure. Henri Fayol was among the most cited theorists of this approach, and in 1916, Fayol defined management roles as (1) planning, (2) organizing, (3) commanding, (4) coordinating activities, and (5) controlling performance.[6] In addition to defining these roles, Fayol delineated several principles of management, ranging from how work should be organized to the degree of job security employees should be offered. **Table 2–1** details Fayol's management principles.[6]

Max Weber was another major contributor to management theory during this era. He advanced the notion that bureaucracies were the most efficient organizational structures and suggested that the best bureaucracies were characterized by[7]

- A system of supervision and subordination.
- Unity of command

TABLE 2–1	Henri Fayol's Management Principles

- **Division of work:** Specialization encourages continuous improvement in skills and the development of improvements in methods.

- **Authority:** Managers have the right to give orders and should be given the power to exact obedience. At the same time, the legitimacy of this authority is only possible when managers provide good leadership.

- **Discipline:** Employees should work hard consistently and rules should not be bent.

- **Unity of command:** Employees should receive direction from only one supervisor.

- **Unity of direction:** People engaged in the same work should have the same goals.

- **Subordination of individual interests:** When employees are at work, they should think about only work.

- **Remuneration:** Employees should receive fair payment for services.

- **Centralization:** Management functions should be consolidated and decisions should be made from the top.

- **Scalar chain (line of authority):** There should be a formal chain of command running from the top to the bottom of the organization.

- **Order:** All materials and personnel have a prescribed place.

- **Equity:** Employees should be treated equitably but not necessarily identically.

- **Stability of tenure:** Employees will work better if they have a sense of job security.

- **Initiative:** Employees should be able to demonstrate their strengths, talents, and innovative ideas.

- **Esprit de Corps:** Management must foster employee morale.

Source: Data from Fayol H. *General and Industrial Management*. Storrs C, trans. London: Pitman & Sons Ltd; 1949.

- Extensive use of written documents
- Training in job requirements and skills
- Application of consistent and complete rules
- The assignment of work and personnel hiring based on competence and experience[7]

Human Relations Movement (Beginning in the 1920s)

The human relations era introduced the notion that social interactions in the workplace mattered. One of the most famous workplace research efforts, the Hawthorne Studies, greatly influenced

ideas about management during this period. The Hawthorne Studies were conducted on female Western Electric employees between 1927 and 1932 and subjected employees to different work schedules, rest breaks, temperatures, and humidity to determine the factors most linked to employee productivity.[8] Curiously, the research revealed that productivity increased during almost every workplace environment change. Elto Mayo and Fritz Roethlisberger, the researchers who managed these studies, determined that being studied, attended to, and cared for positively influenced worker performance.[8] In scientific research, this phenomenon is known as the Hawthorne effect, wherein study participants improve simply because they are observed as part of a study, rather than as a result of an experimental condition. In short, pay attention to your employees, and their performance will improve.

These studies were followed by research related to individual needs and motivation. During the 1940s, Abraham Maslow introduced the hierarchy of needs theory, which asserted that five basic human needs must be satisfied and that the lowest needs must be satisfied in order for higher-level needs to emerge.[9] These five basic human needs, from lowest to highest level, include:[9]

1. Basic physical needs (e.g., hunger, thirst, sleep)
2. Safety and security (need to feel secure and free from threats)
3. Belonging and love (need to belong, to be accepted, to give and receive love)
4. Esteem (need for respect and esteem in the eyes of oneself and others)
5. Self-actualization (need to fulfill one's potential, to be the best one can be)

Although Maslow's hierarchy has been criticized (for example, if safety and security are required for self-actualization, why are there so many starving artists?), the model offers helpful guidance for managers. **Figure 2–1** displays how Maslow's framework can be applied within a pharmacy setting.[9]

Maslow's work was complemented by Frederick Herzberg, who, in 1959, proposed that employees have two different types of needs: (1) *hygiene factors or needs* (factors that affect job dissatisfaction and present in conditions surrounding job), such as job security, pay, physical working conditions, supervision, and relations with coworkers, and (2) **motivation** *factors or needs* (factors that affect job satisfaction and present in work itself), such as opportunities for recognition, achievement, and personal growth.[10] Herzberg was among the first to suggest that, while hygiene factors such as fair pay are important, motivation factors are more tightly linked to employee engagement and satisfaction. For example, a safe environment is required to attract or retain an employee, but offering such things as professional development and the opportunity to move into a more senior role is necessary to keep employees fully engaged.

Douglas McGregor, author of *The Human Side of Enterprise* and another member of the human relations school, explored the effect of management styles on worker performance and categorized managers in one of two ways.[11] He asserted that (1) *Theory X managers* believe that because employees do not like to work, they must be strictly controlled and forced to work; and (2) *Theory Y managers* believe that rigid controls and punishment are not required to ensure worker performance, as employees inherently desire accomplishment(s) and will demonstrate commitment to their organization if their work is satisfying.[11] Extending McGregor's work in the late 1960s, Rensis Likert suggested that there are four basic management approaches:[12]

- *Exploitive-authoritarian*: Managers distrust their direct reports (employees they supervise) and motivate through fear and punishment.
- *Benevolent-authoritative*: Managers are condescending and motivate through rewards and threats of punishment.
- *Consultative*: Managers have a fair amount of confidence and trust in direct reports, but while they request ideas from them, they do not involve them in decision making.
- *Group participative*: Managers have high performance standards, trust, and supportive relationships with direct reports and engage direct reports in decision making. Likert argued that managers who employ the group participative approach are most likely to achieve organizational profits and long-term success.[12]

In the 1980s, William Ouchi took McGregor's typology a bit further and introduced *Theory Z management*, a style observed in the Japanese business culture that emphasizes the value of employee participation, job rotation, continuous learning, and generalization rather than specialization.[13] McGregor, Likert, and Ouchi were among the researchers who formed the foundation of later management approaches that stress the importance of participation, trust, and employee

FIGURE **2–1**   **Applying Maslow's Hierarchy of Needs Within a Pharmacy Setting.**

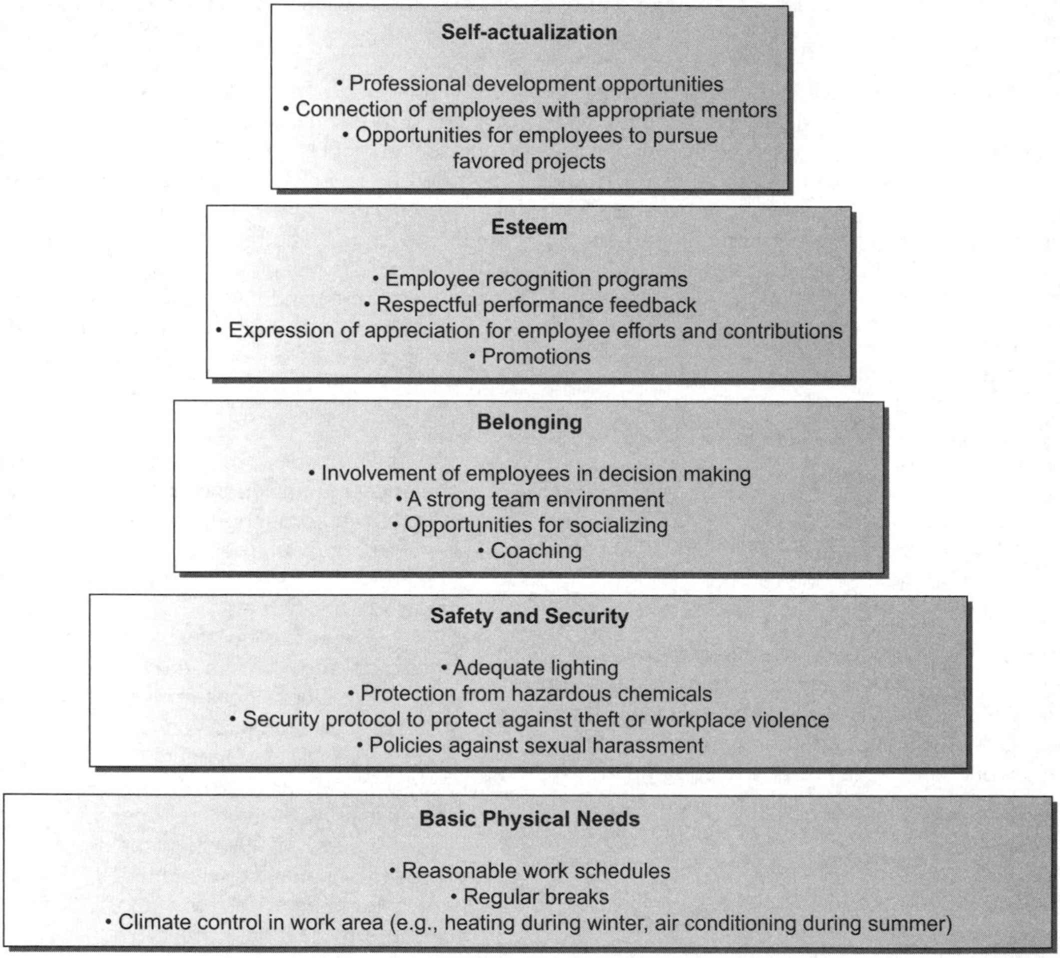

Self-actualization

- Professional development opportunities
- Connection of employees with appropriate mentors
- Opportunities for employees to pursue favored projects

Esteem

- Employee recognition programs
- Respectful performance feedback
- Expression of appreciation for employee efforts and contributions
- Promotions

Belonging

- Involvement of employees in decision making
- A strong team environment
- Opportunities for socializing
- Coaching

Safety and Security

- Adequate lighting
- Protection from hazardous chemicals
- Security protocol to protect against theft or workplace violence
- Policies against sexual harassment

Basic Physical Needs

- Reasonable work schedules
- Regular breaks
- Climate control in work area (e.g., heating during winter, air conditioning during summer)

The figure displays Maslow's hierarchy of needs from lowest (basic physical needs) to highest (self-actualization) and delineates examples of each need in a pharmacy setting.

Source: Data from Maslow AH. A theory of human motivation. *Psychol Rev* 1943;50(4):370–396.

empowerment—elements likely to ensure employee engagement. Refer to Chapter 13 ("Achieving Results Through Others and Strategic Planning") and Chapter 20 ("Creating and Identifying Desirable Workplaces").

Systems Theory (Beginning in the 1950s)

During the past 50 years or so, management theorists have begun to recognize the importance of the interactions between individuals and organizational structures, thus giving birth to a systems thinking approach to management. Theorists such as Peter Senge and Edward Deming advanced the notion that people do not fail, systems do, and argued that policies, processes, and infrastructure can influence employee productivity to a significant degree.[14,15] Deming's 1986 work *Out of the Crisis* is considered one of the true management classics and includes "14 points of management."[14] Among these 14 points are "drive out fear," "remove barriers that rob the hourly worker of his right to pride of workmanship," and "institute a vigorous program of education and self-improvement."[14] These points conflict with certain management approaches explicated by human relations theorists, such as Theory X management, and further emphasize a focus on developing an empowered and engaged workforce through considering the effect of organizational systems. Discussion of how these 14 points might be applied to pharmacy operations is included in Chapter 7 ("Pharmacy Operations: Workflow, Practice Activities, Medication Safety, Technology, and Quality").

Synthesizing the Best from Management Theory

It is beyond the scope of this textbook to address every major management theory; however, the aforementioned schools of thought demonstrate an evolution in the way people view the role of management within organizations. Although beliefs about management have changed over time, there is general agreement that management should focus largely on **human capital**—the employees of an organization—and should create structures and adopt practices that support their success.

ESSENTIAL MANAGEMENT COMPETENCIES

The management theories described thus far have addressed a range of belief systems about how to manage people, but effective managers need more than a management philosophy to be effective; they must also demonstrate a variety of critical management competencies (further described in Table 1–4 of Chapter 1, "Leadership Essentials for Pharmacists"). This textbook addresses each com-

petency, and this chapter provides a foundational review of the most critical and basic pharmacy-associated management competencies (some of which will be expounded on in later chapters), including organizational knowledge, human resource management, communication, organizing meetings, planning for crises, time management, "managing up," and self-insight.

Knowledge of Organizational Context and Environment

❸ *Although management fundamentals may be similar from organization to organization, the most effective managers are those who understand the context in which their organizations exist, the organization's unique culture, and the industry- and organization-specific knowledge required to get things done.* Effective pharmacist managers draw on formal and informal resources to learn who is who, what matters, and how things work. How do they obtain this knowledge? They may forge relationships with people throughout their organization, read corporate reports, analyze who is promoted and why, and note which issues receive the most attention from leadership. To be competent practitioners, improve patient care, and achieve organizational goals, they read pharmacy- and medical-related publications, attend professional meetings, and form and leverage relationships with colleagues. By understanding their internal and external environments, these managers are able to understand organizational decisions and pharmacy-related changes, anticipate emerging needs, and help their employees make sense of new directions.

Human Resource Management

Most pharmacist managers are responsible for personnel management activities, including hiring, motivating, engaging, providing **feedback**, evaluating performance, and **coaching** employees. ❹ *Strong managers surround themselves with talented people and develop these individuals into high-performing team members who can translate vision into reality.*

HIRING EXCELLENT PEOPLE

Organizational success is most likely when a manager makes wise choices about the people who join his or her pharmacy team. Hiring the right people is critical to a manager's success, as the right employees are essential for executing projects and achieving results. Many managers view activities related to the search and hiring process as a distraction from their "real work" and begrudge the time spent on this activity. This is unfortunate, as hiring the wrong people wastes valuable time, thereby requiring managers to spend vital hours addressing the mistakes or bad behaviors of these individuals.

Hiring the right people actually starts before the candidate applies. Chapter 18 ("Successful Recruitment and Hiring Strategies") addresses the various elements required to identify and select outstanding talent. Steps described include writing clear job descriptions, identifying essential competencies, employing targeted recruitment strategies, developing effective screening tools, and making job offers. As that chapter notes, the hiring process does not end once a new employee accepts an offer but continues until the orientation process is complete. Once employees are on board, pharmacist managers must work to ensure that they are satisfied and successful.

MOTIVATING AND ENGAGING EMPLOYEES

In management circles, there is some debate about whether managers have the power to motivate employees. Indeed, some people have suggested that it is a manager's job simply to avoid *demotivating* employees.[16] Several management theorists have attempted to determine the exact factors that promote employee motivation. Management scholar Victor Vroom is among them and is best known for developing the expectancy theory, which asserts that an employee's likelihood of tackling a task is related to the probability of the ability to complete it and the possible outcome or consequence of doing so.[17] According to Vroom's expectancy theory, an employee's motivation is influenced by three key factors:[17]

- *Expectancy*: Does the employee believe that he or she can achieve the task? In a pharmacy setting, expectancy could be influenced by the level of pharmacy-related expertise the employee possesses, support and expectations of colleagues and the pharmacy

manager, and adequate information, equipment, materials, and other resources required to perform the work.
- *Valence*: Does the employee believe that completing the task will be personally beneficial or lead to unfortunate consequences? Examples of positive valence in a pharmacy-related setting may include recognition by peers, appreciation by patients, opportunities to work on new projects, a pay raise, or even a promotion. Negative valence could include being assigned a disliked task, such as ordering supplies just because one demonstrates attention to details, or suffering scorn from coworkers for being the one the pharmacist manager praises for constantly doing more than is required or expected.
- *Instrumentality*: What is the probability that completing the task will lead to the outcome desired by the individual? For example, a pharmacist in a hospital pharmacy setting may consider becoming certified in oncology or in diabetes education to advance to a position managing oncology or diabetes therapy. If the employee receives information that suggests that hiring officials will not consider this certification in the selection process, he may choose not to pursue it. Similarly, if employees observe that employees who do the bare minimum at work are rewarded to the same degree as those who consistently perform at exceptional levels, high performers may cease to demonstrate extra effort.[17]

As experienced pharmacist managers know, motivating employees to complete tasks is not enough to build a successful organization that provides superior patient care. Steps must be taken to engage employees. Engaged employees are excited about their work and see a clear link between their efforts, their future, and the organization's long-term success. According to a 2008 BlessingWhite study on employee engagement, "engaged employees are 'enthused' and 'in gear' using their talents and discretionary efforts to make a difference in their employer's quest for sustainable business success."[18] Thus, engagement enhances performance, increases discretionary efforts, strengthens commitment, and supports retention. Refer to

Chapter 13 ("Achieving Results Through Others and Strategic Planning") and Chapter 20 ("Creating and Identifying Desirable Workplaces").

Given the positive potential of employee engagement, how can pharmacist managers ensure that their employees are fully engaged? ❺ *Although competitive and equitable pay matters, decades of research and hundreds of studies have demonstrated that, while money can be a demotivator, it rarely matters most to employees.*[19] *Many pharmacists enter the profession because they are interested in providing patient care; however, other motivation factors are in play, among them, interesting, challenging, and purposeful work; recognition and appreciation; a sense of accomplishment; and growth opportunities, including the opportunity to acquire new knowledge and build connections with others.*[20,21] **Table 2–2** lists nonmonetary motivators.

Most people, pharmacy personnel among them, are motivated by one of six needs: (1) attainment, (2) power, (3) belonging, (4) independence, (5) respect, and (6) equity; these factors are described in **Table 2–3**.[22] As described in Chapter 20 ("Creating and Identifying Desirable Workplaces"), these needs can be translated into elements of the **employee value proposition**— what an employer offers to its employees in exchange for their effort and commitment.[23] The employee value proposition comprises five key components:[23]

- *Affiliation*: The feeling of belonging to an admirable organization that shares one's values
- *Work content*: The satisfaction that comes from the work one does
- *Career*: Long-term opportunities for development and advancement in the organization
- *Benefits*: Programs that support health, wellness, work–life balance, and financial security
- *Compensation*: Direct financial rewards

The importance of these factors varies by individual, by profession, and even by organizational affiliation. For example, a pharmaceutical sales representative may be motivated by opportunities associated with the pharmaceutical industry (such as travel) more than a pharmacist who chooses to work for a pediatric hospital to care for children or a pharmacist-clinical researcher who enjoys translational science and the autonomy of an academic setting. One's life stage may influence motivational factors as well. New pharmacists may value the opportunity to acquire new skills in order to advance, while senior pharmacists may be more concerned about benefits and job security. Likewise, some employees may be content to focus on their specific work assignments, while others want to understand how their work contributes to larger organizational goals and may enjoy learning about organizational **metrics**, patient care expectations, marketing and advertising tasks, budgets, and financial obligations such as controlling inventory. For example, a medication delivery assistant who delivers medications to nursing units will better appreciate the importance of accurately delivering medications if he or she understands that a key departmental metric is to have 100% "on time" unit delivery of all medications.

What is the best way to determine what motivates your staff? Ask.[22,24] For further details on linking employee responsibilities to organizational goals, refer to Chapter 13 ("Achieving Results Through Others and Strategic Planning").

ESTABLISHING GOALS AND PERFORMANCE STANDARDS, AND PROVIDING FEEDBACK

Employees look to their managers to establish clear expectations regarding work performance and results and want to know which performance standards or outcome measures, including behaviors and metrics, will be used to evaluate their performance. Gallup Organization research has revealed that employees are more likely to be engaged in their work when they know what is expected of them.[1] Orientation programs are often helpful in demonstrating correct application of skills and explaining information systems and processes but generally do not explain what expectations an employee must meet and how performance is measured. Therefore, pharmacist managers should be explicit about standards of performance and provide specific goals and expectations for each project or work assignment.[1,25] To verify that employees understand these goals and expectations, employees should be asked to explain goals and expectations in their own words. A dialogue between manager and employee can clarify

TABLE **2–2**	Examples of Nonmonetary Motivators

Method	Description	Examples in Pharmacy Practice
Recognition	Recognize people's achievements. This lets people know their efforts are appreciated and facilitates work for future recognition.	Publicly recognizing the technician or pharmacist who routinely provides excellent customer service.
Celebration	Celebrate victories along the way. Celebrations do not have to be large scale—they can be as simple as tickets to a ball game or lunch coupons to a local restaurant.	Organize a potluck luncheon with your staff. Everyone can participate in the celebration of their own achievements.
Compelling mission	Create a mission that everyone adheres to. The best creation process incorporates everyone's input to develop a strong mission.	Seek input from your pharmacy staff and others to develop a medication use safety mission statement for the department. Safety is everyone's job, and this will help everyone get on board with achieving this critical task.
Balance of achievement and challenge	People want to accomplish their goals while still knowing there is room to grow. They need achievements as much as they need new challenges. Give employees ways to exert control or influence over their work. Most people have a psychological need to shape their daily lives, rather than react helplessly as crises hit them from all sides. You will not only motivate your staff but also cut their stress level by respecting their ability to call at least some of the shots.	Involve your pharmacists and technicians in the strategic planning of the department and organization. By including them, you will produce buy-in from them as they provide input into the direction of the pharmacy. They will be properly challenged and rewarded as they take notice that their own input was listened to and has provided challenges back to them. Once achieved, the victory will be even sweeter.
Increased responsibility	One of the most often cited reasons for employees to put in extra effort is having responsibility for results. By allowing employees to make decisions and produce results on their own, they will be more motivated to volunteer and go beyond the call of duty.	Create a department report card, and let the staff choose the things they want to be measured on. Help them understand the importance of each metric to the department. Then, make each of them responsible for achieving the best possible scores.

TABLE **2-3**	Factors Influencing Motivation

Factors Influencing Motivation	Strategy
Attainment	Motivate these employees by constantly introducing new tasks that build on one another. Allow them to work toward both short- and long-term goals, thus creating a record of achievement and growth.
Power	Treat these employees like in-house experts, and frequently ask them for advice. This will instantly plug into what makes them feel motivated because they will savor the chance to offer their opinions and see that you take them seriously.
Belonging	Because these individuals find the social aspects of their job to be the most meaningful, you can motivate them by making them feel like they are part of a larger group. For example, arrange meetings where they can collaborate and share ideas, or assign them to project teams. Organize lunches to enable them to connect with others.
Independence	Provide clear goals and allow these employees to find the best way to produce results. When possible, offer them the flexibility to set their own hours and choose projects.
Respect	Recognize the contributions and acknowledge the value of these employees' opinions. Give them time to express their perspective, and do not interrupt them while they are talking. Listen to them carefully and provide them with undivided attention when interacting. If you choose not to follow one of their recommendations, explain your rationale.
Equity	Take care to be fair when making decisions about your staff's work schedules, job titles, scope of responsibilities, pay, and benefits to ensure there are no hints of inequities. Explain your rationale for making decisions so that employees will understand the process you used to make choices. Invite employees to speak up in the event they believe they have been treated inequitably.

Source: Data from Cohen WA. *The Art of a Leader*. Englewood Cliffs, NJ: Prentice Hall; 1990.

potential misunderstandings. As reviewed in **Table 2–4**, all goals for employees should be SMART: **s**pecific, **m**easurable, **a**greed upon, **r**easonable, and **t**ime based.[25]

In addition to setting performance goals and expectations, pharmacist managers should also provide performance feedback. All employees require regular feedback about things that are working well and aspects of their performance that merit attention. However, it is not uncommon to hear employees say that the only time they receive feedback is during their annual evaluation. Although an annual evaluation is an excellent opportunity to review overall performance, there

TABLE **2-4**	SMART Goals

- **Specific**

  Well defined

  Clear to anyone that has a basic knowledge of the project

- **Measurable**

  Know whether the goal is obtainable and how far away completion is

  Know when it has been achieved

- **Agreed upon**

  Agreement with all the stakeholders on what the goals should be

- **Realistic**

  Within the availability of resources, knowledge, and time

- **Time based**

  Enough time to achieve the goal

  Not too much time, which can affect project performance

Source: Data from Gibson CL. *Performance Appraisals*. New York, NY: Barnes and Noble Publishing; 2004.

should be ongoing communication between managers and employees throughout the year. ◆*Feedback serves as both a preventive and a corrective measure; it is a mechanism not only to help identify and develop solutions to potential work-related barriers or problems but also to get assignments back on track when problems arise or when mistakes are made. Therefore, feedback is a critical aspect of managing employees and accomplishing desired results. Failing to provide feedback is a failure to manage.* Ongoing communication allows managers and employees to "trade knowledge"—managers are provided updates, or progress reports, on the status of work assignments, and employees receive advice, guidance, feedback, and support regarding their efforts.[1,25] Ongoing communication also provides the opportunity for managers and employees to modify strategies and performance outcome measures as necessary. As a result, feedback is a

common and expected occurrence in the work environment, rather than a rare, yearly event.

Curiously, providing feedback to employees is a challenge for some managers, and, as discussed in Chapter 19 ("Effective Performance Management"), managers can be feedback averse and reluctant to tell both new and experienced employees how to do their jobs better.[1,25,26] While a fear of upsetting or alienating employees is often the foundation for this reluctance, not providing feedback can have unfortunate consequences. When employees do not know how they are performing, they make assumptions, "filling in the gaps" with their own best guesses. Although short-term results may not be compromised, incorrect assumptions often lead to negative long-term consequences.[1,25,26] Some managers find it easier to provide feedback once they reframe their thinking about it. Rather than providing constructive

TABLE **2–5**	Emotional Intelligence

Emotional Intelligence Is a Skill That Requires:	Description
Developing a high self-awareness	With high self-awareness, you are able to monitor yourself (observe yourself in action) to influence your actions so that they work to your benefit. It is the foundation on which all other emotional intelligence skills are built.
Managing emotions	Unlike suppressing your emotions, which deprives you of valuable information your emotions can give you, managing your emotions means understanding them and then using that understanding to deal with situations productively.
Motivating yourself	When you are self-motivated, you are able to begin a task or assignment, stick with it, and move ahead to completion, all while dealing with any setbacks that may arise.
Developing effective communication skills	Communication is the basis of any relationship. It establishes connections, and connections forge relationships.
Developing interpersonal expertise	This requires deep connections with others to exchange information meaningfully and appropriately.
Helping others help themselves	This means helping others to manage their emotions, communicate effectively, solve their problems, resolve their conflicts, and become motivated.

Sources: Data from Weisinger H. *Emotional Intelligence at Work: The Untapped Edge for Success*. San Francisco, CA: Jossey-Bass Publishers; 1998. Goleman D. *Emotional Intelligence: Why It Can Matter More Than IQ*. New York, NY: Bantam Books; 2005.

criticism, managers can "support employee success by providing work-related advice." Providing feedback in this manner requires using **emotional intelligence** (**Table 2–5**) and **social intelligence**.[25-29] Daniel Goleman, psychologist, journalist, and author of the best-selling books *Emotional Intelligence* and *Social Intelligence* asserts that noncognitive skills can matter as much or more than intelligence quotient (IQ) for workplace achievement.[29,30] Emotional intelligence, defined as the ability to assess and manage the emotions of self and others, and social intelligence, defined as the ability to understand and manage human interactions and relations, require a great deal of maturity and security on the man-

ager's part.[28,31] When managers view feedback as a development opportunity that benefits both the organization and the employee, rather than a punitive measure, they often find it easier to be honest and direct. Further, if employees believe that feedback is offered to help them improve, they are more likely to listen and make the suggested changes. For further details, refer to Chapter 19 ("Effective Performance Management"), Chapter 21 ("Communicating Effectively with Others"), and Chapter 23 ("Managing Conflict and Building Consensus").

As noted in Chapter 19 ("Effective Performance Management"), useful feedback requires a manager to focus on observable actions. Focusing on actions and their consequences rather than perceived motivations minimizes defensive and unproductive reactions. For example, "You have arrived more than 30 minutes late three times this week, and this has made it difficult for us to make patient rounds" is more appropriate and accurate than "You don't care about your coworkers." When providing feedback, managers should[26,32]

- *Be direct.* Some managers try to give criticism by mixing good feedback with negative information—referred to as the "sandwich technique." The premise of this approach is that employees will be more open to negative feedback if it is blended with compliments.[33] For example, "You did a great job organizing the continuing education program; I just wish you'd demonstrate the same attention to detail when marketing our employee prescription program. You can be really focused and organized when you want to, so I hope you work on that." As clever as managers may perceive themselves to be, the sandwich technique does not work. Most employees will see through the ploy and dwell solely on the criticism.[26,32] The sandwich approach also conditions employees to ignore positive feedback when it is provided, expecting it to be followed by some form of criticism.
- *Rely on evidence.* Managers should collect information before expressing concern about a situation.[26,32,33] Assumptions are dangerous and can create unnecessary ill will. As noted in Chapter 23 ("Managing Conflict and Building Consensus"), phrases like "I'm concerned about . . ." and "Can you help me understand . . ." give managers the opportunity to discuss performance concerns in a nonthreatening manner.
- *Talk about the employee, not themselves.* When some managers get nervous, they work to alleviate their anxiety by talking about a more comfortable subject—themselves.[26,33] Rather than describing concerns clearly and proposing a solution that helps an employee perform better, nervous managers may lapse into a monologue in which they discuss their own feelings, worries, or experiences that may or may not relate to the issue at hand.[26,32,33]

- *Provide positive feedback in a public way and negative feedback in a private way.* Good managers know that employees should never be criticized in front of others. The goal of feedback is to increase employee performance, and a sense of confidence and motivation is critical for that to occur.[26,32,33]
- *Let employees propose their own solutions.* Suggestions offer hints, insights, or observations that the listener can choose to embrace or reject. When there are performance issues, this approach is generally more welcome than explicit advice that includes specific steps, actions, and instructions.[33] Effective managers pinpoint the action or behavior of concern, describe the desired behavior or outcome, and then partner with the employee to support his or her success.[33]
- *Express confidence in the employee's ability to be successful.* Employee motivation is significantly influenced by whether they believe they can complete a given task or assignment.[17] Let employees know you believe in their abilities and expect them to succeed.

COACHING TO SUCCESS

When employee performance is less than what it should be, and simple feedback is not enough to improve performance, employees may need more active support to be successful. Just as professional football players benefit from a coach who is trustworthy and credible—someone who identifies individual talents, provides feedback to encourage improvement, strategically positions players in the field, and facilitates team bonding experiences to achieve team goals effectively—employees benefit from coaching to ensure they are doing the right things in the right ways. Coaching is an interactive process through which managers and supervisors aim to enhance employee performance and capabilities.[34] The process relies on collaboration and is based on three components: (1) technical help, (2) personal support, and (3) individual challenge.[34,35] These three coaching elements are held together by a bond between the manager/coach and the direct report/coachee. When coaching is done well, it may actually produce less work for managers in the long run by[7] (1) developing employee skills and enabling managers to

delegate more; (2) increasing productivity by teaching employees how to work smarter and effectively collaborate; (3) improving retention, especially among those employees whom managers most want to retain; and (4) fostering a positive work culture that can increase job satisfaction and motivation.[34] Effective coaching requires identifying specific performance gaps, identifying options to address the performance issue, agreeing on indicators of progress, monitoring progress, and recognizing when improvements have occurred.

Communicating with Impact

❼ *Communication is one of the most important management competencies and includes sharing information through verbal means, body language, written documents, and compelling presentations. Pharmacist managers who master communication have a unique ability to connect with people to achieve organizational results.* Strong communicators understand that there are four basic elements of communication: (1) the sender, (2) the receiver, (3) the message, and (4) the environment. Each of these affects the results and the effectiveness of communication. To be successful communicators, pharmacists and pharmacist managers must take responsibility for each element of the communication.[36] Often, senders want to put the responsibility for successful communication on the receivers rather than accept it themselves. When the message does not get through, senders place the blame on the receiver, rather than admit that their own communication skills may have caused the error. They convince themselves that "I don't know how I could have been clearer." Thus, it is important to understand that

- What you say may not be what the receiver hears. People have "filters," a series of barriers that alter the message as it is delivered. Barriers can be the result of past experiences or simply the unfamiliarity that comes from inexperience.
- The sender and the receiver have different levels of interest in the subject matter. People may not be interested in your message, and as a result, they may not hear it completely. Make your message "stick." You must deliver it in a way that communicates the importance of the message to the listener.
- It is up to the sender to realize that a recipient may not be interested in the message.
- Body language, facial expressions, posture, tone, and inflection greatly influence communication.
- Message "packaging" can enhance or inhibit effective transmission. The way messages are delivered can influence whether information is received or ignored. Effective communicators design their messages with their recipients' needs and interests in mind.
- People differ in the ways they like to receive information. Some prefer extensive detail, while others will only want a general overview.
- People often need to receive a message multiple times and in multiple ways.

Strong communication skills are especially important when there is a need to negotiate with others or resolve conflict.

NEGOTIATING WITH OTHERS

Without even being aware of it, we tend to negotiate all day long. "If you can pick up milk, I can swing by the dry cleaners." "I'd be happy to present at the management team meeting if you can help me with the slides." "I'm not in the mood for Italian tonight. Can we have Chinese food instead?" Although most of us are able to negotiate effectively with friends and family members, negotiating within a work setting can be more challenging. In a pharmacy setting, pharmacists and pharmacist managers may negotiate prices or delivery schedules with vendors, formularies with insurance companies, and schedules and duties with employees. Negotiation is a voluntary attempt, through direct dialogue, to achieve goals or resolve conflicts that arise from competing needs, interests, and objectives.

There are many approaches to negotiation; however, the **principled negotiation** approach supports productive and long-term relationships. Principled negotiation is a process designed to reach mutually acceptable solutions based on using objective standards to address the concerns of the individuals or organizations involved.[37] As reviewed in Chapter 22 ("Negotiation Techniques"), effective principled negotiation is a multistep process that involves[37]

- Identifying your own interests
- Seeking to understand the interests of the other party
- Working together to develop potential options
- Evaluating possibilities
- Reaching agreements that benefit both parties

Effective managers use well-developed negotiation techniques to accomplish work and extend resources. They may also use these techniques when faced with individual or organizational conflict.

MANAGING CONFLICT

Managers with strong negotiation skills are typically more equipped to manage conflict than those without these skills. In a pharmacy setting, opportunities for conflict abound. A patient may be angry about the cost of a medication or its side effects. A vendor may object to your corporate accounts payable practices. An employee may take issue with the way you have planned the week's schedule. The possibilities are endless. Conflict situations can often emerge during times of adversity and stress. The ability to plan and develop contingency plans is one way to minimize conflict in the workplace, and the following strategies can help pharmacists and pharmacist managers prepare for and work through employee conflict:[38-40]

- Treat the other person with respect
- Separate people from the problem
- Confront the problem
- Define the conflict by determining the underlying interests
  - Focus on behaviors or problems, not people
  - Define the conflict as a problem to solve together, not a battle to be won
- Communicate understanding
  - Listen to really understand the other person's feelings, needs, etc.
  - Seek first to understand, then to be understood[41]
  - Step back and try to imagine how the other person sees things
  - Explain how you see the problem after you have talked about it; discuss any changes

you have made in the way you see things or how you feel
- Explore alternative solutions
  - Take turns offering alternative solutions, and list them all
  - Be nonjudgmental of others' ideas
  - Examine consequences of each solution
  - Think and talk positively
- Agree on the most workable solution
  - Agree to a solution you both understand and can live with
  - Work to find a "win–win" solution
  - Be committed to resolving the conflict
- Conduct a postnegotiation evaluation
  - Check on how well the solution is working, and adjust the resolution when necessary

Organizing Team Meetings

Team meetings organized by the pharmacist manager are commonplace in a variety of pharmacy settings. Team meetings set the tone for interactions with employees and, for the first-time manager, serve as the true management initiation. Managers should create a supportive, nonthreatening atmosphere in team meetings.[32,42,43] By making everyone feel comfortable, they can build momentum and instill and maintain confidence in their management abilities. Such meetings should occur regularly to keep the team apprised of relevant information, events, and projects. One strategy to prepare for the meeting is to make a list of questions that employees may ask, which should include issues that individuals have already raised in one-on-one meetings. Managers should then consider responses to each question, noting important points to express. Managers should also ask themselves

- What is the key message?
- What words or phrases will best convey the importance of the message?
- What is the best format to communicate clearly and concisely?

If possible, managers should hold meetings in a conference room where everyone can sit together and arrange the seats in a circle so that all participants are positioned as peers. This fosters a close-knit, collegial feeling. If people are too scattered, retreat into their own space, or form "camps," it will be harder to rally them as a group. A classroom-style setting can create an invisible barrier between manager and staff because the rows of seats may make employees feel like students (and they will perceive the manager as the teacher/taskmaster). This is also true for a U-shaped conference setup with the manager at the head of the table.

SUPPORTING TEAM SUCCESS

Both team and individual employee meetings may be used by managers to identify issues and problems significant to employees.[32,42,43] This information helps to focus efforts and produce results. There is no better way to establish and maintain momentum as a manager than to demonstrate responsiveness to the team's concerns.[33] Ways to address employee concerns and demonstrate support for the success of the team include the following:

- *Remove long-standing irritants.* The longer something has plagued employees, the more heroic the manager will appear if he or she addresses the problem.[44–46]
- *Simplify their lives.* Managers should find ways to make their employees' jobs easier; for example, eliminate a needless policy or procedure.[20,45]
- *Assign team leaders to recommend solutions.* Convening a team every time employees mention a problem can get managers into trouble, especially if they are not ready to act on employees' suggestions. However, managers can use this approach effectively by distributing a precise timetable to each team leader (chosen by teammates, and not necessarily the manager) that outlines when a list of proposed solutions should be submitted *and* commits to a response date.[20,45,46]
- *Provide necessary resources.* To accomplish goals, resources will be required. The type and amount of resources needed are a function of the goal and resources available. Managers should ask what resources are needed to accomplish a task and determine whether the request is within reason. Moreover, managers should review the request and communicate which resources can be obtained.

- *Provide training.* Trained and competent employees are one of the organization's and manager's greatest resources. Pharmacist managers should instill a culture of competency and learning.

Planning for Crises

8 *Effective managers are good planners who manage their time well, establish reasonable budgets, deploy people appropriately, and prepare for contingencies. Managers cannot possibly prevent all emergencies, but they can take steps to minimize surprises.* Refer to Chapter 10 ("Cents and Sensibilities: Understanding the Numbers") and Chapter 14 ("Pharmacy Business and Staff Planning"). Nothing kills momentum like a crisis. It can arise out of nowhere and deplete everyone's energy. Although managers cannot possibly "put out every fire before it ignites," they can take steps to reduce risks. This requires a high level of readiness and preparation. Take, for example, a pharmacy that faces the depletion of an important medication in its pharmacy stock. A prepared manager and department would have a plan in place to obtain emergency supplies. By anticipating what can go wrong and devising strategies to guard against such occurrences, managers are able to impose at least some order on an otherwise disorderly universe of work-related mishaps.[47]

8 *Although crisis-level events are generally considered negative, they can open doors to more positive opportunities and possibilities.* Crises often force us to think creatively and to develop innovative solutions. For example, one retail pharmacy experienced a sharp increase in demand for prescription dispensing just as two staff pharmacists resigned. This crisis threatened to derail the pharmacist manager's plan to implement two new services, immunization and medication therapy management (MTM), for two reasons: (1) the staff pharmacists who resigned were primarily responsible for these new services and (2) the remaining staff pharmacists were already overburdened by the increased prescription-dispensing demand (although two of these individuals were trained and motivated to provide the new services). Rather than allow the crisis to overwhelm her, the manager decided to identify opportunities the crisis presented. To meet the increased prescription-dispensing demand (which was expected to be ongoing), the manager negotiated the purchase and implementation of robotics and other automation that could help meet prescription-filling needs. The installation of this technology allowed the manager to use those staff pharmacists who wanted to be involved in immunizations and MTM services without having to hire more pharmacists. As a result, prescription demand was met in a timely manner and the new services were implemented; in turn, greater income was generated and patient satisfaction increased. Thus, the pharmacist manager was successfully able to create opportunity from crisis. Another strategy the pharmacist manager may have considered was using a regional filling center. As a result of economic challenges, some chain pharmacies implemented regional prescription-filling centers for chronic medications and used local stores for acute and new prescription-filling. A benefit of this approach is that it allows local pharmacies to concentrate the efforts of their pharmacists on more direct patient care services rather than dispensing-only functions.

Managing Time

Demands on pharmacists and pharmacist managers are intense, thus time management skills are an especially important management competency. Managing time requires understanding one's workload, identifying priority tasks, staying organized, and remaining flexible in the face of emergent situations. Managers can employ several strategies to better manage their time, including establishing explicit priorities, using to-do lists, establishing meeting agendas, and using scheduling and organizational tools, such as electronic calendars and personal digital assistants. Additional information on time management is provided in Chapter 24 ("Managing Your Time").

Delegating

Effective delegation is one of the best time management skills a manager can develop, and **Table 2–6** lists some examples of day-to-day activities that may be considered for delegation in a pharmacy. ◆9 *Delegation is most effective when manag-*

ers:[48] *(1)* **entrust** *employees with a job; (2) give employees adequate freedom to get a job done (the act of empowering employees); (3) provide employees with the appropriate level of support to get the job done well, including information, training, and resources; and (4) hold employees accountable to produce desirable outcomes. Thus, managers do not have to be hands-on for the right outcomes to occur, but neither do they have to be uninvolved and unaware of what is occurring.*[49]

As a pharmacist manager, you must accept one hard fact: you cannot do it all. You should resist the urge to finish what your employees start—realize that, even though you may need to wait another hour for someone to complete a task you could have done easily, that hour is a wise investment in the future. Managers save many hours over the long run by giving employees enough time to grapple with tasks and gain the experience they need to be successful. If employees grow and continually sharpen their skills, then they will become more valuable assets and be positioned to perform their work with more enthusiasm and confidence.[50]

Most employees thrive in a culture of autonomy and will work hard to exceed their manager's expectations. The key to autonomy is establishing and communicating clear guidelines and expectations. Managers need to determine (1) which decisions to make versus which decisions to delegate; (2) how frequently to communicate; and (3) goals and performance metrics. If you find it hard to delegate, consider the worst-case scenario if things go awry postdelegation. Errors may occur; but most of the time, you will likely be able to find solutions and take appropriate measures. Delegation is most likely to lead to successful outcomes when the manager is willing to[51]

- *Select qualified individuals.* Ensuring that the employee has the necessary skill set to accomplish the task is critical.
- *Delegate tasks of significance.* Delegating "grunt work," rather than work with meaning and importance, can reduce morale and increase turnover.
- *Exhibit confidence.* Exuding confidence while delegating eases anxiety the employee might

TABLE **2–6**	Examples of Day-to-Day Activities That May Be Delegated in a Pharmacy Setting

- Solving fairly routine patient care and dispensing problems.
- Setting the daily work schedule and work flow.
- Preparing agendas for regular staff meetings.
- Making decisions on situations that employees face in carrying out their responsibilities.
- Handling technical duties—for example, troubleshooting of automation, scheduling, or reconciling time worked.
- Compiling data—for example, medication error tracking, capital expenses, or tracking medication waste.
- Composing administrative reports.
- Conducting research.
- Training new employees.
- Handling vendor-relation issues.

have about completing a new or difficult project.

- *Delegate the proper authority to complete the task and convey accountability for completion.* Clarification of the resources available and expectations of outcomes equip the employee with knowledge of the tools and expectations of the manager.
- *Supervise according to employees' follow-up style.* Know the amount (frequently to rarely) and type (hands-on to hands-off) of supervision that works best for each employee.
- *Give employees room to fail (and then hopefully succeed).* Certain components of projects lend themselves to more latitude for the employee to make decisions, and learning from making a wrong choice can often be a beneficial experience.
- *Provide adequate directions and ensure that the employee understands them.* The manner in which managers provide directions for delegated tasks plays an important role in how

others respond.[52] Many employees need extra time to process instructions and gain confidence that they understand how to follow them. Therefore, managers should make sure they have a suitable amount of time set aside to provide adequate instructions, rather than trying to give instructions while pressed for time. If managers deny employees the opportunity to absorb directions and ask questions, then errors are more likely.[51]

- *Focus on outcomes rather than deadlines.* Effective managers give reasonable deadlines and trust employees to get the work done without excessive follow-up.[51]
- *Treat employees like grown-ups.* Employees are not children and should not be treated as such. Managers must not delegate with the assumption that employees are unable to understand simple directions. If obvious points are repeated needlessly in a condescending tone, employees will almost certainly feel offended and alienated. As a result,

they may spend more energy resenting the manager's communication style than listening to the content of his or her message.[51]

- *Give praise and credit for work well done.* Good managers not only delegate and direct but make certain to acknowledge the efforts of their employees.

Managers who are unable to delegate may have what organizational psychologists refer to as **self-enhancement bias**, a psychological condition in which an individual grows convinced that he or she is the only one who can produce the necessary level of acceptable work.[53] In perpetuating this bias, the individual disregards or discounts employees' skills, attitudes, and contributions. He or she gains an inflated sense of importance by repeatedly claiming to have skills, talents, experience, and intuitive ability that far exceed others. The biased manager eventually concludes that he or she should "just do it all" or else the unit's work will suffer. In truth, self-enhancement bias is detrimental to successful management, as you risk alienating employees and becoming overwhelmed with the amount of work that needs to be done. Relinquishing activities that can be delegated and empowering your staff are quintessential traits of effective pharmacist managers.

"Managing Up"

Managing one's manager is another management competency. ⑩ *"Managing up" is the process of consciously working with your boss to obtain the best possible results for you, your boss, and your organization.*[54] *"Managing" in this context is not the result of formal authority over one's supervisor but rather is a method for developing a positive and effective working relationship with him or her.*[55] Managing up is also a deliberate effort to bring understanding and cooperation to a relationship between individuals who often have different perspectives.[56,57] **Table 2–7** addresses several managing up strategies.[22,24,26,27,33,34,44–46,58–62] Managing up may seem counterintuitive in a world of top-down organizational structures.[63] Many new pharmacist managers often invest significant time and effort in managing the personnel they directly supervise, yet they take a passive approach to managing their supervisors. Doing so can harm personnel and the

organization. For example, failure to manage the boss can result in misunderstandings about what you expect from one another and can cause you to waste time on tasks that are not congruent with organizational goals. Furthermore, career progress and satisfaction rarely occur if pharmacists and pharmacist managers do not manage their respective bosses or supervisors. The following are areas on which you as a pharmacist or pharmacist manager should concentrate to build a solid relationship with your boss:[64–67]

- Clarify roles and expectations so that both you and your boss understand your tasks, responsibilities, and priorities.
- Know and adhere to your boss's work and communication styles to facilitate effective interactions.[64,65] For example, if your boss likes information presented in writing, prepare well-written reports. If your boss prefers brief executive summaries, provide one-page reports with bulleted content rather than lengthier documents with significant amounts of background information.
- Provide your boss with necessary and complete information, all relevant news (whether good or bad), and your concerns/issues/positions, so that he or she can make accurate and beneficial assessments and decisions on behalf of the organization.[64,66,67]
- Develop a trusting relationship with your boss by being dependable and fulfilling your work commitments.[64,65]
- Assist your boss in better managing his or her time by ensuring that requests of your boss's time are necessary, and address issues and problems on your own when it is appropriate to do so.[64,65]
- Provide your boss with sincerely positive comments and express appreciation so your boss will, in turn, develop positive regard for you.[64,65]
- Disagree with your boss tactfully and respectfully when you believe it is appropriate and in the best interest of the organization.[64]

Accurate Self-Insight

Just as managing your boss is important, managing yourself is also critical, and regular requests for

TABLE 2-7	"Managing Up" Strategies

- **Enhance the reputation of your manager.** Your manager cares as much about his or her career as you do about yours and looks to you to make him or her look smart and successful.[45]
- **Never criticize your manager to others.** There is nothing to be gained by doing this, and the consequences could be more negative for you than for your boss.[33]
- **Never "show up" or correct your manager when others are around.** Do not strive to look good at the expense of your boss.[33,44]
- **Be nice to everyone in the department.** New managers may choose to be nice to the VIPs (very important persons) and ignore others, but that is the worst way to go about ingratiating yourself within the department. If you develop a reputation for elitism, it will reflect poorly on you and your boss.[46]
- **Always give credit where credit is due.** Everyone wants to feel as if the job he or she is doing is important. Keeping up morale around the office by crediting employees when appropriate will send the message to the organization that the department is running well and will reflect well on your boss.[33,45,46]
- **Never put others down.** Disrespect and disloyalty will always reflect poorly on you, the department and ultimately your manager.[33,45,46]
- **Honor your commitments.** If your boss asks you to complete an assignment by tomorrow, have it done. Managers do not typically hand out tight deadlines arbitrarily. It is likely that the assignment is due outside the department, and the tight deadline reflects its importance. Failing to meet the deadline will send a poor message.[33,45,46]
- **Present options to your boss.** In decision making, managers like to see alternatives and the consequences associated with each alternative. You were hired for your expertise—share it. This is particularly critical if the decision may put the department or your boss at risk. It is your responsibility to make sure your boss is aware of any hidden risks that may compromise his or her position or the organization.[45]
- **Pay attention to details.** If you are preparing information for your boss to present to external stakeholders, double-check your work. If you put your boss in a situation where he or she looks bad in front of management, you have not only hurt your credibility but also your boss's credibility.[33,45,46]
- **Find out how often and in what manner your manager wants to hear from you.** Does your manager like daily check-ins, weekly meetings, or something different? Does he prefer phone calls to discuss several items or a series of e-mail messages that tackle one issue at a time?
- **Determine your manager's preferred communication style.** Does your manager like information provided in conversations or in writing? Does he or she like a lot of detail or is an executive summary more his or her style? Providing information in the way your manager likes to receive it will make you more effective and your manager more satisfied.
- **Remember your priorities.** You will have many assignments delegated to you. It is your responsibility to keep your boss informed of your priority list so that he or she can readjust or reassign work. It is unacceptable to let a critical assignment fall through the cracks because you allowed your work list to derail your priorities without informing your boss.[45]

(continues)

TABLE **2–7**   (continued)

- **Be a role model.** Be a manager who represents the department/unit well. This will increase your functionality and allow your boss to assign you to more diverse assignments.[26,33,45]

- **Serve as a resource.** Make yourself indispensable by collecting pertinent knowledge. Research more than you need to so you will have information when your boss needs it. Keep him or her updated on organizational and professional events and other news. You are his or her eyes and ears on the ground organizationally.[46]

- **Show initiative.** Figure out what projects are making your boss's life more difficult and volunteer to help. If you pay attention to time-consuming projects that aggravate your boss and come up with creative solutions to those projects, you will increase your value.[26,46]

- **Communicate well.** Do not make your boss work to find out information. Package information well so that he or she can easily repackage it for others.[27,45]

- **Check your ego.** While your boss will give you as much credit as he or she can, there are times when the final product must have only his or her name on it. Accept this.[33,45,46]

- **Seek advice and feedback.** Your boss will not want to give you feedback constantly and will likely only tell you the "big things." This does not mean you cannot improve. Make sure your boss knows you are willing to improve and are interested in the intricacies of your job. Key questions for your boss: How can I improve? How can I get ahead? What can I do to make your job easier? Ask for advice on your daily duties and the long-term projects you are tackling. Your boss can be a good resource as he or she has probably encountered a similar situation. If you listen to your boss, you might learn something from his or her experiences.[45]

- **Watch and learn.** You do not know how to do many things. Do not be afraid to let your boss know you need help. He or she would rather know that up front than get a poorly completed assignment late because you were too embarrassed to admit you did not know how to do something. Your boss does not expect you to know everything. He or she does expect you to be adult enough to say so.[34,62]

- **Look professional.** As a manager, you represent the department, not just when you are on duty, but all of the time. Be mindful of your behavior and your dress. Pay close attention to what the senior administrators wear, and model your dress after them. When in doubt, it is better to be too conservative than too casual.[26]

- **Manage your own conflicts.** Your boss does not want to intervene on your behalf or spend his or her political capital to make things right with others. If you are at odds with a colleague, figure out how to resolve it. If you reach an impasse with the director of another unit, use your negotiation and conflict management skills to reach an agreement. Do not send these issues to your boss.[26]

Sources: Data from Cohen WA. *The Art of a Leader.* Englewood Cliffs, NJ: Prentice Hall; 1990. Bennis WG. The seven ages of the leader. *Harv Bus Rev* 2004;82(1):46–53. Hunsaker PL, Alessandra AJ. *The Art of Managing People.* New York, NY: Simon and Schuster Inc; 1980. Weisinger H. *Emotional Intelligence at Work: The Untapped Edge for Success.* San Francisco, CA: Jossey-Bass Publishers; 1998. Gaynor GH. *What Every New Manager Needs to Know: Making a Successful Transition to Management.* New York, NY: AMACOM; 2004. *Coaching and Mentoring: How to Develop Top Talent and Achieve Stronger Performance.* Boston, MA: Harvard Business School Press; 2004. Straub JT. *The Rookie Manager.* New York, NY: AMACOM; 2000. Betof E, Harwood F. *Just Promoted: How to Survive and Thrive in Your First 12 Months as a Manager.* New York, NY: McGraw-Hill; 1992. Finzel H. *The Top Ten Mistakes Leaders Make.* Trenton, NJ: Nexgen Press; 2000. Raiffa H. *The Art and Science of Negotiation.* Boston, MA: Belknap Press; 2005. Brousseau KR, Driver MJ, Hourihan G, Larsson R. The seasoned executive's decision-making style. *Harv Bus Rev* 2006;84(2):110–121. Michelman P, Kleiner A. Debriefing Art Kleiner: how to lead when your influence goes off the (org) chart. *Harv Manag* 2004;9(5). Hogan R, Curphy GJ, Hogan J. What we know about leadership: effectiveness and personality. *Am Psychol* 1994;49:493–504. White SJ. Will there be a pharmacy leadership crisis? An ASHP Foundation Scholar-in-Residence report. *Am J Health Syst-Pharm* 2005;62:845–855.

employee feedback can reveal opportunities to improve your own effectiveness. This chapter focuses a great deal on providing feedback *to* employees to promote their success, but it is equally important for both new and experienced managers to evaluate their own progress periodically by soliciting feedback *from* others.[20,68] On the basis of this feedback, managers can make needed adjustments and improvements. Three ways to solicit employee feedback effectively are to

- *Seek casual advice.* By showing interest in employees' ideas and opinions, managers can increase employees' willingness to provide honest feedback and offer the manager valuable insights.[47,69]
- *Formalize the process.* Ask employees to submit items of concern.[42,70] This can be done through suggestion boxes, focus groups, or an appointed employee **ombudsman**.[43,44] If a manager chooses to use focus groups, he or she should consider asking a neutral person to facilitate the group, as employees may be inhibited by the manager's presence.[20,45,46] Remember, the goal is to get honest feedback.[47,71]
- *Trace changes in behavior.* Managers should be attentive to changes in employee behavior. For example, do they smile and seem comfortable chatting with the manager? Do they volunteer comments when they run into the manager in the hall? Do they station themselves near the manager in a meeting or try to keep a low profile? Armed with these observations, managers should monitor changes in the first month or two on the job. If they notice that someone no longer seems as eager to stop and chat in the cafeteria, for instance, they may want to get input as to why.[54,69,71]

To open communication channels, managers should prepare to listen without lashing out and accept they may hear things that are surprising and upsetting. However, rather than react negatively, managers must maintain their composure. In this way, they condition employees to be open and honest without fear of recrimination or backlash. Peers and colleagues can also be a valuable source of insight and will often provide specific advice and guidance if they believe you genuinely want to enhance your management skills.

SUMMARY

Pharmacists have the unique ability to practice in a variety of different settings, and whether planned or not, pharmacists will likely have opportunities to become managers in these settings. In addition to reviewing an array of management theories, this chapter addresses key management competencies, such as personnel management, communicating with impact, organizing team meetings, planning for crises, managing time, managing up, and developing accurate self-insight. This chapter also provides specific recommendations to increase effectiveness. Each of these elements will be discussed in a more comprehensive manner in subsequent chapters. Armed with solid management skills, pharmacists will have the opportunity to make a difference in their profession and in the lives of others.

References

1. Buckingham M, Coffman C. *First, Break All the Rules: What the World's Greatest Managers Do Differently.* New York, NY: Simon & Schuster Inc; 1999.

2. Frederick FT. *The Principles of Scientific Management.* New York, NY: Harper and Brothers Publishers; 1911.

3. Gilbreth L. *The Psychology of Management.* New York, NY: Sturgis & Walton Company; 1914.

4. Gantt H. *Organizing for Work.* New York, NY: Harcourt, Brace and Howe; 1919.

5. Ratnayake RM. Evolution of scientific management towards performance measurement and managing systems for sustainable performance in industrial assets: philosophical point of view. *J Tech Manag Innovation* 2009;4(1):152–161.

6. Fayol H. *General and Industrial Management*. Storrs C, trans. London: Pitman & Sons Ltd; 1949.

7. Weber M. *The Theory of Social and Economic Organization*. Henderson and Parsons, trans. New York, NY; 1947.

8. Roethlisberger FJ, Dickson WJ. *Management and the Worker: An Account of a Research Program Conducted by the Western Electric Company, Chicago*. Cambridge, MA: Harvard University Press; 1939.

9. Maslow AH. A Theory of Human Motivation. *Psychol Rev* 1943;50(4):370–396.

10. Herzberg F. *The Motivation to Work*. New York, NY: John Wiley & Sons; 1959.

11. McGregor D. *The Human Side of Enterprise*. New York, NY: McGraw-Hill; 1960.

12. Likert R. *The Human Organization: Its Management and Value*. New York, NY: McGraw-Hill; 1967.

13. Ouchi WG. *Theory Z: How American Business Can Meet the Japanese Challenge*. Reading, MA: Addison-Wesley; 1981.

14. Deming, E. *Out of the Crisis*. Cambridge, MA: MIT Press; 2000.

15. Senge P. *The Fifth Discipline: The Art and Practice of the Learning Organization*. New York, NY: Doubleday Currency; 1990.

16. Sirota D, Mischkind LA, Meltzer MI. Why your employees are losing motivation. HBS Working Knowledge, April 10, 2006. Available at: http://hbswk.hbs.edu/archive/5289.html. Accessed August 22, 2009.

17. Vroom V. *Work and Motivation*. Hoboken, NJ: John Wiley & Sons; 1964.

18. BlessingWhite. Employee Engagement Report 2008. Published April–May 2008. Available at: http://www.blessingwhite.com/EEE__report.asp. Accessed August 22, 2009.

19. Fournies FF. *Why Employees Don't Do What They Are Supposed to Do: And What to Do About It*. New York, NY: McGraw-Hill; 1991.

20. Buckingham M. *The One Thing You Need to Know: About Great Managing, Great Leading, and Sustained Individual Success*. New York, NY: Free Press; 2005.

21. Marshall DR. *The Four Elements of Successful Management*. New York, NY: American Management Association; 1999.

22. Cohen WA. *The Art of a Leader*. Englewood Cliffs, NJ: Prentice Hall; 1990.

23. Mulvey PW, Ledford GE Jr, LeBlanc PV. The rewards of work: how they drive performance, retention and satisfaction. *WorldatWork* (formerly *ACA J*) 2000;9: 6–18.

24. Bennis WG. The seven ages of the leader. *Harv Bus Rev* 2004;82(1):46–53.

25. Gibson CL. *Performance Appraisals*. New York, NY: Barnes and Noble Publishing; 2004.

26. Hunsaker PL, Alessandra AJ. *The Art of Managing People*. New York, NY: Simon and Schuster Inc; 1980.

27. Weisinger H. *Emotional Intelligence at Work: The Untapped Edge for Success*. San Francisco, CA: Jossey-Bass Publishers; 1998.

28. Goleman D. *Emotional Intelligence: Why It Can Matter More Than IQ*. New York, NY: Bantam Books; 2005.

29. Goleman D. *Social Intelligence: The New Science of Human Relationships*. New York, NY: Bantam Books; 2006.

30. Goleman D. *Working with Emotional Intelligence*. New York, NY: Bantam Books; 2000.

31. Thorndike EL. Intelligence and its use. *Harper's Magazine* 1920;140:227–235.

32. Robbins H, Finley M. *The Accidental Leader: What to Do When You Are Suddenly in Charge*. San Francisco, CA: Jossey-Bass; 2004.

33. Gaynor GH. *What Every New Manager Needs to Know: Making a Successful Transition to Management*. New York, NY: AMACOM; 2004.

34. *Coaching and Mentoring: How to Develop Top Talent and Achieve Stronger Performance*. Boston, MA: Harvard Business School Press; 2004.

35. Hill LA. *Becoming a Manager: How New Managers Master the Challenge of Leadership*. New York, NY: Penguin Books; 1992.

36. Robbins S. Seven communication mistakes managers make. *Harv Manag Update* 2009;14(2). Available at: http://blogs.harvardbusiness.org/hmu/2009/03/seven-communication-mistakes-m.html. Accessed August 22, 2009.

37. Fisher R, Ury W, Patton B. *Getting to Yes: Negotiating Agreement Without Giving In*. 2nd ed. New York, NY: Penguin Books; 1991.

38. Gentile M, Gant SB. *Managing Conflict in a Diverse Workplace*. Boston, MA: Harvard Business Publishing; 1995.

39. Barsky AE. *Conflict Resolution for the Helping Professions*. Stamford, CT: Brooks-Cole; 2000.

40. Lundin W, Lundin K. *Working with Difficult People*. New York, NY: American Management Association; 1995.

41. Covey SR. *The 7 Habits of Highly Effective People*. 1st ed. New York, NY: Simon & Schuster, Fireside Division; 1989.

42. Arden P. *It's Not How Good You Are, It's How Good You Want to Be*. New York, NY: Phaidon Press Ltd; 2003.

43. Stettner M. *Skills for New Managers*. New York, NY: McGraw-Hill; 2000.

44. Straub JT. *The Rookie Manager*. New York, NY: AMACOM; 2000.

45. Betof E, Harwood F. *Just Promoted: How to Survive and Thrive in Your First 12 Months as a Manager*. New York, NY: McGraw-Hill; 1992.

46. Finzel H. *The Top Ten Mistakes Leaders Make*. Trenton, NJ: Nexgen Press; 2000.

47. Broadwell MM, Dietrich, CB. *The New Supervisor: How to Thrive in Your First Year as a Manager*. Cambridge, MA: Perseus Books; 1998.

48. Goldsmith M. How can I become better at delegating? *Harv Manag Update* 2007;12(12):1.

49. Johnson LK. Are you delegating so it sticks? *Harv Manag Update* 2007;12(9)3–5.

50. Katzenbach JR, Smith DK. The discipline of teams. *Harv Bus Rev* 2005;83(7/8):162–171.

51. Finzel H. *The Top Ten Mistakes Leaders Make*. Colorado Springs, CO: Cook Communications Ministries; 2000.

52. Kalyanam K, Zweben M. The perfect message at the perfect moment. *Harv Bus Rev* 2005;83(11):112–120.

53. Hill LA. Becoming the boss. *Harv Bus Rev* 2007; 85(1):48–56.

54. Bittel LR, Newstrom JW. *What Every Supervisor Should Know*. New York, NY: McGraw-Hill; 1990.

55. Woodward BW. The journey to professional excellence: a matter of priorities. *Am J Health-Syst Pharm* 1998;55:782–789.

56. Kubica AJ, White SJ. Leading from the middle: positioning for success. *Am J Health-Syst Pharm* 2007;64: 1739–1742.

57. Zilz DA, Woodward BW, Thielke TS, Shane RR, Scott B. Leadership skills for a high performance pharmacy practice. *Am J Health-Syst Pharm* 2004;61:2562–2574.

58. Raiffa H. *The Art and Science of Negotiation*. Boston, MA: Belknap Press; 2005.

59. Brousseau KR, Driver MJ, Hourihan G, Larsson R. The seasoned executive's decision-making style. *Harv Bus Rev* 2006;84(2):110–121.

60. Michelman P, Kleiner A. Debriefing Art Kleiner: how to lead when your influence goes off the (org) chart. *Harv Manag* 2004;9(5).

61. Hogan R, Curphy GJ, Hogan J. What we know about leadership: effectiveness and personality. *Am Psychol* 1994;49:493–504.

62. White SJ. Will there be a pharmacy leadership crisis? An ASHP Foundation Scholar-in-Residence report. *Am J Health Syst Pharm* 2005;62:845–855.

63. *Effective Pharmacy Management*. Kansas City, MO: Marion Merrell Dow Inc; 1993.

64. Gabarro JJ, Kotter JP. Managing your boss. *Harv Bus Rev* 2005;83(1):92–99.

65. Mark SM. Succession planning: the forgotten art. *Hosp Pharm* 2008;43:593–600.

66. Zuber TJ, James EH. Managing your boss. *Fam Pract Manag 2001*. Available at: http://www.aafp.org/fpm/20010600/33mana.html. Accessed February 19, 2009.

67. Pearce C. Ten steps to managing change. *Nurs Manag* 2007;13:25.

68. Thomas KW, Kilmann RH. Thomas-Kilmann Conflict Mode Instrument (A). CPP 2007. Available at: https://www.cpp.com/products/tki/index.aspx. Accessed December 20, 2009.

69. Blanchard K, Bowles S. *Raving Fans: A Revolutionary Approach to Customer Service*. New York, NY: William Morrow and Company Inc; 1993.

70. Mehrabian, A. Communication without words. *Psychol Today* 1968;2(9):52–55.

71. Templar, R. *The Rules of Management: A Definitive Code for Managerial Success*. Upper Saddle River, NJ: Prentice Hall; 2005.

Abbreviations

IQ:	intelligence quotient
MTM:	medication therapy management
SMART:	specific, measurable, agreed upon, realistic, and time based
VIPs:	very important persons

Case Scenarios

CASE ONE: Mark Anderson is the pharmacist manager at a community pharmacy. Raul, his lead pharmacist, works on projects with Mark frequently. Because Mark is a busy person, he relies heavily on Raul to make decisions that will lead to successful execution of the projects. What would you recommend to Raul to help him be more successful in his work with the manager, Mark?

CASE TWO: Cara Douglas, one of the hospital's pharmacists, is suddenly appearing complacent. She does all that is required, but never anything more. Her manager is struggling to figure out what has happened and what can be done to turn it around. When he said to Dr. Douglas point blank, "Cara, You're not your old self," she responded, "That's because I'm bored. How many more days can I count pills and put them in a bottle, and feel like my life has meaning?" How should Dr. Douglas' manager respond?

CASE THREE: You are the assistant pharmacy director at an urban medical center. Your boss, the pharmacy director, recently instituted new operational procedures to which pharmacy staff members have expressed resistance. These staff members have complained to you about the new procedures on several occasions. What strategies might you employ to "manage up" and "down" in this situation?

CASE FOUR: Adam Ryan has recently been thrust into a management position in his pharmacy. He has been around for a long time and understands both the political landscape and major issues facing the department. After Dr. Ryan's first meeting, he realizes there is much work to be done: (1) decreasing the amount of documentation required for simple operations; (2) removing a grumpy, part-time business manager when the job clearly requires a full-time employee; and (3) encouraging staff to focus on patient counseling activities instead of other unnecessary activities, such as nonrequired paperwork. Dr. Ryan quickly needs to build relationships with his team members to create momentum toward achieving desired outcomes. How could he score "quick wins" in order to accomplish this?

CASE FIVE: Kimberly Lewis is a young pharmacist who is highly motivated and a detail-oriented individual. Recently, Kimberly has been asked to lead a high-profile project for the pharmacy. As a manager, you need Kimberly to succeed with this project because, although it is a high-profile project, you have 10 other high-profile projects that are consuming your time. However, you will still be responsible for her success or failure. Discuss how you as a manager will prepare Kimberly to take on the role of project leader and provide Kimberly with clear goals to help her succeed.

Additional Resources Available Online!

Visit the Student Companion Web site at http://healthprofessions.jbpub.com/pharmacymanagement for interactive study tools and additional resources.

See www.rxugace.com to learn how you can obtain continuing pharmacy education for this content.

CHANGE AND INNOVATION

CHAPTER 3

LEADING AND MANAGING CHANGE

MARIE A. CHISHOLM-BURNS, PharmD, MPH, FCCP, FASHP

JOSEPH T. DIPIRO, PharmD, FCCP

BRENNA NEUMANN, PharmD

LEARNING OBJECTIVES

After completing the chapter, the reader will be able to

1. List some change drivers associated with pharmacy and health care.
2. Describe general outcomes associated with failure to change.
3. Cite eight errors common to organizational change efforts and the consequences of these errors.
4. Apply Kotter's eight-stage process for implementing organizational change.
5. Describe why deliberate change methods and processes are important.
6. Explain the critical roles of pharmacy leaders and managers in change.
7. Describe the components of a persuasive campaign for change.
8. Design effective interventions to manage resistance to change.

KEY CONCEPTS

① The ability to respond in a timely manner to emerging threats and opportunities by promoting change is crucial to a pharmacy organization's survival and prosperity and has helped many organizations successfully adapt, strive, and gain and maintain strong market positions.

② A well-thought-out plan and high-quality leadership are required to institute significant organizational change. Without these elements, change can be destructive, often resulting in decreased morale, lost energy and loyalty, and reduced organizational viability.

③ Realizing that change is more likely to fail when the reasons for change are poorly understood and communicated, pharmacy leaders must be able to communicate logical reasons for change while articulating a clear vision.

④ The first step in a transformation may not be about setting objectives, but rather gaining an understanding of the organization and its goals, activities, operations/processes, stakeholders, and so forth.

⑤ It is important to measure change as well as reward desired behaviors and results associated with transformation.

⑥ Open and frequent communication during and after the transformation process may limit the formation of inaccurate perceptions and undesirable employee behaviors.

⑦ Change requires vision, skills, rewards, resources, and an action plan.

⑧ Although upper administrative leaders are needed to facilitate positive change, middle-level leaders and managers have enormous influence in implementing and managing change.

⑨ Pharmacy leaders can only make change happen if they have a coherent strategy for persuasion.

⑩ Many pharmacist managers underestimate the variety of reactions to change and their power to influence those responses. Effective pharmacist managers recognize this and use their influence to facilitate desired outcomes and minimize undesirable effects.

INTRODUCTION

The adage, "the only constant is change," is especially true in the pharmacy profession. During the past few decades, the focus of the profession has shifted from quietly dispensing medications to patient-focused practice in which pharmacists discuss with patients how to take their medications, help with medication selection, monitor therapeutic effects and drug-related outcomes, and make medication adjustments. Likewise, the entry-level pharmacy degree has changed from the Bachelor of Science in Pharmacy to the Doctor of Pharmacy degree. Although each of these changes had significant challenges and resistance associated with them, they also fostered new opportunities and improved patient care.

Transformation, or change, in health care occurs constantly. The impetuses for these changes are multifaceted and include reimbursement models, increased competition, technological advances, and the expectation among consumers for high-quality care. Increasing demands to optimize productivity, promote innovation, and enhance quality while minimizing expenses have become a norm in our culture. Those who embrace these changes and meet these demands will be successful, while those who are resistant to or incapable of adapting will lose competitive edge and **market share**, which, in turn, may result in decreased profit, forced layoffs, and other failures.

One thing is certain: exceptional leadership and management are required to facilitate positive change. This chapter is written for current and future pharmacist managers and leaders. Information within this chapter will also be valuable to those who do not hold management roles because change—whether personal, professional, societal, or organizational—is part of everyone's life. This chapter focuses on organizational change and discusses (1) the importance of change, (2) why most change initiatives fail and common consequences of these failures, (3) a basic framework for implementing change, (4) the mechanics of change, and (5) how to manage common change challenges.

WHY CHANGE?

Change is the law of life. And those who look only to the past or the present are certain to miss the future.

—*President John F. Kennedy[1]*

❶ *The ability to respond in a timely manner to emerging **threats** and opportunities by promoting change is crucial to a pharmacy organization's survival and prosperity and has helped many organizations successfully adapt, strive, and gain and maintain strong **market positions**.* Change may be prompted by new opportunities, such as technological advances, that promote organizational success. For example, change triggers include the availability of robotics and barcoding systems that may facilitate improved pharmacy operations. Such technology may increase productivity and improve medication dispensing, as well as accuracy of medication administration, thus decreasing medication errors. Likewise, threats or perceived dangers that may decrease the success of the pharmacy organization may trigger strong change. For example, the opening of a new retail pharmacy in a small town may be considered a threat to the existing community pharmacy unless the existing pharmacy can offer services that provide a competitive edge. See **Table 3–1** for other events that trigger pharmacy changes and examples of these changes. Change triggers are said to fall into two categories: (1) external (forces outside the organization) and (2) internal (forces inside the organization); however, in actuality, all triggers derive externally.[2] For example, if your customers want improved delivery services and the convenience of picking up medications using a drive-thru window, then that change may occur internally (within the organization);

TABLE 3–1	Events That Trigger Change and Change Examples in Pharmacy

Events	Change Examples
Rapid technology change	New robotics Barcode system Webcams
New innovations	E-prescribing New drug products
Political or economic trends	Legislative policies that impact reimbursement
Threats from competitors	Opening of a new pharmacy in town Generic programs Long-term care pharmacy services contract bidding
Emergent opportunities	Request for partnerships
Competitive strategies that emphasize unique, cutting-edge technology, products, or services	Telepharmacy
Customer or patient requirements and preferences	Delivery services Compliance packaging Drive-thru window
Demands from other stakeholders	Third-party insurance contract requirements Yearly changes in Medicare rules
Regulatory demands	New accreditation standards Change in pharmacy practice act
Globalization of markets and competition	Working with foreign companies or companies with a foreign workforce Canadian drug purchasing

however, the change was driven by an external force (customers). Because change triggers are external, organizations must understand not only their internal environments but also their external environment and influences, including identifying and strategically responding to threats as well as opportunities.

Adaptation involves changes made to cope with these *external* influences, which can include managing or minimizing threats or exploiting opportunities created by shifting needs and expectations of **stakeholders**, new technology, and changing markets. The ability to successfully adapt and change becomes vitally important when (1) the external environment is turbulent and uncertain, such as during economic crises, and (2) the organization is involved in competitive strategies that emphasize unique, cutting-edge products or services. To remain competitive, an organization must constantly innovate in response to the changing environment. Remaining competitive in the pharmaceutical industry requires organizations to be responsive to dynamic preferences, unique products and services, and new technology and initiatives.[3]

CREATING A PLAN FOR CHANGE

Over the years, pharmacy organizations and institutions have undergone many changes as the pharmacy profession has evolved. These changes can be seen in all pharmacy settings, including retail, hospital, and academia. For example, over the past 10 years, many retail pharmacies have focused on medications for special patient populations, such as diabetics, to establish a unique niche, in contrast with a more traditional retail pharmacy approach that provides medications for a wide variety of patients with various disease states. Successful change, such as the transition from a traditional retail pharmacy approach to a more specialized approach, not only depends on having a sound plan for change, including a **SWOT analysis**, but also depends on having strong leadership (SWOT involves analyzing **s**trengths, **w**eaknesses, **o**pportunities, and **t**hreats concerning the change, organization, and environment; refer to Chapter 11 ("Justifying and Planning Patient Care Services") and Chapter 13 ("Achieving Results

Through Others and Strategic Planning"). ❷*A well-thought-out plan and high-quality leadership are required to institute significant organizational change. Without these elements, change can be destructive, often resulting in decreased morale, lost energy and loyalty, and reduced organizational viability.* John Kotter, a well respected authority on leading change, observed transformation efforts of more than 100 companies and concluded that those that fail typically make the following mistakes (**Table 3–2**):[4]

- *Not establishing a great enough sense of urgency*: It has been suggested that at least 75% of management must be convinced that change is necessary to create enough urgency to implement the change successfully. Without a sense of urgency, many people will not give the extra effort that is needed for change.[4] Engaging key pharmacy stakeholders from various levels of the organization is important to help facilitate change.
- *Not creating a powerful enough guiding coalition*: Efforts that do not have a powerful guiding coalition can make progress for a while, but at some point, the stronger opposition will stop the change. The coalition must include most of senior management and those who are powerful in terms of titles, information, expertise, reputations, relationships, and capacity for leadership.
- *Lacking a vision*: Communicating a clear vision within five minutes or less and getting a response that signifies both understanding and interest is critical to gaining support and executing a plan.
- *Under or poorly communicating the vision by a factor of 10 (or more)*: Frequent communication is necessary. This communication comes in both words and deeds, with the latter often being the most powerful.
- *Not removing obstacles to the new vision*: Big obstacles must be confronted and removed if necessary. Avoiding obstacles disempowers employees and reduces change capacity.
- *Not systematically planning for and creating short-term wins*: Short-term wins produce momentum, maintain high urgency levels, and clarify or revise vision(s).

TABLE **3-2**	Common Transformation Mistakes

- Not establishing a great enough sense of urgency.
- Not creating a powerful enough guiding coalition.
- Lacking a vision.
- Under or poorly communicating the vision by a factor of 10 (or more).
- Not removing obstacles to the new vision.
- Not systematically planning for and creating short-term wins.
- Declaring victory too soon.
- Not anchoring changes in the organization's culture.

Source: Reprinted by permission of *Harvard Business Review*. From "Leading change. Why transformation efforts fail." By JP Kotter. 85(1)/2007. Copyright ©2007 by the Harvard Business School Publishing Corporation. All rights reserved.

- *Declaring victory too soon*: Instead of declaring victory, use credibility of short-term wins to tackle bigger problems.[4]
- *Not anchoring changes in the organization's culture*: Change becomes reality when it becomes part of the **organization's culture**.[4]

The consequences of these eight errors often are (1) new strategies are not implemented well, (2) acquisitions do not achieve expected results, (3) reengineering takes too long and costs too much, (4) downsizing does not get costs under control, and (5) quality programs do not deliver desired results.[4]

Kotter used the preceding information to facilitate the development of an eight-stage transformation process that leaders and managers should employ to bring about successful change.[5] This transformation process can be used in pharmacy organizations to promote change and should be implemented in the following sequence:[5]

- Establishing a sense of urgency
- Creating the guiding coalition
- Developing a vision and a strategy
- Communicating the change vision
- Empowering broad-based action
- Generating short-term wins

- Consolidating gains and producing still more change
- Anchoring new approaches in the culture

Figure 3–1 displays the eight stages and their suggested change strategies.[5] Change strategies, defined as how change is to be brought about, are important as well-planned and executed strategies allow for coordinating change activities and processes. They also provide criteria to measure, assess, and alter performance. In addition, strategies force leaders and managers to think about the long-term benefits and drawbacks of change to guide decision making.[6] Strategic planning may be a useful tool for leaders and managers as they prepare to implement a transformation process. Strategic planning involves identifying the organization's strategic direction and developing long-term goals, as well as an action plan for achieving those goals (refer to Chapter 13, "Achieving Results Through Others and Strategic Planning").

UNDERSTANDING THE MECHANICS OF TRANSFORMATION

As depicted in Figure 3–1, transformation is a collection of individual activities arranged into a

FIGURE **3-1** **Eight Stages of Transformation.**

1 ESTABLISHING A SENSE OF URGENCY
➢ Examining the market and competitive realities
➢ Identifying and discussing crises, potential crises, or major opportunities

2 CREATING THE GUIDING COALITION
➢ Putting together a group with enough power to lead the change
➢ Getting the group to work together like a team

3 DEVELOPING A VISION AND STRATEGY
➢ Creating a vision to help direct the change effort
➢ Developing strategies for achieving that vision

4 COMMUNICATING THE CHANGE VISION
➢ Using every vehicle possible to constantly communicate the new vision and strategies
➢ Having the guiding coalition role model the behavior expected of employees

5 EMPOWERING BROAD-BASED ACTION
➢ Getting rid of obstacles
➢ Changing systems or structures that undermine the change vision
➢ Encouraging risk taking and nontraditional ideas, activities, and actions

6 GENERATING SHORT-TERM WINS
➢ Planning for visible improvements in performance, or "wins"
➢ Creating those wins
➢ Visibly recognizing and rewarding people who made the wins possible

7 CONSOLIDATING GAINS AND PRODUCING MORE CHANGE
➢ Using increased credibility to change all systems, structures, and
  policies that do not fit together and do not fit the transformation vision
➢ Hiring, promoting, and developing people who can implement the change vision
➢ Reinvigorating the process with new projects, themes, and change agents

8 ANCHORING NEW APPROACHES IN THE CULTURE
➢ Creating better performance through customer- and productivity-oriented
  behavior, more and better leadership, and more effective management
➢ Articulating the connections between new behaviors and organizational success
➢ Developing means to ensure leadership development and succession

These eight stages should be conducted in the sequence displayed. Change strategies for each stage are listed in the boxes.

Source: Reprinted by permission of Harvard Business School Press. From *Leading Change* by JP Kotter. Boston, MA, 1996, p. 21.

logical sequence. Adcroft, Willis, and Hurst suggest that, to better understand transformation, four areas, or points, in the transformation process require careful and deliberate analysis:[6(p42)]

- *The transformation event*: Understand why the transformation needs to occur and the intended result (*The Problem and Vision*).
- *The transformation program*: Understand how transformation is to occur, and the key management decisions and activities through which change occurs (*The Process/Methods*).
- *The transformation outcome*: Determine the organizational outcomes that emerge from the transformation event and program (*The Results*).
- *The transformation myth*: Understand how the transformation is interpreted and understood externally and internally, not just what happened or the actual results (*Stakeholders' Perceptions of the Transformation*).

Source: Adapted with permission from Adcroft A, Willis R, Hurst J. A new model for managing change: the holistic view. *J Bus Strat* 2008;29(1):40–45.

The Transformation Event (The Problem and Vision)

❸ *Realizing that change is more likely to fail when the reasons for change are poorly understood and communicated, pharmacy leaders must be able to communicate logical reasons for change while articulating a clear vision.* As noted in Stage 1 of Kotter's transformation process (Figure 3–1), defining problem(s) and opportunities should occur early in the change process and involve answering important questions about why change is necessary and urgent. For example, an outpatient oncology clinic of an urban medical center experienced a sharp increase in patients over a five-year period. Providing services to this unit, along with the other units, placed an increased burden on the medical center's main pharmacy. As a result, those with very little experience in oncology pharmacy were expected to participate in distributing these medications to meet increased demand. In turn, a rising number of medication errors occurred among outpatient oncology patients, and a few patients experienced serious adverse drug events. Staff pharmacists were frustrated by the increased workload from the oncology clinic and from other areas of the medical center. They also had serious concerns about the growing oncology medication error rate and other patient safety issues. Thus, it had become clear to staff pharmacists and oncology clinic personnel that a significant and urgent *change* was necessary to reduce medication errors and promote patient safety.

After communicating the need for change, a clear vision and the importance of that vision must be persuasively articulated by the guiding coalition, defined as an influential group of people capable of leading the change process. In the example, the vision proposed was to have an on-site pharmacy in the oncology clinic to facilitate the development of oncology-focused pharmacists and other staff to provide safe and appropriate pharmacy care to oncology outpatients and to discontinue main pharmacy services for the clinic's patients. This example demonstrates (1) why change is necessary and (2) how a sense of urgency can facilitate the change process. Also, at the core of any change program rests the recognition and understanding of the likely repercussions of transformation. In the oncology clinic example, some repercussions of the pharmacy transformation included new staff hires, staff training, individuals transferring from the main pharmacy to the new oncology pharmacy, and remodeling costs. **Table 3–3** further illustrates the progress of the oncology clinic pharmacy example through Kotter's eight-stage transformation process.[5]

The Transformation Program (The Process/Methods)

One of the most difficult parts of any transformation process is knowing where and how to begin. Because every pharmacy-related organization is different, there are no single universal answers to most of the hundreds of questions that might be asked early in the transformation process, including:

- Where should we begin in the transformation process?
- Is the planned change consistent with our mission?

TABLE 3–3	Eight Stages of Transformation as Related to Establishing an Oncology Clinic Pharmacy

Eight Stages of Transformation	Establishing the Outpatient Oncology Pharmacy
Establishing a sense of urgency	• Sharp increase in oncology outpatients over five-year period. • Increased burden on main pharmacy. • Main pharmacy staff with little oncology experience participating in medication distribution. • Increase in oncology medication errors. • Occurrences of serious adverse drug events among oncology outpatients.
Creating the guiding coalition	• Guiding coalition composed of main pharmacy staff pharmacists, oncologists, oncology nurses, and oncology patients and family members.
Developing a vision and strategy	• Proposed vision: to open an on-site pharmacy in the oncology clinic and, within this clinic, facilitate the development of oncology-focused pharmacists and other staff to provide pharmacy care to oncology outpatients.
Communicating the change vision	• Achieve internal buy-in and approval from key stakeholders such as upper administration. • Hold town hall meetings with key stakeholders to discuss need, purpose, development, and implementation of the oncology clinic pharmacy. • Distribute memos describing the need, purpose, development, and implementation of the oncology clinic pharmacy.
Empowering broad-based action	• Empower individuals to remove obstacles, such as — A lack of adequately trained oncology pharmacy specialists. Solutions include hiring pharmacists and pharmacy technicians who specialize in oncology and offering training for those individuals who require it. — Lack of space for the oncology clinic pharmacy. A solution may be to identify appropriate space in the oncology clinic and renovate this space.
Generating short-term wins	• Reduce main pharmacy workload concerning dispensing medications to oncology clinic outpatients. • Improve main pharmacy staff job satisfaction and morale. • Increase patient safety and reduce medication errors. • Increase patient satisfaction with pharmacy services.
Consolidating gains and producing more change	• Use the oncology clinic pharmacy as a model for expanding specialized pharmacy clinics throughout the medical center.
Anchoring new approaches in the culture	• Implement continuous programs (such as staff development) that improve patient care; encourage staff participation in these programs. • Implement a quality improvement program designed to decrease medication errors and increase efficiency.

- Does the program or method of change address the issues that prompted transformation?
- Which stakeholders should be involved in the process?
- How involved do individual stakeholders need to be in the process?

How the transformation should occur and who should lead it is specific to each organization and its external environment. Some organizations may execute a top-down approach, whereas others may use either a grassroots (bottom-up) approach or a mixed approach involving change efforts initiated at multiple levels. Each organization, setting, and situation calls for its own individualized approach. For example, the transformation of the new oncology pharmacy initially used a more grassroots approach because several staff pharmacists, oncologists, oncology nurses, and patients (the guiding coalition) advocated for this specialized on-site service, as they understood the need and urgency for the change. In contrast, the merging of personnel from five retail chain stores to three stores at the behest of the chain's upper administration would be classified as a top-down approach. Regardless of approach, change *must* involve the major stakeholders.

Change strategies are complex. This complexity manifests itself in many ways, the most complex aspect being the relationship between the organization and the environment in which it operates. All pharmacist leaders and managers must realize and respect that pharmacy organizations, like the people who make up these organizations, are complex, as they have perspectives and personalities that define their true nature. ❹ *Thus, "the first step in the transformation may not be about setting objectives but rather gaining an understanding of" the organization, including its goals, activities, processes, stakeholders, and so on which must be involved.*[6(p44)]

The Transformation Outcome (Results)

After transformation occurs, the next step in the change process is the highly anticipated results stage, which includes both short- and long-term wins, or achievements. The results should encompass the entire purpose of the transformation. For example, the establishment of an on-site oncology clinic pharmacy produced many "wins," including (1) decreased medication errors, (2) increased patient safety, and (3) increased patient satisfaction with pharmacy services. In addition, job satisfaction and morale among pharmacy staff increased (Table 3–3).

Following transformation, many questions will arise, and leaders and managers will be expected to have answers. Stakeholders may ask the following:

- Have we dealt with the threats and seized the opportunities that drove the transformation?
- Have we changed in the way that we expected?
- Has transformation made us better or just different?
- Are we better off after transformation than we were before?
- What lessons have we learned?

Leaders and managers should analyze the results of transformation and be able to communicate answers to all of these questions, as this is critical to the entire transformation process, including the "anchoring" or continuation of successful change behaviors within the organization. ❺ *It is important to measure change as well as reward desired behaviors and results associated with transformation.*[6,7]

The Transformation Myth (Stakeholders' Perceptions of the Transformation)

During any change process, managing perceptions is essential. Different stakeholders will have different perceptions, both positive and negative, about the transformation experience, expectations, and outcomes. Although these perceptions do not always equate to objective evidence, they may influence the behaviors of others (employees, customers, etc.). Organizational leaders and managers often find they have little control over the effect of perceptions on *external* stakeholders' behaviors. In contrast, managers involved in change efforts generally invest a tremendous amount of time and effort in controlling the *internal* effect of inaccurate perceptions and rumors, particularly on employees' behaviors. ❻ *Open and frequent communication during and after the transformation process may limit the formation of inaccurate perceptions and undesirable employee behaviors.*[5] In the oncology clinic pharmacy example, a rumor (myth) arose during the transformation process that the main pharmacy's budget would be reduced significantly to provide funding for the new oncology clinic pharmacy, and a high number of layoffs were expected. Although this information was not true, the perception persisted and affected the attitudes of main pharmacy staff toward the implementation of the oncology clinic pharmacy. To combat the inaccurate belief, a systematic communication plan, including town hall meetings and distribution of written material to address the realities of the transformation process, was instituted. Thus, this example reinforces the importance of dispelling myths and providing accurate information through effective communication (Table 3–3).

PRESCRIPTION FOR CHANGE AND OUTCOMES

❼*Change requires vision, skills, rewards, resources, and an action plan.*[8] When at least one of these critical ingredients for change is lacking or inadequate, stakeholders may become confused and resistant to change.[8] Further, they may not understand why change is necessary or the anticipated results of change. For example, if significant changes in the reward system do not occur, leaders, managers, and the organization may be rewarding resistance.[7] Likewise, if appropriate resources and opportunities for using skills are not provided, this will foster frustration and promote anxiety.

CHALLENGES TO CHANGE

> *There is nothing more difficult to take in hand, more perilous to conduct, or more uncertain in its success than to take the lead in the introduction of a new order of things.*
>
> *—Machiavelli*

Machiavelli's quote resonates with many pharmacist leaders and managers responsible for change efforts. ❽*Although upper administrative leaders are needed to facilitate positive change, middle-level leaders and managers have enormous influence in implementing and managing change.* In the change process, leaders are typically involved in vision and direction setting, whereas managers are concerned with intricate operational details or the process of change, which may include budgeting, planning, organizing, staffing, and problem solving of change-related activities.[9] However, both leaders and managers are responsible for confronting and resolving challenges to the change process.

For some, change is exciting, while others find it threatening or even frightening. John D. Rockefeller III described why organizations resist change: "An organization is a system, with a logic of its own, and all the weight of tradition and inertia. The deck is stacked in favor of the tried and proven way of doing things and against the taking of risks and striking out in new directions."[10] Because individuals are the core of organizations, people are generally not in favor of change because of fear or risk aversion and, thus, cling to old, repeated (familiar) patterns, customs, and culture. **Figure 3–2** depicts six common methods employees and other stakeholders use to avoid change:[11(p109)]

- *The dog and pony show must go on.* Organizations focus heavily on process, with little emphasis on achieving results. Because attention is more directed on operations than on outcomes, results are secondary to the perceived need to perform tasks.
- *Ready, aim, aim . . .* A culture of perfectionism exists where mistakes and "rocking the boat" are punished. Thus, a tremendous amount of time is spent trying to analyze the situation instead of implementing change because of fears that the change may be incorrect and result in punitive action.
- *This too shall pass.* Numerous organizational crises in the past have created a "hunker down" attitude, wherein employees ignore new initiatives, work around them, and wait for change efforts to end.
- *After the meeting ends, debate begins.* Seemingly cordial, cooperative meetings regarding the transformation process are followed by resistance to change.
- *A culture of "no."* Resistant individuals, who are overly critical and focus on ways

| FIGURE **3-2** | **Dysfunctional Routines—Six Ways to Avoid Change.** |

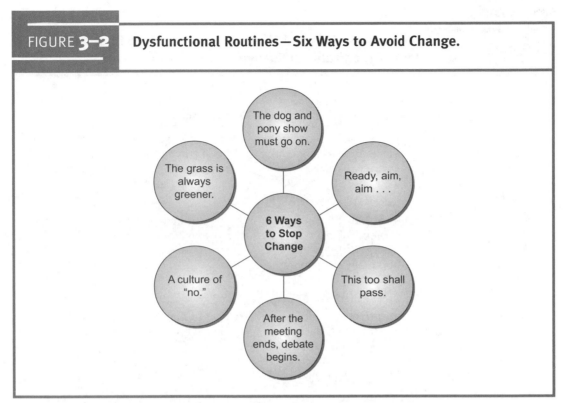

and reasons not to change, dominate organizations.

- *The grass is always greener.* Managers avoid fundamental organizational problems and change by focusing on other items, such as new products, services, etc.

Transition is the mental and emotional transformation that people must undergo to relinquish the old arrangement and embrace the new one.[12] William Bridges, an authority on managing workplace change, indicates that people must undergo transition for change to be successful: "In its most basic function, transition helps one come to terms with change."[13] See **Table 3–4** for potential resistant reactions to proposed pharmacy-related organizational changes and mitigating strategies to address these reactions.[14]

❾ *Pharmacy leaders can only make change happen if they have a coherent strategy for persuasion.*[11] For typical individuals who are resistant to change, all transformation plans look alike. Thus, it is imperative to show employees precisely how your plans differ from predecessors. The four phases of a persuasion campaign are[11(p110)]

- *Phase 1*: Convince employees that radical change is imperative; demonstrate why the new direction is the right one.
- *Phase 2*: Position and frame preliminary plan; gather feedback; announce final plan.
- *Phase 3*: Manage employee mood through constant communication.
- *Phase 4*: Reinforce behavioral guidelines to avoid backsliding.

TABLE 3–4	Resistant Reactions and Mitigating Strategies to Pharmacy-Related Organizational Change	
Proposed Change	**Potential Employee Reaction**	**Mitigating Strategy**
Extend hours of pharmacy operations to 24 hours per day for 7 days a week	Do not want to work more hours per week or work every weekend.	Offer flexible working hours, job sharing, and pay differences for working before 7 a.m. and after 5 p.m., holidays, and weekends.
Implement barcoding inventory management and drug delivery system	Concern that the new system will be too difficult to learn and add too many steps to the process.	Promise training and a reasonable implementation period.
Hire new pharmacy district manager	Concern over work environment, such as schedule, reduction in staff, or less autonomy for store managers.	Involve staff in the interview and selection process of the manager.
Require all pharmacists to become board certified	Expense and time required to gain certification.	Offer to pay for preparatory programs and taking the board certification test.
Institutional mergers	Fear of losing position or stature. Distrust of the "other side." Organizational confusion.	Frequent communications (for example, conducting sessions to clarify organizational structure). Building organizational trust.
Change the curriculum of a pharmacy school	Do not see the need for change. Faculty resentment because teaching assignments changed.	Communicate need for change and vision. Create incentives to try new approaches. Provide opportunities for tradeoffs and compromise.
Require all pharmacy technicians to become certified	Expense of certification. Too much effort. Lack of perceived incentive or reward for achieving certification. Not necessary to perform responsibilities.	Explain necessity to job (for example, allows one to take on additional responsibility). Offer to pay for expenses including preparatory programs, test costs, etc. Offer promotion for those who become certified.

Proposed Change	Potential Employee Reaction	Mitigating Strategy
Reduce operating budget	Fear of losing jobs or programs. Distrust. Organizational confusion.	Frequent communication as to the necessity of actions and anticipated results. Build organizational trust.
Implement medication therapy management service within a pharmacy	Not enough time to provide service. Fear that employees do not have necessary expertise. Pharmacy does not have private area to provide counseling.	Hire more personnel and acquire technology to help address time issues. Offer additional training. Provide renovations that allow private counseling areas.
Implement new robotics-based automation	Fear of losing jobs. Uncomfortable learning a new system.	Communicate need for automation. Provide adequate training and time for learning. Provide adequate technical support.
Close a pharmacy store	Feelings of failure. Rumors develop out of confusion. Anxiety over status of employment.	Communicate reasons for store closing. Meet with each employee individually to determine possibility of job relocation.
Change in wholesale supplier	Confusion over learning new system. Frustration with change in system capabilities.	Provide adequate opportunity for training. Provide adequate technical support. Identify the strengths and capabilities of the new partnership.
Change in benefit structure or offerings	Confusion over details of changes. Feeling less appreciated if benefits are downsized.	Hold staff meetings to detail changes. Allow adequate opportunity and a nonthreatening forum for staff to voice their feelings. Identify reasons for changes in benefits.

Source: Data from Kotter JP, Schlesinger LA. Choosing strategies for change. *Harv Bus Rev* 2008;86(7/8):130–138.

🔟 *Many pharmacist managers underestimate the variety of reactions to change and their power to influence those responses.*[14] Resistance may be unavoidable during the change process. However, the amount of resistance can be mitigated if the organization leads change in a strategic fashion.[15] To be successful, change strategies need to be developed, implemented, analyzed, and fine-tuned. Effective change leaders and managers must

- Set the stage for change by creating urgency, vision, and widespread support among employees, as change in a complex organization cannot be accomplished by a single leader working alone—many people within the organization must participate in change efforts.[3,11,14]
- Demonstrate commitment to the change process.[16,17]
- Provide support throughout and beyond the change process.[16]
- Create the framework for developing methods and strategies to produce desired change and establish metrics to measure and evaluate change (this includes such tasks as **strategic planning**, encouraging innovation, and pacing change).[3,11,16,18]
- Encourage key stakeholders to facilitate change and become engaged (take ownership) in the transformation process.
- Create capabilities to cope with change.[19]
- Manage the mood, as change can be a depressing or an anxiety-generating process, especially when it involves restructuring and downsizing.[11]
- Diagnose the causes of resistance (e.g., individuals protecting self-interests, misunderstanding, lack of trust).[14]
- Deal with resistance, as denying resistance only creates more resistance; educating, communicating, and engaging stakeholders may help reduce resistance.[20]
- Reinforce good behaviors by providing incentives, as the toughest challenge faced by change agents is to avoid backsliding into dysfunctional routines.[11]
- Communicate effectively (see Chapter 21, "Communicating Effectively with Others").
- Avoid pitfalls (refer to the eight common errors of why change fails).[7,16]
- Exercise a high degree of **emotional intelligence** (refer to Chapter 2, "Management Essentials for Pharmacists").[21]

SUMMARY

According to Morley and Eadie, "if changing—personally, professionally, organizationally—were a simple, straightforward process, we would see many more dreams realized, visions actualized, and missions accomplished."[22] Although change is difficult, it occurs out of the necessity to survive. Industries, including pharmacy, are constantly changing to meet growing needs and challenges. Exceptional pharmacist leaders and managers who can be change agents are needed more now than ever before to meet these growing demands. Sarah White, a recognized leader in pharmacy practice, stated that to achieve change, leaders and managers must visualize the desired change and see themselves and the organization as successfully adapting to the change.[23] Pharmacist leaders and managers must "expect to encounter some challenges" and believe that these challenges can be overcome.[23(p2335)] In addition, change leaders and managers must be patient and gentle with themselves, as change efforts take time and require perseverance.[23] This chapter focuses on organizational transformation and reviews the importance of change, strategies to implement change, and the role of pharmacist leaders and managers in facilitating and confronting challenges to successful change.

References

1. BrainyQuote.com. John F. Kennedy quotes. Available at: http://www.brainyquote.com/quotes/quotes/j/johnfkenn121068.html. Accessed September 2, 2009.
2. Oakland JS, Tanner S. Successful change management. *Total Qual Manag* 2007;18:1–19.
3. Yulk G, Lepsinger R. Leading change: adapting and innovating in an uncertain world. *Leadership in Action* 2006;26:3–7.
4. Kotter JP. Leading change: why transformation efforts fail. *Harv Bus Rev* 2007;85(1):96–103.

5. Kotter JP. *Leading Change*. Boston, MA: Harvard Business School Press; 1996.

6. Adcroft A, Willis R, Hurst J. A new model for managing change: the holistic view. *J Bus Strat* 2008;29:40–45.

7. Pritchett P, Pound R. *High-Velocity Culture Change*. Dallas, TX: Pritchett Publishing Co; 2007.

8. Knoster T. Presentation at TASH Conference; Washington, DC; 1991.

9. Kotter JP. *A Force for Change*. New York, NY: Free Press; 1990.

10. Wedge C. Leading change: an exploratory process. *EDUCAUSE Rev* 2006;41:10–11. Available at: http://connect.educause.edu/Library/EDUCAUSE+Review/LeadingChangeAnExplorator/40674?time=1231512757. Accessed January 9, 2009.

11. Garvin DA, Roberto MA. Change through persuasion. *Harv Bus Rev* 2005;83(2):104–112.

12. Management Consulting News. Meet the masterminds: William Bridges on managing transitions. Available at: http://www.managementconsultingnews.com/interviews/bridges_interview.php. Accessed January 23, 2009.

13. William Bridges & Associates Web site. Available at: http://www.wmbridges.com/. Accessed January 23, 2009.

14. Kotter JP, Schlesinger LA. Choosing strategies for change. *Harv Bus Rev* 2008;86(7/8):130–138.

15. Nguyen T. Leading change. Available at: http://www.lce.com/pdf/leadingChangenguyen.pdf. Accessed January 9, 2009.

16. Pearce C. Ten steps to managing change. *Nurs Manag* 2007;13:25.

17. Sirkin HL, Keenan P, Jackson A. The hard side of change management. *Harv Bus Rev* 2005;83:108–118.

18. Abrahamson E. Change without pain. *Harv Bus Rev* 2000;78(4):75–79.

19. Christensen CM, Overdorf M. Meeting the challenges of disruptive change. *Harv Bus Rev* 2000;78:66–76.

20. O'Brien MJ. 5 approaches to leading successful organizational change. *Healthcare Finan Manag* 2008;62:138, 140.

21. Goleman D. What makes a leader? *Harv Bus Rev* 1998;76(6):93–102.

22. Morley J, Eadie D. Leading change. In: Morley J, ed. *The Extraordinary Higher Education Leader*. Washington, DC: National Association of College and University Business Officers; 2001. Available at: http://www.acenet.edu/resources/chairs/docs/Morley_LeadingFMT.pdf. Accessed January 23, 2009.

23. White SJ. Managing change transitions. *Am J Health-Syst Pharm* 2008;65:2334–2335.

Abbreviations

SWOT: strengths, weaknesses, opportunities, threats

Case Scenarios

CASE ONE: An independent community pharmacy in the town of Monticello is being bought out by a small retail drug store. The independent pharmacy, owned by a pharmacist, has eight employees: two pharmacists, three clerks, and three pharmacy technicians. These employees have been working for the independent pharmacy for more than nine years. The independent pharmacy has been the only drug store in Monticello for more than 20 years. The retail drug store has offered all the employees the option to continue working at the store. As part of the purchase agreement, the owner, Marie Wyndom, signed a contract that will not allow her to open a retail pharmacy in Monticello for five years. The owner has no intention of opening a retail pharmacy and is looking forward to retirement. However, she has agreed to work for the retail drug store for six months as store manager to ensure a smooth transition, and the other eight employees are considering working for the retail drug store. What strategies can the retail store and Dr. Wyndom employ to ensure a smooth transition for the employees to the new retail drug store?

CASE TWO: A hospital pharmacy director would like to reorganize his department. He feels that

(continues)

there are too many managers, which leads to inefficiencies, and believes that pharmacy services for the surgical and medical wards should be consolidated under one manager. Rumors begin to spread regarding this possible consolidation, and the pharmacy staff is concerned. Some believe they will be fired, while others are working behind the scenes to have their favored manager appointed to this position. What can the director do to establish a vision for the department? Give examples of communication methods that can be used to counteract the rumor mill. How can the director generate a positive feeling about the change?

CASE THREE: The owner of an established long-term care pharmacy just signed a new hospice contract that will add an estimated 200 new patients starting in 60 days. This will be the pharmacy's first large hospice contract. The pharmacy resides in a suburb of a metropolitan city, and some of the facilities and patient homes are a 40-minute drive from the pharmacy. The existing staff members are concerned about the sudden increase in workload and about how to deal with after-hours prescription orders. How can the owner gain buy-in from staff regarding this new opportunity? What resources are needed to implement the new contract successfully? How can management strategize to implement the new contract within a limited amount of time?

CASE FOUR: A faculty member at a school of pharmacy would like to add a new course to the school's curriculum. The course is on hospital pharmacy management, a specialty area for the faculty member. The faculty member feels very strongly that the school does not teach much in this area and sorely needs this course. The faculty member would like to offer the course next semester but has met with some resistance. Who are the stakeholders that may be interested in the outcome of this issue? What could the faculty member do to lessen resistance to this proposed change? How can a vision for this change be expressed?

Additional Resources Available Online!

CHAPTER 4

INNOVATION AND ENTREPRENEURSHIP

GRANT H. SKREPNEK, PhD, MSc, RPh

JESSE C. FISHMAN, PharmD

LEARNING OBJECTIVES

After completing the chapter, the reader will be able to

1. Define key characteristics of entrepreneurship and intrapreneurship.
2. Contrast micro and macro views of entrepreneurship.
3. Describe the process approaches to entrepreneurship.
4. Differentiate strategy from operational effectiveness.
5. Identify methods to stimulate innovation within organizations.
6. Describe the characteristics of a learning organization.
7. Define the following economic analyses: cost minimization, cost-effectiveness, cost utility, and cost-benefit.

KEY CONCEPTS

❶ Those who innovate have a clear vision and ability to excel in communicating, understanding the environment and organizational culture, inspiring individuals to work together, and persevering through or despite failure.

❷ Entrepreneurs innovate by introducing new products or services, new means of production, or new organizational structures. As such, overcoming barriers associated with implementing innovations may be considered as much a part of entrepreneurialism as is identifying opportunities or conceiving initial inventions or ideas.

❸ Entrepreneurs are often viewed as successful based on the extent to which they systematically assess environments, pinpoint and seize opportunities, analyze innovations, and minimize coincidental risks.

❹ Pharmacy exists as a discipline that offers both services and goods to consumers, which have simultaneously grown as a function of technological advances.

❺ In identifying more specific approaches to stimulate entrepreneurship within organizations, three general variables may promote innovation: (1) cultural, (2) human resource, and (3) structural.

❻ Developing an organization that stimulates innovation ultimately requires an investment in the organization's social capital, referring to the ability to allow individuals and teams to reach their full productive potential by understanding and furthering resources, aptitude, and motivation.

❼ Motivating employees to become innovative requires a thoughtful and multifaceted approach that involves, in part, assessing the needs of individuals, identifying and removing barriers that prevent effectiveness, providing needed resources, and establishing reward systems that acknowledge both innovative activity and outcomes.

❽ A learning organization is defined as one that has developed an ongoing capacity to adapt and change rapidly, often by using highly innovative methods for resolving problems and increasing performance.

❾ It is important to evaluate new innovations using robust methodologies. There are a number of approaches that exist through which an innovation may be evaluated, including cost-effectiveness analysis (CEA), cost-utility analysis (CUA), or cost-benefit analysis (CBA). Collectively, these approaches are comprehensive economic evaluations that compare the costs and various outcome measures associated with a new technology versus those costs and outcomes associated with an alternative technology or intervention.

❿ Organizations may overemphasize identification of innovative solutions for opportunities and underemphasize implementation and diffusion. The diffusion of innovation and subsequent rate of adoption involves understanding characteristics of consumers within the environment, system-/organization-level variables, and attributes of the innovation as perceived by consumers.

INTRODUCTION

The healthcare environment is constantly changing and evolving in response to concerns associated with cost, quality, and access amid new technologies, regulations, scientific knowledge, consumer demands, and outcomes. Thus, pharmacists and pharmacist leaders and managers must prepare for change and be innovative in their efforts to anticipate change (refer to Chapter 3, "Leading and Managing Change"). Peter F. Drucker, an influential management scholar, emphasized the need to be proactive and innovative, stating that "unless it is seen as the task of the organization to lead change, the organization—whether business, university, hospital [small or large] and so on—will not survive."[1] Simply stated, **innovation** is a specific type of change wherein new ideas may lead to either radical breakthroughs that completely transform practice environments or to incremental improvements in existing products, processes, or services.[2] ❶*Those who innovate have a clear vision and ability to excel in communicating, understanding the environment and organizational culture, inspiring individuals to work together, and persevering through or despite failure.*[3] Although the concept of innovation may seem abstract, it is critical to both large and small organizations. Innovation can be as small as changing the way to handle higher call volumes in a steadily growing independent pharmacy, and as large as creating a nationwide electronic prescribing network that interfaces with other electronic health systems.

❷*At the heart of innovation rests the **entrepreneur** who innovates by introducing new products or services, new means of production, or new organizational structures.* **Table 4–1** details some reasons to be an innovator or entrepreneur.[4-6] When applied to both pharmacy and healthcare industries, entrepreneurship has often lagged behind other sectors because of barriers both internal and external to organizations, such as poor economic incentives and provider and payer behaviors.[7,8] ❷*As such, overcoming barriers associated with implementing innovations may be*

TABLE **4-1**	**Reasons to Be an Innovator and/or an Entrepreneur**

- *Economic Growth*

  To promote economic growth, as innovation and entrepreneurial activities may result in new businesses with new opportunities for employment.

- *Organizational Survival and Competitive Advantage*

  To promote organizational survival and create a competitive advantage within a target market, as organizations that become stagnant are at greater risk for failure.

- *Opportunities for Development, Growth, and Creativity*

  To facilitate and enhance opportunities for individual and organizational development, growth, and creativity, as innovation and entrepreneurial activities are likely to prompt expansion or creation of departments, utilization of new knowledge/skills, new ways of approaching solutions to problems, etc.

- *Improved Performance*

  To inspire the improved performance of organizations and individuals, as innovation and entrepreneurial activities may break up boredom, monotony, and inertia experienced by organizations and their employees.

- *Accumulation of Wealth*

  To produce and accumulate wealth, as innovation and entrepreneurial activities are likely to generate higher revenues (sales) and earn greater profits than more commonplace products/services.

- *Improved Human Condition*

  To resolve societal problems and promote the human condition, as innovation and entrepreneurial activities may be used to address issues that undermine human well-being as well as create mechanisms that improve human life.

Sources: Data from Yapps Cohen L. Top 10 reasons why we need innovation. Available at: http://www.amcreativityassoc.org. Accessed June 7, 2009. ASPIRA/Morgan Stanley Entrepreneurial Leadership Initiative. Entrepreneurial Leadership Program Facilitator's Guide. Available at: http://www.scribd.com/doc/296109/Entrepreneurship. Accessed June 7, 2009. Prabhudesai A. Top 10 reasons why you should be an entrepreneur. Available at: http://trak.in/tags/business/2007/08/11/top-10-reasons-an-entrepreneur-start-your-own-business-your-own-boss/. Accessed June 7, 2009.

considered as much a part of entrepreneurialism as is identifying opportunities or conceiving initial inventions or ideas.[9] For example, John Musil, a pharmacist and specialty pharmacy business owner, once faced financial difficulty after opening a number of retail stores.[10] Recognizing the need for change, Musil hired executives to oversee the company's pharmacy operations. With the executives' help, the company identified that national chain pharmacies were not performing niche drug compounding, leaving the practice open to independent pharmacies. Subsequently, the business expanded its therapeutic care to areas that include filling the needs of human immunodeficiency virus (HIV) and veterinary patients, thereby capitalizing in specific niches.

This chapter will describe entrepreneurial processes and approaches, broad categories of entrepreneurial opportunity within the pharmacy arena, methods to promote innovative activity, and basic approaches to evaluate and implement innovations regardless of pharmacy practice setting.

THE CONCEPT OF ENTREPRENEURSHIP

Entrepreneurship, from the French verb *entreprendre*, which means "to undertake" or "to do something," has historically been described as the practice of organizing, managing, and assuming the risk of a business. The role of innovation has expanded to further refine the meaning of entrepreneurship as an activity that seeks to "create purposeful, focused change in an enterprise's economic or social potential."[11,12] This more contemporary description has ultimately led to viewing entrepreneurship as a series of ongoing activities through which growth and progress are achieved. Economist Joseph Schumpeter coined this evolutionary process of innovation as one of **creative destruction**, wherein entrepreneurial approaches of replacing or improving products, processes, or services "incessantly revolutionizes the economic structure from *within*, incessantly destroying the old one, incessantly creating a new one."[3(p83)] Summarizing the vast literature concerning entrepreneurship, Timmons, a leading authority in entrepreneurship, added to the description of this dynamic process:

> *Entrepreneurship is the ability to create and build a vision from practically nothing. . . . It is the application of energy to initiating and building an enterprise or organization, rather than just watching or analyzing. This vision requires a willingness to take calculated risks—both personal and financial—and then do everything possible to reduce the chances of failure. Entrepreneurship also includes the ability to build an entrepreneurial or venture team to complement your own skills and talents. It is the knack for sensing an opportunity where others see chaos, contradiction, and confusion. It is possessing the know-how to find, marshal, and control resources.*[13(p78)]

Applied within pharmacy practice, numerous organizations have developed entrepreneurial visions to expand the role of pharmacy. To illustrate, a joint initiative coined Project Destiny was established by the American Pharmacists Association, the National Association of Chain Drug Stores, the National Community Pharmacists Association, and a number of pharmaceutical companies to extend pharmacy services beyond a dispensary role in order to assume an active role in medication management (including working collaboratively with healthcare delivery and financing systems to focus on managing medications, positively affecting health outcomes, reducing overall healthcare costs, and actively empowering consumers to manage their health).[14] The Wisconsin Pharmacy Quality Collaborative has also sought to build a venture team of pharmacists that provide medication therapy management (MTM) services.[15] Other initiatives, such as the Pharmacy Alliance, seek to improve workplace conditions for pharmacists, while efforts across numerous organizations have created practice-based pharmacy research networks. Collectively, these groups are composed of pharmacist entrepreneurs who are taking calculated risks and building on their own visions of how their practices should develop.

ENTREPRENEURSHIP AND INTRAPRENEURSHIP

Although entrepreneurship is often viewed as a function of a **sole proprietorship**, or small organization, the process may intuitively occur within larger entities as well. Because corporate innovators incur substantially less risk or uncertainty than sole proprietors, they have been termed "**intrapreneurs**," rather than "entrepreneurs."[16] A pharmacist who believes entrepreneurship is an interesting concept but lacks the necessary resources to engage in such activities may still be able to capitalize on his or her unique entrepreneurial abilities by understanding and promoting intrapreneurship. Overall, the process of intrapreneurship consists of five stages: (1) defining the opportunity or problem, including considerable data collection and analysis of the opportunity or problem; (2) building support; (3) mobilizing resources; (4) executing the project (focusing on the start up of the internal corporate venture); and (5) completing the venture. If the venture is successful, the intrapreneur may secure a position of continued project oversight within the corporation.[17]

In comparing entrepreneurship and intrapreneurship,

- Both intrapreneurs and entrepreneurs need autonomy and freedom, but the intrapreneur must work within the existing corporate hierarchy.[17]
- Intrapreneurs have an existing support network; however, entrepreneurs often start without them.
- Entrepreneurs have to locate and obtain resources for the new venture; intrapreneurs can often rely on existing organizational funds and resources.
- Entrepreneurs face personal financial risk, whereas intrapreneurs face career risk in the event of failure.
- In the case of intrapreneurship, the firm can lend its name and reputation to a new venture; in the case of entrepreneurship, image and reputation must be created over time.

When these qualifications are applied to pharmacy practice, an example of intrapreneurship may include the efforts of a medical communications pharmacist manager at a large pharmaceutical consulting firm expanding his department to engage in empirical research and publishing. Therein, forming a team of outcomes researchers to analyze and publish electronic medical records data may require developing a business plan to be presented and evaluated by the pharmacist's colleagues and upper management. Other examples of pharmacy intrapreneurship include (1) creating an immunization administration program within a residency program,[18] and (2) using corporate resources within community chain pharmacies to design pilot programs to expand the pharmacist's role in treating patients with chronic diseases. Such efforts are not limited to community or hospital practice settings. To illustrate, faculty within colleges of pharmacy have recognized the importance of MTM and established successful pharmacist-run centers that provide clinical care

to people with rare diseases or multiple comorbid conditions.

ENTREPRENEURIAL SUCCESS

Entrepreneurs must have diverse skill sets and be successful at several activities to be effective at innovating, catalyzing change, recognizing and seizing opportunities, marketing ideas, providing value, bearing risk, and realizing benefits from efforts (refer to Chapter 3, "Leading and Managing Change," and Chapter 15, "Understanding and Applying Marketing Strategies").[19] Two general approaches used to formally model or describe entrepreneurial success and effectiveness involve (1) assessing internal and external factors, and (2) articulating the processes that are related to successful activities. These are also delineated as "micro" and "macro" views of entrepreneurship, respectively.[19]

Micro and Macro Views of Entrepreneurship

Overall, the *micro view of entrepreneurship* focuses primarily on describing *internal* entrepreneurial characteristics associated with success—particularly those that are within the actual control or direction of entrepreneurs (i.e., an "internal" *locus of control*).[19] This perspective involves three "schools" of thought: (1) entrepreneurial trait, (2) venture opportunity, and (3) strategic formulation.[19]

Proponents of the *entrepreneurial trait* school of thought have attempted to identify traits that are present among historically successful entrepreneurs. One benefit of this approach to a pharmacist or student is that understanding the elements of entrepreneurial traits may allow one to cultivate similar traits to build toward successful entrepreneurship. Traits consistently associated with entrepreneurial activity include achievement, creativity, determination, and technical knowledge. Also, pharmacists and pharmacist managers characterized as having an internal "locus of control" are more likely to assume entrepreneurial rather than employee roles in undertakings.[20] Notably, however, traits alone do not adequately describe all elements of entrepreneurship. To illustrate, according to *venture opportunity*, an entrepreneur's key function involves seeking sources to obtain, develop, and implement products, processes, or services that are either entirely novel or are improvements of existing innovations. For example, an independent pharmacy's purchase of a robotic system to fill prescriptions allows the pharmacist to offer more personalized care and attention to his or her customers while meeting the demands of high-volume prescription filling. An entrepreneurial pharmacist or pharmacist manager who is seeking new opportunities should possess both creativity and market awareness, particularly concerning appropriate timing and the proper match between an innovation and its consumer.[21] *Strategic formulation* emphasizes this process of planning for entrepreneurial effectiveness and is viewed as a central management principle[22,23] (refer to Chapter 3, "Leading and Managing Change," and Chapter 13, "Achieving Results Through Others and Strategic Planning"). In the context of entrepreneurship, this process of planning involves leveraging specific resources to be used explicitly for entrepreneurial functions (e.g., securing **slack resources** and skilled personnel).[24]

Contrasting the micro view, the *macro view of entrepreneurship* focuses on identifying *external* components associated with entrepreneurial effectiveness—particularly those beyond the immediate direction or control of entrepreneurs (i.e., an "external" *locus of control*).[19] The macro view is concerned primarily with the following factors: (1) environmental, (2) financial/capital, and (3) displacement.[19]

The *environmental* component of entrepreneurial effectiveness involves aspects of institutions, including values and norms that create the infrastructure from which entrepreneurs operate.[25] Thus, the degree of success achieved by pharmacist manager entrepreneurs may often be contingent on their work environment. The *financial/capital* perspective stresses the importance of analyzing and acquiring external monetary resources to fund entrepreneurial activity. For example, a start-up business may require **venture capital** or seed monies, while decisions to expand an ongoing operation may require other capital budgeting techniques and cash flow management. Finally, *displacement* involves recognizing that one's

choice to be an entrepreneur may be related to being prevented, redirected, or displaced from conducting other activities.[24] Displacement may be related to political, cultural, or economic factors, such as regulation, perceptions, or recessions that can substantially influence entrepreneurial effectiveness and area of practice. For example, after recognizing the need to serve healthcare clients across the United States regarding guidance, research, advice, strategic planning, and advocacy on health policy and legal issues, pharmacist and lawyer Mary Jo Carden (who had various positions with the American Society of Consultant Pharmacists and cofounded another policy and advocacy firm) founded a healthcare policy and advocacy firm that offers these services.[26] Although Carden was initially prepared for work as a traditional pharmacist and practiced community pharmacy, various political and economic factors likely played a role in her career redirection.

Process Approaches

Beyond the micro and macro views, other models have been used to describe entrepreneurial functions as broad "processes" rather than specific "factors." Instead of identifying specific individual characteristics, these models suggest that various factors must be jointly considered to describe entrepreneurial activity. Three of the more common process approaches include the (1) entrepreneurial events approach,[27] (2) entrepreneurial assessment approach,[21] and (3) multidimensional model of entrepreneurship.[28]

The *entrepreneurial events approach*, presented in **Figure 4-1**, emphasizes that entrepreneurial processes are not isolated activities that occur in succession.[27] More specifically, this model articulates that four distinct events are associated with effective entrepreneurial activities: (1) innovation, (2) triggering events, (3) implementation, and (4) growth. Each of these events is influenced by factors categorized as personal (e.g., risk taking, education, personal values), sociological (e.g., networks, teams), organizational (e.g., strategy, structure), and environmental (e.g., competition, government policy). Other key dimensions of entrepreneurship include team or individual initiative, availability of resources, ability or autonomy to deploy or consume resources, organizational

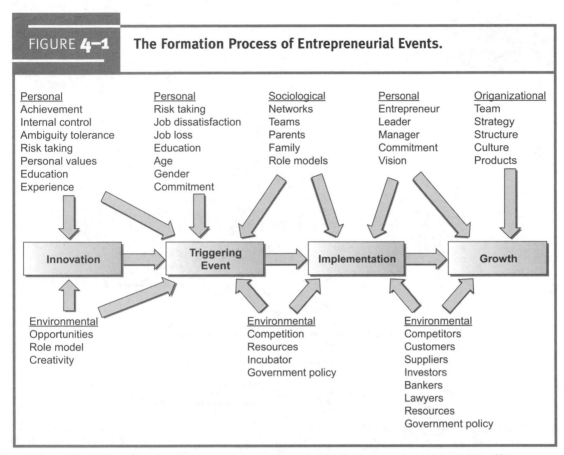

FIGURE **4–1**   **The Formation Process of Entrepreneurial Events.**

This model articulates that four distinct events are associated with effective entrepreneurial activities: (1) innovation, (2) triggering events, (3) implementation, and (4) growth. Each of these events is influenced by factors categorized as personal, sociological, organizational, and environmental.

Source: Courtesy of Bygrave WD. The entrepreneurial paradigm: a philosophical look at its research methodologies. *Entrepreneurship Theory Pract* 1989;4:9.

management, and shared risk taking. For example, two organizations, CVS and the National Council on Aging, are responding to a growing need for attention to the aging U.S. population. Together, these organizations created the Prescription for Better Health program for seniors.[29] After the program's initial positive impact, the organizations announced a three-year extension of their partnership to continue improving the health and well-being of older Americans through pharmacist-led medication management and education.

The *entrepreneurial assessment approach* (**Figure 4–2**) emphasizes the importance of making several assessments (i.e., quantitative, qualitative, strategic, and ethical) according to the type of entrepreneur, environment, and venture involved in an entrepreneurial endeavor.[24] On the basis of these assessments and the **entrepreneurial perspective** of the entrepreneur, an innovative activity or series of activities may then be selected for implementation. Entrepreneurial perspective refers to the comprehensive mix of attributes,

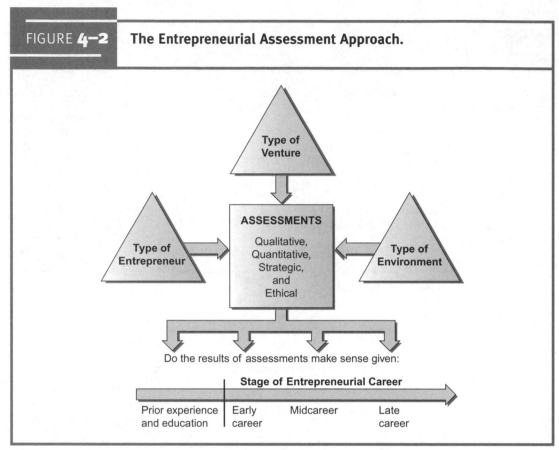

FIGURE **4–2**   **The Entrepreneurial Assessment Approach.**

This approach emphasizes the importance of making several assessments according to the type of entrepreneur, environment, and venture involved in an entrepreneurial endeavor. On the basis of these assessments and the entrepreneurial perspective of the entrepreneur, an innovative activity or series of activities may be selected for implementation. Entrepreneurial perspective is primarily based on the entrepreneur's prior experience, education, and career stage (i.e., early career, midcareer, or late career).

Source: Courtesy of Ronstadt RC. *Entrepreneurship*. Lord Publishing: Dover, MA; 1984.

characteristics, and behaviors that define an individual's entrepreneurial potential[24] and is based primarily on the entrepreneur's prior experience, education, and career stage (early career, midcareer, or late career). Essentially, entrepreneurial perspective embodies the numerous characteristics that are attributed to successful entrepreneurs (e.g., integrity, confidence, perseverance, initiative, creativity, foresight, ability to take calculated risks).[19,24]

The *multidimensional model of entrepreneurship*, presented in **Figure 4–3**, proposes that four broad categories must be considered in assessing the potential success of an entrepreneurial endeavor: (1) individual, (2) environment, (3) organization, and (4) process.[28] This approach emphasizes entrepreneurship as a dynamic process rather than a segmented one.[19] Within the four categories are specific variables, including the entrepreneur's

FIGURE **4–3**

The Multidimensional Model of Entrepreneurship.

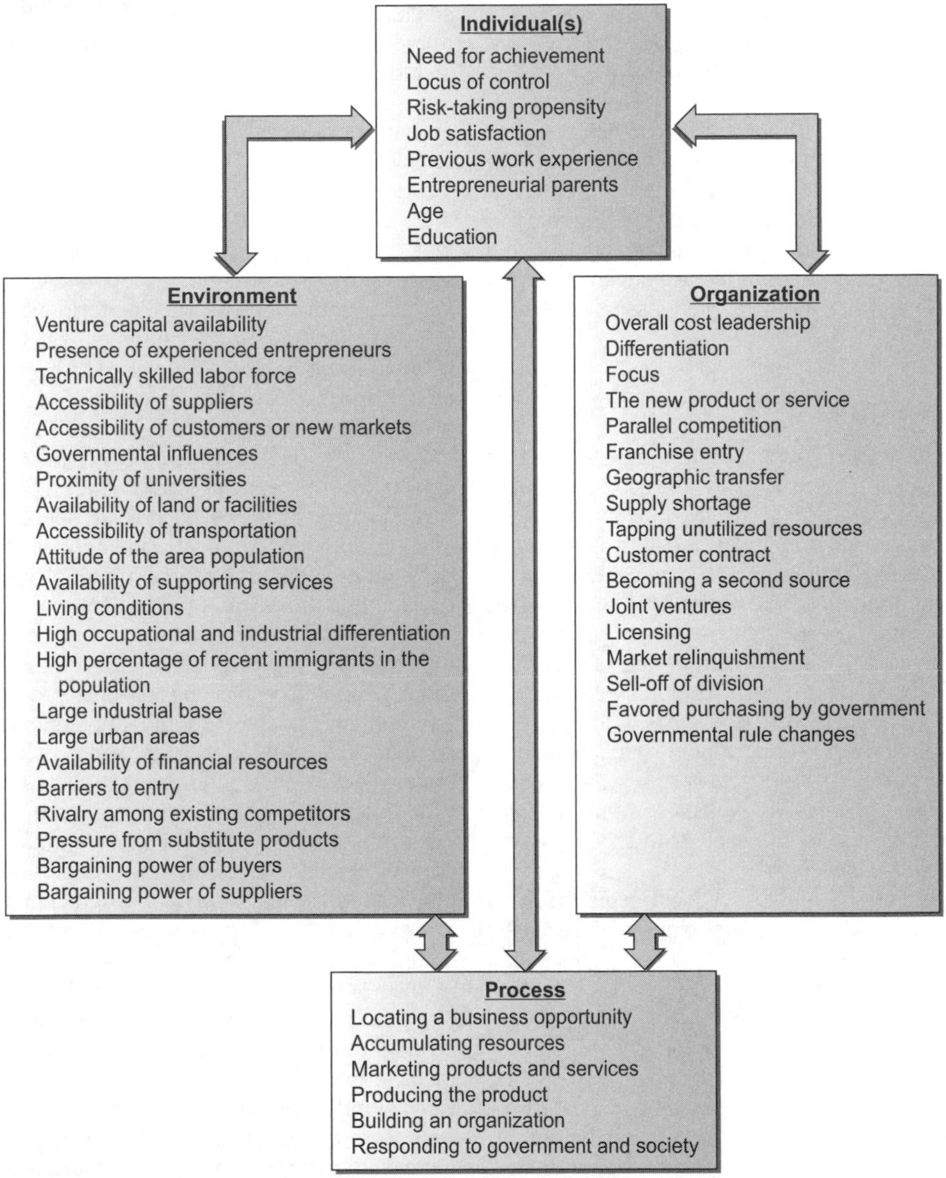

Individual(s)
Need for achievement
Locus of control
Risk-taking propensity
Job satisfaction
Previous work experience
Entrepreneurial parents
Age
Education

Environment
Venture capital availability
Presence of experienced entrepreneurs
Technically skilled labor force
Accessibility of suppliers
Accessibility of customers or new markets
Governmental influences
Proximity of universities
Availability of land or facilities
Accessibility of transportation
Attitude of the area population
Availability of supporting services
Living conditions
High occupational and industrial differentiation
High percentage of recent immigrants in the
    population
Large industrial base
Large urban areas
Availability of financial resources
Barriers to entry
Rivalry among existing competitors
Pressure from substitute products
Bargaining power of buyers
Bargaining power of suppliers

Organization
Overall cost leadership
Differentiation
Focus
The new product or service
Parallel competition
Franchise entry
Geographic transfer
Supply shortage
Tapping unutilized resources
Customer contract
Becoming a second source
Joint ventures
Licensing
Market relinquishment
Sell-off of division
Favored purchasing by government
Governmental rule changes

Process
Locating a business opportunity
Accumulating resources
Marketing products and services
Producing the product
Building an organization
Responding to government and society

This model proposes that four broad categories must be considered in assessing the potential success of an entrepreneurial endeavor: (1) individual, (2) environment, (3) organization, and (4) process. This approach emphasizes entrepreneurship as a dynamic process.

Source: Data from Gartner WB. A conceptual framework for describing the phenomena of new venture creation. *Acad Manag Rev* 1985;10:696–706.

need for achievement (i.e., individual factor), venture capital available outside of the organization (i.e., environmental factor), overall leadership strategy (i.e., organizational factor), and the identification of a business opportunity (i.e., process factor). In contrast to other models, the multidimensional model of entrepreneurship suggests entrepreneurship cannot be explained simply by individual entrepreneurial characteristics or activities but instead involves a complex integration of several factors. Although specific variables within the model may not be equally relevant to every entrepreneurial endeavor, their assessment may be useful.

INNOVATION

A consistent theme within entrepreneurship is that *innovation* is a central tenet to success. Drucker states innovation is "a specific function of entrepreneurship, whether in an existing business, a public service institution, or a new venture started by a lone individual."[30(p67)] He further emphasizes that systematic, rather than piecemeal, approaches to innovation are key determinants of entrepreneurial success.[30] An organization's best innovation policy begins with an analysis of internal and external sources of opportunity. ❸ *Entrepreneurs are often viewed as successful based on the extent to which they systematically assess environments, pinpoint and seize opportunities, analyze innovations, and minimize coincidental risks.*

Organizations must have a strategic focus on innovation and entrepreneurship and explicitly formulate strategies that support endeavors. **Strategy** is defined as the pattern or plan that integrates an organization's major goals, policies, and action sequences into a cohesive whole.[31] A well-conceived strategy is instrumental in guiding an organization to achieve a unique posture or position within the marketplace, given the organization's **s**trengths, **w**eaknesses, **o**pportunities, and **t**hreats (**SWOT analysis**; refer to Chapter 13, "Achieving Results Through Others and Strategic Planning"). Strategy involves asking logical questions about ways to deliver value and quality to customers. In a broad sense, strategy involves **strategic positioning**, which is used to help an organization achieve sustainable **competitive**

advantage, and has been defined as performing different activities from competitors or performing similar activities in different ways.[32-34] There are a number of sources of competitive advantage, including the novel use of unique customer knowledge, shared values within a corporation and among employees, patented technology or processes, and cost leadership. The Walgreens Company, for example, pioneered the concepts of a 24-hour store and drive-thru pharmacy, and it was one of the first drugstore chains to offer prescription drug information in multiple languages.

An organization whose performance excels through changing market conditions often does so by addressing both its strategy and its operational effectiveness. Operational effectiveness, which historically has been a key focus of companies, may be described as conducting activities that are similar to competitors, though offering improvements exemplified by increased speed, higher quality, and reduced cost. Operational effectiveness offers value to consumers through best practice methods, such as total quality management, reengineering, **Six Sigma**, and **benchmarking**.[33,34] One pharmacist manager's Six Sigma project might be improving first-dose processes or, alternatively, overseeing the implementation of computerized physician order entry, which, ultimately, involves the entire healthcare system. When applied to pharmacy, operational effectiveness may involve mitigating or eliminating dispensing errors, while strategy may entail expanding pharmaceutical care services to encompass programs that involve behavioral modifications, complex adherence interventions, or personalized medicine. For example, one large children's hospital conducted a Six Sigma project to decrease errors during pharmacist order processing. The medication safety pharmacist noted that window visits would sometimes prevent the pharmacist from completing an order in its entirety, which increased errors; by moving the pharmacist away from the window, errors decreased. Summarizing the role of operational effectiveness and strategy, Michael Porter, a strategic positioning expert, stated, "A company can outperform rivals only if it can establish a difference it can preserve. It must deliver greater value, or create comparable value at a lower cost, or both. . . . The essence of strategy is choosing to perform activities differently than rivals do."[33]

A comprehensive understanding of the market and the ability to recognize patterns of innovation are critical elements to identify gaps that exist in products and services and to craft strategies necessary to achieve entrepreneurial success.[35–37] Three factors often emphasized to establish an organization's innovative focus are:

- Well-crafted strategies that broadly encompass both the vision and mission of the organization, yet are concise enough to yield tangible objectives and goals.
- An understanding of the environment and consumers.
- Clear articulation of the aforementioned factors across the organization to ensure consistency.[38]

Thus, a commitment to providing quality in health care by developing or implementing novel, cost-effective technologies may require that an organization establish the formal role of innovation within its vision statement. The mission, objectives, and goals would reflect these desired outcomes, and the organization would establish a culture, infrastructure, and reward system that promotes innovative activity (e.g., cross-functional teams, slack resources, pilot programs, innovative bonus packages) and establishes achievable short- and long-term goals.

To systematically aid in the success of entrepreneurial endeavors, one method suggests that organizations specifically identify what they intend to accomplish through innovation activities.[39] Questions to consider include:

- Is **breakthrough innovation** (or disruptive innovation) sought vis-à-vis **incremental innovation** (or sustaining innovation)?
- Is innovation desired to increase the organization's growth, status, or capacity potential?
- Is innovation desired for particular processes?

In this context, breakthrough innovations are typically more difficult to manage through any given structured process. Breakthrough innovations, also called disruptive technologies, are those that often radically alter a frame of reference and transform an entire organization or marketplace. For example, a breakthrough innovation may involve reengineering a healthcare facility to use cost-effective technologies for patients and to develop new ones.[40] Given that breakthrough innovations are often broad in scope and can affect the entire organization, their development typically requires an explicit strategic intent, a team approach, and resources devoted to team research and development activities. In contrast to breakthrough innovations, incremental innovations are characterized by offering improvements to existing products, processes, or services and do not typically or significantly alter established market environments or organizations.[41] As such, these innovations are often used to complement breakthroughs.[40]

Innovation and Entrepreneurial Opportunities in Pharmacy

❹ *Pharmacy exists as a discipline that offers both services and goods to consumers, both of which have simultaneously grown as a function of technological advances.* Value-added services, including compounding, pharmaceutical care, pharmacokinetic monitoring, patient counseling, disease screening, drug utilization review, formulary management, home health care, MTM, wellness programs, and disease state management are considered mainstays of practice in many settings.[42] Emerging opportunities may involve patient risk management programs centered around personalized medicine, specialty pharmacy consultation in certain disease areas, and an array of services associated with biotechnology agents. Furthermore, improvement of patient adherence to medications and medication safety remain important to providers, patients, and employer groups.

Specific categories of entrepreneurial opportunities in the healthcare sector are:

- *The unexpected* (e.g., unintended consequences of healthcare policies: unexpected external events or successes, such as the drug finasteride's unintended side effect of hair growth, which led to remarketing the prostate product for use in male pattern hair loss)

- *System incongruities* (e.g., differences in patient expectations and the delivery of care at the patient versus population level: variation in perceptions versus reality, such as differing patient needs with specialty pharmaceutical products when particular comorbidities are present)
- *Process improvement* (e.g., total quality improvement: information systems such as the implementation of physician order entry or **e-prescribing**)
- *Changes in industry and market structure* (e.g., financing and delivery of health care, such as the implementation of **telepharmacy** in rural hospitals or Medicare Part D allowing pharmacist reimbursement for MTM)
- *Increased aging populations* (e.g., demographic changes, diversity, and disparity: providing a continued need for pharmacists to assume both traditional and nontraditional roles as a large sector of the U.S. population ages)
- *Existing pharmacotherapeutic disparities* (e.g., eliminating disparities related to unequal pharmaceutical treatment among certain populations)[43]
- *Changes in consumer perceptions, mood, and meaning* (e.g., patient autonomy: consumerism, including internet-based social forums or online consumer information compendia)
- *Growth in new knowledge* (e.g., genomics, biotechnology, nonscientific information)[11,30,41]

Promoting Innovation Through Structural, Cultural, and Human Resource Variables

❺ *In identifying more specific approaches to stimulate entrepreneurship within organizations, three general variables may promote innovation: (1) cultural, (2) human resource, and (3) structural.*[2,44] **Structural variables** remain the most thoroughly investigated components that can be readily altered to catalyze innovation and specifically relate to the way the organization is designed. Those specific structural components that have been most commonly associated with innovative successes have been identified as

- Long tenure of management
- Abundance of slack resources
- High levels of intergroup communication

- Presence of organic versus mechanistic organizational structures[2,44]

A long tenure of management often builds legitimacy among employees within organizations and may ensure that key decision makers have acquired sufficient knowledge and experience necessary for task completion. Slack resources provide the means through which an infrastructure exists to purchase materials needed to innovate, to institute and assess various innovations, or to hedge against loss when failures occur in the entrepreneurial process. Organic organizational structures, illustrated in **Figure 4-4**, have been suggested to promote innovation, due in part to characteristics that allow for greater flexibility and adaptability. In contrast to "top-down" mechanistic structures (organizations that possess high job formalizations, fixed duties, centralized decision making, and formal communication channels), organic organizations are characterized by low job formalizations, adaptable duties, participative and decentralized decision making, extensive informal communication channels, and cross-functional teams that collaborate and span across all levels of an organization's hierarchy.

Beyond the actual structure of an organization, both **cultural variables** and **human resource variables** have been identified as other components that are vital in catalyzing innovation.[2,44] Concerning factors involved in shaping an organization's culture, rewarding appropriate risk-taking behaviors, regardless of outcome, and encouraging pilot programs improve successful entrepreneurship. Focusing on human resource factors (i.e., those directly involving employee selection, development, and evaluation), actively training and developing employees, as well as offering higher levels of job security improve innovation. ❻ *Developing an organization that stimulates innovation ultimately requires an investment in the organization's **social capital**, referring to the ability to allow individuals and teams to reach their full productive potential by understanding and furthering resources, aptitude, and motivation.*[2,45] Building social capital within healthcare settings is a key element in creating a working atmosphere where new ideas can be expressed and where relevant innovation can take place. Refer to Chapter 13

FIGURE **4-4**   **Organic Versus Mechanistic Organizations.**

Mechanistic Structure   Organic Structure

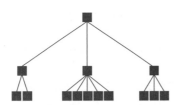 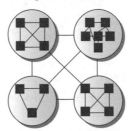

Mechanistic Characteristics   Organic Characteristics

- High horizontal differentiation
- Rigid hierarchical relationships
- Fixed duties
- High formalization
- Formalized communication channels
- Centralized decision authority

- Low horizontal differentiation
- Collaboration (both vertical and horizontal)
- Adaptable duties
- Low formalization
- Informal communication
- Decentralized decision authority

Organic organizations promote innovation, due in large part to characteristics (such as low formalization and collaboration) that allow for greater flexibility and adaptability. In contrast, innovation is more difficult in mechanistic organizations because of high job formalization, fixed job duties, centralized decision making, and formal communication channels.

Sources: From Robbins, Stephen P., *Organizational Behavior: Concepts, Controversies and Applications*, 9th Editions, © 2001. Reprinted by permission of Pearson Education, Inc., Upper Saddle River, NJ.

("Achieving Results Through Others and Strategic Planning") and Chapter 20 ("Creating and Identifying Desirable Workplaces").

❼ *Motivating employees to become innovative requires a thoughtful and multifaceted approach that involves, in part, assessing the needs of individuals, identifying and removing barriers that prevent effectiveness, providing needed resources, and establishing reward systems that acknowledge both innovative activity and outcomes.* Pharmacist leaders and managers must realize that nurturing the entrepreneurial ability of a person requires several levels of attention, often beginning with an assessment of how each person understands and individualizes the process of innovation or their level of **risk aversion**. Encouraging development through continuous learning and studying

and facilitating open dialogue promotes skills development and identification of shortcomings in existing products, processes, and services within an organization. This enhances creative thinking and future development. Pharmacist leaders and managers can promote innovation not only by nurturing and developing employees but also by providing feedback that continues to motivate and promote those who behave in an innovative manner.[45] The more candid the pharmacist leader or manager is about actual issues, goals, and strategies, the greater the employees' potential contributions.[46]

The Learning Organization

❽ *A **learning organization** is defined as one that has developed an ongoing capacity to adapt and*

TABLE **4–2**	Key Characteristics of a Learning Organization

- A shared vision exists that has reached consensus.

- People discard their old ways of thinking and the standard routines that they use for solving problems or doing their jobs.

- Members think of all organizational processes, activities, and functions as part of a system of interrelationships.

- People openly communicate across vertical and horizontal boundaries without fear of criticism or punishment.

- People sublimate their personal self-interests and fragmented departmental interests to work together to achieve the organization's shared vision.

Sources: Data from Senge PM. *The Fifth Discipline*. New York, NY: Doubleday; 1990. Robbins SP. *Essentials of Organizational Behavior*. 7th ed. Upper Saddle River, NJ: Prentice Hall; 2002.

change rapidly, often by using highly innovative methods for resolving problems and increasing performance.[47] A learning organization combines several of the positive aspects of structural, cultural, and human resource variables described previously.[47] The learning organization also embodies several positive characteristics emphasized within the management sciences: continuous improvement, positive forms of conflict, transformational leadership, teamwork, and innovativeness.[2] **Table 4–2** summarizes five of the key characteristics within a learning organization and emphasizes establishing alignment among employees and information channels that transcend the entire organization.[47] By seeking to become a learning organization, entrepreneurial entities may develop numerous competitive advantages due to their capacity to recognize and rapidly adapt to market conditions, a process that has been collectively described as alertness.[48] Jack Welch, former chief executive officer of General Electric, stressed similar characteristics with the creation of the **boundaryless organization**, wherein a large firm could rapidly seize emerging opportunities by removing the constraints of hierarchical barriers.[49]

MANAGERIAL CONSIDERATIONS IN EVALUATING AND IMPLEMENTING INNOVATIONS

❾ *It is important to evaluate new innovations using robust methodologies. There are a number of approaches that exist through which an innovation may be evaluated, including cost-effectiveness analysis (CEA), cost-utility analysis (CUA), or **cost-benefit analysis** (CBA).*[50–53] *Collectively, these approaches are comprehensive economic evaluations that compare the costs and various outcome measures associated with a new technology versus those costs and outcomes associated with an alternative technology or intervention* (refer to **Table 4–3** for additional information regarding economic analyses). In a strictly managerial context (and before a formal economic analysis), if an innovation or new concept has not undergone any formal evaluation, a conservative approach is recommended, and one should "proceed with caution," as resistance may develop that could impede the innovation's adoption.[54]

Recognizing the reality of any business opportunity or innovation can be difficult. A qualitative

TABLE **4–3**	**Economic Analyses**

Consequences of interventions may be classified as economic, humanistic, or clinical outcomes, whereas costs are specified based upon the perspective of a study (i.e., "Costs to whom?"). Costs may be direct (e.g., healthcare utilization), indirect (e.g., productivity), or intangible (e.g., pain and suffering).[50] Economic analyses fall within one of the following categories of full economic analyses (CEA, CUA, CBA), or cost minimization analysis (CMA):[51-53]

- *Cost minimization analysis* may often be regarded as a partial form of economic analysis that measures costs of various technologies but assumes that outcomes are identical across intervention arms. Thus, the CMA ultimately tends to focus on cost assessments alone.

- *Cost-effectiveness analysis* (CEA) compares natural unit endpoints (e.g., clinical measures) and costs across interventions, thus producing a price per unit change, which then must be further examined to determine whether it is worth the resources allocated.

- *Cost-utility analysis* (CUA) is similar to CEA except that it uses an outcome measure that reflects both the quality and quantity of life that result from an intervention. This approach yields an outcome of a quality-adjusted life year (QALY) that combines length of life with a measure of utility.

- *Cost-benefit analysis* (CBA) compares the costs and benefits of intervention alternatives wherein outcomes involve assessing changes in health states that are measured in monetary terms. Thus, CBA allows direct comparisons and provides an absolute value or worth, calculated as benefits minus costs of the alternatives (i.e., CBA is often represented as a net benefit or a net loss but may additionally be presented as a cost-benefit ratio).

Sources: Data from Bungay KM, Sanchez LA. Types of economic and humanistic outcome assessments. In: Barnette D, Bressler L, Brouse S, et al, eds. *Updates in Therapeutics: The Pharmacotherapy Preparatory Course, 2008*. Vol. 2. Lenexa KS, ed. American College of Clinical Pharmacy, 2008; 2:303–350. Drummond M, O'Brien B, Stoddart G, Torrance G. *Methods for the Economic Evaluation of Health Care Programmes*. 2nd ed. Oxford: Oxford Medical Publications; 1997. Gold M, Siegel J, Russell L, Weinstein M. *Cost-Effectiveness in Health and Medicine*. Oxford: Oxford University Press; 1996. Levin H, McEwan P. *Cost-Effectiveness Analysis: Methods and Applications*. 2nd ed. Thousand Oaks, CA: Sage Publications; 2000.

approach to evaluating innovation may be useful to determine whether (1) the new concept is actually novel, (2) the organization can capitalize on the innovation, and (3) there is value for the organization.[50] As part of this evaluation, the entrepreneur must (1) ensure that consumers have been specifically defined, (2) question whether a *broad* consumer base will receive a distinct benefit from the innovation or whether a *niche* is better targeted, (3) evaluate the accuracy of data supporting the innovation's value, and (4) identify what the consumer's willingness to pay may be. The second issue, the organization's ability to capitalize on the innovation, warrants an evaluation of the innovation's uniqueness within the marketplace. This requires an assessment of the competitive advantage of the innovation over time. The final issue requires evaluating the innovation's return on investment. Common approaches involve robust discounted cash flow analyses, such as a **net present value** or internal **rate of return** computation, where full transparency concerning time and cost associated with research, development, and marketing are revealed. Other aspects to evaluate include how the innovation aligns with the broader long-term vision and mission of the organization, how the innovation may stimulate organizational and market growth, and whether there is any potentially unforeseen risk or resistance associated with the implementation of the innovation.

Following the development and assessment of a potentially useful innovation, ❿ *organizations may overemphasize identification of innovative solutions for opportunities and underemphasize implementation and **diffusion**.*[54] *The diffusion of innovation and subsequent rate of adoption involves:*

- *Attributes of the innovation as perceived by consumers (e.g., relative advantage, compatibility, complexity)*[55]
- *Characteristics of consumers within the environment (e.g., behavior; demographics; adopter categories, such as innovators, who are the first to adopt an innovation; **early adopters**, who*

embrace new products/services and follow innovators in adopting an innovation; early majority, who are the first segment of the larger market to adopt the innovation; late majority, who only adopt the innovation after it has been adopted by the majority; and laggards, who are highly conservative and generally the last to adopt the innovation; **Figure 4–5**)[55]
- *System-/organization-level variables (e.g., communication channels, resources, personnel training)*

Inappropriately introducing planned change or being unaware of a potential for resistance may contribute to failure of an otherwise useful innovation (refer to Chapter 3, "Leading and Managing Change").[2,44,56] Creating a particular culture within a pharmacy practice setting may either foster or discourage the diffusion of innovation. At least three considerations are required to create a culture to improve the diffusion of innovation: (1) developing an environment that authorizes, permits, enables, and empowers innovation;

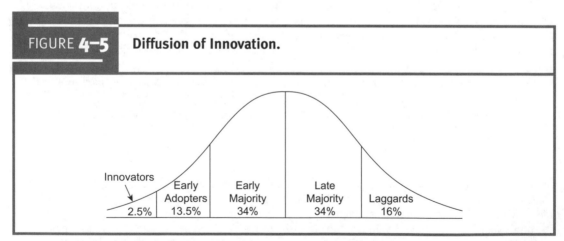

FIGURE **4–5**   **Diffusion of Innovation.**

This figure displays the distribution of innovation adopter categories. Innovators are a small group (2.5%) who are the first to adopt an innovation, followed by the slightly larger early adopter group (13.5%). The early majority (34%) and later majority (34%), respectively, are the next and largest groups to adopt an innovation. The final group to adopt an innovation are the laggards (16%).

Source: Reprinted with the permission of The Free Press, a Division of Simon and Schuster, Inc., from *Diffusion of Innovations*, Fifth Edition by Everett M. Rogers. Copyright © 1995, 2003 by Everett M. Rogers. Copyright 1962, 1971, 1983 by The Free Press, All rights reserved.

(2) nurturing people's abilities within an organization to be innovative; and (3) encouraging people's desire to act in an innovative manner.[2,44] Developing an environment that permits and enables innovation requires building social capital, wherein relationships reach their full productive potential—a vitally important element in the innovation process. Recognizing people's abilities, knowledge, and creativity will foster the diffusion of innovation.[47] Thus, building social capital with one's employees in a healthcare setting is key to creating an environment where new ideas can be expressed and where relevant innovation can take place.

Nurturing a person's ability to be innovative requires several levels of attention. A personal understanding of the process of innovation is necessary. In addition, encouraging continuous learning will improve employee skills and refine their abilities to identify shortcomings of current processes. Moreover, curiosity is a hallmark characteristic of an innovator, and an environment that allows employees to ask questions will nurture innovative capabilities. Finally, the more candid the pharmacist leader or manager is about actual issues, goals, and strategy, the better the contributions will be.[37]

Motivating and encouraging an employee to act innovatively also involves a multifaceted approach. Pharmacist managers and leaders must recognize and remove barriers that prevent employees from conducting themselves in an effective manner. Education must be emphasized at various levels to ensure employee development.

Beyond these considerations, a pharmacist manager must consider aspects of equity and how individuals are rewarded for their day-to-day contributions and for exceptional innovative contributions. Openness to creative thought is a differentiating distinction that fosters success.[47] Thus, a culture of innovation and creativity will flourish if pharmacist managers and leaders consider new possibilities and reward contributions (refer to Chapter 20, "Creating and Identifying Desirable Workplaces").[38]

SUMMARY

This chapter defines innovation and entrepreneurship, describes entrepreneurial processes and approaches, differentiates strategy from operational effectiveness, identifies broad categories of entrepreneurial opportunity, presents methods to promote innovative activity, and describes basic approaches to evaluate and implement innovations. Overall, healthcare organizations must strategically focus on innovation in addition to seeking operational effectiveness. Pharmacists and pharmacist leaders and managers can promote innovation by nurturing employees to continuously identify and seize appropriate opportunities while minimizing risk.

References

1. Drucker PF. *Management Challenges for the 21st Century*. New York, NY: Harper Business; 1999.

2. Robbins SP. *Organizational Behavior*. 9th ed. Upper Saddle River, NJ: Prentice Hall; 2001.

3. Kao J. *Innovation Nation: How America Is Losing Its Innovation Edge, Why It Matters, and What We Can Do to Get It Back*. New York, NY: Free Press; 2008.

4. Yapps Cohen L. Top 10 reasons why we need innovation. Available at: http://www.amcreativityassoc.org. Accessed June 1, 2009.

5. ASPIRA/Morgan Stanley Entrepreneurial Leadership Initiative. Entrepreneurial Leadership Program Facili-tator's Guide. Available at: http://www.scribd.com/doc/296109/Entrepreneurship. Accessed June 7, 2009.

6. Prabhudesai A. Top 10 reasons why you should be an entrepreneur. Available at: http://trak.in/tags/business/2007/08/11/top-10-reasons-an-entrepreneur-start-your-own-business-your-own-boss/. Accessed June 7, 2009.

7. Borkowski N, Gordon J. Entrepreneurial organizations: the driving force for improving quality in the healthcare industry. *J Health Hum Serv Adm* 2006;28: 531–549.

8. Phillips FS, Garman AN. Barriers to entrepreneurship in healthcare organizations. *J Health Hum Serv Adm* 2006;28:472–484.

9. Schumpeter JA. *Capitalism, Socialism, and Democracy*. New York, NY: Harper and Row; 1942.

10. Pharmacist-turned-entrepreneur has the right medicine. *Arizona Republic*, 2008. Available at: http://www.azcentral.com/news/articles/2008/07/16/20080716biz-apothecary0716.html. Accessed April 1, 2009.

11. Drucker PF. *Innovation and Entrepreneurship: Practice and Principles*. New York, NY: Harper and Row; 1985.

12. Schumpeter JA. *The Theory of Economic Development*. Cambridge, MA: Harvard University Press; 1934.

13. Timmons JA. *New Venture Creation*. Homewood, IL: Irwin; 1994.

14. Pharmacy groups unveil findings, future of "Project Destiny." *Medical News Today*, 2008. Available at: http://www.medicalnewstoday.com/articles/99710.php. Accessed April 1, 2009.

15. Wisconsin Pharmacy Quality Collaborative. Available at: http://www.pswi.org/professional/wpqc.htm. Accessed April 1, 2009.

16. Pinchot G. *Intrapreneuring: Why You Don't Have to Leave the Corporation to Become an Entrepreneur*. New York, NY: HarperCollins; 1985.

17. Dollinger M. *Entrepreneurship: Strategies and Resources*. Lombard, IL: Marsh Publications; 2007.

18. Modrzejewski KA, Provost GP. Pharmacists' involvement with vaccinations leads to preventive health care role. *Am J Health-Syst Pharm* 2003;60:1724–1728.

19. Kuratko DF, Hodgetts RM. *Entrepreneurship: A Contemporary Approach*. 4th ed. Fort Worth, TX: Dryden Press; 1998.

20. Inegbenebor A. Pharmacists as entrepreneurs or employees: the role of locus of control. *Trop J Pharm Res* 2007;6:747–754.

21. Rx for success: Pharmacist-entrepreneur melds hometown charm, robotics, and deliveries as he competes with chains. *Bus J*, 2009. Available at: http://triad.bizjournals.com/triad/stories/2009/03/16/smallb1.html?page=1. Accessed May 1, 2009.

22. Porter ME. *Competitive Strategy*. New York, NY: Free Press; 1980.

23. Steiner GA. *Strategic Planning*. New York, NY: Free Press; 1979.

24. Ronstadt RC. *Entrepreneurship*. Dover, MA: Lord Publishing; 1984.

25. Van de Ven AH. The development of an infrastructure for entrepreneurship. *J Bus Venturing* 1993;3:211–230.

26. Millonig MK, Carden MJ. Medicare Part D update: what the pharmacist needs to know. Available at: http://www.rxschool.com/course/info.cfm/course_id/282. Accessed April 1, 2009.

27. Bygrave WD. The entrepreneurial paradigm: a philosophical look at its research methodologies. *Entrepreneurship Theory Pract* 1989;4:7–26.

28. Gartner WB. A conceptual framework for describing the phenomena of new venture creation. *Acad Manag Rev* 1985;10:696–706.

29. CVS Caremark Presents at NCOA-ASA Conference on Company's Commitment to Recruiting and Retaining Mature Workers. Bio-Medicine, 2008. Available at: http://www.bio-medicine.org/medicine-news-1/CVS-Caremark-Presents-at-NCOA-ASA-Conference-on-Companys-Commitment-to-Recruiting-and-Retaining-Mature-Workers-15407-1/. Accessed April 1, 2009.

30. Drucker PF. The discipline of innovation. *Harv Bus Rev* 1985;63(3):67–72.

31. Mintzberg H, Quinn JB. *The Strategy Process: Concepts, Contexts, Cases*. 3rd ed. Upper Saddle River, NJ: Prentice Hall; 1996.

32. Porter M. *Competitive Advantage*. New York, NY; 1985.

33. Porter ME. What Is strategy? *Harv Bus Rev* 1996;74(6):61–78.

34. Hamel G. Strategy as a revolution. *Harv Bus Rev* 1996;74(4):69–82.

35. Henderson B. The origin of strategy. *Harv Bus Rev* 1989;67(6):139–143.

36. Mintzberg H. Crafting strategy. *Harv Bus Rev* 1987;65(4):66–75.

37. Kenichi O. Getting back to strategy. *Harv Bus Rev* 1988;66(6):149–156.

38. Engle P. *The Exceptional Individual: Achieving Business Success One Person at a Time*. New York, NY: St. Martin's Press; 1998.

39. Palmer D, Kaplan SA. Framework for strategic innovation: blending strategy and creative exploration to discover further business opportunities. Internet: www.innovationpoint.com. Accessed November 9, 2008.

40. Marketing Science Institute. Building Long-Term Firm Value Through Innovation. MSI Report No. 06-122. Cambridge, MA: Marketing Science Institute; 2006.

41. Ettlie J, Bridges W, O'Keefe R. Organization strategy and structural differences for radical versus incremental innovation. *Manag Sci* 1984;30:682–695.

42. Shepherd MD. Defining and marketing value added services. *Am Pharm* 1995;NS35(1):46–54.

43. Hall-Lipsy E, Chisholm-Burns MA. Pharmacotherapeutic disparities: demonstrating racial, ethnic, and sex variations in medication treatment. *Am J Health-Syst Pharm*. In press.

44. Robbins SP. *Essentials of Organizational Behavior*. 7th ed. Upper Saddle River, NJ: Prentice Hall; 2002.

45. Kreitner R, Kinicki A. *Organizational Behavior: The Quest for People Centered-Organizations*. Columbus, OH: McGraw-Hill; 2001.

46. Bean R, Radford R. *The Business of Innovation: Managing the Corporate Imagination for Maximum Results*. New York, NY: AMACOM; 2002.

47. Senge PM. *The Fifth Discipline*. New York, NY: Doubleday; 1990.

48. Norton WI, Moore WT. Entrepreneurial risk: have we been asking the wrong question? *Small Bus Econ* 2002;18:281–287.

49. Welch J, Byrne JA. *Jack: Straight from the Gut*. New York, NY: Warner Books; 2001.

50. Bungay KM, Sanchez LA. Types of economic and humanistic outcome assessments. In: Barnette D, Bressler L, Brouse S, et al, eds. *Updates in Therapeutics: The Pharmacotherapy Preparatory Course, 2008*. Vol. 2. Lenexa KS, ed. American College of Clinical Pharmacy, 2008; 2:303–350.

51. Drummond M, O'Brien B, Stoddart G, Torrance G. *Methods for the Economic Evaluation of Health Care Programmes*. 2nd ed. Oxford: Oxford Medical Publications; 1997.

52. Gold M, Siegel J, Russell L, Weinstein M. *Cost-Effectiveness in Health and Medicine*. Oxford: Oxford University Press; 1996.

53. Levin H, McEwan P. *Cost-Effectiveness Analysis: Methods and Applications*. 2nd ed. Thousand Oaks, CA: Sage Publications; 2000.

54. Pinchot G, Pellman R. *Intrapreneuring in Action: A Handbook for Business Innovation*. San Francisco, CA: Berrett-Koehler Publishers; 1999.

55. Rogers EM. *Diffusion of Innovations*. 5th ed. New York, NY: Free Press; 2003.

56. Lewin K. Group decision and social change. In: Swanson GE, Newcome TM, Hartle EL, eds. *Readings in Social Psychology*. 2nd ed. New York, NY: Holt; 1952.

Abbreviations

CBA:	cost-benefit analysis
CEA:	cost-effectiveness analysis
CMA:	cost minimization analysis
CUA:	cost-utility analysis
HIV:	human immunodeficiency virus
MTM:	medication therapy management
SWOT:	strengths, weaknesses, opportunities, threats

Case Scenarios

CASE ONE: Helen Heffernan is a clinical pharmacist who works at an urban teaching hospital that serves a diverse patient population. As she works diligently to monitor and improve patient care by evaluating nonelectronic (paper) medical charts and medical orders, Dr. Heffernan notices an increase in the use of agents designated through national guidelines as third- or fourth-line therapies, which are not cost-effective as drugs of choice. Describe a possible innovation to address the problem Dr. Heffernan has identified. What factors should Helen consider when facilitating the implementation of the innovation?

CASE TWO: Dirk Robert and Lynette Wood are staff pharmacists working at a retail pharmacy in a community in California with a large diabetes patient population. They are both residency trained and are certified diabetes educators. Dirk and Lynette would like to start a diabetes

(continues)

counseling program at the pharmacy as they believe a substantial segment of the pharmacy's patient population needs this service and would be willing to pay for diabetes counseling that includes medication management. Provide recommendations to Dirk and Lynette that will help them achieve success in promoting this innovative value-added service to the owner of the pharmacy.

CASE THREE: In 1886, Dr. John Pemberton, a pharmacist from Atlanta, Georgia, created the Coca-Cola recipe in a three-legged brass kettle in his backyard. The soft drink was first sold to the public in Jacob's Pharmacy in Atlanta on May 8, 1886. One year later, another Atlanta pharmacist and businessman, Asa Candler, bought the formula for Coca-Cola from Dr. Pemberton for $2,300 (i.e., approximately $35,000 in 2010 dollars). By the late 1890s, Coca-Cola was one of America's most popular fountain drinks, largely because of Candler's strong marketing of the product. With Asa Candler in charge, the Coca-Cola Company increased syrup sales by more than 4,000% between 1890 and 1900, in part by selling syrup to independent bottling companies licensed to sell the drink (rather than offering the syrup only within soda fountain pharmacies). What entrepreneurial characteristics do you believe Asa Candler possessed?

Additional Resources Available Online!

Visit the Student Companion Web site at http://healthprofessions.jbpub.com/pharmacymanagement for interactive study tools and additional resources.

See www.rxugace.com to learn how you can obtain continuing pharmacy education for this content.

LAW AND ETHICS

CHAPTER 5
Significant Laws Affecting Pharmacy
Practice Management

CHAPTER 6
Ethical Decision Making

SIGNIFICANT LAWS AFFECTING PHARMACY PRACTICE MANAGEMENT

KENNETH M. DUKE, MBA, RPh

ELIZABETH HALL-LIPSY, JD, MPH

LEARNING OBJECTIVES

After completing the chapter, the reader will be able to

1. Explain the purpose of the Health Insurance Portability and Accountability Act (HIPAA) and how it relates to protected health information.

2. List the elements of a Privacy Notice, as required by HIPAA.

3. Differentiate between permitted, incidental, and nonroutine disclosures under the HIPAA privacy rule.

4. Identify who needs HIPAA training.

5. Discuss the requirements of the Omnibus Budget Reconciliation Act of 1990.

6. Describe the intent of the Prescription Drug Marketing Act, and its effect on the distribution of drug samples by pharmacies.

7. Cite required elements of the Haight Act that must be disclosed on the Web sites of internet pharmacies.

KEY CONCEPTS

❶ The Health Insurance Portability and Accountability Act of 1996 (HIPAA) was enacted primarily to improve access to health care through increased portability and continuity of health insurance, specifically allowing workers and their families to retain health insurance coverage when they changed or lost a job. HIPAA and its Privacy Rule were drafted with an eye toward the increasing use of electronic methods for data storage and use and the need to simplify electronic healthcare transactions.

❷ To ensure compliance with the HIPAA Privacy Rule, covered entities, including pharmacies, must provide training for their employees (as necessary and appropriate given employees' work functions). If a user has access to protected health information (PHI), whether this access is or is not needed to perform his or her duties, then it is necessary to train this person in appropriate use and security of PHI.

❸ To ensure consistency and efficiency throughout the healthcare and health insurance industry, the Department of Health and Human Services adopted national standards to make it easier for health plans, healthcare clearinghouses, physicians, pharmacists, hospitals, and other healthcare providers to process claims and other transactions electronically.

❹ The Omnibus Budget Reconciliation Act of 1990 (OBRA 90) was enacted as a means of controlling the cost of Medicaid reimbursement for prescription medication. As a result, OBRA 90 required each state to design and implement a drug utilization review program to enable pharmacists to provide better information about drugs prescribed and dispensed to their Medicaid patients.

❺ The Prescription Drug Marketing Act (PDMA) was enacted to ensure the safety and effectiveness of prescription drug products purchased by consumers and to avoid the unacceptable risk that counterfeit, adulterated, misbranded, subpotent, or expired drugs were being sold to the American public. Several specific PDMA regulations are related to distributing drug products in the United States, including prohibiting reimportation of prescription drugs that have been manufactured in the United States, restricting the distribution of prescription drug samples, and banning the resale of drugs by hospitals and other entities.

❻ Given the exponential increase in the average health consumer's use of the internet in recent years, pharmacists and pharmacist managers must understand the development of legislation, such as the Haight Act, that governs the internet as a means of drug distribution.

❼ The Haight Act amends the Controlled Substances Act by adding the statement that no controlled substance "may be delivered, distributed, or dispensed by means of the internet without a valid prescription." It further specifies that, for a prescription to be valid, a patient–practitioner relationship must exist; this is consistent with various other provisions in federal and state law.

INTRODUCTION

Several federal laws affect the practice of pharmacy. The chief purpose of these laws is to protect the public by ensuring the safe, efficient, and skilled practice of pharmacy services. This chapter provides a basic overview of four key laws that all pharmacists and pharmacist managers should understand in order to ensure compliance; this overview is needed to comprehend and fully appreciate other sections within this textbook. Specifically, this chapter will provide a brief review of the **Health Insurance Portability and Accountability Act** (HIPAA), Omnibus Budget Reconciliation Act of 1990 (OBRA 90), **Prescription Drug Marketing Act** (PDMA), and Haight Act. This chapter is not a full text of pharmacy law or a guide on legal compliance but rather a brief introduction to the topics previously listed in the context of common pharmacy practice. Consult pharmacy law references for a broader and more comprehensive explanation of pharmacy law topics.

THE HEALTH INSURANCE PORTABILITY AND ACCOUNTABILITY ACT

❶ The Health Insurance Portability and Accountability Act of 1996 was enacted primarily to improve access to health care through increased portability and continuity of health insurance, specifically allowing workers and their families to retain health insurance coverage when they changed or lost a job.[1] Recognizing the increasing importance of protecting the privacy of health information in response to the growing use of electronic information management systems to store, retrieve, and share healthcare information across a broad range of providers, Congress also included a directive within HIPAA to establish guidelines to protect patient health information. Final patient privacy rules ("the HIPAA Privacy Rule") drafted under this directive by the Department of Health and Human Services were issued in 2000 and then later amended in 2002.[2] HIPAA and its subsequent federal regulations have had a significant effect on pharmacy and other healthcare professions, particularly in how health insurers and healthcare providers use and share healthcare information for individual patients. HIPPA and its related regulations will be discussed in terms of how patient information is used and disclosed and how personnel must be trained to ensure appropriate use and protection of this information.

Key Terms

Understanding common HIPAA terminology is an important component of fully comprehending the effect of the HIPPA Privacy Rule, including identifying the parties covered by the rule and the corresponding training that must be undertaken to remain in compliance with the rule. **Protected health information** (PHI), a term coined within the HIPAA Privacy Rule, refers to any individually identifiable information concerning the past, present, or future physical or mental health or condition of an individual. PHI includes prescription files or patient profiles maintained by a pharmacy, as well as electronic data that might be shared with third parties, payers, physician offices, billing records, patients, or others. In addition, PHI can be health information in any form, including that which is transmitted orally, in writing, or electronically. The Privacy Rule prohibits the use or disclosure of PHI except as required or permitted by the rule. A **covered entity** is defined as a person or organization that provides health care or possesses healthcare records; this includes health insurers, healthcare providers, healthcare payers, and healthcare clearinghouses.

Another key term defined in the HIPAA Privacy Rule is "minimum necessary" information. This principle provides that a covered entity must make a reasonable effort to limit the exposure of PHI to the minimum information necessary to accomplish the intended purpose of the use, disclosure, or request. This is best explained in the context of third-party reimbursement. If patient information is required when submitting a claim, sufficient information must be provided to make sense of the claim and to facilitate payment, including patient name, account numbers, prescribed medications, and duration of therapy. However, if a history of previous medication use is not required for the payment decision to be made, it would be inappropriate to provide that information to the payer. In some situations, such as previous therapy failures, past medication history may be relevant to whether a second-tier drug is approved; therefore, it might be necessary for this PHI to be shared with the claims administrator. Exceptions to the principle of minimum necessary information when PHI is disclosed include: disclosures to healthcare providers for treatment purposes, disclosures to the individual who is the subject of the information, disclosures made with the individual's permission, and disclosures required to comply with laws. This is important as it is often necessary to receive or give personal knowledge of a patient's case, beyond the minimum necessary information, to make appropriate treatment decisions. Pharmacist managers must ensure that pharmacy personnel are trained to make these pertinent decisions to maintain all pharmacy operations in HIPAA compliance. Training will be addressed in a later section of this chapter.

When and How to Disclose PHI: Notice, Consent, and Authorization

The HIPAA Privacy Rule permits the disclosure of PHI to carry out treatment, payment, or healthcare operations without first obtaining an individual's authorization. This allows one healthcare provider to communicate with another healthcare provider (e.g., physician to physician, physician to pharmacist) when it concerns patient treatment. One healthcare provider may also consult with another provider who has no direct treatment relationship with the patient—for example, a physician consulting with a laboratory technician concerning lab results. In addition, a covered entity may transmit PHI for payment. Finally, covered entities may disclose PHI for the purpose of carrying out internal healthcare operations, defined as activities associated with quality assessment and improvement, student training, accreditation, certification, licensure activities, medical review and legal services, business planning and development, and activities associated with the sale, transfer, or merger of a covered entity with another covered entity. Disclosure between two healthcare entities for healthcare operations purposes, however, requires that both entities have a treatment relationship with the patient.

Although covered entities are permitted to use PHI for the three tasks described in the previous paragraph, the HIPAA Privacy Rule requires health plans and providers to develop and distribute a **Privacy Notice** with the following elements:

- How the covered entity may use and disclose PHI about an individual.
- The individual's rights with respect to the information and how the individual may exercise these rights, including how the individual may complain to the covered entity.
- The covered entity's legal duties with respect to the information, including a statement that the covered entity is required by law to maintain the privacy of PHI.
- Whom individuals can contact for further information about the covered entity's privacy policies.

This Privacy Notice must be provided directly to the patient during the first patient visit or when services are first provided; in addition, a patient may request a copy of the notice at any time. A covered entity may voluntarily choose, but is not required, to obtain an individual's consent before using and disclosing information about a patient's treatment, payment, and healthcare operations. Under the HIPAA Privacy Rule, a covered entity that uses a consent process has complete discretion to design a process that works best for its businesses and consumers.

An area of concern for pharmacies is providing prescription pick up by someone other than the patient. HIPAA permits friends or family members to pick up prescriptions for a patient. This is an example of something that should be covered in the Privacy Notice. Patients may request that others be prohibited from picking up their prescriptions, or they may permit designated individuals to pick up prescriptions. Patients may make this request during any subsequent interaction. Once requested, the pharmacy must abide by the patient's wishes. A covered entity may also rely on a patient's informal permission to disclose PHI

directly related to care or payment for care to his or her family, relatives, friends, or other identified persons. This provision, for example, allows a pharmacist to dispense filled prescriptions to a person acting on behalf of the patient. If unspecified, the pharmacist or other member of the covered entity must exercise professional judgment about whether release of the prescription is in the best interest of the patient and about what, if any, PHI may be discussed with the patient's agent. The pharmacist could certainly follow up with a telephone call to the patient or ask that the patient call the pharmacy if they have any questions regarding therapy.

Minors' rights are also a frequent topic of controversy regarding the exchange of PHI and are of particular concern to pharmacists and pharmacist managers. The HIPAA Privacy Rule defers to state and other laws to determine the rights of parents to access and control the PHI of their minor children. If state or other law is silent concerning parental control of the minor's PHI, a covered entity has the discretion to provide or deny a parent's access to the minor's health information, provided a licensed healthcare professional exercises professional judgment to make the decision. If the healthcare professional (e.g., pharmacist) believes that the patient might be subject to abuse, domestic violence, or neglect at the hands of a parent, he or she may elect not to treat the parent as the child's personal representative. This exception applies to all personal representatives designated to a patient under a provider's care, not just minor children. The healthcare provider is empowered to exercise professional judgment to protect the patient in those instances in which a professional has a reasonable belief that the personal representative may be abusing or neglecting the individual (patient) or that treating the person as the personal representative could otherwise endanger the individual.

Certain specific circumstances as defined in HIPAA allow a covered entity to provide health information about a patient to third parties. The Privacy Rule permits use and disclosure (**permitted disclosures**) of PHI, without an individual's authorization or permission, for 12 national priority purposes (**Table 5–1**).[3] These disclosures are permitted, although not required, by the Privacy Rule

TABLE **5–1**	Permitted Disclosures Under HIPAA—12 National Priority Purposes

- Required by law
- Public health activities
- Victims of abuse, neglect, or domestic violence
- Health oversight activities
- Judicial and administrative proceedings
- Law enforcement purposes
- Decedents (e.g., disclosure to funeral directors, coroners, or medical examiners)
- Cadaveric eye, organ, or tissue donation
- Research
- Serious threat to health or safety
- Essential government functions
- Worker's compensation

Sources: Data from Public Welfare, 45 CFR §§ 160, 164 (2000).

in recognition of the important uses made of health information outside of the healthcare context. Permitted disclosures are very limited. For example, disclosures may be allowed for public health activities, when the patient may be a victim of abuse, for law enforcement purposes, for certain research, and for reporting adverse effects to the **Food and Drug Administration** (FDA), or other governmental health oversight agencies.[3]

Furthermore, the Privacy Rule does not require that every risk of an incidental use or disclosure of PHI be eliminated. A use or disclosure of this information that occurs as a result of, or as "incident to," an otherwise permitted use or disclosure is permitted as long as the covered entity has adopted reasonable safeguards as required by the Privacy Rule and the shared information was limited to the "minimum necessary," as required by the Privacy Rule. Rules regarding **incidental disclosures** protect healthcare providers who incidentally or accidently expose PHI to others. This type of disclosure might occur in the practice of pharmacy if

someone happens to overhear a pharmacist's discussion with a patient in a semiprivate counseling area or a pharmacist's discussion about a patient with a physician or nurse in a hospital area. The discussion is not considered a violation as long as reasonable attempts have been made to prevent routine disclosure of PHI. The ability of providers and patients to exchange information in a timely and effective fashion in real-world healthcare settings is necessary to provide effective patient treatment.

Any other types of disclosures to anyone without a direct treatment relationship that involves the communication of PHI for any reason other than permitted and incidental are termed **nonroutine disclosures**. Examples of nonroutine disclosures include data collection for research purposes. A release form documenting the patient's permission must be obtained for any nonroutine PHI disclosures, and a patient can request a listing of any nonroutine disclosures six years after an occurrence. In other words, anytime a provider issues information about a patient other than for service reimbursement or discussion of the patient's medical condition with another practitioner, documentation is required, and a patient may request a list of these types of disclosures. For pharmacists and pharmacist managers, this translates to additional record-keeping if anything other than routine disclosures are allowed.

HIPAA Training

A frequent HIPAA-related question pharmacist managers ask is, "Who must be HIPAA trained?" ❷ *To ensure compliance with the HIPAA Privacy Rule, covered entities, including pharmacies, must provide training for their employees (as necessary and appropriate given employees' work functions).* Certainly, pharmacists and support personnel involved in the direct delivery of pharmacy services and patient care must be educated on how to handle patient-identified healthcare information appropriately. However, in certain pharmacy practices, some personnel may not need HIPAA training. For instance, in large chain or department store practice sites, where the need for patient information is limited to the prescription department, certain cashiers or salespeople may not need HIPAA training. Moreover, if strictly clerical personnel are working in other areas of the pharmacy that do not have access to patient PHI, they are not required to be trained. Proper HIPAA training must prevent the inadvertent transmission of PHI to untrained personnel. For example, if PHI is attached to prescription packaging that untrained personnel might need for payment processing, etc., then such information should not be easily read or accessed by the untrained personnel as a part of the transaction. An additional concern would apply to any type of practice in which the computer system might offer access to PHI to various users. ❷ *If a user has access to PHI, whether this access is or is not needed to perform his or her duties, then it is necessary to train this person in appropriate use and security of PHI.* In addition to training, a system of consequences must be developed and applied to employees who violate the entity's policies or requirements regarding the HIPAA Privacy Rule. Accordingly, this will require appropriate administrative, technical, and physical safeguards to protect the privacy of PHI. It may also affect the design of information management systems to limit access to those who need it and are appropriately trained.

Standardization of Information

❶ *HIPAA and its Privacy Rule were drafted with an eye toward the increasing use of electronic methods for data storage and use and the need to simplify electronic healthcare transactions.* At the time HIPAA was passed, health insurers had unique requirements concerning claims. ❸ *To ensure consistency and efficiency throughout the healthcare and health insurance industry, the Department of Health and Human Services (DHHS) adopted national standards to make it easier for health plans, healthcare clearinghouses, physicians, pharmacists, hospitals, and other healthcare providers to process claims and other transactions electronically.*[4] The following transactions were standardized so that the process and format are consistent: (1) claims for reimbursement and patient encounter information, (2) payment for healthcare services and remittance advice, (3) coordination of benefits, (4) healthcare claim status, (5) enrollment and disenrollment in a health plan, (6) eligibility for a health plan (7) health plan premium payments, (8) referral certification and authorization, (9) first report of injury, and (10) health claims attachments. By requiring use of these standards, administered by the Centers for Medicare and Medicaid Services (CMS), electronic recording and claims processing can take place without the paper claim submissions and, most important, without payer-specific or institution-specific formats. With all of its inherent procedural requirements regarding the protection of patient-specific information, this component should be recognized as an overwhelming improvement and advantage to the requirements that were in place before HIPAA. The process of consolidating coding systems and eliminating local and proprietary codes was made somewhat easier by adopting current codes as standards. Examples include the adoption of International Classification of Diseases (ICD-9) codes for specifying diagnosis and problem lists, Current Procedural Terminology (CPT-4) codes for specifying treatment or procedures submitted for reimbursement, and National Drug Code (NDC) to identify drugs provided to patients.

Recently, hospitals have been offered additional incentives to adopt these standards and advance the availability of medical records in electronic format. The American Recovery and Reinvestment Act of 2009 provided economic incentives to increase the availability of electronic health records for patients as a means of increasing the portability and ease of communication of this information between health providers.[4] The long-term goal is improved care and reduced cost of health care.

OMNIBUS BUDGET RECONCILIATION ACT OF 1990

The Omnibus Budget Reconciliation Act of 1990, or OBRA 90, is a massive piece of federal legislation that addresses a variety of topics. The legislation includes 13 chapters, or titles, which cover such topics as student loans, the energy program, and transportation.[5] Included in this legislation, however, are specific items that affect pharmacy practice. ❹ *In particular, OBRA 90 was enacted as a means of controlling the cost of Medicaid reimbursement for prescription medication. As a result, OBRA 90 required each state to design and implement a drug utilization review (DUR) program to enable pharmacists to provide better information about drugs prescribed and dispensed to their Medicaid patients.* OBRA 90 applied only to pharmacists who served Medicaid customers. Most states, however, have extended OBRA 90's DUR requirements to cover all prescriptions, whether or not they are reimbursable by Medicaid.

Under OBRA 90, each state's DUR program must ensure that prescriptions are medically necessary and unlikely to cause adverse medical consequences. At a minimum, OBRA 90 requires each state's DUR program to provide for a drug therapy review before each prescription is filled or delivered to an individual. The review must include screening for potential drug therapy problems due to therapeutic duplication, drug–disease contraindications, drug–drug interactions, incorrect drug dosage or duration of drug treatment, drug–allergy interactions, and clinical abuse/misuse. States that failed to implement an acceptable DUR program by January 1, 1993, automatically forfeited their right to receive matching federal Medicaid funds.

Although specific regulation of pharmacists' duties has been delegated to the states, OBRA 90 lists detailed requirements that a pharmacy or pharmacist must meet to be able to receive Medicaid reimbursement funds. The requirements of OBRA 90 can be divided into the following three categories:[6]

- *Prospective drug utilization review* (Pro-DUR) pertains to the evaluation of a patient's drug therapy to ensure that it is appropriate and that potential adverse effects are anticipated and evaluated in light of a benefit–risk assessment decision. Areas of consideration covered in the Pro-DUR requirements include (1) assessing for duplications in therapy, drug–drug interactions (such as nonprescription medications that a patient may take), and drug–disease state or medical-condition-related interactions; and (2) evaluation of appropriate dosage and duration of therapy, potential for allergies based on patient history, and appropriate use or possibility of misuse of a drug.

- *Patient counseling* guidelines specify the areas and types of information that should be covered during a patient counseling session (**Table 5–2**).[5] Specific counseling requirements depend on state regulation, including who must make the offer to counsel, either the pharmacist or support personnel. When is counseling required by regulation on the filling of a new prescription or on subsequent refills? The answer to this question will vary by state, so practitioners must be familiar with their state laws and board of pharmacy rules. Also, there are specific requirements for documenting patient counseling sessions or patient refusal of counseling. Pharmacists and pharmacist managers must be familiar with their individual state's requirements to ensure that they comply with these regulations.

- *Maintenance of patient records* includes patient drug histories or medication profiles. The availability of this information is critical in providing effective patient counseling as well as Pro-DUR. The minimum areas required in the patient medication profile include patient's name, address, age, gender, list of medications (including regularly taken nonprescription drugs), as well as a list of chronic conditions, allergies, and drug reactions.

TABLE 5-2	Patient Counseling Components of OBRA 90

The pharmacist must offer to discuss with each individual receiving benefits under this title or caregiver of such individual (in person, whenever practicable, or through access to a telephone service that is toll free for long-distance calls) who presents a prescription, matters that in the exercise of the pharmacist's professional judgment (consistent with state law respecting the provision of such information) the pharmacist deems significant, including the following:

• The name and description of the medication.

• The route, dosage form, dosage, route of administration, and duration of drug therapy.

• Special directions and precautions for preparation, administration, and use by the patient.

• Common severe side or adverse effects or interactions and therapeutic contraindications that may be encountered, including their avoidance, and the action required if they occur.

• Techniques for self-monitoring drug therapy.

• Proper storage.

• Prescription refill information.

• Action to be taken in the event of a missed dose.

Note: The inclusion of these specifics in state law is based on actions by each state's board of pharmacy.
Source: From Omnibus Budget Reconciliation Act of 1990, Pub. L. 101-508, 104 Stat. 1388; section codified at 42 USC § 1396r-8(g)(2)(A)(ii)(I).

OBRA 90 requires that these records be maintained for two years after a patient leaves a pharmacy's care. Largely, information management systems, such as on-site computer systems and third-party transaction systems, provide practitioners with support in Pro-DUR and in maintaining patient profiles.

OBRA 90 is designed to improve patient care and the efficiency or expenditures for medications by requiring action by pharmacists. Although many people may view the law as an unwelcome monitoring of pharmacy practice, pharmacists, using their expertise, can significantly improve patient care beyond dispensing the correct drug to the correct patient. The outcome of this legislation is only realized if a pharmacist takes advantage of the opportunity to counsel the patient on the appropriate use of the medication. Pharmacist managers must understand the importance of and facilitate the ability of their pharmacists to counsel their patients effectively. If pharmacists emphasize that they have only complied with the requirement to offer counseling, or otherwise discourage the opportunity for counseling, they may be following the law, but they are not providing the best possible health care for their patients.

PRESCRIPTION DRUG MARKETING ACT

In 1984, G. D. Searle and Company discovered that its Ovulen-21 birth control pills had been counterfeited. The company had received worrisome reports from (1) a pharmacist in Racine, Wisconsin, who noticed that the brand name on some

Ovulen-21 tablets was spelled wrong; (2) a pharmaceutical purchasing agent in Clearwater, Florida, who received complaints that Ovulen-21 birth control pills had caused breakthrough bleeding in some users; and (3) a Chicago pharmacist who inquired as to why the price of his latest order of Ovulen-21 was so much cheaper than previous orders.[7] As a result, G. D. Searle and Company notified the FDA of these complaints, and an investigation was initiated that ultimately involved numerous state, federal, and international law enforcement agencies. Ultimately, 1.5 million counterfeit Ovulen-21 tablets were seized, and seven individuals were sentenced to prison terms and fines. In response to this case, as well as other similar cases, Congress passed the Prescription Drug Marketing Act (PDMA) of 1987, which took effect in 1988.

❺ *The PDMA was enacted to ensure the safety and effectiveness of prescription drug products purchased by consumers and to avoid the unacceptable risk that counterfeit, **adulterated**, **misbranded**, subpotent, or expired drugs were being sold to the American public.*[8] *Several specific PDMA regulations are related to distributing drug products in the United States, including prohibiting reimportation of prescription drugs that have been manufactured in the United States, restricting the distribution of prescription **drug samples**, and banning the resale of drugs by hospitals and other entities.* Specifically, the PDMA restricts the distribution of drugs to only those entities licensed to distribute these products, such as drug wholesalers or suppliers, and with certain exceptions, prohibits the sale of, or offer to sell, prescription drugs that have been purchased by a hospital or other healthcare entity or that have been donated or supplied at a reduced price to a charitable organization.

The PDMA also restricts the sale and resale of drug samples. Drug samples are defined as a unit of a drug that is not intended to be sold and is intended to promote the sale of a drug. These samples are intended for distribution by a physician to encourage a patient to begin a particular drug therapy and then, if the therapy is successful, a patient would receive a prescription to continue therapy using the medication. Promoting prescription drug samples is a widespread pharmaceutical industry practice that can benefit patients, but it

can be potentially risky for manufacturers, representatives, physicians, and pharmacists. During hearings in 1985, Congress focused on the numerous ways that pharmaceutical manufacturers, doctors, and drug wholesalers were abusing the sampling practice, which created considerable health risks. Because neither drug companies nor physicians were required to keep records of the samples they distributed, it was nearly impossible to identify people who had taken products in the event of a recall. Furthermore, drug samples had been improperly diverted to the retail market, and products that were adulterated, expired, and potentially less potent had been dispensed to consumers.

As a result of the PDMA, manufacturers' distribution of drug samples came under increased regulation and control. The PDMA permits sample distribution only to licensed practitioners with prescribing authority. The regulations also permit drug sample distribution to a hospital or other healthcare entity pharmacy, provided a licensed practitioner has clearly indicated at the time of his or her request for samples that those samples should be delivered to the designated pharmacy of a hospital or healthcare entity. A provision in the law enables drugs packaged as "starter packs" to be available so that a patient can try a medication to ensure that it is effective and can be tolerated before a full prescription amount is dispensed.

Individual state laws and institutional policies may vary, but the PDMA provides extensive restrictions to the distribution of prescription drug samples and criminal penalties for violations. A drug sample may be dispensed if the sample is provided by a physician who obtained it through the legitimate sample distribution process for dispensing to that physician's patients on his or her order. Prescription drug samples cannot be sold, purchased, traded, or offered for sale, purchase, or trade. Although samples have been used in the past to provide medications for patients who cannot afford their prescriptions, other mechanisms for getting drugs into the hands of patients who need them have become available. Many pharmaceutical manufacturers offer patient assistance programs that can provide prescription medications directly to patients or their physicians based on various criteria, which include income level and other considerations. For more information on these programs, refer to the Partnership for Prescription Assistance (http://www.pparx.org) or RxAssist: Patient Assistance Program (http://www.rxassist.org).

HAIGHT ACT

❻ *Given the exponential increase in the average health consumer's use of the internet in recent years, pharmacists and pharmacist managers must understand the development of legislation, such as the Haight Act, that governs the internet as a means of drug distribution.* The Haight Act was named for Ryan Haight, who died in 2001 at age 18 years from an overdose of a pain medication containing hydrocodone.[9]

After complaining of back pain from lifting at work, Ryan Haight was found unconscious the next morning and could not be resuscitated. When his parents were told that Ryan's death was due to an overdose of hydrocodone, they were puzzled about how he had obtained the medication. Ryan's friends told his parents that he had purchased the medication over the internet. The family contacted the Drug Enforcement Agency (DEA) and provided Ryan's computer to aid in their investigation. DEA agents were able to confirm that Ryan had visited an online pharmacy, where he completed an online profile and requested medication. The pharmacy Web site forwarded the submitted profile to a doctor for approval. The doctor reviewed the patient's profile and approved and signed the prescription without ever communicating with the patient. The online pharmacy then filled the prescription and mailed it to Ryan's home. The physician and the pharmacist, who was also the Web site owner/operator, were both convicted of federal drug-trafficking offenses;[10] they were sentenced to jail terms and were found civilly liable for professional malpractice.

Both the volume of prescriptions for scheduled substances filled through this Web site without valid prescriptions, and the number of deaths resulting from these practices, raised concerns that the growth of similar Web sites posed a hazard to public health. Legislation was introduced, and the Haight family and others testified before congressional committees about the potential serious and tragic outcomes associated with such uncontrolled access to prescription drugs. The Haight Act was enacted into law in late 2008.[11] Although dissenters of the act feel that any control of access to prescription medications is too much government restriction, the law demonstrates a necessary compromise between those who advocate for enhanced access to pharmaceutical products and those who promote the safety of the public and protection of the legitimate processes of healthcare services.

❼ *The Haight Act amends the **Controlled Substances Act**[12] by adding the statement that no controlled substance "may be delivered, distributed, or dispensed by means of the internet without a valid prescription." It further specifies that, for a prescription to be valid, a patient–practitioner relationship must exist. This is consistent with various other provisions in federal and state law.* New in the stipulation of what constitutes a valid relationship is the requirement that a practitioner must conduct at least one in-person medical evaluation of the patient. The act, however, includes language to ensure that this legislation does not suppress the legitimate practice of telemedicine, as referenced in the Controlled Substances Act. Legitimate pharmacy practices that choose to use the internet to facilitate patient care are subject to the requirements of this law, but the burden is minimal. The enforcement focus is directed toward operations that intend to provide services without acknowledging their location, proper licensure, or the use of existing legitimate practice standards. Specific registration and reporting requirements include (a) display of adherence to the act on the online pharmacy's homepage; (b) compliance with state licensure requirements; (c) disclosure of contact information of the pharmacy, qualifications of its pharmacist-in-charge, and certification of its registration under the act; and (d) notification to the attorney general and applicable state boards of pharmacy at least 30 days before offering to sell, deliver, distribute, or dispense controlled substances over the internet. As the market increases for internet pharmacies, it is critical that pharmacists and pharmacist managers understand how this and similar laws apply to pharmacy practices.

The Haight Act also enhances penalties for unlawfully dispensing controlled substances in Schedules III through V. Before this change, sentencing guidelines were very strict for crimes involving Schedule II drugs, but relatively light for other controlled substance schedules. The act also permits state attorneys general to file a civil action in a federal district court to enjoin (or prohibit) the conduct of an online pharmacy or person operating in violation of this statute and to enforce compliance.

Although the effects of these federal regulations are directed toward "rogue" internet pharmacies, it is certainly a sign of things to come as the use of the internet and other technological advancements to provide pharmacy services increases. Specifically, this act takes steps to regulate online pharmacies. The inclusion of the requirements for a valid physician–patient relationship is already a part of most states' regulations used to determine the validity of a prescription; however, the act was developed to address the technique used by certain internet sites to imply a physician–patient relationship where no traditional face-to-face interaction occurred. There are many legitimate routes by which a prescription might be transmitted, filled, or refilled over the internet, and this legislation does not directly affect these routes. However, regulatory and legislative agencies are now aware of misuse and are acting to prevent harm to the public resulting from abuses. As a manager of pharmacy services hoping to keep up with the latest mechanism of service delivery, it is important to stay current with regulations and how regulations might affect both legitimate and illicit practice.

Patients frequently have questions regarding the sources of their pharmacy services. Internet pharmacies now have certification designations, and pharmacists may encourage patients to look for these certifications in selecting internet-based pharmacy services. As more regulations are developed to govern the specific areas of internet pharmacy services, the importance of accepted certification and accreditation of these internet pharmacies will likely increase. For example, accreditation is available through Verified Internet Pharmacy Practice Sites (VIPPS), a voluntary, for-fee service provided through the National Association of Boards of Pharmacy; internet pharmacies seeking accreditation through VIPPS must comply with licensing and other requirements of their home states as well as all states in which they dispense medications.[13]

SUMMARY

This chapter provides an overview of four important federal laws that affect contemporary pharmacy practice and will be mentioned in later chapters within this textbook: HIPAA, OBRA 90, the PDMA, and the Haight Act. Although beyond the scope of this chapter, it is critical for pharmacists and pharmacist managers to recognize that each state provides additional laws and regulations both in conjunction with and separate from these federal laws. Optimally, pharmacy practice will view federal laws not as a deterrent or complication to the provision of good patient care, but as a structure to protect the public.

References

1. Health Insurance Portability and Accessibility Act of 1996, Pub L No. 104-191, 110 Stat 1936 (1996).

2. Standards for Privacy of Individually Identifiable Health Information: Final Rule, 67 *Fed. Regist.* 53181, 53209 (2002).

3. HIPAA Regulations Regarding Public Health Information, 45 CFR 164.512 (2002).

4. American Recovery and Reinvestment Act. Available at: http://frwebgate.access.gpo.gov/cgi-bin/getdoc.cgi?dbname=111_cong_bills&docid=f:h1enr.pdf. Accessed February 15, 2009.

5. Omnibus Budget Reconciliation Act of 1990, Pub L 101-508, 104 Stat 1388.

6. Vivian JC, Fink JL III. OBRA '90 at sweet sixteen: a retrospective review. *US Pharm* 2008;33(3):59–65.

7. Farley D. Counterfeit pills buy prison time—Lantor Corp. sells phony Ovulen-21. *FDA Consumer Magazine*. December 1990.

8. Prescription Drug Marketing Act of 1987, Pub L No. 100-293, 102 Stat. 95 (1988).

9. McKenna C. Ryan Haight Act will require tighter restrictions on internet pharmacies. *Government Technol* October 2, 2008. Available at: http://www.govtech.com/gt/419355. Accessed November 11, 2008.

10. *US v Fuchs*, 467 F3d 889 (5th Cir 2006).

11. Ryan Haight Online Pharmacy Consumer Protection Act of 2008, Pub L No. 110-425 (2008).

12. Comprehensive Drug Abuse Prevention and Control Act of 1970, Pub L No. 91-513, 84 Stat. 1236 (1970), codified at 21 USC § 801 et seq.

13. National Association of Boards of Pharmacy. Verified Internet Pharmacy Practice Sites. Available at: http://vipps.nabp.net/verify.asp. Accessed September 18, 2009.

Abbreviations

CMS:	Centers for Medicare and Medicaid Services
CPT-4:	Current Procedural Terminology
DEA:	Drug Enforcement Agency
DHHS:	Department of Health and Human Services
DUR:	drug utilization review
FDA:	Food and Drug Administration
HIPAA:	Health Insurance Portability and Accountability Act
ICD-9:	International Classification of Diseases
NDC:	National Drug Code
OBRA 90:	Omnibus Budget Restructuring Act
PDMA:	Prescription Drug Marketing Act
PHI:	protected health information
Pro-DUR:	prospective drug utilization review
VIPPS:	Verified Internet Pharmacy Practice Site

Case Scenarios

CASE ONE: A patient comes into your pharmacy with a prescription for an antiviral drug used in HIV patients. The prescription is left for filling, and later another person comes in to pick up the filled prescription for the patient. What are your responsibilities to provide information for the proper and safe use of the product? How do you ensure that the information is made available to the patient? How is the patient's privacy protected while still providing the needed counseling?

CASE TWO: A pharmacist receives a phone-in prescription from a doctor's office from a nurse. The order is taken as Diabeta (glyburide), 5 mg to be taken daily. The prescription is filled and placed in the will-call area of the pharmacy for pickup by the patient. The patient arrives after a change in shift, signs the "logbook" verifying receipt, and waives the opportunity to be counseled by a pharmacist regarding the medication and its use.

The drug intended by the physician to be prescribed for the patient was Zebeta (bisoprolol), 5 mg to be taken daily. Discuss the implications of this medication error and possible mechanisms by which it may have been prevented.

CASE THREE: Amanda DiFranco, the clinical pharmacist in the medicine clinic, has been given some samples of antihypertensive medications from a pharmaceutical company. She takes the medications to the hospital pharmacy, where an employee indicates that the samples will be repackaged and dispensed to a patient on 7 South (Room 707). Explain why this should not occur, and why the hospital pharmacy cannot charge the patient in Room 707 for these medications.

CASE FOUR: A pharmacist practicing in a community care clinic has a question from a patient about where he might procure the prescribed medications from the least expensive source. Specifically, this patient wants to know about internet pharmacies. What options might the pharmacist provide to help the patient evaluate the various sources of his prescription medications?

Additional Resources Available Online!

Visit the Student Companion Web site at http://healthprofessions.jbpub.com/pharmacymanagement for interactive study tools and additional resources.

See www.rxugace.com to learn how you can obtain continuing pharmacy education for this content.

CHAPTER 6

ETHICAL DECISION MAKING

AMY MARIE HADDAD, PhD

KATHRYN R. MATTHIAS, PharmD, BCPS

LEARNING OBJECTIVES

After completing the chapter, the reader will be able to

1. Describe how the general concerns of ethics, including human dignity, justification, and response to multiple and competing demands, apply to pharmacy practice.

2. Compare and contrast ethical decision making in pharmacy practice on an individual and organizational level.

3. Define and apply the following principles to pharmacy practice issues: respect for autonomy, beneficence, fidelity, justice, and nonmaleficence.

4. Differentiate between principlism, virtue, and care-based ethics.

5. Identify and evaluate the presence or absence of an ethical problem or issue in a clinical pharmacy practice situation.

6. Apply principlism, virtue, or care-based ethics to an ethical problem in pharmacy practice.

7. Judge the contributions of ethics to management and leadership in pharmacy practice.

KEY CONCEPTS

❶ Ethics is a branch of philosophy that poses four fundamental questions: (1) What are the source, meaning, and justification of ethical claims? (2) What kinds of acts are right? (3) How do rules apply to specific situations? and (4) What ought to be done in specific situations?

❷ Applied ethics takes the tools and concepts of ethics and applies them to practical issues, such as those encountered in health care, in general, and in pharmacy management and leadership, in particular.

❸ Ethics involves carefully considering reasons for particular actions so that pharmacists can "act with conviction of conscience."

❹ By sharing ethical concerns with others, we may also determine several "right" answers or different paths to reach an ethical conclusion.

5 Although laws and regulations dictate many activities of the pharmacist, these entities do not take the place of ethics.

6 The "principle-based approach," or "principlism," involves the use of objective moral principles, or action guides to moral behavior. Principlism requires that we systematically reflect on moral principles and their relevance to resolving the ethical problem in question.

7 There are three general criteria for an autonomous decision. First, the action or decision must be intentional, not accidental. Second, the person acting is informed or knows what he or she is doing. Third, the person is substantially free to make a choice.

8 An ethical dilemma involves choosing among equally compelling alternatives.

9 A number of virtues are necessary for leaders in healthcare organizations, such as faithfulness, equanimity, justice, adaptability, and competence.

10 Explicit expectations and organizational norms, as well as regular conversations about decision-making approaches, can support ethical action by building "ethical muscles" and better judgment.

INTRODUCTION

Have you ever felt uncomfortable about providing a prescription for a patient based on your clinical knowledge, concern for abuse, or moral objection? Have you ever read a journal article and wondered whether the results were a function of a biased study design or approach to statistical analysis? Have you ever been concerned about a coworker's or employee's ability to perform a job effectively due to substance abuse, an inadequate knowledge base, or a bad attitude?

During pharmacy school, many ethical issues are discussed on a theoretical level, but a practicing pharmacist must translate theory to practice and be prepared to respond to these types of ethical situations.[1] As a pharmacist, how will you respond to these types of ethical situations?[1] A "Code of Ethics for Pharmacists" (see **Table 6–1**)

offers guidance about how to respond to complex and ethically challenging clinical issues[2–5] and will be referenced in this chapter as principles and approaches that support ethical decision making.

1 *Ethics is a branch of philosophy that poses four fundamental questions: (1) What are the source, meaning, and justification of ethical claims? (2) What kinds of acts are right? (3) How do rules apply to specific situations? and (4) What ought to be done in specific situations?*[6] This basic definition encompasses the traditional understanding of ethics from an objective, universal approach that best answers the moral question, "What is the 'right' thing to do?" Other equally important approaches to ethics are particularly relevant in pharmacy management, which ask such questions as, "What comprises a morally upright character?" and "What should one attend to or care about in life?" **2** *Applied ethics takes the tools and concepts of ethics and applies them to practical issues such as those encountered in health care, in general, and in pharmacy management and leadership, in particular.*[7] Pharmacists and pharmacist managers are often confronted with issues that require the consideration and application of ethical principles. Although words such as "good," "right," and "wrong" are used throughout this chapter, the reader should keep in mind that interpretations of these words may differ based on one's individual perspective. This chapter will provide an overview of ethical concepts and suggest ways in which both pharmacists and pharmacist managers may apply them when faced with difficult decisions.

THREE CONCERNS OF ETHICS

The basic concerns of ethics that are particularly important in health care are respect for persons and **human dignity**, well-developed justification for ethical decisions, and recognition of the multiple and competing demands of the moral life.[8] Almost all ethical traditions include a concern regarding respect for persons and dignity that requires unconditional regard for human beings.[9] Human dignity means that humans possess an absolute, intrinsic worth. Respect for persons is a foundational concept and especially important in a healthcare system that sometimes ignores the voice of the individual.[10] Respect here refers to one of two convictions. The first is that individuals such as patients, but also pharmacists, should be respected for their capacity to make autonomous (self-determined) decisions. The second conviction is a corollary to the first, asserting the requirement to protect those with diminished ability to make their own decisions (**autonomy**).[7,9] Thus, patients who possess the capacity to make informed decisions should be able to do so without undue interference. These two convictions relate to the third statement in the code of ethics (see Table 6–1) that as pharmacists we should respect our patients for their differences and ability to be involved in their healthcare decisions.[2,3]

The second basic concern of ethics is justification, or the "why" of ethics. Pharmacists can develop a possible course of action to resolve an ethical problem but often find it challenging to explain the rationale for their choices. ❸ *Ethics involves carefully considering reasons for particular actions so that pharmacists can "act with conviction of conscience"* (see code of ethics statement number 4 in Table 6–1).[2,3] Examples of ethical situations that involve pharmacists and pharmacist managers may include how they respond to requests to justify dispensing emergency contraceptives and other controversial agents.[11,12]

The third concern of ethics is the recognition of multiple and competing demands on human beings in relationship to others that require a response. We need to be aware that we have many duties or obligations in our lives. Healthcare professionals must juggle patient needs, professional responsibilities, and personal duties to family and friends each day.[8] Healthcare professionals, including pharmacists, face infinite needs with finite resources. We cannot meet all of the needs that we are called on to meet, so we make choices throughout the day. Some of our choices are conscious and some are not. What is important is that a choice is being made and that the choice is based on known or unknown values. We should strive to be aware of the values that influence these choices, especially in relation to maintaining professional competency (see code of ethics statement number 5 in Table 6–1).[2,3,13]

TABLE **6–1**	Code of Ethics for Pharmacists

Number	Statement
1	A pharmacist respects the covenantal relationship between the patient and pharmacist.
2	A pharmacist promotes the good of every patient in a caring, compassionate, and confidential manner.
3	A pharmacist respects the autonomy and dignity of each patient.
4	A pharmacist acts with honesty and integrity in professional relationships.
5	A pharmacist maintains professional competence.
6	A pharmacist respects the values and abilities of colleagues and other health professionals.
7	A pharmacist serves individual, community, and societal needs.
8	A pharmacist seeks justice in the distribution of health resources.

Note: Adopted by the membership of the American Pharmaceutical Association October 27, 1994.
Source: Adapted from the "Code of Ethics for Pharmacists." Washington DC: American Pharmacists Association; 1994. www.pharmacists.com (accessed 2009 March 11). Used with permission.

Three of the most commonly encountered approaches in contemporary **bioethics**—**principlism** ethics, **virtue** ethics, and **care-based ethics**—are presented in this chapter and applied to a case study to highlight their usefulness and limitations. Principlism ethics focus on action guides for moral behavior. Virtue ethics emphasize character rather than actions. Care-based ethics focus on relationships. This chapter begins with a brief examination of the effect that context has on ethics with a specific focus on pharmacy management and leadership.

CONTEXT OF MANAGEMENT AND ORGANIZATIONAL ETHICS

Generally, when we discuss ethics, we think about an individual and his or her actions, character, and concerns. We "do" ethics on an intrapersonal level when we reflect on our value system and the ways we make the choices that we make. The more time we spend thinking about what principles we personally hold most dear, the more insight we will have into what underlies decisions or actions. In addition to personal examination of values and beliefs about what is right or wrong and how we choose, we might also turn to a trusted advisor, colleague, or family member and ask for his or her advice. Conferring with a small number of intimates is "doing" ethics on an interpersonal basis. Although we tend to work with specific individuals and view their challenges and struggles as somewhat individual, when we confer and share experiences with others, we can see the connection between an injustice with a particular patient, for example, to larger injustices within the healthcare system. ◆ *By sharing ethical concerns with others, we may also determine several "right" answers or different paths to reach an ethical conclusion*. These collaborations and consultations relate to the sixth statement in the code of ethics (see Table 6–1), which focuses on the importance of valuing and respecting our fellow colleagues, even if their beliefs differ from our own.[2,3]

Much of what is written about problems in healthcare ethics, regardless of the specific health discipline, addresses the interpersonal level of ethics, an ethical conflict between two moral agents or competent adults, such as a pharmacist

and a patient.[14,15] The pharmacist, in such cases, must determine what is the right thing to do for and with a particular patient. With the pharmacist manager, the focus is no longer solely on patients, but on several other things, including the people who report to the manager. The interpersonal perspective is insufficient to address the complexity of ethical issues encountered at the organizational level. We must move to an organizational perspective that takes into account the individuals that make up the organization and the larger society within which the organization resides.[10,14]

A primary objective of **organizational ethics** is the overall good, or benefit, of the organization, which includes individuals within the organization, such as patients, healthcare professionals, and other staff.[10] Organizational ethics must also attend to the good of society, as organizations are part of the larger community. Principles and tools of ethics that are important at the interpersonal level, such as respect for autonomy, are not as relevant at the organizational level. Other principles, such as **justice** (to be fair) or **nonmaleficence** (do no harm), become more salient at the organizational level.[7] Therefore, a pharmacist in a management or leadership position must develop the capacity to look within to the ethical well-being of the organization and look outside the organization to society and the common good.

Internally, the pharmacist leader must attend to the good of individuals but with an eye toward organizational solutions, which relates to the seventh statement in the code of ethics (see Table 6–1).[2,3,16,17] For example, if an error occurs in dispensing or preparing a certain drug product, treating the error as an isolated event by questioning and possibly educating the pharmacist responsible is not enough. Medication errors are often examples of organizational, not individual, ethics. The approach called for here involves institutional systems and structures. With a focus on the organizational level, care should be taken to ensure the well-being of all those affected by errors, including patients, family members, and healthcare professionals. This means institutionalizing consistent, fair, and effective methods to identify and resolve systemic causes of errors.

Pharmacists and pharmacist managers must also respond to societal-level concerns.[10,16] External ethical concerns include compliance with the law; regulatory bodies, such as the Joint Commission or Occupational Safety and Health Administration (OSHA); requirements of payers on a federal, state, or private level; and general social justice. ❺ *Although laws and regulations dictate many activities of the pharmacist, these entities do not take the place of ethics.* An example of societal ethics is the cost of drugs in the United States. The high cost of drugs is possibly, foremost, a question of social and **distributive justice** in pharmacy management.[7] Among the reasons offered for the high cost of drugs are fair reimbursement for the costs of research and development of new drugs, market economies, and even politics. The cost of drugs is a social justice issue, however, because the remedies for reducing drug costs so that they are more accessible to those who need them most require addressing larger inequities in society and the lack of power of certain vulnerable groups to change how drugs are marketed and distributed.[18,19] In other words, ethically speaking, it is not enough to assist a single patient or even many patients with the necessary paperwork to receive free medication from a pharmaceutical manufacturer. Instead, social justice requires an overall evaluation of the structure of how important and necessary health care is distributed, particularly to those who are most vulnerable. In the code of ethics, statement number 8 (see Table 6–1) relates to the fair and equitable distribution of healthcare resources based on patient and society needs.[2,3]

Case Study

Local community pharmacist Nancy Edwards receives a prescription for Darren Wilson for "ibuprofen 600 mg PO q6hr PRN muscle pain" signed by a local primary care physician. She notices that, the quantity to be dispensed is "420," an unusually high number of tablets for a 30-day supply and that the "4" looks like a different handwriting than the rest of the prescription. Dr. Edwards questions the patient about the quantity written on the prescription, and the patient admits that he changed the prescribed quantity from 120 to 420. Mr. Wilson states, "I am just so tired of making trips to the pharmacy and paying my prescription copay every month. I am barely able to pay for my medications and it would really help if I could get more pills this time." Dr. Edwards contacts the **health maintenance organization** (HMO) and speaks to the patient's physician who states that it is fine to dispense 420 tablets since he trusts the patient not to take more than the prescribed amount of ibuprofen per day. Dr. Edwards fills the prescription with 420 tablets but only bills the patient for a copay based on 120 tablets and does not charge the patient for the other 300 tablets. Dr. Edwards's colleague, Jennifer Adams, overhears these conversations and finds Dr. Edwards's actions objectionable. She asks to speak with you since you are the pharmacy manager.

Before considering how to apply ethical principles to this case (see Case Study box), we must first ask, "How do we know that the case involves an ethical issue or problem?" Two basic questions can be asked to assist in recognizing an ethical issue (see **Table 6–2**).[20] First, is there something wrong personally, interpersonally, or socially? Could the conflict, the situation, or the decision be damaging to people or to the community? Second, does the issue go beyond legal or institutional concerns? What does it do to people, who have dignity, rights, and hopes for a better life together?[20] When we ask the two basic questions, we get an affirmative answer to both. There is a conflict between an individual's good and that of the HMO and the community pharmacy. Potential legal issues here include the patient's alteration of his prescription and an attempt to defraud the HMO, and the pharmacist's decision to dispense 300 "free" ibuprofen tablets, an act that likely violates the pharmacy company's policies related to medication price discounts. This case also includes concerns about how the pharmacy acts as an organization. Ethical issues are also present because the dignity of someone is at stake, specifically Mr. Wilson's. As a member of the HMO and a patient at the pharmacy, Mr. Wilson has rights and has hopes that something would be done to improve his quality of life, albeit with a hidden cost to other members of the HMO and to the pharmacy. Also, Dr. Edwards's actions do have an effect on her coworkers such that one

TABLE **6–2**	**Evaluation of Ethical Pharmacy Situations**

Recognize a Pharmacy Ethical Issue:

1. Could this pharmacy-related situation be damaging to someone or to some group? Does this decision involve a choice between a good and bad alternative?

2. Is this issue about more than what is legal or what is most efficient? If so, how?

Get the Facts:

3. What are the relevant facts of the case? What facts are not known? Can I learn more about the situation? Do I know enough to make a decision?

4. What individuals and groups have an important stake in the outcome? Are some concerns more important? Why?

5. What are the options for acting? Have all the relevant persons and groups been consulted? Have I identified creative options?

Evaluate Alternative Actions:

6. Evaluate the options by asking the following questions:
   — Which option will produce the most good and cause the least harm?
   — Which option best respects the rights of all stakeholders?
   — Which option treats people equally or proportionately?
   — Which option best serves the community as a whole, not just some members?
   — Which option leads me to act as the sort of person I want to be?

Make a Decision and Test It:

7. Considering all these approaches, which option best addresses the pharmacy situation?

8. If I told someone I respect which option I have chosen, what would they say?

Act and Reflect on the Outcome:

9. How can my decision be implemented with the greatest care and attention to the concerns of all stakeholders?

10. How did my decision turn out, and what have I learned from this pharmacy situation?

Source: Adapted from "Making an Ethical Decision." Santa Clara, CA: Markkula Center for Applied Ethics at Santa Clara University; 2009. www.scu.edu (accessed 2009 March 11). Used with permission.

of them, Dr. Adams, felt compelled to go to a higher authority in the organization. Although this case involves potential legal issues, the focus of this discussion will be on ethical issues. Ethical principles can be used to evaluate the various issues raised by this case.

APPROACHES TO ETHICS
Principlism

❻ *The "principle-based approach," or "principlism," involves the use of objective moral principles, or action guides to moral behavior. Principlism requires* *that we systematically reflect on moral principles and their relevance to resolving the ethical problem in question.*[7] The ethical problem in this case study is a conflict between one member's well-being and the good of the entire pharmacy company (and the HMO). The task is to determine a resolution that collectively accounts for the well-being of the individual patient, as well as evaluation of the pharmacist's and physician's actions from the perspective of other members of the patient's HMO, local retail pharmacy, and the retail pharmacy organization.

Using a principle-based approach, the various rights and duties of the parties involved in Dr. Edwards's case are clarified. The principles described in **Table 6–3** offer guidance in analyzing this situation.

RESPECT FOR AUTONOMY

Autonomy literally means "self-rule." Thus, pharmacists are obligated to respect people not only because they are human but also because they respect the healthcare decisions of those who are capable of making such decisions. How can we tell that a decision is an autonomous one and therefore worthy of respect? ❼ *There are three general criteria for an autonomous decision. First, the action or decision must be intentional, not accidental. Second, the person acting is informed or knows what*

TABLE **6–3**	Principles in Pharmacy Ethics

Ethical Principle	Definition	Pharmacist/Patient Example
Autonomy	Ability to make decisions without controlling interference	Pharmacist can individualize drug information for a specific patient during a counseling session. Patient can choose not to take prescribed medication.
Beneficence	Obligation to help other people	Pharmacist provides accurate and up-to-date patient education on the management of asthma or diabetes.
Fidelity	Obligation to keep promises	Pharmacist is trusted to keep a patient's medical information confidential. Patient complies with agreed on treatment.
Justice	Ability to be right and fair within reason	Pharmacist provides medications for costs determined by patients' insurance status.
Nonmaleficence	Obligation to avoid harming other people	Pharmacist must refuse to fill a prescription for penicillin in a patient with a history of a type-1 hypersensitivity (anaphylactic) reaction to penicillin.

Sources: Data from Beauchamp TL, Childress JF. *Principles of biomedical ethics.* 5th ed. New York City: Oxford University Press; 2001. Veatch RM, Haddad A. *Case studies in pharmacy ethics.* 2nd ed. New York City: Oxford University Press; 2008.

he or she is doing. Third, the person is substantially free to make a choice.

Autonomy is a deeply held value within mainstream American culture. We recognize, however, that autonomy is not an absolute. We can restrict the autonomy of a patient for several reasons. For example, we would be justified in restricting a patient's autonomy if an action he wanted to take would severely harm others. In Mr. Wilson's case, it appears that he is capable of exercising autonomy. He freely chose to alter the prescription. He appears to understand that what he did was wrong but still wants to avoid the inconvenience of monthly copays and unnecessary trips to the pharmacy. To a certain degree, we can assume that he autonomously chose his insurer and did so with an understanding of his benefits and obligations such as copays. Because of his agreement with the HMO, Mr. Wilson could rightly expect that he should have access to health benefits. However, there is no health plan that would allow each person enrolled to have access to all the health benefits he or she wanted. There are limits to the individual beneficiary's choices, or actions, because there is an effect on the group that must also be considered. Mr. Wilson has other options that he could freely exercise. For example, he might choose to pay for the ibuprofen himself if he has the resources instead of using the copay prescription plan through his HMO or obtain his medication through a 90-day pharmacy supplier so that he would not need to make as many trips to the pharmacy.

To a certain degree, Dr. Edwards is autonomous as well, as she should abide by the payer agreement with the HMO and the pharmacy company policies. In this case, it appears that she has chosen not to do so to benefit her patient.

BENEFICENCE AND NONMALEFICENCE

For most healthcare professionals, the most obvious ethical principles, or guides, for moral action in clinical encounters are the obligation to assist or help patients and avoid harm. Formally known as the principles of **beneficence** and nonmaleficence, these two duties serve as the ethical foundation of the relationship between people in general and, more important, between health professionals such as pharmacists and patients. In this case, beneficence, or nonmaleficence, applies to the good of all patients who use the retail pharmacy, all patients enrolled in the HMO, the pharmacy employees, and the patient's physician.[7] Although the principles of respect for autonomy, beneficence, and nonmaleficence are important ones in healthcare ethics, they do not play a major role in the case of Mr. Wilson and Dr. Edwards. Because the case rests at the organizational level, the principle of fairness, or justice, becomes more important in reaching a resolution.

JUSTICE

The principle of justice deals with the fair distribution of benefits and burdens. There is an element of fairness in the contractual nature of insurance. For example, beneficiaries agree to pay a certain amount for a certain level of coverage. Within an HMO, as with any type of insured group, there is a need to balance the number and type of covered benefits for members against the need of the HMO to break even financially or make a profit. The good of a single patient and the HMO or the pharmacy organization are not identical and therein lies the conflict. In addition, there is a contractual agreement with the pharmacy and the HMO regarding how the pharmacy will be reimbursed. If every pharmacist within the retail pharmacy acted like Dr. Edwards did, the pharmacy organization would soon be out of business. Dr. Edwards's action is hard to justify according to the principle of justice. Furthermore, Dr. Edwards and Mr. Wilson had other choices that would not have compromised fairness to other patients of the pharmacy or the HMO.

FIDELITY

The principle of **fidelity** requires that, other things being equal, promises should be kept. In Dr. Edwards's case, fidelity is most evident in the contractual agreement between Dr. Edwards and the retail pharmacy in which Drs. Edwards and Adams work. Dr. Edwards's actions, even though they were to benefit her patient, are in breach of this agreement, or promise. To break a promise, there must be strong reasons, and it does not appear that those exist in this case.

If there were a strong reason for breaking the contractual promise but an equally strong reason for keeping the promise, that would constitute an **ethical dilemma**. ◆*An ethical dilemma is choosing among equally compelling alternatives.* One would then have to turn to ethical theories, such as **utilitarianism**, which asserts we should always choose the action that brings about the most good for the most people. Or, one could look at the additional questions listed in Table 6–2, part 6, such as, "Which option best respects the rights of all who have a stake?" This question represents the ethical theory of **deontology**, or duty-based ethics, which is concerned more with the importance of principles themselves, particularly autonomy and honesty, as opposed to outcomes of action.

Virtue Ethics

A second approach to ethics focuses on virtue rather than right action. Virtue ethics is concerned about the moral character of a person rather than, "what a person should do." Thus, it is sometimes referred to as a character-based approach to ethics.[7,21] This interest in moral character best answers the question, "Who should I be?" A virtuous person is dedicated to being a good person. Virtue ethics provides insight into what kind of person you need to be to do the right thing in a leadership or management position. Virtue ethics asserts that the ultimate source of goodness lies within the person. A good pharmacist will be inclined to choose the morally correct action. Briefly put, a virtuous pharmacist is inclined to do good with respect for patients' dignity and privacy, which relates to the second statement in the code of ethics.[2,3]

What sorts of goodness are evident in Dr. Edwards's case? What virtues are needed as a retail pharmacist or for you as a pharmacist manager? What kind of people do the members of an HMO and employees of the retail pharmacy organization require in leadership positions to meet their collective and individual needs? When thinking about what kind of people we would like our pharmacist caregivers and leaders to be, and, in essence, who we would like to be, we are really examining the virtues central to our moral lives. ◆*A number of virtues are necessary for leaders in healthcare organizations, such as faithfulness, equanimity, justice, adaptability, and competence.* Dr. Adams recognizes that there is an obligation to keep the legal or implicit promises made to the pharmacy organization even when it is difficult to do so, which indicates the virtue of faithfulness; however, this was broken by Dr. Edwards. Dr. Edwards expressed her concern about the well-being of the patient, while Dr. Adams expressed her concern for the health of the retail pharmacy as a whole by considering the effect of specific decisions on all concerned, which shows her dedication to justice. The retail pharmacy that employs Dr. Edwards and Dr. Adams can have a direct effect on their virtue by cultivating an environment that encourages them to be "good" pharmacists and leaders through such actions as reinforcing morally good habits.

By exploring the virtues of the individuals involved in a case, we understand those traits that will produce morally correct action. Yet virtues alone might not be enough. For example, if we are virtuous but do not know anything about moral principles that guide right actions, we may not be much help to our patients. In fact, it would appear that there is a moral obligation to know what to do. Conversely, if we know the right thing to do but lack the moral character to do it, we are also unhelpful in resolving an ethical problem or righting an injustice. Virtue also does not provide insight into the moral relevance of the primary relationships in which we care for one another. Care-based ethics require that we include such relationships in our ethical deliberations.[7]

Care-Based Ethics

Care-based ethics emphasizes a responsiveness to particular situations in which morally salient features are perceived with a sensitivity thought to be made possible by the pharmacist leader's emotional stance and openness.[22,23] Care-based ethics asks, "What should one care about in this particular situation?" Furthermore, in Dr. Edwards's case, the particular situation is not about a solitary patient and his needs but about the retail pharmacy patients and employees. The general, objective language of principlism initially might seem better suited to address the problem facing Dr. Edwards until one recognizes that the particulars of the case cause us to look elsewhere for assistance. Care-based ethics asks about the relationships and connections of the individuals involved and feelings, such as compassion or sympathy, that are also components of the moral life, if not the precursor to ethical action.[7] In other words, the "gift of trust" from society and patients to pharmacists and the covenantal nature of the pharmacist–patient relationship could be the starting point for considering a variety of ethical actions as in the first statement of the code of ethics"[2,3] (Table 6–1).

Care-based ethics asks us to identify the problem in context. A care-based orientation often serves as one more perspective that could help break a tie between two or more important principles. You as the pharmacist manager in this case could turn to care-based ethics to determine which principle is the most caring resolution to the problem being addressed. However, care-based ethics have limitations. The overall emphasis on care may not appeal to some who hold a more rational, objective view. An example of these care-based ethical situations relates to the selling of tobacco products in a for-profit retail pharmacy setting.[24] Another example relates to pharmacists' attitudes toward dispensing potentially harmful narcotic medications to a patient with chronic pain issues.[25] Many of these issues or policies are evaluated in pharmacy organizations through **drug utilization review** (DUR) **committees**. Overall, there is the concern that because care-based ethics requires such a deeply personal, singular focus there are no general guidelines or rules to help us truly know what the "most" caring action should be. Regardless, once an ethical situation in pharmacy has been evaluated and a decision for action has been made it is important to evaluate the outcomes and reevaluate the appropriate solution to the situation.

CONTRIBUTIONS OF ETHICS TO MANAGEMENT AND LEADERSHIP IN PHARMACY PRACTICE

An action by someone in a pharmacy leadership position has broader implications compared with an individual decision affecting the one customer in front of you, so awareness of ethical issues and methods to resolve them become more visible. Organizations, should, therefore, provide support for recognizing ethical issues. For example, policies and guidelines that address the most commonly encountered types of ethical problems in the particular healthcare- or pharmacy-specific environment should be available. In general, these guidelines should outline the process for making sound ethical decisions to resolve ethical problems. But no policy manual yet exists that encompasses all of the ethical problems encountered in pharmacy practice. As pharmacists, we are called on to maintain our "gift of trust" from society, despite numerous ethical dilemmas and limited guidelines, through professional competency and honest behavior which are, as stated in the "Code of Ethics for Pharmacists", the "fundamental basis of the roles and responsibilities of pharmacists."[2,3]

SUMMARY

The "Code of Ethics for Pharmacists," professional standards, and organizational policies can offer guidance, but it is incumbent on you as a pharmacy professional to establish a process for analyzing ethical issues. The questions provided in Table 6–2 can offer guidance in this regard. In the event you serve as a pharmacist manager, you will be responsible for helping your staff make regular ethical decisions. ⑩ *Explicit expectations and organizational norms, as well as regular conversations about decision-making approaches, can support ethical action by building "ethical muscles" and better judgment.* Practicing pharmacy requires professionals to navigate complex and nuanced situations, many of which have no apparent right answer. While maintaining our "gift of trust" can be our most challenging task, it can also be our most rewarding.

References

1. Latif D. An assessment of the ethical reasoning of United States pharmacy students: a national study. *Am J Pharm Educ* 2004;68:1–10.

2. Code of ethics of the American Pharmaceutical Association. *J Am Pharm Assoc* 1952;13:721–723.

3. Code of ethics for pharmacists. American Pharmacists Association Web site. Available at: www.pharmacist.com. Accessed March 11, 2009.

4. Dessing RP. Ethics applied to pharmacy practice. *Pharm World Sci* 2000;22:10–16.

5. Dessing RP, Flameling J. Ethics in pharmacy: a new definition of responsibility. *Pharm World Sci* 2003;25:3–10.

6. Veatch RM, Haddad AM, English DC. *Case Studies in Biomedical Ethics.* New York, NY: Oxford University Press; 2008:4.

7. Beauchamp TL, Childress JF. *Principles of Biomedical Ethics.* 5th ed. New York, NY: Oxford University Press; 2001.

8. Kälvemark S, Höglund AT, Hansson MG, et al. Living with conflicts—ethical dilemmas and moral distress in the health care system. *Soc Sci Med* 2004;58:1075–1084.

9. Davis FD. Human dignity and respect for persons: a historical perspective on public bioethics. In: *Human Dignity and Bioethics: Essays Commissioned by the President's Council on Bioethics.* Washington, DC: The President's Council on Bioethics; 2008:19–38.

10. Ozar DT. Taking the lead in developing institutional policies. In: Hester DM, ed. *Ethics by Committee: A Textbook on Consultation, Organization, and Education for Hospital Ethics Committees.* 1st ed. Lanham, MD: Rowman-Littlefield Publishers; 2007:255–256.

11. Fincham JE, Harris CE, Fassett WE, Richards W. Over-the-counter availability of Plan B emergency contraception: further discussion and commentary. *Ann Pharmacother* 2005;39:346–351.

12. Lau HS, Riezbos J, Abas V, Porsius AJ, De Boer A. A nation-wide study on the practice of euthanasia and physician-assisted suicide in community and hospital pharmacies in the Netherlands. *Pharm World Sci* 2000;22:3–9.

13. Fassett WE. Ethics, law, and the emergence of pharmacists' responsibility for patient care. *Ann Pharmacother* 2007;41:1264–1267.

14. Wingfield, Bissell P, Anderson C. The scope of pharmacy ethics—an evaluation of the international research literature, 1990–2002. *Soc Sci Med* 2004;58:2383–2396.

15. Cooper RJ, Bissell P, Wingfield J. A new prescription for empirical ethics research in pharmacy: a critical review of the literature. *J Med Ethics* 2007;33:82–86.

16. Redman BK. The ethics of leadership in pharmacy. *Am J Health-Syst Pharm* 1995;52:2099–2104.

17. Cooper RJ, Bissell P, Wingfield J. Ethical decision-making, passivity, and pharmacy. *J Med Ethics* 2008;34:441–445.

18. Prayle D, Brazier M. Supply of medicines: paternalism, autonomy, and realism. *J Med Ethics* 1998;24:93–98.

19. Veatch RM, Haddad A. *Case Studies in Pharmacy Ethics.* 2nd ed. New York, NY: Oxford University Press; 2008.

20. Velasquez M, Moberg D, Meyer MJ, et al. A framework for thinking ethically. Markkula Center for Applied Ethics Web site. Available at: www.scu.edu. Accessed December 27, 2008.

21. Aristotle. *The Nicomachean Ethics.* Thomson JAK, trans. New York, NY: Penguin Press; 2004. First published by Allen & Unwin, 1953.

22. Key statements, beliefs, and philosophies behind the American Association of Critical-Care Nurses (AACN). American Association of Critical-Care Nurses Web site. Available at: www.aacn.org. Accessed December 27, 2008.

23. Noddings N. *Caring: A Feminine Approach to Ethics and Moral Education.* 2nd ed. Berkeley, CA: University of California Press; 2003.

24. Bentley JP, Branahan BF III, McCaffrey DJ III, Garner DD, Smith MC. Sale of tobacco products in pharmacies: results and implications of an empirical study. *J Am Pharm Assoc* 1998;38:703–709.

25. Harding G, Smith FJ, Taylor KMG. Injecting drug misusers—pharmacists' attitudes. *J Soc Adm Pharm* 1992;9:35–41.

Abbreviations

DUR: drug utilization review
HMO: health maintenance organization
OSHA: Occupational Safety and Health Administration

Case Scenarios

CASE ONE: You are the Director of Pharmacy at a community hospital and are notified that a staff pharmacist approved a prescription written for an expensive monoclonal antibody in an adult immunocompromised patient with a life-threatening viral infection. There are limited and controversial data regarding efficacy of this agent in this situation in the medical literature, and use of the monoclonal antibody in this patient does not meet the hospital's pharmacy and therapeutics committee approved use. The staff pharmacist states he is aware of the hospital policy and limited information for use of this agent in patients with similar conditions, but states that no other options are available for this patient. You are aware that your pharmacy department is over budget for the year and that every large cost is being closely evaluated. You are already concerned that hospital administration will ask for a decrease in pharmacy staff, which may alter pharmacist coverage of numerous patients. You agree that there are limited pharmaceutical options for this patient but do not want to lose pharmacist coverage in the hospital. What strategies can be used to evaluate the ethical issues in this case based on principlism ethics?

CASE TWO: You are the pharmacist at a local community pharmacy, and it is now 10:54 p.m. on a Saturday night. You have worked two shifts in a row and are looking forward to being able to leave at the end of your second shift at 11:00 p.m. The night-shift pharmacist arrives on time but stumbles into the pharmacy area and almost immediately falls asleep at the counter. A coworker had told you last year that the night-shift pharmacist had abused narcotic medications and alcohol previously. What strategies can be used to evaluate the ethical issues in this case based on virtue ethics?

CASE THREE: Dr. Smith is the sole pharmacist in a small town. She receives a prescription for levonorgestrel 0.75 mg (Plan B) for Sandra Rollins, a 23-year-old college student. On the basis of her personal values, Dr. Smith refuses to dispense any emergency contraceptive. Ms. Rollins states that she had unprotected intercourse almost 72 hours ago and needs the prescription filled now. Ms. Rollins asks if there are any other pharmacies in the area. What strategies can be used to evaluate the ethical issues in this case based on principlism ethics?

CASE FOUR: Mr. Juan Escobar is a self-employed, 51-year-old man with a serious, chronic respiratory infection, who has been admitted to the hospital where you work as a staff pharmacist. On the basis of culture and susceptibility testing, his physician recommends long-term therapy with a new oral antibacterial agent. The patient informs you that he does not qualify for any of the state-funded healthcare insurance programs based on his yearly income ($29,000/year), and he will have trouble paying for this new antibacterial agent since his current insurance plan does not have prescription benefits. On the basis of local retail pricing, this antibiotic will cost him approximately $23,000/year. In addition, Mr. Escobar does not qualify for any patient assistance programs because the antibiotic manufacturer limits assistance to those earning less than $15,000/year. His physician is reluctant to discharge Mr.

Escobar from the hospital until the antibiotic cost issue is resolved, and has ordered the continuation of the intravenous antibacterial agent so that Mr. Escobar will qualify for inpatient care. Assuming that the new oral antibacterial agent is the only available option for treatment based on efficacy, what strategies can be used to evaluate the ethical issues in this case based on care-based ethics?

Additional
Resources
Available
Online!

Visit the Student Companion Web site at http://healthprofessions.jbpub.com/pharmacymanagement for interactive study tools and additional resources.

See www.rxugace.com to learn how you can obtain continuing pharmacy education for this content.

PHARMACY OPERATIONS

CHAPTER 7

PHARMACY OPERATIONS

WORKFLOW, PRACTICE ACTIVITIES, MEDICATION SAFETY, TECHNOLOGY, AND QUALITY

TAD A. GOMEZ, MS, RPH

JAMES C. MCALLISTER IV, PHARMD, MS

CHRISTY MONIQUE NORMAN, PHARMD, MS

MARIE A. CHISHOLM-BURNS, PHARMD, MPH, FCCP, FASHP

LEARNING OBJECTIVES

After completing the chapter, the reader will be able to

1. Describe how to conduct a workflow analysis.

2. List some activities that constitute the practice of pharmacy.

3. Define a medication error, identify factors that result in medication errors, and discuss policies and procedures to reduce medication errors.

4. Describe information technology tools, automation tools, and medication delivery systems, and their benefits to pharmacy operations.

5. Determine factors that should be considered when deciding whether to adopt new technology.

6. Define quality and how it can be measured in a pharmacy setting.

7. State the differences between quality assurance, quality control, and continuous quality improvement, and how managers use each to ensure quality.

8. Explain the plan-do-study-act cycle.

9. Describe brainstorming, root cause analysis, and failure mode and effects analysis and their role in the continuous quality improvement cycle.

10. List ways that pharmacists and pharmacist managers can improve quality.

KEY CONCEPTS

❶ One of the fundamental necessities in managing pharmacy operations and services is a firm understanding of the physical and psychological work environment. The environment where work will be performed must be designed to facilitate accuracy, safety, efficiency, and staff and customer/patient satisfaction.

❷ Pharmaceutical care redefined the pharmacist's and the pharmacist manager's roles into the realm of managing and performing collaborative patient care with the responsibilities of assessing patient status, developing and implementing a pharmaceutical care plan, monitoring and documenting health-related outcomes, and assuming responsibility of these outcomes.

❸ Because many pharmacy protocols were developed to reduce errors, deviations from medication safety protocols often result in medication errors and other adverse events; therefore, an important responsibility of the manager is to make sure all employees comply with protocols.

❹ The greatest opportunity for medication error prevention is provided when circumstances or events that have the capacity to cause error are identified, thus allowing organizations to develop action plans for process improvements that prevent the error from recurring.

❺ Effective managers identify methods for monitoring the medication-use system, establishing opportunities for additional safety measures, and developing processes for evaluating errors when they occur. It is imperative that organizations take a systems-based approach to assessing and resolving causes of medication errors.

❻ Pharmacy informatics refers to the use of technology within healthcare systems and settings to access, store, analyze, and disseminate medication-related data and information to optimize patient care, safety, and outcomes. E-prescribing allows prescribers to send an electronic prescription directly to a pharmacy from the point of care, and it is believed to be an important element in improving the quality of patient care and reducing medication errors. As the use of informatics increases within the healthcare field, interfacing capabilities of these information systems are critical.

❼ It is incumbent upon managers and administrators to explain the reasons for implementing technology and its benefits, as employees are more likely to embrace technology changes if they are able to identify the advantages they will personally gain from the technology.

❽ Quality in pharmacy practice can be described as the provision of pharmacy services where all processes are aimed toward the safe delivery of care that increases the probability of desired patient outcomes, reduces adverse outcomes, and has other benefits. Although performing high-quality service is expected of all pharmacists, a major goal of management is to ensure quality by measuring performance and implementing strategies to improve quality.

❾ Continuous quality improvement (CQI) is characterized by a multidisciplinary team or total systems approach to quality. The focus of CQI is not on correcting individual errors after they occur but rather on continually and incrementally improving the individual steps within processes that lead to variation and errors.

❿ Pharmacists are highly encouraged to get involved in quality improvement efforts, share their experiences with others, and network with internal and external colleagues to identify and implement solutions that have proved to be successful. By doing so, they contribute to the improvement of quality and safety for all patients regardless of differences in geographic and practice settings.

INTRODUCTION

The **Institute of Medicine** (IOM) described the quality of U.S. health care as follows: "The American health care delivery system is in need of fundamental change. . . . The care delivered is not, essentially, the care we should receive. . . . Between the health care we have and the care we could have lies not just a gap, but a chasm."[1(p1)] As pharmacists and pharmacist managers and leaders, it is our responsibility to provide optimal pharmacy services to facilitate closing the gap between the current state of health care and the high-quality health care we need. The quality of pharmacy services largely depends on pharmacy operations, which include a vast array of responsibilities and tasks that differ based on the specific pharmacy practice setting. This chapter describes basic concepts of pharmacy operations and management as they relate to pharmacy work environment and workflow, practice activities, medication safety, technology, and assessing and monitoring quality. Whether you are a staff pharmacist or pharmacist manager, understanding these concepts will assist you in connecting day-to-day pharmacy operations to the overall quality of healthcare delivery in your organization and beyond.

PHARMACY WORK ENVIRONMENT AND WORKFLOW ANALYSIS

Pharmacy operations vary according to setting and work environment, each with its own unique cultural, **psychosocial**, and physical composition. For example, the retail community pharmacy environment is different from the home healthcare pharmacy environment. Because pharmacy environments are different and workflow may differ greatly between environments, this section will provide an overview, rather than a site-specific explication, of work environment considerations, as well as basic workflow analysis and its relationship to pharmacy operations.

❶ *One of the fundamental necessities in managing pharmacy operations and services is a firm understanding of the psychosocial and physical environments in which the pharmacy operates. The environment where work will be performed must be designed to facilitate accuracy, safety, efficiency, and staff and customer/patient satisfaction.* A variety of factors heavily influence the psychosocial work environment, including interpersonal and social relations among coworkers, employee attitudes, the degree of individual autonomy, and the organization's culture.[2] These factors can have a profound effect on employee satisfaction, performance, self-esteem, achievement, confidence, and commitment to organizational goals and problem solving.[3]

The physical work environment, which includes elements such as work space, temperature, airflow,

safety systems, and security, is equally important and can affect the psychosocial environment.[2] The physical environment should also contribute to pride, belonging, and respect for others. Most important, factors such as adequate lighting, space, limiting interruptions through spatial design, privacy, and adequate access to information resources are critical to ensuring a practice environment that optimizes patient safety and effectiveness. Designing or modifying the physical work environment is a complex, time-intensive process. In addition to the general layout and amount of space that will be needed to adequately perform tasks, the environment must meet legal and regulatory requirements. Examples of legal requirements may include such things as compliance to building codes, security requirements, and fire safety codes. Examples of regulatory requirements include compliance with state pharmacy boards and standards.

Building or modifying a work environment that conforms to legal and regulatory requirements while concomitantly allowing space for an efficient, logical workflow is often challenging. However, performing a workflow analysis may help. A workflow analysis is a systematic process by which tasks performed in a particular work environment are broken down into their individual steps and then evaluated for variables such as accuracy, safety, efficiency, and customer/patient satisfaction. To conduct a workflow analysis, all essential tasks performed in the environment must be identified. (Although simplistic, **Figure 7–1** describes tasks involved in dispensing a medication in an inpatient pharmacy setting.) Next, the order in which the steps of the process will be performed, along with the environment in which these steps are conducted, should be described and designed. Finally, an analysis of the smaller environments (e.g., decentralized pharmacy) and their flow into other larger environments (e.g., the centralized pharmacy) should be performed.

Another consideration particularly important in workflow design within health care is the adaptability of the environment. Healthcare services are in a constant state of flux, often requiring changes based on a patient's individual needs. Organic workflows, or systems, have the ability

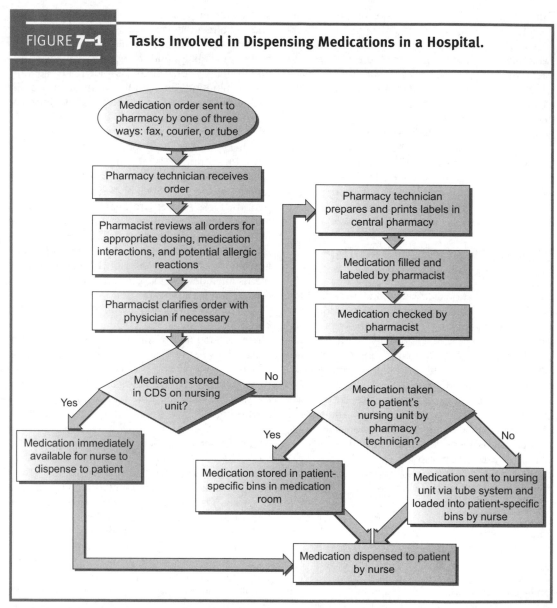

FIGURE **7–1** **Tasks Involved in Dispensing Medications in a Hospital.**

This figure examines the step-by-step process of completing/dispensing a medication order in an inpatient hospital central pharmacy. CDS = computerized dispensing system.

to allow for modification of workflows based on the needs at that time. In contrast, mechanistic workflows are systems that tend to be more rigid. It is essential that workflows are designed to help facilitate the provision of safe, accurate, and efficient practice activities amid the constant changes encountered within the realm of pharmacy and health care.

PHARMACY PRACTICE ACTIVITIES

Since the pharmacy profession's inception, pharmacists have played an essential role in optimizing the integrity of the medication-use process. Early responsibilities of pharmacists included the reliable compounding and distribution of medications to patients, as well as serving as a resource for drug information to patients and healthcare professionals in the community. With increased volume and regulation, large industrial production establishments became the primary source of pharmaceutical compounding. This shift in production allowed pharmacists to explore alternative opportunities for involvement in the medication-use process. Pharmacists began to declare clinical roles, particularly in the hospital setting, and the earliest direct patient care models were created. Pharmacists in the community also participated in direct patient care activities, such as monitoring health (e.g., blood pressure and cholesterol screening) and disease and medication therapy management. Pharmacists and pharmacist managers have continued to maintain responsibility for the safe preparation and distribution of medications while becoming leaders in **pharmaceutical care**, defined as "the responsible provision of drug therapy for the purpose of achieving desirable outcomes that improve a patient's quality of life."[4(p539)] These outcomes include "(1) cure of a disease, (2) elimination or reduction of a patient's symptomatology, (3) arresting or slowing of a disease process, or (4) preventing a disease or symptomatology."[4(p539)] ❷ *Pharmaceutical care redefined the pharmacist's and the pharmacist manager's roles into the realm of managing and performing collaborative patient care with the responsibilities of assessing patient status, developing and implementing a pharmaceutical care plan, monitoring and documenting health-related outcomes, and assuming responsibility of these outcomes.*[5]

Many federal laws influenced pharmacy practice, such as the Omnibus Budget Reconciliation Act of 1990 (OBRA), the **Health Insurance Portability and Accountability Act** (HIPAA), the Prescription Drug Marketing Act, and the Haight Act (for additional details, refer to Chapter 5, "Significant Laws Affecting Pharmacy Practice Management," and pharmacy law textbooks). Further,

state boards of pharmacy typically establish standards for pharmacists' professional practice. Varying degrees of regulation and consistency in defining pharmaceutical services led the National Association of Boards of Pharmacy (NABP) to develop the Model State Pharmacy Act and Model Rules.[6] This model guides states in defining the practice of pharmacy, and it is key that pharmacist managers are familiar with the practice of pharmacy within their state. Pharmacy is diverse and includes various areas of practice. The "Practice of Pharmacy" includes, but is not limited to

- Evaluating and filling **prescriptions** and **medication orders**
- Dispensing medications
- Participating in medicine and device selection and monitoring
- Engaging in specific activities that may include ordering, evaluating, and performing laboratory and related tests; performing physical assessments; and initiating, adjusting, and evaluating drug therapy under **Collaborative Practice Agreements** and/or **Collaborative Drug Therapy Management Agreements** (examples include pharmacist-managed disease management clinics and retail pharmacies where the pharmacist manages/treats the patient's hypertension, diabetes, dyslipidemia, etc.)
- Administering medicines to patients
- Performing medication regimen reviews
- Participating in **telepharmacy** and **telemedicine** programs
- Participating in drug and drug-related research
- Counseling patients
- Compounding and labeling drugs and devices
- Storing medications
- Maintaining medical/medicine records and confidentiality

Federal Pharmacy Law: The Pharmacist and Liability

The expanding role of the pharmacist has resulted in increased opportunity and potential for liability. Two types of liability most applicable to pharmacists are civil and administrative. Civil liability involves malpractice or professional negligence. Administrative liability is determined by governing bodies, such as the state board of pharmacy. In civil liability, the plaintiff must be able to prove that a legal duty to a patient arose, and breach of that duty occurred and caused a distinguishable injury to the patient. Many pharmacists invest in malpractice insurance regardless of whether coverage is provided by their employer. Under pharmacy practice laws, boards of pharmacy are authorized to investigate when complaints about a pharmacist are received from the public. If necessary, boards of pharmacy may issue a wide variety of penalties ranging from a reprimand to license revocation.[7]

Organizational responses to various legal standards include developing protocols, guidelines, and policies for proper medication use. Generally, various individuals develop these documents, and staff education and systems of accountability are essential to ensuring the success of such protocols. Highly regarded evidence-based medicine documents and articles may be used as a resource to develop protocols. Institutions may choose to develop and implement internal protocols or adopt protocols from various professional organizations. ❸ *Because many pharmacy protocols were developed to reduce errors, deviations from medication safety protocols often result in **medication errors** and other adverse events; therefore, an important responsibility of the manager is to make sure all employees comply with protocols.* Regardless of the cause or outcomes, reporting adverse events, such as medication errors, should occur, and managers should encourage this activity.

MEDICATION SAFETY

Medication Errors

The National Coordinating Council for Medication Error Reporting and Prevention defines a medication error as

Any preventable event that may cause or lead to inappropriate medication use or patient harm while the medication is in the control of the health care professional, patient, or consumer. Such events may be related to professional practice; heath care products, procedures, and systems, including prescribing; order communication; product labeling;

packaging; nomenclature; compounding; dispensing; distribution; administration; education; monitoring; and use.[8(p4)]

Errors may occur at any step of the medication-use process. Because there is no single system that will render a pharmacy organization error free, the entire medication ordering, dispensing, and administrating process must be designed with multiple checks and backup systems.

The "five rights" of medication administration include the "right patient, right drug, right dose, right route, and right time."[9] Several factors may contribute to a deviation from the "five rights", and **Figure 7–2** describes examples of different types of medication errors. These errors often occur during the prescribing process, and illegible handwriting is a common cause of medication errors (**Figure 7–3**). Improperly written orders increase the risk that the intended drug, dosage, route of administration, or frequency may be misinterpreted.[9] The Institute for Safe Medication Practices (ISMP) compiles a list of "Error-Prone Abbreviations, Symbols, and Dose Designations" that should never be used when communicating medical information.[10] These abbreviations, symbols, and dose designations have been frequently misinterpreted or have resulted in medication errors. Examples of these types of abbreviations can be found in **Table 7–1**.[9,10] Disruptions in pharmacists' workflow to clarify illegible orders also increase the chances for error.[11] Computerized prescriber order entry systems, or **e-prescribing**, have many potential benefits, including decreasing risk of medication errors due to illegible handwriting.[12]

Additional sources of medication errors include drugs that have names that look or sound alike (**Table 7–2**).[13] If dosage forms overlap, the problem may be further exacerbated. These types of errors may occur if the individual writing the prescription (medication order) inadvertently interchanges the two drugs or when someone misinterprets a poorly written medication order. Failure to read-back and verify verbal orders to prescribers may also result in errors due to hearing the order incorrectly. The implementation of computerized prescriber order entry systems and electronic pharmacy systems can provide clinical warnings for medications with similar names. Designating the purpose of a

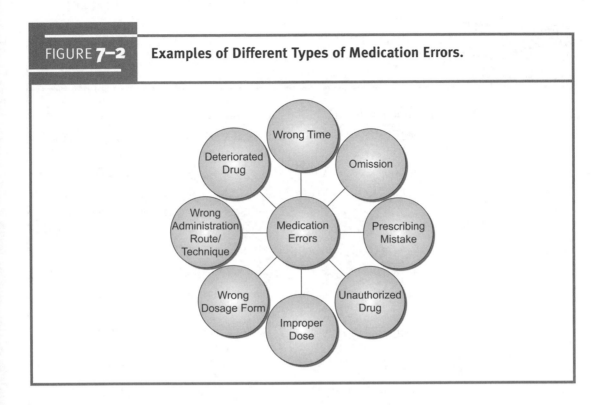

FIGURE 7–2   **Examples of Different Types of Medication Errors.**

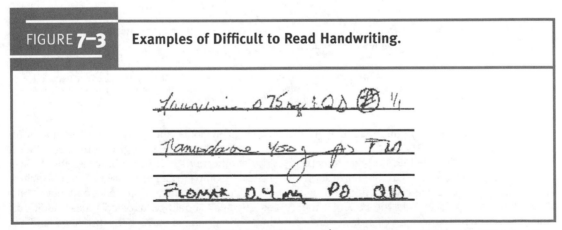

FIGURE 7–3   **Examples of Difficult to Read Handwriting.**

In line 1, "Levoxine" may be mistaken for "Lanoxin." In line 2, "↑ amiodarone" was mistaken for "trazodone." In line 3, "QD" was mistaken for "QID."

Source: Adapted with permission from Cohen MR. *Medication Errors*. 2nd ed. Washington, DC: American Pharmacists Association; 2007:89,162,165.

TABLE 7–1	Abbreviations to Avoid

Abbreviations	Intended Meaning	Common Error
U	Units	Mistaken as zero (0) or four (4), resulting in overdose
µg	Micrograms	Mistaken for "mg," resulting in overdose
Q.D.	Every day	Period after "Q" mistaken for an "I," and drug is given "QID," which is four times daily
Q.O.D.	Every other day	Mistaken as "QD" or "QID"
SC or SQ	Subcutaneous	Mistaken as "SL," sublingual
TIW	Three times weekly	Mistaken as "three times daily" or "twice a week"
D/C	Discharge; discontinue	Patient's medications prematurely discontinued
HS	Half strength	Misinterpreted as "HS," hour of sleep
cc	Cubic centimeters	Mistaken as "U" units
AU, AS, AD	Both ears; left ear; right ear	Mistaken as "OU," both eyes; "OS," left eye; "OD," right eye
IU	International unit	Mistaken as IV (intravenous) Or 10 (ten)
MS, MSO4, MgSO4	Morphine sulfate or magnesium sulfate	Confused for one another

Source: Data from Cohen M. *Medication Errors: Causes, Prevention, and Risk Management.* Sudbury, MA: Jones and Bartlett Publishers; 1999. Institute for Safe Medication Practices. ISMP's list of error-prone abbreviations, symbols, and dose designations. Available at: http://www.ismp.org/Tools/errorproneabbreviations.pdf. Accessed November 8, 2008.

medication by the prescriber may also prevent this type of error.

Ambiguous orders fail to provide complete information to ensure the safe administration of the medication. Complete prescription and medication orders should include the patient's name and any pertinent patient-specific data, such as date of birth (age), allergy information, weight, and height. Generic and brand names may be used for prescribing, although the generic name is generally preferred. Research or chemical names,

chemical symbols, and abbreviations should never be used, and the drug strength should be included. The apothecary system for quantity should never be used. Complete directions for use should include the route of administration and frequency. "Take as directed" should be avoided unless additional instructions are or have been provided and the patient understands how to take or use the medication. It is also helpful to include the purpose of the medication to confirm that the patient received the correct drug for the correct indication.

TABLE **7–2**	Examples of Medications with Similar Names	

Drug Name	Confused Drug Name
Abelcet	Amphotericin B
Acetazolamide	Acetohexamide
Amaryl	Reminyl
Ambisome	Amphotericin B
Avandia	Coumadin
Avinza	Evista
Carboplastin	Cisplatin
Celebrex	Celexa, Cerebyx
Clonidine	Clonazepam
Daunorubicin	Idarubicin
Diabeta	Zebeta
Dopamine	Dobutamine
Ephedrine	Epinephrine
Fentanyl	Sufentanil
Lamisil	Lamictal
Luvox	Lasix
Oxycontin	Oxycodone
Plavix	Paxil
Quinine	Quinidine
Ritonavir	Retrovir
Serzone	Seroquel
Tiagabine	Tizanidine
Vinblastine	Vincristine
Zyprexa	Zyrtec

Sources: Data from Cohen M. *Medication Errors: Causes, Prevention, and Risk Management.* Sudbury, MA: Jones and Bartlett Publishers; 1999. Institute for Safe Medication Practices. List of Confused Drug Names. Available at: http://www.ismp.org/tools/confuseddrugnames.pdf. Accessed November 8, 2008.

If an error occurs, it can be categorized based on the severity of harm caused to the patient (**Figure 7–4**).[14] This classification mechanism allows organizations to track medication errors in a consistent, systematic approach. ◆*The greatest opportunity for medication error prevention is provided when circumstances or events that have the capacity to cause error are identified, thus allowing organizations to develop action plans for process improvements that prevent the error from recurring.* An example of one such opportunity would be the discovery of the amphotericin B conventional in the amphotericin B liposomal bin. The use of amphotericin B conventional to prepare an intravenous solution that was intended to include amphotericin B liposomal could be fatal to a patient. The discovery of this error gives the pharmacy an opportunity to determine strategies to prevent the placement of these products in the same bin. Studies have demonstrated that pharmacist-led programs have been successful in reducing medication errors.[15,16]

Performance Improvement

Performance improvement is essential to the integrity of the medication-use process and the prevention of medication errors. There are both proactive and reactive processes for performance improvement, and effective managers seek opportunities to employ proactive processes to improve performance. ❺ *Moreover, effective managers identify methods for monitoring the medication-use system, establishing opportunities for additional safety measures, and developing processes for evaluating errors when they occur. It is imperative that organizations take a systems-based approach to assessing and resolving causes of medication errors.* Error-reporting must be required on a nonpunitive basis, and placing blame on individuals should generally be avoided because this approach may foster fear, thereby reducing error reporting and reducing quality improvement programs.

Regardless of whether you practice in a community retail pharmacy or in a large teaching hospital, pharmacists and pharmacist managers should use well-established, proactive performance improvement approaches that include a mechanism for monitoring the system while implementing specific protocols, guidelines, and

FIGURE **7-4**   National Coordinating Council for Medication Error Reporting and Prevention Index for Categorizing Medication Errors.

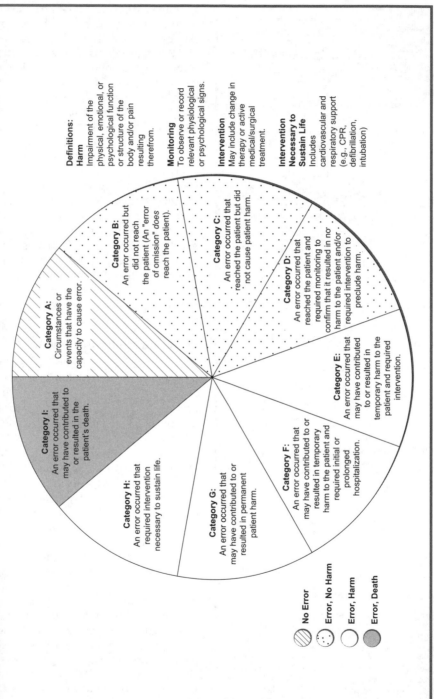

Definitions:

Harm
Impairment of the physical, emotional, or psychological function or structure of the body and/or pain resulting therefrom.

Monitoring
To observe or record relevant physiological or psychological signs.

Intervention
May include change in therapy or active medical/surgical treatment.

Intervention Necessary to Sustain Life
Includes cardiovascular and respiratory support (e.g., CPR, defibrillation, intubation)

Category A:
Circumstances or events that have the capacity to cause error.

Category B:
An error occurred but did not reach the patient (An "error of omission" *does* reach the patient).

Category C:
An error occurred that reached the patient but did not cause patient harm.

Category D:
An error occurred that reached the patient and required monitoring to confirm that it resulted in no harm to the patient and/or required intervention to preclude harm.

Category E:
An error occurred that may have contributed to or resulted in temporary harm to the patient and required intervention.

Category F:
An error occurred that may have contributed to or resulted in temporary harm to the patient and required initial or prolonged hospitalization.

Category G:
An error occurred that may have contributed to or resulted in permanent patient harm.

Category H:
An error occurred that required intervention necessary to sustain life.

Category I:
An error occurred that may have contributed to or resulted in the patient's death.

No Error
Error, No Harm
Error, Harm
Error, Death

The index classifies errors according to the severity of the outcome and assists healthcare practitioners and institutions to track medication errors in a consistent, systematic manner. CPR = cardiopulmonary rescucitation

Source: © National Coordinating Council for Medication Error Reporting and Prevention. All Rights Reserved.

policies. Performance measure guidelines assist organizations in prioritizing which portions of the medication-use process will be monitored for deviations, as deviations help to identify process improvement opportunities. For example, an analysis of error rates in a busy community pharmacy revealed a significant rate of inaccurate medication refills after 4 p.m. each day. An analysis of this deviation revealed that the pharmacy fills almost twice as many prescriptions after 4 p.m., with less than half the staff, than it does from 9 a.m. to 4 p.m. A performance improvement approach could include having more staff available to meet work demands after 4 p.m., or employing the use of technology (robotics and **automation**) to help meet workload demands. Keep in mind that process improvement is continuous and reevaluation is always necessary.

Reactive approaches to process improvement can be conducted as a **root cause analysis**, a process that identifies the root, or initiating causes, of a problem. A successful root cause analysis focuses on systems and processes and looks at why the error occurred. The following three questions may help to identify potential system failures:[17]

- What was the error?
- What was the proximal cause?
- What were the underlying system failures?

Medication Dispensing

Pharmacists are responsible for accurately dispensing medications, and managers should encourage the development and implementation of policies and procedures to prevent dispensing errors. Common dispensing errors include incorrect medication, dosage strength, or dosage form. Additional sources of dispensing errors include dose miscalculation, drug interactions, and contraindications. The following steps should be taken to minimize the risk of medication dispensing errors:[11]

- Ascertaining and assessing the patient's medical and medicine history
- Reviewing and assessing prescription(s) or medication order(s)
- Reviewing patient's profile and ascertaining information from the individual concerning medication allergies, other medications currently taken, and concomitant disease states
- Entering order/prescription and other data into an electronic pharmacy system
- Assessing and acknowledging computer alerts
- Selecting appropriate medication
- Verifying the expiration date of the medicine
- Counting/measuring the appropriate amount of the medication
- Affixing the correct prescription label
- Double-checking the prescription/medication order to ensure accuracy
- Returning the stock medicine container to the appropriate location in pharmacy
- Counseling patients about their medications
- Answering medication-related questions

Proper selection of the medication involves choosing the correct medication for the patient and filling the prescription/medication order correctly. **Barcoding systems** are effective for reducing some medication errors, such as proper selection of medication and proper dose.[18] Barcoding and similar systems are also effective in managing pharmacy inventory (for more information, refer to Chapter 8, "Purchasing and Managing Inventory"). Appropriate labeling of medication should occur after the product is prepared, and the label should include drug name, dosage strength, dosage form, quantity, complete instructions for use, number of refills, and prescriber's name. Auxiliary labels are used to caution medical professionals and patients about warnings for specific medications. Some medications have auxiliary labels provided by the manufacturer, while others do not. Some products may require auxiliary labels to designate the appropriate route of administration (e.g., orally, subcutaneously, intravenously) or any precautions that should be taken (e.g., take medication with food).

Compounding Sterile Preparations

Errors with compounding sterile preparations may be the result of incorrect ingredients, incorrect strengths of ingredients, and contamination with pathogenic microorganisms, pyrogens, or harmful ingredients. Aseptic technique is critical for preventing contamination with microorganisms and pyrogens. The **United States Pharmacopeia** (USP) Chapter <797> provides standards that organizations may adopt to ensure the safe preparation of compounded sterile preparations. These standards include guidance on compounding conditions, **quality assurance** (QA) programs, storage and beyond-use dating, and staff competency.[19] Managers should confirm that pharmacists and support personnel are trained and tested to ensure competency in sterile product preparation.

Patient Education and Counseling

Patients and family members represent the final step in the medication-use process where medication errors can be prevented. Thus, patients play an important role in preventing medication errors. Pharmacists should tell the patient the name of each medication when filling prescriptions, allow patients to view the medication, counsel the patient as to how to take the medication (and test their recall on medication instructions) for the prescribed indication, and describe adverse events associated with the medication(s). Patients who have taken the medication in the past may be able to prevent medication errors if they notice that the medication looks different.[12] Patients must be educated to monitor their response to the drug, be able to recognize signs of an adverse event, and know when to contact a healthcare professional.

TECHNOLOGY IN PHARMACY OPERATIONS

Information Technology, Automation, and Medication Delivery Systems

For more than three decades, information technology, automation, and medication delivery systems have been used to improve medication safety and manage various facets of pharmacy operations. Often, such technologies are considered cost-effective and valuable tools in patient care improvement efforts.[20] Strategic use of information technology and automation will largely define the degree of excellence achieved by pharmacy practice both today and in the future.[21] In addition, successful pharmacist leaders and managers will likely devote attention to information technology and automation at a level similar to the attention given to clinical and financial considerations.[21]

Information technology, in a general sense, encompasses the **hardware** and **software** that are used to enter, retrieve, transmit, or otherwise manipulate information or process data electronically. **Data processing** involves the input, storage, organization, transformation, and extraction of meaningful information from data; levels of data processing range from the very basic to the very complex.[22] The following sections address information technology tools, automated technology, medication delivery systems, and considerations for implementing technology within pharmacy sites.

COMMON INFORMATION TECHNOLOGY TOOLS

The development of information technology tools, such as **pharmacy informatics**, e-prescribing, point-of-care devices, and telepharmacy, has enhanced healthcare access and patient safety efforts and expanded the role of pharmacists in patient care delivery. ❻ *Pharmacy informatics refers to the use of technology within healthcare systems and settings to access, store, analyze, and disseminate medication-related data and information to optimize patient care, safety, and outcomes.*[23] In particular, pharmacy informatics allows for developing an integrated or centralized data system to create continuity of access to patients' medication-related data across healthcare settings. E-prescribing (or electronic prescribing) is an example of the application of pharmacy informatics.

❻ *E-prescribing is the "computer-based electronic generation, transmission, and filling of a prescription, taking the place of paper or faxed prescriptions."*[24] *This increasingly popular application of information technology in health care has the potential to increase patient safety, enhance patient and provider satisfaction, and create tremendous savings in healthcare costs.* Experts believe that more than two million adverse drug events could be avoided each year pending full implementation of e-prescribing, and savings of more than $27 billion in healthcare costs could be achieved in the United States alone.[25] This tremendously positive effect on healthcare delivery in America is recognized by the U.S. Congress and was incorporated into the Medicare Prescription Drug, Improvement, and Modernization Act of 2003. In this legislation, Congress mandated several provisions, including requiring all Medicare Part D plans to support electronic prescription programs, as well as establishing standards for e-prescribing systems, exchange of patient-specific clinical data, security and patient confidentiality, and data interoperability.[26] Barriers to adopting nationwide e-prescribing exist and include the lack of broadband internet connections in some clinical environments; lack of established network connections between clinician offices, pharmacies, and health plans; unwillingness of clinicians to participate; inherent limitations in the system's ability to retrieve current patient information; and the lack of standards for electronic information exchange.[27] Despite these barriers, government and healthcare organizations continue to adopt and refine current e-prescribing systems. As technology and industry standards advance and evolve, these barriers may quickly be overcome, and e-prescribing may consequently become a standard of health care in the United States and a valuable informatics tool used at point of care.

Point-of-care devices, such as personal digital assistants (PDAs), have become more widely used in the healthcare environment. Point-of-care devices are pieces of hardware that enable practitioners to bring technology closer to the patient to improve efficiency, accuracy, and safety. The evolution of point-of-care technologies has grown dramatically with the use of wireless networks, the increased availability of portable devices with expanded memory and operating capabilities, and the availability of pharmacy-related application programs that can be easily downloaded and updated to PDAs. Desirable features for point-of-care devices include access to patient-specific medical information and updated (current) information, memory and processing conducive to data retrieval from database software, and ease of use.

Telepharmacy is the use of communication technology to enable a pharmacist to provide pharmaceutical care to a patient from a distance.[28] Examples of telepharmacy include **videoconferencing**, review of patient medication profiles using computer networks, off-site pharmacist supervision of prescription dispensing and counseling using telecommunication, and interactive Web services in which patients can ask a pharmacist medication-related questions. By reducing the barrier of geographic location, telepharmacy allows pharmacists to provide care to patients who otherwise may not receive these services, and telepharmacy programs have successfully expanded pharmacy services, improved quality of care, and reduced medication-related costs.[29,30]

Automated Technology

The use of automation and robotics to manage pharmacy operations has grown significantly over the past several decades.[31] Automation is any technology, machine, or device linked to a control system, such as using computers to manage machinery and processes.[32] Several types of automation are used to manage pharmacy operations, each with its own purpose, function, benefits, and limitations. Automation can be used in pharmacy in all aspects of the medication distribution process in both inpatient and outpatient facilities.[33–35] Examples include carousel technology, centralized narcotic dispensing technologies, decentralized automated dispensing cabinets, intravenous compounding devices (**Figure 7–5**), **smart pumps**, and unit-dose medication repackaging systems. The appropriate application of automation can allow an organization to achieve outcomes such as improved operating efficiencies, improved safety and quality, provision of high-level customer service, and reduced overall costs.[29,33,34,36–38]

Robotics, a type of automation used in pharmacy, are devices that perform repetitive tasks and functions with minimal need for someone to interact with the device. For example, centralized robots have been used by hospital pharmacies to perform repetitive functions, such as product selection and medication filling (as discussed in the following section, robots are also being used for medication delivery). In this scenario, the robot would be located in a pharmacy and would interface with the pharmacy information system. When a pharmacist enters a new order into the pharmacy information system, the order is automatically transmitted to the robot, which can then select the medication from its inventory, place a patient-specific label on the product, and release the product for delivery (**Figure 7–6**). An application of robotics in pharmacy operations has been in

FIGURE **7–5**   **Intravenous Compounding Device.**

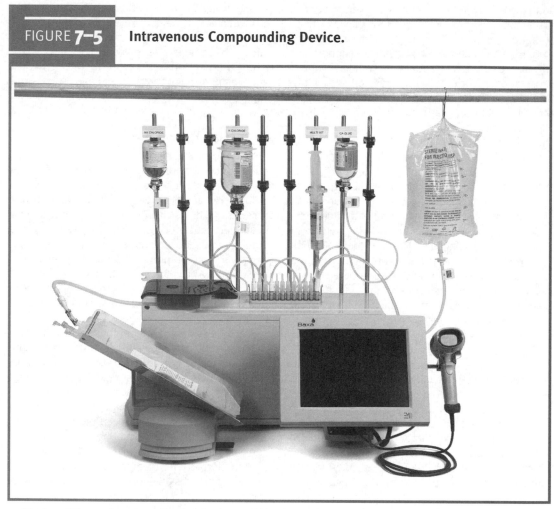

The Baxa EM 2400 is an example of technology used in pharmacies to prepare complex, multi-ingredient intravenous medications, such as total parenteral nutrition and cardioplegia solutions, with tremendous accuracy and precision.

Source: Courtesy of Baxa Corporation.

intravenous admixture preparation. These robots, when interfaced with a pharmacy information system, can select, prepare, label, and dispense a patient-specific product often without a technician or pharmacist to touch the product in any way. The use of robotic intravenous (IV) automation will continue to develop and become more sophisticated. The greatest advantage of using robotics in pharmacy is that tasks can be performed with a high degree of accuracy. Unlike humans, robots are designed to do the same task in the same way, thus minimizing variance, which, in turn, results in reduced medication error rates.[39–41] For example, a study found that robot systems in two hospitals decreased medication dispensing error rates by 50%.[39]

FIGURE **7–6**

| FIGURE **7–6** | **Robotic Technology Used for Dispensing Patient-Specific, Unit-Dose Medications.** |

Following the pharmacist verification of a medication order, this robot will select the medication from its inventory, place it in an envelope marked with a patient-specific label and barcode, and dispense the medication.

Source: Courtesy of McKesson Corporation.

MEDICATION DELIVERY SYSTEMS

Although couriers, clerks, and pharmacy technicians have typically filled the role of "pharmacy delivery person," many organizations have turned to alternate methods of delivering drugs to the patient, and most large facilities now use technology to help deliver medications. Alternatives to human delivery systems in institutional settings include **pneumatic tube systems** and robots.

Pneumatic tube systems are one of the most common nonhuman drug delivery methods many hospitals use (**Figure 7–7**). The cylinders for pneumatic tubes are available in various sizes with differing optimal weight capacities. Many pneumatic tube systems travel at a speed of up to 25 feet per second, which makes these systems excellent for large facilities. However, drawbacks to pneumatic tube systems include the inability to tube large items that will not fit in the cylinder, as well as some protein-based biological medications, blood products, and chemotherapy because of the risk to either the drug or the system if a failure or leak occurred.

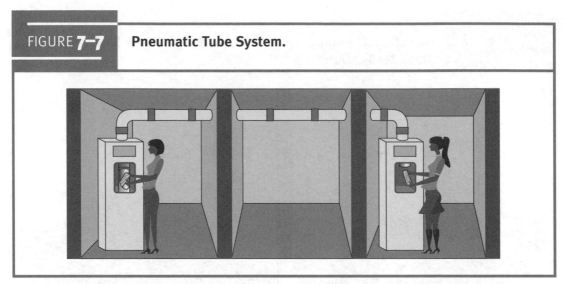

FIGURE **7–7**   **Pneumatic Tube System.**

The medication is put in the cylindrical container propelled by compressed air or by a vacuum through a tube system to a desired location. Pneumatic tube systems are commonly used to transport medications in hospitals from one location to another.

Over the past few years, medication delivery robots have become an increasingly popular method of drug delivery. Aethon's TUG, an automated drug delivery system, is one of the most popular medication delivery robots. TUG connects to existing medication delivery carts and uses a wireless network to navigate efficiently from the pharmacy to patient care units; it requests elevators, opens doors, and announces its arrival (**Figure 7–8**). TUG can operate continuously up to 10 hours at a time without recharging its batteries and can travel up to 5 miles in a day.

TECHNOLOGY IMPLEMENTATION CONSIDERATIONS AND CHALLENGES

Security
Although information systems and automated technology have allowed the healthcare field to improve the quality of care provided to patients, they have also presented a new vulnerability. As an increasing amount of health information is stored electronically, the security of this information and prevention of unauthorized access is an important consideration in the selection of new technology. As part of HIPAA, all healthcare providers are required to ensure that protected health information remains confidential and secure. Methods of accomplishing this include the use of **firewalls** and **encryption software**.

Employee Resistance
As with any major change, resistance by those affected can be overwhelming, and due consideration should be given to this possible challenge to implementation of technology. Refer to Chapter 3, "Leading and Managing Change." New technology may meet the needs of not only the organization as a whole but also the staff and other individuals who will be interacting with or affected by the technology on an ongoing basis. As part of the planning process to implement new technology, administrators should consult with members of the groups that will be using and interacting with the technology; these groups include, but are not limited to, healthcare providers, administrators, and even patients. ❼ *In addition, it is incumbent upon managers and administrators to explain the*

| FIGURE **7–8** | **Aethon's TUG Robot Delivering Medications.** |

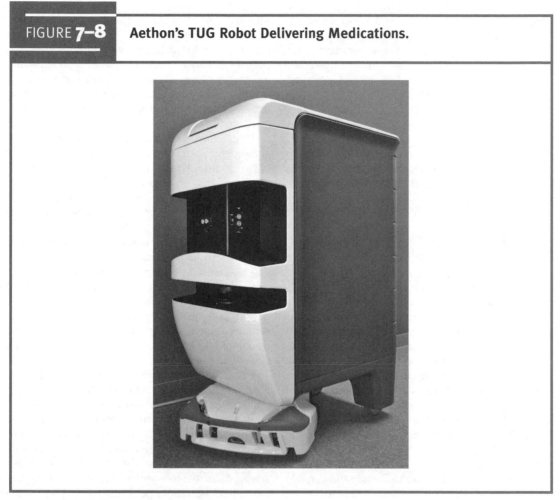

Source: Courtesy of AETHON Inc.

reasons for implementing technology and its benefits, as employees are more likely to embrace technology changes if they are able to identify the advantages they will personally gain from the technology.[32] Also critical to employee acceptance of new technologies, the organization should have in place appropriate and adequate training and education of how to operate or interact optimally with the new technology.[42] If users have not been trained to work with the new technology, frustration will ensue, and the technology's acceptance will be delayed

or may never occur. Technical and operational support, both during implementation and ongoing, is also important and should be available to users of the technology if they encounter problems.

The initial period during which the new technology is implemented can be very stressful for many employees. Implementation of new technology can be done in one of two ways: (1) phased implementation or (2) "big bang" implementation.[43] Phased implementation occurs when the technology is slowly implemented in different areas of the organization over an extended period. Big bang implementation involves a rapid transition from an existing system to the new system. Phased implementations tend to foster quicker acceptance of technology on the part of employees as compared with big bang implementations. Phasing implementation of technology allows individuals who maintain the system to make updates and refinements throughout the early implementation stages (in other words, work out the bugs). Widespread acceptance is enhanced by positive endorsements from early users, and successful users can serve as trainers or consultants for their colleagues.

Documentation

The importance of accurate and timely documentation is essential. Without documentation, there is no record that an action has been taken, and thus no proof that the task was performed. This is an important factor to consider when choosing new technology. Think about the pharmacy that wants to install a new narcotic control system to help with inventory management. Will this new system keep a perpetual electronic record of the number of tablets of each controlled substance placed into or removed from the narcotics control cabinet, or will staff have to keep a written, manual record? Will the system automatically capture and store the identity of the person who accessed the system? When possible, the system should maintain this type of documentation automatically. Regardless of whether the technology is capable of documenting actions automatically, it is important that it facilitates appropriate documentation to ensure safe and accurate pharmacy operations and to comply with legal and regulatory standards.

Cost, Installation, and Maintenance

The overall cost of the technology is another important consideration when deciding what technology to use in pharmacy-related settings, and technology expectations and costs should be clearly stated in the business plan. Overall costs include the cost of the technology, as well as operational costs, such as personnel who may need to be hired to maintain the system and additional pieces of technology that may need to be pur-

chased to maximize the utility of the technology.[44] Although initial costs of purchasing and implementing technology may be expensive, in the long run, it may help the business/program save costs, such as employee time and other resources that would have been expended if the technology was not in place. The technology may also result in increased productivity, which, in turn, may lead to increased revenue (income).

Cost considerations are directly related to equipment selection and choice of vendor or company from which you will acquire technology. The vendor's reputation and experiences with other customers will provide your organization with insight into the vendor's reliability and may serve as a reference to the vendor's degree of service. An additional consideration when evaluating where to purchase equipment is installing and maintaining the technology and the vendor's role and responsibilities within these processes. In many cases, the vendor is responsible for the basic design and installation of the technology. The service agreement between the vendor and the customer should address installation and ongoing system maintenance.

Once the technology has been installed, there is an ongoing need to maintain the technology to optimize its use within the organization. Typically, both the user and the vendor maintain the technology. The user may perform general maintenance tasks, such as software and security updates. The user may also upload electronically stored data to repositories.[35] However, it is preferred that the vendor performs routine, scheduled maintenance of the technology, known as preventative maintenance.[45,46] Most vendors also offer technical support in the form of "help desks" or "hotlines," wherein trained experts troubleshoot issues that arise regarding a specific technology.

Systems Integration

❻ *As the use of informatics increases within the healthcare field, interfacing capabilities of these information systems is critical.* When technology and information systems were first used within health care, they tended to be independent of each other. For example, if a pharmacist needed to review a patient's lab values before initiating therapy with a new medication, he or she might have needed to access two separate electronic systems, the pharmacy system and the lab system. This separation of systems caused more time to be spent processing the medication, resulting in a delay in the delivery of the medication to the patient. With the expanding application of technology in health care and its growing capabilities, it has become important to interface systems to allow for more efficient operations. In the earlier example, if the lab system and the pharmacy system were interfaced, the pharmacist could access necessary information from the lab system with relative ease. This, in turn, would save time and money, promote convenience and customer satisfaction, and improve the overall delivery and quality of patient care.

QUALITY AND QUALITY IMPROVEMENT

In health care, the focus should be on delivering quality patient care. The term *quality* can be defined as a degree or grade of excellence or worth.[47] High patient care quality has been defined by Donabedian as "that kind of care which is expected to maximize an inclusive measure of patient welfare, after one has taken account of the balance of expected gains and losses."[48] Quality is determined by the extent to which patient care programs and services increase the likelihood of desired patient outcomes and decrease undesired outcomes, keeping in mind the existing knowledge base.[49] Pharmacy practice is an essential part of the overall healthcare services that patients receive, and it plays a vital role in patient care quality. ❽ *Specifically, quality in pharmacy practice can be described as the provision of pharmacy services in which all processes are aimed toward the safe delivery of care that increases the probability of desired patient outcomes, reduces adverse outcomes, and has other benefits. Although performing high-quality service is expected of all pharmacists, a major goal of management is to ensure quality by measuring performance and implementing strategies to improve quality.*

Measuring Quality

Patient safety and health, clinical, and humanistic (for example, quality of life) outcomes may be used to measure quality in pharmacy practice. Quality measures related to determining patient safety and outcomes include optimizing health outcomes, limiting the number and type of medication errors and adverse events, minimizing medication turnaround times in a pharmacy setting, and maximizing healthcare access. The key to measuring quality is to *first* define the desired outcome or result, and *then* work in reverse from that point (which is the last step in the process of producing a desired outcome), analyzing each step in the process for potential obstacles to producing the desired outcome until you arrive at the first step in the process. For example, consider the process to measure quality of sterile product compounding in a pharmacy. A desired outcome is that the final compounded sterile product is compounded accurately according to acceptable standards (e.g., the drug label). In this case, the final measure could be either the number of products compounded accurately or the number compounded inaccurately. Once the final measure is defined, potential obstacles should be identified by working in reverse chronological order through the process of compounding a sterile preparation; some potential obstacles may include mislabeling the final product, compounding the final product in the wrong solution or volume, reconstituting the drug incorrectly, selecting the wrong drug strength, or selecting the wrong drug or final solution. By observing and evaluating the final compounded sterile product, one should be able to ascertain and measure the quality of the entire process. An effective manager encourages everyone to ensure quality.

QUALITY ASSURANCE AND CONTROL

The measurement method, or process, described previously with sterile compounding is an example of quality assurance (QA). QA is the systematic process of evaluating a product or service in which actual processes or outcomes are compared with predefined criteria, or requirements, to ensure quality.[50] QA focuses on improving and stabilizing production and processes to avoid or minimize problems that lead to defects; thus, monitoring or evaluating processes is conducted on the final product or service to ensure that it meets a specified quality standard. Any quality problems identified during QA can only be corrected after the fact, as the product has already been produced or the service has already been provided.

In contrast to quality assurance, **quality control** (QC) refers to the systematic use of methods to ensure that a service or product conforms to a desired standard and emphasizes blocking the release of defective products.[50] QC was first used in engineering and manufacturing to ensure that defective products did not enter the market. Although the existence of QA processes may seem to decrease the need for QC, some critical products need QC testing if QA fails. An example of the need for both QA and QC is the production of cardioplegia solutions used during cardiothoracic surgeries wherein the role of the cardioplegia solution is to facilitate temporary cessation of cardiac activity and protect the heart during open-heart surgery. Because of the critical role of the cardioplegia, the pharmacist conducts the normal QA processes while checking the compounding of the solutions; in addition, most (if not all) hospitals, as a QC measure, will send samples to the laboratory to confirm the exact concentrations of potassium and other electrolytes in the final compounded solution.

CONTINUOUS QUALITY IMPROVEMENT

Continuous quality improvement (CQI) is an approach to quality management that brings together established quality assurance methods by emphasizing the organization and systems and focusing on the process rather than the individual. CQI refers to ongoing or repeated enhancements of a product or service, contends that most things can be improved, and endorses the need for objective data to analyze and improve processes.[51] W. Edward Deming, widely regarded as the leading expert in the field of quality management, professed the following philosophy regarding CQI: continuous quality improvement leads to decreased costs as a result of fewer errors, reduced need to redo work, fewer delays, and improved use of employees and resources.[51,52] This, in turn, results in increased productivity, which allows the organization to have a strong market position (offering high-quality services at a lower price).[51,52] Organizations with a strong market position are able to remain operational, with opportunities for expansion and hiring.[51,52] Thus, CQI has a greater effect on the organization beyond improving a particular system or service. Deming proposed the following 14 points of total quality management, which have been adopted by corporations such as the Ford Motor Company:[52(p23–24)]

- "Create constancy of purpose" regarding quality improvement. In other words, quality improvement should be an ongoing (continuous) process.
- Management must actually adopt a continuous improvement philosophy.
- Organizations should reduce dependence on inspections and promote systems and processes that produce quality products.
- Build relationships with reliable, quality suppliers rather than those suppliers that are the least expensive.
- Constantly improve all aspects of operations.
- "Institute training on the job." Integrate employee training into organizational operations.
- "Institute leadership." Leaders are driven to achieve results; they do not settle for a supervisory role.
- "Drive out fear." As stated previously, if employees fear reporting errors, then quality suffers. Leaders and managers should establish a culture in which such communication is encouraged and valued.
- Remove barriers between departments/divisions to facilitate interdepartmental teams that will work toward improving quality.
- Remove slogans, as they are unlikely to affect quality improvement and may alienate employees.
- Focus on achieving quality rather than meeting numerical goals.
- Remove barriers to pride in workmanship, as pride will likely contribute to quality.
- Facilitate employee education, self-improvement, growth, and development.
- "The transformation is everybody's job." In other words, all employees must contribute to the process of quality improvement.[52(p23–24)]

CQI has been used in the manufacturing world more extensively than in health care. For example,

Motorola and General Electric have set reliable goals for the manufacture of their products and services that they describe as the quest for **Six Sigma Quality**.[53] The strategy of Six Sigma quality was invented by Motorola, and the goal of Six Sigma means setting tolerance limits for defective products of fewer than 3.4 defects per million units (opportunities). A defect rate is defined in whatever terms are appropriate and sensible for the process that needs to be improved.[52] For example, the defect rate could be the number of dispensing errors per million prescriptions dispensed. Although CQI principles have been used more in industry, they are becoming a substantial part of the underlying foundation of medicine and health-care delivery and include:

- Observing an occurrence/process
- Isolating variables and changing the process
- Monitoring results
- Taking action

If results are positive, continue with the process change and identify other areas that need to be improved. If results are negative, abandon the changes and implement other approaches believed to meet goals. ◆*Unlike QA and QC, CQI is characterized by a multidisciplinary team or total systems approach to quality* (refer to **Table 7–3** for some of the differences between QA and quality improvement [QI][54]). Total systems means that all persons involved in the system are involved in improving the quality of the system.[55] CQI teams should continue to monitor the results until a pattern of predictable results emerges when performing certain actions. Although variation is present in any process, minimizing variation and deciding when it is natural or when it needs to be corrected are key to quality control.

Any systems, or processes, identified as error prone or high risk are potential candidates for CQI. Because every action of a healthcare professional is performed to help the patient, all processes must be designed to improve care. ◆ *Therefore, the focus of CQI is not on correcting individual errors after they occur but rather on continually and incrementally improving the individual steps within processes that lead to variation and errors.*

Plan-Do-Study-Act Cycle

Among the most commonly used tools for CQI is a four-step quality cycle, or model—the

TABLE 7–3	**Differences Between Quality Assurance and Quality Improvement**

Quality Assurance	Quality Improvement
• Conform to standards	• Improved performance
• Relies on inspection of final product, service, etc.	• Ongoing/occurs repeatedly over time
• Focuses on a single process, item, individual, etc.	• Focuses on systems and their interactions
• Departmental function	• Interdisciplinary function
• Typically retrospective in nature	• Typically prospective in nature
• Usually completed to avoid a problem	• Can be completed without identifying problems

Source: Data from Chassin MR. Is health care ready for Six Sigma quality? *Milbank Quart* 1998;76(4). Available at: http://www.milbank.org/quarterly /746featchas.html.

plan-do-study-act (PDSA) **cycle** (also known as the Deming cycle; **Figure 7–9**):

- *Plan*: Identify an opportunity for improvement and plan a change.
- *Do*: Implement the change on a small scale (pilot).
- *Study*: Collect data on the change and compare to the baseline; study the effect of these changes on the pilot; and (if applicable) show the effects of multiple changes on a process over time.
- *Act*: If the change was successful, implement it on a wider scale and continuously assess

your results; if the change did not work or meet the level of satisfaction, begin the cycle again.

Plan. The first step in planning for quality improvement is to assemble an interdisciplinary team or CQI team. The team should comprise representatives of those areas or divisions that will be involved in or affected by the QI plan to be developed and implemented. It must include staff and management personnel, as well as any subject-matter experts in the area to be studied. To facilitate the success of the QI plan, all members of the CQI team must be engaged in the process. The

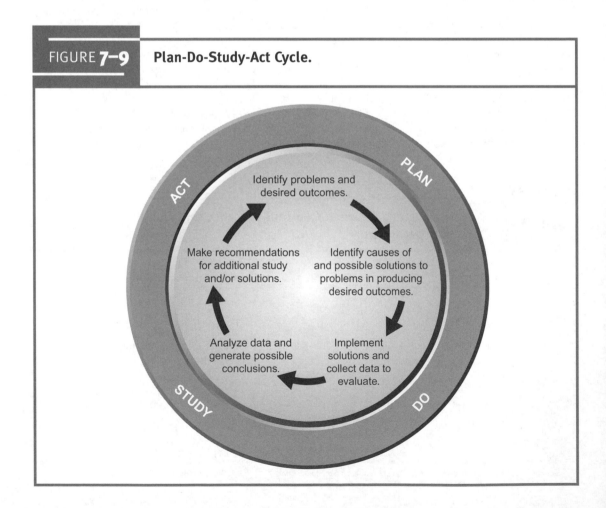

FIGURE **7–9**   **Plan-Do-Study-Act Cycle.**

PLAN

ACT

STUDY

DO

Identify problems and desired outcomes.

Make recommendations for additional study and/or solutions.

Identify causes of and possible solutions to problems in producing desired outcomes.

Analyze data and generate possible conclusions.

Implement solutions and collect data to evaluate.

team's planning goal is to identify both the desired outcome of a process and potential problems hindering achievement of that outcome.[56]

Because the focus of a CQI team can be any existing process, the team may use one or more of the following processes to identify and prioritize target areas of improvement: **brainstorming**, root cause analysis, or **failure mode and effects analysis** (FMEA). Brainstorming allows individual team members to submit ideas, then the group discusses and ranks the ideas, and the consensus

of the team determines the priority. Root cause analysis is a systematic evaluation and problem-solving method with the goal of identifying the root causes (or initiating causes) of problems. As stated previously, it is believed that by directing corrective action against the "root causes," the probability of the problem recurring will be reduced. **Figure 7–10** is a **fishbone diagram** demonstrating the root causes identified in reducing renal transplant recipients' adherence to immunosuppressant medications.[57] Last, FMEA is

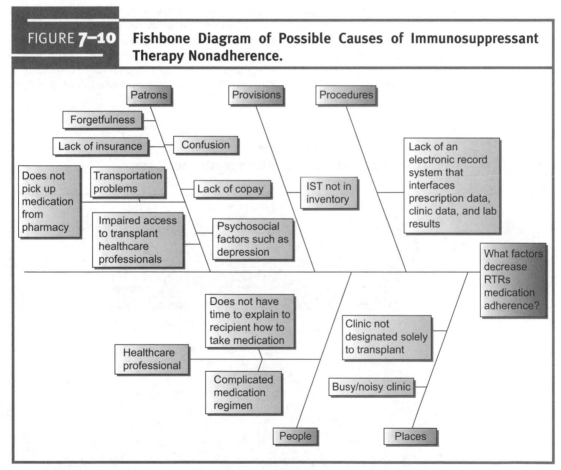

FIGURE 7–10 **Fishbone Diagram of Possible Causes of Immunosuppressant Therapy Nonadherence.**

This fishbone diagram displays possible causes of immunosuppressant therapy (IST) nonadherence among renal transplant recipients (RTRs). Examples of possible causes identified include patients (patrons) forgetting to take IST and not having money to pay their copayment for the drugs.

Source: Courtesy of Chisholm-Burns MA, Spivey CA, Garret C, McGinty H, Mulloy LL.[57]

a prospective means to identify areas for improvement in a process before they occur and involves an analysis of potential failure modes within a system for classification by severity of the effect of failures on the system. A **Pareto chart** is also helpful in identifying causes of problems. A Pareto chart is a bar chart in which the plotted values are arranged in descending order, accompanied by a line graph that shows the cumulative totals of each category (bar). It is developed to illustrate the 80–20 rule—80% of problems stem from 20% of various causes. **Figure 7–11** illustrates a Pareto chart of problems addressed by a clinical pharmacist's recommendations in a clinic setting.[57] Once the team has identified the desired outcome and the problems or threats, possible changes to the process, or operation, are generated to solve the problem. The next step in the PDSA cycle is to put the proposed change into effect.

Do. The second step in the quality improvement cycle is the implementation of a proposed change, or the "do" step. This is generally done on a small scale as a pilot project to test the efficacy of the change.[56] A pilot test is conducted before full-scale implementation to evaluate whether the change will actually benefit the production of the desired outcome. Full-scale implementation of an untested change may result in wasted resources if that change has a neutral or negative effect.

Study. The next step is to determine the efficacy of the change in the pilot project—thus, data are collected and analyzed by the CQI team.[56] The CQI team should identify how the desired outcomes will be measured and analyzed and identify effective methods to demonstrate results and conclusions. Organizations such as **The Joint Commission** (http://www.jointcommission.org/Standards/), **Centers for Medicare and Medicaid Services**

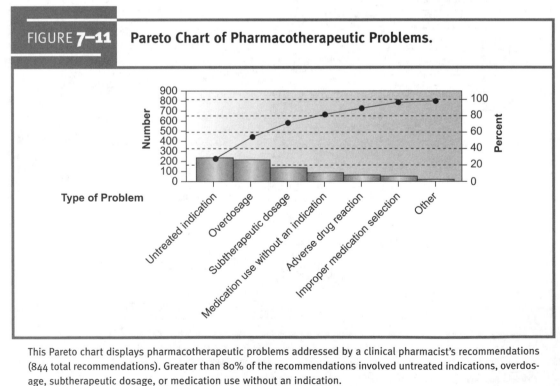

FIGURE **7–11**   **Pareto Chart of Pharmacotherapeutic Problems.**

This Pareto chart displays pharmacotherapeutic problems addressed by a clinical pharmacist's recommendations (844 total recommendations). Greater than 80% of the recommendations involved untreated indications, overdosage, subtherapeutic dosage, or medication use without an indication.

Source: Courtesy of Chisholm-Burns MA, Spivey CA, Garret C, McGinty H, Mulloy LL.[57]

(CMS; http://www.cms.hhs.gov/home/rsds.asp), and the **National Quality Measures Clearinghouse** (http://www.qualitymeasures.ahrq.gov), which includes the **Healthcare Effectiveness Data and Information Set** (HEDIS; http://www.ncqa.org/tabid/59/Default.aspx), are all potential sources to help decide outcomes and which data should be collected.

Often the data to be analyzed are descriptive, and therefore, the use of descriptive statistics may be all that is necessary for data analysis. Descriptive statistics, such as the mean and median, are commonly used in CQI and are easily displayed by using simple charts and graphs. Common charts used in CQI are flowcharts and process charts (such as the chart in Figure 7–1). **Run charts** and **control charts** are also used in CQI. A run chart is a line graph that displays observed performance data in a time sequence (data over time). A control chart is a type of run chart that is used to determine whether a process is in a state of statistical control. If the chart indicates that the process is currently under control, then it can be used with confidence to predict the future performance of the process; however, if the chart indicates that the process being monitored is not in control, the pattern demonstrated can help determine the variation source to be eliminated or a process change that needs to be implemented to bring the process back into control. Although both can be used to monitor performance over time, a control chart also uses upper and lower control limits that provide additional information in terms of compliance with external or internal performance standards. Run and control charts can be made by software such as Excel and Minitab. **Figure 7–12** displays a control chart demonstrating approximately two years of dispensing error rate data of a large retail pharmacy. Other charts and graphs commonly used in CQI include **histograms** (**Figure 7–13**), pie and bar charts, and **scatterplots** (**Figure 7–14**).

Act. This is the final step of the quality improvement model. During this step, full-scale process

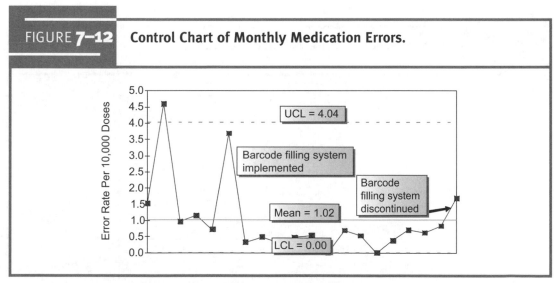

FIGURE **7–12**   Control Chart of Monthly Medication Errors.

This control chart displays monthly medication errors. Before implementing and after discontinuing the barcode filling system, a medication error rate of approximately 0.80 to 4.5 occurred per 10,000 doses dispensed. After implementing the barcode filling system, most of the error rates per 10,000 doses fell below 1. UCL = upper control limit; LCL = lower control limit.

FIGURE **7–13** **Histogram of Costs of Medication.**

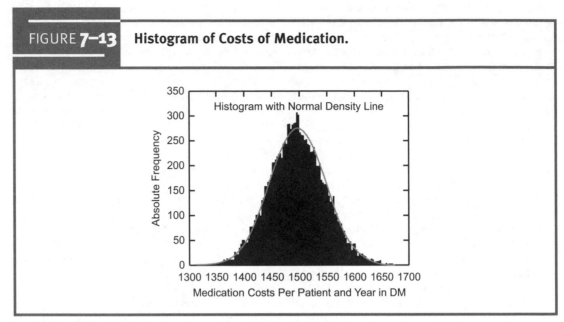

This histogram displays absolute frequencies of the bootstrapped values of costs for medication per patient per year and corresponding normal density line. DM = diabetes mellitus.

Source: Courtesy of Wagenpfeil S, Neiss A, Goertz A, Reitberger U, Stammer H, Spannheimer A, Liebl A. Bootstrap confidence intervals for costs-of-illness of type 2 diabetes mellitus in Germany. *Value in Health* 2002;5:401.

FIGURE **7–14** **Scatterplot of Drug Potency over Time.**

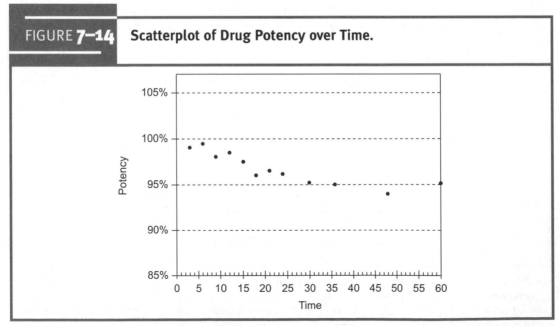

This scatterplot consists of a series of data that measures the potency of a drug (y-axis) at a certain time in minutes (x-axis).

changes are implemented based on the analysis and evaluation of data collected in the study portion of the cycle. The process changes should center on recommendations regarding findings, which are generated by the CQI team. The CQI team should then put their evaluative data, conclusions, implications, and recommendations into a formal report. Typically, CQI projects are reported both up and down the organizational structure, so the key is to ensure that all **stakeholders** can easily understand the report. The report should be concise and should include recommendations for the current CQI cycle as well as future CQI cycles. On the basis of the report, decisions are made about whether the change is beneficial to the production of the desired results and should be adopted into ongoing operations. If the change is not beneficial, a decision may be made to discontinue employment of the change in operations and to continue the PDSA cycle exploring an alternative change to achieve a desired result.[56] The primary benefit of a manager employing a CQI philosophy is the ability to continually and incrementally improve processes that have been identified as problematic or error prone.

ACCREDITATION AND COMPLIANCE STANDARDS

Compliance with national standards and quality improvement measures also plays a key role in organizations that seek to become accredited or to maintain accreditation. The Joint Commission, formerly known as the Joint Commission on Accreditation of Healthcare Organizations, or JCAHO, is the most widely known accreditation organization for healthcare facilities in the United States. The Joint Commission accredits organizations of varying sizes and scope. It offers accreditation programs for ambulatory care, behavioral health care, critical access hospitals, home health care, hospitals, laboratory services, long-term care, and office-based surgery organizations. The Joint Commission is recognized by CMS to accredit healthcare organizations, thus determining which are eligible for federal reimbursement for health care provided to Medicare- and Medicaid-eligible

recipients. In addition to personnel, quality initiatives, and finance, a major responsibility of a pharmacist manager is ensuring that his or her department complies with accreditation standards.

Pharmacists' Role in Improving Healthcare Quality

In addition to advocating for the patient's optimal therapy and health care and competently fulfilling medication delivery, including adhering to all standards of care, pharmacists and pharmacist managers should relentlessly get involved in QI activities within their own organizations. Whether you work in a community, home health, long-term care, hospital, nuclear, or other type of pharmacy, each setting probably has a defined quality improvement team that can benefit from your expertise. Moreover, pharmacists should assume leadership roles on important QI activities related to medication use and safety. Medication error reduction, monitoring high-risk medications, and medication reconciliation are just a few areas in which pharmacists must take the lead to ensure that these quality issues are viewed as top priorities within their organizations. Clearly, pharmacists hold a critical role in providing the infrastructure for the promotion of QI. ❿ *Pharmacists are highly encouraged to get involved in QI efforts, share their experiences with others, and network with internal and external colleagues to identify and implement solutions that have proved to be successful. By doing so, they contribute to the improvement of quality and safety for all patients regardless of differences in geographic and practice settings.*

SUMMARY

Pharmacy services are a vital part of the healthcare system, and pharmacists are legally and ethically responsible for various tasks beyond proper dispensing of medications. Our ultimate responsibility as pharmacists and pharmacist leaders and managers is to deliver optimal quality of health care for all individuals. This chapter briefly reviewed basic concepts of pharmacy operations and pharmacy operations management as they relate to work environment and workflow, pharmacy practice activities, medication safety, technology, quality assurance, quality control, and quality improvement. By applying some of the lessons learned in this chapter, pharmacists and pharmacist managers will perform pharmacy-related tasks while working toward decreasing gaps in medication safety and quality health care.

References

1. Committee on the Quality of Health Care in America, Institute of Medicine. *Crossing the Quality Chasm: A New Health System for the 21st Century.* Washington, DC: National Academy Press; 2001.

2. Moos RH, Billings AG. Understanding and improving work climates. In: Jones JW, Steffy BD, Bray DW, eds. *Applying Psychology in Business: The Handbook for Managers and Human Resource Professionals.* Lexington, MA: Lexington Books; 1991:552–554.

3. Carr JZ, Schmidt AM, Ford KJ, DeShon RP. Climate perceptions matter: a meta-analytic path analysis relating molar climate, cognitive and affective states, and individual level work outcomes. *J Appl Psychol* 2003;88(4):605–619.

4. Hepler DD, Strand LM. Opportunities and responsibilities in pharmaceutical care. *Am J Hosp Pharm* 1990;47:533–543.

5. Manasse HR Jr, Speedie MK. Pharmacists, pharmaceuticals, and policy issues shaping the workforce of pharmacy. *Am J Health-Syst Pharm* 2007;62:e30–e48.

6. National Association of Boards of Pharmacy. Model State Pharmacy Act and Model Rules of the National Association of Boards of Pharmacy. Available at: www.nabp.net/index.asp?target=/law&. Accessed November 8, 2008.

7. Abood R. *Pharmacy Practice and the Law.* Sudbury, MA: Jones and Bartlett Publishers; 2005.

8. The National Coordinating Council for Medication Error Reporting and Prevention. NCC MERP: The First Ten Years "Defining the Problem and Developing Solutions." Available at: http://www.nccmerp.org/pdf/reportFinal2005-11-29.pdf. Accessed November 12, 2008.

9. Cohen M. *Medication Errors: Causes, Prevention, and Risk Management.* Sudbury, MA: Jones and Bartlett Publishers; 1999.

10. Institute for Safe Medication Practices. ISMP's list of error-prone abbreviations, symbols, and dose designations. Available at: http://www.ismp.org/Tools/errorproneabbreviations.pdf. Accessed November 8, 2008.

11. American Society of Hospital Pharmacists. ASHP guidelines on preventing medication errors in hospitals. *Am H Hosp Pharm* 1993;50:305–314.

12. Center for the Advancement of Health. Computerized doctors orders reduce medication errors. Available at: www.sciencedaily.com/releases/2007/06/070627084702.htm. Accessed November 8, 2008.

13. Institute for Safe Medication Practices. List of confused drug names. Available at: http://www.ismp.org/tools/confuseddrugnames.pdf. Accessed November 8, 2008.

14. National Coordinating Council for Medication Error Reporting and Prevention. Index for categorizing medication errors. Copyright 2001. Available at: http://www.nccmerp.org/medErrorCatIndex.html. Accessed November 8, 2008.

15. Brown JN, Barnes CL, Beasley B, Cisneros R, Pound M, Herring C. Effect of pharmacists on medication errors in an emergency department. *Am J Health-Syst Pharm* 2008;65:330–333.

16. Weiner BK, Venarske J, Yu M, Mathis K. Towards the reduction of medication errors in orthopedics and spinal surgery: outcomes using a pharmacist-led approach. *Spine* 2008;33:104–107.

17. Leape LL, Bates DW, Cullen DJ, et al. Systems analysis of adverse drug events. *J Am Med Assoc* 1995;274(1):35–43.

18. Sakowski J, Leonard T, Colburn S, Michaelsen, Schiro T, Schneider J, Newman J. Using a bar-coded medication administration system to prevent medication errors in a community hospital network. *Am J Health-Syst Pharm* 2005;62:2619–2625.

19. Pharmaceutical compounding-sterile preparations (general information chapter 797). In: *The United States Pharmacopeia.* 31st rev. *The National Formulary.* 26th ed. Rockville, MD: United States Pharmacopeial Convention; 2008:319–334.

20. Shekelle PG, Morton SC, Keeler EB. Costs and benefits of health information technology. *Evid Rep Technol Assess (Full Rep)* 2006;132:1–71.

21. Woodward BW. The journey to professional excellence: a matter of priorities. *Am J Health-Syst Pharm* 1998;55:782–789.

22. Darmont J, Boussaid O. *Processing and Managing Complex Data for Decision Support.* Hershey, PA: Idea Group Inc; 2006:viii.

23. Healthcare Information and Management Systems Society. Pharmacy informatics. Available at: http://www.himss.org/ASP/topics_pharmacyInformatics.asp. Accessed January 15, 2009.

24. The basics: what is electronic prescribing? Available at: eHealth Initiative Web site. http://www.ehealthinitiative.org/eRx/basics.mspx. Accessed December 2008.

25. *Pilot Testing of Initial Electronic Prescribing Standards—Cooperative Agreements Required Under Section 1860D-4(e) of the Social Security Act as Amended by the Medicare Prescription Drug, Improvement, and Modernization Action (MMA) of 2003.* 2007. Available at: AHRQ Health Information Technology Web site. http://healthit.ahrq.gov/erxpilots. Accessed January 2009.

26. Bell DS, Friedman MA. E-prescribing and the Medicare Modernization Act of 2003. *Health Aff* 2005; 24(5):1159–1169.

27. Grossman JM, Gerland A, Reed MC, Fahlman C. Physician's experiences using commercial e-prescribing systems. *Health Aff* 2007;26:w393–w404. http://content.healthaffairs.org/cgi/content/abstract/hlthaff.26.3.w393. Accessed January 2009.

28. ASHP Report: Focus group on telepharmacy. *Am J Health-Syst Pharm* 2001;58:167–169.

29. Stubbings T, Miller C, Humphries TL, Nelson KM, Helling DK. Telepharmacy in a health maintenance organization. *Am J Health-Syst Pharm* 2005;62: 406–410.

30. Rose JL. Improved and expanded pharmacy care in rural Alaska through telepharmacy and alternative methods demonstration project. *Int J Circumpolar Health* 2007;66(suppl 1):14–22.

31. Barker KN, Felkey BG, Flynn EA, Carper JL. White paper on automation in pharmacy. *Consult Pharm* 1998;13:256–293.

32. Rough S, Temple J. Automation in practice. In: Brown TR, ed. *Handbook of Institutional Pharmacy Practice.* 4th ed. Bethesda, MD: American Society of Health-System Pharmacists; 2006:329.

33. Kheniene F, Bedouch P, Durand M, Marie F, Brudieu E, Tourlonnias MM, et al. Economic impact of an automated dispensing system in an intensive care unit. *Ann Fr Anesth Reanim* 2008;27:208–215.

34. Lee LW, Wellman GS, Birdwell SW, Sherrin TP. Use of an automated medication storage and distribution system. *Am J Hosp Pharm* 1992;49:851–855.

35. Lin AC, Huang YC, Punches G, Chen Y. Effect of a robotic prescription-filling system on pharmacy staff activities and prescription-filling time. *Am J Health-Syst Pharm* 2007;64:1832–1839.

36. Schwarz HO, Brodowy BA. Implementation and evaluation of an automated dispensing system. *Am J Health-Syst Pharm* 1995;52:823–828.

37. Oswald S, Caldwell R. Dispensing error rate after implementation of an automated pharmacy carousel system. *Am J Health-Syst Pharm* 2007;64:1427–1431.

38. Carmenated J, Keith MR. Impact of automation on pharmacist interventions and medication errors in a correctional health care system. *Am J Health-Syst Pharm* 2001;58:779–783.

39. Franklin BD, O'Grady K, Voncina L, Popoola J, Jacklin A. An evaluation of two automated dispensing machines in UK hospital pharmacy. *Int J Pharm Pract* 208;16:47–53.

40. Slee A, Farrar K, Hughes D. Implementing an automated dispensing system. *Pharm J* 2002;268: 437–438.

41. Fitzpatrick R, Cooke P, Southall C, Kauldhar K, Walters P. Evaluation of an automated dispensing system in a hospital pharmacy dispensary. *Pharm J* 2005;274: 763–765.

42. Lorenzi NM, Riley RT. Managing change: an overview. *J Am Med Inform Assoc* 2000;7(2):116–124.

43. Culp LM, Adams JA, Byron JS, Boyer EA. Phased Implementation. In: Walker JM, Bieber EJ, Richards F, eds. *Implementing an Electronic Health Record System (Health Informatics).* Secaucus, NJ: Springer-Verlag New York Inc; 2005:111.

44. Agency for Healthcare Research and Quality. Planning for technology implementation: infrastructure assessment. Health IT adoption toolbox Web site. Available at: http://healthit.ahrq.gov/portal/server.pt?open=512&objID=1088&&PageID=14307&mode=2&in_hi_userid=3882&cached=true#Answer. Accessed December 2008.

45. Zafar A. Getting started with health IT implementation. [slide presentation]. AHRQ National Resource Center for Health Information Technology. Available at: http://healthit.ahrq.gov/portal/server.pt/gateway/PTARGS_0_3882_825579_0_0_18/Health%20IT%20Implementation.pdf. December 2005. Accessed December 2008.

46. Adler KG. How to select an electronic health record system. *Fam Pract Manag* 2005;12(2):55–62.

47. Fellbaum C. *Wordnet: An Electronic Lexical Database.* Cambridge, MA: MIT Press; 2006.

48. Donabedian A. *Explorations in Quality Assessment and Monitoring.* Vol. 1. *The Definition of Quality and Approaches to Its Assessment.* Ann Arbor, MI: Health Administration Press; 1980.

49. Congress of the United States, Office of Technology Assessment. *The Quality of Medical Care: Information for Consumers.* Washington, DC: US Government Printing Office; 1988.

50. American Society of Health-System Pharmacists. ASHP guidelines on quality assurance for pharmacy-prepared sterile products. *Am J Health-Syst Pharm* 2000; 57:1150–1169.

51. Gitlow HS, Melby MJ. Framework for continuous quality improvement in the provision of pharmaceutical care. *Am J Health-Syst Pharm* 1991;48:1917–1925.

52. Deming EW. *Out of the Crisis.* Cambridge, MA: MIT Press; 1986.

53. Chassin MR. Is health care ready for Six Sigma quality? *Milbank Quart* 1998;76(4). Available at: http://www.milbank.org/quarterly/764featchas.html. Accessed January 7, 2009.

54. Rossi, PA. *Case Management in Health Care: A Practical Guide.* 2nd ed. Philadelphia, PA: WB Saunders; 2003.

55. ASHP report: guidelines on preventing medication errors in hospitals. *Am J Health-Syst Pharm* 1993;50: 305–314.

56. Dartmouth Medical School, Office of Community-Based Education and Research. The clinician's black bag of quality improvement tools. The PDCA cycle. Available at: http://www.dartmouth.edu/~ogehome/CQI/PDCA.html. Accessed January 8, 2009.

57. Chisholm-Burns MA, Spivey CA, Garret C, McGinty H, Mulloy LL. Impact of clinical pharmacy services on renal transplant recipients' adherence and outcomes. *Patient Preference Adherence* 2008;2:287–292.

Abbreviations

CDS:	computerized dispensing system
CMS:	Centers for Medicare and Medicaid Services
CPR:	cardiopulmonary resuscitation
CQI:	continuous quality improvement
DM:	diabetes mellitus
FMEA:	failure mode and effects analysis
HEDIS:	healthcare effectiveness data and information set
HIPAA:	Health Insurance Portability and Accountability Act
IOM:	Institute of Medicine
ISMP:	Institute for Safe Medication Practices
IST:	immunosuppressant therapy
IV:	intravenous
JCAHO:	Joint Commission on Accreditation of Healthcare Organizations
LCL:	lower control limit
NABP:	National Association of Boards of Pharmacy
OBRA:	Omnibus Budget Reconciliation Act of 1990
PDA:	personal digital assistant
PDSA:	plan-do-study-act
QA:	quality assurance
QC:	quality control
QI:	quality improvement
RTR:	renal transplant recipient
UCL:	upper control limit
USP:	United States Pharmacopeia

Case Scenarios

CASE ONE: Jack Reid is a pharmacist practicing in a retail chain pharmacy and has recently been promoted to pharmacist manager. After accepting this promotion, the district manager informs him that she has received multiple complaints from patients over the past several months regarding prescription turnaround time at Dr. Reid's location. Dr. Reid's first charge as manager is to evaluate this problem and identify potential strategies for improving turnaround time. What methods should he employ to analyze the current workflow in the pharmacy?

CASE TWO: Kate Tyler is new pharmacist manager overseeing pharmacy operations at a large, academic medical center. Members of the hospital administration have decided that they want to invest in an electronic medical record computer system. This new system will have programs such as electronic documentation of care by providers, a physician order entry system, a pharmacy information system for medication distribution and order verification, and an electronic medication administration record. Dr. Tyler has been asked to take the lead for the department of pharmacy and to represent it during the selection phase. What considerations should she be sure to address in the selection process from the pharmacy's perspective?

CASE THREE: You have been hired by a national chain of retail drug stores to develop a training course for new pharmacists focused on preventing medication dispensing errors. You have been given access to the company's medication error reporting database and have determined that the most common dispensing errors are incorrect medication, incorrect dosage strength, and dose miscalculations. On the basis of this information, on which aspects of the medication dispensing process will you focus your training and what strategies will you use to minimize the potential for future medication errors?

CASE FOUR: Nina Gomez is the clinical pharmacist in an outpatient comprehensive cancer center. The cancer center comprises multiple physician clinics, an 18-chair infusion area, pharmacy, lab, and other ancillary services. Because of multiple physician and patient complaints regarding long waiting times for chemotherapy, she has been asked by the cancer center manager to lead a continuous quality improvement (CQI) team to examine and improve the throughput of the clinic by decreasing pharmacy turnaround times. On the basis of CQI principles, whom should Dr. Gomez ask to be on her CQI team?

CASE FIVE: You have been contacted by a small community hospital as a medication safety consultant to provide strategies for reducing the incidence of medication errors. The pharmacy order entry system is currently the only electronic system in place. Orders are handwritten by physicians and scanned to the pharmacy. Nurses are responsible for reviewing the chart and transcribing orders to their medication administration record. The hospital has experienced several medication errors related to wrong medication, wrong dosing interval, wrong strength, and wrong patient. As a medication safety consultant, what strategies might you employ to reduce the number of medication errors in this institution?

Additional Resources Available Online!

Visit the Student Companion Web site at http://healthprofessions.jbpub.com/pharmacymanagement for interactive study tools and additional resources.

See www.rxugace.com to learn how you can obtain continuing pharmacy education for this content.

CHAPTER 8

PURCHASING AND MANAGING INVENTORY

ALICIA S. BOULDIN, PhD, RPh

ERIN RENEE HOLMES, PharmD, PhD

DEWEY D. GARNER, PhD, RPh

ANN HEIN DEVOE, RPh

LEARNING OBJECTIVES

After completing the chapter, the reader will be able to

1. Describe the interrelated nature of purchasing and inventory management activities.
2. Discuss the basic objectives concerning good purchasing practice.
3. Calculate stock depth for an item in inventory.
4. Explain the discounts generally available from vendors.
5. Describe factors related to vendor selection.
6. Compare various inventory management methods.
7. Calculate inventory turnover rate.
8. Identify costs associated with poor inventory management.
9. Describe available technologies to assist with inventory management.

KEY CONCEPTS

❶ Because inventory typically represents a pharmacy's largest investment, purchasing is actually an asset management process that merits focused attention and forethought.

❷ Approximately 75% of the overall expenses that a pharmacy outlays to do business may be accounted for by the cost of goods sold (COGS).

❸ Purchasing objectives include obtaining the right products, in the right quantity, at the right time, at the right price, and from the right vendor.

❹ Reduction of the risk of out-of-stock situations is desirable but must be balanced with having an acceptable amount of funds tied up in inventory; this balance between "too much" and "too little" must be determined on an individual basis for each item.

❺ Having product on hand is important, but having safety stock increases the carrying costs associated with inventory.

6 The actual COGS is an important element of the "right price" objective, but other costs, such as procurement costs and inventory carrying costs, must also be considered.

7 An understanding of supply and demand is needed, as the main objective of inventory management is to have available the minimum quantity of goods to meet demands.

8 A variety of mechanisms are used by pharmacy managers to control the level of inventory. These may be grouped into three general method categories: (1) visual methods, (2) periodic methods, and (3) perpetual methods.

9 Inventory management may be evaluated in a variety of ways but most commonly through examining the inventory turnover rate or the rate at which supply of an item is exhausted and replaced.

10 Pareto's law suggests that 80% of the value of inventory is composed of 20% of the actual items in inventory. Managing those 20% "high value" items effectively represents an efficient use of resources (time, personnel, etc.) and may have a more significant effect than attention to those 80% of items with lower monetary or service value.

INTRODUCTION

Have you had experience with purchasing or inventory management? Chances are you have, whether or not that experience was in the workplace. Consider your personal checkbook: the routine tasks of writing checks, balancing the checkbook, and evaluating the amount of money available in your account are "purchasing activities." As for inventory management, consider your sock drawer: evaluating your weekly wardrobe to examine your need for dark socks and then ensuring the appropriate number of pairs are clean and ready to wear are steps required to manage your sock inventory. If you have engaged in these or similar activities, then you have had some experience with purchasing and inventory management.

The two functions, purchasing and inventory, are included in a single chapter of this text because they are so closely interrelated. One cannot make optimal purchasing choices for an organization without having some understanding of inventory needs and availability. Purchasing and inventory management activities are not always accomplished by the same person within the organization, as these functions may be performed by numerous individuals, including staff pharmacists, pharmacist managers, and pharmacy technicians. However, as will be illustrated, these activities do need to be coordinated. This chapter will provide foundational information regarding purchasing, purchasing decisions, managing inventory investment, and evaluating management efficiency pertaining to inventory, including unclaimed prescriptions and inventory management technology. Each function can potentially contribute positively or negatively to the pharmacy's bottom line, as well as other outcomes, including patient satisfaction and patient health, so attention to detail in these matters is essential (refer to Chapter 12, "Achieving and Measuring Patient Satisfaction").

PURCHASING: THE ART OF RIGHT SPENDING

Purchasing is not simply a "support" activity, as it can have profound strategic implications for the organization.[1] **1** *Because inventory typically represents a pharmacy's largest investment, purchasing is actually an asset management process that merits focused attention and forethought.* The word "art" is used in the header for this section, and given the nuances that may be involved in the development of an optimal purchasing plan for an entity, "art" may be an accurate descriptor. Of course, decisions are informed by simple quantitative tools available to the manager; several such tools will be discussed later in this chapter. At the very least, however, organizational values and personal preferences play a part, as they would in any investment strategy. Spending money is relatively easy, but making wise or "right" spending choices to enable an optimal level of service and income is challenging. Although this chapter will cover some of the basic principles behind "right" spending and purchasing activities, it cannot cover everything you might wish to know to develop your own purchasing strategy. Just as with most things in the real world, situations differ and individual strategies vary.

Purchasing and the Bottom Line

Careful attention to the purchasing function may have a significant positive effect on the bottom line, or profit, that a pharmacy is able to reap for the products and services it provides. Likewise, lack of attention to this important task can negatively influence **profit margin**. In an industry where the profit margin (represented as net income) hovers around 3%, and where external influences introduce extra variability into the profit equation, it makes sense to attend well to any activity that can be monitored or influenced by internal practices.

Before goods can be sold from the pharmacy, they must be purchased from a supplier and carried as stock. ❷*Approximately 75% of the overall expenses that a pharmacy outlays to do business may be accounted for by the **cost of goods sold** (COGS).*[2] This percentage of expenses is higher than salaries, rent, and other assumed "high dollar" items. Given a constant sales level, profits can potentially increase or decrease by 15% for every 1% change in COGS.[3] Therefore, close management of this resource may significantly affect the income of the business (refer to Chapter 10, "Cents and Sensibility: Understanding the Numbers").

Purchasing Decisions

The purchasing agent (the individual who is responsible for purchasing inventory) must consider a host of factors when making strategic decisions. What does your **target market** need or want? What are your competitors carrying? From which source are you likely to get the best service? How often do you plan to restock? The answers to questions like these are likely to be slightly different for each business. And while there may be some common answers to these questions for most organizations, no set purchasing formula works for everyone.

❸ *Consider the following purchasing objectives:*[1,4,5]

- *Obtain the right products*
- *Obtain products in the right quantity*
- *Obtain products at the right time*
- *Obtain products at the right price*
- *Obtain products from the right vendor*

Each of these objectives will be discussed in detail in the following sections.

THE RIGHT PRODUCT MIX

In determining the best mix of products, you must consider the following:

- *What breadth and depth of products do your patrons expect to find when they visit your business or institution?*
- *What items meet their expectations with respect to quality and price?*
- *What image do you wish for your business to portray?*
- *What kind of capital do you have to invest in inventory?*

Decisions related to product choice, including both variety and quality, should be driven largely by your clientele, or target market. This includes both prescription and over-the-counter (OTC) considerations. In the community setting, having the right mix of available merchandise is critical for attracting and keeping one's patient base and for competing with other pharmacies. Some marketing research will likely be required to discover the ideal mix of merchandise. Although the thought of taking on "marketing research" may sound ominous, several resources are available (refer to Chapter 15, "Understanding and Applying Marketing Strategies").

Start with your own observations. What have you noticed selling well? What have your patients requested? What do they appear to desire? Technicians and clerks can expand these observations significantly as they may see even more consumption behavior beyond the prescription counter than the pharmacist or pharmacist manager. Scanning popular media and the press may also indicate what patrons may be requesting; managers often see increased sales (and phone calls) on products that are covered by the media. Regarding prescriptions, recall that approximately 50% of these are refills; thus, patient profiles can provide valuable information regarding which prescription medications should be kept in inventory. Also, knowledge of the prescribing habits of physicians in the community can aid in stocking the prescription area wisely.[3-5] For example, if a dermatologist in your immediate area favors a specific steroid cream over the many available, keeping that particular product on hand will facilitate rapid filling of prescriptions from patients who stop at the pharmacy after their clinic (office) visits. Medication therapy management protocols in which your pharmacy participates may also reveal information on prescribing preferences. Establish and keep open lines of communication with the top prescribers in your area. Also, examine product movement reports (these may be generated by software provided by your wholesaler), detail statements from insurance claims, and drug utilization reviews to assess the pulse of stock supply and demand.

Although the demand and expectations of your market are important, so are your own expectations or those of your organization.[3-5] You may desire an **apothecary** ambience or the convenience of a superstore with a wide array of nonprescription and even nonmedication items. You may have interest in stocking **durable medical equipment** (DME), such as wheelchairs, walkers, or crutches but find that you have neither the money nor space to do so. Your hospital may specialize in treating certain disease states, such as end-stage renal disease. Thus, your preferred practice, organization's mission, space restrictions, and budget will further influence stocking decisions.

Beyond preferred stock choices, a variety of factors remain to influence the final decision—to stock or not to stock. For example, managing DME items involves a different set of **procurement costs**, and assessing other factors, such as storage, maintenance, and delivery—hidden costs that can whittle away at profits ("hidden" because they are not directly attached to the price tag of the item itself but are relevant costs nonetheless). Another consideration is that **third-party payments** for DME are typically much slower than for prescription medications and often involve extra personnel hours to ensure proper completion of forms and payment. If patron demand exists, DME can be profitable as long as one accepts the large overhead cost on the front end and has the additional capital to sustain it until a profit comes to fruition (often six months or more). Any of these factors may make a difference when deciding whether a product or product category is right for your business.

The Right Product Quantity

Deciding what to carry must be complemented by deciding how much of each item is the optimal amount to balance supply with demand. Obviously, one would seek to avoid out-of-stock incidents, which result in more than just lost potential revenue. If a product is out of stock when a patient seeks it and an appropriate substitute is not available, then he or she may be forced to seek the product from another pharmacy, possibly resulting in depletion of patient goodwill or the reduction of positive attitude regarding your pharmacy. There could also be health consequences for out-of-stock situations, for example, if a patient needs a specific antibiotic to eradicate an acute infection and treatment is delayed because the antibiotic is not available. In the hospital setting, having medication available may be a matter of life and death, and often time is of the essence; for example, the necessity of having thrombolytics available to dissolve blood clots for acute myocardial infarction patients. ◆ *Reduction of the risk of out-of-stock situations is desirable but must be balanced with having an acceptable amount of funds tied up in inventory; this balance between "too much" and "too little" must be determined on an individual basis for each item.*

The **stock depth** for an item is the quantity at which you may be reasonably certain that the item will be available when needed.[6] How "deep" does your stock of a particular item need to be to accommodate average use? This is sometimes also referred to as the "reorder point." Determining the appropriate depth for each item requires consideration of the timing of review and delivery, as well as the average daily demand:

Stock Depth = (Review Time + Lead Time)
        × Average Demand + Safety Stock

In this formula, *review time* is the time between shelf review or reports on product sales (typically, one day for prescription products in the pharmacy, which are monitored continuously); *lead time* is the time required to obtain product from your vendors once ordered (also typically one day, as most wholesalers distribute the next morning on orders placed the evening before); and *average demand* is the amount of product sold each day. This demand may have seasonal variation for some products, which will alter the stock depth formula at those times. A buffer of **safety stock** may also be included to ensure supply even when demand varies.[1,7] The amount of safety stock you choose for a particular item depends on a variety of factors, including the cost of the item (is a unit so expensive that to have many extra would tie up too much capital?), anticipated fluctuations (was this product recently profiled on a morning news show and thus demand may likely increase sometime soon?), the return policy for the item (if you find you have too much on hand, will it be easy to return?), and the manager's risk tolerance (how willing are you to risk an out-of-stock situation? theft of the product?) among others. Refer to inventory topics in Chapter 10 ("Cents and Sensibility: Understanding the Numbers").

The Right Time to Order

Now that you have determined what to carry and how much, the timing of purchasing and reordering must be orchestrated. Variables in this coordination include all of the factors in the stock depth formula, indicating a close relationship between timing and appropriate quantity or consumer demand. Another significant variable is inventory investment.

🔶 *Having product on hand is important, but having safety stock increases the carrying costs associated with inventory.* **Inventory carrying cost** includes such components as[1,3,4]

- Capital costs (required to finance the inventory, could be invested elsewhere)
- Storage costs (to house the inventory, move the inventory, etc.)
- Cost of risk (insurance, obsolescence, or actual loss)

These carrying costs are also sometimes referred to as "holding costs," reflecting the cost of holding the product in inventory. The timing of purchases, coordinated to keep shelf stock at a minimum, influences minimizing those costs. For example, having Drug A on hand may be essential. However, the cost of goods may be extremely high ($1,000) for a single unit. So while adequate supply is important, the typical community pharmacy would need to evaluate the high carrying costs in maintaining excess shelf stock of such a product. The working capital tied up by expensive safety stock of this item (one aspect of the carrying cost) would yield less available capital for paying bills, paying employees, and buying other stock. If shelf stock of this product were insufficient (and overnight delivery might unnecessarily delay treatment), another community or institutional pharmacy might have supply to meet a patient's needs at that moment. Both formal and informal arrangements generally exist between local businesses to accommodate such product crises for the good of patients.

Ideally, the timing of a purchase should coincide closely with the sale of that item, reducing the need for safety stock. In a perfect world, stock orders will be replaced at the precise point in time when sales just deplete all inventory on hand. This is known as **just-in-time** (JIT) **purchasing**. As the last unit of an item sells, the next unit arrives before it is needed by a patient. In other words, the last bottle of *Medication X* falls off the shelf and into the hands of a consumer at the exact time the replacement bottle arrives in the store. This would mean no need for "extra," or safety stock, thus effecting a reduction in inventory levels and a reduction in the carrying costs of that item in inventory.[8]

Some wholesaling and warehousing practices are already nearing this ideal. With automation and point-of-sale technologies, JIT purchasing is more possible now than before. At any given moment during the day, the computer can provide a report of exactly how many **stock keeping units** (SKUs) of a given product are available within the store (not accounting for theft or other **shrinkage**) because of a running tally kept as barcodes that are scanned at checkout, thus providing support for using automation to help facilitate pharmacy operations (refer to Chapter 7, "Pharmacy Operations: Workflow, Practice Activities, Medication Safety, Technology, and Quality").

An internal practice that can facilitate the approximation of JIT purchases involves communication alongside available technology. This is especially important for medications that tend to be expensive and are dispensed on a monthly basis for a small number of patients. Communication with the patient (e.g., encouraging a patient to notify you a day in advance of his intended pickup of the medication) is key. This communication can also be supplemented with an electronic "note," or alarm, that can be programmed into some pharmacy management systems (computer software for dispensing prescriptions); this electronic reminder notifies the pharmacist when it is time to order the patient's medication. Thus, the expensive stock is available immediately before it is needed and does not incur carrying costs for weeks ahead of dispensing.

THE RIGHT PRICE

When one considers the cost of a product, the price at which that product is purchased from the supplying vendor immediately comes to mind. Most of us appreciate a good deal, an opportunity to make our money go farther, or the chance for improved profit. ❻ *Therefore, the cost of goods to be sold is an important element of the "right price" objective, but other costs must be considered as well, including procurement costs and carrying costs.*

The procurement cost is the cost associated with the act of purchasing. Personnel time is required for placing the order, checking the order, stocking, paying the invoice, and completing other purchasing-related paperwork.[3,8] The more efficient this purchasing function, the less the organization's procurement costs in personnel time will be. Purchasing tools, including technology, may be a value-added service provided by vendors or **wholesalers**, some of whom supply these at little or no cost to the pharmacy to make the purchasing activity faster, easier, or more accurate. (For more information regarding vendors, refer to Chapter 7, "Pharmacy Operations: Workflow, Practice Activities, Medication Safety, Technology, and Quality.")

Another way to minimize costs is by taking advantage of available discounts. Four primary types of discounts may be available from your vendor:

- *Quantity discounts*: Reduction in price gained by buying in quantity, either on a single order

or across a set time period.[1,3,4] Sometimes, the quantity "discount" is actually free goods (e.g., buy 10, get 1 free). Quantity purchases increase inventory, which increase carrying costs and the risk of unsalable merchandise.[6]

- *Cash discounts*: Reduction in price for prompt payment.[1,4] This reduction is usually 1–2% of the net amount of the total amount due on the invoice, if paid within a certain time (e.g., 10 days). Given the slim profit margins in community pharmacy, this can be a significant, perhaps even the most significant, discount.[6] However, making the payment promptly can deplete cash resources for a time. Therefore, as with any investment decision, the overall implications for your cash position need to be considered. Thus, a 1% discount within 10 days represents, in essence, a 36% annual saving, and one could argue that, even if money needed to be borrowed to take advantage of that discount, a loan would almost certainly have a lower interest rate than 36%.

- *Product bundling*: Reduction in price of one item gained by simultaneous purchase of another product, often related. For example, 12 units of amoxicillin 150 mL suspension —a fast-moving item—may be discounted when purchased along with 6 units of amoxicillin infant drops, which are less frequently dispensed. Note that the bundle may not always be a good deal. If the bundle increases carrying costs through the addition of slow-moving items, the benefit of reduced price for certain items in the bundle may not be worth it. Bundling is a less common practice today than in years past.

- *Minimum purchasing*: Reduction in price of a featured generic or brand medication along with a minimum generic order. This method is a "blended" approach, melding product bundling and quantity discounts. Some hard-to-get items are available from smaller vendors in this manner; a certain minimum order of their generic brand may be required to receive the much-needed or heavily discounted product that you seek.

The movement of goods trumps most "deals"; bear this in mind regarding quantity discounts, bundling, and minimum purchases. If by getting a "good price" you are acquiring merchandise that will not sell in a reasonable amount of time (for example, before the returns policy expires or before the capital is needed for other purchases or activities), then chances are the "deal" may not be advantageous in the long run. However, the cash discount may be "worth it" (as described earlier, even a 1% discount for 30 days can yield a significant return).

THE RIGHT VENDOR FOR YOUR NEEDS

Pharmacies make purchases from a variety of vendor types, primarily wholesalers and **buying groups**. Some products, such as biologicals and vaccines, may still be purchased directly from the manufacturer, but this source of supply is more limited than it was in years past. Most purchases are made from wholesalers. Full-service wholesalers provide a variety of tools and services to complement purchasing and accounting functions, including order-entry hardware and distributive technology, detailed reporting software, promotional and advertising assistance, shelf labels, and credit options.

Buying groups are cooperative organizations that may be used by smaller organizations, such as independent pharmacies that can improve their buying power by purchasing larger quantities as a combined entity.[6] Buying in bulk may provide significant reduction in cost. Hospitals may purchase through buying groups known as cooperative group purchasing organizations (GPOs) for similar economies of scale. Chain pharmacies may subscribe to centralized purchasing activities, which function similarly to take advantage of the larger quantities to buy at lower cost.

Before making a choice of vendors, several factors should be considered, among them:[3]

- Delivery schedule (overnight from wholesaler? Or 4–5 days for direct purchase?)
- Frequency of out-of-stock situations (do they have it on hand when you request it?)
- Breadth of merchandise lines and assortment (does the vendor carry all—or most—of the products you would like to have on your shelves?)

- Assistance with product placement and floor layout (merchandising advice and "plan-o-grams")
- Available technology and other services (inventory management software and hardware? provision of reports?)
- Returned goods policies (free to return within a certain time frame? What is the fee thereafter?)
- Financing and credit terms and options (longer terms—better for the pharmacy? or shorter terms?)

One vendor may rise to the top when considering these factors, perhaps surpassing the others by having more deliveries and lower prices available (based on volume); this may serve as your primary vendor. But while the pharmacy may have one primary vendor, it is also considered a wise practice to do some business with a second vendor as well, even if on a limited basis. Not all desired products may be available from a single vendor. Also, having an established relationship with an alternate product provider may prove advantageous, if, for some reason, the supply from your primary vendor is interrupted. Be cautious, however, in entertaining faxed and e-mailed solicitations for purchasing "deals" from unfamiliar vendors. Some of these may come from rogue sites attempting to pass on short-dated (near expiration) or substandard products; if it sounds "too good to be true," it probably is.

PUTTING IT TOGETHER

To optimize the effectiveness of attending to these purchasing objectives, the manager must have a bird's-eye view and examine all factors simultaneously. For example, right quantity, right time, right price, each may have an effect on the other, and balance is needed. The costs associated with procurement (procurement costs) are likely to decrease when an increased quantity is ordered, as may the cost of goods, but the tradeoff is that carrying costs increase. The ideal timing for purchases would occur at the point where total costs are minimized because procurement and carrying costs are equal. This point has been referred to as the **economic order quantity** (EOQ) and is illustrated in **Figure 8–1**.

FIGURE **8–1**   **RELATIONSHIP OF PROCUREMENT COSTS TO CARRYING COSTS.**

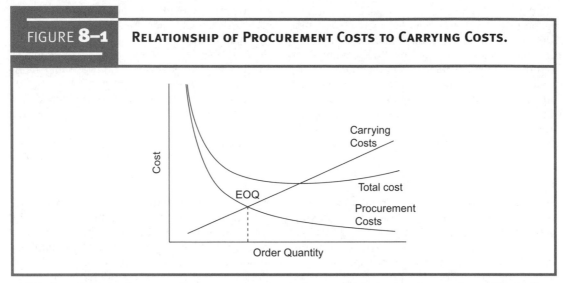

This figure illustrates the concept that as procurement costs decrease (likely due to an increase in quantity order), the carrying costs increase. The point at which total costs are minimized because procurement costs and carrying costs are equal is referred to as the economic order quantity (EOQ).

The EOQ reflects the optimum number of units per order, and may be calculated as follows:[1,9]

$$EQQ = \sqrt{2DP/CI}$$

D = Annual demand for product (in units)
P = Procurement cost per order (in dollars)
C = Unit cost to the business (in dollars)
I = Inventory carrying cost (expressed as a percentage of the investment in inventory; may be estimated to include capital costs, storage, insurance, taxes, other risk)

As an example, if your pharmacy dispenses 75 prescriptions per month of *Product Z* (twice daily dosing) for a total of $75 \times 60 = 4{,}500$ tablets needed per month, and *Product Z* comes in 1,000-count bottles, then the demand is 4.5 bottles per month or 54 bottles per year. If the COGS is $150 per unit (1,000-count bottle), with an estimated carrying cost of 25% and a procurement cost of around $10 (average employee time and expense per order), the optimum quantity of *Product Z* per order would be $\sqrt{2(54)(10)/(150)(0.25)}$, or 5.4. To accommodate all 54 bottles required for the year's time would mean 5.4 per order across 10 orders (translating practically to ordering 5 bottles monthly for 11 months).

In practice today, this EOQ number is rarely calculated by hand. There are limitations to the formula's application, including assumptions of a stable, continuous-use pattern and consistent pricing.[1] Available software (often from the wholesaler) aids in determining the optimal order times and quantities based on these cost factors, ranking, and product sales history at your pharmacy. Fact-driven purchasing tools allow for consistent decisions. Even with these mathematical aids, however, common sense is still an important element in determining your defined balance of the factors related to purchasing.

MANAGING YOUR INVENTORY INVESTMENT

To ensure the best management of your inventory investment, you should consider the following:

- *Do you consider yourself to be a good planner, thinking ahead and anticipating needs?*
- *Do you consider yourself to be a good organizer of time or other resources?*

Planning and organizing are essential to effective inventory management. As the inventory is the largest asset of the pharmacy (nearly $300,000 in independent pharmacies in 2007), effective inventory management is critical.[2,6] Successfully managing inventory can help to accomplish several major goals that facilitate success, including improved customer service, minimized costs, increased profit, and increased cash flow.[6]

❼ *An understanding of supply and demand is needed, as the main objective of inventory management is to have available the minimum quantity of goods to meet demands.*[4] Balancing supply and demand is an important and difficult responsibility, which requires watching and planning for seasonal variability (e.g., flu season, high allergens in spring) and observing product movement to note any changes in usage or clientele. This management task can be time consuming, so one must establish a balance between costs of controlling inventory and the derived benefits. Significant attention is required to maintain inventory at an optimal level. Having too little on hand may result in shortages and emergency orders (which carry additional cost). However, having excess goods increases carrying costs and may also increase other costs as well, including capital costs, or the interest that could be gained from having the capital available to invest elsewhere, and **opportunity costs** of space that could be used for another product.

Inventory Management Methods

❽ *A variety of mechanisms are used by pharmacy managers to control the level of inventory. These may be grouped into three general method categories: (1) visual methods, (2) periodic methods, and (3) perpetual methods.*

VISUAL INVENTORY CONTROL METHOD

This simple inventory control method means visually observing the number of units in an inventory and comparing it with a list of the prescribed number of units that should be carried (your calculated stock depth). When stock falls below the desired number, you order more.[3,4] This control is relatively common in the pharmacy's prescription department, where conducting visual inspections occurs continuously and replacement can be quick—in most cases, overnight. An artifact of this kind of inventory control familiar to many

prescription departments is a "wantbook," or a running tab of product tags, representing units that have recently been depleted or are low. The visual method of control is informal, convenient, and inexpensive, but because it focuses on stock depletions and units only (not cost of those units), it is a less effective mechanism for actual inventory management. Also, the potential for human error or oversight is great: it is relatively easy to miss low stock on a visual inspection or to neglect to add a depleted stock product tag to the wantbook.

PERIODIC INVENTORY CONTROL METHOD

The periodic method of inventory control relies on stock counts at intervals defined by policy and comparing the number on hand to predefined minimums (determined by stock depth).[3,4] Certain slower-moving portions of the pharmacy's inventory (e.g., first aid supplies) may be checked weekly, for example, rather than every day. If the shelf stock is found to be below the desired level, more stock is ordered. Because records are generally kept of these periodic counts and orders, this method allows for some limited analyses to occur (e.g., how fast each item is selling, how many units are generally on hand, and therefore, how much money is invested in that product). This method may require more personnel time than the visual method and measures only a single point in time (a snapshot), rather than a continuous evaluation.

PERPETUAL INVENTORY CONTROL METHOD

As the name implies, perpetual inventory control methods monitor inventory constantly through the use of technology (e.g., point-of-sale scanners at the cashier stations that read barcodes on the products sold). The precision of a perpetual system can generate a report at any moment to reveal precisely the amount of inventory that should be on hand for any product in the system. The technology enables generation of reports and analyses to improve maintaining adequate supply while minimizing extra stock (refer to Chapter 7, "Pharmacy Operations: Workflow, Practice Activities, Medication Safety, Technology, and Quality"). Perpetual inventory control provides the most accurate and comprehensive picture of both units and actual financial investment in inventory, in theory enabling a reduction in procurement costs and inventory carrying costs.

Evaluation of Management Efficiency

❾ *Inventory management may be evaluated in a variety of ways but most commonly through examining the* **inventory turnover rate** *(ITOR), or the rate at which supply of an item is exhausted and replaced.* This performance ratio may be calculated using the following formula:[6,8]

ITOR = COGS / Average Inventory

Average inventory for a year may be calculated as

(Beginning Inventory + Ending Inventory) / 2

The turnover rate of inventory for independent community pharmacies averages around 10 turns per year. That number is somewhat higher (around 12 turns per year) when the prescription department alone is considered.[2] Turnover for an individual item may vary from the overall average for the total inventory. For example, turnover for a popular OTC cold remedy may occur quickly, especially during cough and cold season, whereas the turnover rate for a box of ear-cleaning drops may be much lower, as patrons may have less need for that product (refer to Chapter 10, "Cents and Sensibility: Understanding the Numbers," for examples of ITOR calculations).

Ideally, the turnover rate will be a relatively high number for many reasons. If ITOR is high, that implies a reduced investment in inventory (not too much on the shelf), which frees cash to be used for other services or activities that may contribute to profit. Also, a higher ITOR increases the return on one's inventory investment, which may in turn increase profits.[3,6] However, it is possible for the ITOR to be too high, resulting in out-of-stock situations.

For example, because of a change in local prescribing practices, the turnover of a particular antidepressant may increase in your pharmacy, resulting in an insufficient amount of product to fill a prescription as it arrives. This may result in a partial fill (20 of the required 30 tablets are in stock), with the patient having to return the next day to pick up the balance. In effect, then, this generates two "dispensings" (employee time, pre-scription vial, label, etc.) for a single prescription and a single fee.

VARIABILITY IN INVENTORY

Technology facilitates reports that can provide detailed information on turnover rate and other inventory management indicators. By studying these reports, a manager can forecast future consumer needs. Such reports also make it possible to identify those products among the entire inventory that may need extra attention. Those with highest value to the organization (monetary or service-wise) merit the most focus, as time is limited and cannot be devoted to detailed analysis for every product in inventory.

❿ *Pareto's law suggests that 80% of the value of inventory is composed of 20% of the actual items in inventory.[8] Managing those 20% "high value" items effectively represents an efficient use of resources (time, personnel, etc.) and may have a more significant effect than attention to those 80% of items with lower monetary or service value.[7]* A manager might choose a technique as unsophisticated as the wantbook to manage that 80% of lower-value inventory that generates only 20% of sales. However, more closely managing the turnover of the high-value items (which may be identified through computerized product reports and the manager's experience) can contribute to improved management of the inventory investment. Increasing the turnover rate for those targeted products (resulting in inventory reduction) decreases the amount of investment in inventory,[7] thereby also decreasing carrying costs and improving the profit margin of the business. On the other end of the spectrum, close examination of the low-value (or slow-moving) items might permit deletion of some of those underperformers from the inventory roster.

Other Factors in Inventory Management

RETURNS MANAGEMENT

What happens when your purchaser mistakenly orders 100 units instead of 10? Most wholesalers will allow returns within 48 hours of ordering at no extra cost. Return fees generally apply beyond that period, so catching the error quickly can avert a significant inventory management issue. No matter how closely you monitor your purchasing and management of inventory, your shelves may wind up with unsellable products, especially in the prescription department (partial bottles, whole unused bottles, expired lots, etc.) Thus, it is beneficial to regularly dispense stock from lots with the closest expiration date before others with a longer shelf life to reduce the amount of stock that expires in your inventory. Having proficiency in the return process can improve inventory management, reduce time required to receive credit, and ensure proper credit for returns.

The return goods policies for direct purchases from each manufacturer are listed in the *Red Book*.[6] Those policies differ in terms and conditions. To make accurate business decisions regarding returns or disposal, one needs to be aware of these various policies. Getting credit for returning merchandise (where applicable) carries its own indirect costs, including employee time to prepare and monitor the return transactions and to ensure that proper return credit is received. Sometimes restocking fees are associated with returns.

Larger organizations (chains, hospitals, etc.) have found value in using "returns processors," who coordinate return of goods for multiple entities. Some of these processors even offer on-site services (also referred to as **shelf sweepers**), while others require returns to be mailed to a central processing facility. The processors' fees vary, as do their service levels.[3,10]

Unclaimed Prescriptions

An unclaimed prescription "is any prescription that has been presented in a pharmacy, either by the patient or an agent of the patient, or phoned-in to a pharmacy, whether filled by the pharmacist or not, and for which the patient does not wait or return to pick up the prescription, arrange to have it picked up for him or her, or have it delivered."[11] Unclaimed prescriptions may potentially result in higher inventory and associated costs.[12] Presumably, this is because unclaimed prescriptions hold inventory that could otherwise be used for filling prescriptions that generate sales for the pharmacy.

Efforts to minimize the number of unclaimed prescriptions a pharmacy holds and the length of time they go unclaimed (providing delivery ser-

vices, reminder calls, etc.) may help to negate any potentially adverse effects of unclaimed prescriptions on inventory costs. For those prescriptions that remain unclaimed, pharmacists should develop or be cognizant of policies that dictate how long a prescription will remain unclaimed (two weeks, four weeks, etc.) before (1) contacting the patient and ideally the prescriber; (2) deleting the prescription from the computer record or profile as a dispensed prescription; (3) crediting the third-party payer if applicable; and (4) returning the drug to stock.[13] Pharmacists should verify that their processes for returning drugs to stock comply with state pharmacy practice acts and federal regulations.

Monitoring Shrinkage

Shelf count and record count may not always match. On occasion, the number of items on the shelf is less than the number indicated in your inventory records. This can be the result of "shrinkage," when items are lost, stolen, or misplaced.[1] Merchandise shrinkage, averaging 1.44% of sales according to the National Retail Security Survey,[14] is a potential cause for the inventory cost as a percentage of sales to increase. Be aware that not all shrinkage is the result of external theft or shoplifting; a considerable portion may be due to internal theft (by employees).

Deterrence of Internal Theft

Initial screens, such as checking references or conducting a criminal background check on prospective employees, may aid in ensuring—but cannot guarantee—the integrity of those individuals. In addition to screening for honesty in the recruitment process, additional techniques may be used to minimize the effect of internal theft. Either the manager or another employee should clear employee purchases through a register at a specific time before the employee leaves the pharmacy. Some pharmacist managers require employees to charge all purchases. Other accountability measures include cosigning purchases for another employee (to affirm authenticity) or requiring that another employee actually ring up the sale. Packages carried by employees should be inspected periodically. Storeroom areas should be constructed so that they may be locked and have closely controlled access. Areas where employees could deposit packages and personal belongings before coming into the working area should be provided.

Deterrence of External Theft

Plan the pharmacy layout with deterrence in mind. Maintain adequate lighting in all areas, and install a few security mirrors and perhaps a camera. Avoid high fixtures and tall displays that give visual protection to the shoplifter. Never leave your sales floor unattended. Place a cash register and sales clerk station near the front door, thus providing a barrier between the shoplifter and the exit. Acknowledge everyone who comes into the pharmacy. Shoplifters fear attention; so be observant, and provide individual, friendly, and alert service.

Technology Used in Inventory Management

Many available technologies can increase efficiency and effectiveness of inventory management. Barcoding and use of point-of-sale (POS) scanners are becoming commonplace in pharmacy settings. In the retail setting, this is especially useful for assessing sales of nonprescription merchandise. The use of POS technology as a perpetual inventory monitor is facilitated by integrated reporting software. An interested manager could review sales and stock levels daily, or even more often, if desired. Likewise, automated dispensing systems used in community pharmacies may provide a constant log of prescription product sales (refer to Chapter 7, "Pharmacy Operations: Workflow, Practice Activities, Medication Safety, Technology, and Quality").

Radio frequency identification (RFID) is a technology that stores data in computer chips that are commonly embedded in tags attached to the product. RFID enables the data to be read from a distance, facilitating ease in logging and monitoring. With monitoring scanners at store entries, this technology can also detect a theft as it occurs.[15]

A host of available online applications may enable reporting and monitoring, some of which may allow for shipment tracking and anticipated delivery time (e.g., management software from larger wholesalers and proprietary software for several large chains). Other types of software designed for pharmacy inventory management provide for automatic replenishment of inventory that adapts to changes in product demand due to seasonal changes, etc. (e.g., Cardinal Inventory Manager). These precise tools help the inventory manager move closer to the JIT ideal.

SUMMARY

Purchasing activities and inventory management are integrally related functions that must be coordinated to support optimal product acquisition and distribution. Pharmacists and pharmacist managers should note that these activities have far-reaching strategic implications whose consequences are both tangible (e.g., income or health-related outcomes) and intangible (e.g., maintenance of goodwill). Decisions related to these activities are essentially investment choices and need to be planned with considerable care and attention. This chapter reviews purchasing, purchasing decisions, managing inventory investment, methods of inventory management, and evaluating inventory management efficiency.

References

1. Heinritz S, Farrell PV, Giunipero LC, and Kolchin MG. *Purchasing Principles and Applications*. 8th ed. Englewood Cliffs, NJ: Prentice Hall; 1991.

2. National Community Pharmacists Association (NCPA). *NCPA Digest*. Alexandria, VA: NCPA; 2008.

3. West DS. Purchasing and inventory control. In: *Effective Pharmacy Management*. 9th ed. Alexandria, VA: National Community Pharmacists Association; 2003: Chapter 17.

4. Tootelian DH, Gaedeke RM. Purchasing and inventory control. In: Tootelian DH, Gaedeke RM, eds. *Essentials*

of Pharmacy Management. St. Louis, MO: Mosby; 1993: 357–377.

5. West D. Purchasing and inventory management. In: Desselle SP, Zgarrick DP, eds. *Pharmacy Management: Essentials for All Practice Settings.* New York: McGraw-Hill; 2005: 373–387.

6. Garner DD. Purchasing and inventory control. Module 11. In: *Effective Pharmacy Management Program.* National Association of Retail Druggists Management Institute; 1998.

7. Wild T. *Best Practice in Inventory Management.* New York, NY: John Wiley & Sons; 1997.

8. Muller M. *Essentials of Inventory Management.* New York, NY: AMACOM, American Management Association; 2003.

9. Carroll N. *Financial Management for Pharmacists: A Decision-Making Approach.* Philadelphia, PA: Wolters Kluwer Health/Lippincott Williams & Wilkins; 2006.

10. Hunter TS, Droege M, Marsh WA, Droege WL. Effectively managing pharmaceutical returns and waste. *Drug Top* 2005;149(2):36–43.

11. McCaffrey DJ, Smith MC, Banahan BF, et al. A continued look into the financial implications of initial noncompliance in community pharmacies: an unclaimed prescription audit pilot. *J Res Pharm Econ* 1998;9(2): 33–57.

12. McCaffrey DJ, Wilkin NE. Leveraging community pharmacy to improve patient compliance. In: Banahan BF, ed. *Marketing to Pharmacists: Understanding Their Role and Influence.* New York, NY: Haworth Press; 1998:37–60.

13. Farmer KC, Gumbhir AK. Unclaimed prescriptions: an overlooked opportunity. *Am Pharm* 1992;NS32(10): 55–59.

14. 2007 National Retail Security Survey. Washington, DC: National Retail Federation; 2008.

15. Barbella M, Paul R. RFID tracking system tags drugs at item level. *Drug Top* 2007;151(3):80,83.

Abbreviations

COGS:	cost of goods sold
DME:	durable medical equipment
EOQ:	economic order quantity
GPO:	group purchasing organizations
ITOR:	inventory turnover rate
JIT:	just-in-time
OTC:	over the counter
POS:	point of sale
RFID:	radio frequency identification
SKU:	stock keeping unit

Case Scenarios

CASE ONE: The staff system at the pharmacy that you manage operates closing each day by using a single cashier to "count down" the register drawers each night. Other clerks in the store bring their drawers to this centralized accounting, which occurs in a quiet alcove in the prescription area. The prescription "fast mover" shelf is nearby, behind which the clerks wait for their confirmed count. When each drawer is confirmed, the clerk is free to leave the store; so by the end of the counting, a single clerk is waiting there alone for several moments. One morning the Xanax stock (a fast mover) seems to be 250 tablets short (in the 1,000-count bottle). What are some possible explanations for this missing stock? And how might this discrepancy have been prevented?

(continues)

CASE TWO: One of your pharmacy's patients has chronic medication needs of around $1,200 per month COGS (multidimensional disease profile, including an immune deficiency). The medications that he needs are highly specialized and not commonly used (e.g., slow movers), so to keep them in stock would increase your carrying costs and risk. What are some potential mechanisms for reducing carrying cost and risk but still allowing you to meet the needs of your patient?

CASE THREE: One of the common formulas for striking a balance of supply with demand is "stock depth."

Stock Depth = (Review Time + Lead Time) × Average Demand + Safety Stock

Calculate the stock depth for throat lozenges in your pharmacy during cold and flu season. You typically review your OTC stock once weekly, and most items come overnight from your primary wholesaler. You sell on average four boxes of lozenges per day during the winter season. What should your stock depth be?

Additional Resources Available Online!

Visit the Student Companion Web site at http://healthprofessions.jbpub.com/pharmacymanagement for interactive study tools and additional resources.

See www.rxugace.com to learn how you can obtain continuing pharmacy education for this content.

CHAPTER 9

THIRD-PARTY PAYMENT FOR PRESCRIPTION MEDICATIONS IN THE RETAIL SECTOR

KAVITA V. NAIR, PhD

KENNETH A. LAWSON, PhD, RPh

LEARNING OBJECTIVES

After completing the chapter, the reader will be able to

1. List some of the major third-party payers for retail pharmacies.
2. Describe the medication supply chain and the flow of claims and payments in the retail pharmacy sector.
3. Explain the prescription reimbursement framework used in the retail pharmacy sector and the product cost plus fee reimbursement method.
4. Identify the control mechanisms used by pharmacy benefit managers and other third-party payers to influence prescription drug utilization and expenditures.
5. Define flat rebates and market share rebates and describe the differences between them.
6. Assess the reasons patient cost sharing is used to control expenditures and list cost-sharing mechanisms.
7. Describe the prescription reimbursement process and rebates under Medicaid.
8. Describe Medicaid, Medicare, and the components of a standard Medicare Part D plan.
9. State the goal of the Medicare medication therapy management (MTM) program and describe MTM services.
10. Discuss challenges facing retail pharmacies regarding reimbursement for prescription drugs.

KEY CONCEPTS

◆ Retail pharmacies have a key relationship with third-party payers (TPPs)—entities that reimburse retail pharmacies for prescriptions and services. Third-party payers affect (1) patients' access to and expenditures for prescriptions and related services; (2) reimbursement to pharmacies for prescriptions and services provided to patients; and (3) pharmacies' financial indicators.

❷ Most TPPs pay retail pharmacies for prescriptions and services on a retrospective, fee-for-service basis.

❸ Third-party payers use various mechanisms to control prescription use and expenditures, including payment formulas, formularies, rebates, patient cost sharing, prior authorization, generic substitution, quantity limits, step therapy, and mail service provisions.

❹ A formulary is a list of medications covered by an insurer; the list typically includes both generic and brand-name drugs. Formularies are often organized into "tiers" that indicate the out-of-pocket costs for patients. Medications in a preferred or lower tier will cost the patient less than medications in higher tiers. Medications on a formulary can also be subject to other cost control mechanisms, such as prior authorization, step therapy, and generic substitution.

❺ Rebates from pharmaceutical manufacturers are important considerations for pharmacy benefit managers (PBMs), and these rebates generally take two forms: (1) flat rebates and (2) market share rebates.

❻ Medicaid is a joint federal–state program to provide healthcare services to the low-income population. All state Medicaid programs offer a prescription drug benefit. Each state is responsible for managing its own Medicaid prescription drug benefit within federal guidelines. State Medicaid agencies do not purchase prescription drugs directly; instead, they reimburse retail pharmacies for covered outpatient drugs dispensed to Medicaid beneficiaries. Following federal guidelines, state Medicaid agencies typically reimburse pharmacies for prescriptions on the basis of an estimated product cost plus a dispensing fee.

❼ Medicare was established in 1965 under the Social Security Act as a federally funded system of health and hospital insurance for U.S. citizens age 65 years or older, for younger people receiving Social Security benefits, and for persons needing dialysis or kidney transplants to treat end-stage renal disease. The goal of Medicare Part D, which went into effect on January 1, 2006, is to provide prescription benefits to Medicare beneficiaries, many of whom had no prescription coverage before Part D was implemented.

❽ The role of retail pharmacies under the Part D benefit has become even more visible because of medication therapy management (MTM) services. Under the legislation, all Medicare prescription drug plans must develop MTM services for certain beneficiaries and reimburse healthcare providers for those services.

❾ One of the critical issues facing retail pharmacies is the reduction in reimbursement amounts by both public and private TPPs at a time when retail pharmacies are experiencing increasing operating expenses and medication costs.

❿ An ongoing area of concern for retail pharmacies regarding reimbursement is transparency in PBM contracting and transactions.

INTRODUCTION

Adequate payment for pharmaceutical products and services is critical for the survival of retail pharmacy. A shift has occurred over the past two decades wherein these payments have evolved from primarily cash payments from patients to the current practice in which approximately 80% of payments are made by third-party payers (TPPs).[1] Patients still contribute some payment in the form of **cost sharing**, but retail pharmacies receive most of their prescription revenues from insurance companies or **pharmacy benefit managers** (PBMs). The determination of payment amounts and patient cost share has long been an important issue for payers, patients, and the retail pharmacy industry. This chapter introduces third-party payments for prescriptions in the retail pharmacy setting. Specifically, the following topics are covered:

- Major TPPs for prescriptions provided through community pharmacies
- The channels for medication supply and payment in the retail sector
- The fundamentals of the third-party reimbursement framework
- Outpatient prescription benefits under Medicaid and Medicare
- Key issues that pharmacy managers and pharmacists should consider regarding reimbursement

Pharmacist managers and nonmanagers have a vested interest in reimbursement issues, and this chapter introduces basic principles and challenges of reimbursements as they relate to TPPs.

OVERVIEW OF THIRD-PARTY PAYERS FOR RETAIL PHARMACY

Retail pharmacies are licensed entities that deliver pharmaceutical goods and services directly to patients; they represent the "terminal seller in the channel of pharmaceutical distribution."[2] Retail pharmacies encompass a diverse group, including traditional chain pharmacies, independent community pharmacies, mass merchants, supermarkets, and mail-order pharmacies. Their presence continues to grow; prescription drug sales in the retail sector increased from $120.6 billion in 2000 to $227.5 billion in 2007, an approximately 90% increase.[1] Mail and retail pharmacies do differ on several dimensions that include the mode of delivery, unit cost, number of days supplied and patient cost sharing. However, for the purposes of this chapter, we will refer to all pharmacies as "retail pharmacies" for simplicity and highlight these differences later in the chapter.

🔷 *Retail pharmacies have a key relationship with TPPs—entities that reimburse retail pharmacies for prescriptions and services. Third-party payers affect (1) patients' access to and expenditures for prescriptions and related services; (2) reimbursement to pharmacies for prescriptions and services provided to patients; and (3) pharmacies' financial indicators.* In today's market, TPPs comprise several groups that are either private or public (government) organizations. Private TPPs include privately owned PBMs and health insurance companies. Pharmacy benefit managers are entities that manage and administer the prescription drug benefit for insurers and other plan sponsors; PBMs contract with retail pharmacies to create a network of pharmacies from which patients can purchase their prescriptions. In addition, they are responsible for functions, such as **formulary** development and management, utilization and cost management, claims processing, and provider payment. The major public TPPs are **Medicare** and **Medicaid**. Medicare is a federal healthcare program for individuals 65 years or older, those with end-stage renal disease, and certain disabled individuals. **Medicare Part D** (the Medicare outpatient prescription drug benefit program) went into effect in 2006 because of the Medicare Prescription Drug, Improvement, and Modernization Act of 2003 (MMA). Medicaid is a joint federal–state program for low income individuals that provides coverage for outpatient prescriptions in all states. Federal oversight for Medicare and Medicaid comes from the Centers for Medicare and Medicaid Services (CMS). Low-income elderly individuals who qualify for both Medicare and Medicaid are known as "dual-eligibles." Additional public TPPs include other state and local programs for low-income enrollees.

The importance of TPPs to retail pharmacy has grown in recent years. **Figure 9–1** shows that, for independent retail pharmacies, the proportion of prescriptions covered by TPPs has increased from 80% in 2003 to 88% in 2007.[3] Because TPPs cover a majority of prescriptions dispensed by community pharmacies, these payers are the source of most of the pharmacies' prescription revenues; thus, the payment frameworks and processes established by TPPs are important to pharmacy managers and pharmacists.

MEDICATION SUPPLY CHAIN IN THE RETAIL SECTOR

Several entities are involved in providing prescription medications to patients and payment for those medications under third-party plans in the retail

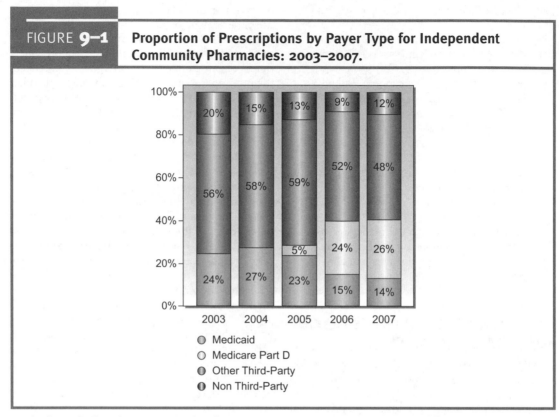

FIGURE 9–1 Proportion of Prescriptions by Payer Type for Independent Community Pharmacies: 2003–2007.

The figure displays the percentage of medication prescriptions by payer type in independent community pharmacies in the United States from 2003 to 2007. Third-party payers covered payment for the majority of prescriptions each year. Since implementing enrollment in late 2005, the proportion of prescriptions covered by Medicare Part D has increased to slightly more than one-quarter of prescriptions filled, and non-third-party payer coverage of prescriptions has declined from 20% in 2003 to 12% in 2007.

Source: Courtesy of National Community Pharmacists Association (NCPA).[3]

sector. **Figure 9–2** shows a flowchart for prescription medications, claims, and payments. The primary supply chain for prescription medications in the retail sector consists of pharmaceutical manufacturers, drug **wholesalers**, conventional retail pharmacies, mail-order pharmacies (often owned and operated by PBMs), and ultimately patients. Drug wholesalers (for example, Ameri-sourceBergen, Cardinal Health, and McKesson) purchase prescription medications from pharmaceutical manufacturers. Conventional chain and independent retail pharmacies and mail-order

pharmacies purchase prescription medications from wholesalers or directly from pharmaceutical manufacturers. Pharmacies then provide prescription medications to patients and file claims with TPPs (often PBMs, such as Medco Health Solutions, Express Scripts, or CVS Caremark) to receive payments for those prescriptions. Patients are usually responsible for some form of cost sharing for the prescriptions they receive under prescription benefit plans.

The PBM, in turn, submits claims for prescriptions dispensed through both the conventional

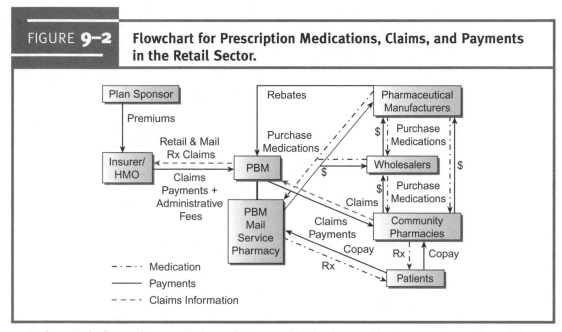

FIGURE **9–2**   **Flowchart for Prescription Medications, Claims, and Payments in the Retail Sector.**

As shown in the figure, pharmaceutical manufacturers and wholesalers provide community pharmacies and pharmacy benefit manager (PBM) mail service pharmacies with prescription (Rx) medications, and in turn, receive payment for those medications. Community pharmacies and PBM mail service pharmacies provide prescriptions to patients and receive payments (copays) from patients that cover a part of prescription costs. For the remainder of prescription costs, pharmacies submit claims to PBMs who, in turn, submit retail and mail prescription claims to insurers/health maintenance organizations (HMOs). Insurers and HMOs receive premium payments from plan sponsors. The insurers/HMOs make claim payments to PBMs who then make claim payments to pharmacies; PBMs also receive rebates from pharmaceutical manufacturers.

retail pharmacies and its mail-order operation to a health plan or insurer (which also may be responsible for providing physician, hospital, and other medical services to enrollees). The plan sponsor (often an employer but also could be a government agency) pays premiums to the health plan/insurer on behalf of its employees or enrollees. The PBM manages the prescription payment and reimbursement process for the health plan/insurer. PBMs receive **rebates** from pharmaceutical manufacturers that may be based on quantity of medications dispensed through the health plan, market share achieved for a particular manufacturer's products, product placement on the plan's formulary, and other factors that are discussed later in the chapter.

The flowchart shown in Figure 9–2 represents a common structure for the provision of and payment

for medications in the retail sector; however, other structures exist. For example, some plan sponsors, such as large employer groups, contract directly with a PBM (eliminating the health plan/insurer as part of the prescription benefit), and some Medicaid agencies act as their own PBM by contracting directly with retail pharmacies and processing claims in-house. These are only a few of the structures that exist in the retail sector.

RETAIL PHARMACY REIMBURSEMENT FRAMEWORK

In 2007, TPPs (public and private) covered 79% ($180 billion) of the $228 billion spent on prescription drugs dispensed through retail outlets.[1] Thus, understanding the nature and process of third-party reimbursement for prescription medications is important. ❷*Most TPPs pay retail pharmacies for prescriptions and services on a **retrospective, fee-for-service** basis.* In this system, the pharmacist files a claim with the payer when dispensing a prescription or rendering a service and collects any specified cost sharing (for example, **copayment**) amount from the patient. At some later time, the payer reimburses the pharmacy for each covered prescription or unit of service provided. For prescriptions, the **product cost plus fee method** is generally used to determine the reimbursement amount. **Table 9–1** shows the components of the product cost plus fee method. The values for each of these components and other payment and participation terms are specified in the contract between the pharmacy and the TPP.

Prescription Payment

The total payment received by the pharmacy for a prescription is equal to the sum of the product cost amount plus the dispensing fee, with the amounts for these two components specified in the contract between the TPP and the pharmacy. The patient makes part of this total payment to the pharmacy (the patient's cost share, which is also specified in the contract), and the remainder is made by the TPP. Each of these components is described in the following sections.

PRODUCT COST AMOUNTS

Several terms may be used in determining or estimating the cost of the medication dispensed (the product cost) for reimbursement purposes or for the pharmacy's internal cost accounting. These terms are generally applied to specific transactions between pharmaceutical manufacturers, wholesalers, retail pharmacies, and TPPs. **Figure 9–3** shows a simplified application of the product cost terms.[4]

Each term is described below based on a Congressional Budget Office report:[4]

- **Wholesale acquisition cost** (WAC). The manufacturers' published catalog (list) price for sale of a drug (**brand name** or **generic**) to wholesalers. However, in practice, wholesalers do not pay WAC for drugs; instead, they pay some lesser amount. WAC may be used

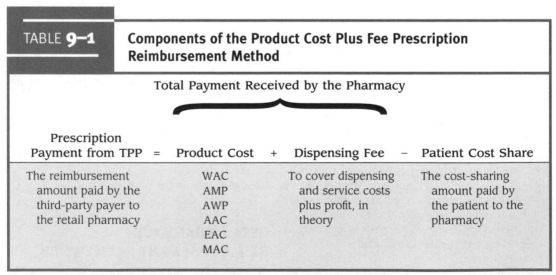

TABLE **9–1**	**Components of the Product Cost Plus Fee Prescription Reimbursement Method**		
	Total Payment Received by the Pharmacy		
Prescription Payment from TPP =	Product Cost +	Dispensing Fee –	Patient Cost Share
The reimbursement amount paid by the third-party payer to the retail pharmacy	WAC AMP AWP AAC EAC MAC	To cover dispensing and service costs plus profit, in theory	The cost-sharing amount paid by the patient to the pharmacy

Note: TPP = third-party payer; WAC = wholesale acquisition cost; AMP = average manufacturers' price; AWP = average wholesale price; AAC = actual acquisition cost; EAC = estimated acquisition cost; MAC = maximum allowable cost.
Source: Modified from Congressional Budget Office.[4]

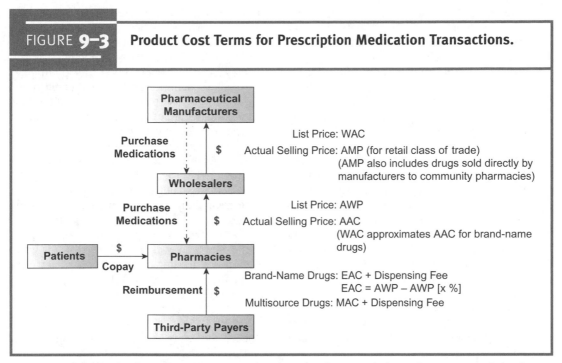

FIGURE **9-3**   **Product Cost Terms for Prescription Medication Transactions.**

Two prices apply to medication purchase transactions between pharmaceutical manufacturers and wholesalers and between wholesalers and pharmacies: (1) list prices and (2) actual selling prices. The actual amounts paid by purchasers (actual selling prices) are usually lower than the list prices. When wholesalers purchase medications from pharmaceutical manufacturers, WAC is the list price and AMP is the actual selling price (for the retail class of trade). When pharmacies purchase medications from wholesalers, AWP is the list price and AAC is the actual selling price. WAC and AWP are often used as pricing indices in calculating EAC. Third-party payers typically reimburse pharmacies for dispensed prescriptions based on EAC plus a dispensing fee (for brand-name drugs) or on MAC plus a dispensing fee (for multisource drugs). AAC = actual acquisition cost; AMP = average manufacturers' price; AWP = average wholesale price; EAC = estimated acquisition price; MAC = maximum allowable cost; WAC = wholesale acquisition cost.

Source: Modified from Congressional Budget Office.[4]

as a basis, or index, for determining contract prices between wholesalers and retail pharmacies. It is a close approximation to the prices that retail pharmacies pay wholesalers for single-source brand-name drugs (brand-name drugs that do not have a generic alternative), but WAC exceeds pharmacies' acquisition costs for generic drugs. Brand-name drug rebates paid by pharmaceutical manufacturers to PBMs are sometimes based on WAC.

- *Average manufacturers' price* (AMP). The average price paid by wholesalers to manufacturers for drugs distributed through retail pharmacies or by retail pharmacies that buy directly from manufacturers. AMP is an average of actual transaction prices. A current proposal to use AMP in determining pharmacy reimbursement for multisource drugs (drug products that are available in both brand-name and generic versions from different manufacturers) under Medicaid is controversial because it is likely to lower reimbursement amounts, in some cases, to levels below the amounts that pharmacies pay for the medications.[5]

- *Average wholesale price* (AWP). A suggested list price for products purchased from wholesalers by pharmacies (both retail and nonretail). This list price is publicly available in industry compendia, including First Data-Bank's *Annual Directory of Pharmaceuticals* (*Blue Book*) and National Drug Data Files, Medi-Spans' *Price Alert* and Master Drug Data Base, and Thomson Reuter/Micromedex *Red Book*. However, in practice, pharmacies usually purchase drugs at an amount lower than AWP. AWP often serves as a pricing index (AWP – 15% is commonly used for brand-name drugs) in the payment formulas used to determine payments to pharmacies under prescription benefit plans.
- *Actual acquisition cost* (AAC). The *actual* amount paid by a pharmacy to a supplier for a product. The AAC for any particular bottle or package of medication is difficult to determine because discounts that affect the AAC may not be known until the purchase invoice is paid by the pharmacy. The AAC is rarely used in determining reimbursement amounts for product costs under prescription benefit plans, but it is used internally by pharmacies for cost accounting purposes.
- *Estimated acquisition cost* (EAC). An estimate of the AAC that is commonly used to determine the reimbursement amount for product cost under prescription benefit plans. EAC is usually expressed as a percentage off AWP (e.g., AWP – 15% of AWP). The Congressional Budget Office estimated EAC for single-source drugs in the retail sector for 2003 as follows:[4]
  Conventional retail pharmacies: AWP – (17% of AWP)
  Mail-order pharmacies: AWP – (22% of AWP)
  (Note: The discount off AWP may be greater than 22% in some cases for mail-order pharmacies, leading to a lower EAC.)

- *Maximum allowable cost* (MAC). A maximum amount per unit of medication that TPPs will pay pharmacies for multisource drugs. Medicaid, PBMs, and other insurers may set their own MACs. The pharmacy's reimbursement for product cost under a prescription benefit plan cannot exceed the MAC amount regardless of the pharmacy's actual cost for the medication. This provides an incentive for the pharmacist to use less expensive generic drugs rather than brand-name drugs. The Deficit Reduction Act of 2005, a federal budget reconciliation act that decreased spending for entitlement programs such as Medicaid, has proposed setting federal MACs (**federal upper limits**, or FULs) at 250% of the lowest AMP; however, this provision is still being litigated by pharmacy organizations and has not yet been implemented at the time of this writing.[5,6]

DISPENSING FEE

In theory, the dispensing fee should be sufficient to cover service/operational costs plus profit. The service/operational costs consist of all of the operational costs (salaries, rent, utilities, etc.) associated with providing the service (e.g., dispensing the prescription, patient counseling, and medication therapy management [MTM] services). One operational expense unique to third-party prescriptions is the transaction fee (up to $0.15 per prescription claim) charged by prescription claims processing "switches" (companies that provide the electronic link between the pharmacy and the PBM to facilitate prescription claims processing). Profit is an amount above the product cost and service/operational cost, which yields a return on the owners' investment in the pharmacy.

PATIENT COST SHARE

Patient cost-sharing provisions are widely used by TPPs to control plan expenditures. The plan expenditure for prescriptions is reduced because patients pay for a portion of the prescription cost, and as such, they are likely to consider the need for the medication more carefully since they are responsible for part of the costs. This is further discussed later in the chapter.

PRESCRIPTION COST AND UTILIZATION CONTROL MECHANISMS

◆ *Third-party payers use various mechanisms to control prescription use and expenditures, including payment formulas, formularies, rebates, patient cost sharing,* **prior authorization***, generic substitution, quantity limits,* **step therapy***, and mail service provisions.* Each of these mechanisms is described in the following sections.

Payment Formulas

As noted previously, TPPs usually pay retail pharmacies using a product cost plus fee formula (Prescription [Rx] Payment = Product Cost + Dispensing Fee – Patient Cost Share). Third-party payers set the product cost, dispensing fee, and cost share amounts to control the plan's drug expenditures. The product cost amount in the payment formula is often calculated as AWP minus a specified percentage discount to estimate the actual product cost the pharmacy incurs. The dispensing fee offered to retail pharmacies is usually a fixed fee. However, the method used to determine the product cost amount and the dispensing fee may vary depending on whether the drug dispensed is a brand-name or generic drug. For single-source drugs, a common reimbursement formula is

Rx Payment = (AWP – [AWP (x%)]) + Dispensing Fee

For example, if the AWP for Drug A is $100, the product cost allowance is AWP – 15%, and the dispensing fee is $3.00; the total payment to the pharmacy would be

Rx Payment = ($100 – [$100 (0.15)] + $3.00

Rx Payment = $85.00 + $3.00

Rx Payment = $88.00

If the copay is $10.00 for this prescription, the patient would pay $10.00 and the TPP would pay $78.00.

The discount percentage for generics or multi-source drugs is much greater than for single-source drugs and can be as high as 50% to 80%. Dispensing fees typically range between $2.00 to $3.00 for brand-name drug prescriptions and $3.00

to $3.50 for generic drug prescriptions.[2] However, a recent study found that the mean cost of dispensing a prescription was $10.50, which is much higher than the $2.00–$3.50 dispensing fee normally reimbursed to retail pharmacies to process a prescription (dispensing fees vary by plan).[7] Profitability in retail pharmacies is complex. For prescriptions, profits may be generated from payment formulas, with product cost allowances that are higher than actual product costs and from dispensing fees that exceed the average cost of dispensing a prescription (a rare occurrence with most TPPs). For overall pharmacy profitability, nonprescription sales, **cost of goods sold**, and operational expenses also must be considered.

Formularies

◆ *A formulary is a list of medications covered by an insurer; the list typically includes both generic and brand-name drugs. Formularies are often organized into "tiers" that indicate the out-of-pocket costs for patients. Medications in a preferred or lower tier will cost the patient less than medications in higher tiers. Medications on a formulary can also be subject to other cost control mechanisms, such as prior authorization, step therapy, and generic substitution.* Recognizing the importance of drug placement on a formulary, pharmaceutical manufacturers give discounts to PBMs in the form of rebates to get a preferred spot on a formulary.

Rebates and Pharmacy Benefit Managers

Rebates are an important cost control mechanism. Because of their close connection with rebates, pharmacy benefit managers are also discussed in this section. PBMs are TPP entities that manage the prescription benefit for employers and health insurance carriers and contract with managed care organizations, self-insured employers, insurance companies, unions, Medicaid, and Medicare to design, implement, and administer outpatient prescription drug benefit programs.[8] They also act as intermediaries between pharmaceutical manufacturers and insurers to negotiate drug prices. PBMs originated in the late 1970s as entities that processed prescription claims for insurers. Merck-Medco Managed Care and PCS Health Systems were formed in the 1970s as PAID Prescriptions and Pharmaceutical Card Systems, Inc., respectively, to function purely as third-party prescription claims processors. The advent of electronic claims processing systems at pharmacies in the late 1980s further fueled the growth of PBMs. In the early to mid-1990s, pharmaceutical companies tried to leverage the concentrated buying power and extensive prescription claims' data of PBMs by acquiring them. Notable examples are the acquisition of PCS Health Systems by Eli Lilly and the acquisition of Diversified Pharmaceutical Services by SmithKline Beecham, among others. These mergers were controversial and resulted in antitrust inquiries by the Federal Trade Commission about competitor pharmaceutical companies being denied fair access to products on the formularies of PBMs owned by rivals. By the early 2000s, all pharmaceutical companies had divested the PBMs they owned. Examples of PBMs are CVS Caremark, Medco Health Solutions, and Express Scripts.

PBM functions are divided into two main categories: (1) administrative functions and (2) control of drug use.[9] Administrative functions include establishing benefit structure and design, maintaining a network of retail pharmacy providers, and processing claims and adjudication. Drug use control functions include establishing policies and programs targeted toward physicians, pharmacists, and patients to monitor and control drug use, such as formulary development and management, drug therapy interchange programs, drug utilization review activities, disease management initiatives, and mail service programs. In this latter category, negotiating rebates and the cost of drugs and contracting with pharmaceutical manufacturers are crucial functions for PBMs. The nature of the rebates obtained by PBMs, to some extent, controls the reimbursement that retail pharmacies receive for medications.

Rebates are given to PBMs by manufacturers to encourage PBMs to increase the market share for a particular medication. ❺ *Rebates from pharmaceutical manufacturers are important considerations for PBMs, and these rebates generally take two forms: (1) flat rebates and (2) market share rebates.* In a flat rebate method, the rebate amount paid by manufacturers to the PBM is based on a fixed percentage of the WAC, which may range from 2% to 27% of the WAC.[2]

Example of a Flat Rebate Calculation

WAC Price = $75

Flat Rebate Percentage = 8%

Number of prescriptions dispensed in reporting period = 10,000

Rebate to the PBM = $75 × 10,000 × 8%
= $60,000

In the market share rebate method, manufacturers make payments to PBMs based on the market share PBMs achieved for the drug product. This market share is increased by the PBM's promotion of the drug using various methods, such as preferred formulary status and lower copays. Market share is calculated by taking the total number of prescriptions or units of a drug dispensed by a plan sponsor and dividing that number by the total number of prescriptions or units for all drug products within that drug class. The rebate percentages offered to the PBM are based on market share achieved by the PBM.

Example of a Market Share Rebate Calculation

WAC Price = $75

Number of prescriptions dispensed by the plan sponsor in the reporting period = 10,000

Rebate Percentages Based on Achieved Market Share Within the Contract Period:
<50% = 2.0%
51% to 75% = 3.0%
76% to 80% = 3.5%
81% to 85% = 4.0%
>85% = 5.0%

Actual Market Share Achieved by the PBM = 82.5%
Rebate Paid to the PBM = $75 × 10,000 × 4%
= $30,000

Pharmaceutical manufacturers do not make rebate payments directly to retail pharmacies, primarily because retail pharmacies belong to networks of several health plans and PBMs that have several different formularies. Therefore, retail pharmacies have a very limited ability to influence which medications are dispensed. Retention rates represent the percentage of all rebates made to PBMs by manufacturers not explicitly passed on to the plan sponsors or retail pharmacies. Rebate retention by PBMs also follows various models and varies considerably, ranging from 25% for smaller PBMs to 91% for larger PBMs.[2]

Patient Cost Sharing

Patients typically must pay for part of the cost of their prescriptions, and patient cost-sharing provisions are often used to control expenditures in prescription benefit plans for two reasons: (1) when patients pay for a portion of overall prescription costs, it reduces the plan's portion of the costs; and (2) when patients pay for part of their prescription costs, they will be more likely to control use to reduce their own expenditures. Prescription cost-sharing mechanisms usually include copayments, deductibles, co-insurance, and maximum payment amount; copayments are the most commonly used (these mechanisms are described in **Table 9–2**).

Combinations of patient cost-sharing types are often used. For example, a deductible and a copay may be used in combination so that the patient is responsible for the first $250 of prescription charges during the plan year and $25 per prescription after meeting the deductible. The standard benefit under Medicare Part D uses all four cost-sharing types. The effects of cost-sharing provisions on the use of and expenditures for prescriptions depend on several factors, including

TABLE 9–2	Patient Cost-Sharing Mechanisms
Mechanism	**Definition**
Copayment	The patient must pay a fixed dollar amount per prescription. Copays may range from $1 or $2 (usually in Medicaid plans) up to $100 or more per prescription in private plans. Prescription benefit plans often use tiered copayments corresponding to the medication's formulary status with lower copays (e.g., $10) for generic medications, higher copays (e.g., $25) for preferred brand medications, and highest copays (e.g., $50) for nonpreferred brand medications.
Co-insurance	The patient must pay a fixed percentage of the cost of each prescription. This percentage is often set at 10% to 20% but may be up to 50%. For example, if the allowable cost of a prescription is $100 and the co-insurance is set at 20%, the patient pays $20 and the prescription plan pays $80 for that prescription.
Deductible	The patient must pay for a specified amount of charges per coverage period before the prescription benefit starts to cover expenses. For example, a $250 deductible for prescription coverage means that the patient must pay the first $250 of charges for prescriptions during each plan year. Insurance will begin paying benefits after the patient pays the first $250 of charges.
Maximum payment amount	The TPP will pay only up to a stated maximum amount for a patient's prescriptions during the plan year (e.g., $1,000). Once prescription charges reach this maximum, the patient must pay out-of-pocket for prescriptions for the remainder of the plan year.

the cost-sharing amounts, the number of prescriptions dispensed for the patient, and the patient's financial status.

Prior Authorizations

Prior authorization programs are used to allow access to certain medications for patients who meet specified criteria. Under prior authorization programs, prescribers must get approval from the plan before patients can receive medications subject to prior approval requirements. Patients with contraindications or allergies to a preferred medication or a prior treatment failure with a preferred medication are among those for whom prior approval may be required. Although prior authorization may reduce the use of certain medications and increase the use of preferred medications, access to medications requiring prior authorization may be delayed or reduced because prescribers must follow prior authorization procedures and, in some cases, will prescribe a non-prior authorization medication to avoid the process, even though this non-prior authorization medication may not be the most appropriate for the patient.

Generic Substitution

Generic medications are usually less expensive than their corresponding brand-name medications. Third-party payers often encourage generic substitution (the use of a generically equivalent medication in place of a prescribed brand-name medication) to reduce plan and patient expenditures. Some generic substitution programs are mandatory; in other cases, incentives, such as lower patient cost sharing, are used to encourage generic substitution.

Quantity Limits

Third-party payers often impose quantity limits on prescription medication coverage. These include limits on the days' supply or number of dosage units (tablets, capsules, etc.) of medication allowed per prescription and limits on the number of prescriptions per month that will be covered per member or enrollee.

Step Therapy

Step therapy uses a prescribing pattern set by protocol based on the stage of illness or treatment

effectiveness. Typically, the most cost-effective drug is used first, followed by alternative therapies.

Mail Service Options

Mail service options are frequently offered by prescription benefit plans. Plan enrollees typically pay lower cost-sharing amounts and are able to obtain greater quantities (days' supply) of medication for prescriptions filled through mail service compared with community pharmacies. As a representative example, plan terms may allow an enrollee to obtain up to a 90-day supply of a medication for a $50 copayment if using the mail service pharmacy or up to a 30-day supply for a $25 copayment at a community pharmacy; this differential results in the enrollee having to pay a total of $75 in copayments to obtain a 90-day supply (three 30-day fills) through the community pharmacy. In 2008, mail service accounted for 6.2% of prescriptions dispensed and 15.8% of prescription sales in the United States.[10]

Although these utilization and cost control mechanisms (i.e., payment formulas, formularies, rebates, patient cost sharing, prior authorization, generic substitution, quantity limits, step therapy, and mail service options) are generally effective in controlling the plan's prescription expenditures, they may reduce patient access to medications, which may, in turn, lead to the use of other expensive healthcare services (e.g., emergency department and hospital services). For example, restrictive formularies and prior authorization programs may prevent some patients from receiving the most appropriate medications, and some patients may not fill prescriptions because they cannot afford the cost-sharing amounts. These control mechanisms are widely used in private and in public prescription drug plans. Two major public plans, Medicaid and Medicare, are described next.

MEDICAID

❻ *Medicaid is a joint federal–state program to provide healthcare services to the low-income population. All state Medicaid programs offer a prescription drug benefit. Each state is responsible for managing its own Medicaid prescription drug benefit within federal guidelines. State Medicaid agencies do not purchase prescription drugs directly; instead, they reimburse retail pharmacies for covered outpatient drugs dispensed to Medicaid beneficiaries.* Federal statute requires manufacturers to enter into an agreement with the secretary of Health and Human Services, on behalf of the states, to provide rebates for covered outpatient prescription drug products paid for by Medicaid through the Medicaid Drug Rebate Program.[11] Manufacturers that do not sign an agreement are not eligible for Medicaid coverage of their products. With the exception of some drug classes, if a Medicaid program opts to cover prescription drugs for their beneficiaries, it must provide coverage and reimbursement for all covered outpatient drug products manufactured by pharmaceutical companies that have entered into a rebate agreement with CMS. Currently, more than 600 pharmaceutical companies and 49 states and the District of Columbia participate in the Medicaid Drug Rebate Program (Arizona has a Section 1115 waiver that exempts it from participating in the Medicaid Drug Rebate Program).[11]

◆ 6 *Following federal guidelines, state Medicaid agencies typically reimburse pharmacies for prescriptions on the basis of an estimated product cost plus a dispensing fee.* Community pharmacies are reimbursed for single-source medications in a manner similar to the previous description: Rx Payment = (AWP – [AWP (x%)]) + Dispensing Fee. Dispensing fees are expected to be "reasonable" and generally range from $3.50 to $5.00 per prescription. Dispensing fees in many states vary, with higher fees paid for generics than for single-source drugs in most states.[12]

Under the Medicaid Drug Rebate Program, manufacturers are required to submit their best price (BP) to CMS for their drug products. The BP is the manufacturer's lowest price offered in the same period to any wholesaler, retailer, nonprofit, or public entity.[13] CMS calculates the rebate amount based on the difference between the AWP and the BP. Rebates for single-source drugs (brand-name drugs with no generic alternatives) are the greater of 15.1% of the AWP or AWP minus BP. Generic manufacturers must rebate a flat 11% of AWP for their products dispensed under Medicaid. Additional rebates are required if the weighted average prices for a manufacturer's single- and

multisource drugs rise faster than inflation as measured by the **consumer price index for all urban consumers** (CPI-U).[13]

For multisource drugs (drug products with at least one generic alternative), the reimbursement rates are somewhat different. State Medicaid programs may only receive matching funds for reimbursements up to a maximum limit known as the federal upper limit, or FUL.[14] Through the FUL program, CMS sets an upper limit reimbursement amount for drugs that meet the following criteria: (1) they are multisource products; (2) at least three therapeutically equivalent drug products are in a drug class; and (3) there are at least three suppliers of the drug product. CMS has historically set the FUL for multisource drug products at 150% of the lowest price of a therapeutic and biologically equivalent version of the drug. CMS used a 150% markup so that FUL prices were high enough to ensure that pharmacies can stock an equivalent product without incurring a loss on acquisition costs while also ensuring that Medicaid pays relatively low prices for prescription drugs on the FUL list.

A state's aggregate payment for all Medicaid prescription drugs on the FUL list must not exceed the total payment levels established by the FUL program. The aggregate cap allows states to increase or decrease the cost of individual prescription drugs in accordance with state or local markets while maintaining the overall savings created by the FUL program.

One concern about the FUL reimbursement methodology for retail pharmacies is the potential adoption of the AMP in determining the product cost reimbursement amounts for pharmacies as outlined in the Deficit Reduction Act of 2005. The Deficit Reduction Act proposes to calculate a multisource drug's FUL as 250% of the lowest AMP among therapeutically equivalent options.[14] The AMP is the average price paid to a manufacturer by wholesalers for drugs distributed to retail pharmacies and is not currently publicly available to retail pharmacies. For multisource drugs, the new FUL reimbursement rate to a pharmacy would be

250% of the Lowest AMP + Dispensing Fee

At the time this change was proposed, it was estimated to cut payments for multisource and generic drugs to pharmacies by $8 billion between 2008 and 2011.[5] Retail pharmacists have expressed concern that the calculation of AMP includes sales, discounts, and rebates to mail-order pharmacies, PBMs, and other outpatient pharmacy sales, including hospitals and clinics. Therefore, the proposed AMP calculation yields a much lower amount than the traditionally used AWP and does not accurately reflect the acquisition costs borne by retail pharmacies. To assess the proposed AMP pricing, the General Accounting Office conducted a study using the first quarter of 2006 Medicaid utilization data and identified 77 multisource products that would be subject to the new FUL pricing methodology.[14] The results showed that the estimated AMP-based FULs for all 77 drugs were, on average, 36% lower than the average retail pharmacy acquisition costs and ranged from 65% lower for high-expenditure drugs to 15% lower for the most frequently used drugs. At the time this chapter was written, the National Association of Chain Drug Stores (NACDS) and the National Community Pharmacists Association (NCPA) had filed a lawsuit against CMS and the Health and Human Services secretary to prohibit the use of AMP in calculating FUL reimbursement rates for multisource drugs.[15]

For generic or multisource drugs, states can also use a state-specific maximum allowable cost (MAC) program to set a cap on payment for brand or generic versions of the same drug. States may establish their own MAC to use to reimburse pharmacies. Under the MAC formula, states establish a single price for each generic regardless of the manufacturer of the generic. Typically, states administering MAC programs will publish lists of generic drugs with the maximum price at which Medicaid will reimburse for those medications. Retail pharmacies generally will not receive payments that are higher than the MAC price. These programs differ from the FUL list, as states have more discretion in determining what drugs to include on the MAC list. State methods for setting MAC prices include the following:

- Setting the MAC at the lowest published price for a generic version of the drug
- Manually setting the MAC based on surveys of pharmacies to determine the actual acquisition costs for generics from manufacturers

- Using the FUL MAC that is updated twice a year

MEDICARE

❼ *Medicare was established in 1965 under the Social Security Act as a federally funded system of health and hospital insurance for U.S. citizens age 65 years or older, for younger people receiving Social Security benefits, and for persons needing dialysis or kidney transplants to treat end-stage renal disease.* The Medicare system was originally administered by the Social Security Administration, but in 1977, management was transferred to the Health Care Financing Administration (renamed the Centers for Medicare and Medicaid Services). Individuals are eligible for Medicare if they are U.S. citizens or have been permanent legal residents for five continuous years and they are 65 years or older or are under 65 years, disabled, and have been receiving either benefits or the Railroad Retirement Board disability benefits for at least 24 months; or they receive continuing dialysis for end-stage renal disease or need a kidney transplant; or they are eligible for Social Security Disability Insurance and have amyotrophic lateral sclerosis (ALS, also known as Lou Gehrig's disease).[16] Many beneficiaries are dual-eligible. This means they qualify for both Medicare and Medicaid. In some states, Medicaid will pay Medicare for premiums and for drugs not covered by Medicare Part D for dual-eligibles with incomes below specified levels.

The original Medicare program has two parts: Part A (hospital insurance) and Part B (medical insurance). Part A covers hospital stays, including stays in skilled nursing facilities. Part B coverage is detailed in **Table 9–3**.[17] In most cases, medication is covered under Part B only if it is administered by the physician during an office visit (there are exceptions such as outpatient immunosuppressant medications for transplant recipients). Part B is optional and may be deferred if the beneficiary or his or her spouse is still employed and covered by an employer's plan. Neither Part A nor Part B pays for all of a covered person's medical costs. The program contains premiums, deductibles, and copays that the covered individual must pay out of pocket. With the passage of the Balanced Budget Act of 1997, Medicare beneficiaries were given the option to receive their Medicare

TABLE **9–3**	**Listing of Some Healthcare Services Covered by Medicare Part B**

- Abdominal aortic aneurysm screening
- Ambulance services
- Ambulatory surgical centers
- Blood
- Bone mass measurement
- Cardiovascular screening
- Chiropractic services (limited)
- Clinical laboratory services
- Clinical research studies
- Colorectal cancer screening, mammograms (screening), Pap tests and pelvic exams, prostate cancer screening
- Defibrillator-implantable automatic
- Diabetes screening, self-management training, supplies, eye exams
- Doctor services, practitioner (nondoctor) services
- Durable medical equipment
- Emergency room services
- Eyeglasses (limited)
- Federally qualified health center services
- Flu shots, hepatitis B shots, pneumococcal shot
- Foot exams and treatment
- Glaucoma tests
- Hearing and balance exams
- Home health services
- Kidney dialysis services and supplies
- Medical nutrition therapy services
- Mental health care—outpatient
- Occupational therapy, physical therapy, speech-language pathology services
- Outpatient hospital services, outpatient medical and surgical services and supplies
- Physical exam (one time)
- Prosthetic/orthotic items
- Rural health clinic services
- Second surgical opinions
- Smoking cessation
- Surgical dressing services
- Telemedicine
- Tests
- Transplant and immunosuppressive drugs
- Travel—health care needed outside the United States
- Urgently needed care

Source: Data from Centers for Medicare and Medicaid Services.[17]

benefits through private health insurance plans instead of through the original Medicare plan (Parts A and B). These programs are known as **Medicare Advantage**, or Part C, plans. Medicare Advantage plans are required to offer a benefit package that is at least as good as Medicare's. For people who choose to enroll in a Medicare Advantage plan, Medicare pays the health plan a set amount every month for each member. Members may have to pay a monthly premium in addition to the Medicare Part B premium and generally pay copays for services.

Medicare Outpatient Prescription Drug Benefit (Part D)

Title I of the Medicare Prescription Drug, Improvement, and Modernization Act (MMA) of 2003 established the Medicare Part D prescription drug program, which is based on a private market model. ❼ *The goal of Medicare Part D, which went into effect on January 1, 2006, is to provide prescription benefits to Medicare beneficiaries, many of whom had no prescription coverage before Part D was implemented.* Anyone with Part A or B is eligible for Part D. To receive this benefit, a person with Medicare must enroll in a stand-alone prescription drug plan or a Medicare Advantage plan with prescription drug coverage. These plans are approved and regulated by the Medicare program but are designed and administered by private health insurance companies. Generally, beneficiaries pay an annual premium for Part D, and unlike original Medicare (Parts A and B), Part D coverage is not standardized. Plans choose which drugs (or even classes of drugs) they wish to cover, at what level (or tier) they wish to cover them, and are free to choose not to cover some drugs at all.

To provide beneficiaries with a choice of plans and sponsors, the MMA requires at least two plans offered by different sponsors to be available in every region. As of February 2009, CMS reported that 26.7 million (59.1%) of the 45.2 million Medicare beneficiaries were enrolled in Part D plans.[18] As shown in **Figure 9–4**, 32% of Medicare beneficiaries had retiree or other prescription coverage while 10% had no prescription coverage.[18]

CMS has developed a "standard Part D" benefit that prescription drug plans and Medicare Advantage with prescription drug benefit plans can adopt or modify as long as the plans are "actuarially equivalent" to the standard Part D plan. The components of the standard Part D plans between 2006 and 2010 are shown in **Table 9–4**, the highlights of which are presented next:[19]

a. *Initial deductible* that a beneficiary has to meet after which the beneficiary pays 25% of covered costs up to the initial coverage limit. The deductible ranged from $250 in 2006 to $310 in 2010.
b. *Initial coverage limit* represents the sum of the beneficiary's out-of-pocket expenses and the health plan's drug costs. When a beneficiary reaches the initial coverage limit, he or she enters the gap phase of the standard Part D benefit. The initial coverage limit ranged from $2,250 in 2006 to $2,830 in 2010.
c. *Total out-of-pocket expenses* represent the total out-of-pocket costs that beneficiaries accrue from the start of the calendar year until they reach the limit that enables them to leave the gap phase. These expenses ranged from $3,600 in 2006 to $4,550 in 2010.
d. *Catastrophic coverage* is in effect after enrollees accrue enough total out-of-pocket expenses to leave the gap phase. Under this phase, beneficiaries paid cost-sharing amounts between $2.00 and $2.50 for generics from 2006 to 2010 and between $5.00 and $6.30 for brand-only drugs between 2006 and 2010.

CMS contracts with prescription-only drug plans and Medicare Advantage plans that then reimburse retail pharmacies for prescription drugs through PBMs. The plans pay retail pharmacies according to the previously noted formula (Prescription Payment = Product Cost + Dispensing Fee – Patient Cost Share).

Medication Therapy Management (MTM) Services

❽ *The role of retail pharmacies under the Part D benefit has become even more visible because of MTM services. Under the legislation, all Medicare prescription drug plans must develop MTM services*

FIGURE **9–4** | **Prescription Drug Coverage Among Medicare Beneficiaries, 2009.**

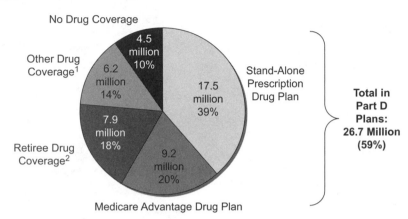

Total Number of Medicare Beneficiaries = 45.2 Million

NOTE: Percentages do not sum to 100% due to rounding. [1]Includes Veterans Affairs, retiree coverage without RDS, Indian Health Service, state pharmacy assistance programs, employer plans for active workers, Medigap, multiple sources, and other sources. [2]Includes Retiree Drug Subsidy (RDS) and FEHBP and TRICARE retiree coverage.
SOURCE: Centers for Medicare & Medicaid Services, 2009 Enrollment Information (as of February 1, 2009).

Approximately 26.7 million Medicare beneficiaries were enrolled in Medicare Part D plans as of February 2009 (the majority of these individuals, 17.5 million, are enrolled in stand-alone prescription drug plans [PDPs] while the other 9.2 million are enrolled in Medicare Advantage plans with prescription drug benefits [MA-PDs]). Of the remaining Medicare beneficiaries (approximately 18.5 million), 7.9 million have retiree prescription (Rx) coverage, 6.2 million have other prescription coverage, and 4.5 million have no coverage.

Source: This information was reprinted with permission from the Henry J. Kaiser Family Foundation. The Kaiser Family Foundation is a nonprofit private operating foundation, based in Menlo Park, California, dedicated to producing and communicating the best possible analysis and information on health issues.

for certain beneficiaries and reimburse healthcare providers for their services.[20] The goal of MTM programs is to "optimize therapeutic outcomes through improved medication use, and to reduce the risk of adverse events, including adverse drug interactions."[20] Pharmacists and other health professionals can provide MTM services, and given the nature of MTM programs, it is clear that pharmacists are ideally suited to perform such services. CMS does not provide any clear MTM guidelines apart from eligibility guidelines, which include Medicare members with multiple chronic disease states, those taking multiple medications, and

those who spend more than $4,000 in a calendar year on prescription medications.[21]

The American Pharmacists Association (APhA) and the NACDS Foundation have constructed a model framework for documenting an MTM visit.[22] A core element is the initial comprehensive medication therapy review (MTR) to determine targeted goals and to assess the appropriateness of the patient's medication therapy. At the end of the MTR, the patient will receive a "personal medication record" of his or her medications, which he or she would bring to the pharmacy for subsequent MTM sessions.[22] The patient will also be given a

TABLE 9-4	Components of the Standard Part D Benefit Between 2006 and 2010					
Standard Part D Benefit Design		2006	2007	2008	2009	2010
Deductible		$250	$265	$275	$295	$310
Initial coverage limit (start of the gap phase)		$2,250	$2,400	$2,510	$2,700	$2,830
Total member out-of-pocket costs through the gap phase		$3,600	$3,850	$4,050	$4,350	$4,550
Catastrophic Coverage Benefit Copays						
Generic/multisource drugs		$2.00	$2.15	$2.25	$2.40	$2.50
Other drugs		$5.00	$5.35	$5.60	$6.00	$6.30

Source: Data from Q1Medicare.com.[19]

"medication action plan" to resolve drug therapy issues. This plan is collaborative and designed by the patient, pharmacist, and other healthcare providers. The patient should be encouraged to bring this plan back for future MTM visits. Any referrals or interventions the patient needs can be conducted by the pharmacist in conjunction with other providers if necessary.[22]

Reimbursement for MTM services is the responsibility of individual plan sponsors, and CMS does not dictate the associated fees for these programs except that fees for MTM services are to be considered separate from dispensing fees for retail pharmacies. However, CMS does require plan sponsors to describe their fee structure as part of the application process, including an explanation of those fees attributable to MTM services. The American Medical Association's Current Procedural Terminology (CPT) panel approved three new billing codes for pharmacists to use to bill TTPs for MTM services, which went into effect in January 2008. These codes are intended to be used only for face-to-face pharmacist–patient interactions and are as follows:[23]

- 99605: Initial face-to-face assessment or intervention with a new patient; 1–15 minutes

- 99606: Initial face-to-face assessment or intervention with an established patient; 1–15 minutes
- 99607: Each additional 15 minutes spent face to face with the patient (this code should be listed separately in addition to code for primary service)

Reimbursement for MTM services appears to be generally based on $1–$2 per minute of the pharmacist's time according to a 2005 review conducted by the Lewin Group and commissioned by APhA with 11 pharmacy stakeholder organizations.[24] Fees differed by the type of pharmacy (independent, supermarket, chain). For example, initial visits at independent pharmacies ranged from $75 to $120 while follow-up visits ranged from $35 to $60. In chain pharmacies, $75 was charged for an initial assessment and $40 for each follow-up visit, while in supermarket pharmacies, $40 was charged for an initial visit, $20 for reviews, and $10 for immunizations.

REIMBURSEMENT ISSUES

❾ *One of the critical issues facing retail pharmacies is the reduction in reimbursement amounts by both public and private TPPs at a time when retail pharmacies are experiencing increasing operating expenses and medication costs.* Medicaid, PBMs, and plan sponsors are reducing reimbursement to retail pharmacies as they are the most visible component of the drug supply chain. Some key issues contribute to the shrinking margins that retail pharmacies face.

First, retail pharmacies have struggled with inadequate dispensing fees. Although Medicaid pays retail pharmacies an average dispensing fee of $4.50 per prescription, the estimated average cost of dispensing a prescription in retail pharmacies is twice that amount, at approximately $10.50 per prescription, and it varies among states: California has the highest cost of dispensing ($13.08 per prescription), and Rhode Island has the lowest ($8.50 per prescription).[7] The continuing reduction in dispensing fees for retail pharmacies has diminished their sustainability.

Second, the growth of mail-order pharmacies has also affected the sustainability of retail pharmacies. In 2003, unit sales growth for retail pharmacies increased by 1.4% while mail-order sales increased by 8.4%.[25] In addition to some of the larger PBMs owning mail-order pharmacies, PBMs are also able to create incentives for patients to purchase drugs from mail-order pharmacies by setting copays for a 90-day supply to be the same as the 30-day supply from a retail pharmacy.

◆10 *Third, an ongoing area of concern for retail pharmacies regarding reimbursement is transparency in PBM contracting and transactions.* An example is "spread pricing," whereby PBMs can earn revenue and profits through the "spread" between the amount charged to a plan sponsor (health plan or insurance company) and the amount paid to the retail pharmacy for a prescription. The spread has been estimated at $0.10 to $0.35 per transaction. In other words, for every prescription dispensed, the PBM keeps $0.10 to $0.35 per claim before it pays the pharmacy.[26] This estimate may prove to be low. Consider an example in which a PBM's contract with a network of pharmacies specifies the following arrangement for brand-name drugs: the pharmacy is to be paid AWP minus 13% plus a dispensing fee, while the PBM's contract with the plan sponsor states that the payer is to be billed AWP minus 10% plus a dispensing fee. If the AWP is $120.00, the PBM will pay the pharmacy $104.40 ($120 − [$120 × 0.13]) plus the dispensing fee. However, the PBM will charge the plan sponsor (insurance company) $108.00 ($120 − [$120 × 0.10]) plus the dispensing fee. Thus, the PBM retains the extra 3% (13% − 10%), or $3.60. A study by Siracuse et al., using data from 2002 to 2004, found that the mean ± standard deviation spread was $12.29 ± $27.93 per prescription, with a range of −$1.67 to $201.65.[27] Retail pharmacies continue to ask for more transparency in the PBM negotiation process with pharmaceutical manufacturers to limit the effect of spread pricing methods PBMs currently use, as they can affect the sustainability and profitability of their businesses.

Fourth, the Deficit Reduction Act of 2005 may result in the use of AMP as a metric for setting a federal maximum on Medicaid reimbursement for generic drugs. Retail pharmacy organizations contend that the use of the lowest AMP as the basis for generic drug reimbursement will significantly reduce reimbursement rates to retail pharmacies and may also influence Medicaid beneficiary access to pharmacies.[5] To prevent future erosion of reimbursements to community pharmacies, the NACDS and the NCPA formally announced the creation of the Coalition for Community Pharmacy Action (CCPA) in 2006. The CCPA is a fully staffed and funded permanent organization dedicated to representing community pharmacy on federal and state legislative and regulatory issues.[28]

Despite the challenges of falling reimbursement rates, there are opportunities such as the advent of MTM programs for retail pharmacies to increase revenue streams while providing services to improve the health of patients (refer to Chapter 4, "Innovation and Entrepreneurship," and Chapter 11, "Justifying and Planning Patient Care Services"). Finally, the growth of specialty pharmacy has been explosive, and currently, more than 500 biologic compounds are being evaluated by the Food and Drug Administration. Although specialty pharmacy models are emerging nationwide, for traditional retail pharmacies, the growth of these products can represent a unique opportunity to increase reimbursement streams.

SUMMARY

The advent of managed care, PBMs, and health insurance programs with prescription drug plans, along with public health programs, such as Medicare and Medicaid, have forced retail pharmacy operations to adapt and evolve to become more competitive in the marketplace. The pressure to provide cost-effective products and patient care services has forced retail pharmacies not only to be more efficient in their operations but also to develop innovative services and improve delivery of cost-effective care to patients. This chapter reviewed TPPs' reimbursement terms and rates, issues concerning PBMs, and challenges pharmacist managers and pharmacists must deal with regarding reimbursement. Those pharmacies that can provide the most value to patients and TPPs will be winners in this very competitive environment.

References

1. Hartman M, Martin A, McDonnell P, Catlin A, the National Health Expenditure Accounts Team. National health spending in 2007: slower drug spending contributes to lowest rate of overall growth since 1998. *Health Aff* 2009;28(1):246–261.

2. Kreling DH. Cost control for prescription drug programs: pharmacy benefit manager (PBM) efforts, effects, and implications. A background report prepared for the Department of Health and Human Services' Conference on Pharmaceutical Pricing Practices, Utilization, and Costs. Leavey Conference Center, Georgetown University; Washington, DC; August 8–9, 2000. Available at http://aspe.hhs.gov/health/reports/Drug-papers/Kreling-Final.htm. Accessed December 4, 2009.

3. National Community Pharmacists Association (NCPA). *2008 NCPA Digest.* Sponsored by Cardinal Health. Alexandria, VA: NCPA; 2008.

4. Congressional Budget Office. Prescription drug pricing in the private sector. January 2007. Available at: http://www.cbo.gov/ftpdocs/77xx/doc7715/01-03-PrescriptionDrug.pdf. Accessed February 4, 2009.

5. National Association of Chain Drug Stores. Implications of federal Medicaid generic drug payment reductions for state policymakers. Issue Brief, May 2007. Available at: http://www.nacds.org/user-assets/pdfs/gov_affairs/Issues/Medicaid/Implications FederalMedicaidGenericDrugPaymentReductions 2007.pdf. Accessed November 24, 2008.

6. The Kaiser Commission on Medicaid and the Uninsured. Deficit Reduction Act of 2005: implications for Medicaid. 2006. Available at: http://www.kff.org/medicaid/upload/7465.pdf. Accessed June 17, 2009.

7. Grant Thornton LLP. *Cost of Dispensing Study: An Independent Comparative Analysis of US Prescription Dispensing Costs.* Commissioned by the Coalition for Community Pharmacy Action; January 2007.

8. Lipton HL, Kreling DH, Collins T, Hertz KC. Pharmacy benefit management companies: dimensions of performance. *Annu Rev Public Health* 1999;20:361–401.

9. Kreling DH, Lipton HL, Collins TC, Hertz KC. Assessment of the impact of pharmacy benefit managers: final report to the Health Care Financing Administration, Pub L No. PB97-103683 (1996).

10. IMS Health, Top-line Industry Data, 2008 U.S. Sales and Prescription Information. Available at http://www.imshealth.com/portal/site/imshealth/menu item.a46c6d4df3db4b3d88f611019418c22a/?vgnextoid =85f4a56216a10210VgnVCM100000ed152ca2RCRD &cpsextcurrchannel=1. Accessed November 30, 2009.

11. US Department of Health and Human Services. *Testimony of Dennis Smith, CMS, on Medicaid Prescription Drug Reimbursement before the House Energy and Commerce Subcommittee on Oversight and Investigations.* December 7, 2004. Available at: www.dhhs .gov/asl/testify/t041207.html. Accessed November 21, 2008.

12. Congressional Research Service Report to Congress. *Prescription Drug Coverage Under Medicaid.* February 6, 2008, by Jean Hearne Specialist in Social Legislation, Domestic Policy Division. Available at http://aging.senate.gov/crs/medicaid16.pdf. Accessed March 21, 2009.

13. Center for Medicare and Medicaid Services. Drug rebate program. Consumer Price Index Urban Values. Available at: http://www.cms.hhs.gov/MedicaidDrug RebateProgram/04_CPIValues.asp. Accessed November 21, 2008.

14. General Accounting Office. *Report to the Committee on Energy and Commerce, House of Representatives. Med-*

icaid Outpatient Prescription Drugs: Estimated 2007 Federal Upper Limits for Reimbursement Compared with Retail Pharmacy Acquisition Costs, December 22, 2006. GAO-07-239R.

15. Kaisernetwork.org. Medicaid judge grants preliminary injunction against rule that would revise Medicaid AMP for Rx drugs, Dec 18, 2007. Available at: http://www.kaisernetwork.org/daily_reports/rep_index.cfm?hint=3&DR_ID=49481. Accessed November 24, 2008.

16. Key milestones in Medicare and Medicaid history, selected years. 1965–2003: a review. *Health Care Financ Rev* 2005–2006; 27(2):1–3.

17. Centers for Medicare and Medicaid Services. Medicare and you 2009. Available at: http://www.medicare.gov/Publications/Pubs/pdf/10050.pdf. Accessed June 16, 2009.

18. Henry J. Kaiser Family Foundation. The Medicare Prescription drug benefit: fact sheet. No. 7044-029. March 2009. Available at: http://www.kff.org/medicare/upload/7044–09.pdf. Accessed May 12, 2009.

19. Q1Medicare.com. What is the outlook for Medicare Part D 2010? Available at: http://www.q1medicare.com/PartD-The-2010-Medicare-Part-D-Outlook.php. Accessed June 17, 2009.

20. American Society of Health-System Pharmacists. CMS finalizes Part D regulations. Available at: http://www.ashp.org/import/news/HealthSystemPharmacyNews/newsarticle.aspx?id=1781. Accessed January 28, 2009.

21. American Association of Colleges of Pharmacy. Medication therapy management services definition and program criteria. Available at: http://www.aacp.org/Docs/MainNavigation/Resources/6308_MTMServicesDefinitionandProgramCriteria27-Jul-04.pdf. Accessed November 25, 2008.

22. American Pharmacists Association and National Association of Chain Drug Stores Association (NACDS). Medication therapy management in community pharmacy practice: core elements of an MTM service. Available at: http://www.aphanet.org/AM/Template.cfm?Section=Search§ion=Pharmacy_Practice_Resources1&template=/CM/ContentDisplay.cfm&ContentFileID=848. Accessed November 24, 2008.

23. National Home Infusion Association. Update to the Medication Therapy Management Service CPT Codes. 2007. Available at: http://www.nhianet.org/documents/20071010MTMCodeUpdate.pdf. Accessed June 17, 2009.

24. American Pharmacists Association. Medication therapy management services: a critical review. Available at: http://www.aphanet.org/AM/Template.cfm?Section=Home&CONTENTID=4230&TEMPLATE=/CM/ContentDisplay.cfm. Accessed November 24, 2008.

25. Federal Trade Commission. Pharmacy benefit managers: ownership of mail order pharmacies. August 2005. Available at: http://www.ftc.gov/opa/2005/09/pharmbenefit.shtm. Accessed June 21, 2009.

26. Mercer Human Resources Consulting. *Navigating the Pharmacy Benefits Marketplace*. Oakland: California Healthcare Foundation; 2003.

27. Siracuse MV, Clark BE, Garis RI. Undocumented source of pharmacy benefit manager revenue. *Am J Health-Syst Pharm* 2008;65(6):552–557.

28. Coalition for Community Pharmacy Action. Available at: http://www.rxaction.org. Accessed November 24, 2008.

Abbreviations

AAC:	actual acquisition cost
ALS:	amyotrophic lateral sclerosis
AMP:	average manufacturer's price
APhA:	American Pharmacists Association
AWP:	average wholesale price
BP:	best price
CCPA:	Coalition for Community Pharmacy Action
CMS:	Centers for Medicare and Medicaid Services
CPI-U:	consumer price index for all urban consumers
CPT:	current procedural terminology

EAC: estimated acquisition cost
FUL: federal upper limit
HMO: health maintenance organization
MAC: maximum allowable cost
MA-PD: Medicare Advantage Plans with prescription drug plans
MMA: Medicare Prescription Drug, Improvement, and Modernization Act
MTM: medication therapy management
MTR: medication therapy review
NACDS: National Association of Chain Drug Stores
NCPA: National Community Pharmacists Association
PBM: pharmacy benefit manager
PDP: prescription drug plan
Rx: prescription
TPP: third-party payer
WAC: wholesale acquisition cost

Case Scenarios

CASE ONE: Jane Smith is the new manager of the In-town Pharmacy. Recently, she received a letter from a new managed care plan that wanted In-town Pharmacy to join its network of pharmacies. The new plan covers one million lives and has contracted out its pharmacy benefit to a pharmacy benefit manager (PBM). After reading the contract, she sees that the product cost reimbursement rate for prescription drugs through this PBM will be AWP – 20%. This reimbursement rate is lower than what has been offered by other PBMs at AWP – 15%. What should Dr. Smith consider in deciding to accept this contract from a new managed care plan to join its pharmacy network?

CASE TWO: Mike Gotell is the manager for a pharmacy that serves a large Medicaid population. He has always enjoyed serving the low income population and works closely with his patients to ensure that they receive the lowest-cost, most appropriate drug. He counsels his clients to switch to comparable generics when appropriate. Recently, however, Medicaid has changed how it reimburses generic drugs, and this change could result in a loss of revenue for the pharmacy. Dr. Gotell is torn. Does he continue to counsel his clients about using generics

when appropriate, or does he try to increase the reimbursement rates for his pharmacy by using brand-name prescriptions for his Medicaid patients?

CASE THREE: Break Even Pharmacy has been a neighborhood pharmacy for several years. Recently, the pharmacy has experienced declining revenues due to PBMs' and Medicaid's reductions in reimbursement rates. Break Even Pharmacy is struggling to stay open. Recently, Dave Brown, the owner, has been approached by the School of Pharmacy to develop an MTM program with his pharmacists and School of Pharmacy faculty. The program would consist of a series of face-to-face consultations with Medicare patients who qualify for these services to optimize their medication therapies. Given the bleak financial situation for Break Even Pharmacy, what should Dr. Brown consider in deciding whether to spend more resources to develop this MTM program?

CASE FOUR: Kate Richardson is a graduate student at the School of Pharmacy and is conducting research on the cost of hypertensive drugs at retail pharmacies in different geographic regions. She does not have access to the amounts that retail pharmacies are charged for their drugs. How can she assess the cost of these hypertensive drugs?

CASE FIVE: Tom Jones is a pharmacist at a health plan and has been tasked to develop an MTM program for the Medicare population. CMS outlines broad criteria for Medicare beneficiaries who could be eligible for an MTM program, one of which is an expected annual drug expenditure of $4,000 or more in a calendar year. How can Dr. Jones estimate what a member's annual drug spending will be for the next calendar year?

Additional Resources Available Online!

Visit the Student Companion Web site at http://healthprofessions.jbpub.com/pharmacymanagement for interactive study tools and additional resources.

See www.rxugace.com to learn how you can obtain continuing pharmacy education for this content.

CENTS AND SENSIBILITY

UNDERSTANDING THE NUMBERS

KEITH NICOLAS HERIST, PharmD, CPA

WILLIAM E. WADE, PharmD, FASHP, FCCP

LEARNING OBJECTIVES

After completing the chapter, the reader will be able to

1. Explain the accounting entity assumption and the importance of accounting.

2. Describe the periodicity concept and the six principles of *going concern, objectivity, conservatism, consistency, matching,* and *materiality* and their role in accounting.

3. Differentiate between real and nominal accounts and where their balances are reflected in the financial statements.

4. Describe the importance of the accounting equation and the concept of double-entry accounting.

5. Master the relationship between debits and credits and their effect on nominal and real accounts.

6. Compare and contrast the major components of a balance sheet and income statement.

7. Describe the utility of financial ratios.

8. Calculate the inventory turnover, a basic financial ratio used by pharmacist managers.

9. Differentiate between the three inventory, cost-flow assumptions, and their effect on the balance sheet and income statement.

10. Identify different types of budgets and cite the five key purposes of budgeting systems.

KEY CONCEPTS

◆ Accounting is often referred to as the universal language of business because all organizations use accounting information to facilitate financial decision making. Accounting is recording, reporting, and analyzing financial transactions of accounting entities, defined as organizations, companies, institutions, or beings that exist for various operational, legal, or taxation purposes.

❷ A financial statement is a written report that quantitatively describes the financial well-being of a company. Four basic financial statements include (1) the balance sheet, (2) the income statement, (3) the statement of owner's equity, and (4) the statement of cash flows. The balance sheet is an itemized statement that lists total assets and total liabilities of a company and is used to portray the company's net worth at any moment in time. The income statement records the company's revenues and expenses for a specified period; the basic income statement equation is: Revenues – Expenses = Net Income. The statement of owner's equity reports how a company's retained earnings have changed over some time period. The purpose of the statement of cash flows is to report all major cash receipts and cash payments during a period and is used to report the short-term viability of a company.

❸ The principles of *going concern*, *objectivity*, *conservatism*, *consistency*, *matching*, and *materiality* are used when accounting systems are developed, implemented, evaluated, and maintained.

❹ Transactions are the basic exchanges of economic considerations between two entities. Although most transactions occur between a company and its customers, there are also many other transactions, such as transactions between different departments within a company.

❺ Accrual basis accounting requires that revenue and expenses are recorded in the period in which they are earned or incurred regardless of whether cash is received or disbursed in that period. However, cash basis accounting is defined as recording revenue and expenses in the period they are actually received or expended.

❻ The accounting equation is a mathematical expression used to describe the relationship between assets, liabilities, and owner's equity accounts of an entity: Assets = Liabilities + Owner's Equity. This equation is made up of real accounts and can be modified/restated as follows: Assets – Liabilities = Owner's Equity.

❼ The process of recording debits and credits is called posting. Simply stated, for every debit entry, there must be a corresponding credit entry; thus, there must be two entries for every transaction recorded in a general journal or the book of original entry. Fortunately, many software programs are used to create and maintain accounting records.

❽ A financial ratio is computed by dividing one financial statement item by another, allowing users to evaluate a company's performance by focusing on specific relationships between various items on the balance sheet and income statement. Three common types of ratios that can be calculated and are used in pharmacy include (1) solvency, (2) liquidity, and (3) profitability. Solvency evaluates a company's long-term ability to meet all financial obligations, while liquidity evaluates the same items in the short term. Profitability measures the company's ability to make money.

❾ The solvency ratio said to be the most important in inventory management is inventory turnover, which is used to assess efficiency in inventory control and is calculated as follows: Cost of Goods Sold ÷ Average Inventory.

❿ Budgetary accounting measures the cost of planned acquisitions and the use of economic resources in the future. The most common type of budget is an operating budget, or forecasted income statement. Closely related to the operating budget is an operating expense budget, which focuses only on a department's expenses for the forecast period. A zero-based budget is perhaps the most difficult to prepare while providing the most detailed information and assumptions. In developing a zero-based budget, the prior period revenues, expenses, or costs are ignored when establishing the future period performance.

INTRODUCTION

◆ *Accounting is often referred to as the universal language of business because all organizations use accounting information to facilitate financial decision making.* Just as pharmacists use specific patient data information in their decision-making process for proper patient care, financial information is critical to enable pharmacist managers and pharmacies to perform optimally. Pharmacist managers exist in all practice settings and must be able to manage a wide range of financial tasks, including developing drug **formularies**, financing equipment purchases, improving operating efficiencies, negotiating insurance contracts for reimbursements, and managing staffing and payroll expenses. Even at the individual patient level, pharmacists are engaged in basic economic decision making. For example, pharmacists have made a substantial impact in the cost-effective prescribing of medications. The fundamentals addressed in this chapter provide necessary tools to understand common financial and accounting terminology and processes as they relate to pharmacy; these tools include **financial statements** prepared in accordance with **generally accepted accounting principles** (GAAPs), **ratio analysis**, and **budgeting**.

ACCOUNTING FUNDAMENTALS

◆*Accounting is recording, reporting, and analyzing financial transactions of accounting entities, defined as organizations, companies, institutions, or beings that exist for various operational, legal, or taxation purposes.* The accounting entity assumption recognizes that information derived from operations of an accounting entity (i.e., company) belongs to the accounting entity and is separate from the owners, employees, and others. A company is an organized group of people with a purpose to perform an activity, either for profit or nonprofit. The three basic legal structures under which a company operates are (1) *sole proprietorship*, (2) *partnership*, or (3) *corporation*. A sole proprietorship is owned exclusively by one person, whereas a partnership has two or more owners. The corporation is the most common form of business enterprise. When a company incorporates, or forms a corporation, the ownership of the company is divided into equal units called shares, or stock. The shares are sold to **shareholders** who become the actual owners of the corporation. Major decisions affecting the management of the company are voted on by **stockholders**, and each share of stock is assigned voting and other rights. Two classes of stock are common and preferred. Common stock is often the most frequently issued and usually has voting rights but is not awarded automatic **dividends**. Preferred stock usually is nonvoting but has automatic specified dividend payments. Major benefits of the incorporation of a company, while different from sole proprietorships and partnerships, are that shareholders are not financially liable for more than the dollar amount that they have invested in the purchase of shares, and **creditors**, by law, cannot file a claim against a shareholder's personal **assets**. Many sole proprietorships and partnerships currently form as limited liability companies (LLC), which combine the taxation benefits of a sole proprietorship and partnership with the limited liability aspects of a corporation.

A company's accounting system is the set of procedures and controls used to identify relevant transactions, or events, within the company. Accounting systems prepare source documents, which accurately reflect the economic outcomes of transactions. All relevant information within a company must be reported to investors, creditors, and management, and this process is referred to as financial reporting. Essential to every accounting system is an internal control system (generated by the top management of every company) that consists of all policies and procedures used to protect company assets, ensure accurate accounting practices, and promote efficient operations of the company.

Financial statements are used to provide critical company financial information to both internal and external users. Internal users are composed of various levels of management within the company, whereas stockholders, lenders, and potential investors are common external users. ❷ *A financial statement is a written report that quantitatively describes the financial well-being of a company.* It is the summary of all the transactions of a company for the entire accounting period. Generally accepted accounting principles, a recognized set of accounting principles, standards, and procedures, guide the preparation of financial statements. Authoritative standards are set by policy boards, most notably the **Financial Accounting Standards Board** (FASB). ❷ *Four basic financial statements include (1) the* **balance sheet***, (2) the* **income statement***, (3) the* **statement of owner's equity** *(also known as statement of retained earnings and statement of shareholder's equity), and (4) the* **statement of cash flows***.* Each of these statements will be described in this chapter.

Managers often oversee the operations and accounting systems of departments responsible for generating reports to evaluate performance. These individuals are responsible for planning, organizing, and controlling resources to ensure that an organization's goals are met. Managerial accounting refers to the various reports and supplemental information supplied to internal users of the accounting system's information. Departments operate with the intent of producing a profit or not (i.e., cost centers), depending on the department's purpose and its place in the overall organizational structure. Profit centers are those sections of a company responsible for producing profits (e.g., most pharmacies). Cost centers, however, are non-revenue-generating sections of a company that are considered critical to the optimal performance of the company's overall operations (e.g., administration outside of profit center departments).

Accounting Period

Because results ultimately have to be reported, determination of an appropriate accounting period over which results are produced is essential. The periodicity concept states that each accounting period has an economic activity associated with it, and that the activity can be measured, accounted for, and reported on. An accounting period is the period for which accounts are prepared and is usually defined as one year or the fiscal year. By convention, the calendar year (January 1 to December 31) is most often used as the accounting period; however, an accounting period may be of any duration and begin and end on any date (e.g., July 1 to June 30). One major determinant of a fiscal year or an accounting period is the natural start and end of a company's revenue process. This

start and end time is also referred to as an operating cycle. For example, assume a company produces an annual influenza vaccine. Because the "flu season" in the United States is usually from November through April each year,[1] inventory levels need to be sufficient to meet demand, which usually begins in late September. As most vaccines are administered by December, a more representative business cycle may begin on May 1 and end on April 30 of the following year (as April 30 coincides with the end of flu season), rather than a calendar year accounting period. Since an entire year is a long time for internal management to operate without financial statements or operating reports, many companies use the **time period principle** and prepare interim financial statements.

Principles of Going Concern, Objectivity, Conservatism, Consistency, Matching, and Materiality

❸ *The principles of going concern, objectivity, conservatism, consistency, matching, and materiality are used when accounting systems are developed, implemented, evaluated, and maintained.* Before discussing how these principles are employed in pharmacy, we will briefly define each:

- The *going concern* principle simply means that any given company plans to remain in existence for the foreseeable future and operate for the long term. The company will maintain proper accounting records from the date it is established to the date it is liquidated; therefore, decisions will be made from the perspective of the long-term interest and viability of the company.
- The *objectivity* principle states that accounting entries will be recorded on the basis of objective evidence. Under this principle, all accounting entries are based on objective fact, not on personal opinions or feelings.
- The *conservatism* principle states that accounting estimates, evaluations, and opinions should be made to neither overstate nor understate the business activities of the company. These estimates, evaluations, and opinions should be fair and reasonable so that decisions will not be made from

financial statements that were prepared unrealistically.

- The *consistency* principle assures financial statement users that similar measurement concepts and procedures for related items within the company's financial statements are applied for the entire accounting period; in addition, the same accounting procedures will be used by the company in future periods. When a change of accounting procedures is encountered from one period to another, an explanation of the change must be clearly noted in the financial statements.
- The *matching* principle is fundamental to accounting and is closely tied to the accounting periods discussed. The matching principle requires that all **expenses** directly associated with the production of **revenues** be reported within the same period on the income statement. The matching process is essential to account for differences in time between earning and receiving revenue, as well as incurring expenses before their actual payment.
- The *materiality* principle acknowledges the significance of various decisions and their ultimate effects on the financial statements, given the magnitude of a company's operations. The primary purpose of financial statements is to fairly present the results of a company's operations, not to assure the user that each and every transaction was recorded properly. This is an important distinction because many companies have millions of small transactions that make up their results but do not individually affect the overall fairness of the reported results. Generally accepted accounting principles (GAAPs) help guide the recording of all material transactions; an item is deemed to be material if the user of the financial statement would make a different decision based on the omission or inclusion of the item.

Transactions

🔸 *Transactions are the basic exchanges of economic considerations between two entities. Although most transactions occur between a company and its customers, there are also many other transactions,* *such as transactions between different departments within a company.* All transactions should be accurately measured and recorded. To facilitate this, the money measurement concept stipulates that all business transactions must be expressed in monetary terms. If an event, or transaction, cannot be measured in these terms, it will not be included in accounting records. In trying to convert certain transactions and events into monetary terms, the six principles of going concern, objectivity, conservatism, consistency, matching, and materiality should be applied.

Real and Nominal Accounts

Another important concept essential to understanding financial statements is the theory of real accounts and nominal accounts. Remember, a company is assumed to exist forever (going concern principle); therefore, real accounts, or permanent accounts, are never closed or reduced to a zero balance. They always exist and have a cumulative balance. The ending balance in real accounts represents the cumulative effect of all transactions recorded in that account since the company began operations. Real accounts are found on the balance sheet and statement of owner's equity, and examples are **cash**, **accounts receivable**, **accounts payable**, and **retained earnings**. However, nominal accounts, or temporary accounts, are closed out and reduced to a zero balance at the end of each period and begin accumulating a balance in the next period. They are found on the income statement and include revenue accounts and expense accounts.

Accrual and Cash Basis of Accounting

🔸 *Accrual basis accounting requires that revenue and expenses are recorded in the period in which they are earned or incurred regardless of whether cash is received or disbursed in that period.* This form of accounting is generally used to prepare financial statements for external users since it conforms to GAAP. An example of accrual basis accounting can be seen in a typical community pharmacy. When prescriptions are paid for by a third-party insurance carrier, the expected payment is recorded immediately as revenue, even though the actual cash reimbursement may not be received for several weeks. The cost, or expense, of the medications is also recorded, whether payment to the medication supplier has been made or not. ❺ *However, cash basis accounting is defined as recording revenue and expenses in the period they are actually received or expended.* Therefore, continuing with the previous example, no revenue would be shown for the dispensed prescriptions until the actual reimbursement from the third-party insurance carrier is received several weeks later, and the medication cost of the prescriptions would be recorded when the actual payment is made to the vendor. Use of cash basis accounting generally is not considered to conform with GAAP, as it does not appropriately reflect the matching principle. Given the oversimplicity of cash basis accounting compared with accrual basis accounting, cash basis accounting is only used in selected situations, such as small companies and, when permitted, for income tax reporting.

The Accounting Equation

Understanding the accounting equation is the last step in mastering the development of financial statements. ❻ *The accounting equation is a mathematical expression used to describe the relationship between assets, **liabilities**, and **owner's equity** accounts of an entity:*

$$Assets = Liabilities + Owner's\ Equity$$

Note that this equation is made up of real accounts, or the accounts that exist in perpetuity and are never closed. It can be modified and restated as follows:

$$Assets - Liabilities = Owner's\ Equity$$

The owner's equity balance includes the net result of all transactions recorded in all nominal accounts.

Debits, Credits, and T Accounts

An understanding of double-entry accounting, a system of recording transactions in a way that maintains the equality of the accounting equation, is essential to follow the path of transactions included in financial statements. The double-entry accounting system records each transaction as both a debit and a credit and forms the basis for a journal entry. Journal entries are the basic elements of the accounting cycle. Recording transactions and their monetary value into accounting

records summarizes information contained on the source documents (bills, receipts, invoices) of each transaction and maintains their traceability.

A debit (abbreviated dr) is defined as an entry on the left side of an account and constitutes an addition to an asset or expense account. Conversely, a debit constitutes a decrease from a liability, revenue, or net worth account. A credit (abbreviated cr) is an entry on the right side of an account. Because the accounting equation must always balance, it is imperative that a credit perform the opposite function of a debit. Therefore, a credit constitutes an addition to a liability, a revenue, or a net worth account, and a deduction from an asset or expense account. **Table 10–1** provides a summary of the effect of debits and credits on balance sheet and income statement accounts.

❼ *The process of recording debits and credits is called posting. Simply stated, for every debit entry, there must be a corresponding credit entry; thus, there must be two entries for every transaction recorded in a general journal or the book of original entry.* The general journal is commonly used to keep track of these entries until they are summarized in the general ledger, which contains all of a company's financial account balances. The chart of accounts is a list of the names of all the financial accounts contained in the general ledger and is used to assist in properly classifying each transaction to the appropriate account.

The format of a general journal is columnar, with a separate column for the date, accounts used, reference number, debit, and credit. Recording an entry begins with the date and then the name of the account to be debited, along with the amount of the debit shown in the "debit" column. Next, the name of the account to be credited is listed, with the amount of the credit shown in the "credit" column. Beneath the account names is a brief description of the details of the transaction resulting in the journal entry. The reference column is left blank until these journal entries are actually recorded, or posted, in the general ledger. At that time, the account numbers of the individual accounts used are referenced. See **Table 10–2** for a sample general journal.

To simplify the effect of numerous entries and their effects on different accounts, one may choose

TABLE 10–1 Effects of Debits and Credits on Accounts

Accounting Equation
Assets = Liabilities + Owner's Equity

DEBITS	=	CREDITS
INCREASE assets		DECREASE assets
INCREASE expenses		DECREASE expenses
DECREASE liabilities		INCREASE liabilities
DECREASE owner's equity		INCREASE owner's equity
DECREASE revenues		INCREASE revenues

Note: A simple way to remember which accounts are increased by debits and decreased by credits is the mnemonic DEA. Remembering **DEA,** you can easily remember **D**ebits increase **E**xpense and **A**sset accounts. Given that the accounting equation has the measure of equality, then the converse is true for credits as they decrease expense and asset accounts. Remember that accounting is the universal language of business, and as such, all companies use the same rules when making entries. So, if the general ledger of Company A indicates an account receivable from Company B for $500, Company B will have an accounts payable to Company A on their own general ledger.

TABLE 10–2 Sample General Journal

Dawgtown Drugs, Inc.
General Journal

Date	Account Name and Description	Reference No.	Debit	Credit
10/26/XX	Inventory		$8,562.13	
10/26/XX	Cash; check 2929			$8,562.13
	To record receipt of drug order and subsequent payment			
10/28/XX	Cash		$6,527.14	
10/28/XX	Prescription dept. sales			$4,857.25
10/28/XX	Photo dept. sales			$565.23
10/28/XX	Front store dept. sales			$1,104.66
	To record cash sales			
10/31/XX	Payroll Expense—pharmacist		$500.00	
10/31/XX	Cash; check 2930			$500.00
	To record wages for pharmacist for the day			

to use a T account. **Table 10–3** illustrates the three basic elements of T accounts: (1) a title, (2) a left side (for debits), and (3) a right side (for credits). For each transaction, an entry in the T account is recorded on the appropriate side of the "T." When the accounting period is closed, a line is drawn across the bottom of the page. All debits and credits, including any beginning balance, are totaled. The lowest total is subtracted from the highest total, and the net remainder is listed as the ending balance. Remember, there are five basic types of accounts, and each has an expected debit or credit balance: (1) assets (debit), (2) liabilities (credit), and (3) owner's equity (credit), which are real accounts, and (4) revenues (credit) and (5) expenses (debit), which are nominal accounts. ❼*Fortunately, many software programs are used to create and maintain accounting records.*

FINANCIAL STATEMENTS

With the foundations of the important principles and concepts for basic accounting and information recording in place, translation into actual financial statements can begin. As stated previously, ❷ *the four basic financial statements used by companies include (1) the balance sheet, (2) the income statement, (3) the statement of owner's equity, and (4) the statement of cash flows.*

The Balance Sheet

❷ *The balance sheet, sometimes called the statement of financial position, is an itemized statement that lists total assets and total liabilities of a company and is used to portray the company's net worth at any moment in time.* Therefore, the balance sheet is always dated "as of" a specific date. The amounts shown on a balance sheet are generally the historic cost of items (amount actually paid) and not their current values. When cost is difficult to determine, as is often the case if a gift is received, or trading of services occurs between two entities, the asset is valued at the **fair market value**. The use of published references and appraisals can help in determining an appropriate fair market value. This process ensures the proper application of the principles of *objectivity*, *conservatism*, and *consistency*.

As illustrated in **Table 10–4**, assets are listed at the top of the balance sheet. An asset is anything owned by an individual or company that has commercial or exchange value. Assets are either tangible or intangible and may consist of specific property or claims against others. Notice that the order of assets ranges from current to long term. A current asset is reasonably expected to be converted to cash, purchased by customers, or consumed during the company's operating cycle, which for most accounting entities is one year. Therefore, cash and **cash equivalents** begin the listing of assets. Inventory, the goods a company owns and expects to sell in its operations, is classified as current assets, as quantities are usually kept at a level needed for less than one operating cycle. Continuing down the balance sheet are the long-term assets, usually named property, plant, and equipment, that are expected to benefit the company over several operating cycles. Examples of long-term assets are the company's building, computer systems, furniture, and fixtures. According to the matching principle, the "usage" of these long-term assets must be recorded in each accounting period as depreciation expense, determined by allocating the cost of buildings and other equipment to periods in which they are used. Because depreciation expense represents the cost of using an asset over several accounting periods, a real account, called accumulated depreciation, contains the total depreciation incurred since the acquisition of long-term assets and represents a reduction in the historical cost. The net difference between historical cost and accumulated depre-

TABLE **10–3**	**Elements of a T Account**
Account Name	
Debit Side	**Credit Side**
Beginning balance	Transaction activity
Transaction activity	
Ending balance	

TABLE **10–4**	**Sample Balance Sheet**

Dawgtown Drugs, Inc.
Balance Sheet
December 31, 20XX

Assets:		
Cash and cash equivalents	$20,000	
Accounts receivable, net	$15,000	
Inventories	$70,000	
Total current assets		**$105,000**
Property and equipment, net	$17,000	
Total long-term assets		**$17,000**
Total assets		**$122,000**
Liabilities:		
Accounts payable	$5,000	
Accrued expenses[a]	$2,000	
Total current liabilities		**$7,000**
Mortgage payable	$14,000	
Total long-term liabilities		**$14,000**
Total liabilities		**$21,000**
Common stock	$10,000	
Retained earnings	$91,000	
Total owner's equity		**$101,000**
Total liabilities and owner's equity		**$122,000**

[a]Accrued expenses: Expenses incurred during a defined accounting period for which payment is delayed.

ciation represents the depreciated value of the long-term assets and is referred to as the net book value.

Continuing down the balance sheet, the accounts on the right side of the accounting equation are listed, beginning with liabilities. Liabilities include loans, expenses, or any other item that must be paid or otherwise honored by an entity. Again, the current and long-term designations are used based on the expected date of maturity or when the actual payment is due. A **mortgage payable** is an example of a long-term liability. Following liabilities on the balance sheet, we have owner's equity. ❻ *The accounting equation defining owner's equity is*

Total Assets – Total Liabilities = Owner's Equity

Components of this total amount are shown separately. Retained earnings are defined as the cumulative profits of the company that have not been paid out to the shareholders as of the balance sheet date. These earnings have been "retained" by the company. At the end of each accounting period, when the nominal accounts contained in the income statement are closed, the net income (or loss) is posted to this account, as either a credit or debit, depending on the results of operations. This account is not a pool of money, even though it reflects historical profits and losses. Profits are not composed of cash, because of the accrual basis accounting concept, which records revenues and expenses in the period in which they provide economic benefit and does not reflect the actual movement of cash.

The Income Statement

Because companies have a natural operating cycle, nominal accounts (revenue and expense accounts) are used to produce the income statement, also known as the profit and loss statement (P&L). ❷ *The income statement records the company's revenues and expenses for a specified period,* *and therefore is dated "for the period ended" of a specific date. All the cumulative transactions of the nominal accounts for a specific time are closed at the end of each period. A sample income statement is shown in* **Table 10–5**.

The basic income statement equation is as follows:

$$Revenues - Expenses = Net\ Income$$

TABLE **10–5**	**Sample Income Statement**	

Dawgtown Drugs, Inc. Income Statement For the Year Ended December 31, 20XX		
Net sales		**$2,000,000**
Cost of goods sold		**$1,550,000**
Gross profit		**$450,000**
Operating expenses		
Salaries[a]	$300,000	
Rent	$40,000	
Utilities	$15,000	
Insurance	$6,000	
Depreciation	$4,000	
Legal and accounting	$5,000	
Advertising	$2,000	
Total general, administrative, and selling		**$372,000**
Operating profit		**$78,000**
Interest expense		**$3,000**
Income tax expense		**$25,000**
Net income		**$50,000**

Note: The income statement summarizes a company's transactions that affect the nominal accounts for a specific period. The order of the accounts listed follows the relative size of the transactions; therefore, net sales will always be listed first. Following net sales, cost of goods sold (COGS) represents the largest use of resources to generate the net sales. Gross profit follows as the amount remaining after COGS is deducted from net sales. Next are the operating expenses, which represent the indirect costs of operating the company to support the generation of the net sales amount. These accounts, while having some commonality between all companies, are specifically tailored to each individual company and the order of their listing may vary slightly between different companies. After all general, administrative, and selling expenses have been listed, another subtotal is shown, called operating profit, which represents the results of operations before the major expenses of interest and income taxes. Interest and income taxes are shown as separate line items because of their importance to the overall efficiency of the company's operations. Net income represents the remaining amount of net sales after all expenses of the company have been presented.
[a]Salaries (payroll, which includes salaries, benefits, etc.).

Revenues, also referred to as sales, are listed at the top of the income statement and represent the inflows of assets from selling goods or providing services to customers. When presented on the income statement, net sales is used, which reflects any discounts, allowances, or sale returns incurred in generating the total sales. Expenses are costs incurred in the normal operating cycle of a company to generate its revenues and represent the amount of assets or services used during that period. The largest expense account is usually cost of goods sold (COGS), which represents the cost of the inventory sold in generating the revenues. Subtracting COGS from net sales results in the gross profit (also known as **gross margin**) and represents the total revenue remaining for other expenses of the accounting period. After all of the operating expenses (known as general, administrative, and selling) have been deducted from gross profit, the resulting balance is called operating profit and reflects the results of operations before **interest expense** and **income tax expense**. After deducting these two expenses, which are shown on separate lines, net income (also called profit, or earnings) is determined. Net income is the amount earned after recording all expenses necessary to generate the sales recorded. When total expenses exceed total revenues, a net loss is incurred.

The Statement of Owner's Equity

❷ *The statement of owner's equity (**Table 10–6**) reports how a company's retained earnings have changed over some time period and is dated "for the period ended" of an accounting period.* The statement is a **reconciliation** of the retained earnings balance at the beginning of the period with the retained earnings balance at the end of the period. Major transactions affecting this statement are the payment of dividends and net income or loss.

The Statement of Cash Flows

❷ *The purpose of the statement of cash flows is to report all major cash receipts (inflows) and cash payments (outflows) during a period.* This includes separately identifying the cash flows related to operating, investing, and financing activities. The statement of cash flows is analogous to reconciling a company's beginning cash balance, accounting for all the "ins" and "outs" for the period, and reconciling to the ending cash balance on the balance sheet. Only sources and uses of cash are included in the statement of cash flows; noncash items are excluded. Because both nominal and real accounts affect cash over an operating cycle, the statement of cash flows is dated "for the period ended" of a specific date. ❷ *The statement of cash flows may be*

TABLE **10–6**	**Sample Statement of Retained Earnings**

	Dawgtown Drugs, Inc. Statement of Retained Earnings for the Year Ended December 31, 20XX		
Retained earnings	**Beginning of year**		**$41,000**
Net income		$50,000	
Dividends		$0	
Retained earnings	**End of year**		**$91,000**

Note: The statement of retained earnings actually serves as the transition from the income statement to the balance sheet. The statement is simply a rolling forward of the prior year retained earnings balance, with the current year's transactions, which affect the retained earnings account shown. For most companies, the current year net income and dividends paid to shareholders represents the entire year's activity.

TABLE **10–7**	Sample Statement of Cash Flows—Direct Method

Dawgtown Drugs, Inc.
Statement of Cash Flows
for the Year Ended December 31, 20XX

Cash provided (or used) by:	
Operating activities	$9,000
Investing activities	$3,000
Financing activities	$0
Net increase (decrease) in cash and cash equivalents	**$12,000**
Cash and cash equivalents at beginning of year	**$8,000**
Cash and cash equivalents at end of year	**$20,000**

used as an analytical tool to assess the short-term viability of a company. Potential external financial statement users, such as lenders, investors, and even employees, all have different interests when reading this statement.

The two methods of preparing a statement of cash flows are direct and indirect. The direct method reports gross cash receipts and payments and then reconciles the beginning and ending cash balances. In contrast, the indirect method begins with net income, makes adjustments for all noncash items, and then adjusts for all cash items and ends with the current cash position. Under either method, the statement of cash flows adjusts net income, as determined by the accrual basis of accounting, to a cash basis of accounting and presents the results of a company's operations in terms of how cash was used during an accounting period. The sample statement of cash flows displayed in **Table 10–7** shows the reconciliation of the prior year's cash balance to that of the current year and attempts to provide answers to the following questions:

- How does the company obtain its cash?
- Where does a company spend its cash?
- What explains the change in the cash balance?

Cash inflows and outflows are determined in the three major categories shown in Table 10–7: (1) operating activities, (2) investing activities, and (3) financing activities. Operating activities include those transactions and events that determine net income, revenue generation, and associated expenses. Investing activities represent those transactions and events that affect long-term assets, most notably the purchase of long-term assets. Financing activities identify those transactions and events that influence long-term liabilities and owner's equity. Transactions that involve the company's owners and creditors, such as cash received from issuing debt or repayment of amounts borrowed, are also shown in the financing activities section.

AN EXAMPLE: DAWGTOWN DRUGS

To bring the principles, concepts, and definitions discussed thus far together in an understandable manner, a community pharmacy can provide a good example. The activities for a typical day at a community pharmacy will be recorded using T accounts, and the net income for that day will be determined. Because the income statement reflects any period, one day is sufficient, and **Table 10–8**

| TABLE **10–8** | **Sample Daily Income Statement from T Accounts** |

Dawgtown Drugs Income Statement for the Day Ended October 31, 20XX from T Accounts

REAL ACCOUNTS

	Cash		Inventory		Accounts Payable	
Beginning Balance	3,000		15,000			2,000
(A) Record daily sales.	4,000					
(B) Record cost of inventory sold.				3,100		
(C) Record the inventory received.			1,200			1,200
(D) Record RPh wages.						600
Ending Balance	7,000		13,100			3,800

NOMINAL ACCOUNTS

	Sales		Cost of Goods Sold		Payroll Expense	
Beginning Balance		0	0		0	
(A) Record daily sales.		4,000				
(B) Record cost of inventory sold.			3,100			
(D) Record RPh wages.					600	
Ending Balance		4,000	3,100		600	

Daily Transactions to Be Recorded for the Day

(A) Prescription sales totaled $4,000. Dawgtown only accepts cash.

(B) Gross margin for Dawgtown is 22.5%; cost of goods sold is 77.5% of sales.

(C) Inventory costing $1,200 received from wholesaler; charged to Dawgtown.

(D) A temporary pharmacist worked; payment of $600 for his services will be at a later date.

NET INCOME (LOSS) for the ONE-DAY Period

Total sales	$4,000
Cost of goods sold	3,100
Payroll expense	600
Net income	$300

Note: PRh = pharmacist.

illustrates the recording of the day's transactions. Beginning balances have been assumed for the real accounts. The nominal accounts, by definition, start with a zero balance on October 31, 20XX (this is the beginning and ending of the accounting period).

You have offered your services as a licensed pharmacist to Dawgtown Drugs, a community pharmacy, for October 31, 20XX. Your shift at the pharmacy will be for the entire day at an agreed rate of $600, to be paid next week. Dawgtown Drugs is usually busy, and at the end of the day, the total prescription sales were $4,000. All sales are in cash, as this pharmacy accepts no third-party insurance plans. Using T accounts, transactions representing the day's activities will be recorded. For simplicity, the daily prescription sales are summarized and recorded as simply one summary transaction of $4,000. The prescription sales entry will be to a debit to the cash T account for $4,000 and a credit of $4,000 to the sales T account and is noted as transaction (A). Once the daily sales activity has been recorded, the matching principle requires the recording of the inventory. Dawgtown Drugs has a gross margin of 22.5%; therefore, the COGS percentage will be 77.5% of sales, or $3,100. A debit entry to the COGS T account for $3,100 is recorded, with a corresponding credit of $3,100 to the inventory T account as shown in transaction (B). When new inventory is delivered to Dawgtown Drugs from the **wholesaler**, the receipt of this inventory must be reflected in the accounts. Assume the shipment received on October 31, 20XX, was valued at $1,200. Dawgtown Drugs has an account with the wholesaler and will eventually make payment for this inventory shipment. Recording the transaction, noted as (C), requires a debit of $1,200 to the inventory T account and a credit to the accounts payable T account. Next, the matching principle dictates that all costs associated with generating revenue be matched with the expenses necessary to generate that revenue. Therefore, the expense for you, as the pharmacist, known as payroll expense, must be included in the net income calculation. Again, for simplicity, all other payroll for the day is ignored. Dawgtown's owner will write a check for you for $600 when he returns next week. Transaction (D) records this expense (and future

payment) with a debit entry of $600 to the payroll expense T account along with the credit entry of $600 to the accounts payable T account. For simplicity, all other transactions related to the day's operations are ignored, such as utilities, rent, overhead, and payroll tax expenses.

To calculate the net income for October 31, 20XX, all the activity in the six T accounts must be summarized and the ending balances noted. Net income is calculated as follows:

$$\text{Sales} - \text{Cost of Goods Sold} - \text{Expenses} = \text{Net Income}$$

Completing this equation noted with the ending T account balances, the following result is obtained: $4,000 – $3,100 – $600 = $300.

The $1,200 inventory shipment received on October 31, 20XX, has no effect on the day's net income since inventory is a real account and, therefore, has no effect on the expense accounts until it is actually sold. Conversely, the credit entry of $1,200 to the accounts payable account also has no effect on the determination of net income, as neither will affect the ultimate cash payment of the accounts payable. Of course, the income statements of many pharmacies are much more complex. **Table 10–9** shows the national average of independent pharmacy income statements, reported on a percentage of sales basis, for 2005–2007.[2]

T account analysis is useful in many different instances encountered each day. For instance, many banks provide their customers with **automated teller machine** (ATM) cards, also known as debit cards, which have become an essential part of completing daily transactions in lieu of carrying large amounts of cash. In T account analysis, cash decreases the balance, and a credit entry is necessary to the T account labeled "Cash," both on the customer's accounts as well as on the bank's accounts. As can be seen in **Table 10–10**, when customer cash is deposited in the bank, the bank records a debit in the T account for cash and the corresponding credit to the T account for customer accounts payable, a liability on the bank's accounts. A withdrawal of cash results in a credit entry to the T account for cash, but a debit entry must be recorded to the T account for customer accounts payable. Note, the name "debit card" comes from

TABLE 10–9 Historical Income Statement Analysis of Average Independent Pharmacies

National Average of Independent Pharmacy Income Statements

	2005		2006		2007	
	$	%	$	%	$	%
Prescription sales	3,210,239	92.1	3,169,010	92.4	3,344,896	92.8
All other sales	275,363	7.9	260,654	7.6	259,517	7.2
Total sales	**3,485,602**	**100.00**	**3,429,664**	**100.00**	**3,604,413**	**100.00**
Cost of goods sold						
Prescription costs	2,481,749	71.2	2,486,506	72.5	2,605,991	72.3
All other costs	181,251	5.2	161,195	4.7	162,199	4.5
Total cost of goods sold	2,662,000	76.4	2,647,701	77.2	2,768,190	76.8
Gross profit	**822,602**	**23.6**	**781,963**	**22.8**	**836,223**	**23.2**
Operating expenses						
Payroll expenses						
Salaries, wages	404,330	11.6	408,130	11.9	425,321	11.8
Payroll taxes and benefits	62,741	1.8	58,304	1.7	68,483	1.9
Payroll expenses	**467,071**	**13.4**	**466,434**	**13.6**	**493,804**	**13.7**
Other operating expenses						
Advertising	17,428	0.5	17,148	0.5	18,022	0.5
Insurance	13,942	0.4	13,718	0.4	10,813	0.3
Supplies—containers, labels	13,942	0.4	13,718	0.4	14,417	0.4
Office postage	3,485	0.1	3,429	0.1	3,604	0.1
Delivery service	6,971	0.2	6,859	0.2	7,208	0.2
Pharmacy computer expense	13,942	0.4	10,288	0.3	14,417	0.4
Rent	41,827	1.2	41,155	1.2	43,252	1.2
Utilities, telephone	17,428	0.5	17,148	0.5	18,022	0.5
All other operating expenses	97,599	2.8	96,035	2.8	104,532	2.9
Total other operating expense	**226,564**	**6.5**	**219,498**	**6.4**	**234,287**	**6.5**
Total operating expenses	**693,635**	**19.9**	**685,932**	**20.0**	**728,091**	**20.2**
Net operating income	**128,967**	**3.7**	**96,031**	**2.8**	**108,132**	**3.0**

Source: Adapted with permission from National Community Pharmacists Association (NCPA). *2008 NCPA Digest*, sponsored by Cardinal Health. Alexandria, VA: NCPA; 2008: 14.

TABLE **10–10**	T Accounts Analysis for Debit Card Activity

Bank's T Account Entries for Sample Customer

	Cash		Customer Accounts Payable	
Beginning Balance	257.61			257.61
(A) Record deposit of paycheck.	385.98			385.98
(B) Record ATM withdrawal.		202.00	202.00	
Ending Balance	441.59			441.59

Sample Customer's T Account Entries

	Cash		Retained Earnings	
Beginning Balance	257.61			257.61
(A) Record deposit of paycheck.	385.98			385.98
(B) Record ATM withdrawal.		202.00	202.00	
Ending Balance	441.59			441.59

Transactions to Be Recorded for Sample Customer and the Bank

(A) Sample customer deposits paycheck for $385.98 at the bank.

(B) Sample customer withdraws $200.00 for the weekend. Bank charges a $2.00 ATM fee.

Note: ATM = automated teller machine.

recording of the debit entry made by the bank to reduce the customer's accounts payable. On the bank's accounts, customer deposits not only are an asset on the balance sheet but also represent a liability account, as the bank is simply acting as custodian for those deposits.

RATIO ANALYSIS

Although financial statements provide the user with a vast amount of information, additional tools are needed to comprehend the financial performance of a company. A company's performance can be analyzed in-depth by using ratio analysis. By converting the financial numbers of a company into ratios, or ratio analysis, comparisons can be made between a company's historical performance and an established, expected performance or industry norm. Better decision making can occur when the operations and performance of a company are fully understood.

◆⑧ *A financial ratio is computed by dividing one financial statement item by another, allowing users to evaluate a company's performance by focusing on specific relationships between various items on the balance sheet and income statement.* Financial ratio analysis affords pharmacist managers an easy and valuable way to interpret and understand the results of operations and identify possible areas for improvement within a company. **Vertical financial analysis** refers to the process of comparing the financial ratios of a single company over time, relating current results to historical performance as well as future performance. **Horizontal financial analysis** provides managers with essential information as it compares the financial results of one company's ratios to the ratios of other similar companies, as well as to standard average industrial ratios and the internal deviation of these ratios. Comparing and analyzing a company's financial performance with that of other companies or industry standards, known as **benchmarking**, can be effective in either vertical or horizontal financial analysis.

◆⑧ *Three common types of ratios that can be calculated and are used in pharmacy include (1) solvency, (2) liquidity, and (3) profitability. Solvency evaluates a company's long-term ability to meet all financial obligations, while liquidity evaluates the same items in the short term. Profitability measures the company's ability to make money.* Numerous solvency (short-term and long-term) and profitability measures are listed in **Tables 10–11** and **10–12**, respectively. Pharmacy has ratios specific to its practice, and these are shown in **Tables 10–13** and **10–14**.

Controllable expenses are subject to management discretion. As pharmacist managers, the most controllable balance sheet account is the inventory account, and proper inventory management is critical for several reasons. The resource dollars devoted to inventory are often a significant portion of a pharmacy's department budget (refer to Chapter 8, "Purchasing and Managing Inventory"). Inventory represents a use of cash, and increases in the inventory balance between accounting periods are shown on the statement of cash flows. Maintaining proper inventory control is essential in any pharmacy setting. Obviously, the availability of sufficient quantities of goods must

be maintained to meet patient needs, yet maintaining inventory that cannot be sold before its expiration date must be avoided. The most common obsolete inventory item in pharmacies, or inventory that can no longer be sold, is expired medication.

Given that medications for most patients are reimbursed by third-party insurance carriers, management of the drug formulary can be challenging, both in terms of meeting financial constraints and patient needs. ◆⑨ *The solvency ratio that is said to be the most important in inventory management is inventory turnover, which is used to assess efficiency in inventory control and is calculated as follows:*

Cost of Goods Sold ÷ Average Inventory

Average inventory is calculated by the following equation:

(Beginning Inventory Account Balance + Ending Inventory Account Balance) ÷ 2

Using the information shown in **Table 10–15**, the pharmacy's actual inventory turnover of 10.5 for the year is determined by dividing the COGS ($1,233,072) by the pharmacy average inventory ($117,435). A separate turnover can be calculated for front store inventory in the same manner: COGS ($564,998) divided by the front store average inventory ($73,388) yields the turnover 7.7. Of course, the corresponding combined inventory turnover of 9.4 is simply the combined COGS ($1,798,070) divided by the combined average inventory ($190,823).

The inventory turnover ratio measures how many times the inventory of a company is sold and replaced over a specific period. It is expressed as "turns per period" and varies based on industry; however, the higher the inventory turnover, the better. In community pharmacy practice, an inventory turnover of 12 for prescription drug inventory is considered optimal and indicates that, on average, the inventory is replaced every month.[2] A company's inventory turnover is compared with prior periods to determine whether inventory has improved or deteriorated. In addition, a company's inventory turnover should also be compared with the industry average. These comparisons provide important information to company managers. Inventory turnover that is slower than prior periods

TABLE **10–11**	Various Liquidity and Solvency Ratios

Liquidity and Solvency	Method of Computation	Use
Working capital[a]	Current Assets – Current Liabilities	To indicate the ability to meet currently maturing obligations
Current ratio[b]	Current Assets ÷ Current Liabilities	To indicate the ability to meet currently maturing obligations
Acid–test ratio[c]	Quick Assets ÷ Current Liabilities	To indicate instant debt-paying ability
Accounts receivable	Net Sales on Account ÷ Average Accounts Receivable	To assess the efficiency in collecting receivables[d] and in the management of credit
Number of day's sales in accounts receivable	Accounts Receivable (EOY) ÷ Average Daily Sales on Account	To assess the efficiency in collecting receivables and in the management of credit
Inventory turnover	Cost of Goods Sold ÷ Average Inventory	To assess the efficiency in the management of inventory
Number of day's sales in inventory	Inventory (EOY) ÷ Average Daily Cost of Goods Sold	To assess the efficiency in the management of inventory
Ratio of fixed assets to long-term liabilities	Net Fixed Assets ÷ Long-Term Liabilities	To indicate the margin of safety[e] to long-term creditors
Ratio of liabilities to stockholder's equity	Total Liabilities ÷ Total Stockholder's Equity	To indicate the margin of safety to creditors
Number of times interest charges earned	(Income before Income Tax Expense and Interest Expense) ÷ Interest Expense	To assess the risk to debt holders in terms of the number of times interest charges were earned

Note: EOY = end of year.

[a]Working capital: Current assets minus current liabilities at a given point in time.

[b]Current ratio: Ratio used to determine a company's ability to pay short-term obligations, calculated by dividing current assets by current liabilities.

[c]Acid–test ratio: Ratio used to asses a company's ability to settle its current debt with its most readily available assets; defined as quick assets (cash, short-term investments, and current receivables) divided by current liabilities.

[d]Collection of accounts receivable is measured in days outstanding. An account receivable is created when a sale is generated and credit is extended to the purchaser in lieu of cash. Terms of repayment can vary, but traditional terms dictate repayment within 30 days of the date of sale. Therefore, analysis is performed in days outstanding, with results at or near the 30-day mark. Efficiency measures in collecting receivables will use this mark as their goal.

[e]The margin of safety refers to the resulting ratio. A higher ratio means that there are fewer long-term liabilities in relation to fixed assets, meaning that the fixed assets are owned by the company rather than creditors.

TABLE **10–12**	**Various Profitability Ratios**

Profitability	Method of Computation	Use
Ratio of net sales to assets	Net Sales ÷ Average Total Assets (excluding long-term investments)	To assess the effectiveness in the use of assets
Rate earned on total assets	(Net Income + Interest Expense) ÷ Average Total Assets	To assess the profitability of the assets
Rate earned on total stockholder's equity	Net Income ÷ Average Stockholder's Equity	To assess the profitability of the investment by stockholders
Rate earned on common stockholder's equity	(Net Income – Preferred Dividends) ÷ Average Common Stockholder's Equity	To assess the profitability of the investment by common stockholders
Earnings per share[a] on common stock	(Net Income – Preferred Dividends) ÷ Shares of Common Stock Outstanding	To assess the profitability of the investment by common stockholders
Price-earnings ratio[b]	Market Price per Share of Common Stock ÷ Earnings per Share of Common Stock	To indicate future earnings prospects, based on the relationship between market value of common stock and earnings
Dividends per share of common stock	Dividends ÷ Shares of Common Stock Outstanding	To indicate the extent to which earnings are being distributed to common stockholders
Dividend yield	Dividends per Share of Common Stock ÷ Market Price per Share of Common Stock	To indicate the rate of return to common stockholders in terms of dividends

[a]Earnings per share: The amount of net income (less dividends on preferred stock) earned per the average outstanding shares of a company's common stock.
[b]Price-earnings ratio: Ratio of a company's existing market value per share to its earnings per share; also called P/E ratio.

or industry average indicates higher levels of inventory that is not turning over. When the inventory turnover is higher, it may indicate that managers are efficient in their operations—the incoming inventory replaces the sold inventory, fewer inventory items are actually idle on the shelves, and generally less company cash is tied up in inventory as compared with before. Refer to Chapter 8 ("Purchasing and Managing Inventory") for further discussion.

The term "shrinkage," sometimes referred to as "shrink," is often encountered when analyzing

TABLE **10–13**	**Typical Pharmacy Ratios Related to Prescription Activity**	
Ratio	Calculation	Discussion
Number of prescriptions dispensed per day	Number of prescriptions filled for each day	Indicator of overall pharmacy operations and aids in determination of staffing requirements
Average prescription sales price	Total Prescription Sales ÷ Number of Prescriptions Dispensed	Indicator of the relative mix of the medications dispensed. Very high ratio would indicate a specialty pharmacy (e.g., HIV, fertility, cancer)
Percent third party	Dollar Amount of Prescriptions Paid by Third Parties ÷ Total Amount of Prescription Sales	Indicator of the amount of dependence on patients with insurance. Third-party payments usually have a much lower gross margin than cash-paying patients.
Percent generic	COGS of Generic Medications Dispensed ÷ COGS of Total Medications Dispensed	Indicator of efficiency in dispensing generic medications, which traditionally have a higher gross margin than brand medications

Note: COGS = cost of goods sold; HIV = human immunodeficiency virus.

inventory and inventory turnover. Shrink is the reduction in the inventory account balance caused primarily by shoplifting and employee theft, and pharmacist managers should strive to keep shrinkage to a minimum (refer to Chapter 8, "Purchasing and Managing Inventory"). It can be expressed in a dollar amount or as a percentage of the total inventory balance. To explain further, the accounting system records inventory purchases to the inventory account, and as sales are recorded, there is a corresponding credit to the inventory account. The inventory account balance continues to increase because of continued drug purchases at the pharmacy, but no corresponding increase in sales reduces the inventory account balance. Assume that the amount of drugs ordered is appropriate in relation to the current stock on the shelves; theft could be the reason. Remember, the physical flow of the inventory and recording these transactions are separate.

The numerator in the inventory turnover ratio, COGS, is also a major expense on the income statement. In a **retail** company, items are purchased in a condition in which they may be immediately resold, and COGS represents the total purchase price of inventory sold during any given time period. In a pharmaceutical manufacturing company, determining COGS may be a bit more complicated. Because raw materials are purchased and time and effort are spent on converting these to a finished good, we must add these additional costs in accordance with the matching principle. Consequently, COGS for a manufacturing company is the cost of the raw materials as well as factory

TABLE **10–14**	Typical Pharmacy Ratios Related to Payroll Expense

Ratio	Calculation	Discussion
Full-time employee per prescription dispensed	Number of FTEs ÷ Number of Prescriptions Dispensed	Indicator of FTE staffing levels relative to prescription dispensing volume
Full-time employee per patient day	Number of FTEs ÷ Number of Patients in Hospital per Day	Indicator of staffing levels relative to total number of patients in the hospital
Total payroll per prescription dispensed	Total Payroll ÷ Number of Prescriptions Dispensed	Indicator of total staffing (FTE and PTE) levels relative to prescription dispensing volume
Prescription sales per store hour open	Total Prescriptions Dispensed ÷ Total Store Hours of Operations	Indicator of prescription activity relative to each hour of operation. Aids in determining hours of operation of the store or pharmacy department
Prescriptions filled per pharmacist per hour	Number of prescriptions dispensed by each pharmacist per hour	Indicator of the efficiency of each pharmacist on duty each day

Note: FTE = full-time employee; PTE = part-time employee. FTE ratios include PTE on a prorated basis.

TABLE **10–15**	Sample Inventory Turnover Analysis Report

For the Year Ended December 31, 20XX			
Description	Actual	Budget	Last Year
Average inventory			
Pharmacy	$117,435	$98,392	$108,308
Front store	$73,388	$58,723	$54,874
Combined	$190,823	$157,115	$163,182
Cost of goods sold			
Pharmacy	$1,233,072	$1,180,706	$1,131,833
Front store	$564,998	$432,634	$348,532
Combined	$1,798,070	$1,613,340	$1,480,365
Inventory turnover			
Pharmacy	10.5	12.0	10.5
Front store	7.7	7.4	6.4
Combined	9.4	10.3	9.1

labor (**direct costs**) and overhead (**indirect costs**).

To establish inventory value, there are three inventory cost-flow assumption methods used to assign cost to the inventory. Each method assumes a particular process for how costs flow through the inventory account. Depending on the method chosen by management, reported amounts for inventory, COGS, gross profit, net income, current assets, and other accounts will be different. Note that the actual physical flow, or movement, of the inventory items does not always match the cost-flow assumption. The physical inventory dispensed should always be based on the earliest expiration date of individual inventory items. The first-in, first-out (FIFO) method assumes inventory items are sold in the order in which they are acquired. Under the FIFO method, the earliest inventory items purchased are the first inventory items sold. FIFO attempts to match the cost of the inventory value on the balance sheet with the actual flow, or physical movement, of the inventory items. The last-in, first-out (LIFO) method assumes the last inventory items purchased are the first inventory items to be sold. Under the LIFO method, COGS is reflected with the current replacement cost of inventory items. Therefore, LIFO provides a closer match of the replacement cost of inventory to increased selling prices of that inventory during periods of **inflation**. The net effect of LIFO, in comparison to FIFO, is a reduction in net income during inflationary periods. Although companies often switch to LIFO during inflationary times to reduce income and the corresponding income taxes, it is a permanent change and cannot be reversed during times of **deflation**. Accordingly, the balance sheet will reflect less than current replacement costs for the inventory values, but the income statement reflects a more accurate net income. The weighted average cost (WAC) method dictates that the weighted average cost per unit of inventory is determined at the time of each sale and yields values between FIFO and LIFO. The WAC is used to minimize the effects of fluctuating inventory prices. **Table 10–16** illustrates the effects of FIFO, LIFO, and WAC on ending inventory and COGS.

Another determinant of COGS in the income statement is the type of inventory system used. A perpetual inventory accounting system is most commonly used to keep track of inventory. Under this system, detailed records, also called the "book inventory," are continuously updated for all purchases and relieved for all sales. A daily record is maintained of both the dollar amount and the physical quantity of each inventory item on hand. In theory, the quantity totals indicated in the book inventory should exactly match the inventory items physically located on the shelves in the pharmacy. Because shrinkage, obsolescence, and damages can alter quantities, a physical inventory or actual count should be taken periodically. The extended physical inventory lists every item in inventory, the quantity counted, and the cost associated with that item. After multiplying each inventory item's quantity by its cost, the extended physical inventory is totaled and then reconciled to the book inventory. The difference between the book inventory value and the extended physical inventory is the shrinkage for that period.

A periodic inventory system is an inventory accounting system in which no book inventory is maintained. Instead, all inventory purchases made during the accounting period are recorded to the inventory purchases account. At the end of the period, a physical inventory is taken. The extended physical inventory total is the final inventory account balance for the balance sheet. An entry is recorded to close the inventory purchases account to zero and adjust the inventory account balance to the extended physical inventory total, and the other side of the entry is the COGS for the period on the income statement. Small-business owners usually use this method because of its bookkeeping simplicity. The various methods of managing inventory purchases are discussed in further detail in Chapter 8, "Purchasing and Managing Inventory."

BUDGETING

A budget is simply a tool used to forecast events as part of the planning process for future periods. ❿ *Contrary to financial accounting, budgetary accounting looks forward: it measures the cost of planned acquisitions and the use of economic resources in the future. Additionally, an evaluation of*

TABLE **10–16**	Effects of FIFO, LIFO, and WAC on Ending Inventory and COGS

Dawgtown Drugs Inventory Detail Lipitor 10-mg tablets; 90-count bottles			
Month	Bottles Purchased	Cost/Bottle	Total Cost
January	4	$275.00	$1,100.00
May	5	$298.00	$1,490.00
September	6	$325.00	$1,950.00
December	3	$313.00	$939.00
Total purchases	**18**	**$304.39 (average cost)**	**$5,479.00**

Inventory Valuation Method	Ending Inventory Calculation	Ending Inventory Value
FIFO	(3 bottles × $313.00/bottle) + (1.5 bottles × 325.00/bottle)	$1,426.50[a]
LIFO	(4 bottles × $275.00/bottle) + (0.5 bottle × $298.00/bottle)	$1,249.00[b]
WAC	(4.5 bottles × $304.39/bottle)	$1,369.75[c]

Inventory Valuation Method	Cost of Goods Sold Calculation (Beginning Inventory + Purchases – Ending Inventory = COGS)	COGS Amount
FIFO	0 + $5,479.00 – $1,426.50	$4,052.50
LIFO	0 + $5,479.00 – $1,249.00	$4,230.00
WAC	0 + $5,479.00 – $1,369.75	$4,109.25

[a]First-in, first-out (FIFO) calculates the cost of the last 4.5 bottles purchased at their respective purchase price.
[b]Last-in, first-out (LIFO) calculates the cost of the first 4.5 bottles purchased at their respective purchase price.
[c]Weighted average cost (WAC) calculates the cost of the remaining 4.5 bottles at the average cost per bottle for the period.
The following information has been generated by the accounting system for Dawgtown Drugs: The beginning inventory balance on January 1, 20XX, for this inventory item was zero. A perpetual inventory system is used and indicates a quantity of 4.5 bottles on hand as of December 31, 20XX (ending inventory). Notice how the different inventory valuation methods result in different ending inventory values as well as cost of goods sold amounts. Therefore, each method also produces a different net income.

actual performance is made against the budget as part of the analysis of that period. The most common type of budget is an **operating budget***, or forecasted income statement.* An operating budget is an itemized listing of the amount of all estimated revenue that a given company anticipates receiving, along with a listing of the amount of all estimated costs and expenses that will be incurred in obtaining the above-mentioned income during a given period, typically for one business cycle or year. A cash budget shows a company's cash flow for the period and is usually derived from important information contained in the operating budget. Larger companies will also typically prepare a **capital budget**,

TABLE **10–17** **Chain Community Pharmacy Operating Report and Analysis**

Traditional Chain Pharmacy
Operating Report and Analysis

Current Month						
Actual ($)	% Sales	Budget ($)	% Sales	Last Year ($)	% Sales	Description
Sales						
201,633	68.86%	212,241	72.89%	184,828	70.02%	Pharmacy
91,167	31.14%	78,945	27.11%	79,124	29.98%	Front store
292,800	**100.00%**	**291,186**	**100.00%**	**263,952**	**100.00%**	**Combined**
Cost of Goods Sold—By Division and Combined						
144,362	71.60%	150,300	70.82%	155,272	84.01%	Pharmacy
57,271	**28.40%**	**61,941**	**29.18%**	**29,556**	**15.99%**	**Gross profit**
56,371	61.83%	45,678	57.86%	27,439	34.68%	Front Store
34,796	**38.17%**	**33,267**	**42.14%**	**51,685**	**65.32%**	**Gross profit**
200,733	**68.56%**	**195,978**	**67.30%**	**182,711**	**69.22%**	**Combined**
92,067	**31.44%**	**95,208**	**32.70%**	**81,241**	**30.78%**	**Gross profit**
Payroll Expense—By Division and Combined						
20,037	9.94%	19,703	9.28%	17,353	9.39%	Pharmacy—REG
0	0.00%	0	0.00%	0	0.00%	Pharmacy—OT
2,326	1.15%	1,554	0.73%	0	0.00%	Vacation/holiday
22,363	**11.09%**	**21,257**	**10.02%**	**17,353**	**9.39%**	**Total**
6,837	7.50%	7,448	9.43%	8,727	11.03%	Front Store—REG
0	0.00%	0	0.00%	0	0.00%	Front Store—OT
497	0.55%	933	1.18%	0	0.00%	Vacation/holiday
7,334	**8.04%**	**8,381**	**10.62%**	**8,727**	**11.03%**	**Total**
29,697	**10.14%**	**29,638**	**10.18%**	**26,080**	**9.88%**	**Combined**
6,515	**2.23%**	**6,742**	**2.32%**	**5,172**	**1.96%**	**Employee benefits**
36,212	**12.37%**	**36,380**	**12.49%**	**31,252**	**11.84%**	**Total**
Gross Profit Less Payroll Expense and Benefits						
55,855	**19.08%**	**58,828**	**20.20%**	**49,989**	**18.94%**	
Direct Store Expenses						
8,484	2.90%	6,019	2.07%	7,151	2.71%	Rent
2,804	0.96%	424	0.15%	1,334	0.51%	Telephone
998	0.34%	1,213	0.42%	76	0.03%	Utilities
833	0.28%	833	0.29%	0	0.00%	Taxes/licenses
1,359	0.46%	1,621	0.56%	1,636	0.62%	Depreciation
2,718	0.93%	3,467	1.19%	3,257	1.23%	Other
17,196	**5.87%**	**13,577**	**4.66%**	**13,454**	**5.10%**	**Total**
Operating Profit Before Indirect Allocations						
38,659	**13.20%**	**45,251**	**15.54%**	**36,535**	**13.84%**	
Indirect Store Expenses						
4,244	1.45%	4,364	1.50%	4,247	1.61%	Advertising
851	0.29%	1,026	0.35%	2,083	0.79%	Administrative
767	0.26%	755	0.26%	675	0.26%	Transportation
3,300	1.13%	3,150	1.08%	10	0.00%	Warehousing
9,721	3.32%	9,488	3.26%	5,422	2.05%	Other overhead
18,883	**6.45%**	**18,783**	**6.45%**	**12,437**	**4.71%**	**Total**
Operating Profit						
19,776	**6.75%**	**26,468**	**9.09%**	**24,098**	**9.13%**	

Note: Although the analysis may appear confusing at first glance, very important information is displayed in a very logical format. The net income statement format is shown, beginning with sales at the top, followed by cost of goods sold (COGS), payroll expenses, and direct expenses and indirect expenses. Expense account names are listed in the center. Year-to-date activity, both actual and budget, is shown on the right side, and current month activity, both actual and budget, is shown on the left side. Each expense is shown as a percentage of sales and is the basis for comparison. Prior year actual amounts, for the current period and year-to-date periods, are also shown for comparison purposes.

		Year to Date			
Actual ($)	% Sales	Budget ($)	% Sales	Last Year ($)	% Sales
1,694,238	67.00%	1,715,492	69.96%	1,615,340	68.86%
834,348	33.00%	736,690	30.04%	730,339	31.14%
2,528,586	**100.00%**	**2,452,182**	**100.00%**	**2,345,679**	**100.00%**
1,233,072	72.78%	1,180,706	68.83%	1,131,833	70.07%
461,166	**27.22%**	**534,786**	**31.17%**	**483,507**	**29.93%**
564,998	67.72%	432,634	58.73%	348,532	47.72%
269,350	**32.28%**	**304,056**	**41.27%**	**381,807**	**52.28%**
1,798,070	**71.11%**	**1,613,340**	**65.79%**	**1,480,365**	**63.11%**
730,516	**28.89%**	**838,842**	**34.21%**	**865,314**	**36.89%**
173,977	10.27%	167,858	9.78%	153,909	9.53%
373	0.02%	0	0.00%	0	0.00%
12,267	0.72%	12,833	0.75%	0	0.00%
186,617	**11.01%**	**180,691**	**10.53%**	**153,909**	**9.53%**
61,059	7.32%	70,042	9.51%	66,558	9.11%
4	0.00%	0	0.00%	0	0.00%
4,918	0.59%	5,952	0.81%		0.00%
65,981	**7.91%**	**75,994**	**10.32%**	66,558	9.11%
252,598	9.99%	256,685	10.47%	220,467	9.40%
55,007	2.18%	57,730	2.35%	42,861	1.83%
307,605	**12.17%**	**314,415**	**12.82%**	**263,328**	**11.23%**
422,911	**16.73%**	**524,427**	**21.39%**	**601,986**	**25.66%**
66,283	2.62%	48,156	1.96%	55,125	2.35%
5,688	0.22%	3,392	0.14%	4,529	0.19%
9,284	0.37%	8,127	0.33%	7,487	0.32%
6,674	0.26%	6,875	0.28%	0	0.00%
12,267	0.49%	12,968	0.53%	14,704	0.63%
29,748	1.18%	31,220	1.27%	43,400	1.85%
129,674	**5.14%**	**110,738**	**4.52%**	**125,245**	**5.34%**
293,237	**11.60%**	**413,689**	**16.87%**	**476,741**	**20.32%**
35,567	1.41%	36,390	1.48%	36,197	1.54%
17,044	0.67%	9,450	0.39%	19,224	0.82%
6,832	0.27%	5,829	0.24%	6,009	0.26%
28,965	1.15%	24,929	1.02%	27,506	1.17%
81,476	3.22%	107,124	4.37%	123,444	5.26%
169,884	**6.72%**	**183,722**	**7.50%**	**212,380**	**9.05%**
123,353	**4.88%**	**229,967**	**9.38%**	**264,361**	**11.27%**

which shows the estimated amounts planned for capital assets in a given period. Although the capital assets will benefit the company over several future periods, the capital budget consists of only the current-year expenditures.

10 *Closely related to the operating budget is an operating expense budget, which focuses only on the expenses for a department for the forecast period.* This type of budget is usually prepared by institutional pharmacies or national chain community pharmacies, where controlling expenses is critical and the responsibility for revenue generation is not a primary function of the pharmacy. Therefore, containment of all expenses noted in the operating expense budget is important, while still providing proper patient care, and is the major factor in evaluating management performance. However, pharmacist managers working in independent pharmacies must also be concerned about revenue generation in addition to controlling expenses. The proper provision of good customer service and appropriate patient care can result in additional sales, thereby increasing net income. A manager's performance is evaluated on the complete operations, or net income, of the pharmacy. Thus, in this setting, the pharmacist manager must consider both the appropriate management of operating expenses as well as revenue streams.

Five key purposes for the development and use of budgets follow:

- Planning
- Supporting communication and coordination
- Assigning resources
- Benchmarking
- Assessing performance

An operating budget is critical in the planning process of any company to achieve its overall financial goals. Planning includes providing pharmacist managers with specific goals for their departments. The accounting department can complete the development of various budgets with input, desirably from departmental managers. Proper coordination and communication of the budget's importance are essential for budget control and ensuring that current operations are carried out as planned. Allocation of resources should be decided in accordance with the budget.

Several methods can be employed in budget development. The simplest method is to replicate the prior year's budget without any changes or use the actual performance of the current period as the next year's budget. If using the current period, you would base next year's budget on the current year's budget until the month the budget is being prepared (the remaining months should be accounted for using data from the prior year or estimated based on most appropriate data); for example, if you are preparing the fiscal year 2015 budget in November 2014, then you would base the budget on actual performance in January–October 2014 and November–December 2013. More commonly, the prior year actual performance is used with an anticipated percentage increase, decrease, or no change in each line item based on certain assumptions or goals set by management. An operating budget can be developed by using the historical data of an individual company over many years, which is then adjusted for key assumptions determined by management about the upcoming period. **10** *A zero-based budget is perhaps the most difficult to prepare while providing the most detailed information and assumptions. In developing a zero-based budget, the prior period revenues, expenses, or costs are ignored when establishing the future period performance.* Each revenue and expense category starts with a zero balance, and all budget line items within the budget must be justified as being necessary and realistic.

Budgets, however prepared, are only estimates and are not perfect. Management is often evaluated with budget performance reports, which compare actual performance to that shown in the budget. Benchmarking compares one company's actual performance, or budget, to other companies within the industry as a standard. Having a basis of comparison with competitors throughout the industry can provide management with valuable insight to their company's performance.

In dealing with budgets, controllable expenses become important. Controllable expenses are those expenses subject to control, or manipulation, by management. Many company expenses can be delayed, eliminated, and even accelerated by management. In a pharmacy, the most controllable expense is payroll, evidenced by the strict control over the amount of hours budgeted for pharmacists and technicians.

Cost allocation, or the equitable assignment of the expenses of the general and administrative (i.e., non-revenue-generating) departments, must be considered in overall budget development. As the name implies, the amount allocated is not controllable by most pharmacist managers since they are not directly involved in the operations of most departments (e.g., distribution warehouses, corporate advertising, executive management salaries). The expenses of services provided by these general and administrative departments are a vital part of the operation of the company and must be allocated to the revenue-generating departments within the company on an equitable basis. For example, a large national chain pharmacy maintains a warehouse that services the southern region of the United States. The warehouse generates expenses of $2,500,000 annually for ordering, warehousing, and delivering inventory to 200 pharmacies located throughout the southern region. Therefore, each of these individual pharmacies might receive a warehousing allocation of $12,500 ($2,500,000 ÷ 200) in their annual operating budget. The services provided by the warehouse are a vital part of the operations of the company, and recognizing the corresponding expenses is necessary in the budget. **Table 10–17** illustrates a traditional chain community pharmacy actual-to-budget operating report.

SUMMARY

Optimal financial performance is an expectation of all pharmacist managers, and an understanding of basic accounting principles by pharmacist managers is essential to surviving and maintaining a competitive edge. This chapter reviews accounting fundamentals, such as basic financial statements, the principles of going concern, objectivity, conservatism, consistency, matching, and materiality, real and nominal accounts, accrual and cash basis of accounting, the accounting equation, debits and credits, ratio analyses, and budgeting. The basic accounting principles reviewed in this chapter along with proper and timely financial reporting provide the necessary tools to help pharmacist managers meet these expectations.

References

1. Centers for Disease Control and Prevention, Seasonal flu page. Available at: http://www.cdc.gov/flu/about/qa/fluvaccine.htm. Accessed October 28, 2008.

2. National Community Pharmacists Association (NCPA). *NCPA Digest.* Alexandria, VA: NCPA; 2008.

Abbreviations

ATM:	automated teller machine
COGS:	cost of goods sold
cr:	credit
dr:	debit
EOY:	end of year
FASB:	Financial Accounting Standards Board
FIFO:	first-in, first-out
FTE:	full-time employee
GAAP:	generalized accepted accounting principle
HIV:	human immunodeficiency virus

LIFO:	last-in, first-out
LLC:	limited liability corporation
P&L:	profit and loss statement
PTE:	part-time employee
RPh:	pharmacist
WAC:	weighted average cost

Case Scenarios

CASE ONE: Like many towns in rural America, Anytown, USA, exists because of the presence of a large automobile manufacturer. There is one independently owned pharmacy in Anytown, and nearly 100% of the pharmacy's customers are employees of the automobile manufacturer. The automobile manufacturer is changing health carriers to reduce pharmacy-related healthcare costs for their employees. Currently, the pharmacy earns a gross margin percentage of 24% on prescription sales. The new insurance carrier for the automobile manufacturer offers a plan that will lower the gross margin percentage to 17%. The pharmacy has annual prescription sales of $4,000,000 and employs two full-time pharmacists and three full-time pharmacy technicians. The building has no mortgage, and there is only a small over-the-counter section despite the significant free space within the store. Current hours of operation are 9 a.m. to 9 p.m. weekdays and 9 a.m. to 6 p.m. on weekends. Given the drastic reduction in the pharmacy's gross margin percentage, discuss the various implications in regard to the pharmacy's balance sheet, income statement, and staffing requirements. Propose some alternative courses of action the pharmacy's pharmacist managers can implement in response to the recent changes.

CASE TWO: You are the pharmacist manager at a hospital with 220 beds and an open formulary system. One of the ratios calculated by the hospital and used for your employee performance bonus is drug inventory cost per adjusted patient days. This ratio evaluates the drug inventory cost for the entire hospital against the total hospital census. The ratio is developed from financial information from the prior year, and any decreases in this ratio greater than 10% results in the elimination of your annual bonus. Currently, the ratio is $38.47 per adjusted patient day. Recently, the hospital has granted admitting privileges to a neurosurgeon specializing in treating brain tumors. His reputation is outstanding, and he soon begins to admit many patients. One of the primary medications used in his practice is Gliadel Wafers, which are expensive, at approximately $23,000 each. As the pharmacist manager, you are apprehensive about including these expensive items in your inventory, which can slow the inventory turnover if they are not used often. However, your concerns lessen once you learn that the manufacturer allows the hospital to purchase them on consignment, meaning they will only buy Gliadel Wafers when they are ordered and used by the physician. Therefore, there are no carrying costs, and you think that your bonus will not suffer from this addition. After the first year of having Gliadel Wafers used in your hospital, the drug cost per adjusted patient day is reported to you at a much higher $58.21 per adjusted patient day. Along with this report, the human resources department also informs you that your annual performance bonus will not be paid due to this increase. What was wrong with your assumptions about inventory turnover and other financial ratios? What could have been done to prevent this situation from happening?

CASE THREE: You are the pharmacist manager for a large hospital in a rapidly growing metropolitan area. Upper management has asked various managers throughout the hospital for input in reducing current operating expenses, as well as help planning for increased demand for hospital services from the surrounding area in the future. You have investigated a new inventory robot that will manage the top 1,000 medications for the hospital. The robot will cost $1,000,000 and has a useful life of 20 years. The company selling the robot offers a 5-year, no-interest financing plan with five equal annual payments. The efficiencies of the robot will result in eliminating two pharmacy technician positions, currently $35,000 each, including benefits on an annual basis, during the first two years, as well as a third position in future years. You are asked to make a presentation to the board of directors regarding purchase of the robot. Discuss the financial impact on the balance sheet, the income statement, and the effects on the cash flow of the hospital for the next five years.

CASE FOUR: You have just returned from your first national professional pharmacy association meeting where the term "cost of dispensing" a prescription was used in a continuing education program. Having never heard the term before, you were interested to note that it is an important tool used by pharmacist managers to determine the expenses associated with dispensing medications, other than the drug cost itself (COGS). Cost of dispensing is defined as the total of all costs allocated to a pharmacy department divided by the total number of prescriptions dispensed; the national average is $10.89. Knowing the cost of dispensing a prescription allows a pharmacist manager, as well as other users of the financial statements, to determine the average of all costs associated for a particular pharmacy in relation to the volume of prescriptions dispensed, which can be compared with other pharmacies and help evaluate the efficiency of overall pharmacy operations. Knowing the cost of dispensing a prescription is also vital when determining prescription pricing, as it must be added to the COGS to help meet the indirect costs of the pharmacy (staffing, rent, utilities, etc.). Note the cost of dispensing a prescription does not contain any profit or net income.

Since you are graduating in just a matter of months and plan to join the pharmacy staff at Dawgtown Drugs, Inc., you decide to perform a bit of financial analysis before beginning your employment just to make sure Dawgtown can afford to employ you. Using the information provided in Table 10–5, you try to determine the cost of dispensing a prescription for Dawgtown Drugs, Inc. Since there are no data on the number of prescriptions dispensed on the income statement, you call the owner and are told that the prescription dispensed volume was 30,000. You have negotiated an annual part-time salary for your 32 hours per week of $125,000 (which includes the total cost of salary, benefits, etc.), and the owner also tells you that all other employees are receiving an increase of 5% (includes salary, benefits, and other expenses paid by employer). All other expenses will remain constant in the following year except payroll. This fact troubles you since you know that Dawgtown Drugs, Inc., currently only has a net income of $50,000, and your employment with them alone would create a net loss of $75,000 ($50,000 [Current Net Income] – $125,000 [Your Salary] = –$75,000). Even so, the owner has assured you that there will be an increase of 20,000 prescriptions dispensed because a competitor has closed in the area, and these additional prescriptions will be similar to the current prescription sales (selling price, COGS, gross margin, etc.). Calculate the cost of dispensing for Dawgtown Drugs, Inc., and the affect your employment and the additional prescription volume will have.

CASE FIVE: You are currently working as manager of all consultant pharmacists with a regional long-term care facility. During the annual meeting, the chief financial officer (CFO) discussed plans for the company, as well as three important operational changes. First, the company will issue an additional 10,000 shares of common stock, all of which are expected to sell at $100 per share by the end of the year. Second, since no annual pay raises will be given because of decreased company profits, an extra week of vacation (amounting to $200,000 in additional payroll) is granted (accrued) to all employees, although it cannot be taken until the following year. Finally, inventory levels at all

(continues)

locations must be reduced by 25%, even though patient care volume and use of inventory is not expected to decrease. To achieve this reduction, a new contract with the wholesaler has been negotiated, and there will now be deliveries at all locations twice weekly, instead of the current weekly schedule. Your employees are paid an annual bonus based on the company's net income and inventory turnover for the year. Describe the implications of these corporate changes to the company's financial statements so you can adequately explain them to the employees you supervise. In addition, predict what effect these changes, in general, will have on their annual bonus.

Additional Resources Available Online!

Visit the Student Companion Web site at http://healthprofessions.jbpub.com/pharmacymanagement for interactive study tools and additional resources.

See www.rxugace.com to learn how you can obtain continuing pharmacy education for this content.

CHAPTER 11

JUSTIFYING AND PLANNING PATIENT CARE SERVICES

JoAnn Stubbings, MHCA, RPh

Mary Ann Kliethermes, PharmD

LEARNING OBJECTIVES

After completing the chapter, the reader will be able to

1. List examples of pharmacist patient care services.
2. Formulate a plan to justify a pharmacy patient care service.
3. Explain the fundamentals of performing a needs assessment for a service.
4. Describe the difference between primary and secondary research data sources.
5. Determine key components of a pharmacist patient care service plan.
6. Differentiate the two models of reimbursement for pharmacist patient care services.
7. Recommend the most appropriate payment model for a pharmacist patient care service.

KEY CONCEPTS

❶ Patient care services provided by pharmacists should address a significant patient need. This can be done by providing an entirely new service or by providing an existing service in a different way, such as higher quality, easier access, or less expense.

❷ To justify a service, pharmacists should always consider future goals and know whether the patient base or other pertinent factors (e.g., revenue streams) will grow, decline, or remain constant.

❸ After deciding on the types of pharmacist patient care services to be provided, the next step is to justify the proposed service needs.

❹ Results of the SWOT analysis should provide objective information as an indication to support or to not support the planned proposal, as well as identify the weaknesses and threats that need to be addressed.

❺ The pharmacist patient care service should be clearly defined, and mission and vision statements are powerful tools to provide focus for a service or program.

❻ Organization structure may be viewed as two distinct components: (1) the structure of the program and (2) the reporting structure for employees within the program. Establishing the structure of the program leads to the development of policies and procedures, or the guidelines and rules of how the service will run.

❼ Policies and procedures should be developed for all pharmacist patient care services.

❽ Documentation of patient care and services provided is an essential component of every pharmacist patient care service plan.

❾ Demonstrating the ability to be paid for a service is a vital part of justifying pharmacist patient care services.

❿ To determine the amount to be billed, the pharmacist should assess what it costs to provide the service.

INTRODUCTION

Numerous studies have shown that pharmacists can improve patient care and outcomes.[1-4] As a result, pharmacist patient care services have been implemented in many practice areas, such as long-term care, hospitals, clinics, managed care, and community settings (**Table 11-1**).[5-25] To financially support these services, it is imperative that all pharmacists (whether managers or not) understand how to justify and plan patient care services. Thus, this chapter will focus on the process of justifying and planning pharmacist patient care services.[26-29] A case study based on a medication therapy management service/program (MTM, MTMS, or MTMP) in an independent community pharmacy will illustrate this process.

Case Study

Jill Stewart, PharmD, works in a community pharmacy in Anytown, Florida. The pharmacy serves a population of 25,000, of whom 5,000 are 65 years or older. Of the patients 65 years or older, 2,500 have **Medicare Part D**, another 2,300 have prescription drug coverage through their former employers, and 200 do not have any prescription drug coverage. Dr. Stewart observes that many patients in her practice have difficulty adhering to their medications, experience drug-related problems, receive care from multiple prescribers, or have issues with limited health literacy or limited cognition. Dr. Stewart wants to develop an MTM service to address these issues and improve outcomes in this patient population. She intends to justify the need for the service to the pharmacist owner and demonstrate that her time spent on this service will be beneficial from a clinical and an economic perspective. She will also develop a plan for delivering the service.

Medication Therapy Management

MTM services, or programs, are pharmacy-related patient care services that were established by the Medicare Prescription Drug, Improvement, and Modernization Act of 2003 and further defined in the Medicare Prescription Drug Benefit Final Rule.[30-31] The Medicare Drug Benefit is commonly known as Medicare Part D. The Centers for Medicare and Medicaid Services (CMS) require plan sponsors, such as prescription drug benefit managers or Medicare Advantage organizations, to develop and administer MTM programs. CMS states that pharmacists are logically the primary healthcare providers to assume responsibility for these services. The pharmacy community, through the Pharmacy Provider Coalition, established a comprehensive definition of MTM services.[32] Services provided should include but are not limited to a comprehensive assessment of patient medication-related needs and developing a medication treatment plan. These plans ensure that the patient is receiving the most optimal medications by addressing access and adherence, monitoring the patient for therapeutic response and real or potential drug-related problems, taking action on any identified medication issues, coordinating the patient's care with other healthcare providers, educating the patient and other caregivers with regard to medications and the medication treatment plan, and documenting the care provided.

TABLE **11–1**	Examples of Pharmacist Patient Care Services

Pharmacy Practice Sites	Pharmacist Patient Care Services

Community or ambulatory settings	Medication therapy management
	Disease state management
	  Diabetes
	  Heart failure
	  HIV
	  Asthma/COPD
	  Hyperlipidemia
	  Hypertension
	  Immunization
	Anticoagulation
	Medication reconciliation
	Medication adherence

Hospital or health system	Intensive care unit services
	Anticoagulation
	Emergency room services
	Medication reconciliation
	Infectious disease
	  Infection control
	  Antibiotic stewardship
	Nutritional support
	Adverse drug event monitoring
	Preventative care
	  Immunizations
	  Fall risks

Long-term care	Drug regimen review
	Preventative care
	  Immunizations
	  Fall risks

Managed care/physician clinic	Anticoagulation Medication therapy management Disease state management Medication adherence

Note: COPD = chronic obstructive pulmonary disease; HIV = human immunodeficiency virus.
Sources: Kliethermes MA, Schullo-Fuelner AM, Tilton J, et al;[5] Hassol A, Shoemaker SJ;[6] Doucette WR, McDonough RP, Klepser D, McCarthy R;[7] Wubben D, Vivian E;[8] Koshman SL, Charrois TL, Simpson SH, et al;[9] March K, Mak M, Louie S;[10] Benavides S, Rodriquez JC, Maniscalco-Feichtl M;[11] Machado M, Nassor N, Bajcar JM, et al;[12] Green BB, Cook AJ, Ralston JD, et al;[13] Loughlin S, Mortazavi A, Garey K, et al;[14] Chiquette E, Amato MG, Bussey HI;[15] Schnipper JL, Kirwin JL, Cotugno MC, et al;[16] Murray MD, Young J, Hoke S, et al;[17] Kaboli PJ, Hoth AB, McClimon BJ, et al;[18] Leape LL, Cullen DJ, Clapp MD, et al;[19] Locke C, Raynan SL, Patel R, et al;[20] Szczesiul JM, Fairbanks RJ, Hildebrand JM, et al;[21] Gums JG, Yancey RW Jr, Hamilton CA, Kubilis PS;[22] Maack B, Miller DR, Johnson T, et al;[23] Christensen D, Trygstad T, Sullivan R, et al;[24] Witt DM, Sadler MA, Shanahan RL.[25]

NEEDS ASSESSMENT

The first step in justifying pharmacist patient care services is to clearly define the need that will be addressed with the proposed service to determine whether a market exists and whether the service can be justified. In other words, a **needs assessment**, defined as the collection of data to assess the need for a particular service or product within a defined population or community, should be conducted. This may sound intuitive, but often pharmacists skip this step and develop services that interest them without assessing the need. It is also strongly suggested that a business/program plan be developed, and many service-related topics discussed in this chapter complement the business/program plan (refer to Chapter 14, "Pharmacy Business and Staff Planning"). For example, in Dr. Stewart's pharmacy, her elderly patient population has problems with medication management. She has also observed that many patients have hyperlipidemia, heart failure, risk of falls, and asthma or chronic obstructive pulmonary disease (COPD). There is also a small population that needs assistance with human immunodeficiency virus (HIV) medications. Therefore, before deciding to develop an MTM service, Dr. Stewart must identify and define the major needs in her patient population and then determine how the needs compare to one another in size, severity, and current service delivery. When a needs assessment has been completed, the pharmacist will be able to select the service that best meets patient needs.

For the needs assessment, there are three basic questions to ask:

- What is the patient need or problem to be addressed?
- How large is this problem, and what are the trends?
- How well is the patient need being addressed?

If a service is developed without a thorough assessment of patient needs (which may or may not be the needs of the pharmacist or pharmacy), the service may not attract the desired number of patients, may not obtain adequate reimbursement, or, at worst, may fail. Well-planned research will lead to ideas for developing the service and

will provide the necessary evidence to justify or not justify the service. The stepwise approach explained next should answer the three basic questions.

What Is the Patient Need or Problem to Be Addressed?

❶ *Patient care services provided by pharmacists should address a significant patient need.* Patient needs may be related to disease prevention, disease management, access to pharmaceuticals, and access to pharmacy services. Pharmacists often identify patient needs in the normal course of their work or education, and they should conduct **primary** and **secondary research** to identify and describe the need for services. In Dr. Stewart's case in Anytown, Florida, one of the identified patient needs is for MTM among people age 65 years and older. Dr. Stewart should use personal experience, community or business data, and published literature to confirm whether this need really exists, and to determine the current and future prevalence of the problem and the most up-to-date services to help manage or decrease the problem.

PRIMARY AND SECONDARY RESEARCH

Primary research is original research conducted to answer the question at hand. To answer a question about the need for MTM, Dr. Stewart may examine patient medication profiles, survey patients, conduct personal interviews, or perform group interviews (also known as **focus groups**) of patients at her site. This type of primary, qualitative research helps to describe the need or problem. For example, Dr. Stewart may ask, "Have you ever experienced a reaction to medications?" or "Have you ever *not* taken your medication according to instructions?" Answers from patients can provide rich insight and understanding. She may also contact physicians or other providers to discuss the need for medication management among their patients. Physicians and nurses are important **stakeholders** in any pharmacy service, and it is wise to include other healthcare practitioners during the research phase. Dr. Stewart may conduct an observational study of patients in her pharmacy, such as selecting a day or week in which she monitors medication refills or performs medication therapy reviews. This will help determine the frequency of the problem or the need. Another common primary research tool is the study of pharmacy refill records or a chart review to analyze problems or patterns. To do this, a sample of patients is selected and data from their records are collected, such as medications prescribed, dates prescriptions were filled, drug interactions, and other notes from the profile or record. This will quantify the magnitude of the problem in a select patient group. The value of primary research is that it provides information about the specific patient population and can identify patterns.

Although time constraints may prevent many pharmacists from conducting secondary research, it may be beneficial for Dr. Stewart to also conduct secondary research to define the overall benefit of MTM. Secondary research is research that has already been conducted for another purpose and is usually publicly available. Articles from literature reviews, Web searches, information obtained from continuing education programs, and reviews of databases are examples of secondary research. Sources of secondary research data include the Centers for Disease Control and Prevention, local health agencies (such as epidemiologic and special studies), and the U.S. Census Bureau. Through secondary research, Dr. Stewart finds that Medicare Part D beneficiaries fill an average of 3.2 prescriptions per month.[33] Eighty-three percent of Medicare beneficiaries have at least one chronic condition, and 38% have three or more chronic conditions.[34,35] Twenty-nine percent of Medicare beneficiaries have some kind of cognitive or mental impairment, and 48% have an income of less than 200% of the federal poverty level (**Table 11–2**).[33,36] Previous studies have also found that problems with medication management have been shown to increase with age, number of chronic conditions, number of medications, cognitive impairment, and lower socioeconomic status. On the basis of secondary research, Dr. Stewart estimates that up to 50% of the population 65 years and older may have problems with medication management. Excellent secondary information on MTM as a pharmacy service are available from the American Pharmacists Association (http://www.apha.com), American Society of Health-

TABLE **11–2**	**2009 Federal Poverty Guidelines**
Number of Individuals in Family	**Poverty Guideline ($)[a]**
1	10,830
2	14,570
3	18,310
4	22,050
5	25,790
6	29,530
7	33,270
8	37,010[b]

[a]This table applies only to the 48 states within the continental United States and the District of Columbia. Alaska and Hawaii each have slightly different poverty guidelines.
[b]For families with more than eight members, $3,740 should be added for each additional person.
Source: Data from US Department of Health and Human Services.[36]

System Pharmacists (http://www.ashp.org), American College of Clinical Pharmacy (http://www.accp.com), Academy of Managed Care Pharmacy (http://www.amcp.org), and the American Association of Colleges of Pharmacy (www.aacp.org), and are cited in the literature.[5,37] Secondary research can provide understanding of the nature of the patient need and its cost to society in terms of healthcare costs, clinical outcomes, and quality of life.

How Large Is the Problem, and What Are the Trends?

Once Dr. Stewart identifies the patient need for MTM, the next step is to determine whether enough patients in her pharmacy's service area (community) can justify the time a pharmacist will spend on an MTM service by answering the question, "How large is the problem, and what are the trends?" She should again use primary and secondary sources to quantify the problem and determine the trends. It is usually helpful to use secondary sources to extrapolate the size of the potential patient base to the clinic or community the pharmacy serves. The following example shows a typical extrapolation using secondary and primary research:

- *Secondary research*. On the basis of a review of the literature, Dr. Stewart learns that up to 50% of people older than 65 years are possible candidates for MTM because of multiple chronic conditions, multiple medications, and other factors. Given that Dr. Stewart's pharmacy serves approximately 5,000 people age 65 years and older, to extrapolate the literature findings to Dr. Stewart's pharmacy, multiply 50% by 5,000. Thus, 2,500 people in the pharmacy may be MTM candidates.
- *Primary research*. Dr. Stewart found through her primary research that 40% of her patients age 65 years and older are potential candidates for MTM. As stated previously, Dr. Stewart's pharmacy serves approximately 5,000 people age 65 years and older. Thus, to extrapolate the primary research findings regarding potential MTM candidates to Dr. Stewart's pharmacy, multiply 40% by 5,000. Thus, 2,000 people served by Dr. Stewart's pharmacy may be candidates for MTM.

In the previous example, the results of Dr. Stewart's secondary and primary research are different. This is not unusual. When possible, conduct both primary and secondary research to estimate the need for a pharmacy service. When justifying the service, Dr. Stewart should state that "approximately 2,000 to 2,500 people age 65 years and older are potential candidates for MTM services in the pharmacy population."

Quantify patient trends to determine the growth potential of the service. To do this, secondary sources provide data on population trends and **incidence** and **prevalence** of disease or complications. For instance, if the population of people older than 65 years in the community served by the clinic or pharmacy is growing by 2% each year, the trend would indicate a potential growth in the patient base. Likewise, if the incidence of people with MTM problems is increasing and if it is greater than the number of patients losing their MTM services for some reason, the patient base will increase. ❷ *To justify a service, pharmacists should always consider future goals and know whether the* *patient base or other pertinent factors (e.g., revenue streams) will grow, decline, or remain the same.*

How Well Is the Patient Need Currently Being Addressed?

❶ *Typically, a pharmacist patient care service addresses a significant unmet patient need. This can be done by providing an entirely new service or by providing an existing service in a different way, such as higher quality, easier access, or less expense.* Understanding how the service is new or different requires a good understanding of "competitors," or other providers, who already provide the service or who may potentially provide the service. In Dr. Stewart's case study, competitors may be physicians, nurses, other pharmacists, pharmacy benefit management companies, or even family members who are relied on to assist with MTM. Be specific regarding competitors, and be able to describe how well they currently meet the patient need. For example, physicians or nurses may provide MTM services but may not have enough time to monitor adequately desired outcomes and adverse medication events. Thus, a niche may be to provide medication monitoring services (refer to Chapter 14, "Pharmacy Business and Staff Planning").

The Needs Assessment Grid

Figure 11–1 shows a needs assessment grid, or gap analysis, that compares various patient needs for different pharmacist patient services, based on the size of the need in terms of numbers of patients and how well the need is currently being met. A need in the first quadrant (large number of patients, high unmet need by the pharmacy) presents the greatest opportunity for a service, whereas a need in the fourth quadrant (low number of patients, low unmet need by the pharmacy) presents the least opportunity for a service. Dr. Stewart assessed different patient needs in her pharmacy and determined that the need for MTM affected a high number of patients and has a large unmet need. This grid is useful for pharmacists or managers trying to decide among various competing patient needs and the allocation of limited resources. Data for completing the grid are gathered during the needs assessment. Once the patient needs are assessed, the next step is to justify the service.

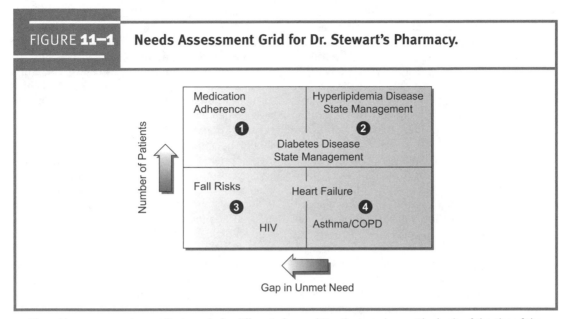

FIGURE **11–1**   **Needs Assessment Grid for Dr. Stewart's Pharmacy.**

The grid compares various patient needs for different pharmacist patient services on the basis of the size of the need (number of patients) and how well the need is met by Dr. Stewart's pharmacy. The first quadrant presents the greatest need for a service, whereas the fourth quadrant presents the least need for a service. COPD = chronic obstructive pulmonary disease; HIV = human immunodeficiency virus.

JUSTIFICATION

Systematically evaluating the needs of the organization and identifying the needs of the patients, or customers, is a strategy to identify patient care services that should be considered for development. For example, Dr. Stewart's pharmacy's needs may be (1) to be one of the first pharmacies (an **early adopter**) in Anytown to develop, implement, and be reimbursed for MTM services for individuals 65 years or older, or (2) to develop and implement services that differentiate Dr. Stewart's pharmacy from other pharmacies in Anytown. The needs identified for the pharmacy's customers may be MTM or, more specifically, improved adherence, resolution of drug-related problems, improved coordination of care with medications, improvement in various disease states, and reduction of hospitalizations. ◆ *After deciding on the types of pharmacist patient care services to be provided, the next step is to justify the proposed service needs.*

SWOT Analysis

A critical evaluation of the internal and external factors that may affect the success of the service is needed, and a method commonly used to perform this type of assessment is called a **SWOT analysis (S**trengths, **W**eaknesses, **O**pportunities, and **T**hreats). The SWOT analysis is used to (1) evaluate strengths the organization currently possesses that increase the chances to initiate and perform the service successfully; (2) understand areas of weakness that may create barriers or make it difficult to provide the service; (3) identify opportunities that will allow the service grow; and (4) understand threats (perceived dangers to the solvency of a service/program) that may put the planned service at risk. Strengths and weaknesses involve an internal assessment of characteristics of the particular service or organization. Opportunities and threats are external forces that may affect the program. Internal analysis of strengths and weaknesses will revolve around staff skills, internal support from the organization, facilities to provide the service, availability of internal resources, and technological resources. Questions to be considered for assessment include: What do you do well? What needs to be improved to provide the proposed services successfully? What sources of revenue will be generated by performing these services, and will they support the program?

Dr. Stewart's SWOT analysis identified many strengths. The top two are (1) highly trained pharmacy staff with experience in providing patient care services and (2) a loyal elderly customer base. Weaknesses include the available space for patient care services is small and not accessible to patients with ambulatory challenges, and the pharmacy currently has no patient care documentation system. External analysis of threats include concerns that reimbursement for the service may not meet the cost of the service and the pharmacy's ability and experience to secure contracts with payers (a **willingness to pay** [WTP] **analysis** may be helpful to address this concern). Opportunities include other healthcare providers identifying adherence as a large medication problem currently not adequately addressed and growth of the elderly population.

❹ *Results of the SWOT analysis should provide objective information as an indication to support or to not support the planned proposal, as well as identify the weaknesses and threats that need to be addressed.* By using objective data, the SWOT analysis may reveal that the service is not justified, and thus, it will not be in the best interest to continue planning the service. However, the SWOT analysis may provide supporting data that the service may be justified and worth further consideration. For example, the analysis may provide data on how the proposed service differs or offers advantages over currently available care. The service can be justified by showing how the proposed program will:

- Increase revenue
- Decrease costs to key stakeholders or customers (patients, insurance company, etc.)
- Improve health (clinical) outcomes
- Improve humanistic outcomes

Communicating the results of the SWOT analysis to key stakeholders is important. Although many pharmacist managers may influence the future direction of pharmacies' services, often the decision maker is not a pharmacist; therefore, the rationale for the service should be explained so that nonpharmacists will understand. Different stakeholders will have different interests; for example, managed care organizations and payers should be interested in reducing the burden of inappropriate medication use. Managed care employers may be interested in improved patient outcomes, better formulary adherence, reduction in hospitalization and emergency room visits, and reduced healthcare cost. Physicians in a medical group practice may be interested in improved clinical outcomes, new revenue streams, increased efficiency, and decreased costs. The pharmacy owner, who may or may not be a pharmacist, will be interested in many factors already mentioned, in addition to increased return on investment and **revenue projections**. Pharmacists will be interested in all of these, as well as increased job satisfaction and new career opportunities.

In Dr. Stewart's case study, she must justify the MTM service to the pharmacy owner and to local physicians she hopes will refer patients to her for the MTM service. Dr. Stewart should compile the results of her needs assessment, showing the problems associated with medication adherence among her customers, as well as review her site-specific data, review the literature, and describe other MTM programs that have been implemented and the clinical and economic outcomes of these programs.[5] From her SWOT analysis, she should demonstrate that other health providers identify medication adherence as a major problem not currently well managed and then explicate how her proposed program will increase revenue, decrease costs, and improve clinical and humanistic outcomes.

SERVICE PLANNING

❺ *The pharmacist patient care service to be provided as well as the scope of the service should be clearly defined.* It is important for customers and referral sources to understand clearly what essential services the program provides, as ambiguity and uncertainty may affect referral of customers and the ability of the program to prosper. Describing the program also helps with regulatory and program approval as state pharmacy practice acts and any applicable federal regulations need to be reviewed to ensure the program meets legal requirements and parameters. In the case study, Dr. Stewart will need to define the scope of services to be offered as part of the pharmacy's MTM program. Services may include adherence evaluations, use of certain adherence aids, monthly or quarterly evaluations for drug effectiveness and drug-related problems, patient disease state and drug education with provision of patient action plans, and provision and maintenance of a current medication list for patients and their providers.

◆ *Mission and vision statements are powerful tools to provide focus for a service or program.* Effective mission and vision statements will help guide the details of creating the service. A mission statement describes the purpose of the program and why it needs to exist in a clear, concise, and informative manner. Its creation should have input from key members of the team involved in the program's formation and maintenance. The vision statement defines the program's and service's direction and its goals and achievements at some future time, usually at an interval of 5 to 10 years. The value of the service or program should be articulated in the vision statement (refer to Chapter 14, "Pharmacy Business and Staff Planning"). An example of a mission statement for Dr. Stewart's MTM clinic may be "The Medication Therapy Management Clinic's mission is to provide superior care to patients in the management of their drug therapy to improve health and to prevent or minimize drug therapy–related problems." The vision statement may be, "Our vision is that by being medication-use specialists and patient care providers, our patients will have optimal health as measured by their clinical, economic, and humanistic outcomes."

Well-defined goals set service measures that result in objective data to determine the value and success of the service over time. Program goals should address the interests of key stakeholders (for example, customers) and other key areas, including financial survival, growth and improvement, and overarching organizational goals. Specific goals will depend on the type of service and

its purpose. Using the case example, Dr. Stewart may select the following goals for her MTM service: improve patient adherence rates to a minimum of 90%, decrease hospitalization rates of patients by 20%, and increase number of patient referrals from physicians by 10% each year. A continuous threat to the service that should be considered when planning is that the market is dynamic and that other pharmacies may implement and duplicate successful services. Thus, it will be essential to consistently improve, augment, or enhance the service to maximize **competitive edge**.

Organizational Structure

◆ *Organization structure may be viewed as two distinct components: (1) the structure of the program and (2) the reporting structure for employees within the program. Establishing the structure of the program leads to the development of policies and procedures, or the guidelines and rules of how the service will run.* Reporting structure should clearly define the reporting chain for employees, define individual roles and responsibilities, and set parameters for decision making. Program structure may include items such as (1) hours of operation; (2) the setting for services, such as in person only, on the telephone, or both; (3) who may or may not be eligible for services; and (4) appointment length, facility, and equipment needs and procurement. It is also necessary to plan and manage growth of the program. For example, the points at which new staff will be added or an expansion of physical facilities will be needed are important planning issues that will affect the structure of the organization (refer to Chapter 14, "Pharmacy Business and Staff Planning").

Policies and Procedures

◆ *Policies and procedures should be developed for all pharmacist patient care services.* Policies and procedures are guidelines for program operations to ensure a standard of practice and a consistent level of service is performed regardless of the employee providing care. Depending on the type of service, any existing standards of care or practice should be reviewed and incorporated into the program's policies and procedures. A suggested outline of items to address in pharmacy service policies is listed in **Table 11–3**.

TABLE 11–3	Outline of Items to Address in Pharmacy Service Policies

- Patient entry into the program
  - Referral or entry process
  - Criteria for entry
- The patient encounter and movement through the program
  - Patient visit procedures
  - Process for services to be provided
    - Collaborative practice agreement
    - Tools to be used (adherence aids)
    - Point-of-care testing processes
    - Standards of care
    - Routine care versus periodic care (e.g., blood pressure assessed every visit versus influenza immunizations to be given or inquired about yearly)
    - Patient receivables, such as medication lists and self-care action plans
    - Patient education
  - Management process for complications or unexpected events
  - Patient follow-up
- Patient exit from the program
- Documentation of patient care
  - For other healthcare providers
  - For the patient
  - Availability of documentation
  - Standards for documentation
- Continuity of care and communication of care
  - Communication to referral source
  - Communication to other providers
    - Timeliness of communication
- Reimbursement for services
  - Process for reimbursement
    - Billing
    - Collecting
  - Process for determining charges
- Staff qualifications
  - Job descriptions
  - Certification and credentialing
- Quality and improvement
  - Procedures for collecting and analyzing outcome measures
  - Procedures for collecting and analyzing program goal measures
- Miscellaneous
  - Regulatory bodies/agencies
    - OSHA (Occupational Safety and Health Administration)
    - CLIA (Clinical Laboratory Improvement Amendments)
- Research and quality improvement

COLLABORATIVE PRACTICE AGREEMENT

A **collaborative practice agreement** is a voluntary written agreement in which a prescriber (usually a physician) authorizes a pharmacist to perform certain activities of patient care under his or her authority.[38,39] The agreements are guidelines, or protocols, that describe the activities that the pharmacist is authorized to perform and under what conditions and limitations. Authorized activities may include physical assessment, ordering or performing laboratory tests, medication administration, or initiating and modifying patients' drug therapy. In developing pharmacist patient care services, the feasibility of acquiring a collaborative practice agreement with prescribers serviced by the organization should be evaluated. The purpose of such agreements is to optimize patient care such that the care is efficient, effective, and safe. Collaborative practice agreements are used for a wide variety of pharmacist patient care services from inpatient nutritional support and pharmacokinetic dosing to medication management and specific disease state or drug therapy management (diabetes, lipid therapy management, hypertension, smoking cessation, pain therapy, anticoagulation, etc.). The essential components of pharmacist collaborative practice agreements are listed in **Table 11–4**.

A review of state pharmacy practice laws, regulations, and organizational policies will need to be performed to confirm the availability of collaborative practice for pharmacist patient care management. If allowed, then close cooperation with an appropriate physician or physician group will need to occur. The type and scope of pharmacist patient care services will dictate the appropriate medical group. The agreement must be written, and parameters defining the scope of practice should be clear; the skills of the pharmacist needed to perform this practice must be well delineated. The agreement should be reviewed and renewed at regular appropriate intervals for accuracy and updating. In Dr. Stewart's MTM service, obtaining a collaborative practice agreement that allows the pharmacist to adjust medication dosages should be considered.

Staffing

The organization will need to evaluate carefully the skills required to provide the intended patient service and develop a human resource plan that addresses the service's staffing needs. Staffing considerations include the number of individuals needed for the service, the roles and responsibilities of these individuals (not only when they are providing the service but also when they are not), and the expected time commitment of staff as they pertain to both medication dispensing and other responsibilities, such as MTM services. Time demands may require that nondispensing services be delivered on a schedule or by an appointment. The desired education level, experience, and professional qualifications of staff (such as training, licensure, and certification) should also be addressed. In particular, a number of specialized pharmacist patient care practice categories have independent board certification, certificates, or other mechanisms to attain competency and special recognition. It is important to clearly define the professional qualifications expected (refer to Chapter 14, "Pharmacy Business and Staff Planning").

Documentation

A common statement used in health care is "If you didn't document it, you didn't do it." Lack of documentation has an effect on quality of patient care, liability of the patient services provider, and reimbursement for those services. ❽ *Therefore, documentation of patient care and services provided is an essential component of every pharmacist patient care service plan.* Several different formats are used for healthcare documentation, from a free format, or unstructured documentation, to highly structured templates using accepted formats, such as the **"SOAP" method** (**S**ubjective, **O**bjective, **A**ssessment, and **P**lan). Structured formats are most commonly used not only for pharmacists but also for other healthcare providers because of the vast amount of patient data/information routinely collected and the need for standardized communication among providers. Whatever format is used, documentation should be clear, concise, legible, nonjudgmental, patient focused, and standardized, and it should ensure patient confidentiality.[40]

When considering the details and structure of documentation, recognize that documentation serves as:

TABLE 11–4	Essential Components of Pharmacist Collaborative Practice Agreements

1. Statement naming the pharmacist(s) and physician(s) who agreed to work together under a signed agreement to provide patient services further specified in the agreement under the authority of the physician(s) and delegated to the pharmacist(s).
2. Definition of the knowledge, skills, and ability or defined competency for the pharmacist(s) to perform the authorized functions.
3. Allowance and definition of the access of the pharmacist(s) to medical records and information for referred patients.
4. Identification of the patient population, diseases, and drugs authorized for pharmacist management in the collaborative practice.
5. Definition of protocol, guidelines, and scope of practice (should include methods, procedures, and decision criteria) for the authorized activities or functions. Examples of authorized activities may include the following:
   a. Initiation, modification, and monitoring of patient's drug therapy
   b. Ordering, performance, and evaluation of laboratory tests
   c. Actions or activities (e.g., physical exam) to assess patient response to therapy
   d. Patient education
   e. Administration of medications
6. Communication and documentation procedures, including authority to document activities in the medical record.
   a. Manner of communication
7. Guidelines for feedback and reporting to the authorizing physician(s).
8. Description of how pharmacist(s) will be supervised by the physician(s) and the accountability for assuring quality for the services provided.
9. Defined methods and amount of compensation for activities.
10. Defined time period for the agreement (e.g., yearly) and procedures for changing or adjusting protocol.

Note: State laws and Board of Pharmacy and Medicine rules should be reviewed as specific criteria or limits may exist in a particular state.

- A means to communicate with other healthcare providers caring for the patient (both external and internal communication)
- A legal record describing the patient interaction and services and instructions provided to the patient
- A marker for critical thinking and judgment
- Justification for reimbursement
- A tool to collect data on the program for **quality improvement** activities and research or administrative purposes[40]

Evaluating the purpose of documentation will help decide the critical items to include in documentation. Guidance on contents of documentation is available (though not pharmacy specific) from federal and state laws or regulations governing billing and various other organizations.

Program Evaluation

The quality of any **patient-centered care** program should be characterized by patient outcomes and reflect the processes that convey current standards of practice.[41] It is essential that all pharmacist patient care service programs plan and implement ongoing and robust evaluation and quality improvement programs. Such programs provide opportunities to learn and to improve one's practice and are key to promoting accountability for activities. Improvement can be geared toward the structure, processes, or outcomes of the program. The ECHO (**E**conomic, **C**linical, and **H**umanistic **O**utcomes) model is often used to measure outcomes:

- *Economic*: Monetary value of the program (cost/benefit)
- *Clinical*: Measures of the patient's health status, including primary outcomes, such as morbidity and mortality, and secondary outcomes that relate to a disease or treatment, such as measures of blood pressure, cholesterol, adherence, etc.
- *Humanistic*: Measures that evaluate customers' (usually patients') satisfaction with the program, possibly including the service's effect on the patients' well-being or functioning (refer to Chapter 12, "Achieving and Measuring Patient Satisfaction")

Dr. Stewart conducted an evaluation of her MTM service and found two areas where quality improvement efforts would be useful: (1) documentation of medication adherence and (2) insulin and beta-blocker therapy that cause the highest number of adverse drug events. Her quality improvement strategies include standardizing methods for documentation of adherence and implementing a new education process for insulin and pulse measurement performed on all patients on beta-blockers at each visit. For further details, refer to Chapter 7 ("Pharmacy Operations: Workflow, Practice Activities, Medication Safety, Technology, and Quality").

PAYMENT

◆ *Demonstrating the ability to be paid for a service is a vital part of justifying pharmacist patient care services.* Indeed, the best service may not be viable if it cannot be financially sustained. Many pharmacist services have been paid by the **gross margin**

generated from dispensing prescriptions. When justifying pharmacist patient care services, the product-driven model is limited. First, the model links the pharmacist service to the success of dispensing a prescription. Many services, however, may result in the reduction of prescriptions dispensed, which may curb the financial success of the model. Second, the model depends on a sufficient gross margin to cover the cost of the service—margins for prescription dispensing are shrinking because of reduced reimbursement from third-party payers and price competition (refer to Chapter 9, "Third-Party Payment for Prescription Medications in the Retail Sector").

Pharmacists should be paid for services as a separate transaction instead of through the prescription transaction. This service-driven model requires that pharmacists be recognized as providers of services by **Medicare Part B** (supplemental medical insurance that currently pays for services from physicians, nurse practitioners, physician assistants, and others), Medicaid, and other public or private third-party payers. At present, Medicare Part B pays for a limited scope of services by pharmacists, namely, immunizations, durable medical equipment, outpatient diabetes self-management training, and laboratory tests waived by Clinical Laboratory Improvement Amendments (CLIA).[42] A collaborative practice agreement may facilitate reimbursement through Medicare Part B. Medicare Part D recognizes pharmacists as providers of MTM services, but payment is made by private prescription drug plans or Medicare Advantage plans, not by Medicare.[31] Numerous attempts have been made to introduce amendments to the Social Security Act that would recognize pharmacists as providers under Medicare Part B, but none have passed Congress. The American Medical Association has approved billing codes that pharmacists will use to bill Medicare Part B in the event that Medicare Part B recognizes pharmacists as providers. These billing codes are known as Current Procedural Terminology (CPT) codes and are described in **Table 11–5**.[43] Currently, pharmacists use these codes to bill Medicare Part D prescription drug plans or other payers for MTM services. Once pharmacists are recognized as providers by Medicare Part B, these bill codes may be used by pharmacists to bill Medicare for MTM services, and

TABLE 11–5	Current Procedural Terminology (CPT) Codes for Medication Therapy Management
CPT Code	**Description**
99605	Medication therapy management service(s) provided by a pharmacist, individual, face to face with patient, initial 15 minutes, with assessment, and intervention if provided; initial encounter
99606	Initial 15 minutes with an established patient
99607	Each additional 15 minutes

Source: Data from American Medical Association.[43]

payment will be more consistent and standardized than it is with Medicare Part D. In addition, Medicare Part B sets the precedent for payment, and when Medicare Part B recognizes pharmacists as providers, others, such as Medicaid and private third-party payers, are likely to follow.

Cost Terminology

🔟 *To determine the amount to be billed, the pharmacist should assess what it costs to provide the service.*[28] Costs can be fixed or variable. **Fixed costs** include costs incurred regardless of the volume of the service, such as the cost of equipment. **Indirect costs** (overhead costs such as utilities and room rentals) of providing the service should also be included and can be estimated through cost accounting methodology. **Variable costs** are directly related to the service volume and increase as the service volume increases. Examples of variable costs are salary dedicated to the time spent in the delivery of the service, benefits, or materials used in the delivery of the service. The unit cost of providing the service should be calculated, and payment should be established that covers the cost of the service and provides a margin for future investment.

Billing Models

Two common payment models for pharmacist patient care services that provide compensation separately from the prescription include direct billing and indirect billing.[42,44]

DIRECT BILLING

In the direct billing model, the pharmacist submits a bill for a service directly to a patient (a first-party payer) or a third-party payer and gets paid. The pharmacist is the provider and is paid directly for the service. This is the most straightforward method for pharmacists to be compensated for services. Examples of activities that pharmacists can directly bill include the following:

- Medicare Part B for flu shots
- Medicare Part B for outpatient diabetes self-management training (special training and certification is required)
- A Medicare Part D prescription drug plan for MTM services
- A patient "brown bag" medication assessment
- A private third-party payer for a diabetes monitoring service
- A long-term care facility for consulting pharmacy services
- Another third-party payer, such as an employer, union, or government entity for an asthma management service
- State Medicaid agencies (in some states) for MTM services

The direct billing model depends on the patient's or the payer's willingness to pay (WTP) for the service. For some payers and services, the WTP is already established because the payer recognizes the pharmacist as a provider of the service and has established a fee. For example, Medicare Part B pays properly certified pharmacists to administer flu shots or for outpatient diabetes self-management training. Medicare Part D plan sponsors pay-contracted pharmacists for MTM services for eligible Part D beneficiaries. For many other payers and services, the WTP is not established because pharmacists are not yet recognized as providers of the service. As an example, most third-party payers are not prepared to pay pharmacists for disease management services, such as diabetes or asthma management. When direct billing a third-party payer, such as a private insurance plan, the pharmacist must establish the payer's WTP by getting the payer's approval to bill for the service and negotiating payment rates. The same process must be followed when a pharmacist intends to bill a patient directly for a service. Studies have shown that patients are increasingly willing to pay for pharmacist services, especially those that reduce the risk of medication-related problems or for diseases perceived as higher risk.[45-47] The direct billing model is most commonly used by pharmacists in such outpatient settings as community pharmacies, medical clinics, hospital outpatient pharmacies, and long-term care facilities. Remember that patients must be informed of the fee and terms of payment before receiving services; preferably, this information should be acknowledged in writing.

Dr. Stewart's MTM service will use a direct billing model because she will bill Medicare Part D prescription drug plans or Medicare Advantage plans directly for patients who have Medicare Part D. She will be required to contact the Part D plan in advance to determine the payment rates and billing method for qualified patients. Each plan differs in the way pharmacist-provided MTM services are paid. For patients who do not have Medicare Part D, Dr. Stewart can directly bill the patient for the service, or she can directly bill the patient's third-party payer, if there is one. Again, Dr. Stewart will need to contact the third-party payer to negotiate a payment agreement. As you can see from this case, the direct billing model may present some difficulties to Dr. Stewart because she will have to negotiate payment with individual Part D plans, patients, and third-party payers. Dr. Stewart should investigate whether the program can be self-sufficient in covering the program cost.

INDIRECT BILLING

Indirect billing refers to the situation in which a pharmacist submits a bill to Medicare Part B indirectly, as through a physician. This is commonly known as "incident-to-physician billing" and has specific requirements for billing Medicare Part B. For example, the pharmacist must work under the supervision of the physician and must have an agreement with the physician for the provision of services. The services must be deemed medically necessary by the physician and must be performed in the physician's office suite. Indirect billing has also been referred to as a "back door" approach to getting paid. It allows pharmacists to be paid for services for which they cannot directly bill. Payment is made to the physician who negotiates the agreement with the pharmacist. Pharmacists can indirectly bill Medicare Part B for medically necessary services, such as

- Asthma management services
- Anticoagulation monitoring services
- Any other medically necessary services that can be performed by a pharmacist

Other third-party payers, such as private insurance plans, may allow indirect billing for pharmacy services on a case-by-case basis. The indirect billing model is most commonly used by pharmacists who work in medical clinics or hospital-based outpatient clinics and who provide services in the physician's office suite.

Justifying Services by Cost Avoidance

The **cost avoidance** model for justifying services does not bill for a service. Instead, pharmacists justify their service to the organization by demonstrating the costs avoided. Cost avoidance refers to action taken to reduce future expenditures, such as a pharmacist providing interventions that improve blood glucose, which reduces hospitalizations and decreases other adverse sequelae. Real costs of providing services may be higher in the short term, but in the long term, the services will save money. Pharmacists can use a cost avoidance model alone or in conjunction with a direct or indirect billing model. Cost avoidance has been demonstrated for many patient services, including

- Hospital-based anticoagulation service[22]
- Hospital-based intravenous to oral medication conversion service[48]
- Managed care-based medication management service[49]
- Hospital-based infectious disease service[22]

The goal in the cost avoidance model is that the costs avoided by the organization can offset the expenses of performing the services.

SUMMARY

Pharmacy practice is evolving to include more patient care services, and pharmacists and pharmacist managers should be prepared to justify and carefully plan their services to deliver quality care that responds to patient needs and results in positive clinical, economic, and humanistic outcomes. This chapter described the steps necessary to justify and plan pharmacist patient care services. A case study of a community pharmacy-based medication therapy management service was used throughout the chapter to explain the process, challenges, and opportunities of justifying and planning patient care services. Examples of pharmacist patient care services and references were provided. Several tools and techniques were introduced, specifically the needs assessment grid, the SWOT analysis, mission and vision statements, collaborative practice agreements, SOAP documentation, the ECHO evaluation model, and billing models. Pharmacists and pharmacist managers in any practice setting, including the community, hospitals, clinics, managed care, and long-term care, can use these tools to justify and plan their services.

References

1. Donovan JL, Drake JA, Whittaker P, Tran MT. Pharmacy-managed coagulation: assessment of an in-hospital efficacy and evaluation of financial impact and community acceptance. *J Thromb Thrombolysis* 2006;22:23–30.

2. Kaboli PJ, Hoth AB, McClimon BJ, Schnipper JL. Clinical pharmacists and inpatient medical care: a systematic review. *Arch Intern Med* 2006;166:955–964.

3. Kane SL, Weber RJ, Dasta JF. The impact of critical care pharmacists on enhancing patient outcomes. *Intensive Care Med* 2003;29:691–698.

4. Blenkinsopp A, Anderson C, Armstrong M. Systematic review of the effectiveness of community pharmacy-based interventions to reduce risk behaviors and risk factors for coronary heart disease. *J Pub Health Med* 2003;25:144–153.

5. Kliethermes MA, Schullo-Fuelner AM, Tilton J, et al. Model for medication therapy management in a university clinic. *Am J Health-Syst Pharm* 2008; 65(9):844–856.

6. Hassol A, Shoemaker SJ. Exploratory research on medication therapy management: final report. July 8, 2008. CMS. Available at: http://www.cms.hhs.gov/Reports/Downloads/Blackwell.pdf. Accessed April 2, 2009.

7. Doucette WR, McDonough RP, Klepser D, McCarthy R. Comprehensive medication therapy management: identifying and resolving drug-related issues in a community pharmacy. *Clin Ther* 2005;27:1104–1111.

8. Wubben D, Vivian E. Effects of pharmacist outpatient interventions on adults with diabetes mellitus: a systematic review. *Pharmacotherapy* 2008;28:421–436.

9. Koshman SL, Charrois TL, Simpson SH, et al. Pharmacists care of patients with heart failure: a systematic review of randomized trials. *Arch Intern Med* 2008;168:687–694.

10. March K, Mak M, Louie S. Effects of pharmacists' interventions on patient outcomes in an HIV primary care clinic. *Am J Health-Syst Pharm* 2007;64:2574–2578.

11. Benavides S, Rodriquez JC, Maniscalco-Feichtl M. Pharmacist involvement in improvement in improving asthma outcomes in various healthcare settings: 1997 to present. *Ann Pharmacother* 2009;43:85–97.

12. Machado M, Nassor N, Bajcar JM, et al. Sensitivity of patient outcomes to pharmacist interventions. Part III: Systematic review and meta-analysis in hyperlipidemia management. *Ann Pharmacother* 2008;42: 1195–1207.

13. Green BB, Cook AJ, Ralston JD, et al. Effectiveness of home blood pressure monitoring Web communication and pharmacist care on hypertension control: a randomized controlled trial. *J Am Med Assoc* 2008;299: 2857–2867.

14. Loughlin S, Mortazavi A, Garey K, et al. Pharmacist-managed vaccination program increased influenza vaccination rates in cardiovascular patients enrolled in a secondary prevention lipid clinic. *Pharmacotherapy* 2007;27:729–733.

15. Chiquette E, Amato MG, Bussey HI. Comparison of an anticoagulation clinic with usual medical care: anticoagulation control, patient outcomes, and healthcare costs. *Arch Intern Med* 1998:158;1641–1647.

16. Schnipper JL, Kirwin JL, Cotugno MC, et al. Role of pharmacist counseling in preventing adverse drug events after hospitalization. *Arch Intern Med* 2006; 166:563–571.

17. Murray MD, Young J, Hoke S, et al. Pharmacist intervention to improve medication adherence in heart failure: a randomized trial. *Ann Int Med* 2007;146: 714–725.

18. Kaboli PJ, Hoth AB, McClimon BJ, et al. Clinical pharmacits and inpatient medical care: a systematic review. *Arch Intern Med* 2006;166:955–964.

19. Leape LL, Cullen DJ, Clapp MD, et al. Pharmacist participation on physician rounds and adverse drug events in the intensive care unit. *J Am Med Assoc* 1999;282:267–270.

20. Locke C, Raynan SL, Patel R, et al. Reduction in warfarin adverse events requiring patient hospitalization after implementation of a pharmacist-managed anticoagulation service. *Pharmacotherapy* 2005;25:685–689.

21. Szczesiul JM, Fairbanks RJ, Hildebrand JM, et al. Survey of physicians regarding clinical pharmacy services in academic emergency departments. *Am J Health-Syst Pharm* 2009;66(6):576–579.

22. Gums JG, Yancey RW Jr, Hamilton CA, Kubilis PS. A randomized, prospective study measuring outcomes after antibiotic therapy intervention by a multidisciplinary consult team. *Pharmacotherapy* 1999;19(12): 1369–1377.

23. Maack B, Miller DR, Johnson T, et al. Economic impact of a pharmacy resident in an assisted living facility-based medication therapy management program. *Ann Pharmacother* 2008;42:1613–1620.

24. Christensen D, Trygstad T, Sullivan R, et al. A pharmacy management intervention for optimizing drug therapy for nursing home patients. *Am J Geriatr Pharmacother* 2004;2:248–256.

25. Witt DM, Sadler MA, Shanahan RL. Effect of a centralized clinical pharmacy anticoagulation service on the outcomes of anticoagulation therapy. *Chest* 2005;127:1515–1522.

26. Harris IM, Baker E, Berry TM, et al. Developing a business-practice model for pharmacy services in ambulatory settings. *Pharmacotherapy* 2008;28(2): 7e–34e.

27. Epplen K, Dusing-West M, Freedlund J, et al. Stepwise approach to implementing ambulatory clinical pharmacy services. *Am J Health-Syst Pharm* 2007;64: 945–951.

28. Schumock GT, Stubbings JA. *How to Develop a Business Plan for Pharmacy Services*. Lenexa, KS: American College of Clinical Pharmacy; 2007.

29. Snella KA, Sachdev GP. A primer for developing pharmacist-managed clinics in the outpatient setting. *Pharmacotherapy* 2003;23(9):1153–1166.

30. US Congress, Amendment to Title XVIII of the Social Security Act, PL 108–173. Medicare Prescription Drug, Improvement, and Modernization Act of 2003. Available at: http://www.treas.gov/offices/public-affairs/hsa/pdf/pl108–173.pdf. Accessed January 20, 2008.

31. US Department of Health and Human Services, Centers for Medicare and Medicaid Services. Federal Register 42 CFR Parts 400, 403, 411, 417, and 423 Medicare Program; Medicare Prescription Drug Benefit; Final Rule. Available at: http://www.cms.hhs.gov/EmployerRetireeDrugSubsid/Downloads/MMAFinalTitleIFederalRegister.pdf. Accessed October 30, 2008.

32. Pharmacist Provider Coalition. Medication therapy management services definition and program criteria. July 27, 2004. Available at: http://www.pharmacist.com/AM/Template.cfm?Section=Home&CONTENTID=4577&TEMPLATE=/CM/ContentDisplay.cfm. Accessed April 1, 2009.

33. Centers for Medicare and Medicaid Services. Medicare releases Part D data for 2006 and 2007 at Medicare prescription drug benefit symposium. Part D Data Symposium Fact Sheet. Available at: http://www.cms.hhs.gov/PrescriptionDrugCovGenIn/Downloads/PartDSymposiumFactSheet_2008.pdf. Accessed January 5, 2009.

34. Anderson GF. Medicare and chronic conditions. *New Engl J Med* 2005;353(3):305–309.

35. Kaiser Family Foundation. Characteristics of the Medicare population, 2006. Fast Facts. Available at: http://facts.kff.org/chart.aspx?ch=377. Accessed January 5, 2009.

36. US Department of Health and Human Services. The 2009 HHS poverty guidelines. Available at: http://aspe.hhs.gov/POVERTY/09poverty.shtml. Accessed May 4, 2009.

37. Simenson ST, Somma McGivney M. Creating a patient care process for MTM in your practice. Module 4 in *Medication Therapy Management Services*. American Pharmacists Association; 2007.

38. Hammond R, Schwartz A, Campbell MJ, et al. Collaborative drug therapy management by pharmacists—2003. *Pharmacotherapy* 2003;23:1210–1225.

39. Pharmacy Access Partnership, Public Health Institute. Collaborative practice agreements. Available at: http://www.go2ec.org/CollabPracticeAgreements.htm. Accessed April 2, 2009.

40. Zierler-Brown S, Brown TR, Chen D, et al. Clinical documentation for patient care: models, concepts, and liability considerations for pharmacists. *Am J Health-Syst Pharm* 2007;64:1851–1858.

41. Lurie JD, Merrens EJ, Lee J, et al. An approach to hospital quality improvement. *Med Clin N Am* 2002;86:825–845.

42. Nutescu EA, Klotz RS. Basic terminology in obtaining reimbursement for pharmacists' cognitive services. *Am J Health-Syst Pharm* 2007;64(2):186–192.

43. American Medical Association. Current Procedural Terminology. Available at: http://www.ama-assn.org/ama/pub/category/3113.html. Accessed January 5, 2009.

44. Snella KA, Trewyn RR, Hansen LB, et al. Pharmacist compensation for cognitive services: focus on the physician office and community pharmacy. *Pharmacotherapy* 2004;24(3):372–388.

45. Schuh MJ, Droege M. Cognitive services provided by pharmacists: is the public willing to pay for them? *Consult Pharm* 2008;23(3):223–230.

46. Issa AM, Tufail W, Hutchinson J, et al. Assessing patient readiness for the clinical adoption of personalized medicine. *Public Health Genomics* 2009;12(3):163–169.

47. Barner JC, Branvoid A. Patients' willingness to pay for pharmacist-provided menopause and hormone replacement therapy consultations. *Res Social Adm Pharm* 2005;1(1):77–100.

48. Ho BP, Lau TT, Balen RM, et al. The impact of a pharmacist-managed dosage form conversion service on ciprofloxacin usage at a major Canadian teaching hospital: a pre- and post-intervention study. *BMC Health Serv Res* 2005;5:48.

49. Bhosie MJ, Reardon G, Camacho FT, et al. Medication adherence and health care costs with the introduction of latanoprost therapy for glaucoma in a Medicare managed care population. *Am J Geriatr Pharmacother* 2007;5(2):100–111.

Abbreviations

CLIA:	Clinical Laboratory Improvement Amendments
CMS:	Centers for Medicare and Medicaid Services
COPD:	chronic obstructive pulmonary disease
CPT:	Current Procedural Terminology
ECHO:	economic, clinical, and humanistic outcomes
HIV:	human immunodeficiency virus
MTM, MTMS, MTMP:	medication therapy management (system/program)
OSHA:	Occupational Safety and Health Administration
SOAP:	subjective, objective, assessment, and plan
SWOT:	strengths, weaknesses, opportunities, and threats
WTP:	willingness to pay

Case Scenarios

CASE ONE: You are working in the inpatient pharmacy of a large medical center. The chief pharmacist asks you to develop a clinical pharmacy service that would result in earlier conversion of intravenous to oral medications among inpatients. How do you justify the service?

CASE TWO: As a pharmacist at an independent, clinic-based community pharmacy that is located on the first floor of a multispecialty medical group practice, you enjoy an excellent relationship with the physicians and other providers in the group practice. You have a devoted group of regular pharmacy customers; however, you have lost some business to mail-order pharmacy. You want to identify new services to improve patient care, attract new customers, retain customer loyalty, and increase revenue to the pharmacy. The pharmacy practice act in your state allows collaborative practice agreements. What are some options for services, and suggest methods of payment?

CASE THREE: You have been asked to establish a pharmacist-run anticoagulation therapy clinic within a large outpatient ambulatory clinic affiliated with a health system. Your clinic will be located within the cardiology clinic. Currently, the cardiologists in the clinic follow approximately 800 anticoagulation patients. What are the steps you need to take to justify and set up the clinic?

Additional Resources Available Online!

Visit the Student Companion Web site at http://healthprofessions.jbpub.com/pharmacymanagement for interactive study tools and additional resources.

See www.rxugace.com to learn how you can obtain continuing pharmacy education for this content.

CHAPTER 12

ACHIEVING AND MEASURING PATIENT SATISFACTION

TRINA J. VON WALDNER, PHARMD
STEVEN R. ABEL, PHARMD, FASHP

LEARNING OBJECTIVES

After completing the chapter, the reader will be able to

1. Identify four conceptualizations of patient satisfaction.
2. Determine the importance of patient-centered care in promoting patient satisfaction.
3. List factors that contribute to patient satisfaction.
4. Define the categories of the ECHO model.
5. Cite issues that should be addressed when measuring patient satisfaction.
6. Describe factors that should be considered when developing a patient satisfaction instrument.

KEY CONCEPTS

❶ Patient satisfaction refers to the degree to which a consumer perceives a healthcare good or service (or delivery of said good or service) to be valuable, beneficial, useful, appropriate, and effective.

❷ To provide excellent consumer service and increase patient satisfaction, pharmacists and pharmacist managers must engage the patient in his or her care—a strategy known as patient-centered care, in which patients take on a significant role (in other words, more active involvement) in healthcare management and decision making.

❸ Patient satisfaction with pharmacy services has been demonstrated across healthcare settings and disease states.

❹ The ECHO model suggests a multimodal approach to evaluating value and quality of a healthcare good, product, or service by examining economic, clinical, and humanistic outcomes. Multiple outcome measures across the ECHO categories should be used by pharmacist managers to conduct a well-rounded, informative assessment of pharmacy service quality.

❺ Economic, clinical, and humanistic outcomes, such as decreased healthcare costs and improved quality of life, are critical components of determining the efficacy of pharmacy services; however, patients who achieve other optimal outcomes may not achieve complete satisfaction with their care and vice versa.

6 To optimize future success in pharmacy practice, the pharmacist manager's approach to measuring patient satisfaction requires addressing myriad considerations, including patient satisfaction conceptualization, pharmacy setting, prevalent disease states, available services, and location.

7 Although appropriate pharmacy-related patient satisfaction measures may be identified through a search of the pharmacy literature, often an instrument must be adapted or developed to be used for a particular pharmacy setting or disease state service.

INTRODUCTION

Quality has been previously defined in this text as the extent to which programs and services increase the likelihood of desired patient outcomes and decrease undesired outcomes, given the current knowledge base.[1] Pharmacists in all practice settings are uniquely qualified and poised to offer needed services, resources, and education to improve quality health care in the United States. The Pharmacy Quality Alliance (PQA), a collaboration of association and industry representatives, has proposed a series of pharmacy quality indicators (**Table 12–1**) largely reflecting **adherence** and use of appropriate medications in selected patient populations (for example, patients with diabetes or dyslipidemia).[2] Other quality indicators, in addition to those proposed by the PQA, should also be considered when assessing the effect of pharmacists on patient care. In particular, **patient satisfaction**, a humanistic (sociobehavioral)

TABLE **12–1**	**Pharmacy Quality Indicators**
Type of Indicator	**Example**
Proportion of Days Covered	The percentage of patients who were dispensed a diabetes medication and were estimated to have medication at least 80% of the measurement period. (Refilled late.)
Gaps in Therapy	The percentage of patients receiving medication for dyslipidemia who experienced a significant gap in therapy (>30 days). (Refill missed.)
Suboptimal Control or Treatment	The percentage of patients with persistent asthma who were dispensed more than five canisters of a short acting beta$_2$ agonist inhaler over a 3-month period. (Poor control.)
High-Risk Medications	The percentage of patients over the age of 65 years who received one or more prescriptions for a high-risk medication. (Inappropriate use.)

Source: Adapted with permission from Pharmacy Quality Alliance.[2]

outcome defined as the perception that a good or service is useful and beneficial, represents an important indicator pharmacy and other healthcare providers and health plans (including Medicare) use to evaluate the quality of health services.[3-5] Optimizing patient satisfaction with pharmacy goods and services is central to the operation and success of any pharmacy or pharmacy department, as patients who are satisfied with particular goods or services are more likely to continue using them.[4,6-8] Pharmacists and pharmacist managers are responsible for identifying ways to assess and enhance satisfaction, promoting health outcomes, and maintaining a successful pharmacy environment. This chapter will address (1) patient satisfaction, its key characteristics, and its relationship to other outcomes; and (2) approaches to measuring patient satisfaction.

A note about terminology used in this chapter: although the chapter primarily considers patient satisfaction relative to pharmacy services, the concepts discussed may also be applicable to satisfaction as it pertains to goods or products (and often, patient perceptions of goods or products and pharmacy services are interrelated). Also, there have been many debates about whether healthcare providers should substitute the term "customer" or "consumer" for "patient" or vice versa, as this word choice and orientation may influence how we think about service provision and outcomes. In this chapter, we will use the terms "patient" and "consumer" (referring to someone who uses or consumes a good or service) interchangeably. The term "stakeholder" is also used, as it represents the range of people and entities affected by healthcare services. Examples of **internal stakeholders** and **external stakeholders** of pharmacies are listed in **Table 12–2**.[9] Although this chapter focuses on meeting the needs of patients as consumers, the roles of other pharmacy stakeholders should be considered when evaluating patient satisfaction.

DEFINING PATIENT SATISFACTION

❶ *Patient satisfaction refers to the degree to which a consumer perceives a healthcare good or service*

TABLE **12–2**	Examples of Pharmacy Stakeholders	
Pharmacy Type	**External Stakeholders**	**Internal Stakeholders**
Community	Patients and family	Pharmacists
	Physicians and nurses	Technicians
	Pharmacy benefit managers	Clerks
	Third-party payers	Other employees
	Other customers	
Hospital	Patients	Pharmacy staff
	Third-party payers	Physicians and nurses
	Auditors	Hospital managers
	Patient family and friends	Other hospital staff

Source: Adapted from *Effective Pharmacy Management*, Eighth Edition, NARD 1996, http://www.ncpanet.org.

(or delivery of said good or service) to be valuable, beneficial, useful, appropriate, and effective. Patient satisfaction is measured to examine the performance level of healthcare services and providers and the extent to which consumer needs are met.[4,10] Ultimately, the goal of conducting patient satisfaction assessments is to allow pharmacist managers and pharmacists to: (1) identify gaps or deficits in service provision to meet consumer needs and (2) implement improvement strategies in response to these gaps or deficits. The decision to use patient satisfaction as an outcome measure must begin by determining the dimension or conceptualization of satisfaction most relevant to the evaluation conducted by the pharmacist or pharmacist manager. Schommer and Kucukarslan describe four service-related conceptualizations of patient satisfaction as follows (**Table 12–3**):[4]

- *Performance evaluation*: Refers to determination of satisfaction with characteristics of a particular service, such as interactions with the pharmacist (e.g., pharmacist's friendliness, empathy, communication skills, competence, knowledge, and skills) or the physical environment (e.g., location, cleanliness, privacy, noise level, and security) of the pharmacy; however, performance evaluation may capture assessment only of those service characteristics readily identifiable by consumers. Items 1–3 of the patient satisfaction instrument presented in **Table 12–4** pertain to service performance evaluation.[11]
- *Disconfirmation of expectations*: Refers to a psychological process in which consumers evaluate the gap between their expectations regarding a service and their perceptions of the actual experience of the service. When experience meets or exceeds expectations, the consumer is likely to be satisfied. Likewise, when experience fails to meet expectations, dissatisfaction may occur. Consider the dynamic nature of service delivery—consumer expectations and, in turn, satisfaction levels are likely to change based on prior experiences or encounters with a particular service. For example, a patient with low expectations of a first counseling encounter with a

community pharmacist who receives valuable insights during the course of the counseling conversation may be highly satisfied at the conclusion of that encounter. As a result, this patient will probably enter the next counseling appointment with much higher expectations, and it may be more difficult for the pharmacist to meet or exceed these expectations despite offering the same quality service. Items 4–6 of Table 12–4 pertain to disconfirmation of expectations.[11]
- *Affect-based assessment*: Refers to the emotional reaction, such as pleasure or displeasure, a consumer may experience as a result of the service. Items 7–9 of Table 12–4 pertain to affect-based assessment.[11]
- *Equity-based assessment*: Refers to a consumer's perceptions of fairness in the provision of services, including inputs and outcomes; generally based on comparison to another individual's service experience.[3] See items 10–12 of Table 12–4, which pertain to equity-based assessment.[11]

Pharmacy organizations, such as community pharmacies and clinic pharmacies, may address one or more of these conceptualizations when assessing patient satisfaction. The conceptualization used largely depends on the question the organization attempts to answer regarding patient satisfaction, such as, "What are our patients' feelings regarding their service experience?"[4] In this case, an affect-based assessment of satisfaction would be most appropriate. In another example, a community pharmacy desiring to evaluate patient satisfaction with certain aspects of a medication therapy management service may find that a performance evaluation-based satisfaction assessment is more appropriate when compared with other conceptualizations.

Promoting Patient Satisfaction in Pharmacy

❷ *To provide excellent consumer service and increase patient satisfaction, pharmacists and pharmacist managers must engage the patient in his or her care—a strategy known as* **patient-centered care**, *in which patients take on a significant role (in other words, more active involvement) in healthcare*

TABLE **12–3**	Conceptualization of Patient Satisfaction

Conceptualization	Focus	Strengths	Weaknesses
Performance Evaluation	Salient characteristics of a service	Can evaluate specific characteristics of a service	Characteristics are selected by the inquirer/researcher, which might limit patients in their expression of concerns; the process of evaluation is not assessed; the measure might be invalid if the service is ambiguous to respondents
Disconfirmation of Expectations	Cognitive appraisal of a service experience	Provides an understanding of the psychological process of service evaluation	Standardization of key variables and processes has not been achieved; results are sensitive to the type and level of the expectations used for the study
Affect-Based Assessment	Emotional response to a service and resultant consumer actions	Allows the investigation of the emotional responses to services; particularly useful when consumer expectations are not formed or used for service evaluation	Provides a limited view of consumer evaluation of services; might be applicable to discrete service encounters but not to long-term evaluations
Equity-Based Assessment	Fairness in what is gained compared with what it cost the consumer	Allows investigation of the relationship between inputs and outputs of consumer and provider	Assumes that fairness is the key determinant of patient satisfaction; few examples of measures for pharmacy are available; measures are cognitively complex for respondents

Source: Originally published in Schommer JC, Kucukarslan SN.[4] © 1997, American Society of Health-System Pharmacists, Inc. Reprinted with permission. (R0911)

TABLE 12–4	Schommer et al.'s Patient Satisfaction Instrument

1.   This service is convenient for me to use.

2.   This service can be relied on to meet my needs.

3.   This service allows me to get the help that I need.

4.   The quality of this service exceeded my expectations.

5.   The service I received did not live up to my standards.

6.   My experience with this service was better than expected.

7.   I am pleased with this service.

8.   I am thankful for this service.

9.   I am delighted with this service.

10. If this service would have cost me $50, I would have received a fair return for my money.

11. Compared with the time I invested in receiving this service, I received a fair return.

12. If this service cost me $50, it would be a good value.

Note: The full version of this patient satisfaction instrument also includes three items pertaining to self-efficacy. A 7-point Likert scale is used in which 1 = "very strongly disagree" and 7 = "very strongly agree."
Source: Adapted from Schommer JC, Wenzel RG, Kucukarslan SN.[11]

management and decision making.[12] Patient-centered care is defined as the sharing of disease management between a patient and his or her healthcare team and relies on the provision of specific, evidence-based medical information to a patient/consumer or caregiver to support decision making.[13] As depicted in **Figure 12-1**, four changes in health care in recent years have served to engage the patient at the center of care, and centering care on the informed patient enhances satisfaction.[13] Aspects of patient-centered care are reflected in Geoffrey James's "12 Laws of Customer Satisfaction," including listening to and understanding the consumer (patient) as well as valuing, appreciating, and showing interest in the consumer (patient).[14] Furthermore, patient-centered care and, in turn, patient satisfaction require both professional competence (e.g., the prescription was filled correctly) and personal service (e.g., staff was courteous and respectful). Other pharmacy-related factors needed to achieve patient sat-

isfaction are described in **Table 12-5**.[15–17] Thus, to promote patient satisfaction, pharmacist managers should facilitate provision of patient-centered, professional, courteous, and convenient pharmacy care services.

Patient satisfaction is associated with the performance of pharmacy-related tasks, such as patient counseling, patient education (including medication adherence promotion), and medication therapy management services (including maximizing therapeutic effects and minimizing adverse events). ❸ *Patient satisfaction with pharmacy services has been demonstrated across healthcare settings and disease states* (**Table 12-6**).[18–27] For example, a randomized, controlled trial of a community pharmacy-based medication management program found greater patient satisfaction among coronary heart disease patients who received pharmacist services compared with those who did not receive such services.[28] In another community pharmacy-based

FIGURE **12–1**   **Health Change and the Patient.**

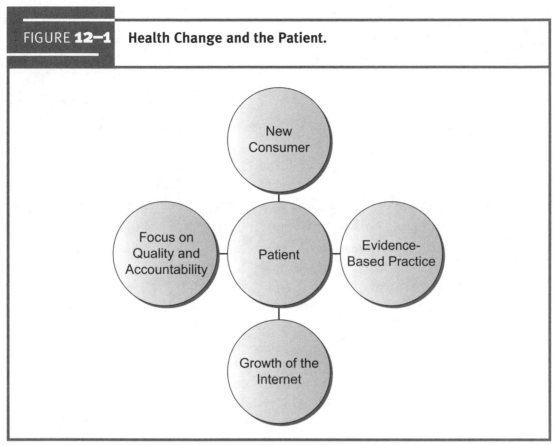

Four recent changes in health care have engaged the patient at the center of care; centering care on the informed patient enhances satisfaction. With increasing frequency, patients reflect new-age consumers who are informed and active participants in their care. Growth of the internet has enabled patients to access a plethora of information related to virtually all health conditions. This information must be balanced with evidence-based practice, empowering the patient to better understand the rationale behind recommended care. The emphasis on quality and accountability for healthcare professionals and patients enhances satisfaction as care outcomes are better understood and shared accountability becomes the norm.

Source: Data from Kemper DW, Mettler M.[13]

program, Fera and colleagues found that patient satisfaction with overall diabetes care increased among patients following enrollment in a diabetes care program that included consultation with pharmacists and health status monitoring.[29] An emergency department–based, pharmacist-managed program (services included patient education) for patients with venous thromboembolism produced a patient satisfaction level of greater than 96%,[20] and a home-based medication therapy management service conducted by a pharmacist resulted in a satisfaction level (classified as either "very satisfied" or "somewhat satisfied") of 94%.[30] Thus, pharmacy care may have a significant, positive effect on patient satisfaction. In turn, as stated previously, satisfied patients are more likely to continue using pharmacy services, substantially contributing to the ongoing success and viability of pharmacy services and organizations.[4,6–8]

TABLE **12–5**	**Pharmacy-Related Factors Needed to Achieve Patient Satisfaction**

- Pharmacist demonstrates professionalism and competence by being
  - polite
  - knowledgeable
  - culturally sensitive
  - respectful and treating consumer with dignity

- The pharmacy location is convenient.

- Pharmacy services and needed medications are accessible.

- Pharmacy services are reliable and dependable.

- Pharmacy services (such as medication-related education and instruction) are accurate and provided in a timely manner.

- The pharmacy's physical environment is clean and safe.

- The pharmacy's physical environment allows for privacy when interacting with the pharmacist.

- Medications are labeled correctly.

- Medications are dispensed in a timely manner.

Source: Data from Johnson KA, Parker JP, McCombs JS, Cody M;[15] Pope CR.[16]

The ECHO Model

Although patient satisfaction is the primary focus of this chapter, it represents only one of several possible pharmacy quality indicators, as detailed in the ECHO model. ❹ *The ECHO model suggests a multimodal approach to evaluating value and quality of a healthcare good, product, or service by examining economic, clinical, and humanistic outcomes.*[31,32] A further elaboration of these three outcome categories follows:

- *Economic*: The costs (direct, indirect, and intangible) related to healthcare utilization.[31]
- *Clinical*: Biological (therapeutic) outcomes, such as mortality and measures of blood pressure, blood glucose, and cholesterol levels.
- *Humanistic*: Sociobehavioral outcomes, such as medication adherence, patient knowledge, quality of life, and patient satisfaction.

The positive effect of pharmacy care services on economic, clinical, and humanistic outcomes is documented in the pharmacy literature (examples are provided in Table 12–6[18–27]). For example, the Asheville Projects, which focused on community-based pharmacy care services (disease management services) for patients with diabetes, hypertension, dyslipidemia, and asthma, demonstrated positive clinical outcomes among patients receiving pharmacist disease management services (compared with care received by these patients before enrollment in these services), including decreased risk of a cardiovascular event and improved blood glucose levels, hemoglobin A_{1c}, blood pressure levels, cholesterol levels, and asthma control.[33–35] The Asheville Projects also suggested decreased direct healthcare expenditures, as well as reduced number of days used for work-related sick leave.[33–35] Humanistic

TABLE 12-6 Studies of Patient Satisfaction with Pharmacy Services

Study	Conceptualization of Satisfaction	Setting	Measurement of Satisfaction	Satisfaction Results	Other Results
Davis et al. 2008[18]	Performance evaluation	Hospital inpatient with follow-up telephone survey	Two validated surveys were used to help develop survey items—the Patient Satisfaction with Insulin Therapy Questionnaire and the Diabetes Treatment Satisfaction Questionnaire	Increased patient satisfaction and continuation of the method of insulin administration used in the hospital at home by patients who received insulin pens compared with conventional insulin vials and syringes (74% vs. 45%).	A substantial cost saving was projected for patients in the insulin pen group if insulin pens had been dispensed during their entire hospital stay.
Malfair et al. 2008[19]	Performance evaluation	Pharmacy in outpatient cancer treatment center	Survey of satisfaction with counseling on a Likert 5-point scale	Increase in overall patient satisfaction associated with routine counseling on natural health products.	Minimal increase in workload and cost (9 minutes and CDN$7.49, respectively).
Zed and Filiatrault 2008[20]	Performance evaluation	Pharmacist outpatient treatment program	Twenty questions with yes/no answers	The pharmacist-managed, ED-based outpatient treatment program for VTE disease is able to achieve a high level of patient satisfaction.	The pharmacist-managed, ED-based outpatient treatment program for VTE disease is safe and effective.

(continues)

TABLE 12–6   (continued)

Study	Conceptualization of Satisfaction	Setting	Measurement of Satisfaction	Satisfaction Results	Other Results
Murray et al. 2007[21]	Unable to determine	Pharmacist intervention to improve medication adherence in heart failure	An internally developed and validated 12-item instrument	Overall improvement in patient satisfaction from baseline to 12 months was greater in the intervention group than in the usual care group (1.0 vs. 0.7; $P = .022$).	The intervention group had statistically greater overall refill adherence; increase of 4.2% ($P = .007$).
Kumar et al. 2007[22]	Disconfirmation of expectations	Patients presenting with new prescriptions to retail pharmacies	Validated survey—Treatment Satisfaction Questionnaire for Medications (TSQM version 1.4)	A positive experience was strongly associated with satisfaction, and satisfaction was strongly associated with intent to continue using new medication ($P < .001$).	The value of the patient's experience and its contribution to satisfaction is associated with intended continued use of the newly prescribed medication.

Christensen et al. 2007[23]	Performance evaluation	Medication Therapy Management for North Carolina State Health Plan enrollees	Pretested, nonvalidated survey questionnaire; 5-point Likert scale	90% of respondents were satisfied with the amount of time pharmacists spent evaluating medications. 80% to 89% were satisfied or highly satisfied with the medication evaluation, quality of information provided, and courteousness and respectfulness of the pharmacist during the visit.	Approximately two-thirds of respondents agreed or strongly agreed that the pharmacist was able to "clear up problems" related to their medications.
Collins et al. 2006[24]	Performance evaluation	Veterans Affairs outpatient clinic	Nonvalidated questionnaire; 14 questions, used 5-point Likert scale	91.4% of patients were strongly or somewhat satisfied with the services provided by the pharmacist-managed lipid clinic.	82.9% of patients felt their LDL cholesterol, total cholesterol, and triglyceride levels had improved.
Scott et al. 2006[25]	Unable to determine	Community care center	Used validated survey; Diabetes Quality of Life (DQOL) Questionnaire	Quality-of-life measures, including satisfaction, were assessed at baseline and 9 months for intervention group vs. controls. Satisfaction score increased 13.7% vs. 6.4% (net increase 7.6%, $P < .005$).	Worry about disease quality-of-life measure also showed a net improvement of 11.6% for intervention group vs. controls ($P = .0027$).

(continues)

TABLE 12–6 (continued)

Study	Conceptualization of Satisfaction	Setting	Measurement of Satisfaction	Satisfaction Results	Other Results
Chan et al. 2006[26]	Performance evaluation	Outpatient anticoagulation clinic, Hong Kong	Validated survey instrument—Patient Satisfaction Questionnaire (PSQ-18); uses 4-point rating scale	The overall mean scores of the pharmacist-managed group (3.8 ± 0.2) were significantly higher than the physician-managed group (3.6 ± 0.3; $P < .001$).	The cost per patient per month in the pharmacist-managed group was lower than in the physician-managed group ($76 vs. $98, $P < .001$).
Law and Shapiro 2005[27]	Performance evaluation	Independent community pharmacy	Pre-post design awareness study developed from literature and experience; 4-point Likert scale	92% of the 103 respondents reported that they were "very satisfied" with the pharmacist interaction.	81% of respondents reported that the pharmacist "helped a lot" in raising awareness of osteoporosis risk factors and treatment

Note: CDN = Canadian; ED = emergency department; LDL = low-density lipoprotein; VTE = venous thromboembolism.
Sources: Davis E, Christensen C, Nystrom K, Foral P, Destache C;[18] Malfair Taylor S, de Lemos M, Jang D, et al;[19] Zed PJ, Filiatrault L;[20] Murray M, Young J, Hoke S, et al;[21] Kumar R, Kirking D, Hass S, et al;[22] Christensen DB, Roth M, Trygstad T, Byrd J;[23] Collins C, Kramer A, O'Day M, Low M;[24] Scott D, Boyd S, Stephan M, Augustine S, Reardon T;[25] Chan F, Wong R, Lau W, Chan T, Cheng G, You J;[26] Law A, Shapiro K.[27]

outcomes, such as the effect of asthma on the lives of patients and patient satisfaction, were also investigated and found to be improved as a result of pharmacy care services.[35,36] ◆4 *As suggested by the Asheville studies, multiple outcome measures across the ECHO categories (such as patient satisfaction in combination with prescription costs, blood pressure levels, and patient knowledge of hypertension) should be used by pharmacist managers to conduct a well-rounded, informative assessment of pharmacy service quality.*

Patient Satisfaction and Other Outcomes

◆5 *Economic, clinical, and humanistic outcomes, such as decreased healthcare costs and improved quality of life, are critical components of determining the efficacy of pharmacy services; however, patients who achieve other optimal outcomes may not achieve complete satisfaction with their care and vice versa.* Although it is not always possible to reach various treatment goals concurrently, it is more likely when patient-centered care is used, patients are educated appropriately concerning their medications and disease states, and goals of treatment are communicated effectively. The following examples demonstrate the situations in which disparities in outcomes may be reconciled through effective communication, education, and consideration of the consumer's needs.

Example 1. A 51-year-old male presents to your pharmacy with newly diagnosed type 2 diabetes and a prescription for a 3-month supply of metformin. Because you recognize the importance of patient education, you provide information about managing the disease. You stress that controlled blood glucose (sugar) is the most important indicator of a well-managed patient and explain that blood glucose should be monitored at least daily. In addition, you explain that the patient may feel no different after starting metformin but advise him that when it is taken correctly, this drug (in combination with lifestyle modifications, such as diet and exercise) should help improve his blood glucose levels and reduce disease progression. The patient seems to understand and agrees to take metformin as directed. However, three months later, the patient returns complaining that the metformin is causing severe gastrointestinal disturbance. He remembers that you said something

about stomach upset as a possible side effect but did not realize the effect it could have on his daily life and well-being. You ask to see his blood sugar journal and notice that his readings have been in or near the desired range, a great therapeutic improvement since beginning metformin. Yet the patient is dissatisfied both with you as the pharmacist and with the medication; he considers stomach upset to be a negative outcome and desires to stop taking the medication. You, however, view the improvement in blood glucose control as a successful outcome, though you are, of course, concerned about the gastrointestinal symptoms. You question the patient further regarding his medication-taking behaviors and learn that he has not been taking metformin with food as you previously recommended. To improve patient satisfaction and maintain therapeutic success, you reiterate your suggestion that he take metformin with meals to minimize stomach upset, and he agrees to try this strategy. After making these modifications and clarifying with the patient your goals of care, you hope to align achievement of positive therapeutic outcomes with a satisfied patient.

Example 2. In the clinic setting, the pharmacist is constantly reminded of the delicate balance of patient satisfaction and having to achieve positive therapeutic outcomes. For example, a 16-year-old renal transplant patient who is two years post-transplant experiences gingival hyperplasia due to her immunosuppressant therapy. The patient has undergone several gum clippings and blames the transplant team, especially the transplant clinical pharmacist, for the undesirable appearance of her gums even though her immunosuppressant therapy has prevented the patient from rejecting her kidney—the overriding therapeutic goal. Immunosuppressive serum concentrations suggest that the teenager has resorted to decreasing her adherence to therapy, and although the transplant pharmacist does not want to risk graft (kidney) rejection, a shared decision between the healthcare provider and the patient is made to discontinue one of the immunosuppressive agents and to start the patient on another immunosuppressant agent that is less likely to cause gingival hyperplasia. This treatment results not only in desired therapeutic effects, including graft survival and decreased adverse events (no more gingival hyperplasia), but also in increased patient satisfaction. Thus, this example further emphasizes that to improve patients' satisfaction, as well as adherence to therapy and achievement of therapeutic goals, patients should be included in the treatment decision-making process.[37-39]

MEASURING PATIENT SATISFACTION

Measuring patient satisfaction begins with considering four practical issues: (1) choosing a method of distribution or administration of the instrument (also referred to as survey, questionnaire, or measure) used to collect patient satisfaction data; (2) deciding how often patient satisfaction data should be collected; (3) selecting the population of study; and (4) determining the instrument that will be used for data collection. Regarding administration, surveys may be administered to patients using such mechanisms as U.S. mail, e-mail, internet survey Web sites, telephone, and on-site distribution (e.g., pharmacy clinic). Selection of an administration method is generally influenced by factors such as costs (e.g., mailing costs), time to complete instrument (e.g., is the survey too long to complete in-store?), and convenience (e.g., would it be more convenient for patients to complete survey at home and return by U.S. mail?). Related to administration is how often satisfaction should be measured. Depending on the objectives of the pharmacist manager, patient satisfaction may be assessed at one point in time (for example, to determine satisfaction with a special event, such as a health fair) or on an ongoing basis (e.g., every three months) to determine trends or stability in satisfaction levels among patients. Satisfaction may also be compared before and after implementation or modification of a particular pharmacy service.

Another key issue in patient satisfaction assessment is determining whose satisfaction you would like to measure (the target population)—patients receiving a particular service, patients with a specific disease state, all patients who patronize the pharmacy, etc. Once the particular patient population of interest has been identified, decide whether the instrument will be distributed to the population as a whole (for example, to all patients receiving medication therapy management services) or whether a sample will be selected from that popula-

tion to receive the instrument (a sample is a subset of a defined population, for example, 300 patients selected from 1,000 total retail pharmacy patients).

Instrumentation is one of the most critical issue to address when planning to measure patient satisfaction. Patient satisfaction with pharmacy services has historically been measured by indicators such as whether the provider was kind and courteous, provided timely care, shared appropriate educational information in an understandable, respectful manner, and ensured the lowest prescription cost. ❻ *However, to optimize future success in pharmacy practice, the pharmacist manager's approach to measuring patient satisfaction requires addressing myriad considerations, including patient satisfaction conceptualization, pharmacy setting, prevalent disease states, available services, and location.* Instruments used to assess patient satisfaction may address any number of elements, including (but not limited to) pharmacy location, timeliness of service provided, perceived competency of the pharmacy staff, avoidance of adverse events, characteristics of the pharmacist–patient interaction (shared goals, communication, follow-up), and optimal disease or symptom control.

Several instruments have been developed to measure patient satisfaction.[8,17,40-43] Prominent among these measures is Ware et al.'s Patient Satisfaction Questionnaire (PSQ), which uses a **Likert scale** to assess patient rating of agreement or disagreement with items related to interpersonal manner, technical quality, accessibility or convenience, finances, efficacy or outcomes, continuity, physical environment, and availability.[40] However, the PSQ has limited application in pharmacy, as the wording of items is oriented to care provided by physicians. As a result, MacKeigan and Larson adapted the PSQ for general use in determining patient satisfaction with pharmacy services.[41] The MacKeigan and Larson instrument also uses a Likert scale to rate agreement or disagreement with 44 items related to the following pharmacy service satisfaction dimensions: explanation, consideration, technical competence, financial aspects, accessibility, drug efficacy, over-the-counter product availability, and quality of the drug product.[41] Because of changes in pharmacy practice (specifically, the advent of pharmaceutical care services, such as medication therapy management), Larson, Rovers, and MacKeigan updated this instrument, resulting in 20 items related to two dimensions of pharmaceutical care: (1) friendly explanations and (2) managing therapy (**Table 12–7**).[42]

◆*Although appropriate pharmacy-related patient satisfaction measures, such as the Larson et al. instrument, may be identified through a search of the pharmacy literature, often an instrument must be adapted or developed to be used for a particular pharmacy setting or disease state service.* When adapting or developing items for a patient satisfaction instrument, certain factors must be considered, including the following:[4]

- *The conceptualization of patient satisfaction measured.* Clearly identify what it is you want to measure. Performance evaluation is generally the most common conceptualization used in constructing patient satisfaction instruments.
- *The format for the patient satisfaction instrument, in particular the type of response (e.g., Likert scale, yes/no, multiple choice, fill in the blank, open ended).* For example, will the items be a series of questions the patient must provide yes/no answers to, or will the items be a series of statements the patient must rate his or her level of agreement or disagreement with by using a Likert scale?
- *Possible items for the instrument.* Specify which topics (for example, convenience of service, helpfulness of service) you believe are important to be measured. Item content should reflect the conceptualization of patient satisfaction measured.
- *The wording of instrument items or questions.* Wording should be kept as simple as possible so that consumers completing the instrument are not confused and the data they provide is as accurate as possible. Avoid using[44]
  ○ Jargon, or informal terminology commonly used among members of a particular field or profession that may not be known to individuals external to the field (for example, rather than "bid" use the phrase "twice daily")
  ○ Compound statements, or statements that contain two or more ideas (for example,

"The pharmacy is clean and the staff is friendly.")
  ○ Leading or biased statements, or statements that suggest how you want the consumer to respond (for example, "I agree the pharmacist who provided the service is knowledgeable.")
  ○ Slang, or informal language that may be common to a particular group (such as adolescents) but is less commonly known to other groups (for example, "My BFF [best friend forever] texts me every day to remind me to take my meds.")
- *Barriers pertaining to the target audience of the patient satisfaction instrument, such as reading level and time to complete the instrument.*
- *Demographic items (e.g., gender, age, ethnicity, income level) to gain a better understanding of patients who complete the instrument and how satisfaction levels may vary based on certain demographic characteristics.* Consider including an item asking the person completing the instrument to identify himself or herself as the patient or a caregiver acting on behalf of the patient, as this may be an important distinction when considering the results of satisfaction measurements.

Once the instrument has been constructed, it should undergo rigorous **reliability** and **validity** testing to determine that the same data are collected by the measure each time it is used and that the instrument is actually assessing the concept it purports to assess. On the basis of such testing, the instrument may be revised and refined as needed and appropriate. Although further discussion of instrument construction and reliability or validity evaluation is beyond the scope of this chapter, we encourage readers to consult texts related to these topics to enhance understanding of instrument development.

Examples of the adaptation or original construction of patient satisfaction instruments are commonplace in the pharmacy literature. Zed and Filiatrault were unable to locate an appropriate patient satisfaction measure applicable to a pharmacist-managed, emergency department–based

TABLE 12–7 Larson, Rovers, and MacKeigan's Patient Satisfaction with Pharmaceutical Care Instrument

	Excellent	Very Good	Good	Fair	Poor
1. The professional appearance of the pharmacy	☐	☐	☐	☐	☐
2. The availability of the pharmacist to answer your questions	☐	☐	☐	☐	☐
3. The pharmacist's professional relationship with you	☐	☐	☐	☐	☐
4. The pharmacist's ability to advise you about problems that you might have with your medications	☐	☐	☐	☐	☐
5. The promptness of prescription service	☐	☐	☐	☐	☐
6. The professionalism of the pharmacy staff	☐	☐	☐	☐	☐
7. How well the pharmacist explains what your medications do	☐	☐	☐	☐	☐
8. The pharmacist's interest in your health	☐	☐	☐	☐	☐
9. How well the pharmacist helps you to manage your medications	☐	☐	☐	☐	☐
10. The pharmacist's efforts to solve problems that you have with your medications	☐	☐	☐	☐	☐
11. The responsibility that the pharmacist assumes for your drug therapy	☐	☐	☐	☐	☐
12. How well the pharmacist instructs you about how to take your medications	☐	☐	☐	☐	☐
13. Your pharmacy services overall	☐	☐	☐	☐	☐
14. How well the pharmacist answers your questions	☐	☐	☐	☐	☐
15. The pharmacist's efforts to help you improve your health or stay healthy	☐	☐	☐	☐	☐
16. The courtesy and respect shown to you by the pharmacy staff	☐	☐	☐	☐	☐
17. The privacy of your conversations with the pharmacist	☐	☐	☐	☐	☐
18. The pharmacist's efforts to ensure that your medications do what they are supposed to	☐	☐	☐	☐	☐
19. How well the pharmacist explains possible side effects	☐	☐	☐	☐	☐
20. The amount of time the pharmacist offers to spend with you	☐	☐	☐	☐	☐

Note: When scoring the instrument, excellent = 5, very good = 4, good = 3, fair = 2, and poor = 1.

Source: Adapted with permission from Larson LN, Rovers JP, MacKeigan LD. Patient satisfaction with pharmaceutical care: update of a validated instrument. *J Am Pharm Assoc* 2002;42(1):47. ©American Pharmacists Association (APhA). Reprinted by permission of APhA. This patient satisfaction instrument is protected under copyright. To use this instrument, please contact the publisher and request permission to use this material.

venous thromboembolism management program; therefore, they developed their own 18-item, performance evaluation–based patient satisfaction instrument (**Table 12–8**).[20] Briesacher and Corey used the physician-oriented Visit-Specific Satisfaction Questionnaire as their model for the Pharmacy Encounter Survey (PES), which examines the following dimensions of satisfaction related to a community pharmacy visit: interpersonal manner,

technical quality, telephone accessibility, and location convenience.[17] To assess patient satisfaction with diabetes management services provided in community pharmacy settings, Krass and colleagues integrated original items and adapted items from an existing measure, the Diabetes Measurement and Evaluation Tool, to produce the Diabetes Disease State Management Questionnaire (DDSM-Q; **Table 12–9**).[8]

TABLE **12–8**	Zed and Filiatrault's Outpatient Venous Thromboembolism Treatment Program Patient Satisfaction Survey

Please place a check in the circle of your choice.

1. At the time the blood clot was diagnosed, were you satisfied with the explanations given to you about:
   a) Why procedures or tests were being done?   ○ Yes   ○ No
   b) What was wrong with you (diagnosis)?   ○ Yes   ○ No
   c) Your follow-up arrangements in the outpatient DVT program?   ○ Yes   ○ No

2. Do you understand why your condition was treated at home rather than having to stay in the hospital?   ○ Yes   ○ No

3. Do you feel you should have been admitted to the hospital?   ○ Yes   ○ No

4. Were any questions you had regarding your treatment adequately answered by hospital staff?   ○ Yes   ○ No

5. It was more convenient to return to the hospital to get your injections than having to stay in the hospital?
   ○ Yes, strongly agree
   ○ Yes, agree
   ○ Neutral
   ○ No, disagree
   ○ No, strongly disagree

6. When you returned for treatment on the weekend, how satisfied were you with how long you had to wait to receive treatment in the emergency department?
   ○ Very satisfied
   ○ Satisfied
   ○ Neutral
   ○ Unsatisfied
   ○ Very unsatisfied

7. Was the emergency department staff courteous and understanding?   ○ Yes   ○ No

8. When you returned for treatment on weekdays, how satisfied were you with how long you had to wait to receive treatment in the medical daycare center?
   ○ Very satisfied
   ○ Satisfied
   ○ Neutral
   ○ Unsatisfied
   ○ Very unsatisfied

(continues)

| TABLE **12–8** | (continued) |

9. Was the medical daycare staff courteous and understanding?	○ Yes	○ No
10. Did you have any problems finding the medical daycare center?	○ Yes	○ No
11. Was it convenient to be called at home to receive information on what dose (how many pills) of warfarin to take?	○ Yes	○ No
12. Were there any days during your treatment with warfarin when you were not sure what dose or how many pills you were supposed to be taking?	○ Yes	○ No
13. Were the written instructions and information provided in the DVT package clear and easy to read and understand?	○ Yes	○ No
14. How satisfied were you with the teaching provided by the clinical pharmacist?	○ Very satisfied ○ Satisfied ○ Neutral ○ Unsatisfied ○ Very unsatisfied	
15. Were you comfortable having your condition treated as an outpatient?	○ Yes	○ No
16. Overall, how satisfied were you with the treatment you received in the outpatient DVT program?	○ Very satisfied ○ Satisfied ○ Neutral ○ Unsatisfied ○ Very unsatisfied	
17. Should you develop another clot, would you want to take part in the same outpatient DVT program?	○ Yes	○ No
18. If taught, would you be willing to give yourself injections at home?	○ Yes	○ No
19. Comments (including suggestions for improving our service)		

Note: DVT = deep vein thrombosis.
Source: Courtesy of Zed PJ, Filiatrault L. Clinical outcomes and patient satisfaction of a pharmacist-managed, emergency department-based outpatient treatment program for venous thromboembolic disease. *Can J Emerg Med* 2008;10(1):17. The patient satisfaction instrument presented in Table 12-8 is protected under copyright. To use this instrument, please contact the publisher and request permission to use this material.

	Strongly Agree	Agree	Neither Agree nor Disagree	Disagree	Strongly Disagree
1. I am satisfied that the pharmacist was helpful during the service.	☐	☐	☐	☐	☐
2. I am satisfied with my understanding of when I should check my blood sugar levels.	☐	☐	☐	☐	☐
3. The service gave me confidence to deal with my diabetes.	☐	☐	☐	☐	☐
4. I was satisfied with being able to reach the pharmacist when needed.	☐	☐	☐	☐	☐
5. The pharmacy was too hard to get to.	☐	☐	☐	☐	☐
6. I am satisfied with my understanding of how things (e.g., stress and blood pressure) can change my blood sugar levels.	☐	☐	☐	☐	☐
7. I appreciated receiving the service from the pharmacist.	☐	☐	☐	☐	☐
8. I am more compliant with my medications since participating in the service.	☐	☐	☐	☐	☐
9. The pharmacist was unfriendly and unsupportive during the service.	☐	☐	☐	☐	☐
10. I was satisfied with the convenience of the location during the service.	☐	☐	☐	☐	☐
11. I am thankful for the time the pharmacist gave up to provide the service.	☐	☐	☐	☐	☐

(continues)

TABLE **12–9** (continued)

	Strongly Agree	Agree	Neither Agree nor Disagree	Disagree	Strongly Disagree
12. I have improved my lifestyle (diet and exercise habits) since participating in the service.	☐	☐	☐	☐	☐
13. I am satisfied with my understanding of what I should eat to control my diabetes.	☐	☐	☐	☐	☐
14. I am pleased with the service I received.	☐	☐	☐	☐	☐
15. I feel a sense of accomplishment after achieving my goals and participating in the service.	☐	☐	☐	☐	☐
16. I am satisfied with my understanding of the types and amounts of physical activity I can do to control my diabetes.	☐	☐	☐	☐	☐
17. The service motivated me to stay in control of my diabetes.	☐	☐	☐	☐	☐
18. I monitor my blood glucose level before meals and bedtime on different days of the week since participating in the service.	☐	☐	☐	☐	☐
19. I do not know what types of exercise are beneficial to control my diabetes.	☐	☐	☐	☐	☐

Note: When scoring the instrument, strongly disagree = 1, disagree = 2, neither agree nor disagree = 3, agree = 4, and strongly agree = 5.

Source: Reprinted (adapted) from *Research in Social and Administrative Pharmacy*, vol. 5, Krass I, Delaney C, Glaubitz S, Kanjanarach T. Measuring patient satisfaction with diabetes disease state management services in community pharmacy. Page 37, 2009, with permission from Elsevier. The patient satisfaction instrument presented in this table is protected under copyright. To use this instrument, please contact the publisher and request permission to use this material.

Each of the preceding examples illustrates common approaches to determining or constructing an instrument that may be used in a patient satisfaction assessment. In addition to identifying an already existing measure, a pharmacist manager may (1) adapt an already existing measure; (2) use a combination of originally developed items and items adapted from an already existing measure; or (3) develop an original measure. The approach used depends greatly on a clear explication of patient satisfaction conceptualization, purpose of the assessment, pharmacy practice setting (location, service type, etc.), consumer population, and disease state. As stated previously, when planning a patient satisfaction assessment, pharmacist managers should carefully consider each of these factors to design and implement an effective measurement process.

SUMMARY

Quality patient care is the goal of the U.S. healthcare system, and pharmacists are well positioned to promote quality healthcare products and services. Patient satisfaction is a key quality indicator in pharmacy and other healthcare settings. Efforts to promote patient satisfaction, in conjunction with optimization of economic, clinical, and humanistic outcomes, may facilitate and enhance the success of pharmacy goods, services, or organizations. This chapter defines patient satisfaction and discusses its key characteristics and relationships to other outcomes, as well as provides practical information on how to design and measure patient satisfaction.

References

1. Donabedian A. *The Definition of Quality and Approaches to Its Assessment.* Vol. 1. Ann Arbor, MI: Health Administration Press; 1980.

2. Pharmacy Quality Alliance. Measure descriptions for demonstrations. Available at: http://www.pqaalliance.org/files/PQA_MeasureDescriptionsForDemonstrations.pdf. Accessed May 7, 2009.

3. Hospital compare—a quality tool for adults, including those with Medicare. Available at: http://www.hospitalcompare.hhs.gov/Hospital/Search/Welcome.asp. Accessed September 25, 2008.

4. Schommer JC, Kucukarslan SN. Measuring patient satisfaction with pharmaceutical services. *Am J Health-Syst Pharm* 1997;23:2721–2732.

5. Gourley GA, Portner TS, Gourley DR, et al. Humanistic outcomes in the hypertension and COPD arms of a multicenter outcomes study. *J Am Pharm Assoc* 1998;38(pt 3):586–597.

6. Ware JE, Wright WR, Snyder MK, et al. Consumer perceptions of health care services: implications for academic medicine. *J Med Educ* 1975;50:839–848.

7. Ross CK, Frommelt G, Hazelwood L. The role of expectations in patient satisfaction with medical care. *J Health Care Mark* 1987;7:16–26.

8. Krass I, Delaney C, Glaubitz S, Kanjanarach T. Measuring patient satisfaction with diabetes disease state management services in community pharmacy. *Res Soc Admin Pharm* 2009;5:31–39.

9. Shepherd MD. Development of innovative services. In: *Effective Pharmacy Management.* 8th ed. Alexandria, VA: NARD; 1996:515–543.

10. Dearmin J, Brenner J, Miglini R. Reporting on QI efforts for internal and external customers. *J Qual Improv* 1995;21:277–288.

11. Schommer JC, Wenzel RG, Kucukarslan SN. Evaluation of pharmacists' services for hospital inpatients. *Am J Health-Syst Pharm* 2002;59:1632–1637.

12. Silow-Carroll S, Alteras T, Stepnik L. Patient-centered care for underserved populations: definition and best practices. Economic and Social Research Institute. 2006. Available at: http://www.esresearch.org/documents_06/Overview.pdf. Accessed April 28, 2009.

13. Kemper DW, Metzler M. *Information Therapy: Prescribed Information as a Reimbursable Medical Service.* 1st ed. Boise, ID: Healthwise; 2002.

14. James G. The twelve laws of customer satisfaction. Available at: http://blogs.bnet.com/salesmachine/?p=462&tag=nl.rSINGLE. Accessed May 7, 2009.

15. Johnson KA, Parker JP, McCombs JS, Cody M. The Kaiser Permanente/USC patient consultation study: patient satisfaction with pharmaceutical services. *Am J Health-Syst Pharm* 1998;55:2621–2629.

16. Pope CR. Consumer satisfaction in a health maintenance organization. *J Health Soc Behav* 1978;19:291–303.

17. Briesacher B, Corey R. Patient satisfaction with pharmaceutical services at independent and chain pharmacies. *Am J Health-Syst Pharm* 1997;54:531–536.

18. Davis E, Christensen C, Nystrom K, Foral P, Destache C. Patient satisfaction and costs associated with insulin administered by pen device or syringe during hospitalization. *Am J Health-Syst Pharm* 2008;65(14):1347–1357.

19. Malfair Taylor S, de Lemos M, Jang D, et al. Impact on patient satisfaction with a structured counselling approach on natural health products. *J Oncol Pharm Pract* 2008;14(1):37–43.

20. Zed PJ, Filiatrault L. Clinical outcomes and patient satisfaction of a pharmacist-managed, emergency department-based outpatient treatment program for venous thromboembolic disease. *Can J Emerg Med* 2008;10:10–17.

21. Murray M, Young J, Hoke S, et al. Pharmacist intervention to improve medication adherence in heart failure. *Ann Intern Med* 2007;146(10):714–725.

22. Kumar R, Kirking D, Hass S, et al. The association of consumer expectations, experiences, and satisfaction with newly prescribed medications. *Qual Life Res* 2007;16(7):1127–1136.

23. Christensen DB, Roth M, Trygstad T, Byrd J. Evaluation of a pilot medication therapy management project within the North Carolina State Health Plan. *J Am Pharm Assoc* 2007;47(4):471–483.

24. Collins C, Kramer A, O'Day M, Low M. Evaluation of patient and provider satisfaction with a pharmacist-managed lipid clinic in a Veterans Affairs medical center. *Am J Health-Syst Pharm* 2006;63(18):1723–1727.

25. Scott D, Boyd S, Stephan M, Augustine S, Reardon T. Outcomes of pharmacist-managed diabetes care services in a community health center. *Am J Health-Syst Pharm* 2006;63(21):2116–2122.

26. Chan F, Wong R, Lau W, Chan T, Cheng G, You J. Management of Chinese patients on warfarin therapy in two models of anticoagulation service—a prospective randomized trial. *Brit J Clin Pharm* 2006;62(5):601–609.

27. Law A, Shapiro K. Impact of a community pharmacist-directed clinic in improving screening and awareness of osteoporosis. *J Eval Clin Pract* 2005;11(3):247–255.

28. The Community Pharmacy Medicines Management Project Evaluation Team. The MEDMAN study: a randomized controlled trial of community pharmacy-led medicines management for patients with coronary heart disease. *Fam Pract* 2007;24:189–200.

29. Fera T, Bluml BM, Ellis WM, Schaller CW, Garrett DG. The Diabetes Ten City Challenge: interim clinical and humanistic outcomes of a multisite community pharmacy diabetes care program. *J Am Pharm Assoc* 2008;48:181–190.

30. Moultry AM, Poon IO. Perceived value of a home-based medication therapy management program for the elderly. *Consult Pharm* 2008;23:877–885.

31. Gunter MJ. The role of the ECHO model in outcomes research and clinical practice improvement. *Am J Manag Care* 1999;5(4, suppl):S217–S224.

32. Kozma CM, Reeder CE, Schulz RM. Economic, clinical, and humanistic outcomes: a planning model for pharmacoeconomic research. *Clin Ther* 1993;15:1121–1132.

33. Cranor CW, Bunting BA, Christensen DB. The Asheville Project: long-term clinical and economic outcomes of a community pharmacy diabetes care program. *J Am Pharm Assoc* 2003;43:173–184.

34. Bunting BA, Smith BH, Sutherland SE. The Asheville Project: clinical and economic outcomes of a community-based long-term medication therapy management program for hypertension and dyslipidemia. *J Am Pharm Assoc* 2008;48:23–31.

35. Bunting BA, Cranor CW. The Asheville Project: long-term clinical, humanistic, and economic outcomes of a community-based medication therapy management program for asthma. *J Am Pharm Assoc* 2006;46:133–147.

36. Cranor CW, Christensen DB. The Asheville Project: short-term outcomes of a community pharmacy diabetes care program. *J Am Pharm Assoc* 2003;43:14–159.

37. Loh A, Leonhart R, Wills CE, Simon D, Härter M. The impact of patient participation on adherence and clinical outcomes in primary care of depression. *Patient Educ Couns* 2007;65:69–78.

38. Loh A, Simon D, Wills CE, Kriston L, Niebling W, Härter M. The effects of a shared decision-making intervention in primary care of depression: a cluster-randomized controlled trial. *Patient Educ Couns* 2007;67:324–332.

39. Naik AD, Kallen MA, Walder A, Street RL Jr. Improving hypertension control in diabetes mellitus: the effects of collaborative and proactive health communication. *Circulation* 2008;117:1361–1368.

40. Ware JE Jr, Snyder MK, Wright WR, Davies AR. Defining and measuring patient satisfaction with medical care. *Eval Prog Plan* 1983;6:247–263.

41. MacKeigan LD, Larson LN. Development and validation of an instrument to measure patient satisfaction with pharmacy services. *Med Care* 1989;27:522–536.

42. Larson LN, Rovers JP, MacKeigan LD. Patient satisfaction with pharmaceutical care: update of a validated instrument. *J Am Pharm Assoc* 2002;42:44–50.

43. Malone DC, Rascati KL, Gagnon JP. Consumers' evaluation of value-added pharmacy services. *Am Pharm* 1993;NS33(3):48–56.

44. Rubin A, Babbie E. *Research Methods for Social Work.* 4th ed. Belmont, CA: Wadsworth; 2001.

Abbreviations

CDN:	Canadian
DDSM-Q:	Diabetes Disease State Management Questionnaire
DQOL:	Diabetes Quality of Life
DVT:	deep vein thrombosis
ECHO:	economic, clinical, humanistic outcomes
ED:	emergency department
LDL:	low-density lipoprotein
PES:	Pharmacy Encounter Survey
PQA:	Pharmacy Quality Alliance
PSQ:	Patient Satisfaction Questionnaire
TSQM:	Treatment Satisfaction Questionnaire for Medications
VTE:	venous thromboembolism

Case Scenarios

CASE ONE: SuperCo Pharmacy fills 149,240 prescriptions per year and offers immunization services at a cost of $25/injection. It also provides medication therapy management (MTM) for hypertension and disease state management for diabetes on request, and both are reimbursed through third-party payers or by patients ($45/hour). Appointments for these services are offered between 8 a.m. and 12 p.m., Monday through Friday. On the basis of refill records, SuperCo patients average 68% adherence with medications prescribed for chronic illnesses. Demand for MTM and disease state management has declined recently, and patient surveys indicate decreased patient satisfaction over the past two years. If you were hired as a consultant to SuperCo, how would you improve services to increase patient satisfaction?

CASE TWO: MedMart, a retail pharmacy, implemented a specialized management service for consumers with HIV and AIDS six months ago. The service includes medication counseling and education, disease state education, adherence counseling and reminders, and provision of information regarding other support services available in the community. The pharmacist manager of MedMart would like to know whether the new service is meeting patient needs and expectations. Identify the conceptualization(s) that should be used in a patient satisfaction assessment of MedMart's HIV/AIDS

(continues)

management service. Specify factors that may be addressed in the patient satisfaction instrument.

CASE THREE: You have been employed in a small rural hospital for 15 years. The pharmacy department has made great strides in automation with dispensing cabinets in each patient care area, electronic medication administration records, and bedside charting. The pharmacy computer system offers up-to-date drug information sheets for patients on all formulary drugs. The discharge process includes issuance of an electronic list of medications to the nurse with generic and brand names and a link to the patient information sheet. However, patient satisfaction surveys for your hospital consistently reflect low scores for medication education on discharge. Currently, nurses are the primary healthcare professionals performing discharge counseling, and the nursing department has requested assistance from the pharmacy department. What can you do as a pharmacist to ensure that patients receive adequate information about their medications on discharge from the hospital and are more satisfied with their discharge education?

Additional Resources Available Online!

Visit the Student Companion Web site at http://healthprofessions.jbpub.com/pharmacymanagement for interactive study tools and additional resources.

See www.rxugace.com to learn how you can obtain continuing pharmacy education for this content.

PLANNING

ACHIEVING RESULTS THROUGH OTHERS AND STRATEGIC PLANNING

GLENN Y. YOKOYAMA, PharmD, FCSHP, FAPhA

CHRISTINA A. SPIVEY, PhD

LEE C. VERMEULEN, MS, RPh, FCCP

LEARNING OBJECTIVES

After completing the chapter, the reader will be able to

1. Determine the role of stakeholders in setting organizational goals.
2. Identify human capital management drivers (facilitators) and practices.
3. Formulate strategies for engaging pharmacy employees to achieve results.
4. Recommend approaches to improve communication between pharmacist managers and employees.
5. List the primary components of a strategic plan.
6. Explain the value of an organizational SWOT (strengths, weaknesses, opportunities, and threats) analysis.
7. Discuss requirements for successful execution of strategic plans.

KEY CONCEPTS

❶ To achieve desired results, effective pharmacist managers must be able to negotiate individual differences and leverage individual strengths so that employees are able to demonstrate their best talents. Managers must also effectively create a workplace culture and organizational norms conducive to high performance.

❷ Key stakeholders should be identified and involved in setting desired organizational goals, as they may have critical information or ideas for establishing the direction of the organization.

❸ To ensure the success of the organization, a qualified and dedicated employee base is essential, as the operation of an organization depends on employees at every level adequately completing their assigned duties.

❹ To promote human capital management, pharmacist managers should assess leadership practices, employee engagement, knowledge accessibility, workforce optimization, and learning capacity.

⑤ Establishing and maintaining effective, consistent communication between pharmacist managers and employees is necessary for employees to participate actively in decision making.

⑥ Participative management develops cooperation between employees and managers; such cooperation may lead to increased participation in execution, higher performance level, and better-quality results.

⑦ Strategic planning is a tool that may be used to pursue and achieve organizational goals and desired results.

⑧ The goals of great strategic plans cannot be achieved without great execution. Strategic execution refers to the act of putting action strategies developed as part of the strategic plan into practice. Planning without execution is essentially an exercise in futility.

INTRODUCTION

Vincent Lombardi, the well-known professional football coach, once said, "The achievements of an organization are the result of the combined effort of each individual."[1] Like football, the operation of the pharmacy is a team endeavor, as one person alone cannot attain organizational success. Pharmacy leaders, managers, and staff have specific responsibilities and tasks that must be fulfilled to achieve desired results. Like a football coach, the pharmacist leader or manager must procure results through the work of his or her players, or employees. **❶** *To achieve desired results, effective pharmacist managers must be able to negotiate individual differences and leverage individual strengths so that employees are able to demonstrate their best talents. Managers must also effectively create a workplace culture and organizational norms conducive to high performance.*[2] Managers should ask the following:

- What results do we want to achieve?
- Why do we want to achieve these results?
- How will we achieve these results?

- Who are the stakeholders, and at what level should they be engaged in achieving results?
- Who needs to be involved in achieving results?
- What is the time frame to achieve results?
- What resources are available to achieve results?
- How will we know the results have been achieved?

This chapter describes the fundamental elements needed to answer the preceding questions. As noted in **Figure 13–1**, these elements include understanding **stakeholder** needs, hiring, engaging, and evaluating the right people, and identifying and using resources. In addition, this chapter will discuss **strategic planning**, a tool that may be useful to pharmacist leaders and managers in achieving results through others.

STAKEHOLDER NEEDS

The initial step in achieving results through others is to establish exactly what results or outcomes need to be achieved relative to a specific organizational issue or problem. To identify desired results, we must first understand the needs and demands of stakeholders, defined as people or entities who may be affected by an organization's practices and/or policies.[3] Stakeholders may include customers, patients, employees, shareholders/owners, and the community from which the organization derives its resources and clients.[3] **❷** *Key stakeholders should be identified and involved in setting desired organizational goals, as they may have critical information or ideas for establishing the direction of the organization.* Because key stakeholders will vary by organization, a stakeholder analysis may be useful in identifying stakeholders and their specific interests in an organizational issue and then assessing or ranking the importance of each stakeholder to that particular issue.[4] Interviews with managers and employees may be part of this analysis. After key stakeholders are identified, discussions should be held regarding their organization-related needs and desires; this information may then be used to help develop the organization's goals. Following identification of organizational goals, the next step is to make sure the right people are in the right place to achieve these goals.

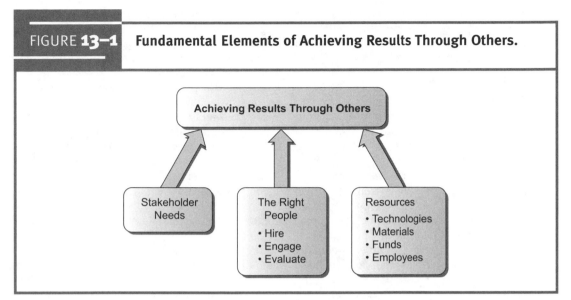

FIGURE **13–1**   **Fundamental Elements of Achieving Results Through Others.**

The elements required to achieve results through others include understanding stakeholder needs, hiring and engaging the right people, and identifying available resources. These elements provide the foundation necessary for achieving desired results through others.

THE RIGHT PEOPLE

❸ *To ensure the success of the organization, a qualified and dedicated employee base is essential, as the operation of an organization depends on employees at every level adequately completing their assigned duties.* Thus, organizations must hire, engage, and evaluate the right people—individuals who are most qualified and have the right attitude to perform needed actions and achieve results.

Hiring Employees

Pharmacy organizations should strive to "hire the right people in the right positions with the right skills at the right time."[5(pp45-46)] In other words, organizations should create jobs (positions) to fill identified needs and hire the best individuals to fill those positions. A critical step in identifying qualified individuals is defining the requirements of the position, as well as characteristics and qualities necessary to attain success in that position (refer to Chapter 14, "Pharmacy Business and Staff Planning," and Chapter 18, "Successful Recruitment and Hiring Strategies"). Leaders and managers then identify, recruit, and hire the

candidate who represents the "best fit" with the organization—the candidate who has the necessary and desired qualifications, experience, characteristics, drive to be a successful part of the organization, and temperament/personality to work well with fellow employees within the existing organizational structure. For example, a pharmacist manager is interested in recruiting an inpatient pediatric pharmacist. Candidate A completed a pediatric pharmacy residency and has worked in an inpatient pediatrics unit at a well-known medical center for four years. Candidate B also completed a pediatric pharmacy residency and has worked as a pediatric pharmacist for two years. The two candidates have equivalent education. During the interview process, the pharmacist manager and the pediatrics team are unable to establish rapport with Candidate A, but do so easily with Candidate B. Although Candidate A has slightly more experience than Candidate B, there are concerns that Candidate A's personality will inhibit effective interactions with staff, patients, and parents or guardians. Therefore, Candidate B is viewed as the better fit and is offered the position. As illustrated in this example, job candidates who are considered a good organizational fit generally demonstrate a balance between desired qualifications/experience and other favorable characteristics.

Putting Employees to Work

After the right people have been hired, these individuals should receive a thorough orientation to ensure that they understand the duties of their position. The orientation process should also provide new employees with a sense of organizational values, culture, and expectations and introduce them to the people and systems they will need to be successful (refer to Chapter 18, "Successful Recruitment and Hiring Strategies"). Pharmacist managers should facilitate and foster effective working relationships both with employees and between employees and provide these individuals with (1) clear work assignments, (2) a description of expected results, (3) time frames for completing assignments, (4) resources necessary to complete assignments, and (5) indicators that will be used to evaluate job performance.[6,7] Refer to Chapter 19 ("Effective Performance Management"). Without these details, many will have trouble producing desired results. Ensuring that employees have this information and other tools and resources necessary to do their jobs in an effective and efficient manner is referred to as **human capital management** (HCM).[6]

HUMAN CAPITAL MANAGEMENT

As employees provide organizations with a competitive advantage, organizations that neglect or devalue their employees imperil opportunities for success.[6] ◀④ *To promote HCM, pharmacist managers should assess the following five HCM drivers: (1) leadership practices, (2)* **employee engagement***, (3) knowledge accessibility, (4) workforce optimization, and (5) learning capacity.*[6] HCM drivers are broad categories of organizational practices that "drive," or promote, the success of operations and employee performance. Leadership practices, the first driver, are those actions and behaviors of leaders and managers that contribute to improved working conditions for employees. Employee engagement practices promote employees' investment in their work and in the organization. Knowledge accessibility, workforce optimization,

and learning capacity practices represent efforts to augment work conditions, promote performance, and build on employee strengths to achieve results. Specific practices related to each HCM driver are further described in **Table 13–1**.[6]

Strong HCM practices may provide a foundation through which employee performance can be maximized and outcomes can be realized, while weak HCM practices will inhibit employee performance and achievement. As an example, two hospital pharmacies install a new computerized dispensing system, and different approaches are taken to train employees to use the new system. The manager of Pharmacy A arranges a one-day training program for pharmacists and pharmacy technicians. By the end of training, all employees demonstrate a moderate-to-strong ability to navigate the new system. Pharmacy B's manager distributes copies of the new system's instruction manual but does not offer formal training. Because the manual is full of technical jargon, employees have difficulty understanding and using the new system. In this example, Pharmacy A exhibited a stronger approach than Pharmacy B in the HCM practice of training. Organizational leaders and managers should develop and implement efforts to improve and maintain HCM strengths to facilitate the success of employees and, ultimately, the success of the organization.

Engaging Employees

Engaged employees are invested in and committed to what they are doing—they are employees who care about the quality of their work and recognize their jobs as valuable and contributing to the organization's purpose.[8] Employees who do not care about the results of their work are not likely to put forth their best effort and produce desired outcomes. The Corporate Leadership Council (CLC), a membership of senior executives committed to advancing human resources management, conducted a study of employee engagement among more than 50,000 employees from 59 organizations worldwide.[8] The CLC found that strongly engaged, committed employees were 87% less likely to leave their positions and 57% more likely to work harder and try to perform at a high level compared with less engaged and committed employees.[8] Therefore, leaders and managers

TABLE 13-1 Human Capital Management Drivers and Practices

HCM Drivers / HCM Practices	Leadership Practices	Employee Engagement	Knowledge Accessibility	Workforce Optimization	Learning Capacity
	Communication Management's communication is open and effective.	*Job design* Work is well organized and taps employees' skills.	*Availability* Job-related information and training are readily available.	*Processes* Work processes are well defined, and training is effective.	*Innovation* New ideas are welcome.
	Inclusiveness Management collaborates with employees and invites input.	*Commitment* Jobs are secure, employees are recognized, and advancement is possible.	*Collaboration* Teamwork is encouraged and enabled.	*Conditions* Working conditions support high performance.	*Training* Training is practical and supports organizational goals.
	Supervisory skills Managers eliminate barriers, provide feedback, and inspire confidence.	*Time* Workload allows employees to do jobs well and enables good work/life balance.	*Information sharing* Best practices are shared and improved.	*Accountability* High performance is expected and rewarded.	*Development* Employees have formal career development plans.
	Executive skills Senior executives eliminate barriers, provide feedback, and inspire confidence.	*Systems* Employee engagement is continually evaluated.	*Systems* Collection systems make information easily available.	*Hiring* Hires are chosen on the basis of skill; new hires complete a thorough orientation.	*Value and support* Leaders demonstrate that learning is valued.
	Systems Leadership development and transition systems are effective.			*Systems* Employee performance management systems are effective.	*Systems* A learning management system automates aspects of training.

Note: HCM = human capital management.

Source: Reproduced with permission from *Harvard Business Review.* From "Maximizing your return on people" by Bassi L, McMurrer D. 85(3)/2007. Copyright ©2007 by the Harvard Business School Publishing Corporation.

must take steps to engage employees in the work process and its outcomes.

Four HCM practices described in Table 13–1 provide the foundation for employee engagement and include: (1) well-organized job design that uses employee skills; (2) job security, recognition, and advancement; (3) reasonable timelines for job and work/life balance; and (4) continual assessment or staying in touch with employees to make sure they are actively involved in their work.[6] Each practice is designed to promote employee satisfaction with and commitment to their position, thereby increasing engagement. The CLC study identified additional priority elements in facilitating engagement, including effective management and leadership; equitable, performance-based compensation; benefit plans that address employee needs; purposeful, clearly defined work; opportunities for learning and development; and an organizational culture committed to community, integrity, equity, diversity, and flexibility.[8] Leaders and managers should also consider using the following strategies as they engage employees:

- Defining organizational mission, vision, and values[5,9]
- Facilitating good communication[10,11]
- Sharing decision making, or practicing participative management[11,12]

DEFINING MISSION, VISION, AND VALUES

Organizations develop mission, vision, and values statements to provide employees and other stakeholders with information regarding the organization's purpose, goals, and priorities. Each statement should facilitate employee engagement by creating an intellectual and emotional connection to the organization.[13] The **mission statement** briefly describes the purpose of an organization (i.e., why the organization exists) and should provide value to the work employees perform.[5,9] Take, for example, *Pharmacy X's* mission, which reads as follows:

We are a successful neighborhood pharmacy that offers affordable products and services consumers need to lead healthy and satisfac-

tory lives. Delivery of services is a collaborative effort by our caring and knowledgeable staff members who are committed to providing our consumers an excellent pharmacy experience.

While a mission statement defines why an organization exists, a **vision statement** captures its aspirations;[9] for example, *Pharmacy X's* vision may be "to be a national leader in providing affordable and accessible high-quality pharmaceutical products and services to eliminate healthcare disparities among patients." The vision statement provides employees with a long-term goal to work toward; it is not something that can be achieved easily or within a brief period. The vision is intended to inspire and create emotional investment among employees who should *want* to achieve this future state.

The organization's mission and vision generally reflect the organization's **values**, or central priorities.[9,11] For example, *Pharmacy X's* values include valuing the lives of consumers, encouraging staff members to pursue development and growth opportunities, winning through collaboration and teamwork, and a commitment to respect, professionalism, diversity, and **cultural competence**. Values help define organizational culture and provide an employee with general expectations of how the organization operates and how they should operate as representatives of the organization.

COMMUNICATION

Effective communication (verbal, nonverbal, or written) between pharmacist managers and employees supports organizational success by promoting performance, enhancing work conditions, clarifying assignments/tasks, setting expectations, identifying needed resources, resolving conflicts, building relationships, etc.[11] To enhance communication, pharmacist managers should[10]

- Use simple, straightforward language (in other words, use language and terminology that is common to the workplace and familiar to employees, and avoid jargon as much as possible).

- Be prepared. Know what needs to be communicated and why.
- Tell the truth. Truth promotes trust between managers and employees.
- Make sure the person receiving the communication understands the message. Use examples to better illustrate the point, if needed. Ask for confirmation of understanding by requiring a response indicating comprehension.
- Be consistent in communications. Do not provide conflicting information to groups or individuals within the organization, and avoid communicating more or less information to different individuals.
- Try to be brief. The longer the communication, the greater the probability that you will stray from the topic or lose audience attention.[10]

❺ *Establishing and maintaining effective, consistent communication between pharmacist managers and employees is necessary for employees to participate actively in decision making.*

DECISION MAKING AND PARTICIPATIVE MANAGEMENT

Employees should be part of the decision-making process that affects their work for two reasons: (1) they are likely to have information and ideas that will help facilitate sound decisions and (2) such collaboration with managers will further enhance employee investment in their work and results. **Table 13–2** details actions that enhance or deter the quality of decisions,[14] and **Table 13–3** provides questions that may help guide the decision-making process.[15] Involving employees in decision making is a critical aspect of **participative management**, which requires managers and employees to share

---

TABLE 13–2   Actions That Improve or Deter the Quality of Decision Making

The quality of the decision improves when one:
- Clearly defines the issue
- Gathers accurate, reliable, timely information/data
- Seeks outside consultation when appropriate
- Identifies or develops possible solutions
- Assesses possible solutions
- Evaluates consequences of possible solutions
- Selects the best solution
- Sleeps on it when appropriate

The quality of the decision suffers when one:
- Makes decisions too quickly
- Does not have all the information/data necessary
- Does not seek outside consultation when needed
- Overanalyzes
- Involves too many decision makers in the process
- Bases decision on past experience rather than current situation
- Tries to satisfy too many stakeholders
- Uses intuition rather than fact

Source: Data from McGuire R.[14]

TABLE **13–3**	Questions to Guide Decision Making

1. What are the key issues?

2. Do you have interim checkpoints, and, if so, what is the timeline and deadline?

3. What is the deadline for completion, and is this the drop dead date?

4. Do you have all the facts and information you need?

5. Who are the stakeholders, and is there a way of involving them in the decision?

6. Are there others affected by the decision?

7. Do you need to ask for outside help or counsel?

8. Is this a long-term decision, or will an interim or stopgap decision be sufficient?

9. What are the implications of your decision on others?

Source: Adapted with permission from Fleming I.[15]

responsibility, authority (ownership), and accountability for work efforts and results. ⑥ *Participative management develops cooperation between employees and managers; such cooperation may lead to increased participation in execution, higher performance level, and better-quality results.* Thus, participative management has "enormous potential for raising productivity, bettering morale, and improving creative thinking."[12(p55–56)]

Evaluating Employees

Performance can be summarized in the equation:[5]

$$Performance = Ability \times Motivation \times Support$$

Monitoring and **evaluating** are key mechanisms by which pharmacist managers (1) galvanize desired employee performance; (2) provide **feedback** that encourages development, improvement, and use of the employee's abilities and strengths; (3) communicate support for employee work efforts; and (4) motivate employees to take ownership of their work, thereby creating accountability. A four-pronged approach to monitoring and evaluating employee performance includes the following:[5]

- Making interpersonal contact by observing employees and keeping in touch with them (e.g., through informal conversations, e-mail).[5]
- Measuring individual performance by monitoring and reviewing individual performance against desired results.[5] Formal evaluation of employee performance should take place at least once annually. Before individual performance evaluations, employees should be informed of the measures that will be used to assess performance.[16,17]
- Being visible and accessible outside of one's office by walking around the unit/department, interacting with employees, asking good questions, and answering the questions of employees.[5]
- Keeping a scorecard. Managers should monitor and measure the performance of the unit or department as a whole against established performance metrics (the "scorecard").[5]

RESOURCES

Resources are those materials, funds, technologies, and people needed to conduct work assignments and achieve desired results.[9] Few assignments within a pharmacy organization can be accomplished without providing resources to employees. For example, up-to-date drug information resources are necessary for providing efficacious patient care, and pharmacist managers should acquire current and relevant drug information resources for their staff. Pharmacist managers and employees should collaborate on identifying resources needed to enable effective employee performance, with due consideration given to the cost involved in acquiring these resources.

THE STRATEGIC PLAN

Developing a strategic plan "involves deciding where you want to go, how you can get there, what you have to watch out for, and what it is likely to cost you."[11(p117)] ❼ *While business planning provides a model for the structure and operation of the business, strategic planning is a tool that may be used to pursue and achieve organizational goals and desired results.* Refer to Chapter 14, "Pharmacy Business and Staff Planning." A logical, realistic fit should exist between the elements of the strategic plan and the structure of the organization.[10] In other words, the strategic plan should reflect the organization's purpose, represent the interests of stakeholders, and consider the organization's human capital and other resources. The strategic planning process involves the following steps:[9,11,18]

1. Organizing a strategic planning team, including key stakeholders
2. Identifying the organization's strategic direction
3. Conducting a strategic analysis
4. Defining major goals
5. Developing an action plan
6. Developing a monitoring and evaluation system, which includes identifying metrics for success
7. Communicating the plan to others

Each step in the planning process (discussed in the following sections) is necessary to further the development of a cohesive, realistic plan designed to promote the organization's success. **Figure** 13–2 provides a strategic planning template, and **Figure 13–3** depicts an example of a strategic plan developed by *Pharmacy X* to address the implementation of cognitive pharmacy services (please note, this is a simplified example of a strategic plan; actual strategic plans developed by organizations are generally more detailed and complex). The strategic planning process should be followed by strategic execution, or implementation, of the plan.

Organizing a Strategic Planning Team

Individuals throughout the pharmacy organization have much to contribute to strategic planning ideas, information, and experience. Internal stakeholders such as pharmacist managers and employees who are directly involved in the day-to-day operation of the organization generally have a strong grasp of what may or may not be needed and, therefore, contribute balance and practicality to the strategic planning process. In addition to internal stakeholders, external stakeholders tend to contribute unique perspectives and valuable input to the strategic plan due to their position outside the organization. Stakeholders may serve on the strategic planning team, or may be surveyed or interviewed to gather input. In the *Pharmacy X* example, the owner included both external stakeholders (community physician, longtime consumer) and internal stakeholders (pharmacist manager, staff pharmacist, technician) on his strategic planning team.

Identifying Strategic Direction

To provide planners with a trajectory of where the organization is heading, the strategic planning process should begin by identifying the overall purpose of the organization, its future direction, and its priorities—its vision, mission, and values.[9] The strategic plan should move the organization toward achieving its vision, fulfilling its mission, and representing those values the organization considers important. For example, **cost-effective** cognitive services may contribute to achieving *Pharmacy X's* vision (the elimination of health disparities in their patient population). In addition, these services would likely help *Pharmacy X* fulfill its mission (providing access to medications and services) and represent the organization's values, particularly valuing the lives of consumers.

FIGURE **13–2**   Strategic Plan Template.

Strategic Direction

Mission:

Vision:

Values:

Strategic (SWOT) Analysis

Strengths:

Weaknesses:

Opportunities:

Threats:

Long-term Goals

Goal 1:

Goal 2:

Action Plan

Objective 1:

   Strategy 1:

     Tactic 1a:

     Tactic 1b:

Objective 2:

   Strategy 2:

     Tactic 2a:

     Tactic 2b:

Monitoring and Evaluation Plan

Monitoring Strategies:

Evaluation:

   Schedule:

   Metrics:

FIGURE **13–3**   **Strategic Plan of *Pharmacy X.***

Strategic Direction

Mission: To be a successful neighborhood pharmacy that offers access to affordable products and services needed by consumers to lead healthy and satisfactory lives. Delivery of services is a collaborative effort by our caring, committed, and knowledgeable staff members in order to provide an excellent pharmacy experience.

Vision: To be a national leader in the provision of affordable and accessible high-quality pharmaceutical products and services in order to eliminate healthcare disparities among patients.

Values: Valuing the lives of consumers, encouraging staff members to pursue development and growth opportunities, winning through collaboration and teamwork, and a commitment to respect, professionalism, diversity, and cultural competence.

Strategic (SWOT) Analysis

Strengths: One of only three retail pharmacies in a community with approximately 5,000 patients with chronic diseases (primarily diabetes, hypertension, and asthma; *Pharmacy X* serves 60% of this population). A loyal consumer base. Strong relationships with community physicians; high patient referral rates from these physicians. Good cash flow.

Weaknesses: Need additional pharmacists on staff. Current space allocation/design of pharmacy not conducive for cognitive pharmacy services (for example, lack of private area to provide services).

Opportunities: Consumers are willing to pay for cognitive pharmacy services. Incidence of chronic disease states (diabetes, hypertension, asthma) is increasing in the community. Other pharmacies in the community do not provide cognitive pharmacy services.

Threats: Two recent pharmacy graduates in the community are considering opening a retail pharmacy. Their plans include offering cognitive pharmacy services.

Long-term Goals

Goal 1: Establish cognitive pharmacy services for patients with diabetes, hypertension, and asthma within one year.

Goal 2: Increase provision of cognitive pharmacy services by 30% within three years.

(continues)

FIGURE **13–3**   (continued)

Action Plan

Objective 1: Hire two new pharmacists within six months.
   Strategy 1: Recruit potential competitors (two recent pharmacy graduates) as new hires.
      Tactic 1a: Have meetings with recent pharmacy graduates to discuss their goals. Point out alignment of their goals with those of *Pharmacy X*.
      Tactic 1b: Offer sign-on bonuses.
      Tactic 1c: Offer incentives such as performance-based bonuses, increased vacation time, funding for development activities, and opportunities to buy into the pharmacy (and eventually become partners in the business). This latter incentive may be particularly appealing to the recent pharmacy graduates as they currently have little capital to start their own business.

Objective 2: Renovate pharmacy within six months to provide designated space for cognitive pharmacy services.
   Strategy 2: Transition a portion of the open space waiting area into a closed office where cognitive pharmacy services will be performed.
      Tactic 2a: Hire an architect to draft a plan/blueprint for the office space.
      Tactic 2b: Hire a contractor to complete the renovation.

Objective 3: Implement marketing and advertising plan within 9 months.
   Strategy 3: Use well-established community resources and venues to inform patient population of the new services.
      Tactic 3a: Purchase ad space in the highly circulated local Sunday newspaper. Ad should run at least once every month for a one-year period. Ad will describe the cognitive pharmacy services (components, time offered, how to set up appointment, etc.).
      Tactic 3b: Ask community physicians to distribute pamphlets describing the cognitive pharmacy services to patients who might benefit from the services.

Objective 4: Establish billing plan for services within 3 months.
   Strategy 4: Draft a billing policy that considers services covered by commonly used third-party payers (such as Medicare), as well as payment plans for patients with limited medical coverage (such as paying for services in installments).
      Tactic 4a: Consult with accountant or other financial planner to determine billing options.
      Tactic 4b: Review data on payment methods of current consumers to determine what billing options may be feasible.

Objective 5: Develop and implement cognitive pharmacy services training program for staff pharmacists within nine months.
   Strategy 5: Conduct a one-day seminar on cognitive pharmacy services (offer seminar on three different dates to accommodate staff schedules).
      Tactic 5a: Review literature on cognitive pharmacy services and put together information packets that will be distributed during training.
      Tactic 5b: Consult with a pharmacist currently providing cognitive services and ask him/her to participate in training.

Monitoring and Evaluation Plan

Monitoring Strategies: Individual performance of staff pharmacists participating in the cognitive pharmacy services program will have regular performance evaluations. The scorecard or metrics of the program will be monitored and measured. The pharmacy owner and pharmacist manager will keep in touch with staff pharmacists involved in the program to informally assess resource needs, answer questions regarding the program, discuss any problems or issues that may arise in the program, etc.

Evaluation:
  <u>Schedule</u>: Evaluation of staff pharmacists involved in the cognitive pharmacy services program will be conducted biannually (in January and July).
  <u>Metrics</u>: Program metrics include the following: (1) for those staff pharmacists involved in the cognitive services program, 20% of weekly work effort will be devoted to providing cognitive services; (2) within one year of enrollment, 80% of patients will be fully adherent to medication therapy regimens; (3) within two years of program enrollment, patients' emergency department visits will decrease by 30%; (4) within two years of enrollment, 70% of diabetic patients will achieve target hemoglobin A_{1c} levels for at least three consecutive months; and (5) within two years of enrollment, 75% of patients with hypertension will achieve target blood pressure levels for at least three consecutive months.

This figure depicts an example of a strategic plan. In this scenario, *Pharmacy X*, a community retail pharmacy, is planning for the development and implementation of cognitive pharmacy services. Responsibility for conducting the majority of the tactics in the action plan will be assigned to the pharmacist manager and members of the *Pharmacy X* staff; however, the pharmacy owner will remain involved executing the plan, particularly in the hiring process and the renovation of the pharmacy.

Conducting a Strategic Analysis

Early in the strategic planning process, it is necessary to assess and analyze the internal and external factors and influences that may affect the organization and strategic plan. A **SWOT analysis** (**Figure 13–4**) is used to assess an organization's internal **s**trengths and **w**eaknesses and external **o**pportunities and **t**hreats.[9,14] Strengths refer to those factors that will be beneficial or conducive to achieving the goals of the strategic plan.[18] In contrast, weaknesses are those characteristics, or factors, that may detract from achieving the goal.[18] Opportunities are those factors that may help the organization achieve goals, while threats are those factors that may hurt the organization's position or performance.[18] With *Pharmacy X*, multiple strengths, weaknesses, opportunities, and threats were identified (Figure 13–3), including a loyal consumer base (a strength), a need for additional pharmacists (a weakness), consumers willing to pay for cogni-

tive services (an opportunity), and potential competition (a threat). The information provided in the SWOT analysis allows strategic planners to determine whether potential goals are achievable given external and internal conditions/situations. If a potential goal is *not* realistically achievable, planners should consider other possible goals that are both attainable and beneficial to the organization.

Defining Major Long-term Goals

With the strategic direction and analysis of the pharmacy organization in mind, planners should define the goals of the strategic plan—what results do we want to achieve? Long-term goals (often several years into the future) are organizational outcomes that reflect the mission of the organization and provide substantial movement toward realizing the vision.[11] McNamara, a strategic planning expert, recommends designing SMARTER goals.[9] In other words, goals should be **s**pecific,

FIGURE **13-4**   **SWOT Analysis Diagram.**

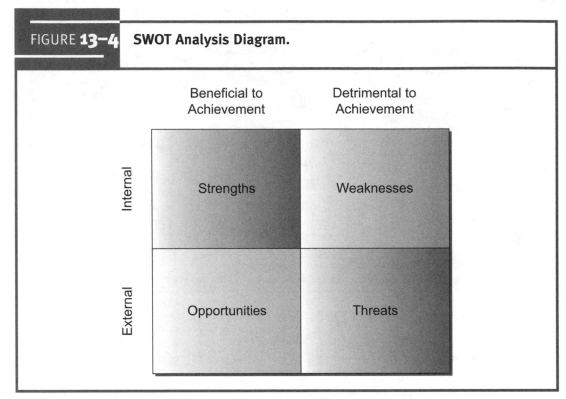

This figure displays an example of how a SWOT (strengths, weaknesses, opportunities, threats) analysis might be organized. Each element of the analysis should consider internal and external factors that may affect organizational success.

measurable, **a**cceptable (to those responsible for achieving goals/objectives), **r**ealistic, **t**ime-based (a time period should be specified for completion or achievement), **e**xtending (working to achieve goals should develop the capabilities of those involved), and **r**ewarding.[9] Pharmacy X's strategic planning team set forth two SMARTER goals: (1) establishing cognitive services within one year and (2) increasing cognitive services by 30% within three years. A critical aspect of strategic planning is the development of strategies and tactics (i.e., actions) that will result in the attainment of goals.

Action Planning

The action plan details strategies—those overarching activities that ensure an organization accomplishes the goals of the strategic plan. Because goals are generally long term, the action plan should include objectives, defined as interim or short-term milestones, that signify progress toward achieving goals (like goals, objectives should be SMARTER), as well as the tactics necessary to accomplish these objectives.[9,19] Tactics are a series of actions deployed when a strategy is implemented; in other words, they are the actions/tasks taken to execute a strategy and achieve a result (objective).[9] **Figure 13-5** represents the relationship between vision, mission, goals, objectives, strategies/tactics, and results and, more specifically, the evolution from an overarching, guiding vision to specific results of the strategic plan. In *Pharmacy X*, establishing cognitive services will require achieving multiple

---

| FIGURE **13-5** | **Relationship Between Vision, Mission, Goals, Objectives, Strategies/Tactics, and Results.** |

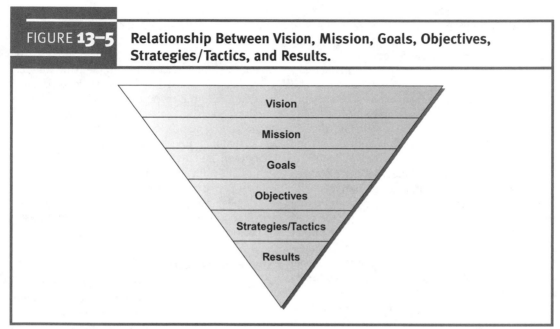

This figure displays the evolution from overarching vision and mission statements that establish the direction and purpose of the organization to more specific goals established during strategic planning, the objectives and corresponding strategies/tactics to accomplish these goals, and the results of strategies/tactics.

objectives, including hiring two additional staff pharmacists. A strategy to accomplish this objective is to recruit two recent pharmacy graduates in the community who are considering opening their own pharmacy. Thus, *Pharmacy X's* owner may use the following tactics: (1) offer sign-on bonuses; (2) provide incentives, such as performance-based bonuses and increased vacation time; and (3) fund development activities.

The action plan should also set the timeline for accomplishing objectives, and responsibility for carrying out tactics and strategies should be assigned to the employee or group/team of employees best equipped with knowledge, skills, and experience to conduct the needed work.[9] Available resources need to be identified as part of the development of strategies and tactics; the plan should include a description of those resources (money, technology, materials, people), why they are needed to achieve objectives, when they will be used or deployed, and how they will be used to

get results. Budgets may be used to describe the costs of needed resources and how these resources will be funded.[9]

Monitoring and Evaluating

Following the development of the action plan, a plan for monitoring and evaluating execution of the action plan and achievement of strategic results should be designed for comparing actual performance to planned performance—in other words, to determine whether the organization is fulfilling the strategic plan's goals and objectives.[9] Elements of the monitoring and evaluation plan include (1) determining which monitoring strategies will be predominately used; (2) establishing the measures, or metrics, that will be used to evaluate progress toward achieving strategic goals and objectives; and (3) setting a schedule for conducting evaluations. Figure 13–3 details the monitoring and evaluation plan of *Pharmacy X*; specific elements of the plan include establishing a biannual performance evaluation schedule and defining metrics, such as devoting 20% of weekly work effort to cognitive services.

To their detriment, few organizations actually implement an ongoing, routine monitoring and evaluation plan, which may compromise decision-making regarding the optimal use of resources and progress toward the vision.[19] To explain further, managers should monitor work to understand what is being done, how it is being done, the success of what is being done, and the resources being used. While monitoring, a manager may realize that a strategy is not effective or is not producing desired results. The manager then has the opportunity to alter that strategy before further resources are wasted. In this way, tactics/strategies may be modified to optimize outcomes. Keep in mind that a plan cannot exist in a vacuum; as conditions change, the strategic plan must allow a degree of fluidity or deviation to compensate and maintain progress toward the achievement of objectives.[18]

Communicating the Plan

The strategic plan should be communicated, both verbally and in writing, to employees responsible for completing tactics/work assignments and other stakeholders.[9] Employees who participated as strategic planning team members may be particularly well suited to communicate the plan to their colleagues. They are positioned to describe how the plan was developed, why it is important (its purpose), and how achieving the plan will benefit the community, the organization, and stakeholders, including employees. It is likely, however, that multiple individuals (employees, managers, leaders) will be involved in communicating the plan. For example, *Pharmacy X's* owner held a staff meeting in which he presented the plan to employees; he also asked the staff pharmacist and pharmacy technician members of the strategic planning team to hold both formal and informal discussions regarding the plan with their fellow employees. These multiple communicators should use similar language to be consistent in how they present the plan. They should also be careful about adding their own opinions or conjectures about ideas, objectives, actions, etc., as this may result

in the delivery of contradictory messages and lead to confusion about the plan. Thus, communication of the plan should include a clear, concrete, straightforward description of the actions to be taken, the timeline to complete the plan, the outcomes (also referred to as the work product) expected, and the resources available. Employees should understand exactly what is expected of them (setting standards for the work product) and know that their performance and outcomes will be monitored and evaluated. This type of effective communication helps create "buy-in," wherein employees become engaged, or invested, in accomplishing the plan's outcomes. The more invested employees are, the more likely they are to perform at a high level to achieve results.

Strategic Execution

❽ *The goals of great strategic plans cannot be achieved without great execution. Strategic execution refers to the act of putting action strategies developed as part of the strategic plan into practice. Planning without execution is essentially an exercise in futility.* Organizations generally actualize only 60% of the value of their strategic plans—a 40% deficit in maximization generally attributed to a disconnect between planning and execution.[20] Successful strategic planning and execution relies on the fundamentals discussed in this chapter: understanding the needs of stakeholders to identify desired results; hiring, engaging, and evaluating employees; and providing needed resources. In addition, the following four requirements are needed for effective strategic execution:[20]

- Realistic expectations of outcomes
- Sound judgment of those executing the strategic plan
- Implementation of the monitoring and evaluation plan
- Promotion of high employee performance

REALISTIC EXPECTATIONS

Forecasts, or outcome (often financial) projections, are generally the result of negotiation between managers and leaders (each with their own biases regarding what the possible forecasts should look like), with managers usually arguing for more conservative short-term expectations and leaders advocating for grander long-term expectations to satisfy key stakeholders.[19] For example, a home healthcare company plans to implement a new pharmacy service. The pharmacist owner of the home healthcare company may overestimate his forecast by projecting a 25% profit margin within three years of implementation, while the pharmacist manager may underestimate her forecast by projecting the new service will break even the first year, with a possible 5% profit margin the second year. Rather than negotiate forecasts, which are subject to bias, depending on the roles of the negotiators, pharmacist leaders and managers should critically develop and use assumptions based on long-term economic and market realities, as well as the performance of the organization in comparison to its competitors.[20] Following agreement on assumptions, realistic forecasts and expectations regarding work product can be made. In the home healthcare example, the pharmacist owner and pharmacist manager should examine profit data from pharmacy services provided by other home health organizations in regions similar to their own and use this data for forecasting. Many organizations may set expectations slightly higher than reasonable to challenge employees and extend their performance, as high-performance employees are likely to rise to such challenges. Expectations can also be developed when implementing clinical programs. For example, in implementing medication reconciliation programs, expectations, or goals, might be set for having pharmacists conduct medication discharge teaching for 30% of patients in the first year of the program and for 100% of patients within three years.

Sound Judgment

A strategic plan establishes a course of action to achieve objectives and goals; however, within the execution of those actions, managers and employees are responsible for decision making and judgments and for taking steps to ensure that strategies are employed effectively and efficiently.[20] With that responsibility must come the understanding that not every decision or step is critical or deserves equal time and attention. The "big picture" should not get lost in the day-to-day operation of the

action plan. There are certain high-priority steps, or decisions, that will play an important role in strategic plan outcomes and should receive more time and attention than other, lower-priority items.[20] Priorities, such as resource deployment, should be set during the planning process and communicated to workers who will then be expected to execute plans according to priority order.

Monitor and Evaluate Performance

Although a monitoring and evaluation plan is developed during the planning process, managers are ultimately responsible for putting that system into effect. Pharmacist managers should monitor the work process on an ongoing basis and implement a schedule to review and evaluate performance, action processes, resource deployment, and results against the expectations stated in the plan, allowing for plan adjustments and reallocation of resources.[20] Engaging staff in the identification of performance metrics and performance goals is an important step in ensuring their commitment to succeed.

Promotion of Employee Performance

Employees should receive training and development opportunities to maximize the use of their skills and knowledge.[20] Training and development can be provided through internal and external programs. Employees should also be provided with a supportive and motivating work environment (refer to Chapter 20, "Creating and Identifying Desirable Workplaces").

Each of these four requirements—(1) realistic expectations, (2) sound judgment, (3) monitoring and evaluation, and (4) performance promotion—is designed to facilitate the successful execution of the strategic plan. Thus, the four requirements should promote realistic and understandable application of the plan's strategies to ensure that employees know and fulfill their roles by accomplishing desired results.

SUMMARY

The success of an organization largely depends on the work of its employees and the use of a sound, realistic plan to guide work efforts. These two ingredients for organizational success—achieving desired results through others (employees) and strategic planning and execution—are significant considerations in the professional lives of pharmacist managers and leaders. Although there is no one "right" mechanism or formula for achieving results through others, this chapter discusses certain key elements, including (1) identifying stakeholder needs; (2) hiring, engaging, and evaluating employees; and (3) acquiring and deploying appropriate resources. This chapter also delineates the strategic planning process and recommends strategies to enhance execution of strategic plans. Thus, the chapter provides pharmacists with the foundation to facilitate and promote employee success, effective use of strategic plans, and overall organizational success.

References

1. Official Web site of Vince Lombardi. Quotes by Vince Lombardi. Available at: http://www.vincelombardi.com/about/quotes4.htm . Accessed February 1, 2009.

2. Drucker PF. Managing oneself. *Harv Bus Rev* 2005; 83(1):3–13.

3. Mitchell RK, Agle BR, Wood DJ. Toward a theory of stakeholder identification and salience: defining the principle of who and what really counts. *Acad Manage Rev* 1997;22:853–886.

4. Golder B, Gawler M. Cross cutting tool. Stakeholder analysis. World Wildlife Federation. 2005. Available at: http://assets.panda.org/downloads/1_1_stakeholder_analysis_11_01_05.pdf. Accessed April 15, 2009.

5. Longenecker CO, Simonetti JL. *Getting Results*. San Francisco, CA: Josey-Bass; 2001.

6. Bassi L, McMurrer D. Maximizing your return on people. *Harv Bus Rev* 2007;85(3):115–123.

7. White SJ. Working effectively with people. *Am J Health-Syst Pharm* 2007;64:2221, 2224–2225.

8. Corporate Leadership Council. *Driving Employee Performance and Retention Through Engagement: A Quantitative Analysis of the Effectiveness of Employee Engagement Strategies*. Washington, DC: Corporate Executive Board; 2004.

9. McNamara C. *Field Guide to Nonprofit Strategic Planning and Facilitation*. 3rd ed. Minneapolis, MN: Authenticity Consulting, LLC; 2007.

10. Ramsey RD. Achieving results with communication. *Supervision* 2006;67:10–12.

11. Gratto Liebler J, McConnell CR. *Management Principles for Health Professionals*. 5th ed. Boston, MA: Jones and Bartlett; 2008.

12. Davis K. The case for participative management. *Bus Horizons* 1963;6:55–60.

13. Katzenbach JR, Santamaria JA. Firing up the front line. *Harv Bus Rev* 1999;77(3):107–117.

14. McGuire R. Decision making. *Pharm J* 2002;269: 647–649.

15. Fleming I. *Time Management Pocketbook*. 4th ed. Hampshire: Management Pocketbooks; 1997.

16. Clausen TS, Jones KT, Rich JS. Appraising employee performance evaluation systems. *CPA J* 2008; 78(Feb):64–67.

17. Meyer C. How the right measures help teams excel. *Harv Bus Rev* 1994;72(3):95–103.

18. Foundation for Community Association Research. Strategic planning. 2001. Available at: http://www.cairf.org/research/bpstrategic.pdf. Accessed November 25, 2008.

19. Armstrong JS. The value of formal planning for strategic decisions: review of empirical research. *Strateg Manag J* 1982;3:197–211.

20. Mankins MC, Steele R. Turning great strategy into great performance. *Harv Bus Rev* 2005;83(7/8): 65–72.

Abbreviations

CLC: Corporate Leadership Council
HCM: human capital management
SMARTER: specific, measurable, acceptable, realistic, time-based, extending, rewarding
SWOT: strengths, weaknesses, opportunities, threats

Case Scenarios

CASE ONE: You are a dispensing pharmacist in a clinic pharmacy in a busy urban hospital whose mission is to help increase healthcare access to the underserved. You have noticed that many patients seen at the clinic do not get their prescriptions filled because, as they put it, they "cannot afford it." Consequently, these patients experience adverse events due to disease state progression (e.g., amputations due to progressively worsening diabetes, increased asthma attacks). Your pharmacist manager is familiar with a program that has reduced adverse events due to decreased access to medications and would like for you to implement such a program in the clinic. What strategic planning steps should you take to help the clinic fulfill its mission?

CASE TWO: Jill Stewart, PharmD, works in a community pharmacy in Anytown, Florida. The pharmacy serves a population of 25,000, of whom 5,000 are 65 years old or older. Dr. Stewart observes that many patients in her practice have difficulty with adherence to their medications, experience drug-related problems, receive care from multiple prescribers, or have issues with limited health literacy or limited cognition. Dr. Stewart has developed a medication therapy management (MTM) service to address these issues and improve outcomes in this patient population. As she prepares to implement the MTM service, what human capital management practices can she use to prepare staff to deliver the new service?

CASE THREE: Nick Spencer is a pharmacist manager in an independent community pharmacy. As a result of several recent medication errors, medication safety has become a high priority. The pharmacy owner has requested that Dr. Spencer lead a team to develop a strategic plan to address this problem. Who will participate as members of the strategic planning team? What factors might the team consider when conducting a SWOT analysis? What is the goal of the plan? What are the objectives and tactics of Dr. Spencer's action plan?

CASE FOUR: Bess Carter is pharmacist manager responsible for budgeting and financial management at a large community hospital. Dr. Carter has been tasked to identify opportunities to cut the medication budget and develop a plan for accomplishing specific cost-containment targets. She recognizes that the success of the plan she is considering will require the active involvement of staff pharmacists. What steps should Dr. Carter take to involve staff in this assignment?

CASE FIVE: As the owner of a busy community pharmacy that serves several long-term care facilities as well as the patients of an adjacent medical clinic, you oversee a staff of 8 pharmacists and 12 technicians. Over the past several months, you have had a problem retaining your staff: 2 pharmacists and 4 technicians have resigned. You are increasingly concerned that the quality of your services and the profitability of your business may be negatively affected by this staff turnover. What actions should you consider to deal with this situation effectively?

Additional Resources Available Online!

Visit the Student Companion Web site at http://healthprofessions.jbpub.com/pharmacymanagement for interactive study tools and additional resources.

See www.rxugace.com to learn how you can obtain continuing pharmacy education for this content.

CHAPTER 14

PHARMACY BUSINESS AND STAFF PLANNING

Tad A. Gomez, MS, RPh

Mark D. Boesen, PharmD

James C. McAllister IV, PharmD, MS

Christy Monique Norman, PharmD, MS

Marie A. Chisholm-Burns, PharmD, MPH, FCCP, FASHP

LEARNING OBJECTIVES

After completing the chapter, the reader will be able to

1. Assess the importance of having a business plan.
2. Cite items that should be included in a business plan.
3. Define three types of organizational structure.
4. Define sensitivity analysis and how it can be used as a planning tool.
5. Describe the process of developing job descriptions.
6. Discuss the importance of implementing a strategic human resources plan.
7. Explain the steps of a proactive human resources plan.
8. Discuss components of professional and cultural competence.

KEY CONCEPTS

❶ Pharmacist leaders and managers should devote significant time and energy to planning, as it is a necessary component to achieving successful pharmacy operations.

❷ A business plan is a formal document that contains background information about the intended opportunity (e.g., business, program, project) and key participating members, as well as describes and details supporting information concerning attaining goals. Business

plans are decision-making tools and, if done correctly, will provide objective data to assess the challenge level of achieving goals while assessing and balancing risk tolerance.

❸ Good business plans cover at least five major content areas, including (1) background and general information, (2) marketing, (3) operations, (4) finances, and (5) a discussion or narrative of the decision-making criteria used to approve or deny the business venture.

❹ A mission statement describes the overall purpose of the business. The vision statement is an illustrative description of what the business or program would like to achieve or accomplish in the mid- to long-term future, and it serves as a clear guide for choosing current and future courses of action.

❺ People are the greatest resource of any business, and good pharmacist managers and leaders know how to achieve results through others.

❻ All positions in the organization should have a clear explication of authority and responsibility. Clarifying the organizational structure and clearly defining employees' roles and responsibilities are useful in describing how employees fit within the business's workflow, or work process.

❼ Human resources planning involves identifying and addressing staffing implications of current and future business plans and specific business strategies.

❽ Professional competence (the capacity to perform the duties of one's profession at an acceptable and appropriate level) and cultural competence (the ability to interact effectively with people of different cultures) are important aspects of staffing and training personnel. In the areas of professional and cultural competence, pharmacist managers are responsible for demonstrating a commitment to lifelong learning and ensuring that they and their staff participate in development activities.

INTRODUCTION

Larry Elder, a political radio and television personality, stated that "a goal without a plan is just a wish," and to achieve goals, plans are not only important but also necessary.[1] **❶** *Pharmacist leaders and managers should devote significant time and energy to planning, as it is a necessary component to achieving successful pharmacy operations.* This chapter focuses on planning; specifically, the chapter provides an overview of how to write a pharmacy **business plan** (in this chapter,

"business" also refers to projects and programs) and reviews staff planning. Although these skills are necessary for pharmacist managers and leaders, they are also important for pharmacists who do not hold formal managerial or leadership positions, as these individuals may be requested to write business plans or assess staff planning strategies. Pharmacy students and pharmacists may also find certain planning strategies discussed in the chapter applicable to their own career planning.

BUSINESS PLANNING

Whether one is starting a pharmacy-related business/program/project, is a manager at an established enterprise, or is a staff pharmacist proposing an expanded service, planning is critical to success. **❷** *A business plan is a formal document that contains background information about the intended opportunity (e.g., business, program, project) and key participating members, as well as describes and details supporting information concerning attaining goals.* Although many people fail to prepare a business plan before engaging in pharmacy business opportunities or operations (such as implementing new or extending services in any pharmacy setting whether retail, home health care, or institutional), success is generally greater for those with solid business plans bolstered by good data and rigorous research.[2] **❷** *Simply put, business plans are decision-making tools and, if done correctly, will provide objective data to decide the challenge level of achieving goals while assessing and balancing **risk tolerance**.* The following is a concise list of additional benefits supporting why pharmacists should develop business plans before engaging in new pharmacy-related opportunities:

- Assists in developing a sound business concept with a unique niche in a stable and, preferably, growing industry
- Helps to focus on objectives/goals and facilitates understanding of the target market using appropriate data and analyses
- Identifies strengths, weaknesses, and omissions in an initial assessment of the business or program

- Serves as a selling tool in dealing with important relationships, including target market, staff, investors, and lenders (banks, etc.)
- Provides detailed written information in one document about the business so you can solicit opinions and start engaging **stakeholders** (refer to Chapter 15, "Understanding and Applying Marketing Strategies," and Chapter 16, "Advertising and Promotion")[2]

Parts of the Business Plan

◆ *Good business plans cover at least five major content areas, including (1) background and general information, (2) marketing, (3) operations, (4) finances, and (5) a discussion or narrative of the decision-making criteria used to accept or deny the business venture.*[3] Preparing a business plan requires a flexible state of mind and may involve many different disciplines, including finance, human resources management, intellectual property management, **supply chain management**, operations management, and marketing.[3] **Table 14–1** provides an overview of the contents of a business plan.[2,4–7] Although the order of business plan sections may vary slightly, the first element of the plan is usually the executive summary, which is an overview of the key points of the plan. As noted in Table 14–1, the executive summary is generally followed by the business profile.

Business Profile

The profile should provide data that defines and describes your intended business, program, or project, and its niche in the marketplace. In addition, emphasis should be placed on how goals are to be achieved, as well as a time schedule of when these goals are expected to be achieved. **Gantt charts** are useful in visually displaying time schedules and may be beneficial to include in your plan (**Figure 14–1**). The profile should also include the business's mission and vision statements, as well as a business description. ◆ *A mission statement, in its simplest form, describes the overall purpose of the business. By contrast, the vision statement is an illustrative description of what the business or program would like to achieve or accomplish in the mid- to long-term future, and it serves as a clear guide for choosing current and future courses of action.* These statements should be concise, yet descriptive, and should serve as a reference and guide to stakeholders. For example, the mission of the Medication Access Program (MAP), a nonprofit pharmacy program, is to increase access to medications for solid-organ transplant patients by serving as a central medication information source.[8] MAP's vision is to become the country's leader in increasing medication access for individuals who have received a kidney, liver, heart, lung, or pancreas transplant (C. Garrett, MAP business manager, oral communication, February 2009). The business description is generally a narrative that expounds on the mission and vision of the organization. The description should be parsimonious, completed within one page, and verbally expressed in less than one minute.

Products and Services

Following the business profile, the business plan should clearly describe the products or services the business will provide. This section should address research and development efforts involved in design and development, need, and benefits of the products or services to consumers.[4] A **market analysis** is useful in determining need and benefit of products or services in relation to similar products or services that may already be available.

Market Analysis and Strategies

There is an inherent assumption by almost every business that it provides superior products and services. After all, if your business was not providing something superior to what already exists in the market, what would be the lasting attraction to patronize your organization? A market analysis is one of the most important elements of a successful business plan. The market analysis should include a description of the industry, the specific sector for which your business intends to compete, a **SWOT analysis**, which includes investigating and detailing the strengths, weaknesses, opportunities, and threats of the business (see Chapter 13, "Achieving Results Through Others and Strategic Planning"), and a **competitive analysis**. A competitive analysis identifies competitors and assesses their strengths and weaknesses relative to those of your business

TABLE 14–1	Parts of a Business Plan

- **Executive Summary:** This is a brief summary of the highlights of the business plan and should be less than two pages.

- **Business Profile:** Define and describe your intended business and how you plan to achieve goals. Stay focused on your niche or opportunities in the market. Include time lines to accomplish tasks and review the plan. See Chapter 15, "Understanding and Applying Marketing Strategies." Also include mission and vision statements; these are concise statements of your business purpose and future goals.

- **Products/Services:** Define what products/services will be offered by the business.

- **Marketing Analysis and Plans:** Provide an overview/analysis of your target market, including identification of competitors and how you intend on marketing your business as well as expanding it. This should include a SWOT analysis. See Chapter 15, "Understanding and Applying Marketing Strategies."

- **Operations and Management:** Describe intended organizational structure and operations (functioning of the business), including assigned responsibilities and tasks, workflow, and required resources and expenses (including technology). Address staffing/personnel plans. Focus on how your prior experiences, as well as the experiences and qualifications of your employees or planned personnel, are applicable to your business. Address any personnel gaps or needs. Include résumés.

- **Financials/Economic Assessment:** Provide a complete assessment of the economic environment in which your business will become a part. Include a one-year cash flow assessment that will incorporate your capital requirements. Include your assessment of what could go wrong and how you plan to handle problems.

- **Summary/Conclusion:** This is the concluding section and should highlight critical points of the proposal; it should be less than one page.

- **Appendices:** This includes supporting documents and other materials that can support the proposal.

Note: An exit strategy, defined as a method for withdrawing from or leaving the business or program in a financially solvent manner, should also be considered, and may or may not be included in the official business plan.

(a competitive analysis worksheet template is available from SCORE [http://www.score.org/index.html] at the following Web site [as of 2010]: http://www.score.org/downloads/Competitive%20Analysis.doc).

On the basis of the market analysis, a marketing strategy, or plan to enter and grow within the market, should be developed that includes a concrete description of the target audience and marketing process (distribution, advertising, etc.).[4] The success of your marketing strategy and, ultimately, your business, is based on the business's **brand**, ability to identify a target client/patient base (niche), and effectiveness in developing successful

FIGURE **14–1** **Example of Gantt Chart.**

Medication Therapy Management Service in *Pharmacy X*

Project Lead: John Doe
Today's Date: 2/24/2010 (Wed) (vertical line)
Start Date: 1/5/2010 (Tue)

WBS	Tasks	Task Lead	Start	End	Duration (Days)	% Complete	Days Complete	Days Remaining
1	Business Planning	John	1/03/10	3/17/10	74	80%	59	15
1.1	Develop service profile		1/03/10	1/20/10	18	100%	18	0
1.2	Describe service including need of and benefits to consumers (may involve conducting needs assessment)		1/21/10	2/19/10	30	95%	28	2
1.3	Conduct market analysis including SWOT and competitive analysis		1/22/10	2/10/10	19	95%	18	1
1.4	Develop marketing strategy for service		2/10/10	3/18/10	37	50%	18	19
1.5	Describe operations and management of service, including personnel needs, organizational structure, workflow, and resources		2/12/10	3/03/10	20	60%	13	7
1.6	Assess financials and conduct economic assessment		2/15/10	3/06/10	20	50%	10	10
2	Staffing Planning	Jane	3/01/10	5/11/10	72	13%	9	63
2.1	Outline organizational chart of service		3/01/10	3/17/10	17	50%	8	9
2.2	Conduct job analyses and skills inventories		3/01/10	3/17/10	17	30%	5	12
2.3	Develop job descriptions		3/18/10	4/25/10	39	0%	0	39
2.4	Develop human resources plan that addresses current and future staffing needs of service		4/15/10	5/12/10	28	0%	0	28
3	Workflow Analysis	Bill	4/25/10	8/31/10	129	0%	0	129
3.1	Assess physical and psychosocial work environment where service will be conducted		4/25/10	5/11/10	17	0%	0	17
3.2	Analyze work process (service activities) to determine effectiveness and efficiency		5/12/10	5/28/10	17	0%	0	17
4	Technology Implementation	Mary	5/29/10	7/04/10	37	0%	0	37
4.1	Assess technological needs of service		7/05/10	8/02/10	29	0%	0	29
4.2	Determine costs of technology and identify preferred vendor		8/02/10	8/10/10	8	0%	0	8
4.3	Negotiate purchase of technology		8/10/10	8/15/10	7	0%	0	7
4.4	Install technology and train personnel in use of technology (be sure to address security and documentation issues)		8/20/10	9/01/10	13	0%	0	13

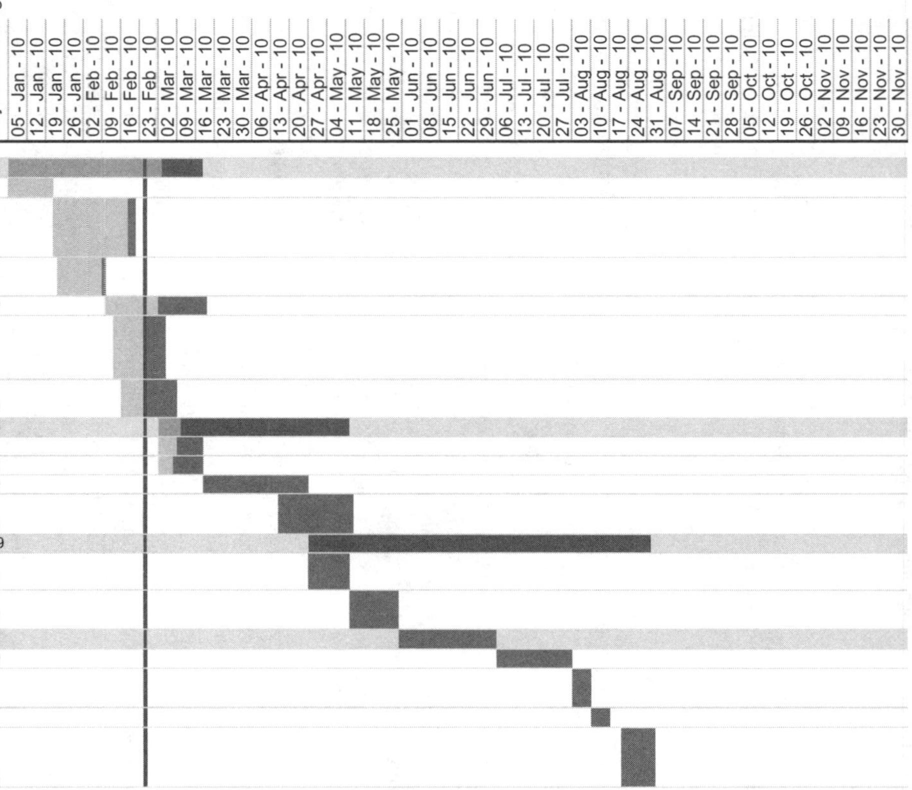

Timeline columns (weeks): 05 – Jan – 10, 12 – Jan – 10, 19 – Jan – 10, 26 – Jan – 10, 02 – Feb – 10, 09 – Feb – 10, 16 – Feb – 10, 23 – Feb – 10, 02 – Mar – 10, 09 – Mar – 10, 16 – Mar – 10, 23 – Mar – 10, 30 – Mar – 10, 06 – Apr – 10, 13 – Apr – 10, 20 – Apr – 10, 27 – Apr – 10, 04 – May – 10, 11 – May – 10, 18 – May – 10, 25 – May – 10, 01 – Jun – 10, 08 – Jun – 10, 15 – Jun – 10, 22 – Jun – 10, 29 – Jun – 10, 06 – Jul – 10, 13 – Jul – 10, 20 – Jul – 10, 27 – Jul – 10, 03 – Aug – 10, 10 – Aug – 10, 17 – Aug – 10, 24 – Aug – 10, 31 – Aug – 10, 07 – Sep – 10, 14 – Sep – 10, 21 – Sep – 10, 28 – Sep – 10, 05 – Oct – 10, 12 – Oct – 10, 19 – Oct – 10, 26 – Oct – 10, 02 – Nov – 10, 09 – Nov – 10, 16 – Nov – 10, 23 – Nov – 10, 30 – Nov – 10

This figure provides an example of a Gantt chart used in planning a medication therapy management service in *Pharmacy X*. The specific tasks involved in business planning, staffing planning, workflow analysis, and technology implementation are organized, and the time schedule for and progress (noted in the "% Complete" column) of each task is detailed.

campaigns to attract business patrons. See Chapter 15 ("Understanding and Applying Marketing Strategies") and Chapter 16 ("Advertising and Promotion").

OPERATIONS AND MANAGEMENT

The business plan should describe key elements of the business's operations and management, including personnel and organizational structure, work environment and workflow, and resources. Keep in mind, operations are determined by business objectives, products, or services; as these elements evolve or change, so will operations. For example, a service may be added to the business that requires additional personnel and resources. Therefore, the business plan should allow for modification to accommodate changes or revisions in operations over time.

❺ *People are the greatest resource of any business, and good pharmacist managers and leaders know how to achieve results through others.* See Chapter 13, "Achieving Results Through Others and Strategic Planning". If you have highly qualified, key personnel who will participate in the business, include that in the proposal. In addition, you should also spend time describing *your* qualifications and why you are the best person to head the business, program, or project; indicate how your prior experiences will be applicable to the new business. It may be beneficial to include résumés in this section.

❻ *For the sake of clarity and transparency, all positions in the organization should have a clear explication of authority and responsibility.* Whether the business is a "one-man operation" or is several hundred members strong, a description of organizational structure is critical for delineating responsibilities and holding people accountable. An **organizational chart** is commonly used to display an organization's structure and illustrates formal lines of authority, as well as relationships between positions within the organization. Lines in an organizational chart represent direct relationships between superiors and subordinates, and when boxes/positions are located laterally, this indicates that the relationship between different units/departments are on the same hierarchical level. The type of organizational structure selected is highly specific to the organization. The three different types of organizational charts (structures) are hierarchical, matrix, and flat, and each has its own advantages and disadvantages:

- A **flat organization** (also known as horizontal organization) refers to an organizational structure with few or no levels of intervening management between staff and managers. One of the driving concepts behind having flat organizations is the belief that employees are more productive when they are more directly involved in the decision-making process, rather than being removed and closely supervised by many layers of management. Other advantages include increased coordination and distribution of information, improved communication, and increased self-actualization among employees; possible disadvantages of flat organizations include limited individual employee growth potential (in other words, fewer opportunities for advancement) and greater role ambiguity.
- Unlike flat organizations, a **hierarchical organization** is structured so that every entity in the organization, with limited exceptions, is subordinate to at least a single other entity. Advantages of this type of organization include clearly delineated authority and responsibility, defined mechanisms for promotion, effective use of specialized knowledge, and loyalty to department; however, possible disadvantages include being slow to change to meet identified needs of consumers or employees, poor communication across hierarchical boundaries, and placement of departmental needs over the needs of the organization as a whole. Most large companies are hierarchical organizations.
- A **matrix organization** uses a team structure wherein team members are brought together from different disciplines and departments within the organization to work together on a project or process; these individuals retain their original positions in their respective departments while functioning as part of this team. Authority in a matrix organization is both horizontal (e.g., project managers across

departments) and vertical (e.g., employees report to department heads). The advantages of the matrix organization include resource sharing, diversity of expertise, improved communication across departments, and minimization of project costs; disadvantages include difficulties in coordinating tasks and identifying responsibility for failures. **Figure 14–2** displays generic hierarchical and matrix organizational charts.

Most large pharmacies belong to organizations with hierarchical organization structures, although flat or matrix organizations are plentiful in pharmacy-related businesses. In organizations with hierarchical structures, pharmacy directors or managers are usually at the top of the pharmacy's reporting structure, and most directors or managers report to chief executive officers (CEO) within the organization. Below the director or manager are the line managers or supervisors who typically have direct supervisory responsibility, or line authority, for pharmacists, pharmacy technicians, pharmacy interns, clerks, delivery personnel, and others. Below the line managers or supervisors are the staff pharmacists, pharmacy technicians, pharmacy interns, clerks, delivery personnel, and others. Many pharmacies do not have more than three layers of personnel; however, in some larger, more complex organizations of more than 100 **full-time equivalents** (FTE), additional layers may exist (**Figure 14–3**). See **Figure 14–4** for an example of an organizational chart for a privately held network of community retail pharmacies.

❻ *Clarifying the organizational structure and clearly defining employees' roles and responsibilities are useful in describing how employees fit within the business's workflow, or work process.* The operations section should include an outline or narrative of the sequence or patterns of activities that compose the work process, as well as information regarding the environment in which those

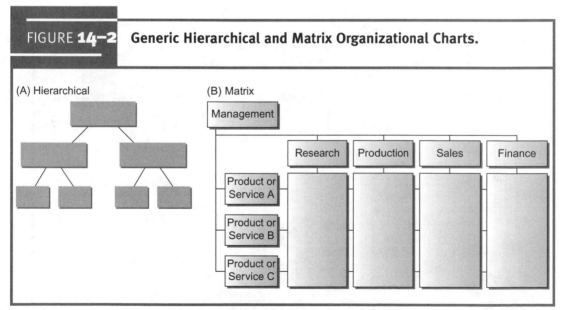

FIGURE **14–2**   **Generic Hierarchical and Matrix Organizational Charts.**

(A) A hierarchical organization is structured so that every entity in the organization, with few exceptions, is subordinate to at least one other entity. (B) A matrix organizational structure has employees with similar skills pooled for work assignments.

FIGURE **14–3**   Organizational Chart of a Complex Pharmacy Organization.

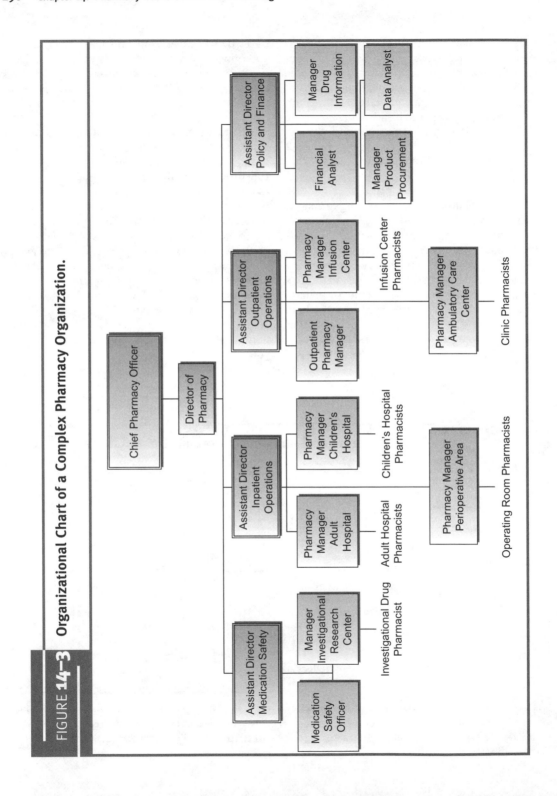

FIGURE **14–4**   **Apothecary Shop Organizational Chart.**

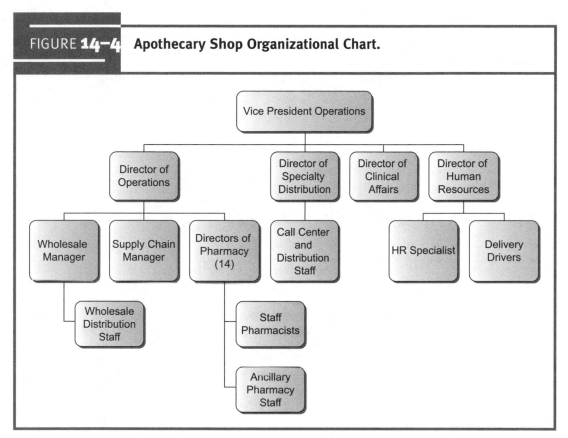

The apothecary shops are a privately held network of community retail pharmacies.
Note: HR = human resources; VP = vice president.

activities take place (as the conditions of the environment may help or hinder workflow). In addition, a description and delineation of needed resources, such as information technology and **automation**, required to effectively conduct work activities should be included in the plan.

FINANCIALS AND ECONOMIC ASSESSMENT

The financial and economic assessment section of a business plan should include an economic analysis describing a complete assessment of the economic environment the business or program will become a part of. It should also include a one-year

cash flow assessment (which is usually a **pro forma statement** since the actual business, program, or project has not been implemented) that will incorporate your capital requirements and other **start-up costs**. In the cash flow section, include an assessment of what could go wrong and how those problems would be handled. You may want to perform a **break-even analysis**[9] (**Figure 14–5**), which refers to the point where total revenue (TR) received equals the total costs (TC) associated with the sale of services or products, TR = TC, and include it in your business plan.[10] For example, if TC to provide a service (e.g., a wellness program) is $200,000 annually, and the

---

FIGURE **14-5** **Break-Even Analysis Graph.**

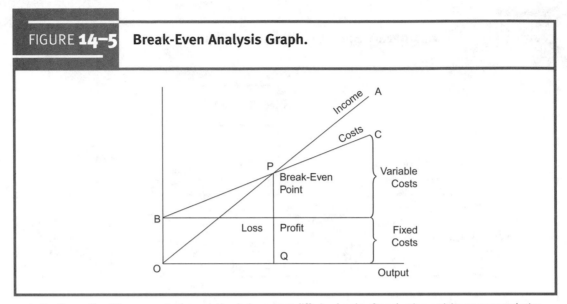

In the figure, line OA represents the variation in income at differing levels of production activity or revenue/sales ("output") — income increases as output increases. Line OB represents the total fixed costs in the pharmacy business. As output increases, variable costs (those costs that are not constant, meaning they vary depending on the level of production activity) are incurred, meaning that total costs (Fixed + Variable) also increase. At low levels of output, costs are greater than income. At the point of intersection, P, costs are exactly equal to income and, hence, neither profit nor loss is made. This is known as the break-even point.

---

charge for each unit of service is $100, approximately 2,000 service units must be performed to cover all service-related expenses (in other words, when TR is $200,000, the break-even point has been reached); anything more than 2,000 units would be considered profit. To determine a range of outcomes associated with lower and upper charges for the service, you may also want to conduct a **sensitivity analysis** (defined as an examination of how projected performance may vary based on changes in the assumptions on which performance projections are determined); for example, to compare how many service units must be performed if the service costs $250,000 annually instead of the previous assumption of $200,000, approximately 2,500 units of service must be performed annually to cover costs. SCORE provides tools and templates for performing 12-month cash flow, break-even, and start-up analyses at the following Web sites (as of 2010):

- 12-month cash flow analysis: http://www.score.org/business_toolbox.html
- Break-even analysis: http://www.score.org/downloads/Break-Even%20Analysis.xls
- Start-up analysis: http://www.score.org/pdf/Start-up%20Expenses_08.xls

The most difficult hurdle to overcome in developing a business is not just developing a budget but funding that budget. Program or business funding entities, such as banks, individuals, institutional administration, etc., can be friendly during times of economic prosperity but may be conservative and critical during economic recessions. A traditional avenue for many small-business start-ups is the Small Business Administration (SBA). At a minimum, the SBA is an excellent resource for healthcare professionals who need a quick education in business financing.

Other sources of funding include community banks, lenders, and individual investors.

If you are considering buying an existing pharmacy business, work with the current owner to uncover mutually beneficial options (refer to Chapter 22, "Negotiation Techniques"). Often, the current owner may be interested in self-financing the takeover. Many businesses, including pharmacy-related businesses, have grown from relationships between previous owners and new owners through partnership arrangements in which the previous owner "carries the loan" for the new owner for a predetermined period. Under the partnership arrangement, the previous owner agrees to a slow takeover by the new owner, eventually dissolving the partnership at some future point when the "loan" is paid off in full. This type of "partnership" between old and new owners is commonly seen in selling and purchasing independent community pharmacies or other businesses.

Another possible relationship that may lead to business ownership is "junior partnership" in which an employee (the "junior partner") in a pharmacy business acquires or takes ownership of the business from the "senior partner" (the current owner) over a specified time.[11] During this time, the junior partner increases his or her share in the business, as well as his or her management responsibilities.[11] The senior partner may provide managerial support, mentorship, and training to the junior partner to enhance the transfer of ownership experience.

BUSINESS PLAN SUMMARY AND CONCLUSION

Business or program plans should conclude with a brief summary or conclusions section that highlights critical elements of the plan. In the end, be creative and passionately communicate your plan to appropriate stakeholders. The business that succeeds generally brings something unique to the market. Whether the innovation is a new pharmacy service or product or a new way of delivering an existing service or product, individuals will not gravitate to your venture and you will not maintain large market shares unless an added value is recognized. A business plan template is available from SCORE at the following Web site (as of 2010): http://www.score.org/pdf/Business%20Plan%20for%20Startup%20Business_08.pdf.[12] Once your

business or program plan is under way, the next essential step involved in planning operations is detailing staffing plans.

STAFF PLANNING

⑤ *As touched on in the "Business Planning" section of the chapter, the number one resource of any business, including pharmacy-related businesses, is its employees.* The expansion of pharmacy services from drug delivery and dispensing to include providing direct patient care services supports the need for recruiting, training, and retaining highly competent staff. Pharmacist managers and pharmacists must understand the basics of developing accurate job descriptions, strategic human resource planning, and competent and diverse staff (personnel). The next several sections of the chapter will discuss each of these topics.

Job Analysis

The development of job (position) descriptions and, ultimately, the staffing plan relies heavily on analyzing responsibilities that need to be filled and the skills needed to complete those assignments or tasks. A **job analysis** is the process used to collect information about the duties, responsibilities, necessary skills, outcomes, and work environment of a particular job. Typical aspects of the job analysis include reviewing job responsibilities; analyzing work duties, tasks, and responsibilities that need to be accomplished; and preparing a statement of the most important outcomes or contributions needed from the position. Job analyses may also be useful to job seekers who are attempting to better understand positions they are considering applying for. Refer to Chapter 18, "Successful Recruitment and Hiring Strategies." See **Figure 14–6** for a job analysis template.

SKILLS INVENTORY

A **skills inventory** is a tool used by job seekers and employers to determine the necessary attributes to fulfill the expectations developed in the job analysis.[13] Typically, candidates (e.g., pharmacist candidates) will identify common skills required for particular positions and use the list to emphasize how their skills and qualifications adequately meet the demands of the position.[13]

FIGURE **14–6** **Job Analysis Template.**

Position: _____

Part A. Job Analysis Worksheet for Tasks

Task	Source	Importance	Frequency

Importance Scale	Frequency Scale
How important is this task to the job?	How often is this task performed?
1 = Not Important	1 = Every few months to yearly
2 = Somewhat Important	2 = Every few weeks to monthly
3 = Important	3 = Every few days to weekly
4 = Very Important	4 = Every few hours to daily
5 = Extremely Important	5 = Hourly to many times each hour

Part B. Job Analysis Worksheet for Competencies

Competency	Source	Importance	Need at Entry	Distinguishing Value

Importance Scale	Need at Entry Scale	Distinguishing Value Scale
How important is this competency for effective job performance?	When is this competency needed for effective job performance?	How valuable is this competency for distinguishing superior from barely acceptable employees?
1 = Not Important	1 = Needed the first day	1 = Not Valuable
2 = Somewhat Important	2 = Must be acquired within the first 30 days	2 = Somewhat Valuable
3 = Important	3 = Must be acquired within the first 3–6 months	3 = Valuable
4 = Very Important	4 = Must be acquired within the first year	4 = Very Valuable
5 = Extremely Important		5 = Extremely Valuable

Source: Adapted from the U.S. Office of Personnel Management. *Delegated Examining Operations Handbook: A Guide for Federal Agency Examining Offices.* May 2007.

Likewise, employers may use the same exercise to identify which skills and attributes they desire in the individual occupying a particular position and develop a job description that features these skill sets and qualities.

Job Description: Content and Format

Job descriptions should be based on the information gathered through the job analysis, an understanding of the competencies and skills required to accomplish needed tasks, and other needs of the pharmacy. Job descriptions clearly distinguish and explain the responsibilities of a specific job and also include information about working conditions, equipment used, knowledge and skills needed, and lines of authority. For additional information, please refer to Chapter 18 ("Successful Recruitment and Hiring Strategies"). The most useful job descriptions are dynamic and are updated periodically as responsibilities change. The best job descriptions do not restrict employees but, more accurately, cause them to stretch their practice, enhance their skills, and develop their own abilities to better contribute to the overall performance of the pharmacy and the entire organization. Managers should also use well-written job descriptions as a recruitment tool by giving potential employees a realistic view of the responsibilities and duties of the position for which they are applying.

Human Resources Planning

❼ *Human resources planning involves identifying and addressing staffing implications of current and future business plans and specific business strategies.* Staffing must be addressed from a proactive, planning perspective and should focus on positions that are critical to the pharmacy's success. The following sections will discuss the steps of a proactive human resource planning process.

"Where Are We Now?"—Current Environment

After developing overall operational goals, the first step in human resources planning is to complete an assessment of the current environment. This self-assessment should include strengths and weaknesses of the current staff, the current staffing plan, and environmental factors that may affect the current staffing model. However, managers must be careful not to let assessment of the current state of business interfere with their judgment or restrict creative thinking about how things will have to be done in the future, as doing so will inhibit growth.

"WHERE DO WE WANT TO GO?" —FORECASTING

Business plans are built on forecasting, defined as calculating or predicting future events, needs, or trends based on past data; thus, plans should be useful in estimating numbers and types of employees who may be needed in the future to accomplish goals. Some factors to consider include staff turnover, retirements, technology, and planned movement of current staff. The final steps in the forecasting process are to identify the difference between anticipated demand and forecasted supply and to develop and implement staffing plans necessary to close talent gaps and eliminate staffing surpluses.

"HOW DO WE WANT TO GET THERE?" —TRANSITION

The transition steps include taking the number of employees and talent mix needed to accomplish the pharmacy's goals, as determined in the forecasting step, and developing recruitment strategies for each position or group of positions. The focus of the transition should be on how to put the recruitment strategies into action. Time should also be spent on how recruitment strategies will be measured in terms of success or failure. In larger organizations, managers will typically have the benefit of consulting with trained human resources specialists who can assist in human resource planning.

Professional Competence, Cultural Competence, and Staff Development

❽ *Professional competence (the capacity to perform the duties of one's profession at an acceptable and appropriate level) and* **cultural competence** *(the ability to interact effectively with people of different*

cultures) are important aspects of staffing and training personnel. For healthcare professionals, including pharmacists, professional competence involves "habitual and judicious use of communication, knowledge, technical skills, clinical reasoning, values, and reflection in daily practice for the benefit of the individual and community being served."[14(p226)] To maintain licensure, a certain number of continuing education hours must be obtained. In addition to continuing education, pharmacy organizations may have programs that they encourage personnel to attend to help achieve organizational goals. Other than pharmaceutical, pharmacotherapy, and pharmacy-specific knowledge and skills, components of professional competence include:[14]

- Cognitive components, such as knowledge acquisition, communication skills, and problem solving
- Technical skills
- Integration of reasoning, judgment, and knowledge
- Understanding of context
- Management of relationships
- **Emotional intelligence**
- Cultural competence

Cultural competence should be considered a critical characteristic of professional competence, as one's ability to understand, communicate, and effectively interact with people of different cultures is paramount in today's global society. Cultural competence comprises four major components:[15]

- *Awareness*: Awareness of one's own cultural worldview
- *Attitude*: Attitude toward cultural differences
- *Knowledge*: Knowledge of different cultural practices
- *Skills*: Cross-cultural skills

Pharmacists and pharmacy staff should be trained in cultural competence, and measures related to cultural competence, should be evaluated during regular performance evaluations of all staff. Further, organizational leaders and managers should demonstrate a commitment to diversity and facilitate activities promoting cultural competence among employees.

Cultural competence is also one of the key components in closing the disparities gap in health care. Pharmacy and other health services that are respectful and responsive to health beliefs, practices, and cultural and linguistic needs of diverse patients can help bring about positive health outcomes. Accreditation bodies recognize the importance of diversity. For example, **The Joint Commission** now mandates that organizations seeking accreditation offer cultural and linguisti-cally appropriate services (CLAS) as part of their standards. The Office of Minority Health, a division of the U.S. Department of Health and Human Services, has also published a set of 14 national CLAS standards (**Table 14–2**).[16] Organizations that seek federal funds (reimbursement or otherwise) are strongly recommended to comply with all 14 standards but are *required* to comply with 4 of the standards (4, 5, 6, and 7).

❽ *In the areas of professional and cultural competence, pharmacist managers are responsible for demonstrating a commitment to lifelong learning*

TABLE 14–2   **The Office of Minority Health's Culturally and Linguistically Appropriate Services (CLAS) Standards**

Standard 1
Healthcare organizations should ensure that patients/consumers receive from all staff members effective, understandable, and respectful care that is provided in a manner compatible with their cultural health beliefs and practices and preferred language.

Standard 2
Healthcare organizations should implement strategies to recruit, retain, and promote at all levels of the organization a diverse staff and leadership that are representative of the demographic characteristics of the service area.

Standard 3
Healthcare organizations should ensure that staff at all levels and across all disciplines receive ongoing education and training in culturally and linguistically appropriate service (CLAS) delivery.

Standard 4[a]
Healthcare organizations must offer and provide language assistance services, including bilingual staff and interpreter services, at no cost to each patient/consumer with limited English proficiency at all points of contact, in a timely manner during all hours of operation.

Standard 5[a]
Healthcare organizations must provide to patients/consumers in their preferred language both verbal offers and written notices informing them of their right to receive language assistance services.

Standard 6[a]
Healthcare organizations must ensure the competence of language assistance provided to limited English proficient patients/consumers by interpreters and bilingual staff. Family and friends should not be used to provide interpretation services (except on request by the patient/consumer).

(continues)

TABLE 14–2   (continued)

Standard 7[a]
Healthcare organizations must make available easily understood patient-related materials and post signage in the languages of the commonly encountered groups or groups represented in the service area.

Standard 8
Healthcare organizations should develop, implement, and promote a written strategic plan that outlines clear goals, policies, operational plans, and management accountability/oversight mechanisms to provide CLAS.

Standard 9
Healthcare organizations should conduct initial and ongoing organizational self-assessments of CLAS-related activities and are encouraged to integrate cultural and linguistic competence-related measures into their internal audits, performance improvement programs, patient satisfaction assessments, and outcomes-based evaluations.

Standard 10
Healthcare organizations should ensure that data on the individual patient's/consumer's race, ethnicity, and spoken and written language are collected in health records, integrated into the organization's management information systems, and periodically updated.

Standard 11
Healthcare organizations should maintain a current demographic, cultural, and epidemiological profile of the community, as well as a needs assessment, to accurately plan for and implement services that respond to the cultural and linguistic characteristics of the service area.

Standard 12
Healthcare organizations should develop participatory, collaborative partnerships with communities and use a variety of formal and informal mechanisms to facilitate community and patient/consumer involvement in designing and implementing CLAS-related activities.

Standard 13
Healthcare organizations should ensure that conflict and grievance resolution processes are culturally and linguistically sensitive and capable of identifying, preventing, and resolving cross-cultural conflicts or complaints by patients/consumers.

Standard 14
Healthcare organizations are encouraged to regularly make available to the public information about their progress and successful innovations in implementing the CLAS standards and to provide public notice in their communities about the availability of this information.

[a]Denotes the CLAS mandates, which are current federal requirements for all recipients of federal funds.
Source: Adapted from U.S. Department of Health and Human Services, Office of Minority Health.[16]

and ensuring that they and their staff participate in development activities. Thus, staff development and continuing education are key components of maintaining overall competence. Developing and maintaining professional competence and respect for cultural differences are caveats of the Code of Ethics for Pharmacists.[17] The American Society of Health-System Pharmacists states: "Next to integrity, competence is the first and most fundamental moral responsibility of all health professions. . . . After the degree is conferred, continuing education is society's only real guarantee of the optimal quality of health care."[18] According to the American Pharmacists Association and American Association of Colleges of Pharmacy,

at the core of patient-pharmacist relationships is a pledge to the patient (or covenant) that the pharmacist will exercise competent judgment and place the patient's safety and welfare above all other considerations. It is a privilege to practice as a pharmacist and, as such,

requires not only competence in the specialized knowledge and skills unique to our profession, but a continuing commitment to excellence, a respect and compassion for others, and adherence to high standards of ethical conduct.[19(p4)]

Pharmacist managers should provide support and incentives for their pharmacists to participate in continuing education programs, as well as to pursue additional certifications, such as those offered through the Board of Pharmaceutical Specialties, the National Certification Board for Diabetic Educators, and the National Asthma Educator Certification Board.

It is essential that pharmacist managers and leaders encourage continual learning among their staff. **Figure 14–7** depicts the four steps of the cycle of continual learning.[20] The steps of the continual learning cycle are (1) learn, (2) analyze, (3) question, and (4) act. *Learning*, the first step, represents the ongoing acquisition of new infor-

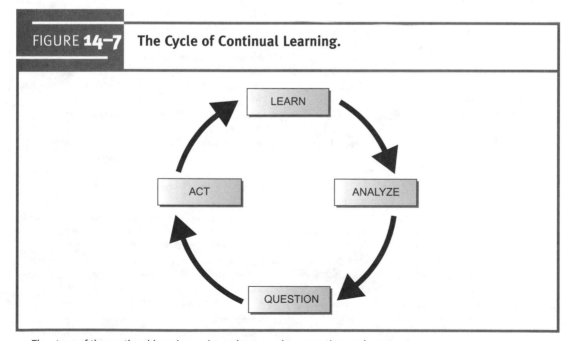

FIGURE **14–7**   **The Cycle of Continual Learning.**

The steps of the continual learning cycle are learn, analyze, question, and act.

Source: Originally published in Woodward BW. The journey of professional excellence: a matter of priorities. *Am J Health-Syst Pharm* 1998;55:784. ©1998, American Society of Health-System Pharmacists, Inc. All rights reserved. Reprinted with permission. (R0910)

mation to address new assignments, problems, and challenges.[20] Step 2, *analyze*, refers to the evaluation of information, thoughts, and options obtained during the learn step.[20] To *question* (Step 3) is to take a closer look at the conclusions produced in the analyze step—to compare against previous existing data, ask further questions, and delve deeper.[20] Questioning requires looking past what is known on the surface to search for additional information, meaning, or data that may have been overlooked or ignored. The fourth step, *act*, requires the leader to take action based on the previous steps.[20] Keep in mind, the fourth step is not the final step—thus, it is important for managers to make sure the cycle is continuous.

SUMMARY

Failure to plan is a plan to fail. According to author A. A. Milne, planning is "what you do before you do something, so that when you do it, it is not all mixed up."[21] In other words, lack of planning may result in disorganization and loss or waste of resources at best and utter chaos, including financial or professional ruin, at worst. Thus, adequate planning is essential to effective development and implementation of pharmacy operations. This chapter reviews the importance and components of business and staff planning and builds on planning as a foundation to promote success in pharmacy operations.

References

1. Brainy Quote. Larry Elder quotes. Available at: http://www.brainyquote.com/quotes/quotes/l/larryelder192362.html. Accessed February 17, 2009.

2. My Own Business. Session two. Business plan. Available at: http://www.myownbusiness.org/s2. Accessed January 12, 2009.

3. Siegel ES, Ford BR, Bornstein JM. *The Ernst & Young Business Plan Guide*. New York, NY: John Wiley and Sons; 1993.

4. US Small Business Administration. Small business planner. Available at: http://www.sba.gov/smallbusinessplanner/index.html. Accessed January 9, 2009.

5. Rich SR, Gumpert DE. How to write a winning business plan. *Harv Bus Rev* 1985;63(3):156–166.

6. Sahlman WA. How to write a great business plan. *Harv Bus Rev* 1997;75(4):98–108.

7. Abrams R. *The Successful Business Plan*. 4th ed. Palo Alto, CA: Planning Shop; 2003.

8. Medication Access Program. About us. Available at: http://www.mapuga.com/about.html. Accessed January 12, 2009.

9. Tutor2u. Introduction to break-even analysis. Available at: http://tutor2u.net/business/production/break_even.htm. Accessed March 17, 2009.

10. Horngren C, Sundem G, Stratton W. *Introduction to Management Accounting*. Upper Saddle River, NJ: Prentice Hall; 2002.

11. Sax B. Partnership programs—a win-win for community pharmacies. *Pharm Times* 2007. Available at: http://www.pharmacytimes.com/issues/articles/Careers_2007-10_7584.asp. Accessed March 17, 2009.

12. SCORE. Business plan for a startup business. Available at: http://www.score.org/downloads/Business%20Plan%20for%20Startup%20Business.doc. Accessed January 12, 2009.

13. Reiter-Palmon R, Young M, Strange J, Manning R, James J. Occupationally-specific skills: using skills to define and understand jobs and their requirements. *Hum Resource Manage Rev* 2006;16:356–375.

14. Epstein RM, Hundert EM. Defining and assessing professional competence. *J Am Med Assoc* 2002;287:226–235.

15. Martin M, Vaughn BE. Cultural competence: the nuts and bolts of diversity and inclusion. *Strateg Div Inclus Manage Mag* 2007;1(1):31–38.

16. US Department of Health and Human Services, Office of Minority Health. *National Standards for Culturally and Linguistically Appropriate Services in Health Care—Final Report*. Washington, DC; March 2001.

17. American Pharmacists Association. Code of ethics for pharmacists. Available at: http://www.pharmacist.com/AM/Template.cfm?Section=Search1&template=/CM/HTMLDisplay.cfm&ContentID=2903. Accessed March 23, 2009.

18. American Society of Hospital Pharmacists. ASHP statement on continuing education. *Am J Hosp Pharm* 1990;47:1855.

19. American Pharmacists Association Academy of Student Pharmacists and American Association of Colleges of Pharmacy Committee on Student Professionalism. Pharmacy professionalism toolkit for students and faculty. 2004. Available at: http://

www.pharmacist.com/AM/Template.cfm?Section=Download_Toolkit. Accessed March 23, 2009.

20. Woodward BW. The journey of professional excellence: a matter of priorities. *Am J Health-Syst Pharm* 1998;55:782–789.

21. ThinkExist.com. Planning quotes. Available at: http://thinkexist.com/quotations/planning/. Accessed April 2, 2009.

Abbreviations

CEO:	chief executive officer
CLAS:	culturally and linguistically appropriate services
FTE:	full-time equivalent
HR:	human resources
MAP:	Medication Access Program
SBA:	Small Business Administration
SWOT:	strengths, weaknesses, opportunities, threats
TC:	total costs
TR:	total revenue
VP:	vice president

Case Scenarios

CASE ONE: You are an entrepreneur pharmacist and have been approached by an independent retail pharmacy owner who wants you to purchase her pharmacy because she is considering retirement. Because this has been your dream since you started pharmacy school, you investigate the offer thoroughly and decide that you would like to purchase the pharmacy. However, to secure the business loans necessary to complete the purchase, your potential investors are requiring you to prepare a business plan for the pharmacy. What should you include in your business plan to demonstrate to your potential investors that this is a sound investment and worthy of their financial backing?

CASE TWO: You have been working at a busy community pharmacy since graduation from

pharmacy school five years ago. You have developed a relationship with several of your patients who have diabetes and you help many of your patients with nutritional support in addition to medication and disease counseling. From your experience, you developed an idea to start a medication therapy management program to support the services you have been providing to your patients. The reimbursement you receive from the service can also help you expand the program to serve more patients. On the basis of your discussion with your district manager who likes the idea, you were asked to prepare a business plan for the corporate office. Outline the business plan for your proposed medication therapy management program.

CASE THREE: You have just started a staff pharmacist position at a small community hospital. Although the hospital provides excellent care,

(continues)

you observe a need for a clinical pharmacist to support the hospital's intensive care unit (ICU). You have seen the value a clinical pharmacist can add to the ICU during your clinical clerkships and your residency program and, therefore, have decided to approach the pharmacy director with your idea. The pharmacy director asks you to put together a personnel plan to support this proposed position. What elements should be included in the personnel plan for the ICU clinical pharmacist position?

Additional Resources Available Online!

Visit the Student Companion Web site at http://healthprofessions.jbpub.com/pharmacymanagement for interactive study tools and additional resources.

See www.rxugace.com to learn how you can obtain continuing pharmacy education for this content.

MARKETING

UNDERSTANDING AND APPLYING MARKETING STRATEGIES

GLENN ROSENTHAL, EdD, MA, MBA

DANA REED-KANE, PharmD, FIACP, FACA, NFPPhC, FCP

LEARNING OBJECTIVES

After completing this chapter, the reader will be able to

1. Define marketing and list key marketing priorities.
2. Differentiate between patient wants, needs, and demands in pharmacy goods and services.
3. Explain the importance of the four P's of marketing.
4. Distinguish between a market segment and a market niche.
5. Provide examples of niche markets within pharmacy practices.
6. Discern the elements of a strong brand.
7. Explain the value of relationship marketing.

KEY CONCEPTS

❶ Pharmacist managers must meet patient and customer expectations, but this is only possible when those needs and preferences are understood.

❷ Marketing focuses on wants, needs, and demands.

❸ The marketing mix includes the four "P's" of marketing: product, place, price, and promotion.

❹ A market niche is a narrower segment of a population that needs or desires specialized goods or services.

❺ Pharmacist managers should consider which market segments hold the most promise and employ strategies to attract and retain individuals within these segments.

❻ Niche marketing is an increasingly appropriate strategy for pharmacy practices, as it offers opportunities to meet needs that are not being fulfilled by existing products and services.

❼ Once a target market has been identified, the organizational leadership must consider how it wants its products and services to be viewed by others. It can do this by developing a recognizable brand.

❽ Given that the majority of pharmaceutical services are for patients with chronic conditions, relationship marketing holds promise as a strategy for long-term patient retention.

❾ Although acquiring new patients is an essential business strategy for most pharmacy practices, existing patients are usually less expensive to serve, as they do not typically require an orientation to your products and services or new record-keeping.

❿ Healthcare providers are key partners in generating referrals, and building relationships with these individuals is essential.

INTRODUCTION

Well-managed and collaborative relationships with patients and healthcare providers are critical for maintaining demand for pharmacy services on a consistent and long-term basis. A thoughtful and well-organized **marketing strategy** is critical to be competitive.[1] **❶** *Pharmacist managers must meet patient and customer expectations, but this is only possible when those needs and preferences are understood.* This holds true regardless of the pharmacy setting (e.g., hospital, retail, independent, or mail order), as success in understanding patient and **stakeholder** needs will determine whether business is directed to your organization or to someone else's. Pharmacy stakeholders are numerous and may include patients, physicians, and other healthcare providers, insurance companies, regulatory agencies, stockholders, vendors, and members of the public—each with differing needs and interests in pharmacy products and services. Regardless of whether they have management responsibilities, pharmacists should be familiar with **marketing** principles and how to apply these principles to

maintain pharmacy market share while optimizing new pharmacy endeavors. This chapter will review essential marketing principles and describe effective methods of applying these principles in pharmacy settings.

DEFINING MARKETING AND MARKETING STRATEGY

What is marketing? In a 2007 memo to its membership, the American Marketing Association (AMA) described marketing as "the activity, set of institutions, and processes for creating, communicating, delivering, and exchanging offerings that have value for customers, clients, partners, and society at large."[2] Marketing theorist Philip Kotler defines marketing as "the science and art of exploring, creating, and delivering value to satisfy the needs of a target market at a profit."[3] Kotler asserts that marketing's key priorities are to (1) identify new opportunities, (2) develop new products, (3) attract customers, (4) retain customers and build loyalty, and (5) fulfill orders.[3]

Marketing focuses heavily on communicating notions of "value" to current and potential consumers. So, what makes a product or service especially valuable in a pharmacy setting? The answers can vary by individual or population and may include such things as the quality of products or services; the expertise of the pharmacists; convenience of the pharmacy's hours of operation, location, or distribution options (e.g., pickup window or home delivery); customer service; the opportunity to purchase other items while picking up prescriptions; and the amount of time it takes to receive a service and or product. It is essential to understand the difference between real value and perceived value and to understand that perceived value may influence consumer satisfaction and willingness to purchase now or in the future.

DETERMINING NEEDS, WANTS, AND DEMANDS

❷ *Marketing focuses on wants, needs, and demands.* A need is a basic requirement for health, safety, and well-being. A want is not required for survival, but the recipient is happier if the want is satisfied. An example of a need is transportation to get to work, something that could be satisfied by a subway, a bicycle, or one's own feet. A transportation want could be a BMW or a personal driver. In the world of marketing, wanting something and getting it are two different things—a distinction that brings us to the notion of demand, a want that is supported by the willingness or ability to pay.[4] In a pharmacy context, pediatric patients may need antibiotics and may want them to be pleasantly flavored, but if cherry or bubblegum-flavored Augmentin suspension is considerably more expensive than the unflavored suspension, demand for the product may be low. Pharmacist managers must be able to distinguish between wants, needs, and demands because patients may want several things, but if they cannot afford or are unwilling to pay for them, there will be little pharmacy demand for them. This may affect how pharmacist managers staff their pharmacies and the inventory they maintain.

An automated telephone ordering system is a classic example of a pharmacy meeting a patient want. These systems offer patients convenience by enabling them to request medications by phone from an off-site location and thus avoid unnecessary waiting within the pharmacy setting. In-pharmacy health clinics are another example of meeting a patient want. These clinics offer diagnosis and prescription filling services and medication dispensing under one roof. Pharmacy-based clinics represent the public's growing interest in convenient and accessible one-stop healthcare services available outside of standard physician offices and, in most cases, provide quicker, more convenient, and affordable care.[5] Given the variety of choices patients and customers have, astute pharmacists and pharmacist managers use marketing skills to create wants and respond to demands.

THE FOUR "P'S" OF MARKETING

When considering the purchase of a good or service, consumers are typically influenced by elements of what is called the **marketing mix**. ❸ *The marketing mix concept was first established in 1960 and includes the four P's: product, price, place, and promotion.*[6]

The Four P's: Product

Product is the good or service provided to meet patient or customer needs.[6] In terms of pharmaceutical products, marketing may be used to determine the color, size, and shape of labels on products, whether to color tablets red or purple, and even what to name the medication. Consumers may be consulted for feedback on their preferences.

Because most chain and private pharmacies sell similar items, they must differentiate themselves based on quality or type of service to gain a competitive edge. Several chain stores sell food items, such as milk, frozen dinners, and other non-pharmaceutical products, to provide additional convenience to customers. Others have set up in-store clinics to provide healthcare services beyond medication dispensing (refer to Chapter 11, "Justifying and Planning Patient Care Services"). Medication therapy management, a partnership between the pharmacist, patient, and healthcare provider designed to promote the safe use of medication and to support the achievement of the desired outcomes of medication therapy, is emerging as a valuable service for managing common conditions, such as hypertension, asthma, anticoagulation, and diabetes, and provides some pharmacies with the opportunity to differentiate themselves from competitors.[7] Many pharmacies have implemented compounding services as a means to satisfy needs unmet by commercially available medications. The compounding services are often coupled with consultation services in a variety of specialty areas, such as pain management and women's and men's health in which compounded preparations are commonly prescribed.

The Four P's: Price

Price refers to charging appropriately for a product or service.[6] Medication pricing can be especially complex in a pharmacy setting because health insurance coverage plans tend to mask true costs (refer to Chapter 9, "Third-Party Payment for Prescription Medications in the Retail Sector"). When a patient has prescription insurance benefits, only a copayment is typically required, thereby obscuring the real costs of a medication to the patient.

Given that most pharmacies accept the same copays, it can be difficult to differentiate on the patient portion of pricing; despite this, several pricing strategies are used in a pharmacy setting:

- *Cost-plus pricing* involves adding a percentage of profit over and above the cost of the product or service to the pharmacy.[8]
- *Valued-based pricing* uses the patient's perception of the value of the product or service to establish a price. When patients or customers perceive high quality, or even prestige, they will often be willing to pay more.[8]
- *Competitive pricing* tends to mirror the pricing strategy used by competitors.[8]
- *Closeout pricing* involves offering steep discounts on excess inventory items to avoid having to discard or store it. This strategy focuses on minimizing loss rather than making a profit.[9]
- *Discount pricing* uses tools, such as coupons, to reduce the cost of a product or service.[8]
- *Membership pricing* can be used to offer cost reductions through loyalty programs.[9]
- *Loss-leader pricing* involves reducing the price of one product to attract customers and making up for this lost revenue by encouraging purchases of other items.[8] This strategy is often used to attract patients without comprehensive prescription coverage.
- *Psychological pricing* strives to make a price more attractive to a consumer. For example, a $9.99 item is often perceived to be a better value than a product that costs $10.00.[8]
- *Bundling and quantity discounts* can be offered to individuals or organizations that buy several items at once.[9]

Focusing exclusively on medication pricing is not always a wise strategy. While some people assume that consumers seek the lowest possible price, this may not always be true. In some cases, low prices are associated with inferior quality, and consumers are often willing to pay more for a product if it is accompanied with better service or a more pleasant experience. Many private pharmacies incorporate the cost of providing more counseling, more staff, or the labor involved in compounding into their prices, and patients are often willing to pay more to receive these services.[10] In a pharmacy setting, price, or "cost," may extend beyond out-of-pocket expenditures to include such things as the inconvenience of long wait times, expensive parking, or an inaccessible location.

The Four P's: Place

Place refers to making the product or service available in the most accessible way.[6] Place includes the organization's physical location, as well as how its products are displayed and distributed. This component of marketing can encompass mail-ordering systems and home delivery options. Many physician offices have pharmacies located within their buildings, and some are installing drug-dispensing machines in their offices so that as soon as they write a prescription, the patient can get the prescription filled in these convenient locations if they choose (**Figure 15-1**).[11] Enhancing patient access to products and services through means such as 24-hour service, drive-thru windows, and delivery services can increase competitiveness.

The Four P's: Promotion

Promotion is a set of strategies designed to make customers or patients aware of goods and services.[6] Advertising, personal selling, publicity, and public relations campaigns are all strategies to promote goods and services and to create a positive impression.[12] Depending on their budgets, some pharmacies may hire salespeople or promotional companies to help market their products and services, while others may create promotional materials themselves. Examples of promotional materials may be flyers, bag-stuffers, newspaper or television advertisements, brochures, newsletters, and in-store signage.

ADDITIONAL P'S OF MARKETING

While marketing professionals typically talk about the four P's of marketing (product, price, place,

FIGURE **15–1**   **Drug-Dispensing "Vending" Machine.**

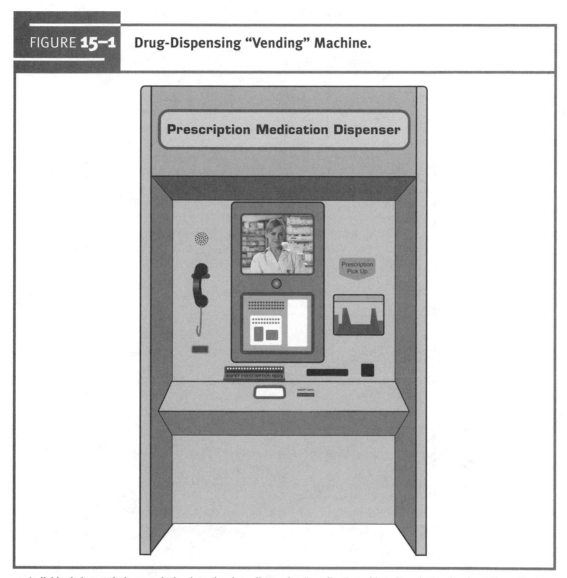

Individuals insert their prescription into the drug-dispensing "vending" machine. By using technology, the patient receives counseling on the medication and the actual medication is dispensed through a hole located at the bottom or on the side of the machine.

Source: © Diego Cervo/ShutterStock, Inc.

and promotion), additional P's are sometimes discussed in terms of the marketing mix. Additional P's include the following:

- *Participation*: Actively engaging with one's customer base through dialogue or patient counseling.[13]

- *Positioning*: The process used to create an image or brand of the product or service.[4,14]
- *People*: The type of people the organization employs and how they behave.[15]

Table 15–1 provides examples of each component of the marketing mix.

TABLE 15–1 Marketing Mix Strategies

Product	Price	Place	Promotion	Participation	Positioning	People
Appearance	Value-based pricing	Product distribution channels	Advertising	Knowledge of patient needs	Provide a sense of belonging	Expertise
Quality	Competitive pricing		Personal selling			Knowledge
Labeling	Closeout pricing	Pharmacy location	Public relations	Involvement in patient care	Establish a perception of luxury	Customer service orientation
Product name	Discount pricing	Product displays	Publicity		Meet a specialized need	Longevity
Accompanying services	Membership pricing					
Effectiveness	Loss-leader pricing	Where patients are counseled	Internet ads		Create a sense of security	Appearance
	Psychological pricing		Web pages			Reliability
	Bundling pricing	Atmosphere	Yellow pages		Enhance a feeling of being special or important	
	Quantity discounts		Health screenings			
			Coupons			

Sources: Data from Kotler P, Keller KL;[4] McCarthy EJ;[6] Ehmke C, Fulton J, Lusk J;[8] Kyle B;[9] Duron M;[13] Ries A, Trout J;[14] Bitner MJ.[15]

MARKET RESEARCH AND ANALYSIS

Savvy pharmacist managers conduct **market research** and complete a **market analysis** before moving into new market segments. Porter's Five Forces Analysis can be helpful in this regard.[16] The five forces include the following:

- *Bargaining power of suppliers* (e.g., How might suppliers drive up your costs? How many suppliers exist?). When there are just a few suppliers of a given product, these suppliers may not be interested in negotiating on such things as price or service because they face little competition.
- *Bargaining power of customers* (e.g., What is the size of your potential customer base? What is their price negotiating power?). Are there enough potential customers to make your organization profitable, and do they have other options that may force you to lower your prices or offer expensive extra services?
- *Threat of new entrants* (e.g., How likely are competitors to enter the market?). If others are likely to enter the market, there may not be an adequate patient or customer base to make your organization viable.
- *Threat of substitute products* (e.g., Do reasonable alternatives to your product or service exist?). If patients or customers can obtain comparable products or services from a mail-order program or a large retail chain pharmacy, they may not choose to patronize your independent pharmacy.
- *Competitive rivalry within an industry* (e.g., How many competitors do you have? Is your product or service fundamentally different than theirs?). Chances of success are highest when an organization has little market competition and unique and highly valued products and services.

Although pharmacist managers may not be expected to conduct market research or analysis, they must be able to make decisions using market analysis data and understand how the data were derived. Pharmacist managers will be more effective if they understand the fundamental tools used to forecast sales and analyze current and emerging markets. Information regarding how to conduct a market analysis is available in Chapter 11 ("Justifying and Planning Patient Care Services"), Chapter 13 ("Achieving Results Through Others and Strategic Planning"), and Chapter 14 ("Pharmacy Business and Staff Planning").

MARKET SEGMENTATION AND MARKET NICHES

Before making decisions about product, price, place, or promotion, an organization must first decide who it wants to target in its marketing efforts. A **market segment** refers to a subgroup of individuals or organizations that have one or more similar characteristics or similar needs or interests.[17] ❹ A **market niche** *is a narrower segment of a population that needs or desires specialized goods or services.*[18] In a pharmacy setting, children are a market segment, and children with asthma are a market niche within the entire pediatric patient population. Men older than age 50 years are years a segment of the market, and men older than age 50 years with chronic hypertension are a market niche. Pharmacies may also segment markets based on factors such as income level, ethnicity, or geographic location. **Table 15–2** provides additional examples of market segments and market niches. ❺ *Pharmacist managers should consider which market segments hold the most promise and employ strategies to attract and retain the individuals within these segments.* A pharmacy practice's location, resources, and staff expertise will often influence the ability to respond to various market segments. For example, a pharmacy whose staff has expertise in geriatric care can target this patient population in ways that other pharmacies cannot.

❻ *Niche marketing is an increasingly appropriate strategy for pharmacy practices, as it offers pharmacy services an opportunity to meet needs that are not being fulfilled by existing products and services.* Niche markets are smaller than the entire market segment and focus on individuals with common needs and characteristics.[18] For a niche market to be profitable, it must

- Be sufficient in size
- Have growth potential
- Not be well served by other organizations

TABLE 15–2	Examples of Market Segments and Market Niches in a Pharmacy Practice	

Characteristic	Market Segment	Market Niche
Age	Pediatric	Asthma patients Patients with ADHD Patients undergoing chemotherapy Patients with autism
Age	Elderly	Patients with hypertension Patients with diabetes Patients on anticoagulation medications Pain management Patients with elevated cholesterol
Gender	Men	Men with prostate cancer Men with erectile dysfunction
Gender	Women	Women with osteoporosis Postmenopausal women New mothers
Species	Animals	Domestic animals (dogs, cats, birds) Large animals (horses)
Income Level	Low income	Patients without health insurance Patients without transportation
Income Level	High income	Patients who want home delivery Patients who want lifestyle prescriptions

Note: ADHD = attention-deficit/hyperactivity disorder.

- Have adequate purchasing potential
- Demonstrate a need and interest for special treatment or distinction[18]

A select group of pharmacies have applied niche marketing strategies by focusing on the needs of specialized patient populations.[19] Kids 'N Cures Pharmacy, with three locations in Ohio, focuses on pediatric patients and uses the slogan, "The family pharmacy that helps parents raise healthier children from conception to college."[20] The pharmacy specializes in products for children and new mothers, such as flavored medications and promethazine morning sickness gels. A free online "Mother and Children's Newsletter" is one of the many ways it promotes products and services and strengthens relationships to clientele.[20] The 50-Plus Pharmacy in Kansas City, Missouri, takes a similar approach but focuses on older adults. It employs a cadre of geriatric-certified pharmacists and is known for providing detailed counseling and services, such as blood pressure and blood glucose checks.[19] Compounding pharmacies are another example of how some entrepreneurial pharmacists have filled a market niche. By offering customized preparation of medicines, not otherwise commercially available, compounding pharmacies can respond to specialized patient needs.[21] Consider the following situations:

- A patient is allergic to dyes or binders often found in many off-the-shelf medications.
- A medication is no longer available because it is no longer profitable to manufacture.
- A patient requires a tailored dosage strength.
- A patient cannot ingest, absorb, or receive maximum benefit from a medication in its commercially available form and requires a different administration, such as a cream, ointment, or solution.

Given the growing number of people who do not respond to the "off-the-shelf," one-size-fits-all prescription medicines provided by most pharmacies, compounding pharmacists fill a vital market need.[21] These services tend to create extraordinary customer goodwill by demonstrating responsiveness and a commitment to individualized care.

What if the patient is an animal who cannot swallow pills, cannot tolerate the taste of standardly prepared medications, or requires special dosing? Many compounding pharmacies work with veterinarians and pet owners to offer customized dosage forms or strengths for animals in which commercial medications are unavailable or not dispensed in the desired form or strength.[22]

Individualized care can also be provided by pharmacist consultation. Pharmacies are increasingly offering fee-based consultation services by appointment in response to the demand from patients for more comprehensive information about their medications and disease states. Patients dissatisfied with the lack of time some healthcare providers have available to answer questions and address concerns are more frequently turning to pharmacists because of their accessibility and knowledge and are willing to pay reasonable fees for quality time and service.[10] Other healthcare providers are also recognizing the value of these services and are referring patients to pharmacists for consultations.[23] Common examples of pharmacist consulting are women's health (e.g., infertility, perimenopause, menopause, osteoporosis), men's health (erectile dysfunction), pain management, asthma, diabetes, hyperlipidemia, hypertension, nutrition, compounding, and drug regimen reviews.

Branding

❼*Once a target market has been identified, the organizational leadership must consider how it wants its products and services to be viewed by others. It can do this by developing a recognizable brand.* The word "brand" is derived from an ancient Norse word meaning "to burn"[24] and refers to the experiences and associations of an entity that have been "burned" into an individual's psyche. To illustrate the importance of **branding**, consider how patients and consumers differentiate between an independent and a chain pharmacy. Does one entity provide services or products that the other does not? Is the experience of visiting one different from the other? Likewise, what might prompt someone to purchase Bayer aspirin instead of a generic brand with the same ingredients? When it comes down to the actual product or service, there may not be much difference between the choices, but a solid brand can create preferences and loyalty. Organizations can use a number of techniques to establish and strengthen their organizational brand. The way they provide service, the kind of people they hire, the processes they employ, their flexibility and the prices they charge can all influence perceptions of the organization's brand. Company names are also part of a branding strategy.

For example, when Custom Care Pharmacies sought to increase its visibility and reputation for innovation and quality, it rebranded itself as AnazaoHealth Corporation. *Anazao* is a Greek word that means "to recover life; to come to life again; be alive again; live again; revive." The new name was accompanied with a new graphic identity and tagline: "Create, Heal, Live."[25] AnazaoHealth's branding campaign is an example of **integrated marketing communication** (IMC) strategy, a key component of a branding campaign. IMC seeks to ensure consistency among the various elements of a marketing strategy and asks, "Does our name reflect the image we are trying to project?" "Are the choices of colors, text fonts, layouts, and images consistent from publication to publication?" "Is the voice consistent from message to message?" "Is our logo used in a consistent fashion?" IMC seeks to create a core message and recognizable overall image to enhance positive associations, increase awareness, and reduce confusion.[26]

Relationship Marketing

Maintaining and growing a patient base can be supported by a marketing strategy that focuses on building relationships with others. When **relationship marketing** emerged, it was viewed as a systematic approach for tracking and building market share. According to Copulsky and Wolf, the relationship marketing process includes the following:[27]

- Using databases to manage current and potential customers
- Delivering differentiated messages to various market segments
- Tracking customer behavior to analyze the value of acquiring and maintaining various customer segments

Databases tend to track such things as customer demographics, frequency of visits, types of products or services purchased or used, and average amounts spent. These data points can then be used to develop differentiated messages, promotional campaigns, or programs to reward the most profitable customers.

The traditional view of relationship marketing is that it is transactional and focused on tracking the volume of goods and services with targeted customers. A broader and more strategic view of relationship marketing in a pharmacy setting focuses on developing long-term and mutually beneficial relationships with both patients and business and clinical partners.[1] In short, relationship marketing encompasses "all marketing activities directed toward establishing, developing, and maintaining successful relationships."[27] **8** *Given that the majority of pharmaceutical services are for patients with chronic conditions, relationship marketing holds promise as a strategy for long-term patient retention.*[1] Practicing principles of relationship marketing requires pharmacists and pharmacist managers to understand the fundamentals of all relationships: communication, commitment, and common interest.[28] Relationship marketing employs several key concepts, among them are the following:

- *Identifying and responding to market segments.* Rather than trying to provide comprehensive goods and services to all potential patients, pharmacies that use relationship marketing focus on providing high-quality and specialized goods and services to a select group of patients or partners.[1]
- *Personalizing marketing.* A one-on-one approach designed to respond to a patient's individual needs, personalized marketing may include listening for patient's unmet health needs and recommending products or services to meet those needs. McDonough and Doucette describe a five-step model that begins with collecting patient information and then includes (1) assessing patient information, (2) asking probing questions, (3) presenting product/service features and benefits, (4) addressing concerns, and (5) offering the product or service.[29]
- *Retaining patients.* Instead of focusing on one-time events to get patients to visit pharmacies to purchase products (e.g., coupons, flu shots, blood pressure screenings), pharmacies that engage in relationship marketing employ efforts such as drug therapy assessment programs to encourage patients to return on a regular basis.[1] They may also employ loyalty programs that offer special offers or discounts to their best customers to reward desired behavior and to provide customers with a sense of exclusivity.[30]
- *Taking a longer-term view.* Relationship marketing emphasizes long-term relationships with patients and stakeholders.[1] For example, pharmacies that specialize in transplant medication therapy often develop relationships with transplant patients, their families, and physicians before the patients receive new organs. Given these patients' ongoing medication needs, these relationships often continue throughout the patients' lives.

Trust is a critical component of all relationships, and it is crucial to relationship marketing as well. How do pharmacy practices maintain patient trust to sustain relationships with them? Pharmacist managers and pharmacists should do three things: (1) make realistic promises, (2) keep those promises, and (3) enable their staff and systems to keep promises.[15] Before offering a service or promising a product, it is important to ensure that it can be consistently delivered. For example, if disease management counseling cannot be consistently provided, it is better not to advertise this service. Likewise, promising to dispense prescriptions within 15 minutes can certainly attract new patients, but failure to meet that time goal by even a minute or two will cause disappointment and harm the pharmacy's reputation, as will offering blood pressure screening but failing to maintain the equipment needed for accurate readings.

Although we often think about the power of relationship marketing to increase repeat purchases and referrals, this strategy increases profitability in other ways as well. ❾ *Although acquiring new patients is an essential business strategy for most pharmacy practices, existing patients are usually less expensive to serve, as they do not typically require an orientation to your products and services or new record-keeping.* Relationship marketing can also reduce the costs of employee turnover, as the opportunity to build a sense of connection and community with returning patients and customers can increase employee satisfaction.[30]

Although we have focused our discussion on building relationships with patients, building relationships with healthcare providers is essential as well. ❿ *Healthcare providers are key partners in generating referrals, and building relationships with these individuals is essential.* Collaborative Practice Agreements (CPAs), a practice whereby physicians and, in some states, nurse practitioners, authorize

pharmacists to adjust and initiate drug therapy, reflect a strong mutually beneficial relationship and exemplify the power of relationship marketing[31] (refer to Chapter 7, "Pharmacy Operations: Workflow, Practice Activities, Medication Safety, Technology, and Quality"). Relationship marketing is extremely important when pharmacists provide consultation services in their pharmacies. To provide these services to patients, the pharmacy and pharmacist must gain the respect and trust of the provider. The relationship with the provider may start with one patient referral and, if handled well, may lead to multiple referrals and a true working relationship.

SUMMARY

When a patient describes symptoms to a pharmacist, the pharmacist connects disparate pieces of information and draws on experience and sound scientific medical knowledge to make treatment suggestions. This interaction requires effective listening and a deep knowledge of drug action and its effects on the body. Like good patient care, effective marketing requires listening. In the pharmacy field, marketers, like good clinicians, work to understand their stakeholders' needs, wants, and demands and try to align their products and services accordingly. In doing so, they create a sense of trust and build a foundation for long-term relationships. Marketing principles, especially niche marketing and relationship marketing, hold promise for building and sustaining a viable pharmacy practice.

References

1. Doucette W, McDonough R. Beyond the 4Ps: using relationship marketing to build value and demand for pharmacy services. *J Am Pharm Assoc* 2002; 42(2):183–194.

2. AMA memo to Academic Leadership and AMA membership. December 17, 2007. Available at: http://www.marketingpower.com/Community/ARC/Pages/Additional/Definition/default.aspx. Accessed March 10, 2009.

3. Dr. Kotler answers your questions on marketing. Available at: http://www.kotlermarketing.com/phil_questions.shtml. Accessed July 25, 2009.

4. Kotler P, Keller KL. *Marketing Management*. 12th ed. Upper Saddle, NJ: Pearson Prentice-Hall; 2006.

5. Palmer I. Quick clinics find niche in health market. *ACP Internist*. 2006;October. Available at: http://www.acponline.org/journals/news/oct06/clinics.htm. Accessed April 3, 2009.

6. McCarthy EJ. *Basic Marketing: A Managerial Approach*. Homewood, IL: Irwin; 1960.

7. The Lewin Group. Medication therapy management services: a critical review. *J Am Pharm Assoc* 2005;45(5):580–587.

8. Ehmke C, Fulton J, Lusk J. The 4 P's of marketing: first steps for entrepreneurs. Purdue Extension Agricultural Innovation & Commercialization Center. Available at: http://www.ces.purdue.edu/extmedia/EC/EC-730.pdf. Accessed July 18, 2009.

9. Kyle B. Pricing strategies that improve profit. Available at: http://www.websitemarketingplan.com/techniques/pricing2.htm. Accessed July 17, 2009.

10. Ukens C. Earning their keep: patients will pay for R.Ph. services, study finds. *Drug Top* 1996;140:42.

11. Sipkoff M. Automated dispensing machines hit doctors' offices. *Drug Top* September 18, 2006. Available at: http://drugtopics.modernmedicine.com/drugtopics/article/articleDetail.jsp?id=372288. Accessed July 24, 2009.

12. American Marketing Association Dictionary. Available at: http://www.marketingpower.com/_layouts/Dictionary.aspx?dLetter=P. Accessed March 19, 2009.

13. Duron M. The 5 P's of marketing. Available at: http://www.personalbrandingblog.com/the-5ps-of-marketing. Accessed July 26, 2009.

14. Ries A, Trout J. *Positioning: The Battle for Your Mind*. New York, NY: McGraw-Hill; 2001.

15. Bitner MJ. Building service relationships: it's all about promises. *J Acad Market Sci* 1995;23:246–251.

16. Porter ME. *Competitive Strategy: Techniques for Analyzing Industries and Competitors*. New York, NY: Free Press; 1980.

17. American Marketing Association Dictionary. Available at: http://www.marketingpower.com/_layouts/Dictionary.aspx?dLetter=M#market+segmentation. Accessed July 24, 2009.

18. Dalgic T, Leeuw M. Niche marketing revisited: concepts, applications, and some European cases. *Eur J Market* 1994;28(4):39–55.

19. Aungst H. Niche pharmacies serve children and the elderly. *Drug Top* 2009;February 1. Available at: http://drugtopics.modernmedicine.com/drugtopics/author/authorInfo.jsp?id=47404. Accessed April 4, 2009.

20. Kids 'N Cures Pharmacy website. Availalable at: http://www.kidsncures.com/about.htm. Accessed April 4, 2009.

21. International Association of Compounding Pharmacies. Frequently asked questions. Available at: http://www.iacprx.org/site/PageServer?pagenAQs. Accessed March 9, 2009.

22. Papich M. Compounding for veterinary patients. *AAPS J* 2005;7(2):E281–E287.

23. AHRQ Innovations Exchange. Clinical pharmacists provide outpatient medication management to patients with severe diabetes and those on anticoagulants, leading to improved outcomes and lower costs. Available at: http://www.innovations.ahrq.gov/content.aspx?id=2359. Accessed July 25, 2009.

24. Adamson A. *BrandSimple: How the Best Brand Keep It Simple and Succeed*. New York, NY: Palgrave Macmillan; 2006.

25. Custom Care Pharmacy announces name change and new branding program custom Care Pharmacy is now AnazaoHealth Corporation. Available at: http://www.anazaohealth.com/LatestNewsArticleView/tabid/143/smid/526/ArticleID/19/reftab/142/t/Custom-Care-Pharmacy-Announces-Name-Change-and-New-Branding-Program/Default.aspx. Accessed April 10, 2009.

26. Brannan T. *A Practical Guide to Integrated Marketing Communications*. London: Kogan Page Ltd; 1995.

27. Copulsky J, Wolf JM. Relationship marketing: positioning for the future. *J Business Strategy* 1990;July/August:16–20.

28. Morgan RM, Hunt SD. The commitment-trust theory of relationship marketing. *J Marketing*. 1994;58:20–38.

29. McDonough RP, Doucette WR. Using personal selling skills to promote pharmacy services. *J Am Pharm Assoc* 2003;43:363–722.

30. Newell F. *The New Rules of Marketing: How to Use One-on-One Relationship Marketing to Be the Leader in Your Industry*. New York, NY: McGraw-Hill; 1997.

31. Hammond R, Schwartz A, Campbell A, et al. ACCP position statement: collaborative drug therapy management by pharmacists—2003. *Pharmacotherapy* 2003;23(9):1210–1225.

Abbreviations

ADHD: attention-deficient/hyperactive disorder
CPAs: Collaborative Practice Agreements
ED: erectile dysfunction
IMC: integrated marketing communication

Case Scenarios

CASE ONE: For almost 60 years, Taylor's Pharmacy was the only retail pharmacy in a working-class neighborhood outside of Baltimore, Maryland. Pharmacy personnel knew customers by name and were even known to provide medication "on credit" to ensure that customers received the treatments they needed. Although the neighborhood demographics have not made the Taylor family wealthy, the pharmacy has enjoyed a consistent and dedicated clientele and has been perceived as a vital part of the neighborhood and business community. This reputation and market position have been challenged during the past few years as successful neighborhood revitalization efforts have attracted both retirees and young professionals to the neighborhood. Hoping to capture an expanding market, a handful of chain pharmacies have moved into the area and established pharmacy/mart stores that allow customers to pick up grocery items, such as milk, soup, and ice cream while picking up prescriptions. They are also offering services such as free home delivery, flu shots, medication counseling, and insurance claims assistance. Given that Taylor's Pharmacy lacks the corporate resources of its new competitors, how can it remain profitable?

CASE TWO: You have recently been hired as a pharmacy manager for a well-regarded pediatric hospital. As part of your orientation process, you have been reviewing the last five years of revenue trend data and have found a disturbing trend. Although inpatient medication prescriptions seem in line with patient growth, prescriptions for outpatient prescriptions have been declining for the past three years. Given the convenience of your on-site pharmacy, this decline is perplexing. Considering the four P's of marketing, what questions might you ask to explain this downward trend?

CASE THREE: David Noble has been charged with opening a retail pharmacy in a largely Spanish-speaking community on the Texas-Mexico border. Although his research has not revealed anything remarkable about the prescription-ordering trends in this community, he senses a market share possibility by responding to the needs and wants of the Spanish-speaking members in this area. How should Dr. Noble decide how to differentiate his pharmacy to achieve maximum profitability?

CASE FOUR: You have been hired by an independent pharmacy and charged with developing a fee-based consultation service within it. The pharmacy currently accepts third-party insurance, and reimbursement is dwindling. Compounding currently makes up about 25% of the pharmacy's business and is much more profitable and rewarding than the third-party business; that is why the owner wants to grow this part of the business. The majority of the current compounding business involves compounding hormone replacement therapy for women's and men's health. Currently, taking care of these patients consumes the majority of the pharmacist's time. The idea is to create a consultation service for the women and men interested in and

(continues)

currently receiving compounded prescriptions for hormone replacement therapy. The creation of these services will serve many purposes: to provide more comprehensive information to these patients, to recoup the cost of an extra pharmacist to provide this service, to provide more time with these patients, to grow this segment of the business, and to emerge as experts in this area. How will you design the pharmacy, change the workflow, and market this service to existing customers and providers, as well as attract new customers? In addition, how will you convince those customers, who already receive these services for free, that these services are worthy of a fee?

Additional Resources Available Online!

Visit the Student Companion Web site at http://healthprofessions.jbpub.com/pharmacymanagement for interactive study tools and additional resources.

See www.rxugace.com to learn how you can obtain continuing pharmacy education for this content.

CHAPTER 16

ADVERTISING AND PROMOTION

MELANIE B. OATES, PhD, MBA, RN
PRACHI D. BHATT

LEARNING OBJECTIVES

After completing this chapter, the reader will be able to

1. Define advertising and promotion and explain their relevance to the practice of pharmacy.
2. Cite the pros and cons of various advertising approaches.
3. Evaluate the pros and cons of various advertising venues.
4. Discuss the role and effect of direct-to-consumer advertising (DTCA) as it relates to patient education and demand.
5. Describe strategies to obtain publicity.
6. List the steps of the Consumer Decision-Making Process, and explain how it can be applied within a pharmacy context.
7. Describe the Health Belief Model, and how it applies to advertising and promotion.
8. Define personal selling and the strategies used in personal selling.

KEY CONCEPTS

❶ Advertising and promotion are the principle vehicles used as part of a marketing plan to convey information about products or services.

❷ In an increasingly competitive, information-rich environment, it is a challenge to get people's attention; therefore, targeted and strategic advertising and promotion are crucial.

❸ Advertising is one of many promotional tools used to increase awareness, recognition, and positive perceptions of products or services and is intended to change the usage (i.e., utilization) or sales of those products or services.

❹ Given changes in the way people receive their news and acquire information, internet advertising is an increasingly attractive strategy for the promotion of those goods and services.

⑤ The importance of direct-to-consumer advertising for the pharmacist lies in recognizing that, for many patients, it may represent a key source of information and may lead them to request medications that may or may not be appropriate for their conditions.

⑥ Publicity is one component of promotion, and it works in a manner similar to advertising, except that it is not paid for or controlled like advertising. Publicity tends to cost less and is more credible, but it is difficult to control.

⑦ Deciding through which channel to advertise is as important as deciding what the content should be. A brilliant creative strategy sent out through the wrong channel may be just as ineffective as a bad creative strategy.

⑧ The Consumer Decision-Making Process can serve as a road map for those engaged in advertising and promotion. It may offer guidance about how to reach consumers who are at different stages of the purchasing process. Knowledge of this process allows one set of strategies to focus on encouraging consumers to try a new product and another to encourage current consumers to feel good about their choice after a purchase has been made.

⑨ The Health Belief Model attempts to predict the health behaviors of patients and consumers. It also attempts to explain how patients perceive their disease, their susceptibility to the adverse effects of the disease, and their perceptions of the potential costs and benefits of changing their behavior to avoid those adverse effects. The Health Belief Model complements the Consumer Decision-Making Process and can also be used to design and stage advertising and promotion efforts.

⑩ Unlike traditional and impersonal advertising campaigns, personal selling involves getting to know patients to identify unmet health needs and to provide appropriate products and services. Personal selling requires strong questioning and listening skills.

INTRODUCTION

Advertising and **promotion** may not seem relevant to the daily practice of the patient-centered pharmacist; however, advertising, promotion, and patient care are quite interrelated. Every television commercial for a medication, every promotion for a product, and every word-of-mouth referral to a pharmacy is an intersection of patient care and product or service promotion.

❶ *Advertising and promotion are marketing communication tools used as part of a marketing plan to convey information about products or services.* If you are in charge of increasing business to a pharmacy, you may employ advertising and promotion to increase patient volume and sales. Even if you are not involved in advertising and promotion, your work as a pharmacist or pharmacist manager will be affected by the advertising and promotional efforts of others (e.g., pharmaceutical companies promoting the use of their medications). **❷** *In an increasingly competitive and information-rich environment, it is a challenge to get people's attention; therefore, targeted and strategic advertising and promotion are crucial.* This chapter complements Chapter 15 ("Understanding and Applying Marketing Strategies") and reviews the principles of advertising and promotion—strategies that can support the effective operation of a pharmacy.

THE PURPOSES OF PROMOTION

Promotion is one of many tools that advance the goals of a marketing strategy and can be used for many purposes in a pharmacy context, among them to

- *Create awareness of a product or service.*[1] For example, making consumers aware of a newly introduced cholesterol medication or the 24-hour services of a newly opened retail pharmacy could create awareness.
- *Encourage patients or consumers to try something new.*[1] An example might include informing patients about a highly effective new medication to treat fibromyalgia or enticing local residents to visit a new community pharmacy as a strategy to increase individual sales.

- *Enhance confidence in a product or service.*[2] A branding effort designed to establish a particular image of a product or service can increase consumer interest. Announcements about enhanced packaging to prevent product tampering can reassure consumers, for example.
- *Maintain market share by encouraging the continued purchase of a product or use of a service.*[1] This can be done by creating positive feelings about a brand of pain reliever to ensure brand loyalty or making patients feel like they are part of a community pharmacy's "family."
- *Encourage recommendations and word-of-mouth marketing.* This involves providing the patient with either an incentive or desire to spread the word about products or services. A patient referral program that provides discounts or cash incentives to current patients who refer new patients is one way to encourage recommendations and increase traffic to a pharmacy site or ordering service.

ADVERTISING

Advertising is one form of promotion and is defined by the American Marketing Association as "the placement of announcements and persuasive messages in time or space, purchased in any of the mass media by business firms, nonprofit organizations, government agencies, and individuals who seek to inform and/or persuade members of a particular target market or audience about their products, services, organizations, or ideas."[3]

❸ *Advertising is one of many promotional tools used to increase awareness, recognition, and positive perceptions of products or services and is intended to change the usage (i.e., utilization) or sales of those products or services.*

Advertising Strategies and Venues

When deciding to advertise, sponsoring organizations have several options; among them are television, radio, newspapers, newsletters, flyers, magazines, direct-mail pieces, Yellow Pages, magazines, conference programs, professional or trade journals, clothing, bus benches, subway signs, bus or taxi signs, Sunday newspaper supplements, **Web banners**, **contextual adver-**

tising, and social media outlets, such as Facebook and Twitter. These devices are typically part of a broader advertising strategy designed with specific objectives in mind.

Advertisers have many approaches and venues from which to choose, as discussed in the following paragraphs.

National advertising refers to advertising of a trademarked brand that is distributed widely. It is designed to create awareness and demand. Prices are rarely mentioned and locations are seldom cited.[1] For instance, television commercials for sleep aids are typically national advertisements.[1]

Retail (local) advertising is designed to sell a product and encourage consumers to visit a specific store. Retail advertising tends to emphasize price, provide store hours, and communicate other factors that may distinguish it from its competitors.[1] Sunday newspaper inserts that advertise sales by a chain of retail pharmacies may be examples of retail or local advertising. This form of advertising may be especially appropriate for national companies seeking to target specific market segments based on geographic differences. For example, a retail pharmacy may advertise mid-winter cold and flu products in the Midwest but not in Florida, California, or Arizona.

Direct-response advertising is designed to reach consumers directly and to encourage them to buy a product.[1] An advertisement that encourages patients to call a toll-free 800 number to obtain a discount for a weight-loss aid is an example of direct-response advertising.

Trade advertising includes ads placed in journals and trade papers read by pharmacy managers and is designed to encourage pharmacies to stock certain kinds of products.[1] An example of trade advertising is an ad placed in a trade paper promoting a new glucometer that requires less blood than the competitors' meters.

Professional advertising may be more indirect and is targeted to professionals, such as physicians or pharmacists, to encourage them to prescribe or recommend medications.[1] Testimonials from healthcare providers in a professional journal are examples of professional advertising.

Institutional advertising is not designed to sell a product but rather to create goodwill and positive perceptions about an organization.[1] A pharmaceutical firm may advertise its discount drug programs for low-income people, or a retail pharmacy chain may advertise that it donates a portion of its annual profits to community groups.

Internet advertising is often used to reach consumers who are seeking information about a product, service, or situation. ◆ *Given changes in the way people receive their news and acquire information, internet advertising is an increasingly attractive strategy for those promoting goods and services.* Continuing declines in local newspaper readership and circulation are reducing traditional communication options.[4] The expansion of Web-based news services is creating new opportunities. The challenge is that, unlike hard-copy publications with established circulation numbers, Web viewers are more difficult to quantify and analyze in terms of their demographic attributes. Despite this, internet advertising has several advantages. First, the internet is available 24 hours a day. There is no down time for promotional materials on the internet, as customers can access them whenever they wish. In addition, the number of people who can see one Web site over the life span of that site is infinite. Internet advertising can be less expensive than more traditional advertising. Its reach is far and wide and may open up global markets in a way other advertising channels cannot. Perhaps most important, the internet is often the first place patients go when looking into a disease state or medication.[5] When patients are in this active stage of seeking information, it is easier to convey information to them. Interactive marketing takes advantage of this. If the consumer can interact with the marketing medium and provide feedback and input, then the marketing message can be more easily tailored to the needs of the consumer.

The most common Web-based advertising approaches are Web banners and contextual advertising. Web banners are horizontal strips that appear at the top of a Web page, which are related to the content of the page.[6] For example, a search on "impotence" may result in a Web banner that links to erectile dysfunction treatments or antidepressants. Contextual advertising uses the key words on a Web page or search engine results to present an advertisement on a related topic (i.e., "pop-ups").[7] For example, typing "arthritis" into a search engine results in various advertisements for such things as glucosamine and local pain specialists. **Table 16–1** describes the pros and cons of various advertising approaches.[5-6]

Direct-to-consumer advertising (DTCA) has emerged as a popular and profitable strategy for promoting pharmaceutical products directly to the people who will use them.[8,9] Television and magazine advertisements increasingly promote the powers of arthritis medications, cholesterol-lowering drugs, and depression treatments. Opponents of DTCA claim this advertising approach can give patients unrealistic expectations about healing and health or may lead people to believe that a particular medication can heal or reverse the effect of a disease more than is really possible.[8] For many medications, the marker of clinical success is not a complete reversal to the patient's predisease state but simply a reduction, or an alleviation, of symptoms. For example, pain, which is the most common patient complaint, is not always completely relieved by medication use; sometimes, the best that can be achieved is a reduction in the severity of pain.

Consumers have not always had access to pharmaceutical advertising, and it is not available in most countries.[10] DTCA became available in the United States in 1996, when the U.S. Food and Drug Administration changed its regulatory language to allow marketers to create advertising directly aimed at the patient rather than focusing promotional efforts on prescribing physicians.[11] When DTCA was first introduced, it was controversial and remains so today. Some see DTCA as a means of empowering patients with critical information and encouraging appropriate medication use. Many believe DTCA creates awareness of options and even enhances adherence among people with chronic conditions.[9] Critics of DTCA counter that these advertisements give patients unrealistic health goals and prompt patients to request medications they do not need.[12-15] Opponents also claim that DTCA may lead patients to pressure their physicians to prescribe certain products.[15] Studies related to the effect of DTCA are decidedly mixed; some have found that physicians serve as appropriate gatekeepers, and others have reported that physicians' prescribing habits are heavily influenced by patient requests.[16,17]

TABLE **16–1**	Pros and Cons of Various Advertising Venues	
Venue	**Pros**	**Cons**
Professional Conference Programs	Easy to target a particular therapeutic area and its thought leaders	Advertising efforts intended to educate are often perceived as insincere Conference coordinators have a degree of control over the advertising
Contextual Advertising	Patient is already thinking about the desired topic so is more receptive to information	May lead to information overload so patients may ignore it
Direct Mail Pieces	Directly target specific patients and geographic regions	May be tossed out as junk mail
Magazines	Ability to segment markets	High cost Need for advanced planning (i.e., ad copy typically provided six to eight weeks in advance)
Newspapers	Wide reach	Has no specific audience target
Professional Journals	Target healthcare professionals when they are seeking information and are more receptive	Credibility of the journal will affect perception of advertisement
Public Transit Signs	Wide, general reach that moves through different geographic regions, increasing exposure	Requires simpler advertisements because of short viewing time
Radio	Ability to segment audiences Low cost per contact Inexpensive creative production	Lack of visual element Decline in radio listenership Difficulty in obtaining reliable listener statistics
Web Banners	Easy to customize for each Web site and its audience	Overabundance of Web banners can lead to being lost in background noise of Web advertising

Sources: Data from Russell JT, Verill G, Lane WR;[1] Web developers notes;[6] Wise Geek.[7]

❺ *The importance of DTCA for the pharmacist lies in recognizing that, for many patients, it may represent a key source of information and may lead them to request medications that may or may not be appropriate.* As DTCA influences product or service demand, pharmacist managers and staff pharmacists must be cognizant of current advertising campaigns, local patterns of use, and DTCA effectiveness to ensure that their inventory is adequate to respond to patient demands. **Table 16–2** details arguments for and against DTCA.[11–16]

PUBLICITY

❻ *Publicity is one component of promotion, and it works like advertising, except that it is not paid for* or controlled as advertising.[18] *Publicity tends to cost less and is more credible, but it is difficult to control.*

Although generating publicity is less expensive than advertising, it is not free. Contrary to popular belief, publicity does not just happen without planning and effort. Just as there are advertisers, there are those who handle publicity. Duties of these individuals include maximizing the amount of positive publicity that a product or service receives and developing the source materials sent to media outlets.

Publicity Vehicles

A number of vehicles exist to create exposure and increase interest and awareness. The following is

---

TABLE **16–2**	**Pros and Cons of Direct-to-Consumer Advertising**

Pros	Cons
Provides easily accessible information to the patient in a patient-centered format.	May oversimplify medication indications as well as differential disease diagnoses.
Lends itself to be a "screening tool" for diseases not commonly discussed.	Patients often mistake information as a suggestion to self-treat instead of seeing a healthcare provider for diagnosis and treatment.
Can increase patient awareness of new treatment options.	Patients often mistake "newer" for "better."
Helps patients assess whether their current treatment regimens are appropriate.	Patients may not have medical literacy to assess the validity of advertising content.
Helps to reduce the stigma associated with disease by keeping the topics in the public consciousness.	Less prevalent diseases get less exposure.

Source: Data from Schwartz MI;[11] Donohue JM, Berndt ER, Rosenthal M, Epstein AM, Frank RG;[12] Donohue JM, Cevasco M, Rosenthal MB;[13] Kravitz RL, Epstein RM, Feldman MD, et al;[14] Rosenthal MB, Berndt ER, Donohue JM, Epstein AM, Frank RG;[15] Aikin KJ, Swazsy JL, Braman AC.[16]

a list of several vehicles that can be used to garner publicity:

- *News releases*: Typically single-page stories that announce an event or occurrence that are sent to media outlets. A pharmacy may announce a flu shot clinic or the addition of a pharmacist who specializes in pediatric care. While some news organizations share news releases as written, most publish only excerpts, or use the information as background for a news or a feature story.
- *Press conferences*: Meetings and presentations held for the press to promote a product or even a concept. Pharmaceutical companies may use this technique to introduce a novel drug.
- *Special events*: Events that help highlight a specific product or service. Special events can include having a blood glucose monitoring kit manufacturer sponsor a blood glucose screening event or a "Drug Check Day" wherein pharmacists and pharmacy students meet with patients to review their medication regimens to prevent adverse drug events.
- *Features*: Articles in newspapers or magazines or spots on news or entertainment programs that focus on topics of general interest or explore a topic in detail; they often have a "human interest" angle. Pharmacy-related feature articles might include an interview with a pharmacist about the dangers of **polypharmacy**, or an extensive look at a pharmacy that offers veterinary services, complete with photos of animals and interviews with their owners.
- *Captioned photos*: Photographs with captions describing a product, service, or event often sent to newspapers, journals, or newsletters. A photo of a newly opened compounding pharmacy that focuses on women's health might be used to alert the community to this new resource.
- *Media interviews*: Speaking to a reporter on television, radio, or the internet. When Michael Jackson died in 2009, several pharmacists were asked to comment on the appropriate use of propofol.

- *Letter to the editor*: A letter with a point of view designed for publication in a newspaper's editorial pages. A pharmacist might write a letter about the effect of rising drug costs on patient compliance, for example.
- *Speeches and presentations*: In-person sharing of ideas to a conference or organization. A pharmacist who specializes in women's health could address a professional women's group about treatments for osteoporosis.
- *Sponsorships*: Providing financial or in-kind support to an event to garner goodwill. A community pharmacy may sponsor jerseys for a cycling event designed to raise money for Alzheimer's research or sponsor a table at an American Cancer Society gala.

ADVERTISING AND PROMOTION CHANNELS

❼ *Deciding through which* **channel** *to advertise is as important as deciding what the content should be. A brilliant creative strategy sent out through the wrong channel may be as ineffective as a bad creative strategy.* An advertisement for an acid reflux disease medication placed on the Disney channel would be unlikely to reach people who need such treatment. Likewise, an advertiser would be unlikely to select a sports network as a primary venue for an osteoporosis treatment.

Consider the strategies a community pharmacy could use to promote services provided by pharmacists who specialize in geriatric medications. Ads in a weekly city music guide whose target audience is 18- to 25-year-old single adults would be wasted dollars, while inserts in retirement community newsletters would probably be more successful. Similarly, speaking to an association of eldercare givers would likely result in more referrals than speaking to a business organization. The channel selected must be a venue that is frequently encountered or sought out by the target population; it has to be within the budget established for the promotional campaign; and the image of the venue must be congruent with the desired image or message. Put simply, the way people perceive the channel's credibility and image has to be consistent with the desired perception of the promotional message.

CRAFTING ADVERTISING AND PROMOTIONAL MESSAGES

Our discussion thus far has focused on advertising and promotion strategies rather than on the content of the messages disseminated through these approaches. We will next examine strategies to communicate with the greatest effect.

Stages in the Consumer Decision-Making Process

Before planning or implementing advertising or promotion strategies, it is important to understand the Consumer Decision-Making Process. Patients and consumers pass through several information processing and evaluation stages before committing to a product or service. Advertising and promotion efforts are most effective when they are aligned with each step in the purchasing or commitment process.

Consumers typically begin by recognizing a need for a product. They then begin to collect information about options and evaluate their various choices. Decisions to purchase are often followed by analyzing whether the choice was wise.[19] ❽ *The Consumer Decision-Making Process can serve as a road map for those engaged in advertising and promotion. It may offer guidance about how to reach consumers who are at different stages of the purchasing process. Knowledge of this process allows one set of strategies to focus on encouraging consumers to try a new product and another to encourage current consumers to feel good about their choice after a purchase has been made.*[19] Given that, the Consumer Decision-Making Process can be used to guide message delivery to people at different stages in the decision-making continuum.[19] Applying it to an advertising and promotion campaign involves a five-step process.

Step 1: Create a need. In some cases, a consumer may not recognize the need for a product or service. When that is the case, advertising and promotion strategies can be used to create awareness of a need. Consider a 47-year-old high school science teacher with chronic insomnia. After months of waking at 2:00 a.m., she finds herself snapping at her husband, her two preteen children, and the students in her classes. While she may believe that insomnia is something women her age must endure as they approach menopause, a television advertisement might introduce her to new possibilities. When she sees the television commercial of a woman her age emerging from bed looking refreshed and then enjoying a lively breakfast with her children, she might be compelled by the advertising commentary: *"Having trouble falling asleep or staying asleep? Ask your physician about Slumberesta."*

Step 2: Provide information. In the event the consumer has identified the need for a product or service and is now actively engaged in gathering information about alternatives and possible choices, promotions should provide information and answers to the questions that these consumers are asking. Our science teacher may want to know the following:

- How effective are various sleep aids?
- How quickly do they work?
- Are there side effects?
- Are they addictive?
- How will I feel the day after taking them?

Because her work requires sustained concentration and energy, our science teacher might be especially worried about her ability to be sharp in the morning. An informational component in the advertisement can assuage her concerns: *"Unlike other sleep aids, Slumberesta leaves you feeling refreshed in the morning."*

Step 3: Support the evaluation of options. The next step for the consumer is to evaluate the alternatives identified through the information search. Promotions that help consumers make choices by providing comparative information are effective. Given our science teacher's strong research and critical thinking skills, it is only natural that she would want data related to sleep product efficacy and safety. She might be comforted to learn that *"Clinical studies have shown that 80 percent of Slumberesta users sleep through the night compared with just 50 percent who use other sleep aids and the side effect profile is minimal."*

Step 4: Encourage a purchase. Once a consumer decides to purchase some form of product or service, advertising can be used to encourage selection of a particular brand. This is true whether a consumer is considering the purchase of a refrigerator or a nasal decongestant. Our science teacher is ready to try a sleep aid and has narrowed her interest to a few options; however, she is frugal and worries about wasting money on a product that will not work. Providing a free or low-cost purchasing option might be enough to encourage her to request Slumberesta by name. A magazine advertisement that reads, *"Deciding to use a sleep aid is a big decision. We want to make it easy. Ask your doctor for a free sample of Slumberesta, and download a coupon for $10 off your next prescription,"* may induce her to ask her physician to prescribe Slumberesta first.

Step 5: Evaluate the wisdom of the purchase. In this final stage, the consumer may experience what is known as "buyer's remorse," the feeling that, despite carrying through with all the necessary steps, the decision was not the right one. To prevent this from happening, advertising and promotional materials need to offer reassurance that the decision was a wise one. Although it may seem that the need for advertising and promotion is unnecessary, once the purchase is made, targeting consumers after purchase is just as important. Promoting the feeling of having made a good decision increases the chances that the consumer will be a repeat user of the product or service (i.e., loyalty).

Being strong-willed and highly disciplined, our science teacher feels guilty that she has not been able to control her insomnia. A reminder that she has taken a responsible course may offer the comfort and support to continue product usage: *"If you are among the one million users of Slumberesta, you know the difference a good night's sleep can make. Slumberesta. Sleep tonight. Be ready tomorrow."*

The previous steps are general and can apply to the decision-making process for almost any product or service. The **Health Belief Model** can also prove helpful to those seeking to advertise products or services.

The Health Belief Model

9 *The Health Belief Model attempts to predict the health behaviors of patients and consumers. It also attempts to explain how patients perceive their disease, their susceptibility to the adverse effects of the disease, and their perceptions of the potential costs and benefits of changing their behavior to avoid those adverse effects. The Health Belief Model complements the Consumer Decision-Making Process and can also be used to design and stage advertising and promotion efforts.* Developed by public health theorists in the 1950s, the Health Belief Model asserts that patients will take action to prevent, screen, or seek treatment for medical conditions if they

- Believe they are susceptible to the condition
- Believe the condition is serious
- Believe there is a benefit to taking action, such as reducing susceptibility to the condition or reducing its severity
- Believe the benefits of taking action outweigh the costs of doing so
- Receive information that prompts them to take some form of action
- Feel confident that they will be able to perform the recommended action[20]

When we apply the elements of the Health Belief Model to our science teacher with insomnia, we may find she conducts the following analysis consciously or subconsciously by asking and answering a series of questions:

- *Am I susceptible to the condition?* Yes; I am clearly awake each night for several hours.
- *Is the condition serious?* Yes; I am exhausted and no longer able to meet my students' needs or those of my family.
- *Is there a benefit to taking action?* Yes; I may get necessary rest, feel better, and increase my performance.
- *Do the benefits of taking action outweigh the costs of doing so?* I may experience drowsiness, nausea, or muscle aches. Paying for this medication will require our family to cut back on other expenses. I will also miss having "alone time" during early morning hours to read or watch old movies. However, if I get

the rest I need, I will be less stressed, my family will be happier, and my students will receive the attention they require. Taking a sleep aid seems like a reasonable strategy for managing my condition.
- *Will I be able to maintain a consistent treatment plan?* Treating my insomnia will require me to take one pill a day and to set aside at least eight hours a night for sleep. I won't have trouble remembering to take the pill and will simply have to start going to bed at a reasonable hour. I can do that.

Table 16–3 describes how advertising and promotional strategies may be used to address each component of the Health Belief Model.[3]

PERSONAL SELLING

While our focus thus far has been on traditional advertising and publicity strategies, **personal selling** is an increasingly important promotional strategy in pharmacy settings. ⟨10⟩ *Unlike traditional and impersonal advertising campaigns, personal selling involves getting to know patients to identify unmet health needs and to provide appropriate products and services. Personal selling requires strong questioning and listening skills.* McDonough and Doucette have developed a five-step model of personal selling in a pharmacy context:[21]

- *Preliminary stage: Gathering information.* Before initiating personal selling, a pharmacist must uncover patient needs. This may be done when dispensing a prescription, offering advice about an over-the-counter product, or through contact at a wellness screening.
- *Step 1: Assessing information.* This stage involves asking the patient open-ended questions to understand health needs or concerns that could benefit from pharmacy products or services.
- *Step 2: Asking probing questions.* While Step 1 uses general questions, Step 2 employs more specific questions to understand patient needs. In this stage, questions may range from "What medication are you currently taking?" to "Do you experience nausea when taking your medication?" to "Did you know that a different combination of prescription and over-the-counter medications might actually save you money?"
- *Step 3: Presenting features and benefits.* Once patient needs and concerns are uncovered, the pharmacist may respond with options to

TABLE **16–3**	Using the Health Belief Model to Guide Advertising and Promotional Strategies
Concept	**Advertising/Promotional Strategy**
Perceived Susceptibility	Increase awareness; help individual assess personal risk.
Perceived Severity	Explain consequences of the condition.
Perceived Benefits	Explain positive benefits to taking action.
Perceived Barriers	Offer reassurance about the treatment option.
Cues to Action	Explain how to obtain the medication; offer reminders.
Self-Efficacy	Increase patient confidence by providing instructions about how to use the medication or device.

Source: Data from American Marketing Association Dictionary.[3]

support the patient's improved health care. A pharmacist interested in promoting pain management consultation services or medication review services could explain the services in moderate detail, note the price, and explain the value of the service in enhancing personal health and well-being.

- *Step 4: Addressing concerns.* In the event a patient objects to the cost or questions the value of a suggested service, Step 4 is used to acknowledge the concerns and provide additional information to explain potential benefits.
- *Step 5: Offering the service.* Once all concerns have been addressed, the patient is offered the service and asked to commit to using the service now or in the future.

Personal selling is, as the phrase suggests, "personal." It involves two-way communication in which a pharmacist seeks to understand patients' needs deeply to promote the best possible option. Given the amount of information people are exposed to each day, this personalized approach promises an effective way to promote pharmacy products and services. See Chapter 11, "Justifying and Planning Patient Care Services," and Chapter 12, "Achieving and Measuring Patient Satisfaction."

WORD-OF-MOUTH PROMOTION

No chapter on promotional strategies would be complete without a discussion of **word-of-mouth promotion**, a process by which one person shares positive purchase- or consumption-related information with another.[22] Examples of word-of-mouth promotion include one friend sharing a story about a positive medication counseling session with a friend, creating a customer referral program, or developing a Web-based video designed to be forwarded from one person to the next. Given declines in traditional advertising venues, such as newspapers, the costs of advertising, and a growing distrust of advertising in general, word-of-mouth promotion can be an effective replacement for traditional approaches to promoting products and services. The growth of the internet and virtual communities, the expansion of social media, and the power of personal relationships make word-of-mouth promotion an increasingly important strategy for pharmacist managers to consider.[23]

A few truisms are worth noting when it comes to word-of-mouth promotion, among them: (1) satisfied patients and customers advertise for you free of charge; and (2) people trust their friends' advice more than they trust advertising messages. Delighting your patients and customers and giving them reasons to talk about you can lead to increased satisfaction, business, and market share.[24]

SUMMARY

Understanding the elements of advertising and promotion can benefit the everyday management of a pharmacy practice. These tools can be used to increase awareness about a service, encourage the purchase of a product, drive business to a pharmacy, or even create feelings of goodwill about an organization. Advertising and promotion are important features of a marketing strategy that use media and other channels to carry a persuasive message. Whether or not the pharmacist actively uses advertising and promotion within the context of his or her individual practice, promotional messages are pervasive and have been shown to affect patient behavior. Knowledge about the fundamentals of advertising and promotion can enable pharmacists and pharmacist managers to serve their patients and other pharmacy clientele effectively.

References

1. Russell JT, Verill G, Lane WR. *Kleppner's Advertising Procedure.* 10th ed. Englewood Cliffs, NJ: Prentice Hall; 1988.

2. Tellis GJ. *Effective Advertising: Understanding When, How, and Why Advertising Works.* Thousand Oaks, CA: Sage Publications; 2004.

3. American Marketing Association Dictionary. Available at: http://www.marketingpower.com/_layouts/Dictionary.aspx?dLetter=A. Accessed March 18, 2009.

4. Arango T. Fall in newspaper sales accelerates to pass 7%. *New York Times*. April 27, 2009. Available at: http://www.nytimes.com/2009/04/28/business/media/28paper.html. Accessed July 5, 2009.

5. Fox S, Jones S. The social life of health information. Pew Internet and American Life Project. June 11, 2009. Available at: http://www.pewInternet.org/~/media//Files/Reports/2009/PIP_Health_2009.pdf. Accessed July 7, 2009.

6. Web Developers Notes. Advertising online using Web banners. Available at: http://www.webdevelopersnotes.com/tips/web_promotion/advertising_online_using_web_banners.php3. Accessed July 7, 2009.

7. Wise Geek. What is contextual advertising? Available at: http://www.wisegeek.com/what-is-contextual-advertising.htm. Accessed July 7, 2009.

8. Almasi EA, Stafford RS, Kravitz RL, Mansfield PR. What are the public health effects of direct-to-consumer drug advertising? *PLoS Med* 2006;3(3):e145. Available at: http://www.pubmedcentral.nih.gov/articlerender.fcgi?artid=1420390. Accessed July 9, 2009.

9. Murray E, Lo B, Pollack L, Donelan K, Lee K. Direct-to-consumer advertising: public perceptions of its effects on health behaviors, health care, and the doctor-patient relationship. *J Am Board Fam Pract* 2004;17:6–18.

10. Yan J. DTCA advertising going global, but not without controversy. *Psychiatr News*. 2008;43(10):1. Available at: http://pn.psychiatryonline.org/cgi/content/full/43/10/1-a. Accessed June 5, 2009.

11. Schwartz MI. To ban or not to ban—that is the question: the constitutionality of a moratorium on consumer drug advertising. *Food Drug Law J* 2008;63:1–34.

12. Donohue JM, Berndt ER, Rosenthal M, Epstein AM, Frank RG. Effects of pharmaceutical promotion on adherence to the treatment guidelines for depression. *Med Care* 2004;42:1176–1185.

13. Donohue JM, Cevasco M, Rosenthal MB. A decade of direct-to-consumer advertising of prescription drugs. *J Am Med Assoc* 2007;357:673–681.

14. Kravitz RL, Epstein RM, Feldman MD, et al. Influence of patients' requests for direct-to-consumer advertised antidepressants: a randomized controlled trial. *J Am Med Assoc* 2005;293:1995–2002.

15. Rosenthal MB, Berndt ER, Donohue JM, Epstein AM, Frank RG. Demand effects of recent changes in prescription drug promotion. *Frontiers Health Policy Res* 2003;6:1–26.

16. Aikin KJ, Swazsy JL, Braman AC. Patient and physician attitudes and behaviors associated with DTCA promotion of prescription drugs—summary of FDA survey research results, executive summary. Available at: http://www.fda.gov/downloads/AboutFDA/CentersOffices/CDER/ucm109877.pdf. Accessed August 30, 2009.

17. Sipkoff M. Direct-to-consumer ads garner mixed outcomes. Available at: http://www.managedcaremag.com/archives/0503/0503.dtc.html. Accessed August 29, 2009.

18. American Marketing Association Dictionary. Available at: http://www.marketingpower.com/_layouts/Dictionary.aspx?dLetter=P. Accessed July 13, 2009.

19. Foxall GR. Consumer decision making: process, level and style. In Baker M, ed. *The Marketing Book*. 5th ed. Oxford: Butterworth-Heinemann; 2003:119–141.

20. Rimmer BK, Glanz K. *Theory at a Glance: A Guide for Health Promotion Practice*. 2nd ed. US Department of Health, National Institutes of Health, National Cancer Institute; 2005. Available at: http://www.cancer.gov/PDF/481f5d53-63df-41bc-bfaf-5aa48ee1da4d/TAAG3.pdf. Accessed July 10, 2009.

21. McDonough RP, Doucette WR. Using personal selling skills to promote pharmacy services. *J Am Pharm Assoc* 2003;43:363–372.

22. Söderlund M, Rosengren S. Receiving word-of-mouth from the service customer: an emotion-based effectiveness assessment. *J Retail Consum Sci* 2007;14(2):123–136.

23. Khin AC. Word of mouth marketing. Available at: http://www.slideshare.net/aungck/wordofmouth-marketing-aung-chit-khin-mmkta. Accessed October 8, 2009.

24. Silverman G. *The Secrets of Word-of-Mouth Marketing: How to Trigger Exponential Sales Through Runaway Word of Mouth*. New York, NY: AMOCOM; 2001.

Abbreviations

DTCA: direct-to-consumer advertising

Case Scenarios

CASE ONE: A successful community pharmacy in a largely Russian neighborhood in the northeastern United States is highly valued because its staff speaks Russian, and its inventory includes a variety of herbs and over-the-counter medications favored by this clientele. A large retail pharmacy chain conducted a demographic analysis of the neighborhood and decided that acquiring the community pharmacy would be strategic to increasing local market share. Because the analysis revealed that an increasing number of the local residents were aging and homebound, the chain proposed that this pharmacy offer free prescription delivery services, something offered by no other pharmacy within a 15-mile radius. Given this new service, and the desire to build a largely Russian clientele, how could this pharmacy increase business?

CASE TWO: You have been hired as a consultant for an advertising agency that has a contract to promote the use of low-dose aspirin to prevent cardiac arrest in men age 50 years and older. Using the Health Belief Model, suggest strategies to encourage adherence.

CASE THREE: A new suburban housing development has emerged 17 miles from a metropolitan center. The majority of the residents in this community have children under 12 years old, and new elementary and middle schools were recently built to accommodate the population. A retail chain pharmacy is under construction on the edge of the development, and young families will be its primary target audience. What are some of the promotion and advertising strategies the pharmacy might use to attract its desired clientele?

Additional Resources Available Online!

Visit the Student Companion Web site at http://healthprofessions.jbpub.com/pharmacymanagement for interactive study tools and additional resources.

See www.rxugace.com to learn how you can obtain continuing pharmacy education for this content.

HUMAN RESOURCES

CHAPTER 17

EMPLOYMENT LAW ESSENTIALS

Vicki Gotkin, JD
Leigh Ann Ross, PharmD, BCPS

LEARNING OBJECTIVES

After completing this chapter, the reader will be able to

1. Differentiate between employees and independent contractors and explain why employers must classify workers appropriately.

2. Cite employment laws most likely to affect employees and employers in a pharmacy setting.

3. List the types of preemployment inquiries that may violate Title VII of the Civil Rights Act.

4. Propose a preemployment screening process that includes permissible interview questions and other information-gathering approaches.

5. Describe various conditions of employment and identify options for terminating each.

6. Identify factors that may make a noncompete agreement unenforceable.

7. Describe Fair Labor Standards Act requirements and how they might be applied in a pharmacy setting.

8. Recommend strategies that a pharmacy can implement to avoid liability based on sexual harassment.

9. Discuss the ways in which employment references can create liability.

KEY CONCEPTS

❶ Given the expanding array of laws and regulations that affect the workplace and continuing increases in employee complaints about employment practices, pharmacists and pharmacist managers alike require knowledge of employment-related laws.

❷ Employment laws treat employees and independent contractors differently, so understanding the difference is essential. Under common law rules, the relationship between the worker and the employer must be examined and the degree of independence and control the worker is able to exert must be assessed.

❸ When interviewing, it is generally best to avoid any questions that relate to gender (sex), age, religion, national origin, disabilities, marital status, sexual orientation, ethnicity, and parental status (or intended parental status).

❹ To ensure that they employ only honest and qualified employees, most pharmacist managers use due diligence to review the backgrounds of their employment finalists before extending an employment offer. These reviews may include reference checks with current or former employers, educational degree verifications, criminal records checks, and drug tests. Engaging in rigorous preemployment screening can reveal potential employees' shortcomings, including dishonesty and performance issues, which can forestall future problems.

❺ Employment agreements may be made for an established time period (such as for one year) or on an "at will employment" basis. Most employment contracts are at will and may be terminated by either party for any reason that does not violate public policy and at any time, without liability.

❻ To be enforceable, a noncompete clause must be reasonable in duration and geographic location and may not unnecessarily impede a departing employee's ability to earn a living.

❼ The Fair Labor Standards Act establishes minimum wage, overtime pay, record-keeping, and youth employment standards affecting employees in the private sector and in federal, state, and local governments.

❽ Unlawful harassment includes harassment on the basis of race, religion, color, creed, age, national origin or ancestry, sex, marital status, veteran status, physical or mental disability, sexual orientation, pregnancy, or any other basis made unlawful by law, regulation, or ordinance.

❾ When managers document performance based on measurable, legally defensible criteria, they are best positioned to withstand legal attacks based on their employment decisions.

❿ It is illegal to terminate pharmacists or other employees for refusing to violate a state law or public policy contained in a regulatory agency's rules.

INTRODUCTION

How do you conduct a meaningful employment interview without violating the law? What is the difference between an employee and an independent contractor? What constitutes an employment contract? Which employees are eligible for overtime pay? How does Title VII of the Civil Rights Act of 1964 affect workplace practices? **❶** *Given the expanding array of laws and regulations that affect the workplace and continuing increases in employee complaints about employment practices, pharmacists and pharmacist managers alike require knowledge of employment-related laws.*[1] This chapter provides an overview of the employment-related laws most likely to affect employees and employers in a pharmacy setting.

WHO IS AN EMPLOYEE?

Pharmacist managers typically hire people whom they expect to work on an ongoing basis, but they sometimes use temporary support to cover during vacations or to assist with special projects. **❷** *Employment laws treat employees and* **independent contractors** *differently, so understanding whether an individual is an employee or an independent contractor is essential. Under* **common law** *rules, the relationship between the worker and the employer must be examined and the degree of independence and control the worker is able to exert must be assessed.* Three primary factors are typically analyzed to determine whether an individual is an employee or an independent contractor:

- *The degree of behavioral control.* Does the employer control the way the worker performs his/her work?
- *The degree of financial control.* Are the business aspects of work controlled by the

company or the worker (e.g., tools, how payments are made)?

- *The relationships between the parties.* Are benefits provided? Is there an expectation of a continued relationship?[2]

In general, courts have determined that employees are paid a salary or wages and are under some form of supervision. Independent contractors, however, receive a sum of money for the performance of discrete services or completion of projects and may decide, without direct supervision from the "employer," how that work is performed. A staff pharmacist who works for a hospital pharmacy on an ongoing basis would typically be considered an employee. A pharmacist who spends two weeks on-site analyzing an inventory management system could be considered an independent contractor. Pharmacist managers can look to Internal Revenue Service publications for guidance on classifying workers.[2]

Even though an employer may intend to hire a pharmacist as an independent contractor, rather than an employee, if a dispute arises regarding the relationship, the courts will look to the factors listed earlier to determine whether the individual is an independent contractor or an employee. If, despite the intentions of the parties, the individual is treated as an employee, then all protections afforded other employees will be available to the so-called independent contractor. Therefore, it matters whether an individual is an employee rather than an independent contractor. Employers must withhold and contribute to appropriate federal, state, and local taxes, such as those that fund Social Security, Medicare, and unemployment compensation. The distinction is also important in terms of certain federal protections, such as those offered that regulate the number of hours an employee may work and protections afforded to people with disabilities, as employees are covered by these laws in a way that independent contractors are not.[3,4]

BEGINNING THE EMPLOYMENT RELATIONSHIP

Assuming that an organization wants to hire an individual as an employee, it will typically evaluate candidates using a variety of criteria. As described in Chapter 18 ("Successful Recruitment and Hiring Strategies"), employers have a number of screening tools available to them, and using them appropriately is critical. Hiring practices are affected significantly by the following:

- Title VII of the Civil Rights Act prohibits employment discrimination based on race, color, religion, sex, and national origin.[5]
- The Age Discrimination in Employment Act (ADEA) protects persons 40 years of age or older from discrimination on the basis of age.[6]
- The Americans with Disabilities Act of 1990 (amendments to which became effective in January 2009), which is now referred to as the **Americans with Disabilities Act Amendments Act** (ADAAA), protects individuals with disabilities against discrimination and requires reasonable accommodation for employees with disabilities.[7]
- **The Fair Labor Standards Act** (FLSA) establishes a minimum wage, regulates overtime pay, and establishes standards for record-keeping and youth employment.
- The Family and Medical Leave Act (FMLA) offers unpaid leave to qualified employees for the birth or adoption of a child, to manage the care of a serious health condition experienced by an employee or an employee's family member, or to support an immediate family member who is on active military duty or is called into service.[8]

Familiarity with these laws can help pharmacist managers and others involved in hiring processes avoid screening techniques that could result in legal challenges.

The Interview Process

The interview is a critical point in the hiring process. Managers must assess not only the education and work experience of potential employees but also their intelligence, motivation, personal qualities, and ability to communicate. Managers may be curious about an applicant's personal life, such as whether he or she is married, has children, has disabilities, or has family obligations that may "interfere" with the employee's ability to carry out his or her job duties, all of which may influence the hiring decision. Many managers believe that asking questions related to an applicant's personal life during the interview enables them to make the best decisions about the capabilities of their employees and avoid unnecessary worries for the future. However, these curiosities can lead to lawsuits in the event an employer discovers "personal" characteristics through illegal interviewing, which result in a candidate not landing a sought-after job. ❸ *When interviewing, it is generally best to avoid any questions that relate to gender (sex), age, religion, national origin, disabilities, marital status, sexual orientation, ethnicity, and parental status (or intended parental status).* The following list, which is not comprehensive, represents some questions pharmacist managers (or those acting on their behalf) should avoid:

- *Are you pregnant or do you intend to have children?*[9] Discriminating on the basis of pregnancy, childbirth, or related medical conditions is unlawful sex discrimination under Title VII of the Civil Rights Act of 1964. Pregnant women and women affected by pregnancy-related conditions are protected by Title VII and must be treated no differently than any other worker. Similarly, although a pharmacy manager may believe that a pregnant woman should not be exposed to certain chemicals/components or be on her feet for extended periods, it is unlawful to limit a pregnant woman's job duties *because of* her pregnancy. It is therefore best to avoid discussing any issues related to pregnancy, either during an interview or during the employment relationship, even if the woman's pregnancy is obvious. Managers must focus on the job duties and the applicant's ability to perform those duties, rather than drawing conclusions about her condition and her ability to carry out her duties based on her medical condition.
- *Are you now, are you planning to, or have you ever been married? What does your spouse do for a living?* These questions are not job related, violate an applicant's rights to privacy, and may lead to claims of sex-based discrimination.

- *Do you have any children? If so, how many are living at home?* Similar to marital status–related questions, asking whether an individual has or plans to have children violates civil rights statutes and is impermissible in a job interview.
- *How old are you? When did you graduate from high school or college?* As mentioned earlier, the Age Discrimination in Employment Act of 1967 (ADEA)[6,10] protects persons 40 years old or older from discrimination on the basis of age. Although guidance from the Equal Employment Opportunity Commission (EEOC) states that the ADEA does not specifically prohibit an employer from asking an applicant's age or date of birth before hire, doing so may discourage older workers from seeking employment, and may also trigger claims that the employer sought the information for unlawful purposes.
- *Are you a U.S. citizen? Where were you born?*[5,11] These questions violate Title VII of the Civil Rights Act and may give rise to claims of national origin discrimination. If you are trying to determine whether someone is authorized to work in the United States, you may ask, "Are you authorized to work in the United States?" which is the legally permissible way to seek the answer.
- *Are you disabled? Can you stand for an entire shift? Have you ever filed a worker's compensation claim?*[7,12] A manager may not ask disability-related questions in an interview, even if the individual is obviously disabled.[12] Managers may ask applicants whether they can perform the **essential functions** of the job. Essential functions are the duties and outcomes most critical to the job. If an applicant has an apparent disability, an employer may ask him or her to describe how he or she would perform the essential functions of the job, as distinguished from those duties that are marginal and are not required on a regular basis. For example, while it might seem reasonable to ask a pharmacist applicant if she can stand for at least eight hours a day, standing is not an essential function of the position. Ensuring that patients receive correct medications and counseling patients are the

functions that matter most, and both can be performed by a person who may not be able to stand for an entire shift or who uses a wheelchair. Failing to offer a qualified candidate employment because of his or her disability is a violation of the ADAAA.

- *Did you regularly use all of your sick leave in your previous employment?*[8] Not hiring a candidate because he or she took advantage of Family and Medical Leave Act protections offered by an employer to care for him/herself or a family member is impermissible.
- *Have you ever been arrested?* This question impinges on the presumption of innocence and raises the potential for disparate impact discrimination.[13] Employers may ask a prospective employee whether he or she has been convicted of an offense, because once convicted, the presumption of innocence no longer exists. Employers are advised to ask potential employees about prior convictions rather than arrests. How an employer should evaluate conviction information will be addressed later in the chapter.
- *Do you own a car?* Although this is not specifically prohibited by employment discrimination laws, this question is not job related and tends to screen out low-income candidates. If trying to determine whether an employee can get to work on time, the manager should ask instead whether the employee is able to meet the established work schedule.

See Chapter 18 ("Successful Recruitment and Hiring Strategies") for additional interview guidance.

Additional Preemployment Screening Strategies

❹ *To ensure that they employ only honest and qualified employees, most pharmacist managers use **due diligence** to review the backgrounds of their employment finalists before extending an employment offer. These reviews may include reference checks with current or former employers, educational degree verifications, criminal records checks, and drug tests. Engaging in rigorous preemployment screening can reveal potential employees' shortcomings, including dishonesty and performance issues, which can fore-* *stall future problems.* If a pharmacist manager uses outside agencies to conduct background checks, these screenings must comply with state and federal laws related to fair credit reporting and privacy. Background checks are covered by the Fair Credit Reporting Act (FCRA),[14] which requires employers who use third-party screening agencies to obtain the applicant's written consent before conducting a background check. In some states, the employer also must make the report it receives following such a check available to the prospective employee. If the employer uses information it obtains from a background check conducted by a third party to take an adverse employment action, such as denying employment or rescinding a job offer, then the individual may be entitled to challenge negative information the employer obtains through this process.

Criminal background checks may be conducted in many ways. A pharmacist manager may check public records or rely on an outside company or investigator to conduct a more intensive records review. In some cases, organizations require prospective employees to submit to preemployment fingerprinting to take advantage of state and federal databases that use fingerprints to match criminal history records. State laws govern whether and how these fingerprint checks may be conducted.[15] Pharmacist managers who conduct criminal background checks and learn that a prospective employee previously was convicted of an offense may find themselves in a quandary. They must consider whether the nature, timing, and seriousness of an offense that a prospective employee committed in the past are job related and would therefore preclude the individual from employment. Pharmacist managers should consider whether hiring someone with a criminal record would adversely affect the workplace, their patients' safety, or the employee's ability to perform his or her assigned duties. Individuals may challenge the hiring decision if they are not hired because of a prior conviction unrelated to the position for which they have applied.[13] Managers should weigh the value of the information they receive against the potential costs to the business of conducting such background investigations.

Healthcare providers are often subject to checks through the National Practitioner Data Bank, the

Healthcare Integrity and Protection Data Bank, and the Drug Enforcement Administration (DEA). These organizations maintain information related to whether an applicant holds an appropriate healthcare license, whether the applicant has been convicted or has pending civil judgments against him or her, or whether more comprehensive interviews may be required before extending an offer. The Federal Controlled Substances Act prohibits a registrant for DEA licensure from employing someone who has been convicted of a felony related to controlled substances or who has lost his or her DEA registration, unless the DEA issues a waiver.[16]

As part of the preemployment screening process, employers also may require prospective employees to submit to preemployment drug testing. Because pharmacy personnel have convenient access to medications, including controlled substances, screening for illegal or illicit drug use as part of the hiring is required for most pharmacy position finalists.[17]

In addition to conducting criminal background checks, some organizations may consider conducting preemployment medical exams. The ADAAA places limitations on preemployment medical screening. First, medical screenings must be job related, may not simply be imposed to eliminate from consideration individuals with health problems or disabilities, and must be required of all employees. The ADAAA also governs the sequence in which employers may seek certain information, including medical information, from their employees or prospective employees. For example, if a prospective employer requires a medical exam before conducting other preemployment screening processes, the employer may be held liable under the ADAAA for disability discrimination.[18] A preemployment medical examination designed to ensure that an employee is qualified to perform the work required is permitted only after an employer makes a "real" employment offer and conducts all other preemployment screening.

Negotiating the Terms of an Employment Agreement

Once the screening process is complete and the organization is ready to make an offer of employment, it is time to negotiate the terms of an employment agreement. To constitute a valid employment contract, a "meeting of the minds" must occur between the offeror (the employer) and the offeree (the potential employee). The parties must have a common understanding of the terms of the contract—what the job entails, what the employer expects, salary, benefits, work hours, and the like. To achieve a meeting of the minds, one party makes an offer to the other, and the other party accepts the offer. If, however, one of the parties makes a counteroffer, the terms of which differ from the original offer, then no contract exists until the parties agree on all material terms of the contract. When both parties agree on the terms of employment, it is wise to reduce the final agreement to writing and include a statement, such as "This letter constitutes the full terms of our employment offer and supersedes all other commitments either written or verbal that may have been made to you." This avoids the potential for later litigation in which one party attempts to suggest that other promises were made, which were not included in the written agreement.

TYPES OF EMPLOYMENT AGREEMENTS

❺ *Employment agreements may be made for an established time period (such as for one year), or on an "**at will employment**" basis. Most employment contracts are at will and may be terminated by either party for any reason that does not violate public policy and at any time, without liability.*

What would violate public policy? Terminating an at will employee because of disability, race, religion, or any other legally protected characteristic would violate public policy. Terminating an employee for reporting an incident of sexual harassment or a pharmacy's practice of distributing medication without prescriptions would also be a violation of public policy.

The type of employment contract is determined by the terms of the agreement, policy manual provisions that govern the employment relationship, state law, and public policy considerations. Some employment agreements are for a definite term, for example, one or more years. For contracts that extend beyond one year, many states' **statutes of frauds** require the agreement be in writing.

Moreover, when an employment agreement is for a definite term, an employer may be required to have **just cause** before it can terminate the employee's employment.[19] Often these agreements contain **noncompete clauses**, or **restrictive covenants**. Medical groups and pharmacies often use noncompete clauses to prevent an employee from opening a competing practice in the same or nearby vicinity for a specified time period. For instance, small-town pharmacy owners may wish to restrict competition by prohibiting a pharmacist from resigning and thereafter soliciting their patients, thereby diluting the pharmacy owner's business opportunities. Because noncompete agreements constitute a restraint of trade, courts do not look on them favorably and require them to be reasonable.[20]

❻ *To be enforceable, a noncompete clause must be reasonable in duration and geographic location and may not unnecessarily impede a departing employee's ability to earn a living.* For example, it might be reasonable to restrict a former employee from opening another pharmacy within a 10-mile radius in a county of 10,000 people, but it would be unreasonable to bar him or her from doing so in New York City, where the population is large and customers would be unlikely to travel 10 miles for pharmacy services.

Noncompete clauses must also be accompanied by adequate additional consideration (something of value the employer gives in exchange for the promise by the applicant to sign such a clause) and be supplementary to a lawful employment agreement. Because courts are reluctant to enforce agreements they perceive to be overreaching, many employers are inserting **liquidated damages** provisions in their employment contracts, instead of requiring prospective employees to sign noncompete agreements. Sometimes these damages can be a set amount or based on a formula, which generally is tied to the individual's salary for a set period and is paid directly to the former employer.[21]

LAWS THAT AFFECT THE EMPLOYMENT RELATIONSHIP

This chapter has discussed, in general, some of the elements that lead up to an employment relationship. Some of the same laws also govern employers' obligations to their employees during the relationship. The following pages will discuss some of these laws and others in more detail and describe how they are relevant within pharmacy settings.

The Fair Labor Standards Act

❼ The *FLSA establishes minimum wage, overtime pay, record-keeping, and youth employment standards affecting employees in the private sector and in federal, state, and local governments.*[3] This law is relevant to pharmacy practices in many ways. For example, the FLSA requires that all employees be paid at least the federal minimum wage. In states that have established a rate higher than the federal minimum, the state minimum applies.

The FLSA also distinguishes between **exempt** and **nonexempt** employees and requires certain employees (those who are nonexempt) to be provided additional compensation when they work more than 40 hours in one workweek. In the private sector, nonexempt employees who work overtime must be paid 1.5 times their regular rate of pay for each hour over 40. In the public sector, employees may earn **compensatory time** at 1.5 hours for each extra hour worked in lieu of receiving overtime pay. While some employers offer overtime pay to exempt personnel who work more than 40 hours a week, they are not legally required to do so. **Table 17–1** documents the factors that determine whether an employee should be classified as exempt or nonexempt.

When the FLSA was originally established in 1938, one of its concerns was protecting children from abusive working conditions. Those concerns persist today, and the FLSA limits youth under age 18 years from working in hazardous environments and places restrictions on the hours they may work and the type of work they can do, although there are some exceptions for family members who work in family-owned businesses. State laws also may impose restrictions on hiring youthful employees.

How would FLSA apply in a pharmacy setting? Among other things, the law would affect the way a pharmacist manager schedules pharmacy technicians and cashiers; maintains records of hours worked; and selects and assigns employees for

TABLE **17–1**	Criteria That Enable Employees to be Exempt from the FLSA Overtime Provisions

To be exempt, an employee must qualify under one or more of the following tests:

- **Executive exemption test**
  - Employee is paid at least $455 a week on a salary basis.
  - Employee supervises two or more full-time employees.
  - Employee has authority to hire and fire or meaningfully recommend hiring and firing.
  - Employee manages a recognized department or subdivision.
- **Administrative exemption test**
  - Employee is paid at least $455 a week on a salary basis.
  - Employee's primary duty is performance of office work directly related to the management of general business operations of the employer or its customers.
  - Employee is expected to exercise discretion and independent judgment in matters of significance.
- **Professional exemption test**
  Learned professional exemption
  - Employee is paid at least $455 a week on a salary basis.
  - Employee's primary work is intellectual in character, requiring the exercise of discretion and independent judgment.
  - Employee's advanced knowledge is in a field of science or learning.
  - Employee's advanced knowledge is customarily acquired through specialized instruction (e.g., undergraduate or graduate education).
  Creative professional exemption
  - Employee is paid at least $455 a week on a salary basis.
  - Employee's primary duty requires invention, imagination, originality, or talent in a recognized field of artistic or creative endeavor.
- **Computer exemption test**
  - Employee is paid at least $455 a week on a salary basis or at least $27.63 on an hourly basis.
  - Employee performs work in the computer field performing duties such as.
    - Application of systems analysis techniques and procedures.
    - Design, development, documentation, analysis, creation of systems or programs.
    - Testing or modification of computer systems or programs.
- **Outside sales employee exemption test**
  - Employee's primary duty is making sales (as defined in the FLSA), or obtaining orders or contracts for services.
  - Employee typically works away from the employer's place(s) of business.
- **Highly compensated employee exemption test**
  - Employee is paid $100,000 per year or more (which must include at least $455 per week paid on a salary or fee basis).
  - Employee regularly performs at least one of the duties of an exempt executive, administrative or professional employee identified in the standard tests for exemption.

Note: FLSA = Fair Labor Standards Act.
Source: Data from U.S. Department of Labor. Fact Sheet 17A: Exemption for executive, administrative, professional, computer and outside employees under the Fair Labor Standards Act (FLSA). Available at: http://www.dol.gov/esa/whd/regs/compliance/fairpay/fs17a_overview.pdf.

summer or after-school jobs. For example, to help minimize compensation expenditures required by FLSA, a pharmacist manager would want to ensure that technicians and cashiers are not scheduled for more than 40 hours a week to prevent the need to pay overtime costs. FLSA regulations, as well as state laws limiting the type of work young employees may perform and the hours they may work, would bar the pharmacist from requiring late-night shifts for certain teenage employees.

Federal Educational Rights and Privacy Act

Pharmacists who contribute to pharmacy education must be aware of another law—the Federal Educational Rights and Privacy Act of 1974 (FERPA), a law that protects the accuracy and privacy of students' education records.[22] While FERPA is not an employment law, it does affect pharmacists who train pharmacy students (e.g., preceptors in experiential training and lecturers in didactic courses) as a part of their work. FERPA has several components, but pharmacists and pharmacist managers will be concerned primarily with the FERPA provisions that require student educational records to be accurate and that bar the release of student information unless authorized by the student. Applied in an experiential learning situation, FERPA would enable a pharmacy student to contest a poor evaluation from a preceptor if the student believed the reports about his or her performance were inaccurate and bar a pharmacist from releasing student evaluations to anyone other than the student or authorized college or university officials.

Sexual and Other Forms of Unlawful Harassment

❽ *Unlawful harassment includes harassment on the basis of race, religion, color, creed, age, national origin or ancestry, sex, marital status, veteran status, physical or mental disability, sexual orientation, pregnancy, or any other basis made unlawful by law, regulation, or ordinance.* Although **sexual harassment** has been the focus of the courts in recent years, and therefore is highlighted in this chapter, sexual harassment, like other forms of unlawful harassment, is a form of employment

discrimination.[23] Other forms of unlawful harassment constitute discrimination if they are based on a protected characteristic, such as those enumerated earlier.

There are two kinds of sexual harassment: "***quid pro quo* harassment**," where submission to unwanted sexual activity is explicitly or implicitly made a term or condition of the employee's employment (e.g., "if you go out with me, I will consider you for promotion"); and "hostile environment harassment," in which the harassment is "sufficiently severe or pervasive 'to alter the conditions of employment and create an abusive work environment.'"[24] Subjecting a coworker to unwelcome lewd comments, viewing pornographic Web sites in the proximity of others, or engaging in inappropriate and unwelcome sexual banter with colleagues are activities that might lead to **hostile work environment** claims. A **plaintiff** does not have to prove that she or he was injured psychologically to prove hostile environment sexual harassment. Rather, the existence of such harassment depends on the totality of circumstances, which may include the frequency of the behavior, its severity, whether it is physically threatening or humiliating, and whether it unreasonably interferes with the employee's work performance or conditions of employment. Psychological harm might be relevant to the determination of whether a particular situation created a hostile work environment and the amount of damages the employee might receive.

A victim of sexual harassment cannot recover damages under federal law unless the conduct is severe or pervasive, such that it creates an objectively hostile or abusive work environment. This means that the fact finder (either jury or judge) would have to conclude that a *reasonable* person would find the conduct to be hostile or abusive. Further, if the alleged sexual harassment victim does not perceive the environment to be abusive, then the conduct has not actually altered the conditions of his or her employment and cannot constitute a basis on which he or she can prevail in a discrimination lawsuit.

Where a "tangible employment action," such as termination of employment, loss of a promotion, or salary reduction, is related to sexual harassment, the employer will be liable for quid pro quo sexual harassment by its supervisor, regardless of whether the employer knew the harassment occurred or took preventative measures to avoid the harassment. Where no tangible employment action occurs, the employer can avoid liability for the sexually harassing acts of its supervisors by raising an **affirmative defense** to the charge of sexual harassment *only* if the employer proves both of the following:

1. It took reasonable steps to prevent and promptly correct the sexual harassment.
2. The victim *unreasonably* failed to take advantage of the employer's preventive and corrective procedures or otherwise attempt to avoid the harm (e.g., failed to report sexual harassment in accordance with established and well-communicated policies).

To take advantage of this affirmative defense, the employer must have a program in place that notifies its employees of the process for accepting and investigating complaints of sexual harassment and promises that it will take appropriate, swift, and remedial action in cases in which sexual harassment occurred. Only if the employee knew of the avenues to complain about sexual harassment and *unreasonably failed* to take advantage of these avenues to complain will the employer be able to assert the affirmative defense in cases in which their supervisory employees engaged in sexual harassment. Employers must routinely train their employees and managers to ensure that sexual harassment does not become part of the workplace milieu.

The U.S. Supreme Court emphasized the importance of having a clear sexual harassment policy outlining complaint procedures and processes to address these complaints. Once an employer receives a sexual harassment complaint or is put on notice that discrimination has or is occurring in the workplace, it must act swiftly to investigate and address the conduct. If the employer has a written sexual harassment policy in place that includes an effective complaint procedure that is communicated to all employees, if the employer follows that procedure, and if the harassment does *not* result in termination of employment, reduction in pay, denial of a deserved promotion, or another

tangible employment action, then an employer may assert the affirmative defense and avoid liability for the sexually harassing acts its supervisors perpetrate.

In sexual harassment cases, supervisor behavior can significantly influence the degree to which employers can be held liable for their employees' actions.[25] When we think about sexual harassment, we often imagine the "perpetrator" to be a supervisor or a coworker, but an employee can be harassed by others—for instance, individuals the employer invites into the workplace. An employer would still be held responsible for sexual harassment. Consider a pharmaceutical sales representative who repeatedly makes unwanted overtures to a pharmacy technician. The pharmacy technician tells the representative that she is not interested and informs the pharmacist manager. Because the representative assists the pharmacy to obtain special pricing, the pharmacist manager takes no action and the behavior persists. This failure to act could result in the employer (the pharmacy in this case) being held liable for the actions of its vendor. Pharmacist managers and other supervisory personnel are obligated to protect employees from unlawful sexual (and other discriminatory) harassment from their supervisors, coworkers, vendors, and even customers.

EVALUATING EMPLOYEE PERFORMANCE

Giving employees timely and accurate feedback about their performance is essential to maintain a productive workplace. When an employee consistently fails to perform as expected, it is sometimes necessary to sever the employment relationship. However, wrongful termination lawsuits may occur in response to such actions. To avoid claims of unlawful or wrongful termination, managers must fulfill their obligations to evaluate their employees' performance regularly. A well-developed job description, coupled with reasonable expectations and regular feedback, can assist managers in preparing written evaluations that reflect reasoned decisions about their employees' job performance. Employee manuals also assist in defining employee expectations, rules and regulations, and consequences for violating those rules.

◆9 *When managers document performance based on measurable, legally defensible criteria, they are best positioned to withstand legal attacks based on their employment decisions.*

TERMINATING THE EMPLOYMENT RELATIONSHIP

When a pharmacist manager decides to terminate an employee, the nature of the employment relationship must be considered before taking action. As mentioned earlier, an employee whose employment is at will may be terminated without cause and without any form of process, as long as the reason for the termination is not unlawful. An employee who fails to meet performance expectations may often be terminated "for cause" based on the terms of the employment agreement. Determining "cause" can be complicated, however.

◆10 *It is illegal to terminate pharmacists or other employees for refusing to violate a state law or public policy contained in a regulatory agency's rules.* In *Kalman v. Grand Union Co.*, Kalman, a pharmacist, questioned his employer's practice of keeping the pharmacy open on a holiday without a licensed pharmacist on duty.[26] Kalman was fired because he objected to his employer's "stay open" practice and reported this practice to the State Board of Pharmacy. After losing his case for wrongful termination initially in a lower court, Kalman appealed. On appeal, he argued that the regulation requiring a pharmacist to be on the premises at all times when the pharmacy is open to the public was an expression of public policy, rather than simply a rule serving the interests of the pharmacy profession. The court agreed and found that Kalman's discharge for questioning this practice constituted wrongful discharge.

The court found that lack of supervision of the pharmacy area posed a significant risk to the public because the public would have access to potentially dangerous substances dispensed by unlicensed and unqualified individuals. Therefore, Kalman's discharge conflicted with (1) the regulatory and statutory scheme requiring a pharmacist to be on duty whenever the premises were open and (2) the pharmacist's code of professional responsibility. The holding in this and other similar cases underscores that, when there is a conflict between state or federal law, a pharmacist's obligations under his or her professional conduct codes, and an employer's policies, the pharmacist must resolve the conflict in favor of following the law.

Courts are also confronting cases in which pharmacists, based on claims of "conscience," refuse to dispense contraceptives or other medications to patients. In the case of *Noesen v. State Dept. of Regulation and Licensing, Pharmacy Examining Bd.*, a pharmacist refused to fill a prescription for an oral contraceptive and was disciplined by the state licensing board for unprofessional conduct.[27] The court upheld the disciplinary action, finding that the pharmacist who refused to fill or transfer a patient's prescription for an oral contraceptive violated standard of care, and his actions did, or could have, harmed his patient. The court found that the pharmacist engaged in unprofessional conduct, subjecting him to discipline. The pharmacist was on notice that he was obligated to help patients find an alternate method to obtain prescriptions he refused to fill, yet he abandoned the steps necessary to perform in a "minimally competent" manner under any standard of care. The pharmacist's determination not to fill a patient's prescription resulted in her missing the first day's dose of her medication, and the patient suffered emotional harm from the stress of worrying about a possible unplanned pregnancy. Whether an employer's decision to discipline a pharmacist for refusing to carry out assigned duties, which results from a religious or moral belief, will be actionable will largely depend on the laws of the jurisdiction in which these cases arise.

POSTTERMINATION ISSUES

Not all employment relationships end negatively. Family issues may require employees to relocate or secure other employment locally. More often, employees simply want to explore new opportunities to acquire new skills, advance their careers, improve their schedules, or earn more money. When seeking to secure other employment, pharmacy employees may request references or letters from their pharmacist manager. In many cases, pharmacist managers receive calls or written inquiries from prospective employers who wish to hire the current or former employee.

Defamation Versus Negligent Referral

In the past, employers had no qualms about giving references for former employees. However, in the late 1980s, employers began to adopt policies permitting disclosure of only basic information regarding their former employees, in part, because negative references that destroyed career opportunities led to charges of defamation and interference with business opportunities. Nevertheless, background checking, including checking references, is an essential component of responsible hiring (i.e., due diligence). Concerns about preventing theft and workplace violence have made reference checking especially important.

Former employers can be held civilly liable for providing negligent references. In other words, if they fail to disclose critical and complete information about a former employee, then these former employers can be held liable for ensuing injuries to the new employer or the parties the employee injures (whether physically or financially). If an employer receives a positive reference about a former employee with a propensity for violence or for dipping into the cash drawer and subsequently hires this individual and suffers harm as a result (e.g., the employee assaults a customer or steals money), then the subsequent employer can sue the former employer for negligent referencing.

Defamation currently is a cause of action that former employees use against former employers to challenge a negative reference that results in the individual not getting a sought-after position. These claims often accompany claims of wrongful termination. To succeed in a defamation case, the former employee must prove that the former employer made an "unprivileged publication of false statements to third parties that tends to harm the plaintiff's reputation in the community."

Truth has always been an absolute affirmative defense to a defamation claim; however, once the employee raises a defamation claim, it becomes the employer's burden to prove the statement's truth. In addition, if this is a public (government) employer, then an employee may claim that, even

though truthful, the employer's statement violated his or her rights to privacy, infringing on the employee's civil rights and violating constitutional provisions. Consent is also an affirmative defense to a claim of defamation. If an employee consents to his former employer's giving a reference by signing a release and waiver of liability, the employer, who has an obligation under such circumstances to be candid and complete in his or her answers, should be able to support this defense. Finally, there may be a defense of "qualified privilege." This privilege arises when an employer (1) believes in good faith that the information it provided was true when given; (2) provides information that served a legitimate business purpose; and (3) provides the information to someone who had a legitimate business interest in receiving the information.

Some states have promulgated "blacklist statutes"[28] or similar laws that provide immunity to employers who provide references, even if the information results in an employee missing out on a job opportunity. However, to avail itself of this defense, the employer may be required to satisfy certain preconditions, which need to be published and disseminated to all employees.

An inaccurate negative reference may also result in a former employee filing a Title VII action for retaliation against his or her former employer. An example of this may occur when an employee, who has filed a charge with the EEOC alleging unlawful discrimination, thereafter terminates his or her employment and then receives a negative reference. The negative reference may be considered retaliation for complaining to the EEOC, which may be the basis for liability against the former employer.

When a former employer gives a reference, the reference must be complete. Often, when a working relationship is strained, a pharmacist manager may want to give a good reference to a departing employee, to help him or her find some other place to work, rather than reveal the employee's shortcomings to a new employer. However, when a former employee has not been a productive worker or has engaged in conduct that could be harmful if repeated in another employment setting and the former employer fails to reveal this information to a subsequent employer who asks, then the former employer could be liable for damages where subsequent predictable harm occurs. Because no law requires an employer to give any reference whatsoever, when an employer gives a reference or makes a recommendation, and knows, but fails to reveal potentially damaging but relevant information about a former employee, the former employer may be liable for subsequent harm.

Employers who have policies about providing references should ensure that their managers are aware of those policies. Deviating from company policy may result in liability if supervisors provide positive, yet untruthful, information about their former employees.

Negligent Hiring/Negligent Retention

This is a relatively new theory on which courts base liability in the employment arena.[29] The emergence of this **tort** has also increased the frequency of criminal background checking. Negligent hiring/retention cases are brought by individuals who are injured by acts of an employee for whom a thorough background check would have revealed prior convictions, poor performance, or dangerous propensities, but on whom an employer did not do a thorough background check. The cause of action is premised on common-law concepts that an employer owes a general duty to protect its customers, employees, and

visitors from harm another employee causes. However, the employer either must have known or *should have known* of the potential for this harm, which arguably a more thorough background check would have revealed. Pharmacist employers can reduce their exposure to liability by routinely conducting thorough preemployment background checks on all prospective employees.

SUMMARY

A number of laws and regulations govern the practice of pharmacy. Employment relationships are governed by a wide range of laws and regulations as well. Employment laws are designed to protect employees from unfair or unreasonable treatment in the workplace, and this chapter reviewed some of the employment-related laws most likely to affect a pharmacy practice. Pharmacist managers need not be employment law experts; however, a basic familiarity with these laws will help them reduce potential claims and lawsuits. Using legally defensible strategies to select employees, paying employees appropriately, creating a safe and fair work environment, properly documenting employees' performance, and providing appropriate references for current and former employees are among the strategies pharmacists and pharmacist managers can use to create a productive workplace and reduce unnecessary legal exposure.

References/Notes

1. *See, e.g.*, US Equal Employment Opportunity Commission (EEOC) Enforcement Statistics and Litigation. For example, in fiscal year 1997, the EEOC received 80,680 charges; in fiscal year 2007, the EEOC received 82,792 charges. Most of these charges related to race, followed by sex, national origin, religion, retaliation (all statutes), retaliation (Title VII only), age, disability, and the Equal Pay Act. Available at: http://www .eeoc.gov/stats/charges.html. Accessed August 12, 2008.

2. IRS Publication 15-A. Employer's supplemental tax guide, supplement to Publication 15 (Circular E) employer's tax guide; 2009. Available at: http://www .irs.gov/pub/irs-pdf/p15a.pdf. Accessed August 26, 2009.

3. 29 USC § 201, *et seq*. Specific provisions related to the work performed by independent contractors may be found at 29 USC § 203.

4. 42 USC § 12111 requires an employee–employer relationship for coverage under the *ADAAA*. Independent contractors are not covered under the ADAAA. *Eyerman v Mary Kay Cosmetics Inc*, 967 F.2d 213, 219 (6th Cir 1992). However, determining whether an individual is an employee or an independent contractor will be based on the facts of the case. *See, e.g., Chadha v Hardin Memorial Hospital*; 202 F.3d 267 (6th Cir 2000).

5. Title VII prohibits employers from hiring, refusing to hire, firing, or laying off an individual because of his or her race, color, religion, sex, or national

origin. It also makes illegal any attempt to segregate, classify, or limit the opportunities of any employees for such reasons. This includes promotion, compensation, job training, or any other aspect of employment.

6. 29 USC 621, *et seq*. Age Discrimination in Employment Act (ADEA) prohibits employment discrimination against persons who are 40 years old and older. The Older Workers Benefits Protection Act (Pub L No. 101–433) amended the ADEA, as did Section 115 of the Civil Rights Act of 1991 (Pub L No. 102-166, which amends section 7[e] of the ADEA [29 USC 626(e)]).

7. 42 USC 12101, *et seq.*, which includes changes made by the Americans with Disabilities Amendments Act of 2008 (Pub L No. 110–325), effective January 1, 2009.

8. 29 USC § 2601, *et seq.*, 29 CFR Part 825, The Family and Medical Leave Act of 1993, Final Rule, November 17, 2008.

9. The Pregnancy Discrimination Act amended Title VII to prohibit an employer from "discriminat[ing] against any individual with respect to . . . compensation, terms, conditions, or privileges of employment, . . . because of or on the basis of pregnancy, childbirth, or related medical conditions." 42 USC §§ 2000e-2(a)(1); 42 USC § 2000e(k). *See Anderson v. GSF Mortg. Corp.*, 543 F.2d 869 (ND Ill 2008).

10. Equal Employment Opportunity Commission. Age discrimination. Available at: http://www.eeoc.gov/types/age.html. Accessed September 2, 2009.

11. 8 USCA § 1324, *et seq.*, Pub L No. 101-649 (Act of November 29, 1990).

12. 42 USC 12101, *et seq.*, which includes changes made by the ADA Amendments Act of 2008 (Pub L No. 110–325), effective January 1, 2009.

13. Austin R. Crime statistics. Disparate impact analysis, and the economic disenfranchisement of minority ex-offenders, race, and society. 2001;4(2):177–193. Available at: http://www.sciencedirect.com/science?_ob=ArticleURL&_udi=B6W5Y-48J48XT-2&_user=56761&_rdoc=1&_fmt=&_orig=search&_sort=d&view=c&_version=1&_urlVersion=0&_userid=56761&md5=0ce659426a845d9922fd0682587d1c54. Accessed September 1, 2009.

14. Fair Credit Reporting Act, 15 USC § 1681, *et seq.*

15. *See, e.g.*, ARS § 15-1881, which requires health sciences students and residents who participate in clinical training to obtain fingerprint clearance cards as a condition of admission to such programs. *See also, e.g.*, ARS § 15-1649, which requires fingerprinting academic and nonacademic personnel who are hired into security-sensitive positions.

16. 21 USCA § 801, *et seq.*

17. University of Utah Policy 5-114. Drug Testing. Available at: http://www.regulations.utah.edu/human Resources/5-114.html. Accessed September 12, 2009.

18. *Leonel v American Airlines Inc*, 400 F.3d 702 (9th Cir. 2005).

19. To overcome presumption of employment at will, the party must present sufficient proof either of contractual provision for definite term of employment or provision forbidding discharge absent just cause. *See Rood v General Dynamics Corp*, 444 Mich. 107, 507 N.W.2d 591 (Mich 1993).

20. *See Mertz v Pharmacists Mut Ins Co*, 261 Neb. 704, 625 N.W.2d 197 (Neb. 2001), where Nebraska Supreme Court struck down a covenant not to compete because it was broader than reasonably necessary to protect the employer's legitimate interest in customer goodwill and covered a greater-than-necessary geographic area. The court held that an "employer has a legitimate business interest in protection against a former employee's competition by improper and unfair means, but is not entitled to protection against ordinary competition from a former employee." In *Allen v Rose Park Pharmacy*, 237 P.2d 823 (1951), the Utah Supreme Court upheld a noncompete clause that restricted a departing pharmacist from opening a competing pharmacy within a 5-mile radius of his former employer. In that case, the pharmacist was terminated by the employer, and the employee sued to undo the noncompete clause. The court held that the anticompetition clause was supported by sufficient consideration and upheld the restraint.

21. Caesar N. A too-tough noncompete clause could defeat its own purpose. Available at: http://www.managedcaremag.com/archives/9611/MC9611.legal.shtml. Accessed August 13, 2008.

22. 20 USC § 1232g; 34 CFR Part 99. "Education records" are those records that are "directly related to a student" and "maintained by an educational agency or institution or by a party acting for the agency or institution."

23. Harassment on the basis of race, color, religion, national origin, disability, etc., all would form causes of action under Title VII of the Civil Rights Act of 1964, as amended by the Equal Employment Opportunity Act of 1972 and state laws prohibiting discrimination on those grounds. These statutes govern private employers engaged in industry that affects interstate commerce and that employ at least 15 employees. They also govern state, federal, and local government employees. In addition to prohibiting discrimination on these bases, they prohibit retaliation for engaging in "protected activity," such as asserting one's rights

under these laws or opposing unlawful employment practices by employers covered by these laws.

24. The US Equal Employment Opportunity Commission issued guidelines in which it defined two kinds of sexual harassment: (1) "quid pro quo," in which "submission to or rejection of [unwelcome sexual] conduct by an individual is used as the basis for employment decisions affecting such individual," and (2) "hostile environment," in which unwelcome sexual conduct "unreasonably interfer[es] with an individual's job performance" or creates an "intimidating, hostile or offensive working environment." 29 CFR §§ 1604.11(a)(2) and (3).

25. *Burlington Industries Inc v Ellerth*, 524 US 742 (1998), and *Faragher v City of Boca Raton*, 524 US 775 (1998), extended liability to employers for the acts of its supervisory employees who engaged in sexual harassment.

26. *Kalman v Grand Union Co*, 443 A.2d 778 (NJ Super App Div 1982). *See also*, *Ryan v Dan's Food Stores Inc*, 972 P.2d 395 (Utah, 1998), in which the court found that, although his employer told him during an interview that he could not be fired "for following the law," this did not negate the express terms of the employee manual, for which the plaintiff signed and agreed to the terms, and in which it confirmed that his employment was "at will."

27. *Noesen v State Department of Regulation and Licensing, Pharmacy Examining Bd*, 311 Wis.2d 237, 751 NW2d 385 (Wis.App 2008).

28. *See, e.g.*, Arizona Revised Statutes (ARS) § 23-1361, which provides that "it is not unlawful for a former employer to provide to a requesting employer, or agents acting in the employer's behalf, information concerning a person's education, training, experience, qualifications and job performance to be used for the purpose of evaluating the person for employment." However, to raise an absolute defense to a claim that a former employee was "blacklisted," the employer must have a well-published policy related to giving references.

29. *See Ruelas v Staff Builders Personnel Services*, 199 Ariz 344, 18 P.3d 138 (Ariz.App 2001). A patient brought a vicarious liability and negligent hiring/retention claim against a general nursing staffing agency after the patient was abused by nurses while the plaintiff was being given an enema. The court held that the agency was not vicariously liable for the nurses' actions, because at the time of the injury, the nurses were under the direct supervision of the healthcare facility, which was their special employer. The court held that, to be liable for negligently hiring the nurses, Staff Builders would have had to hire those nurses; because it had not done so, it could not have been liable for their negligent hire.

Abbreviations

ADAAA: Americans with Disabilities Act Amendments Act
ADEA: Age Discrimination in Employment Act
DEA: Drug Enforcement Agency
EEOC: Equal Employment Opportunity Commission
FCRA: Fair Credit Reporting Act
FERPA: Federal Educational Rights and Privacy Act of 1974
FLSA: Fair Labor Standards Act
FMLA: Family and Medical Leave Act

Case Scenarios

CASE ONE: You manage a growing pharmacy and are responsible for hiring new pharmacists. You have been employed in other pharmacies in which employees seemed to abuse sick leave, take extended lunches, and require time off to take care of sick children or attend school functions. You want to ensure that the pharmacists you hire do not engage in similar "abuses." In addition, you are looking for "new blood," because you believe newly graduated pharmacists are highly energized and more open to

(continues)

using technology. You are preparing your interview questions, which you believe will ferret out individuals whose life circumstances may make them less suitable than others for a fast-paced pharmacy practice like yours. What are strategies you may use and interview questions you may develop that will ensure a productive workforce without violating antidiscrimination laws?

CASE TWO: You are a pharmacy manager who employs 40 people, including pharmacy technicians, clerks, and pharmacists. You observe that one of the pharmacists seems to be engaging in conduct that you believe constitutes sexual harassment, but you have received no complaints from other employees nor do you feel comfortable approaching the offending pharmacist to address his behavior, because he is both well-liked by patients and productive. What are some strategies you can implement to ensure that all of your employees are aware of their rights and obligations to prevent workplace sexual harassment and other forms of discrimination and avoid liability for the acts of your supervisors?

CASE THREE: You are a busy pharmacy manager in a small town. There has been a lot of turnover in your pharmacy, including pharmacists, technicians, and others. You are trying to devise ways not only to get employees to stay but also to prevent them from leaving and "stealing" your customers. You decide that, when hiring pharmacists, you will include noncompete clauses as a term of the agreement. To be effective, what terms may you include in such provisions? Is it a good idea to include such provisions in your employment agreements? What considerations might lead you to explore other means of retaining employees?

CASE FOUR: You are the manager of a pharmacy with two pharmacist employees. On the basis of the prescription volume, only one pharmacist is on duty at any given time. You have recently received several complaints that the pharmacist on duty refused to fill a prescription for birth control pills based on "religious beliefs," and the patients/customers were turned away as there was no one else there to fill the prescription. As the pharmacy manager, you feel the pharmacy is losing business because of the pharmacist's refusal to fill these prescriptions and you are considering terminating the employee. What are important considerations in addressing this concern or in making a decision to terminate the pharmacist?

Additional Resources Available Online!

Visit the Student Companion Web site at http://healthprofessions.jbpub.com/pharmacymanagement for interactive study tools and additional resources.

See www.rxugace.com to learn how you can obtain continuing pharmacy education for this content.

SUCCESSFUL RECRUITMENT AND HIRING STRATEGIES

CHRISTOPHER D. LEE, PhD, SPHR

LYNETTE R. BRADLEY-BAKER, PhD, RPh

LEARNING OBJECTIVES

After completing the chapter, the reader will be able to

1. Prepare a thorough plan for filling a vacancy within a pharmacy practice setting.
2. Describe the information needed to produce a job description.
3. Differentiate between recruiting and advertising.
4. Recommend effective employment screening and evaluation methods.
5. Explain elements of a competitive employment offer.
6. Develop a plan for on-boarding and training a new employee.

KEY CONCEPTS

❶ A strategic approach to recruiting and screening candidates can aid in attracting quality candidates and reducing employee turnover.

❷ When the wrong person is hired, performance problems may occur, and the organization may be exposed to unnecessary liability.

❸ A well-designed job description is an important foundation for recruitment, selection, compensation, training requirements, and performance evaluation parameters.

❹ Essential functions are tasks and responsibilities that are fundamental to doing a particular job.

❺ A key component of a successful hiring process is to determine who will be involved in the process, how they will be involved, and when they will be involved.

❻ A sourcing strategy refers to the set of approaches an organization uses to seek applicants for vacancies.

❼ Advertising involves informing individuals of the position opening to encourage them to apply.

❽ Work samples are the most valid and reliable screening technique because they assess applicants' ability to perform the work required by the job.

9 On-boarding is a process that attempts to get new hires up to speed quickly and effectively with training and support programs designed to orient them to their work, the organization, and coworkers.

INTRODUCTION

"What kind of people do we want to join our workforce?" The answer is one of the most important decisions an organization can make. One way that great organizations set themselves apart from their competitors is by hiring the right people,[1] so careful attention to bringing new employees on board is critical to an organization's success.

Pharmacists work in a variety of settings, and in each practice environment, a number of people are usually involved in selecting new team members. Because each person who joins a team influences the work of everyone else, all teammates are invested in the success of each new hire. Although a pharmacy manager generally has ultimate responsibility for making hiring decisions, staff pharmacists are often called on to assist in recruiting, selecting, and hiring pharmacy support staff members and fellow pharmacist colleagues. Therefore, every pharmacist should be aware of the strategies most likely to result in a quality hire.

Hiring good people is a challenge for all employers; however, pharmacy practices face severe competition for scarce professional talent.[2] Pharmacists have many opportunities, which make them highly marketable and mobile. Finding qualified pharmacy technicians can also be difficult; therefore, pharmacy practices often find it hard to attract and maintain optimal staffing levels. **1** *A strategic approach to recruiting and screening candidates can aid in attracting quality candidates and reducing employee turnover.*

THE HIRING PROCESS

Effective hiring is a multistep process with eight key components. Whenever faced with a hiring decision, pharmacist managers should do the following:

1. Evaluate current staffing needs.
2. Define position requirements.

3. Decide who will be involved in the hiring process.
4. Develop a **sourcing** strategy.
5. Design a screening and evaluation process.
6. Negotiate a competitive employment offer.
7. Provide a thorough and welcoming orientation experience.
8. Evaluate the effectiveness of the hiring process after a candidate is on the job.

A good hiring process contains several interconnected elements that build a complete framework to identify a rich pool of applicants, select the best candidates, and make the right hire. Using a well-designed process is the best assurance of a quality outcome each time.[3] The following section expands on the elements of an effective hiring process.

Step One: Evaluate Current Staffing Needs

When a vacancy occurs, there is often a desire to fill it quickly. However, rushing to hire a replacement can result in filling a role that is not actually needed or placing a person poorly matched for the job or the environment. **2** *When the wrong person is hired, performance problems may occur and the organization may be exposed to unnecessary liability.*[3] Although it is often assumed that a vacancy should be filled the way it was filled before, this may not always be a smart approach. Before moving to fill a vacancy, some questions should be answered:

- What work do we need accomplished?
- What would happen if we chose not to fill this position?
- Can work be reorganized, streamlined, or automated to minimize the need for this position?
- What kind of skills and abilities are required to do this work? Are they different from what was required in the past?
- What level of position is required to meet our needs?
- How much time is required to fulfill these duties (e.g., do we need someone to work full time or part time)?

Table 18–1 provides a more comprehensive list of questions to assess staffing needs. Investing

TABLE **18–1**	Questions to Evaluate Staffing Needs

- Why did this position become vacant? Were there organizational issues that prompted the vacancy (downsizing, change of leadership, change of work requirements, frequent turnover)?
- What would happen if this position were not filled/refilled?
- Could this position be half time, part time, seasonal, etc.?
- Should there be an interim or acting appointment made before a regular search?
- What changes have occurred with this position over time, such as new or different duties, increases of responsibility, etc.?
- What has changed in the department/company?
- What has changed in the general workplace or in society that influences how this position works (changes in technology, computer and security requirements, labor shortage in this discipline/field, change in legal requirements, etc.)?
- What institutional initiatives, goals, or strategic aims are affected by or could be affected by this position?
- Are the title, classification, and compensation still accurate for this position?
- Does this vacancy represent an opportunity to increase the diversity of our staff?
- What unique characteristics did the past incumbent have that are likely not to be replaced?
- Are there internal candidates who can be promoted or trained for this opportunity without a regular search?
- Could there be an internal search only?
- Is there an affirmative action plan or other employment strategy the organization has that affects how the recruitment is conducted?
- Should we consider waiting six months before filling the position to review and analyze whether the work can be eliminated, reshaped, absorbed, or reorganized?

Source: Data from Occupational Information Network—http://www.onetcenter.org.

a reasonable amount of time considering the organization's staffing requirements and engaging in a thoughtful hiring process can result in better decisions and the acquisition of new talent committed to the organization.

Step Two: Define Position Requirements

One of the most overlooked aspects of the employment process is the need to clearly and definitively document the duties, tasks, and responsibilities critical to a position's success. These duties are typically described in a **job description** or, as it is sometimes called, a "position description." ❸ *A well-designed job description is an important foundation for **recruitment**, selection, compensation, training requirements, and performance evaluation parameters.* When duties, required skills, education and experience, and performance expectations are clear, it is easier to recruit qualified people, assess their ability to perform the work, compare their work against others to determine a fair rate of pay, ensure necessary training, and develop and articulate reasonable performance expectations.

One mistake many managers make is to dust off the old job description and write an advertisement based on it. When this approach is used, managers miss important opportunities to make the new role more relevant. For example, a pharmacist position description written 10 years ago would not include the need to be a certified immunizer for influenza administration, but this is a common requirement today, depending on the practice site and expected duties.[4] It is important to evaluate the current demands of the position, note changes in technology that may have occurred since the last job description was developed, and incorporate new skills or duties that are now required. Online resources such as O*Net, a comprehensive online repository of job- and employment-related information produced by the U.S. Department of Labor, can provide the information required to prepare or update a new job description.[5] See **Table 18–2** for an O*Net excerpt of a pharmacy technician position.

TABLE **18–2**	Sample Pharmacy Technician Duties and Responsibilities

	O*NET SAMPLE DATA
Tasks	• Receive written prescription or refill requests and verify that information is complete and accurate. • Answer telephones, responding to questions or requests. • Clean and help maintain equipment and work areas, and sterilize glassware according to prescribed methods. • Receive and store incoming supplies, verify quantities against invoices, and inform supervisors of stock needs and shortages.
Tools	• Filling or sealing auger dose machines—Automatic unit dose-strip packaging machines; tube-filling and crimping machines. • Laboratory balances—Equal-arm balances; single-beam balances; torsion balances; unequal-arm balances.
Technology	• Accounting software—Billing and reimbursement software. • Label-making software—Cardinal Health Pyxis CII Safe.
Skills	• Active listening—Giving full attention to what other people are saying, taking time to understand the points presented, asking questions as appropriate, and not interrupting at inappropriate times. • Mathematics—Using mathematics to solve problems.
Work Activities	• Interacting with computers—Using computers and computer systems (including hardware and software) to program, write software, set up functions, enter data, or process information. • Processing information—Compiling, coding, categorizing, calculating, tabulating, auditing, or verifying information or data.
Work Context	• Contact with others—How much does this job require the worker to be in contact with others (face to face, by telephone, or otherwise)? • Importance of being exact or accurate—How important is being very exact or highly accurate in performing this job?

Source: Data from Occupational Information Network. Available at http://www.onetcenter.org. Accessed January 7, 2010.

A key component of a position description is a set of requirements called **essential functions** of the job. ◆ *Essential functions are the tasks and responsibilities that are fundamental to doing a particular job*. They should be explicit and used to draft job advertisements and to develop selection criteria. Defining essential functions is an important required step to ensure compliance with the Americans with Disabilities Act Amendments Act (ADAAA) provisions, which protect people with disabilities from employment discrimination. This act prohibits discrimination in hiring or evaluation of otherwise qualified individuals who can perform the essential functions of a job, with or without **reasonable accommodation**.[6] A reasonable accommodation is a modification of the job to allow an otherwise qualified person to perform the job. The test for what is "reasonable" is the source of considerable debate; nonetheless, the degree to which a job is altered, the cost of the alterations,

and whether the changes do not alter the basic work elements are some criteria to consider when evaluating this standard. An example of a reasonable accommodation would be to buy a special chair for a pharmacist who cannot stand for eight hours a day. The purchase of the chair would clearly be reasonable, while providing computational aids for someone without the facility to do the math required of a pharmacy professional would not be reasonable. The tasks that are essential for the job should be detailed in the job description development process. **Table 18–3** provides a list of typical essential functions for a pharmacist position.

Step Three: Decide Who Will Be Involved in the Hiring Process

Once it is clear how the position should be designed, it is time to decide who will be involved

---

TABLE **18–3**   **Essential Functions of a Pharmacist Position**

- Review prescriptions to ensure accuracy and to evaluate their suitability.

- Compound and dispense medications by calculating, weighing, measuring, and mixing ingredients, or oversee these activities.

- Provide patients, caregivers, and other healthcare providers with information and advice regarding drug interactions, side effects, dosage, and proper medication storage.

- Plan, implement, and maintain procedures for mixing, packaging, and labeling pharmaceuticals, according to policy and legal requirements to ensure quality, security, and proper disposal.

- Analyze prescribing trends to monitor patient compliance and to prevent excessive usage or harmful interactions.

- Supervise the provision of care by nonlicensed personnel, and oversee the work of pharmacy technicians.

- Offer health promotion and prevention activities, such as blood pressure monitoring and guidance on glucose level testing.

- Oversee ordering and purchasing of pharmaceutical supplies, medical supplies, and drugs.

- Maintain patient profiles, charge system files, inventories, control records for radioactive nuclei, and registries of poisons, narcotics, and controlled drugs.

in the hiring process. ◆❺ *A key component of a successful hiring process is to determine who will be involved in the process, how they will be involved, and when they will be involved.* The individual empowered to make the hiring decision will often solicit the support of several colleagues to help make a selection decision. Although some organizations leave it to one person to make the final decision, many use interview panels or involve multiple managers and peers to screen and evaluate candidates.

One model of involvement is described as **diagonal selection**, a process by which participants are chosen from across the organization and at various levels. The goal is to get a multidimensional and complete picture of the work performed, and supervisors, direct reports, peers, and customers of the work performed can help detail the requirements needed for success in a given position. Providing clarity about each stakeholder's role in the hiring process is critical. Are participants expected to provide feedback on candidates? Rank them? Determine whether the candidate is a good match for the position? Is their role advisory, or are they expected to reach consensus to make a selection? The actual evaluation process expectations should be clear as well. Will stakeholders provide technical assistance in reviewing written materials, share impressions of the candidates, or participate in interviews? Clarity from the beginning is important to ensure that participants do not exceed their boundaries or develop unreasonable expectations about their role in selecting the final candidate.

HIRING OFFICIAL

Organizations differ in who is granted the authority to make an employment offer. Sometimes the direct supervisor of the position makes the decision; in other situations, it might be the unit manager with budgetary authority; and in others, it may require a vice president or another authorized executive to make a financial commitment on behalf of the organization. Most pharmacy personnel are selected and hired by the direct supervisor of the position—who is most often a pharmacist—or the manager of the pharmacy. Depending on the level of a position, the hiring official may or may not manage the hiring process,

but instead, he or she may delegate it to others to conduct. In these circumstances, the person who conducts the recruitment will make a recommendation to the hiring official. A pharmacist might be asked to lead the search and recruitment for a new pharmacy technician even though the technician would not have a direct reporting relationship to that pharmacist. Given the myriad ways in which hiring efforts are managed, all members of a pharmacy practice must understand the elements of a good hiring process.

COWORKERS, MANAGERS, AND OTHERS

Peers and other managers are often asked for input into the recruitment process. Their contributions might be to advise the hiring manager about the job duties for the position, to screen application materials, to participate in panel interviews, or to do a combination of these and other tasks. It is common for subordinates for a unit head or similar position to serve on an interview panel for that position as well.

THE HUMAN RESOURCE MANAGER

Some organizations are large enough to have a human resources department. When that is the case, a representative from this department can ensure that participants in the hiring process are aware of company policies, procedures, laws, and regulations related to recruitment and selection, offer guidance about effective recruitment strategies, describe labor market trends, and provide guidance related to screening techniques and total compensation packages. When there is no human resources department, pharmacy members must manage the process without this guidance, and this chapter provides information to support fair, legal, and successful hiring decisions.

Step Four: Determine the Sourcing Strategy

◆❻ *A sourcing strategy refers to the set of approaches an organization uses to seek applicants for vacancies.* These activities may vary depending on the position, labor market conditions, and time frame for the search. Some typical sourcing strategies include networking, advertising in professional journals, seeking employee referrals, attending career fairs, engaging search firms, or developing an apprenticeship program with a local community college. Training, developing, and promoting internal applicants are also viable sourcing strategies, depending on the position. Frequently used methods for sourcing pharmacy-related positions are noted in **Table 18–4**.

It is important to be familiar with pharmacy-related recruiting patterns, where good candidates are produced and found, and how competitors source their candidates. For example, some organizations hire new college graduates for all entry-level positions, while others attempt to promote and train from within. Still other organizations aggressively recruit pharmacy professionals from their direct competitors by offering higher than market salaries or other **perquisites** (e.g., a work schedule without night or weekend hours, a company car). Most large pharmacy employers, such as chain pharmacies, use a combination of strategies for sourcing qualified candidates.

DETERMINING THE RECRUITMENT AREA

Before developing a sourcing strategy, the geographic area from which candidates will be recruited must be determined. This is typically influenced by the position's level within the organization, compensation, prestige, and the number of new employees needed. Generally, the more senior the position and the more competitive the pay, the more likely candidates will relocate to accept a given opportunity. The recruitment area grows from local or regional to national and even international for different types of jobs. As examples, pharmacy technicians are generally local hires, pharmacists are likely to be local or regional hires, and searches for professors in colleges of pharmacy or directors in the pharmaceutical industry often generate a national pool of candidates. The more specialized the position, the larger the recruitment area required.

SOURCING STRATEGY: ADVERTISING

❼ *Advertising involves informing individuals of the position opening to encourage them to apply.* Although advertising has intuitive appeal, it is a more passive process than other sourcing strategies and should be part of a more comprehensive recruitment process that seeks to cultivate applicants from the universe of qualified applicants, whether or not they are actively pursuing new employment opportunities.

Advertising consists of placing ads in newspapers, journals, and Web sites. There are a number of types of advertisements (ads) that can be used to attract the right applicants. They are column, block, Web, and image ads, as well as **position announcements**.[7] In-column ads are the traditional "help wanted" announcements that contain a brief description of the requirements of a position. A block ad is commonly referred to as a display ad and is larger, usually contains a logo, and often contains information about the company advertising a vacancy. In-column and display ads are most often print-only advertisements and are limited in their size because of the cost of buying the advertisement.

Web ads are not typically restricted in size like printed advertisements and therefore are often lengthier and contain more information about a position. Web ads may contain links to other information pertinent to the job seeker, such as a description of the community where the job is located, background information on the organization and their financial status, and links to the job description for the position. Many organizations are now using generic in-column ads or small display ads that direct applicants to detailed Web ads for more information about vacancies. This can be a cost-effective advertising strategy.

Position announcements provide detailed information about an opening, the location of the organization, and the type of candidate the organization is seeking. This type of advertisement also may be used within an organization to announce opportunities to current employees. Position announcements can be simple one-page documents suitable for posting on bulletin boards or professionally printed trifold brochures designed to be mailed. Electronic position announcements with embedded hyperlinks are now being used as clever recruiting and advertising devices because they can easily be e-mailed. Position announcements can be sent electronically to employees or colleagues who are then asked to forward the announcement to anyone who might be interested in a position. In their many forms, advertisements are designed to call attention to a position vacancy. Advertising and other recruiting efforts must be

TABLE 18–4	Potential Sourcing Methods for Pharmacy Positions

- Newspaper classified ads
- Ads in professional journals, newsletters, etc.
- Internet job search sites (e.g., RxInsider.com, Monster.com)
- Posting announcement on organization Web site
- Employee referrals
- Open-house events within an organization
- Internal bulletin boards, newsletters, and memos
- Continuing education seminars
- Job fairs/career fairs
- Competitor store visitations ("cold-calling")
- Online employment chat rooms
- Window advertisements
- School, campus, training programs
- Professional organizations (American Pharmacists Association, American Association of Pharmacy Technicians, National Pharmacy Technician Association, American Society of Health-System Pharmacists, American College of Clinical Pharmacy, etc.)
- Board of Pharmacy Web sites (to obtain mailing addresses for registered and certified persons authorized to work in the state)
- Direct advertisement mailers
- National pharmacy conferences
- Professional networking (past and current coworkers/colleagues, acquaintances, word of mouth, "a friend-of-a-friend")
- Apprenticeship programs and internships
- Search firms/headhunters

Source: Data from Lee CD.[7]

intensified as the specialization of positions increase. For example, a retail pharmacist is generally easier to recruit than a clinical pharmacist with transplant expertise.

Image advertising is another approach sometimes used to create interest or excitement about an employer rather than a specific position. Image ads are designed to highlight the employer as a great place to work with the hopes that candidates will be predisposed to openings at that employer in the future.[8] Ideally, image advertising builds the company's *employment brand*. As an example, CVS

Pharmacy, a large retail pharmacy organization, ran nationwide ads that included testimonials from some of their actual pharmacists who spoke about their unique approach to providing service to their patients. These images may have sparked interest in CVS by pharmacists who had not considered CVS or a retail pharmacy as an employment option. Image ads can appear in the employment section of printed media, as well as news or information sections to reach candidates not currently seeking a new employment opportunity. See Chapter 20 ("Creating and Identifying Desirable Workplaces"), which details elements that make organizations especially appealing.

Image ads can sometimes be used to emphasize an organization's commitment to **diversity** to attract more heterogeneous employment candidates when openings occur. A progressive diversity posture recognizes and promotes the business case that the best organizations are the ones that use the inherent richness of people from many different backgrounds because their unique skills, values, and perspectives give the organization a competitive advantage in the marketplace by responding to a broad range of organizational challenges and opportunities.[9]

SOURCING STRATEGY: USING NETWORKS

A deliberate and organized approach to maintaining contact information for talented people can be an exceptional recruitment strategy. Savvy managers make an effort to meet and stay in touch with people they meet at professional association gatherings and other interactions to have a pool of potential candidates to contact when openings occur. These individuals may be invited to apply for vacancies or called on to recommend others who would be suitable. A less personal but sometimes effective approach is to use professional organization mailing lists to notify members of existing openings. Networking is also a hallmark activity of diversity efforts when managers are proactive and make an effort to reach out to a wide variety of candidates from traditional and nontraditional recruiting sources.

SOURCING STRATEGY: SEARCH FIRMS

One sourcing option to consider is search firms or professional recruiters—sometimes called **head-hunters**. Although search firms are typically used for senior positions, such as vice presidents or chief executive officers, they are also used to hire in competitive fields warranting additional expertise and support. They can also be helpful when an organization needs to hire a large number of candidates for professional positions in a short period of time, to staff companies in hard-to-fill geographic areas (e.g., rural areas where there is a paucity of pharmacy professionals), and for highly technical pharmacy positions (e.g., nuclear pharmacy-trained professionals), in addition to general pharmacy staffing needs.

Charges for these services can vary significantly depending on the type of position, the level of the position, and the market conditions for sourcing talent in that area but are typically 20–30% of the total estimated first year's income for a pharmacist or pharmacy technician candidate. These fees usually have some guarantee provision should the candidate fail to perform and be released within a designated period. Most large pharmacy organizations have the talent and expertise to use internal staff to manage their recruitment efforts and, therefore, only use external support in special circumstances.

ANALYZING YIELD RATIOS

"How did our top candidates find out about our opening?" "Which sources produced the most unqualified applicants?" The answers to these questions should guide future recruiting efforts. Determining the effectiveness of various sourcing strategies can reduce costs and increase recruitment success. A critical component of this analysis is the calculation of a **yield ratio**, which details the relative success of one particular sourcing activity compared with others.[7,8] A yield ratio analysis includes several components: how much it cost to advertise or recruit applicants, the number of applicants generated by the source, and a comparison of the percentage of interview and job offers accepted by candidates coming from that source.

Two examples illustrate the importance of evaluating a sourcing strategy. Placing ads in a professional journal may cost $2500 and garner an average of 10 applicants for a vacant position, compared with placing an ad in the large regional newspaper for $1,200 that produces an average of 15 applicants. Although the average cost to attract applicants for the journal is almost twice as high as the local newspaper, the most important factor is the number of hires that traditionally come from the journal compared with the newspaper. If the analysis determines that three of the last five hires came from the journal, the cost involved is actually lower because of the effectiveness of this advertising source. Similarly, recruiting applicants from prestigious pharmacy training programs might sound like a smart strategy, but it may be more effective to recruit candidates from direct competitors if more applicants from the second strategy accept employment offers with your organization than the former.

Step Five: Develop a Screening and Evaluation Process

Once sourcing strategies have produced a pool of qualified candidates from which to select, it is time to determine which applicants are viable candidates for employment. Various screening and evaluation strategies are available to conduct this assessment, and each technique has its advantages and disadvantages. For example, written materials such as résumés are indispensable for the information they provide, but applicants may not represent themselves as well in person as they do on paper. Conversely, some candidates may be well prepared for the interview and make a good impression but may not be as capable as other candidates. With this in mind, it is wise to use multiple screening methods to make a sound decision about whom to hire.[10]

Choosing which types of screening methods to use should be done carefully. Deciding how much weight each screening technique will be given should also be determined in advance. Another important consideration is which type of decision-making process will be used to eliminate candidates or to advance them to the next round of screening. A screening matrix allows reviewers to compare the qualifications of one applicant against others at a glance. A quantitative approach to screening candidates involves assigning each candidate a number representing how well his or her background measures up to a given standard. The total points that a candidate accumulates

determines his or her relative ranking in comparison to others. Those who favor more qualitative approaches may describe candidates holistically by outlining their relative strengths and weaknesses and how these are advantages or disadvantages for the position for which they are applying and for the hiring organization. Some hiring managers and committees simply divide applicants into "acceptable," "possible," and "unacceptable" as a quick way to winnow down the applicant pool. Regardless of the screening approach used, each candidate should be evaluated by the same set of objective criteria by everyone involved in the screening process to ensure quality, consistency, and fairness. A sample screening matrix is displayed in **Table 18–5**.

Screening Tool: Application Materials

The selection process typically starts with a review of written or electronic application materials—résumé, cover letter, credentials, transcripts, and application—by those involved in the selection decision. Applicants are evaluated based on how they compare with the objective criteria documented in the job description and described in job advertisements. They are also evaluated against one another.

Screening Tool: Face-to-Face Interviews

Aside from a systematic review of written application materials, interviews are the second most commonly used screening technique.[8] Although interviews are an important part of the hiring process, research reveals that they are less reliable than many other selection methods. Therefore, they should not be used as the sole method for making decisions and should be structured to enhance their effectiveness.[8,11] Structured interviews involve a predefined slate of questions and a standardized method of evaluating responses to them. A structured interview ensures that a degree of rigor and fairness is infused into the interviewing process. Rigor comes by following a well-planned protocol for conducting the interview and by asking the right questions. Fairness and consistency are built into the process by using a common slate of questions based on the duties, tasks, responsibilities, essential functions, goals, and other requirements of the position.[12] These

TABLE **18–5**	Sample Pharmacy Technician Applicant Matrix				
Candidate	Degree(s)	CPhT Certification	Years of Experience	Type of Pharmacy Practice Experience	Remarks
Chu	B.S. Biology	Yes	9	Hospital, retail	Assisted in developing a pharmacy technician quality assurance program at her current place of employment
Erickson	Associate of Science	No	3	Independent	Currently enrolled in a state board of pharmacy approved training program
Garcia	N/A	Yes	4	Hospital	Plans to apply to pharmacy school next year
Sanchez	A.A. Business	Yes	17	Retail, Independent	Has been employed by the same company for 17 years—desires a change in pharmacy practice setting
Star	N/A	No	3	Retail	Is planning to take the CPhT exam this spring
Zane	B.A. Chemistry	Yes	9	Independent	Has trained more than 10 pharmacy technicians (who have become certified) throughout her career

Note: CPhT = certified pharmacy technician.

requirements are then translated into terms that define the competencies a candidate must possess to perform effectively the requirements of the position.

A **competency** is a demonstrated knowledge, skill, or attitude that enables one to perform the activities of a given occupation or function to the standards expected in employment; effective interviews use competency-based questions.[10] In addition to pharmacy-related subject-matter expertise, employees within a pharmacy practice typically need to be able to demonstrate initiative, teamwork, professionalism, and effective communication. How can these "soft skills" be evaluated? Several approaches may be employed.

Situational interview questions ask the candidate how he or she might respond to a hypothetical scenario. These types of questions help determine how well the candidate might perform the essential functions or core elements of the job.[11] To analyze judgment, a candidate might be asked, "Imagine that one of your regular patients drops by on Friday evening to pick up her Dilantin prescription only to find that payment has been rejected by her insurance company. An investigation to determine the problem will have to wait until Monday when insurance company representatives will be available, but your customer says she took her last pill this morning. How would you handle this situation?" The interviewer in this case will be looking for the candidate to demonstrate compassion as well as sound clinical, ethical, and financial judgment.

Behavioral interview questions are predicated on the assumption that past behavior is the best predictor of future performance so they ask the interviewee to respond to questions by indicating what he or she has done in the past in a similar circumstance.[11] Some examples of typical behavioral questions include the following: "Tell us about a time when . . . ?" "How did you react to . . . ?" "Have you ever had to . . . ?" To assess interpersonal communication skills, an interviewer might ask, "Tell us about a time in which a patient became very angry. What were the circumstances and how did you respond?"

Informational interview questions are fact-based questions used to gather or clarify pertinent information necessary to evaluate candidates. Common examples of information questions are as follows: "Why have you changed jobs several times in the past seven years?" "You changed positions while you worked at Great West Home Health Care; was that a promotion or a lateral assignment?"

A **case study question** may not have a right or wrong answer; however, it has the goal of uncovering how the candidate approaches problem-solving, decision-making, or other critical thinking activities. With case study questions, candidates are asked to react to a complex scenario that has multiple layers of interrelated facts. **Table 18-6** provides examples of various interview question approaches. The most informative screening processes use a combination of screening techniques to assess and compare each candidate's capabilities.

Screening Tool: Telephone and Video Interviews

Telephone interviews are a popular means of screening a large number of qualified applicants down to a more manageable number of finalists. Telephone interviews are also used to manage the costs of searches by reducing travel costs. Telephone interviews are a screening device similar to on-site interviews in that they take a structured interview approach using a common slate of questions and an established protocol.[7] They differ in that they tend to be shorter and are not used to make a final selection of a candidate but to determine who is chosen for an on-site interview. It is usually imprudent to make a final hiring decision based on a telephone interview without meeting a candidate face to face.

Interviews by videoconferencing, an interactive telecommunication technology that allows two or more locations to interact using two-way video and audio transmissions simultaneously, serve the same purpose as telephone interviews but enable candidates and hiring managers to see and hear one another and establish a better rapport than a telephone interview.[11] Candidates are asked to travel to a prearranged facility at a designated time to participate in a videoconference with the hiring official or interview team. Both telephone and video interviews can save considerable time and expense in reducing the number of applicants in

TABLE **18–6**	Interview Questions to Assess Customer Service Competencies

Informational Question: Have you ever worked in a customer service position?

Behavioral Interview Question: Tell us about a time when you did not have complete information but were asked to respond to a customer's complaint on behalf of the work that someone else performed?

Situational Interview Question: What would you do if a customer demanded a full refund for the generic medicine that you had dispensed because she thought that it did not work as well as the brand version she had used in the past?

Case Study Question: The pharmacy is filled with customers because of an outbreak of the flu. An obviously ill patient is getting agitated from waiting; a mother with a crying child keeps getting in and out of line, which is annoying other customers; an elderly man, who is one of your best customers, calls you by name and asks if he can just pick up his regular prescription; meanwhile, the telephone continues to ring, someone in the pharmacy just spilled a bottle of capsules on the floor, and the customer you just assisted does not speak English clearly and is asking you for more information about the medications in her prescription bag. What would you do first in this situation?

regional or national searches. Candidates who do well become finalists and are then typically invited to on-site interviews.

Screening Tool: Airport Interviews

In some cases, organizations will conduct what are called "airport interviews" to meet with several national candidates face to face in an efficient manner. When this is done, the hiring authority or team schedules a conference room at an airport or nearby hotel and flies in several candidates to interview. Candidates often fly in and out the same day. This approach reduces the need to pay for hotel stays and to manage other logistics of longer visits.

Screening Tool: Work Samples

Each profession uses unique techniques or tools that help to evaluate candidates in that particular field. Artists are asked to submit a portfolio of their work, chefs are asked to prepare a meal, and cashier candidates may be asked to demonstrate their ability to provide proper change for a purchase. A work sample is a screening technique that uses actual work activities as a test to evaluate candidate's knowledge, skills, and abilities for a given job. ❽ *Work samples are the most valid and reliable screening technique because they assess an applicant's ability to perform the work required by the job.*[8,10] For example, a pharmacy instructor may be asked to teach a class and a hospital pharmacy technician candidate may be asked to write out the entire process (including calculations and aseptic technique) for preparing an intravenous order.

Screening Tool: Medical Exams

Candidates for positions that require significant physical exertion should be evaluated for their physical ability to perform the essential functions of the job. Medical evaluations are standard practice in these instances. However, the ADAAA prohibits medical examinations from being administered *before* an employment offer is made. Therefore, an offer can be extended contingent on the applicant's ability to pass the medical examination. Language such as "Your offer of employment is contingent upon successful completion of a medical evaluation, drug test, and **criminal background check**" may be incorporated into letters of offer.

Screening Tool: Evaluating Organizational Fit

Screening for "organizational fit" is a frequently used and often misunderstood concept. Organizational fit assesses many things, including whether a person would work well, considering the organization's culture, coworkers, and approach to work.[7,8] It can also assess whether a candidate is able to get along with others and has the right kind of style, personality, sense of humor, taste, or disposition. Organizational fit can also be a clever guise for illegal discrimination. Using organizational fit at the interview stage after all other objective criteria have been exhausted can be a useful and defensible screening technique provided that it is used legally and with appropriate cautions and safeguards built into the process and does not screen for **protected-class** criteria (sex, race, national origin, etc.).

Screening Tool: Reference, Drug, and Background Checks (Preemployment Screening)

Until reference and background checks are conducted, all of the information about a candidate comes from the candidate. Therefore, due diligence is required to verify the identity, work experiences, and accomplishments of candidates as documented in their application materials and described during their interview. To some degree, reference and background checks are honesty tests. According to the Society for Human Resource Management, up to 61% of résumés contain some inaccurate information,[13,14] so verifying information provided by the candidate is a critical component of the hiring process. Background checks can verify or reveal a great deal about a candidate, as noted in **Table 18–7**.

Reference and background checks are usually the last screening technique to evaluate candidates for employment and are generally conducted only on a single finalist. Organizations that do not conduct reference and background checks can be sued for *negligent hiring*.[10] This may occur if an employee with a criminal, violent, or marred history harms someone, and it is subsequently found that the injury to others could have been prevented if the organization had uncovered the information in an appropriate reference and background check (refer to Chapter 17, "Employment Law Essentials"). Most pharmacy employers require a drug test and criminal background check of finalists for pharmacy positions because of the access to controlled substances and the level of public trust attributed to the profession.

Illegal and Inappropriate Questions

Care must be taken not to ask inappropriate, unethical, or illegal questions in the interview process,[6,8] as questions perceived to discriminate against members of protected classes can result in complaints to local, state, or federal agencies. A rule of thumb is limit questions to those that relate to the essential functions of the job or to how a person might work within a given environment.

TABLE 18–7	Types of Background Checks

Reference check	Motor vehicle records
Criminal history records	Social security number check
Drug screening	Sexual offender record registry
Degree/licensure verification	Credit history
Employment verification	Military records

Typically, biographic or demographic questions are not pertinent to job performance and may lead to complaints of discrimination on grounds such as religion or national origin. Although it is not exhaustive, **Table 18–8** includes several questions that should not be asked during the interview process. Another piece of good advice is to ask colleagues or the human resource manager for sample questions that have been used effectively in the past for similar positions. Starting from a repository of tried-and-true questions for similar positions is a smart approach to establishing a good slate of questions.

Step Six: Negotiate a Hiring Offer

Once a final candidate has been selected, a competitive offer package must be created. Candidates should be made aware of the intangible benefits of working in the organization, such as its important mission, its reputation in the community, career advancement opportunities, and the collegiality of its employees. They should also be informed about the total compensation package offered by the organization, including salary; sign-on bonuses; **retention bonuses**; performance-related incentives; stock options; retirement plans; health, dental, life, and disability insurance; and other perquisites. If candidates are not made aware of the dollar value of benefits or informed that salaries are increased after successful completion of a probation period, they may accept an employment offer from a competitor that offers a slightly higher initial salary but lower total compensation. Intangibles that may enrich the **employee value**

TABLE **18–8**	**Examples of Illegal or Inappropriate Interview Questions**

What is the origin of your name?

What is your ethnicity?

Where were you born?

What is your age/birth date?

What is your religion?

Do you have a disability?

Is this your maiden name? Are you married?

Do you have child-care responsibilities, or do you have any children?

What church do you attend?

Have you ever been arrested?

What is your race or ethnic origin?

What is your political affiliation?

Have you ever served in the military?

Do you have a car?

Have you ever been treated for a substance abuse problem?

Sources: Data from Steingold FS;[6] Lee CD.[7]

proposition for candidates are flexible work schedules, generous vacation and sick leave options, child-care services, transportation subsidies, relocation packages, and even the amount of support provided for advanced education or professional development. Since employment offers are legally binding, hiring managers should follow any verbal offer with a written letter confirming the terms of conditions of employment but should use the standard language or form letter required by their human resources department or legal counsel.

Step Seven: Develop an On-Boarding and Training Program

❾ *On-boarding attempts to get new hires up to speed quickly and effectively with training and support programs designed to orient them to their work, the organization, and coworkers.*[15] Once an employee is hired, it is the start of a new adventure, and although it is exciting, it can also be filled with anxiety. For the hiring manager, it is time to make the necessary preparations to ensure that the employee becomes successful in his or her new role. The singular goal of this process is to facilitate a smooth transition for the employee.

ORIENTATION

Just as first-year students receive **orientation** into pharmacy school before classes start, new employees should receive a structured orientation to their new responsibilities and the organization for which they will work. Some orientation programs provide so much information that employees complain of information overload. Orientation planners must be careful to focus on essential information to provide a strong foundation for the future, which is vital to ensuring the individual's happiness with work and commitment to the culture of the organization. Orientation sets the groundwork for retention and success.[16]

A proper orientation starts as soon as the candidate accepts the position. The hiring manager is often responsible for the on-boarding process, but these responsibilities are sometimes assigned to a coworker. When an organization has a human resources department, this department often conducts the formal part of orientation and addresses such matters as employee benefits and organizational policies and expectations. In small businesses, it may be the sole responsibility of the manager and other employees to help facilitate a smooth transition for the new employee. **Table 18–9** provides a list of common activities that occur during an orientation program.

A comprehensive on-boarding process will extend beyond the candidate's first day on the job and may last for several months. It is an opportunity to learn about the organization (its history, organization, future directions, etc.), the role the employee's department has in the organization, the role of his or her position within the department, and how other departments and programs fit within the organization. This process helps the new employee embrace the organization's mission, vision, and values. New employee orientation and on-boarding processes can be time consuming to plan and execute effectively but are necessary components to provide a solid foundation for a new employee.

TRAINING

The initial training provided to a new employee is important to ensure proper preparation for the new role. Even a veteran pharmacist will still need to undergo training on the unique requirements of a new position and organization for the transition to be as smooth and comfortable as possible. Initial training offered to new employees often includes mandatory, **hard skill**, and **soft skill training**.

Mandatory training must be completed to meet federal, state, or local statutes, such as an introduction to the Health Insurance Portability and Accountability Act (HIPAA) for pharmacists (refer to Chapter 5, "Significant Laws Affecting Pharmacy Practice Management"). Likewise, many employers require new employees to complete a sexual harassment awareness program. Hard skill training refers to the skill-based knowledge necessary to operate equipment, technology, and processes for a specific task, such as prescription computer entry. Soft skill training refers to competency-based practical skills, such as time management or customer service training. A holistic training approach would contain all three training types to ensure that the on-boarding process is effective.

TABLE **18-9**	**Typical Elements of an On-Boarding Process**

Orientation to Position
- Position description
- Review of performance expectations and standards
- Notification of job schedule and hours
- Schedule of upcoming pertinent meetings
- Initial job assignments
- Training plan

Orientation to Department
- Organizational chart
- Introductions to the team and department staff, mentor (if applicable)
- Department/facility orientation

Orientation to Organization
- Review key company policies (e.g., probationary period, dress code, e-mail, and internet usage)
- Employee benefits
- Employee policies
- Pay and benefits information
- Tour of facility (bulletin boards, parking, office supplies, emergency exits)
- Follow-up orientation plan

Soft skill training, by its nature, can be offered and completed by a new employee after they have been working in their role for some time. Table 18–9 details common elements of an on-boarding process.

Step Eight: Review Outcomes of the Hiring Process

After a candidate has been hired and successfully oriented to the new position, it is good practice to review the hiring process to determine whether the process served its intended purpose. This can be best accomplished after a new employee has worked for a while and received a performance review. The success of the hiring process can be validated when the selected candidates are determined to be successful employees.[9,17] If the selected employees do not perform well over time, the hiring process should be reviewed and revamped.

SUMMARY

Building an effective work team requires a deliberate and systematic approach to recruiting and screening employment candidates. A successful hiring process contains several interconnected elements that together build a complete framework to identify a pool of applicants, select the best candidate, and make the right hire. The best hiring decisions tend to occur when employment openings are announced widely, candidates are clear about the duties and expectations of the position, multiple screening tools are used to assess their ability to perform job duties, and a variety of people have an opportunity to provide feedback about the candidates. The hiring process does not end when an employment offer is made and accepted, however. On-boarding and orientation programs are essential to ensure that new employees become productive and are comfortable in their new environment. Recruiting and selecting candidates for employment is among the most important activities that any organization under-takes, and all pharmacists are likely to participate in this process multiple times regardless of whether they are in formal management positions.

References

1. Collins J. *Good to Great: Why Some Companies Make the Leap and Others Don't*. New York: HarperCollins; 2001.

2. Pharmacist Manpower Workforce Survey, 2005. Midwest Pharmacy Workforce Research Consortium. Available at: http://www.aacp.org/Docs/Main Navigation/Resources/7295_final-fullworkforcereport .pdf. Accessed December 7, 2008.

3. Rothman J. *Hiring the Best Knowledge Workers, Techies, and Nerds*. New York, NY: Dorsett House Publishing; 2004.

4. Hogue MD, Grabenstein JD, Foster SL, Rothholz MC. Pharmacist involvement with immunizations: a decade of professional advancement. *J Am Pharm Assoc* 2006;46(2):168–182.

5. Occupational Information Network. Availabe at: http://www.onetcenter.org. Accessed November 16, 2008.

6. Steingold FS. *The Employer's Legal Handbook*. 8th ed. Berkeley, CA: Nolo; 2007.

7. Lee CD. *Search Committees: A Toolkit for Human Resources Professionals, Administrators, and Committee Members*. Knoxville, TN: College and University Professional Association for Human Resources; 2000.

8. Aamodt MG. *Introduction to Organizational Psychology: An Applied Approach*. 5th ed. Belmont, CA: Thomson Wadsworth; 2007.

9. Arthur D. *The Employee Recruitment and Retention Handbook*. New York, NY: AMACOM; 2001.

10. Kleinman LS. *Human Resource Management: A Managerial Tool for Competitive Advantage*. 4th ed. Cincinnati, OH: Atomic Dog Publishing; 2007.

11. Noe RA, Hollenbeck JR, Gerhart B, Wright PM. *Human Resource Management: Gaining a Competitive Advantage*. 5th ed. Boston, MA: McGraw-Hill Irwin; 2005.

12. Marchese T, Lawrence J. *The Search Committee Handbook*. Washington, DC: American Association for Higher Education; 2005.

13. Minton-Eversole T. *Background Screens Even More Crucial During Economic Slump*. Alexandria, VA: Society for Human Resource Management; July 2008. Available at: http://www.shrm.org/ema/ library_published/nonIC/CMS_026257.asp. Accessed November 16, 2008.

14. Tuna C, Winstein KJ. Economy promises to fuel résumé fraud practices vary for vetting prospective employees, but executives usually face tougher background checks. *Wall Street Journal* Online; 2008. Available at: http://online.wsj.com/article/ SB122671047127630135.html. Accessed November 16, 2008.

15. Tai B, Lockwood NR. *Organizational Entry: On-Boarding, Orientation, and Socialization*. Alexandria, VA: Society for Human Resource Management; November 2006. Available at: http://www.shrm.org/ research/briefly_published/organizational%20entry _%20onboarding,%20orientation%20and%20 socialization.asp. Accessed November 16, 2008.

16. Overman S. *Onboarding: Making a Connection Beyond Orientation*. Alexandria, VA: Society for Human Resource Management; February 2005. Available at: http://www.shrm.org/ema/library_published/nonIC/ CMS_011337.asp. Accessed November 16, 2008.

17. Adler L. *Hire with Your Head: Using Performance-Based Hiring to Build Great Teams*. 3rd ed. Hoboken, NJ: Wiley; 2007.

Abbreviations

Ad:	advertisement
ADAAA:	Americans with Disabilities Act Amendments Act
CPhT:	certified pharmacy technician
HIPAA:	Health Insurance Portability and Accountability Act
O*Net:	Occupational Information Network

Case Scenarios

CASE ONE: You are the pharmacist owner of two independent community pharmacies located 30 miles apart. The pharmacy technician who opened your initial store with you five years ago is relocating to another part of the state and will be unable to commute to your store. There are three independent pharmacies and five chain pharmacies within 15 miles of the store where you now have a vacancy. What strategies could you employ to find a replacement?

CASE TWO: Anne Thomas is the newly promoted pharmacy manager of the division of pediatric pharmacy services of a large metropolitan hospital. This division, which is one of six pharmacy divisions in the hospital, is responsible for preparing all pediatric prescriptions (including compounds and total parenteral nutrition [TPN]) that are dispensed on an inpatient basis in the hospital. Dr. Thomas has a budget for four full-time pharmacists, and the department currently has an opening for one. What steps should she take to develop an accurate job description and job advertisement for the vacant position?

CASE THREE: As one of three staff pharmacists, you are part of a team working to design a screening process for pharmacy technician candidates. You have been assigned to evaluate candidates' integrity through behavioral interview questions, situational interview questions, and reference check questions to former employers. What kinds of questions might you ask?

Additional Resources Available Online!

Visit the Student Companion Web site at http://healthprofessions.jbpub.com/pharmacymanagement for interactive study tools and additional resources.

See www.rxugace.com to learn how you can obtain continuing pharmacy education for this content.

CHAPTER 19

EFFECTIVE PERFORMANCE MANAGEMENT

MARY L. MAHER, MA
NATHAN D. POPE, PharmD

LEARNING OBJECTIVES

After completing the chapter, the reader will be able to

1. Discuss the importance of performance management.
2. Distinguish between performance management and performance evaluation.
3. Describe the components of a performance management approach.
4. Explain the S.C.O.R.E. approach to performance management programs.
5. List common barriers to effective performance management.
6. Discuss legal challenges of performance management systems.
7. Develop defensible performance standards.
8. Compare several performance evaluation methods.

KEY CONCEPTS

❶ Performance management is an ongoing process of communication between a manager and an employee to support accomplishing strategic objectives.

❷ Performance management should be viewed as a process, not a one-time or occasional activity.

❸ Research reveals that two of the strongest manager-influenced high-performance strategies are (1) clarifying employee performance expectations and (2) providing fair and accurate feedback.

❹ Increasing employees' knowledge and understanding of the performance standards by which they are measured and how they support organizational success can result in significant improvements in their performance.

❺ It is critical for pharmacist managers to set aside time and develop systems to provide employees with necessary coaching and to obtain adequate data to provide useful feedback.

❻ When a pharmacist manager is able to link an employee's contributions to larger organizational goals, the employee's work has even greater meaning.

❼ Effective, results-oriented managers know that failing to address concerns or delaying their transmission is a poor way to manage performance.

❽ Performance management systems must be developed with care to withstand possible legal challenges.

❾ Four basic considerations should be used to measure a manager's development of performance standards: (1) strategic relevance, (2) criterion deficiency, (3) criterion contamination, and (4) reliability.

❿ No matter which system or process is selected, an effective performance management process should provide managers and employees with important measurement information related to the strategic alignment of the employee's performance outcomes with the goals and objectives of the organization.

INTRODUCTION

Given the pressure on pharmacy organizations to cut costs while enhancing care, a deliberate approach to managing people, processes, and procedures is essential.[1] As a pharmacist manager, managing the performance of others will be one of your key responsibilities. But even those without management responsibilities are often called on to provide **feedback** on the performance of their peers, coworkers, and, in some cases, their direct supervisors. Knowledge of **performance management** approaches will support effective management and enable individual contributors to meet organizational expectations while supporting the development of others.

What is performance management exactly? Despite beliefs to the contrary, performance management is not synonymous with "performance evaluation." Formal performance evaluations, sometimes called "performance appraisals" or "performance reviews," are but one component of performance management. ❶ *Performance management is an ongoing process of communication between a manager and an employee to support accomplishing strategic objectives.* While performance evaluations document the past,[2] performance management is a more future-oriented process that includes the following:

- Establishing and clarifying expectations
- Linking an individual's work to larger organizational goals
- Setting performance objectives
- Providing feedback and **coaching**
- Offering training and development if necessary to build capacity
- Removing obstacles to ensure that objectives can be achieved
- Evaluating results

❷ *Performance management should be viewed as a process, not a one-time or occasional activity.* When focusing on results, engaging in performance management activities throughout the performance period leads to better outcomes than relying on a once-a-year performance evaluation.[3]

Case Study

Celestino Ortiz was known throughout the company as the first one to complete his annual **performance evaluations**. Although some people assumed this was because he was an efficient manager, the truth was that Celestino despised the annual process and simply tried to get through it as soon as he could. "The sooner these things are over, the better," he said to his wife over dinner.

"Why do you hate them so much?" his wife asked.

"What's to like?" Celestino replied. "People always get mad, and then I have to deal with weeks of sulking afterward. I'm sure if I had lower standards they would be easier, but I expect a lot from my people."

Celestino recognizes that, for organizations to deliver on their promises, people must be productive and act in alignment with organizational goals. He also understands that people, systems, and processes must be well coordinated to accomplish all that is expected of them. That is why he is dreading his upcoming conversation with Kaitlin James, one of his pharmacy technicians. When Kaitlin was hired almost 12 months ago, she aced the interview process. She had great experience from a hospital across town, was progressing well in her PharmD program, and had an outgoing personality. Her former employer described her as well organized. Celestino hired Kaitlin just before terminating Keith Regis, a long-term pharmacy technician who had been hired by Celestino's predecessor. Keith was known for his bad attitude and inability to follow even the simplest of instructions. Celestino was confident Kaitlin would be an excellent addition to the pharmacy team, but after almost a year on the job, she had been a tremendous disappointment. "What is it with technicians?" he thought to himself. He had wanted to talk to Kaitlin for some time, but some help was better than no help at all, and he didn't want to get into an argument with her. Enough was enough, however, and it was time to be explicit about his frustration. Celestino rolled his shoulders to reduce the tension in them. He knew this was going to be a hard conversation.

EVALUATION VERSUS ONGOING PERFORMANCE MANAGEMENT

When performance management is equated with a once-a-year formal evaluation, the pressure on both the manager and the employee is intense, and so much is held in the balance: the possibility of a pay increase, positioning for a promotion, or even feedback that one's job is in jeopardy because performance has been disappointing. It is no wonder that employees often feel like victims of authority when they receive their formal performance evaluation. Although employees tend to dislike the evaluation process, managers report similar discomfort at the prospect of evaluating an employee's performance. They often worry, understandably, about offending an employee whose continuing cooperation and engagement is important to business success.[4] Given how much people seem to dislike performance evaluation, one might

think less would be better than more, but that is not the case. In a survey asking workers about performance appraisals, respondents generally indicated they wanted more feedback than they had received.[5] This desire for more feedback makes sense on many levels. Most people want to do well, so periodic check-ins offer opportunities to break down complex objectives into manageable tasks, praise good work, and correct patterns before they become ingrained. More frequent feedback sessions also reduce the anxiety associated with one big, all-or-nothing meeting that surprises either party at the end of the evaluation period. When performance management is viewed as an ongoing process designed to support both individual and organizational success, both employees and the organization benefit.[3]

The most effective performance management efforts share the following components known as S.C.O.R.E.:

- **S**trategic: Performance management is linked to business goals to achieve a competitive advantage.
- **C**ommunication: Coaching and feedback techniques are used to promote open, honest dialogue.
- **O**pportunity: Key contributors for advancement are identified based on achievement measures associated with performance development/management.
- **R**ecognition: Reward programs are tightly coupled with performance.
- **E**ngagement: Performance management is perceived as a shared responsibility between employee and manager.

These considerations give an alternative meaning to what many performance appraisal programs generate as the end product of a performance evaluation—the **performance S.C.O.R.E.** Taken in this new context, incorporating these measures into an organization's performance management program may well result in a value-added process that rewards time and effort with achievement and opportunity.

Considering the powerful pressures to achieve results, managers face substantial demands on their time. Most managers, including pharmacist managers, acknowledge the critical role their employees serve in meeting strategic objectives, while at the same time admitting they may not be leveraging the right kinds of efforts to influence their employees' success in the pursuit and achievement of these objectives. Given the sheer number and diversity of activities a pharmacist manager could employ in managing the performance of a workforce, which activities yield the strongest results?

❸ *Research reveals that two of the strongest manager-influenced high-performance strategies are (1) clarifying employee performance expectations and (2) providing fair and accurate feedback.*[6] Given this, pharmacist managers have a substantial effect on both performance improvement and organizational achievement. Moreover, pharmacist managers influence the environment in which the work is performed because they are the primary link between their employees and the organization. In one sense, this dual role aligns the employee with the organization's strategic goals while simultaneously demonstrating to the employee the organization's commitment to their development to further position the employee toward success in future opportunities. Thus, a manager's actions enable performance while simultaneously affecting employees' attitudes and commitment to their jobs, teams, managers, and organization. **Discretionary effort**—how hard employees work, how well they perform, and how long they intend to stay with an organization—is driven by that employee commitment (refer to Chapter 20, "Creating and Identifying Desirable Workplaces").[6]

When successfully managing employee work and performance, managers focus their daily employee interactions on activities with the highest impact on performance and engagement. Management succeeds in these efforts when they *S.C.O.R.E.*:

- *Strategically define and align performance expectations and standards resulting in specific, measurable, and outcome-focused performance achievements.* One of the most powerful actions a manager can take when engaging in the performance management review process is to clarify and align performance expectations in specific, outcome-focused detail.

Pharmacist managers should also explain the options an employee has to contribute to organizational success, explaining the "big picture" and demonstrating how the employee's efforts contribute to such success. When the manager clearly establishes and maintains the link between employee work objectives and organizational strategy, both employee effort and **employee retention** increase.[6] ❹*Increasing employees' knowledge and understanding of the **performance standards** by which they are measured and how they support organizational success can result in significant improvements in their performance.*[6] For example, if maintaining medication stock is expected, be explicit about both the expectation (e.g., being able to fill greater than 98% of all "fast moving" medication prescriptions without customers having to wait for medications to come in with the next order) and the procedure required to maintain adequate inventory.

- *Communicate fair and accurate coaching and feedback from knowledgeable sources and measures.* Day-to-day, informal feedback is a powerful strategy for improving employee performance and enhancing employee attitudes that indirectly contribute to performance. Fair, accurate, and regular feedback can increase both employee engagement and discretionary effort. For informal feedback to be powerful, it must be based on a knowledgeable source of employees' performance and contain information that helps employees do their jobs better. "Chris, if you gather all of your supplies at once, it's easier to prepare the IV preparations; here, let me show you how I do it"—this a better approach than chiding Chris for being inefficient.

- *Opportunity can be created by leveraging an employee's skills, knowledge, and abilities, carefully matching employees to jobs, and promoting employee ownership and enjoyment.* Employees normally perform at higher levels when they are doing work they enjoy and for which they are particularly suited. Career development and the opportunity to use talents are two factors tightly linked to job satisfaction, so attention to ongoing development is critical. Employee opportunities can also be enhanced by connecting employees with other skilled coworkers and colleagues, thereby supporting the creation of a high-quality network that can contribute to successful project completion, new idea development, informed work groups, **competency development**, and increased awareness of organizational opportunities. Employees rarely perform in a vacuum and often depend on information and guidance from a broader network of internal employees and external contacts. Often management support in identifying these skill networks and connecting employees to talented coworkers from across the organization increases performance and provides the foundation for increased engagement and reduced turnover. Providing travel funds to enable a pharmacist to attend a national conference to meet new colleagues and enhance skills is an example of creating opportunity.

- *Recognize employee strengths and achievements, and acknowledge and reward performance.* Regular performance-related conversations are ideal for discussing, recognizing, and reinforcing performance strengths and outcomes, promoting stronger identification with work, and reinforcing performance-enhancing behaviors, resulting in the potential for positive change. In addition, focusing the discussion on identifying future skills, performance, and career targets brings with it the potential for performance improvement. "Patricia, I appreciated that you noticed that Mr. McHenry seemed confused about how to take his medication" will be more meaningful than, "Great job today."

- *Engage employees in finding tangible, immediate solutions to specific work challenges, while encouraging continued effort and commitment.* Effective coaching that enables performance and engages employees should focus on uncovering problems and solutions, attaining needed information and resources, breaking down projects into manageable efforts, converting long-term goals into step-by-step plans, and clearly communicating expectations. Imagine a retail pharmacy in which the average prescription wait time has increased from 20 minutes to 40 minutes. Inviting pharmacy staff to identify the factors that have led to the increased wait times would be one way to increase engagement and buy-in, and asking them to propose and implement solutions to reduce wait times would be another.

To keep employees interested and motivated, managers sometimes change projects and assignments frequently to "keep things interesting." This can actually lower employee performance if not done with care. A manager must provide guidance at the start of projects and ensure that needed corrections are timely, clear, and understood. There is, of course, a difference between regular feedback and constant feedback. The former can be helpful, and the latter can feel like oppressive micromanagement. Balancing supportive feedback against employees' interest in autonomy is critical. When done well, providing employees with new and challenging assignments, as well as the support necessary to be successful, can foster increased engagement and overall organizational success.

BARRIERS TO EFFECTIVE PERFORMANCE MANAGEMENT
Lack of Training

Although some organizations offer managers support in the art and science of managing performance, many do not. Without proper training, many managers believe that performance management is a once-a-year activity during which faults should be revealed. This lack of training can also result in a number of errors in conducting the formal performance review. Typical mistakes range from leniency to harshness.[7] **Table 19-1** lists common performance evaluation errors.

Lack of Time and Information

An important requirement of performance management is accurate data about employee performance. Collecting these data can challenge pharmacist managers for several reasons. For example, many pharmacist managers often have to step in to assist in dispensing medications and

TABLE 19–1	Common Performance Evaluation Rating Errors

- Halo effect (one positive trait influences all ratings)
- Central tendency (everything is average)
- Strict rating (being overly harsh)
- Lenient rating (being overly generous)
- Latest behavior (rating influenced by recent actions—good or bad)
- Spillover effect (letting past evaluations influence current ones)

Source: Data from Pynes J. *Human Resources Management for Public and Nonprofit Organizations*. San Francisco, CA: John Wiley & Sons Inc; 2009.

counseling patients, a demand that can make it difficult to spend focused time with employees. Physical separation between staff and manager may also make communication difficult. In large health systems or nationwide community pharmacy chains, the manager may be in a different building or in a different city. Within the pharmacy, the manager may only share a few hours of working time with an employee because of business hours, varied employee schedules, and other responsibilities of the pharmacist manager, as it is common for pharmacist managers to have staffing roles in addition to their management roles. ❺ *It is critical for pharmacist managers to set aside time and develop systems to provide employees with necessary coaching and to obtain adequate data to provide useful feedback.*

Failure to Link Individual Performance to Organizational Aspiration

Goal setting is best described as ensuring **line of sight** (visibility) between the employee's achievement and the employer's overall business goals.[6] An employee's line of sight between business goals and what the employee accomplishes day to day, enhanced by a manager's coaching and feedback, helps illustrate the interconnectedness of the employee's and the employer's goals. ❻ *When a pharmacist manager is able to link an employee's contributions to larger organizational goals, the employee's work has even greater meaning.* When

employees feel like their job is to "stock shelves" or "fill pharmacy orders," the work may not be as meaningful as when they believe their role is to "support patients to achieve their wellness goals." Effective managers are able to describe how their employees' work translates into larger organizational or societal objectives (refer to the Chapter 13, "Achieving Results Through Others and Strategic Planning").[5] When managers fail to do that, their employees are often disengaged and unproductive (refer to Chapter 20, "Creating and Identifying Desirable Workplaces").

Fear of Negative Consequences

Many pharmacist managers fear that honest but critical feedback will dampen employee enthusiasm, lead them to "act out," prompt them to quit, or even lead them to engage in sabotage. Given these concerns, managers often feel uncomfortable providing feedback and "save up" their concerns until it is time for a formal performance appraisal. Sometimes they fail to reveal their performance concerns. This unproductive approach denies employees an opportunity to be successful and denies the organization the benefit of optimized performance from employees.

Imagine a piano teacher who meets each Wednesday afternoon with a young student and listens to her play a piece of music. Knowing that the tempo is off and the student tends to confuse F-sharps with C-sharps, the teacher nods and smiles week after week. Then, at the holiday recital, in front of everyone, the student is horribly embarrassed by a bad performance. "I'm not surprised this went so badly," the teacher might say. "It's clear you haven't really mastered the art of reading notes. Maybe you will do better next year." Just as providing coaching and instruction to music students is essential for them to be successful, coaching and direction are required for employees to achieve superior results. One does not learn how to read music through dependability or trustworthiness; one learns by explicit instruction and constant feedback. A good music teacher would never deny a student the feedback required to master an instrument, yet managers often deny employees the opportunity to master their jobs by failing to give appropriate and timely feedback. ◆ *Effective, results-oriented managers know that failing to address concerns or delaying their transmission is a poor way to manage performance.*

Consider a new pharmacist who is counseling a patient about a new prescription for alendronate. The pharmacist manager observes that the new pharmacist fails to inform the patient that the medication he has dispensed should be taken with a full glass of plain water first thing in the morning, at least 30 minutes before the first food, beverage, or other medication, and the patient should not lie down for at least a half an hour. Rather than getting angry with the pharmacist for failing to share that information or waiting until several patients have been given inadequate advice, the pharmacist manager should quickly insert, "I'm not sure if (pharmacist's name) reviewed this yet, but we're seeing several patients who aren't following the advice about taking this medication on an empty stomach and who are lying down directly after taking the medication and that is causing some severe throat discomfort, so I want you to understand the importance of this." Once the patient has been provided with this information, you can pull the pharmacist aside and stress the importance of adequately counseling the patient about how to best achieve desired therapeutic response while minimizing adverse events. In this case, waiting to share one's disappointment until a formal performance review would be a disservice to both patients and the employee. A formal performance evaluation should never be a surprise. Instead, it should be a process that docu-

ments progress and conversations that have occurred throughout the review period, outlines development opportunities for the months ahead, and describes goals to be achieved in the future.

Developing Legally Defensible Performance Evaluation Systems
WITHSTANDING LEGAL CHALLENGES

◆ *Performance management systems must be developed with care to withstand possible legal challenges.* As long as performance evaluations are used to influence workforce-related activities—pay increases, promotions, and the like—these programs must meet certain legal requirements. In a landmark case involving test validation—*Albemarle Paper Company v. Moody*—the U.S. Supreme Court found that employees had been rank ordered (placing employees in sequential order based on their performance) against ambiguous performance standards. The court stated that "there is no way of knowing precisely what criteria of job performance the managers are considering, whether each manager was considering the same criteria, or whether indeed, any of the managers actually applied a focused and stable body of criteria of any kind."[8] This key decision prompted organizations to eliminate as much vagueness as possible in descriptions of performance-related traits, such as attitude, cooperation, initiative, dependability, and leadership. Reducing subjectivity by using measurable and quantifiable standards improves the entire process. In addition, when performance standards are accurately defined and measured, they translate organizational goals and objectives into job requirements that result in determining satisfactory and unsatisfactory levels of employee performance.

◆*Four basic considerations should be used to measure a manager's development of performance standards:* (1) **strategic relevance**, (2) **criterion deficiency**, (3) **criterion contamination**, *and* (4) **reliability**.

- *Strategic relevance* is the extent to which a standard relates to the organization's strategic objectives.[9] For example, if providing prompt customer service is an organizational value, a pharmacist may be evaluated against his record of ensuring that "90 percent of all refill prescriptions will be available within 30 minutes." If conducting quarterly unit audits is an expectation, the quality and completeness of such audits would be a reasonable factor to evaluate during a formal review.

- *Criterion deficiency* is the extent to which performance standards fail to describe the total range of an employee's responsibilities.[9] When performance standards focus on a single criterion (e.g., number of prescriptions filled) to the omission of other important and possibly less quantifiable performance aspects (e.g., customer service), criterion deficiency results. In short, criterion deficiency refers to the failure of a manager or performance management system to consider the total scope or breadth of an employee's responsibilities.

- *Criterion contamination* is the extent to which factors outside the employee's control influence his or her performance.[9] Comparing two years of sales records for a pharmacist manager when the community in which the pharmacy exists experienced a population surge or population exodus would be an example of criterion contamination. Similarly, holding a pharmacist manager accountable for dispensing a certain number of daily prescriptions, but failing to provide adequate inventory, would be another example of criterion contamination.

- *Reliability* is the extent to which performance is evaluated consistently among raters.[9] If one pharmacist rates a technician highly and another evaluates that same employee poorly, the reliability of the performance tool or standards will be called into question. If a manager rated an employee highly one year and then rated her poorly the next year though nothing about her performance had changed, the reliability of the performance management system would be deemed unreliable.

Retaliation

When providing performance feedback, also ensure that evaluations are not punitive. In the event an employee files a discrimination complaint and then receives a negative evaluation after years of demonstrating acceptable performance, a charge of retaliation could result. Providing specific examples of unsatisfactory performance will be especially important in these circumstances.[10]

Discriminatory Language or Differentiation

Language that could be perceived as discriminatory can lead to legal challenges, so care should be taken in how evaluation language is phrased.[10] Comments such as "Her productivity has suffered since the birth of a new child"; "The staff are uncomfortable when she speaks to her work friends in Spanish"; or "His insistence on attending Friday prayer services has forced the staff to change their lunch schedules" could subject the organization to legal challenges. Discriminatory comparisons can cause problems as well. Evaluating women based on their demonstration of empathy while evaluating men on their ability to solve problems is an example of gender discrimination that could result in a legal challenge.

Case Study (continued)

Celestino pulled up the performance evaluation template on his desktop and began composing the thoughts in his head. "This form is useless," he muttered to himself. Celestino disliked the hospital performance evaluation template, as it asked managers to evaluate employees based on traits such as dependability, safety, and cleanliness of the work area. Kaitlin was just fine in those areas, but the form lacked space to address the issues that caused Celestino the most concern—her inefficiency and lack of organization. "Well," Celestino thought to himself, "I owe it to Kaitlin and the rest of the team to be completely straight about her inferior performance," and he began typing her evaluation. While hospital performance evaluation protocols strongly encourage managers to have employees complete a self-evaluation before writing a final review, Celestino decided to skip this step. "What's the point?" he thought.

Performance Evaluation Methods

A key challenge faced by both the employee and manager is that typically neither participant is able to choose the performance evaluation system required. Understandably, a standardized performance evaluation system is typically designed with the intention to provide a fair and even playing field from which to apply consistent standards in the evaluation of each employee in a particular job. In addition, the performance evaluation form and process may be a key building block for the organization's other human resource programs, including compensation, workforce and **succession planning**, career development, and work design. Nonetheless, research reveals that the majority of managers and employees are dissatisfied with their organization's performance evaluation system.[7]

The success or failure of performance management programs depends on the values and beliefs underlying them and the attitudes and skills of those engaged in participating in them, regardless of whether they receive or give performance feedback and coaching. A variety of methods can be used to collect an employee's performance information and productivity outcomes; however, gathering information is only the beginning, as this information must be reviewed and evaluated in the context of organizational needs and then communicated to employees to further engage and encourage higher levels of performance and productivity.

⑩ *No matter which system or process is selected, an effective performance management process should provide managers and employees with important measurement information related to the strategic alignment of the employee's performance outcomes with the goals and objectives of the organization.* Such a measurement system allows employees to see themselves as key strategic contributors and helps establish **accountability**. With a measurement system, the employee has direction and focus; without such a system, the individual lacks clarity and connection.[11]

Although documenting an employee's performance has many benefits, among them memorializing contributions, documenting progress, and justifying pay increases or promotions, the performance management approach described thus far is an ongoing process rather than a once-a-year evaluation. However, given that a formal evaluation is an accepted component of performance

TABLE **19–2**	**Some Performance Evaluation Measures**

- Evaluating traits
- Evaluating behavior
- Evaluating results
- Multi-tool performance communication and development
- 360-degree feedback
- "No appraisals" approach

management in most organizations, which evaluation tools yield the best results? Pharmacist managers have many approaches from which to choose and often combination approaches are used (**Table 19–2**).

Evaluating traits: Trait approaches to performance evaluation measure the extent to which an employee possesses and demonstrates certain characteristics, such as creativity, dependability, and leadership.[7] If not designed on the basis of job analysis, trait-measured evaluations can be biased and subjective. Measuring traits remains the most used approach, despite its inherent subjectivity. **Figure 19-1** provides an example of a performance tool focused on traits.

Evaluating behavior: Behavioral approaches ensure more action-oriented information and can best be used when focusing on employee development.[4] Behavioral methods specifically describe which actions should or should not be demonstrated on the job. Focusing on specific appropriate or problematic behavior is more effective than general comments about a person's intentions. "You fail to consistently demonstrate good patient care" is less meaningful than "I was disappointed when I observed you telling Mrs. Chung that she could take her alendronate with meals and at night." Using examples such as this is known as a **critical incidents** method.[7] **Figure 19-2** provides an example of a behavioral approach to performance evaluation.

FIGURE **19—1**   **A Trait-Based Performance Evaluation Tool for a Pharmacist in a Long-Term Care Facility.**

5: Serves as a role model to others

4: Consistently exceeds expectations

3: Regularly meets expectations

2: Performance needs improvement

1: Unsatisfactory performance

Traits	5	4	3	2	1	Comments
Dependability						
Effectiveness						
Empathy						
Customer service						
Initiative						
Problem-solving ability						
Interpersonal communication skills						
Job knowledge						
Punctuality						
Team work						

Overall Performance Score: _____

Development Needs:

Evaluating results: In 1954, management expert Peter Drucker proposed a philosophy of management that sought to evaluate performance on the basis of successfully achieving objectives established through discussions between managers and employees. He called this approach **management by objectives** (MBO).[12] Managers who use this approach focus on goals to be achieved rather than on activities employees perform or the traits they exhibit related to their assigned jobs. A positive aspect of MBO is its focus on achieving results. A negative aspect is the potential for an employee to accomplish results using inappropriate tactics, or at the expense of duties or behaviors not explicitly measured. If a pharmacist is measured on the number of medications dispensed daily but not on the accuracy of medications dispensed or the quality of patient care provided, the pharmacist

FIGURE **19-2** **A Behavior-Based Performance Evaluation Tool for a Pharmacist Technician in a Community Retail Setting.**

BEHAVIORS	Always 5	Usually 4	Frequently 3	Seldom 2	Never 1
DEPENDABILITY					
Can be counted on to arrive to work on time					
Completes assigned tasks and projects in a timely way					
When an absence is required, follows call-in procedures so that proper coverage is possible					
Average dependability score: _____					
TEAMWORK					
Willingly works with others to achieve goals					
Offers assistance to others					
Demonstrates flexibility					
Average teamwork score: _____					
CUSTOMER SERVICE					
Treats patients and customers with courtooy					
Listens to customers to understand their concerns					
Takes action to resolve customer/patient concerns					
Average customer service score: _____					
ACCURACY					
Provides accurate information to patients					
Handles cash exchanges properly so that the end-of-shift drawer balances					
Enters prescription properly in computer					
Fills prescription properly					
Average accuracy score: _____					

Comments:_____

_____

and, therefore the organization, will not truly be meeting patients' needs; instead, they will facilitate harm and liability. The value of a results-oriented approach is also compromised when organizations hold employees responsible for results that are not readily achievable given available resources or systems. For example, holding a pharmacist accountable for running a busy specialty clinic (e.g., oncology, infectious disease) without adequate training, a computer system, inventory, and technician support is an unrealistic expectation.

Successful results-oriented programs should meet several requirements: (1) inclusion of both short- and long-term quantifiable and measurable objectives; (2) expected results within the employee's control with goals consistent across each employee level (executive, senior, mid-level, supervisory management, individual contributor); (3) identified and specific time frames for goal(s) review and evaluation; and (4) a description accompanying each goal of how that goal will be accomplished. An example of a results-oriented evaluation tool is displayed in **Figure 19–3**.

Multi-tool performance communication and development: A considerably more contemporary approach is a ***multi-tool performance communication and development*** method determined by both the manager and employee using a blend of these tested methods while offering various combinations of optional performance management tools. This approach focuses on results as well as the traits and behaviors expected for the employee to be successful within the organization. This perpetual performance management approach encourages inclusion and empowerment of the employee in ongoing performance communication and relationship development with his or her manager. Written summaries of performance-related formal and informal conversations between the manager and employee are routinely documented by the employee and reviewed or revised by the manager, ensuring key accomplishments and development needs are clearly identified and understood by these key participants. Guided discussions, formalized work plans, performance development and improvement plans, mentoring and succession plans, etc., are various tools contained within this approach, permitting the implementation and

coordination of additional employee-specific performance tools to encourage responsive and results-focused strategies to meet organizational goals, objectives, mission, vision, values, and culture. A sample work plan is displayed in **Figure 19–4**. A performance discussion guide follows in **Figure 19–5**. **Figure 19–6** provides an example of a performance development plan.

360-degree feedback: **360-degree assessment** tools differ markedly from the approaches described thus far, as they seek feedback from people who surround the employee. In addition to the direct supervisor, feedback may be provided by direct reports, peers, project team members, customers, patients, or clients. A 360-degree approach is valuable because of its ability to provide a comprehensive review of an employee's strengths and weaknesses.[13] Individuals who meet patient needs at the expense of their coworkers' needs will often be exposed. Direct reports may be aware of their managers' communication patterns in a way that direct supervisors are not. When taken together, feedback from a wide variety of perspectives can be enlightening for both the employee and the supervisor.

360-degree tools are not without their controversy. While research organizations such as the Center for Creative Leadership argue that 360-degree tools should be used as management development tools,[14] some organizations use these tools to evaluate performance or guide promotion decisions. When this is the case and raters are aware of this, they may be overly critical or overly gentle in their feedback to influence the final outcome. Regardless of whether 360-degree assessments are used for development or for formal evaluation, the information contained within them can be difficult for employees to receive. As a result, some organizations contract with outside performance coaches or ask organizational development professionals to review findings with the employee. Sample elements of a 360-degree evaluation tool are provided in **Figure 19–7**.

A "no appraisals" approach to enhancing employee performance: A review of the approaches available to evaluate performance would not be complete without acknowledging that some experts question whether any formal evaluation process has merit. Those who argue against formal appraisal

FIGURE **19–3**   **A Results-Oriented Self-Evaluation Tool for a Pharmacist Manager in a Retail Setting.**

3: Exceeds expectations

2: Meets expectations

1: Below expectations

EXPECTATIONS	Review Period Goals	Progress Toward Goals	Self-Rating
Staffing	Fill all vacant positions and hire two on-call pharmacists	Hired Zelda Zachary, a pharmacist with significant pediatric experience; Raul Baez, a pharmacy technician with both hospital and retail experience; and Kim Lee, a pharmacy technician with an RN degree who is pursuing her PharmD. Still seeking a weekend pharmacist and second on-call pharmacist.	2
Staff Development	Made sure that all pharmacists had the opportunity to receive 15 hours of continuing education	Provided opportunity for continuing education by two major methods: (1) providing registration and travel assistance to attend local and state continuing education programs; and (2) partnered with the local pharmacy school to provide on-site continuing education programs for pharmacists.	2
Budgeting	Reduce operating expenses by 6%	Reduced evening staffing and increased use of on-call technician support on weekends. Reduced lighting during early morning and late evening hours to save electricity. Reduced overall expenses by 5.9%.	2
Operations Management	Implement a new inventory management system	Completed without incident.	3
Revenue Generation	Increase overall store revenue by 4%	Launched monthly wellness checks, expanded grocery products, and offered senior discounts on Thursday afternoons. Achieved revenue increase of 5.2%.	3

OVERALL SELF-RATING: 2.4

FIGURE **19-4**   **Performance Work Plan.**

I. Strategic Alignment

Staff Member	Staff ID	Title
Department	Supervisor	Senior Reviewer

Performance Summary Period: _____ to _____ Date/Initials of Plan Reviewer(s)

<u>**Applicable Organizational Strategic Initiative(s):**</u>

<u>**Applicable Departmental Strategic Initiative(s):**</u>

<u>**Applicable Unit/Staff Person's Initiative(s):**</u>

II. Work Plan

1. %FTE   Strategic Initiative/Goals   Key Partners/Beneficiaries

Activities

Measurements/Performance Standards

Results

Coaching/Feedback Notes *(Date and initial each entry)*

2. %FTE   Strategic Initiative/Goals   Key Partners/Beneficiaries

Activities

Measurements/Performance Standards

Results

Coaching/Feedback Notes *(Date and initial each entry)*

3. %FTE   Strategic Initiative/Goals   Key Partners/Beneficiaries

Activities

Measurements/Performance Standards

Results

Coaching/Feedback Notes *(Date and initial each entry)*

Note: FTE = full time equivalent.

FIGURE **19–5**   **Performance Discussion Guide.**

- ❑ Discuss staff member's performance on primary responsibilities, both anticipated and accomplished.
- ❑ Discuss staff member's contributions to the success of the unit and the success of the initiatives, both anticipated and accomplished.
- ❑ Discuss staff member's competencies and opportunities for competency development.
- ❑ Discuss staff member's customer focus and collaborative teamwork approach.
- ❑ Discuss barriers and/or challenges to effective performance and job satisfaction.
- ❑ Discuss recurring tasks and processes. Identify things that could be streamlined or improved.
- ❑ Discuss staff member's suggestions and feedback for supervisor.

Employee: Please summarize discussion points and date(s) of discussion(s). Each dated entry should be initialed by both Staff Member and Supervisor.

Summary of Discussion(s)

Date: _____   **Initials:** Staff Member's: _____   Supervisor's: _____

FIGURE **19–6**   **Performance Development Plan.**

Staff Member's Name:_____ **Staff ID:** _____

Plan Begin Date:_____

Department:_____

Supervisor: _____ **Plan Completion Date:**_____

Major Area of Responsibility	Performance Expectation(s)	Areas for Development	Action Plan

Summary Notes/Dates:

tools assert that performance evaluation ratings can be arbitrary, they are rarely as legally defensible as people believe, they demotivate employees, and they focus on rankings at the expense of providing employees with feedback about how to be more successful. In their book *Abolishing Performance Appraisals*, Tom Coens and Mary Jenkins argue that a confidential and multisource development feedback system is far more valuable than a formal performance evaluation. If an organization insists on conducting evaluations, Coens and Jenkins urge managers to eliminate rankings or at least adopt a pass/fail scoring system to shift the emphasis from grading to development.[15]

When we consider the drivers of fair process—(1) how much input employees have in decision making, (2) how decisions are made and implemented, and (3) the degree to which managers explain the rationale for their decisions[16]—it is clear that poorly managed performance evaluations create opportunities for disappointment and dissent.

Case Study (continued)

Kaitlin arrived in Celestino's office at 2:00 on Thursday afternoon as scheduled, and Celestino got right down to business. "I've given your per-

FIGURE **19–7** **Sample Items from a 360-Degree Performance Assessment Tool for a Manager in Pharmaceutical Industry.**

Developing Organizational Talent	N/A	Serves as an Exemplar	Area of Particular Strength	Consistent Performer	Some Improvement Required	Significant Improvement Necessary
Selects and grooms high performers.						
Provides frequent coaching to support employees to achieve their goals.						
Ensures that each employee receives professional development opportunities.						

Comments: _____

Building Relationships	N/A	Serves as an Exemplar	Area of Particular Strength	Consistent Performer	Some Improvement Required	Significant Improvement Necessary
Works cooperatively with others.						
Recognized for reaching out to members of the local community.						
Establishes mutually beneficial relationships with people at all levels of the company.						
Active in relevant professional organizations.						

Comments: _____

(continues)

FIGURE **19–7**   (continued)

Communication	N/A	Serves as an Exemplar	Area of Particular Strength	Consistent Performer	Some Improvement Required	Significant Improvement Necessary
Writes clear and compelling documents.						
Engages groups when delivering public presentations.						
Listens well.						
Effectively translates technical information for lay audiences.						

Comments: _____

formance a great deal of thought and I hope you have too," He began. "I hope our mutual perspectives are similar."

"I don't know about mutual perspectives," Kaitlin responded, "but I have to admit that I wish I had more time to talk with you during my shifts. I have a lot of ideas about how things could be improved, but you're always busy, so I don't want to take up your time."

"I'm happy you have ideas about improvement," said Celestino, "but until you can master the basics of your job, I don't know that you are in a position to be suggesting much of anything."

"Excuse me?" Kaitlin responded.

"I think we both know what I'm talking about," Celestino continued. "The long lines, your refusal to restock shelves, the misplaced prescriptions. . . . I'm not sure you appreciate the prob-

lems you are creating for patients and for your coworkers."

Kaitlin was stunned. "I've been here for a whole year," she said, "and this is the first time you have given me one sentence of feedback. I can't believe you didn't say anything before. But beyond that, I have no idea what you are talking about."

"How can you be surprised?" Celestino asked in disbelief. "The pharmacy is constantly backed up when you're on duty and you seem to care more about gabbing with people about their pets or who's getting married than you do about getting medicine into people's hands."

"Are you serious?" Kaitlin responded. "When I went through the interview process you made it crystal clear that customer service was your number one priority. I believe your exact words were, 'We want every person who walks into this pharmacy to feel special.' That's what I do. I remember people. I talk to people. I make them feel special."

"I do want every person who walks into the pharmacy to feel special," Celestino responded, "but I don't want lines out the door or 20-minute waits at the cash register."

"The only time lines are backed up like that are between 5:00 and 7:00," Kaitlin responded. "I've told you before that we need at least two technicians in the early evening and you never listen to me."

"Long wait times are just part of the problem," Celestino added. "The pick-up orders are constantly in a state of disarray. When your shift is over, the next technician has to alphabetize every package in the bin. It's alphabetizing; how hard can that be?"

"I cannot believe what I'm hearing." Kaitlin responded. "First of all, I am the one who has to reorganize packages at the beginning of each shift. I don't know whose bright idea it was to organize the packages by time and date of order, but I seem to be the only one who knows how to do it properly. Changing to a completely alphabetical system was going to be one of my suggestions."

"You are filing prescriptions time and date of order?" Celestino responded. "When did I ever give you the impression that this is how I wanted things done? I never gave you those instructions."

"You never gave me any instructions," Kaitlin responded. "When I started, you were preparing for some kind of visit from corporate and told me that Keith would tell me everything I needed to know. I followed all of his instructions exactly," Kaitlin responded.

"And your refusal to stock shelves at the end of your shift?" Celestino asked almost sheepishly.

"I'm supposed to stock shelves?"

As we consider the components of an effective performance management system, it is clear where things went awry:

- Did Celestino establish and clarify expectations? *No.*
- Did Celestino set objectives or performance standards? *No.*
- Did Celestino identify goals for the pharmacy as a whole or for Kaitlin in particular? *No.*
- Did Celestino provide Kaitlin with feedback or coaching to support her success? *No.*
- Did Celestino train her on the techniques used to manage the pharmacy's operation? *No.*
- Has Celestino considered factors beyond her control, such as the volume of customers between 5:00 p.m. and 7:00 p.m.? *No.*
- Did Celestino evaluate the results? *Yes, but those results would have been so much better had Celestino taken the time to alert Kaitlin to his concerns months ago.*

Celestino's failure to alert Kaitlin to his concerns denied her an opportunity to modify her work style to perform to Celestino's standards. More important, Celestino's failure to provide Kaitlin with a proper orientation and necessary training set her up to be unsuccessful from the start. Celestino could have taken a very bright and promising future pharmacist and dampened her morale and enthusiasm, but Kaitlin James was no ordinary employee, and she refused to accept defeat.

Case Study (continued)

"Listen," Kaitlin told Celestino. "I need a successful track record here on my résumé and you need to reduce turnover among your technicians. I have a proposal. How about we set this performance evaluation aside and you spend the next three months actually being honest with me? If I do something that is wrong or annoying, you say so. If I do something right, you share that as well. Then, 90 days from now, we'll come back into this room and you can tell me how I am doing."

"It's a deal," Celestino replied shaking her hand. "What you're suggesting is very fair."

(continues)

Ninety days later Celestino and Kaitlin met in his office. "Kaitlin," Celestino began, "I want to thank you for standing up to me when we had our first performance meeting. I owe you an apology for failing to share my concerns from the start."

"Well," Kaitlin replied, "when you ripped up the evaluation and said, 'Let's try this again in 90 days,' I felt good about things."

"I feel good about things as well," Celestino replied. "And I feel even better about providing you with an excellent performance review. None of what I'm about to say is going to be a surprise, but let's review your key accomplishments...."

SUMMARY

Pharmacy practice environments and the people who receive their products and services benefit most from employees who are engaged and empowered. Employee engagement is most likely to occur when employees understand how their performance and achievements are related to organizational strategic goals and objectives. Engagement and effective performance are also enhanced when managers enlighten and recognize employees, consistently and respectfully identify and communicate performance needs, remove obstacles, and provide the training and resources to support their employees' current and future success. When these elements are in place, employees are more likely to partner and to perform. Effective performance management systems assume that employees have the organization's best interests in mind and provide the tools, resources, feedback, and rewards necessary to help employees feel valued and be successful. Performance management is more than a periodic and formal written review; it is an ongoing process that builds on past successes and positions employees to take on new and ever-challenging assignments.

References

1. Roberts MB, Keith MR. Implementing a performance evaluation system in a correctional managed care pharmacy. *Am J Health-Syst Pharm* 2002;59(11):1097–1104.

2. McKenna PJ, Maiser DH. *First Among Equals*. New York, NY: Free Press; 2002.

3. Swan W. *How to Do a Superior Performance Appraisal*. New York, NY: John Wiley & Sons Inc; 1991.

4. Pulakos ED. *Performance Management: A Roadmap for Developing, Implementing and Evaluating Performance Management Systems*. Alexandria, VA: Society for Human Resource Management Foundation; 2004.

5. Clausen TS, Jones KT, Rich JS. Appraising employee performance evaluation systems: how to determine if an overhaul is needed. *CPA J* February 2008. Available at: http://www.nysscpa.org/cpajournal/2008/208/essentials/p64.htm. Accessed December 20, 2008.

6. BlessingWhite. The state of employee engagement 2008: American overview. Available at: http://www.blessingwhite.com/%5Ccontent%5Creports%5C2008EmployeeEngagementNAOverview.pdf. Accessed May 22, 2009.

7. Pynes J. *Human Resources Management for Public and Nonprofit Organizations*. San Francisco, CA: John Wiley & Sons Inc; 2009.

8. *Albemarle Paper Company v Moody*, 422 US, 405 (1975).

9. Wigdor AK, Green BF. *Performance Assessment for the Workplace*. Vol. 1. Washington, DC: National Academy Press; 1991.

10. Deblieux M. *Performance Appraisal Source Book*. Alexandria, VA: Society for Human Resource Management; 2003.

11. Jones S, Moffett RG III. Measurement and feedback systems for teams. In: Sundstrom E, ed. *Supporting Work Team Effectiveness*. San Francisco, CA: Jossey-Bass; 1999.

12. Drucker PF. *The Practice of Management*. New York, NY: Harper & Brothers; 1954.

13. Edwards MR, Ewen AJ. *360° Feedback*. New York, NY: AMACOM; 1996.

14. Velso E, Leslie J, Fleenor J. *Choosing 360: A Guide to Evaluating Multi-rater Feedback Instruments for*

Management Development. Greensboro, NC: Center for Creative Leadership; 1997.

15. Coen T, Jenkins M. *Abolishing Performance Appraisals*. San Francisco, CA: Berrett-Joehler Publishers Inc; 2000.

16. Brockner J. Why it's so hard to be fair. *Harv Bus Rev*. 2006;March:122–129.

Abbreviations

FTE: full time equivalent
MBO: management by objectives
S.C.O.R.E.:   strategic, communication, opportunity, recognition, engagement

Case Scenarios

CASE ONE: You are the pharmacist manager of a community pharmacy. One day while you are working on some paperwork, you hear Grace Chen and Rose Almozara, two new employees of less than a year, chatting about their previous work environments. Each one came to your pharmacy from other non-pharmacy careers. Grace tells Rose that she never received any feedback from her previous supervisor. Rose says she received feedback from her supervisor but only "negative stuff," and all her coworkers hated when they were called into his office for annual reviews. "I hope that doesn't happen here," says Grace. As their manager, what would you do to relieve Rose and Grace's fear of performance reviews?

CASE TWO: Despite your best efforts, you can't seem to convince your pharmacist in charge that his behavior is alienating other members of the team. You have spoken with him about the need to listen, the importance of modulating his voice, and the degree to which you value harmony in the workplace. Despite this, he insists there is nothing wrong with his behavior and that his consistently superior results should be all that is required. What strategies might you use to get through to him?

CASE THREE: It is approximately one month away from your hospital's performance review period. Your employer has determined the mechanism with which you will review your employees. The leaders of the hospital require a written performance review along with an interview with the employee about that review. How will you make the performance review process helpful and productive?

Additional Resources Available Online!

Visit the Student Companion Web site at http://healthprofessions.jbpub.com/pharmacymanagement for interactive study tools and additional resources.

See www.rxugace.com to learn how you can obtain continuing pharmacy education for this content.

CREATING AND IDENTIFYING DESIRABLE WORKPLACES

ALLISON M. VAILLANCOURT, PhD, SPHR

MARIE A. CHISHOLM-BURNS, PharmD, MPH, FCCP, FASHP

DIANA I. BRIXNER, PhD, RPh

LEARNING OBJECTIVES

After completing the chapter, the reader will be able to

1. Assess the effect of pending labor shortages on pharmacy management.
2. Cite attributes that make a workplace appealing to employees.
3. List five key components of the employee value proposition.
4. Recommend strategies to create a sense of inclusion.
5. Explain the primary factors that drive perceptions of fairness.
6. Identify factors that lead to undesired employee turnover.
7. Propose approaches to support employee development.
8. Describe the value of work-life programs.
9. List popular benefit options that are offered to employees, and describe the importance of understanding and communicating the value of benefit offerings.
10. Differentiate between base and variable pay.

KEY CONCEPTS

❶ Organizations with reputations for exceptional quality and progressive human resources practices enjoy substantial benefits, including the ability to increase employee commitment, minimize employee turnover rates, and attract employees who are not currently seeking new positions. They also tend to outperform competitors in terms of profitability.

❷ Individual managers have enormous influence when it comes to creating conditions that make employees want to give their best to their organization, thereby enhancing productivity, accuracy, creativity, and innovation and strengthening relationships with customers, patients, and coworkers.

❸ Effective pharmacist managers promote admirable attributes that differentiate their organizations from competitors to bolster recruitment efforts and enhance organizational pride among current employees.

❹ Values are beliefs that guide behavior and decisions, and managers increase their success and credibility by using an organization's stated values to drive hiring decisions, assess performance, and offer rewards and advancement opportunities.

❺ Effective pharmacist managers explore opportunities to make all employees feel valued and included. They also hire employees committed to working productively with diverse groups of people.

❻ Managers play a key role in establishing organizational norms and engendering a sense of trust by being proactive and promptly and assertively preventing and confronting rude, dismissive, abusive, or harassing behavior. Managers also play a critical role in ensuring workplace safety and security.

❼ Explaining to employees how their work is essential to the organization's short- and long-term success increases employee commitment. This can be done in several ways, including using job descriptions to detail how an employee's duties are tied to broader organizational goals, using the organization's strategic plan to develop individual performance objectives, and having senior leaders formally recognize employees for their contributions to larger organizational results.

❽ Strong managers understand that "promotability" does not happen by chance and are intentional in their approach to preparing employees for new and expanded roles. These managers tend to have a process for identifying and grooming employees for new roles and are therefore able to posi-

tion excellent employees for expanded responsibilities.

❾ When employees are unable to manage their work roles and non-work responsibilities, they may experience significant stress that can lead to illness, increased healthcare costs, unscheduled absences, lower productivity, reduced satisfaction, and higher employee turnover.

❿ Effective pharmacist managers understand that high performers expect to be recognized for their accomplishments, provided with more flexibility than others, compensated to a greater extent than lower performers, and provided with multiple opportunities to develop and advance.

INTRODUCTION

Although opportunities for pharmacist managers have never been greater, these managers face considerable challenges in recruiting and retaining excellent employees. As the United States' population grows and continues to age, pharmacists will be needed to meet healthcare demands (**Table 20–1**).[1] As the need for skilled workers increases and millions of baby boomers retire, forecasters estimate that those who serve in support roles alongside pharmacy professionals will also be in demand in the next decade.[2] As a result, pharmacy professionals will have wider employment options and pharmacist managers will be challenged to compete for talent. Given these labor market trends, organizations will have to differentiate themselves from other employers to attract and retain high-quality employees.

Several attributes may make an organization particularly appealing to prospective healthcare employees: being recognized as a leader in quality and innovative healthcare services, offering comprehensive work-life programs, maintaining a strong **market position**, demonstrating leadership stability, supporting a diverse workforce, and providing opportunities for professional development and career advancement.[3] ❶ *Organizations with reputations for exceptional quality and progressive human resources practices enjoy substantial*

| TABLE **20–1** | Estimates of Projected Need for Pharmacists in the United States |

	Use of Pharmacists in 2001	Projected Need for Pharmacists in 2020
Order Fulfillment	136,400	100,000
Primary Services	30,000	165,000
Secondary/Tertiary Services[a]	18,000	130,000
Indirect/Other Services	12,300	22,000
Total	196,700	417,000
Total Estimated Supply		260,000
Shortfall		157,000

[a]Secondary/tertiary services mainly consist of acute care services offered to institutionalized patients. This also includes hospital-based pharmacy services involving the entire patient population, such as establishment and oversight of medication safety systems and drug policy issues.
Note: These figures are estimates of the need for pharmacists in 2020 and forecasts of market demand or jobs for pharmacists.
Source: Reprinted from Knapp DA. Professionally determined need for pharmacy services in 2020. *American Journal of Pharmaceutical Education* 2002:66:421–429, with permission.

benefits, including the ability to increase employee commitment, minimize **employee turnover rates**, *and attract employees who are not currently seeking new positions.*[4] *They also tend to outperform competitors in terms of profitability.*[5]

Creating a uniquely desirable workplace takes a focused and deliberate strategy. Managers who understand factors that motivate employees will be well positioned to craft programs and implement practices aligned with employees' and employers' needs and interests. While upper administrative or corporate-level support may be required to implement some strategies, ❷ *individual managers have enormous influence when it comes to creating conditions that make employees want to give their best to their organization, thereby enhancing productivity, accuracy, creativity, and innovation and strengthening relationships with customers, patients, and coworkers.* While this chapter is geared toward current and future pharmacist managers, the information will also be valuable to those who do not hold management roles, as it will describe the elements of an appealing organization and help pharmacists evaluate whether a prospective employer's attributes are likely to support their satisfaction and success.

This chapter focuses on strategies designed to achieve sustained organizational success through **employee engagement**, defined as the extent to which employees commit to something or someone in their organization, how hard they work, and how long they stay as a result of that commitment. Employee engagement is tightly linked to an employer's **employee value proposition**, which is what an employer offers to its employees in exchange for their effort and commitment. The employee value proposition includes five key components (**Figure 20–1**):[6]

- *Affiliation*: The feeling of belonging to an admirable organization that shares one's values
- *Work content*: The satisfaction that comes from the work one does

FIGURE **20–1**   **The Employee Value Proposition.**

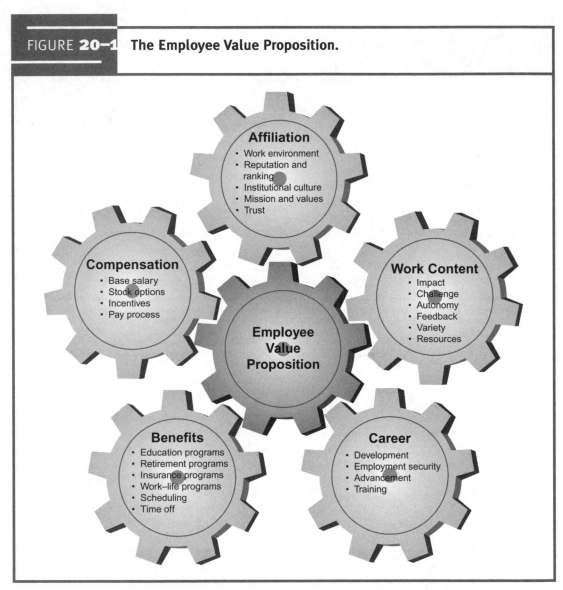

Integral to achieving employee engagement, the employee value proposition (the central cog) is comprised of five basic elements (represented by the outer cogs): (1) affiliation, (2) work content, (3) career, (4) benefits, and (5) compensation. To engage employees successfully, organizational leaders and managers should address factors associated with these five basic elements.

Source: Adapted with permission of The Segal Group, Inc. parent of The Segal Company and its Sibson Consulting Division. ©2008. All rights reserved.

- *Career*: Long-term opportunities for development and advancement in the organization
- *Benefits*: Programs that support health, wellness, work–life balance, and financial security
- *Compensation*: Direct financial rewards

The relative value of these components may vary based on organizational attributes and their individual employees. Few organizations excel in all five areas and must therefore tailor their practices and resource investments to meet the needs of their unique workforces. This chapter reviews each component of the employee value proposition, poses key questions employees ask related to these components, and provides an array of strategies that pharmacist managers can employ to support employee engagement. To implement such strategies successfully requires the time and commitment of managers and organizational leaders.

AFFILIATION

- *What makes this organization unique and impressive?*
- *Are this organization's mission and values aligned with my own?*
- *Will I be accepted here?*
- *Can I trust leaders and coworkers?*

Affiliation Strategy 1: Emphasize a Distinctive Organizational Mission

❸ *Effective pharmacist managers promote admirable attributes that differentiate their organizations from competitors to bolster recruitment efforts and enhance organizational pride among current employees.* Although employees join an organization for what might be considered rational motives, such as better compensation, benefits, or career opportunities, they remain and demonstrate effort based on emotional factors. A sense of connection to an organization's mission is an essential component of employee commitment. A compelling mission statement can convey the "essence" of an organization in a sentence or two.[4] An organization's mission describes why it exists (for example, "We

provide high-quality pharmaceutical care services and medications at the lowest possible price"; "We develop lifesaving pharmaceuticals for the global community"). Employees are attracted to organizations that are superior and unique, and they take special pride in affiliations with organizations admired by others for their market position, social responsibility, employee talent, quality healthcare/pharmacy services, innovation, use of assets, financial soundness, and management quality.[3]

Affiliation Strategy 2: Communicate a Compelling Vision

Although organizational mission statements describe why an organization exists, vision statements describe aspirations for the future and support employee engagement. Employees want to know where their organizations are headed and how they fit in as individual contributors.[7] Vision statements should be ambitious and compelling—for example, "We will be recognized as a top 25 hospital within five years"; "We will double our pharmacy locations by the year 2015"; or "Our success in developing new therapeutics will reduce the morbidity rate of colon cancer by 30% by the year 2020."

Providing employees with detailed information about the organization's strategies and goals for the future enables them to understand how their individual efforts contribute to organizational success. It also creates a sense of excitement about what lies ahead. Refer to Chapter 13, "Achieving Results Through Others and Strategic Planning."

Affiliation Strategy 3: Be Explicit About Organizational Values

❹ *Values are beliefs that guide behavior and decisions, and managers increase their success and credibility by using an organization's stated values to drive hiring decisions, assess performance, and offer rewards and advancement opportunities.*[8] Values statements differ from employer to employer, and words used in formal documents should describe the culture an employee can expect. At CVS Caremark, for example, one of the organizational values statements describes the work atmosphere as one in which employees are expected to "work as a team . . . committed to act with integrity."[9]

At Genentech, a biotherapeutics firm, informality is valued, and the organizational values statement describes "an environment of casual intensity where people enjoy coming to work every day."[10] Both CVS Caremark and Genentech are well-regarded organizations, but their values statements speak to their different cultures.

Affiliation Strategy 4: Create a Culture of Inclusion

When employees feel welcomed, valued, respected, accepted, and supported, they are more likely to put forth exceptional effort. In fact, individuals with close social ties at work demonstrate greater commitment, less absenteeism, and higher productivity.[11] Recognizing this, ❺ *effective pharmacist managers explore opportunities to make all employees feel valued and included. They also hire employees committed to working productively with diverse groups of people.* When one considers the myriad ways in which employees can be diverse, creating a culture of inclusion requires an intentional approach.

When diversity is raised, many people think primarily of gender, race, and ethnicity, and the composition of the American workforce is certainly changing in that regard. One of every 10 people living in the United States was born outside the country, and the nation's racial and ethnic makeup is increasingly heterogeneous.[12] Increased demographic diversity among health professionals, including pharmacists, supports greater access to health care in minority patient populations, improved patient options and satisfaction, better communication between healthcare professionals and patients, and more dynamic educational experiences.[13] Therefore, it is important to recognize and value demographic diversity, as well as other attributes that differentiate employees from one another. Employees bring to their organizations different experiences and perceptions based on their gender, **gender identity**, age, religion, marital status, parental status, geographic origin, sexual orientation, political affiliation, socioeconomic background, learning style, physical ability, communication preferences, intelligence, educational level, language proficiency, decision-making preferences, and a host of other attributes. **Table 20–2** provides a list of possible actions pharmacist

managers can take to establish an inclusive environment and support a productive and diverse organizational culture.

Affiliation Strategy 5: Create a Safe Work Environment

In addition to building a culture of inclusion, creating desirable workplaces also means ensuring that all individuals feel safe and free from hostile behavior. ❻ *Managers play a key role in establishing organizational norms and engendering a sense of trust by being proactive and promptly and assertively preventing and confronting rude, dismissive, abusive, or harassing behavior. Managers also play a critical role in ensuring workplace safety and security.* Pharmacist managers should encourage the development of systems that limit the diversion and abuse potential of medications, including high-cost medications and controlled substances, thus reducing the risk of workplace violence by decreasing the likelihood that these products will be the targets of theft.[14] For example, pharmacist managers may require drug screenings before hiring individuals, enforce random drug screenings among pharmacy employees, and implement a double-check dispensing system for controlled, high-cost medications wherein the quantity of medication dispensed and the quantity of medication remaining are counted by at least two people. Pharmacist managers may also want to consider minimizing the visibility of where controlled medications are stored—in other words, managers should consider storing controlled medications out of public view and in less visible areas if possible. Pharmacists who are not in management roles can help enhance workplace safety by suggesting improvements to current practices and alerting organizational leaders to deviations from established protocols.

Affiliation Strategy 6: Focus on Fairness

Employees want to be treated equitably, and effective managers pay special attention to decisions related to work assignments, compensation, honoring promises, development and promotional opportunities, and job security.[15] There are three primary factors that drive perceptions of fairness. The first is the degree of input employees have in

TABLE **20–2**	**Practices Managers Can Employ to Establish an Inclusive Environment and Support a Diverse Organizational Culture**

- Actively recruit diverse employees.
- Allow employees the option to swap common religious holidays (e.g., Christmas, Easter) for dates aligned with their own religious beliefs.
- Analyze hiring, evaluation, mentoring, and promotion practices for unintended bias, and correct if necessary.
- Analyze the reasons for employee turnover by demographic type to identify opportunities to address concerns of specific employee populations (e.g., women, minorities).
- Ensure that diverse people and perspectives are included on project and leadership teams.
- Ensure that meeting spaces on and off site are accessible to those with physical disabilities.
- Ensure that partners as well as spouses are invited to social events.
- Ensure that vegetarian meal options are available at employer events.
- Establish clear expectations about respectful behavior, and deliver consequences for those who fail to meet these expectations.
- Feature diverse people in organizational publications and presentations.
- Identify diversity as a core organizational value.
- Offer day care and summer programs for children of employees.
- Offer flexible dress codes to support ethnic and religious expression.
- Offer flexible schedules to accommodate employees whose children are in school or day care.
- Promote work–life balance.
- Provide benefits to domestic partners.
- Provide private restrooms to support individuals undergoing gender transitions.
- Provide private rooms and flexible schedules to accommodate religious practices.

the decision-making process: "Did I have an opportunity to share my perspective? Was my opinion considered?" The second is how decisions are made: "What influenced the decision? Were reliable data used to inform the final choice? Was the decision based on impartial evidence or as the result of preferential treatment?" The third factor is related to the way managers behave: "Was the rationale for the decision explained? Was I treated respectfully during the decision-making process?"[16]

Effective pharmacist managers use well-articulated values and consistent criteria to make and explain decisions. When employees perceive that they are being treated fairly, they are more likely to trust organizational leaders, support decisions and new directions, and demonstrate commitment.[16] When it comes to perceptions of fairness, the *content* of a decision—what is decided—is typically less important than the decision *process*, or how the decision was made. For example, for many employees the amount of funding available for continuing education is less important than how those dollars are allocated. Similarly, who was promoted matters less than an assurance that the selection was based on a valid and consistent set of criteria. When people believe they have been treated fairly, they are more likely to accept results and less likely to file complaints or pursue litigation. In one study, for example, researchers found that those who were not given an explanation of why they were dismissed were 10 times more likely to report suing their former company than employees given a complete explanation.[17] They also found that poor treatment during the termination process was the factor that best predicted whether an employee filed a wrongful termination lawsuit. Thus, to promote and demonstrate fairness, pharmacist managers should be transparent, consistent, and respectful—decision-making processes should be clear and applied consistently to all employees, and decisions, whether favorable or unfavorable, should be communicated in a respectful manner.

WORK CONTENT

- *Will I be successful here?*
- *Will I have the opportunity to demonstrate my unique talents?*
- *Will my work have meaning?*
- *Will I be trusted to accomplish my responsibilities without interference or excessive oversight?*
- *Will I receive feedback to support my success?*
- *Will I have the resources I need to accomplish my responsibilities?*

Work Strategy 1: Ensure a Match Between Employees and Their Jobs

People choose to leave organizations for many reasons, but two of the top reasons are (1) discovering that the job or workplace was not what the employee expected and (2) feeling that there is a mismatch between employees and their jobs.[18] To ensure success through role alignment and organizational fit, defined as the fit between the work to be done and an employee's qualifications to do that work, skillful managers engage in a rigorous preemployment screening process in which they explore potential employees' strengths, preferred working conditions, and career aspirations. They also ensure that these candidates get to know the organization, its culture, and the scope and conditions of work to establish a good cultural fit, defined as the fit between the environment in which the work will be done and what the employee needs to work in an effective and productive manner. Some organizations require candidates to participate in multiple interviews with a variety of employees and may even ask candidates to spend some time observing the work site or interacting with potential colleagues before an offer of employment.[18]

Often, work and working conditions that initially attracted an employee to a position change over time. Frequent communication with employees about the elements of their work they enjoy most and least provides opportunities to assess the feasibility of new or modified assignments. As with many healthcare professionals, pharmacists may prefer to work in certain specialty areas, such as pediatrics, geriatrics, internal medicine, acute care, or community practice. Assessing and addressing these preferences may prove to be an essential factor influencing attraction to, acceptance of, and remaining in a position.

Work Strategy 2: Link Work Efforts to Organizational Mission

Although the effect and importance of an employee's work to the larger organizational mission is typically evident to managers, it is not always as clear to others. ❼ *Explaining to employees how their work is essential to the organization's short- and long-term success increases employee commitment. This can be done in several ways, including using job descriptions to detail how an employee's duties are tied to broader organizational goals, using the organization's strategic plan to develop individual performance objectives, and having senior leaders formally recognize employees for their contributions to larger organizational results* (refer to

Chapter 13, "Achieving Results Through Others and Strategic Planning"). For example, an organization's mission might include optimizing health through appropriate medication use, with pharmacists playing a key role in clinical activities that reduce medication errors and medication-related problems. Pharmacists with outstanding contributions to this overall mission may be recognized for their work by receiving awards, honors, or other forms of recognition, such as monetary supplements, certificates, "employee of the month" designation, or supplementary annual leave (e.g., compensatory time). In addition, research has revealed that pharmacists engaged in increased clinical activities experience greater job satisfaction, which may, in turn, result in greater employee commitment.[19]

Work Strategy 3: Offer Autonomy

Employees tend to thrive when given space and time to do their work without unnecessary interference. Talented and disciplined employees do not require excessive supervision and tend to resent micromanagement. Managers can offer autonomy and ensure consistent results by being clear about what is expected and specific about how success will be measured, as well as addressing underperformance and recognizing those who meet or exceed expectations[20](refer to Chapter 19, "Effective Performance Management"). Although it is sometimes difficult for managers to offer autonomy to employees—managers may be reluctant to share power, or they may find it easier to complete a task rather than assigning it to someone else— effective managers recognize the abilities of their employees and use those abilities to achieve tasks and objectives. Mary Ann Allison, a business executive, organizational consultant, and author, offers the following advice to managers and organizational leaders: "Hire the best. Pay them fairly. Communicate frequently. Provide challenges and rewards. Believe in them. Get out of their way and they'll knock your socks off."[21]

Work Strategy 4: Provide Regular Feedback

Employees crave feedback. They want to know how they are doing and appreciate assurances that

their future career prospects are being considered. A Saratoga Institute study of 20,000 employees found that "too little coaching and feedback" and "feeling unrecognized and undervalued" were among the top reasons for employee turnover.[16] This may hold particularly true for pharmacists and support personnel whose work assignments and responsibilities become more routine and perhaps less challenging and rewarding over time. The best managers understand that a once-a-year performance evaluation is one of the least useful mechanisms for providing feedback and engage in regular coaching and feedback sessions (refer to Chapter 19, "Effective Performance Management"). During both formal and informal feedback sessions, effective managers seek to understand employees' evolving interests and career aspirations, as well as potential barriers to their success. They may ask about an employee's long-term career goals to identify learning opportunities to support them. They may also explore opportunities to help an employee achieve greater success, such as better time management practices or better writing skills. They communicate behaviors and actions that make employees effective, describe actions and behaviors that appear to be limiting success, and suggest approaches that will increase professional effectiveness.[22] According to John Mole, an authority on business culture, "Making sure that everyone in the organization knows exactly what his [or her] job is and what its purpose is and how it fits in—and how you know you are doing well—is an arduous and never ending process, but it's the single most important element in managing people."[23]

Work Strategy 5: Provide Resources and Infrastructure Required for Success

Overly bureaucratic policies, antiquated and unreliable data and prescription filling systems (including cumbersome order entry), inadequate computing equipment and other resources, and impractical protocols are among the things that make it difficult for employees to achieve success at work. Managers play an important role in identifying these barriers and ensuring that adequate systems and resources are in place to support optimal employee performance.[9]

CAREER

- *How secure is my job?*
- *How will my manager support my career growth?*
- *Will I have an opportunity to develop new skills and abilities?*

Career Strategy 1: Offer Employment for the Long Term

The expectation that employment will continue if performance meets organizational standards is a key criteria for fostering organizational commitment.[24] Job security is one of the top five job-related characteristics for employees regardless of age, gender, or race and ethnicity.[25,26] The Employers Resource Council found that job security ranked highly as both an attractor (an organizational attribute that attracts an individual to a position) and as a motivator (an organizational attribute that motivates an individual to perform well in a position).[24] Thus, providing a sense of job security may be used as a tool to support recruitment and increase organizational commitment. Although the competitive market for pharmacists may make job security less of a concern for these individuals, prospects for long-term employment tend to be more acute for those in support roles.

Career Strategy 2: Promote from Within

Feeling secure about long-term prospects for employment is not enough to maintain the commitment and enthusiasm of all high performers, however. These individuals want to know that outstanding performance will lead to new opportunities. Evidence suggests that the most successful organizations promote from within, and several studies have found that this strategy leads to better long-term results.[27–29] One study in particular found that 90% of the most successful companies promoted their chief executive officer from within, as compared with 50% of less successful competitors.[30] Choosing an internal candidate increases the likelihood that the person selected understands the culture, has built advantageous internal relationships, demonstrated critical organizational values, and established a level of trust that will provide support for future endeavors.[30] It also sends a message that talented employees can look forward to growth and advancement opportunities without having to move to another employer. Many retail chain pharmacies promote successful staff pharmacists to lead pharmacists who may then be promoted to district managers and other upper management positions. Similarly, in hospital practices, staff pharmacists and technicians may be promoted from within to pharmacist and technician managers and other internal leadership positions.

Of course, sometimes hiring from outside the organization is a more appropriate strategy. When new ideas or skills are needed, if dramatic change is required, or if an outsider is significantly more competent than an inside candidate, hiring from outside may be a more strategic approach.[31] In addition, an external candidate may be more aggressively pursued than an internal candidate and often receives greater resources, such as space, increased personnel, or salary increases for staff.

Career Strategy 3: Create Opportunities to Grow and Develop

Benjamin Franklin stated that "an investment in knowledge pays the best interest,"[32] and top organizations recognize the value of investing in their employees. Organizations offer clues about their commitment to growth and advancement through their approach to professional development and succession planning. ❽ *Strong managers understand that "promotability" does not happen by chance and are intentional in their approach to preparing employees for new and expanded roles. These managers tend to have a process for identifying and grooming employees for new roles and are therefore able to position excellent employees for expanded responsibilities.*[33] In recognizing the need for good leadership in pharmacy practice and education, many national professional pharmacy organizations, such as the American Society of Health-System Pharmacists, the American College of Clinical Pharmacy, and the American Association of Colleges of Pharmacy, offer leadership training.

Development can occur in many ways. Employers can provide tuition assistance to support degree attainment or certification, send employees to internal or external professional development programs, or support other continuing education opportunities. Formal or informal **mentoring** is another way to develop an employee's talents and can be especially helpful in honing interpersonal skills and increasing organizational acumen. For example, a mentor might provide guidance on how to negotiate organizational politics, give constructive feedback about public speaking skills, or identify key people for an employee to get to know. Formal and informal feedback can be an especially powerful tool if the process is constructive and provides the employee with specific suggestions for improvement. **Executive coaching**, a benefit that can be offered to senior-level personnel, involves matching the employee with an experienced coach from outside the organization to provide objective feedback related to one's leadership style and communication and interpersonal skills. **Stretch assignments**, challenging assignments that provide opportunities to learn new things, can prepare employees for larger and more complex roles. For example, a manager may request that an employee create a business plan for a new project the organization is considering. Increasing an employee's scope of responsibility can provide employees with an opportunity to demonstrate expertise or leadership potential.[34] Committee assignments, temporary assignments, and internships are additional options to support development and prepare employees for advancement opportunities.

BENEFITS

- *Is there support for work–life balance?*
- *Will my employer's insurance programs protect my health and assets?*
- *Will my employer's retirement program enable me to retire with adequate financial resources?*

Benefits Strategy 1: Support Employees' Work–Life Balance

Twenty-nine percent of U.S. workers consider work–life balance and flexibility to be the most important factor when considering job offers.[35] ◆ *When employees are unable to manage their work roles and personal responsibilities, they may experience significant stress that can lead to illness, increased healthcare costs, unscheduled absences,* *lower productivity, reduced satisfaction, and higher employee turnover.*

A number of factors lead to work–life stress. Healthcare professionals often work long hours and are required to be on-call during non-work hours. Being constantly connected by cell phones, pagers, and e-mail has increasingly blurred the lines between one's work and one's personal time. Longer work commutes and child care may also lead to work–life stress. While we often think of child-care issues as a stressor for working mothers, it is an increasing concern for working fathers as well. Child care is not the only dependent care issue—eldercare needs are on the rise as the workforce ages, thereby prompting a new set of concerns and resource needs.[36] Employees' interests in life outside of work can also prompt work–life balance concerns. These interests can range from attending graduate school, playing in a community orchestra, or playing on a softball team. Rigid schedules or excessive workloads that impede employees' ability to have a life after work can easily increase stress and reduce commitment.

Although some organizations offer more resource options than others when it comes to such benefits as child- and eldercare services, managers often have the power to address some of employees' most pressing needs through simple scheduling changes. In other instances, having additional employees to provide adequate coverage may be required.

Although **telecommuting** is usually not seen in traditional pharmacy settings, such as retail establishments or hospitals, its use is growing. Telecommuters work from home and stay connected to their workplace through telephone, videoconferencing, other electronic means, and occasional on-site meetings. Some telecommuters work at home exclusively, while others work at home a few days a week, and others just occasionally. Telecommuting may reduce stressful and expensive commuting, may decrease the need for establishing an office/workspace on-site, and may accommodate family or personal interests by providing flexibility to focus on getting work done rather than on where it gets done. This option is only for employees whose work does not require a constant on-site presence, such as some drug information specialists who can consult by phone or by electronic means and pharmacists who review prior authorization requests for insurance plans. Information technology professionals and administrative personnel who support inpatient and outpatient pharmacy practices may also find telecommuting to be a viable option. Other examples of telecommuting typically seen in pharmacy include consultants and freelance writers.

Compressed workweeks allow employees to work longer hours in return for more days off. Typical models include four 10-hour days each week and nine days over a two-week period. Many hospital pharmacy programs have used schedules for pharmacists that include seven days on followed by seven days off, thus ensuring consistency in work activities and allowing employees several consecutive days off to accommodate personal commitments.

Flextime permits employees to arrive early in the day or to stay later in the evening, depending on needs and preferences. Typically, presence during "core hours" is required (e.g., between 10:30 a.m. and 2:30 p.m.) to support meeting attendance or coworker interaction. Many pharmacies enjoy the added benefit of having at least two pharmacists on duty at the same time to cover busy periods or to exchange important data concerning patient care.

Job sharing is a less common but often appealing approach that enables two individuals to divide the responsibilities of a single job. They work together to ensure adequate coverage and delivery of project or task results, typically working different days or hours. This can be a particularly appealing option for pharmacists who want to work fewer hours to accommodate family responsibilities.[37]

For many employees, workload and schedule flexibility may also be an important benefit before retirement. As employees age, more organizations are beginning to offer **phased retirement** options. These arrangements typically allow employees to reduce their work hours over a period of a few years to transition into retirement. The employee gets the benefit of a reduced work schedule and the opportunity to ease into retirement, while employers are able to retain critical talent and enjoy adequate time to secure a replacement.

Although flexible options are appealing to employees, few organizations have formal programs or policies associated with flexible working options, and if they exist, the policies tend to be ad hoc and poorly communicated. As a result, these arrangements are underused and employers miss an opportunity to provide a highly desirable benefit.[38] Managers who package and promote these benefits will have a competitive advantage over those who do not. However, pharmacist managers and leaders must consider the structure of the organization, the work environment, and the nature of the work when considering flexible work schedule options. While some organizational settings are conducive to more flexible work schedules, others are not, and leaders and managers must be aware of these limitations. For example, a community pharmacy setting needs a licensed pharmacist to be on-site to dispense medications during set hours. There is little room for flexibility within this requirement; thus, physical presence during these hours is expected and part of the pharmacist's job duties.

Benefits Strategy 2: Offer an Array of Benefit Options to Meet Employees' Different Needs and Life Stages

Ask a 25-year-old and a 56-year old to describe their ideal set of benefits, and their responses will probably differ markedly. Younger employees tend to express interest in paid time off, flexible schedules, and tuition remission options, while older employees tend to be attracted to comprehensive health insurance options, retirement plans, and eldercare resources to support aging relatives.[39] Managers should seek to understand which benefits tend to matter most based on employee life stage and then emphasize the value of those benefits during the recruitment and retention process.

While benefit offerings tend to be designed at the corporate level or by organizational leaders, managers should be alert to their employees' satisfaction with current programs and services and share this information with plan designers. **Table 20–3** provides a list of popular benefit options.

Benefits Strategy 3: Communicate the Value of Benefit Offerings

In many organizations, benefits can represent a significant percentage of an employee's total

---

TABLE **20-3**	**Popular Employee Benefits**

Educational Programs
Continuing education funds
Scholarships
Tuition assistance/reimbursement for
  employees and dependents

Financial Security Programs
Dependent care spending accounts
Discounts to area businesses
Financial education
Financial planning services
Healthcare spending accounts
Legal services
Retirement plans

Health and Wellness Programs
Employee assistance programs
Fitness center affiliations
Health-risk assessments
On-site fitness centers
On-site meditation, yoga, weight reduction
  and stress-reduction programs
Wellness fairs

Insurance Programs
Dental insurance
Health insurance
Identity theft insurance
Life insurance
Long-term disability insurance
Malpractice insurance
Pet insurance
Short-term disability insurance
Vision care insurance

Leave Programs
Holiday pay
Paid or unpaid parental leave
Sick pay
Vacation pay

Parenting and Family Resources
Adoption assistance
Child-care discounts
Child-care resource and referral services
Eldercare resource and referral services
Lactation rooms for nursing mothers
On-site child care
Sick and emergency child-care services

---

compensation package. For pharmacists, benefits typically constitute approximately 25–35% of an individual's total compensation package (and this percentage might be higher for technicians). Unfortunately, few employees are aware of this and tend to focus almost exclusively on their salary or wages. Likewise, when employees consider benefits, they tend to focus on health insurance or retirement plans, not appreciating the variety of options available to them. Reminding employees of the array of benefits offered (Table 20–3) and the value of each can contribute significantly to enhanced employee satisfaction and commitment.

COMPENSATION

Is my pay competitive?
Are top performers recognized more than average performers?
Are pay processes fair?

Compensation Strategy 1: Develop and Communicate a Compensation Philosophy

A **compensation philosophy** represents an organization's stated approach to allocating compensation dollars. Some organizations seek to pay salaries above market, some strive to pay

TABLE 20–4	The Employee Value Proposition and Employee Engagement Strategies

Components of Employee Value Proposition	Employee Engagement Strategies
Affiliation	Be explicit about organizational values.
	Communicate a compelling vision.
	Create a culture of inclusion.
	Create a safe work environment.
	Emphasize a distinctive organizational mission.
	Focus on fairness.
Work Content	Ensure a match between employees and their jobs.
	Link work efforts to organizational mission.
	Provide constant feedback.
	Provide resources and infrastructure required for success.
	Offer autonomy.
Career	Create opportunities to grow and develop.
	Offer employment for the long term.
	Promote from within.
Benefits	Communicate the value of benefit offerings.
	Offer an array of benefit options to meet employees' different needs and life stages.
	Support employees' work–life balance.
Compensation	Develop and communicate a compensation philosophy.
	Pay attention to pay processes.
	Pay attention to top performers.
	Use pay strategically.

Source: Adapted from The Segal Group, Inc., parent company and its Sibson Consulting Division. © 2008. All rights reserved.

salaries comparable to their competitors, and still others intentionally pay less than the market, knowing that their benefits or organizational climate will be sufficient to attract quality talent. A comprehensive compensation philosophy should describe how pay will be calibrated internally and externally, and what factors will be rewarded (such factors may include exceptional performance, longevity, and proficiency or the acquisition of new skills). The compensation philosophy should also clearly and explicitly state the link between compensation and organizational values. Many *employees* believe pay should be linked to seniority, while many *organizations* value performance and proficiency over longevity. A compensation philosophy statement can help managers explain the principles that guide how salaries and wages are established and modified.

Compensation Strategy 2: Use Pay Strategically

Managers have an array of financial reward options based on their organization's culture and practices. **Base pay** programs provide employees with regular and expected wages and salaries. **Variable pay programs** link one-time rewards to the accomplishment of certain goals or tasks. Stock options provide employees with the opportunity to acquire company stock and realize returns based on organizational performance. **Merit increases** raise base pay according to performance. **Cost-of-living allowances** increase pay based on changes in the consumer price index. Sign-on bonuses can be used to attract new employees, and **retention bonuses** can be used in return for a commitment not to leave an organization. All of these financial incentives are commonly used to attract, reward, and retain pharmacy personnel. Refer to Chapter 18, "Successful Recruitment and Hiring Strategies," for additional information.

Compensation Strategy 3: Pay Attention to Top Performers

10 *Effective managers understand that high performers expect to be recognized for their accomplishments, provided with more flexibility than others,* *compensated to a greater extent than lower performers, and provided with multiple opportunities to develop and advance* (refer to Chapter 19, "Effective Performance Management"). They also understand that top performers have more employment options and pose a greater "flight risk" than their underperforming counterparts. Armed with this knowledge, they pursue several strategies to reward and retain key employees.

Compensation Strategy 4: Pay Attention to Pay Processes

The importance of fairness and consistency was emphasized in the earlier discussion of strategies that bolster a sense of organizational affiliation. While employees value fairness in all matters, the perceived fairness of financial rewards is especially important to employee commitment. Research studies have revealed that the amount of pay employees receive typically matters far less than the way pay decisions are made.[40,41] Clear and consistent explanations about how salaries are established and pay increases are awarded augment employees' confidence in decision-making processes.

SUMMARY

Although organizations differ in their missions, values, and unique employee value propositions, their distinct attributes play a significant role in making workplaces desirable to current and potential employees. Pharmacist managers who assess their employees' diverse needs and interests and act in accordance with organizational values will enjoy a significant advantage in a competitive labor market. And pharmacists who evaluate prospective employers against the strategies described in this chapter will gravitate toward employers most likely to offer a positive and enriching work environment. This chapter reviewed basic principles of employee engagement and provided practical strategies (**Table 20–4**) to create desirable workplaces that attract, retain, and inspire quality employees committed to achieving organizational goals.

References

1. Knapp D. Professionally determined need for pharmacy services in 2020. *Am J Pharm Educ* 2002; 66:421–429.

2. US Department of Labor, Bureau of Labor Statistics. Tomorrow's jobs. *Occupational Outlook Handbook*. Available at: http://www.bls.gov/oco/oco2003.htm. Accessed May 30, 2008.

3. The list of industry stars. *Fortune Magazine*. March 13, 2008:77–84.

4. Corporate Leadership Council. *Managing for High Performance and Retention: The Key Drivers of Employee Engagement*. Arlington, VA: Corporate Executive Board; 2008.

5. Great Places to Work Institute. Available at: http://www.greatplacetowork.com/great/graphs.php. Accessed May 30, 2008.

6. Mulvey PW, Ledford GE Jr, LeBlanc PV. The rewards of work: how they drive performance, retention and satisfaction. *WorldatWork* (formerly *ACA J*) 2000;9: 6–18.

7. Lencioni P. *Obsessions of an Extraordinary Executive*. San Francisco, CA: Jossey-Bass; 2000.

8. McMulland T, Stark M. The role of line managers and HR in rewarding effectiveness. *WorldatWork* 2008;2: 30–43.

9. CVS CareMark. Our vision, mission, and values. Available at: http://www.cvscaremark.com/our-company/our-culture/vision-mission-values. Accessed June 30, 2008.

10. Genentech. Our values. Available at: http://www.gene.com/gene/careers/culture/values.html. Accessed June 30, 2008.

11. Buckingham M, Coffman C. *First Break All the Rules*. New York, NY: Simon and Schuster; 1999.

12. US Census. Available at: http://quickfacts.census.gov/qfd/states/00000.html. Accessed May 30, 2008.

13. Institute of Medicine. *In the Nation's Compelling Interest: Ensuring Diversity in the Healthcare Workforce*. Washington, DC: Academic Medicine; 2004.

14. American Society of Health-System Pharmacists House of Delegates Session 2008. *Board of Directors Report on the Council on Public Policy*. Available at: http://www.ashp.org/s_ashp/docs/files/HOD_PublicPolicy.pdf. Accessed June 10, 2008.

15. Sirota D, Mischkind L, Meltzer M. Stop demotivating your employees! *Harv Manage Update* 2006;11:1–4.

16. Brockner J. Why It's So Hard to Be fair. *Harvard Bus Rev* 2006;March:122–129.

17. Lind EA, Greenberg J, Scott KS, Welchans TD. The winding road from employee to complainant: situational and psychological determinants of wrongful-termination claims. *Adm Sci Q* 2000;45:557–590.

18. Branham L. *The 7 Hidden Reasons Employees Leave*. New York, NY: AMACOM; 2005.

19. Olson DS, Lawson KA. Relationship between hospital pharmacists' job satisfaction and involvement in clinical activities. *Am J Health-Syst Pharm* 1996;53: 281–284.

20. Anderberg M, Froeschle R. Becoming an employer of choice: strategies for worker recruitment and retention. *Benefits Compens Digest* 2006;43. Available at: http://www.ifebp.org/pdf/webexclusive/06apr.pdf. Accessed May 30, 2008.

21. Allison MA, Allison E. *Managing Up, Managing Down*. New York, NY: Simon and Schuster; 1986.

22. Dale J, Potts H. Improving employee performance through performance coaching. *Workspan* 2007;111: 23–27.

23. Mole J. *Management Mole: Lessons from Office Life*. London: Bantam Press; 1998.

24. Elling B. What distinguishes the outstanding HR executives from others. In: Losey M, Meisinger S, Ulrich D, eds. *The Future of HR Management*. Hoboken, NJ: John Wiley & Sons; 2005:126–133.

25. Chao GT, Gardner PD. Importance characteristics of early career jobs: what do young adults want? Available at: http://ceri.msu.edu/publications/pdf/JobChar4-16.pdf. Accessed June 10, 2008.

26. Employers Resource Council. 2005 Job attributes importance survey results. Available at: http://www.northcoast99.com/reports/2005_jais_report.pdf. Accessed June 10, 2008.

27. Rauch JE. Leadership selection, internal promotion, and bureaucratic corruption in less developed polities. *Can J Econ* 2001;34:240–258.

28. Cannella AA Jr, Shen W. So close and yet so far: promotion versus exit for CEO heirs apparent. *Acad Manage J* 2001;44:252–270.

29. Bayo-Moriones A, Ortin-Angel P. Internal promotion versus external recruitment in industrial plants. Working Paper 200303, Department of Business Economics, Universitat Autonoma de Barcelona; 2003.

30. Collins J. *Good to Great*. New York, NY: HarperCollins; 2001.

31. Ulrich D, Smallwood N. *Why the Bottom Line Isn't!* Hoboken, NJ: John Wiley & Sons; 2003.

32. Becker GS. Human capital and the economy. *Proc Am Philos Soc* 1992;136:85–92.

33. Ready D, Conger J. Make your company a talent factory. *Harv Bus Rev* 2007;June:68–77.

34. O'Brien D. Moving beyond mentoring: developing high-potential employees. *Workspan* 2008;April: 26–29.

35. Hudson Institute. *In the Game of Hiring, Flexible Employers Win.* Press release; February 12, 2008.

36. Dychtwald K, Erickson T, Morison R. *Workforce Crisis: How to Beat the Coming Shortage of Skills and Talent.* Boston, MA: Harvard Business School Press; 2006.

37. Finks S, Rogers K. Job sharing. *Am J Health-Syst Pharm* 2008;65:69–72.

38. Hewitt Associates. Lack of consistency, communication and measurement tools around workplace flexibility leads to under-valued programs. Available at: http://www.hewittassociates.com/Intl/NA/en-US/AboutHewitt/Newsroom/PressReleaseDetail.aspx?cid=5074. Accessed May 30, 2008.

39. Redebaugh G, Hillard T. Aging of Aquarius. Presented at the College and University Professional Association for Human Resources Northwest Regional Conference; Boise, Idaho; April 14, 2008.

40. Sanfey A, Rilling J, Aronson J, et al. The neural basis of economic decision-making in the ultimatum game. *Science* 2003;13:1755–1758.

41. Ermanno T. Worker satisfaction and perceived fairness: result of a survey in public, and non-profit organizations. Working Paper 0604, Department of Economics. Department of Economics, University of Trento, Italia; 2006.

Case Scenarios

CASE ONE: You are struggling to compete for pharmacists for your nonprofit children's hospital and suspect it is because you cannot offer the salaries, sign-on bonuses, or stock options available from your retail and industry counterparts. You have worked for this hospital for 18 years, and although you know that you could earn a larger salary in the for-profit sector, you stay because you value the opportunity to be affiliated with a nationally recognized organization with such an important mission. Given how competitive the market is for pharmacists, what strategies might you employ to attract pharmacists who could easily secure larger compensation packages elsewhere?

CASE TWO: You are the pharmacy manager of a store that has been designated as "underperforming." As a result, you need to close your store within 3 months and will not be able to offer employment in other locations to anyone other than your pharmacists. Your corporate leadership has tied your employment security to your ability to keep your store open and profitable during its final three months. Because there are few job opportunities in your community, you are concerned that the closure will result in negative publicity, and you are worried about your employees' future employment prospects. What strategies might you use to keep the store running while honoring the contributions of its soon-to-be-jobless employees?

CASE THREE: You are a staff pharmacist at the University Medical Center (UMC). A few days ago you overheard Molly Bryant, a pharmacy technician and part-time university student, complaining about her salary to a coworker. According to Molly, she could earn a higher salary by going to work for another hospital across town. She is an excellent technician and a valuable employee, and it would be difficult for the pharmacy to lose her. The UMC pharmacy has allowed her to work evening shifts so that she may attend classes during the day and provided her with tuition reimbursement. With this knowledge in hand, what could you do as a staff pharmacist to help the pharmacy retain this valuable technician?

CASE FOUR: Hannah Lee is a brilliant pharmacist, but she is rude and abusive to her employees and coworkers. She seems to delight in

(continues)

embarrassing new employees and is famous for asking, "What? Are you really that stupid?" whenever someone asks her a question she deems too simple. Despite her questionable interpersonal skills, Dr. Lee is an otherwise excellent employee. She is, without question, the smartest pharmacist on your staff—physicians respect her and patients like her. She is highly regarded for catching potentially dangerous drug interactions and protecting patients from unnecessary harm. You rely on her more than any other member of your team and have been willing to ignore her behavior because of her value to you. You know that a couple of employees have left because they couldn't deal with her, and it appears that more might be on their way. A few have confided to you, "It's her or us." What are your options?

CASE FIVE: You have two exceptional staff members. Sanjay Singh graduated from a college

of pharmacy two years ago. Despite being new to the profession, he has forged exceptional relationships with customers and vendors. His strong connections have saved you both time and money and occasionally enabled you to receive discounts and emergency shipments that would not have otherwise been possible. Marissa Lewis, a pharmacy technician, reorganizes inventory systems and databases "for fun" and, as a result, your pharmacy has been exceptionally organized and efficient since she arrived 14 months ago. You should be delighted to have two talented and motivated employees, but you worry constantly that they will find better offers and leave. What options might you explore to retain them both?

Additional Resources Available Online!

Visit the Student Companion Web site at http://healthprofessions.jbpub.com/pharmacymanagement for interactive study tools and additional resources.

See www.rxugace.com to learn how you can obtain continuing pharmacy education for this content.

COMMUNICATION

COMMUNICATING EFFECTIVELY WITH OTHERS

DONNA S. WEST-STRUM, PhD, MS, RPh

JAN K. HASTINGS, PharmD, FAPhA

LEARNING OBJECTIVES

After reading this chapter, the reader will be able to

1. Explain why effective communication skills are important to pharmacist managers.
2. Describe the sender–receiver model of communication.
3. Explain how relationships affect communication.
4. Identify the importance of verbal and nonverbal communication.
5. List communication barriers.
6. Apply active listening skills.
7. Tailor messages appropriately for the intended audience.
8. Define authentic voice and its use in pharmacy management.
9. Determine when passive language is more appropriate than active language.
10. Detail the pros and cons of various mediums of communications (e.g., print, phone, e-mail).

KEY CONCEPTS

❶ Research on employee engagement has revealed that employees who have regular and respectful communication with their supervisors are more likely to be productive, provide excellent customer service, be satisfied with their employment, and remain loyal to their employer.

❷ A person's perception of a situation is his or her reality, so managers must be careful about the words and approaches they use to communicate with others and must be sensitive to the physical, semantic, personal, and time barriers that may impede effective communication.

❸ Effective communication occurs when the sender and receiver interpret the meaning of the message in the same way.

❹ Any face-to-face communication contains three elements: (1) words, (2) tone of voice, and (3) body language. Collectively, these three aspects are often referred to as the "Three V's": verbal, voice, and visual.

❺ Nonverbal communication includes body language, facial expressions, and even one's clothing choices.

❻ Physical communication barriers can often be more symbolic than real.

❼ Semantic barriers occur when people assign different meanings to words.

❽ Sensitivity to cultural and gender-related communication styles is an essential competency for members of the pharmacy profession.

❾ E-mail is appropriate for the one-way dissemination of easy-to-understand messages.

❿ Employees are more likely to accept difficult news if they understand the rationale behind it.

INTRODUCTION

Pharmacists have long understood the importance of good patient communication skills and their effect on patient outcomes. The National Health Quality Report encourages providers to adopt a patient-centered model of healthcare delivery because of the positive effects of this type of relationship on patient morbidity and mortality, as well as overall costs to the healthcare system.[1] The principles that apply to patients apply to employees as well. ❶ *Indeed, research on employee engagement has revealed that employees who have regular and respectful communication with their supervisors are more likely to be productive, provide excellent customer service, be satisfied with their employment, and remain loyal to their employer.* Alternatively, managers with poor communication skills tend to cause their employees to disengage. Poor communication between a manager and an employee can lead to confusion about expectations, resentment, and ultimately poor performance and employee turnover.[2] In fact, poor communication is often cited as a key factor prompting employees to leave their jobs.[3]

Poor communication can take many forms. Employees may report that no one asks their opinion; they don't have a sense of the organization's direction; or they do not understand messages that are conveyed. A statement from a manager such as, "We are going to have to cut costs around here" could be interpreted to mean that jobs are in jeopardy when the manager only intended to convey the importance of managing inventory more efficiently. ❷ *A person's perception of a situation is his or her reality so managers must be careful about the words and approaches they use to communicate with others and must be sensitive to the physical, semantic, personal, and time barriers that may impede effective communication.*[4,5] This chapter will provide the reader with tools to overcome a variety of communication barriers and to discuss strategies for conveying information effectively.

COMMUNICATION PROCESS
Sender–Receiver Model

Communicating with employees, patients, and clients requires a fundamental understanding of the communication process, which includes a sender, a receiver, barriers, and feedback.[4,5] In the communication process, one person is the sender and one person is the receiver. The sender is the person who conveys the message word and nonverbal cues. The receiver decodes the words and symbols to interpret the message and then becomes the sender by giving feedback on the message to the receiver (who originated the message). There can be barriers to the communication process on the part of the sender, the receiver, or both. Because these barriers can block or confuse the intended message, the sender must transmit the message in a way that allows it to be accurately received. The same is true when the receiver gives feedback to the sender. ❸ Effective communication *occurs when the sender and receiver interpret the meaning of the message in the same way.*

The association between the sender and the receiver is important to the effectiveness of the communication process. Every time two people have a communication transaction, a relationship is formed. Sometimes, the transaction results in positive feelings, and sometimes it results in negative feelings. These feelings, or residuals of the transaction, are present the next time the two people communicate with each other and affect the new transaction.[6] Given this, pharmacist managers should work to establish good rapport with their employees.

Pharmacist managers must encourage **open communication** and create a culture that promotes a free exchange of ideas. Employees need to know that honesty is valued. Some managers will state that they have an open-door policy, meaning they want employees to come by and talk to them about anything, ranging from problems and concerns to new ideas. This type of openness tends to promote goodwill among employees and provides the manager with important and timely insights. A pharmacist manager who claims to have an open-door policy but fails to be open to occasional drop-in conversations compromises his or her credibility.

Verbal and Nonverbal Communication

In the communication process, pharmacist managers should ensure congruence between verbal and nonverbal messages. ❹ *Any face-to-face communication contains three elements: (1) words, (2) tone of voice, and (3) body language. Collectively, these three aspects are often referred to as the "Three V's": verbal, voice, and visual.*[7] Mixed messages occur when a person says one thing, but the body language, tone, or other nonverbal cues suggest something different. Attention to verbal and **nonverbal communication** can reduce mixed messages.

VERBAL COMMUNICATION

Verbal communication relies on words and sounds to deliver a message,[8] and the way these messages are received can be influenced by voice qualities, such as rate, volume, and intonation.[5] Voice pitch, tone, and rate can elicit positive or negative perceptions.

Warmth and genuineness are positive, while hesitancy and tension tend to be perceived negatively. Rapid speech may be perceived as bossy or dismissive. A few seconds of silence to gather one's thoughts are generally better received by the audience than interrupters, such as "uh" and "you know," which tend to minimize the effect of messages and make the speaker appear unconfident or ill prepared. Although most speakers focus on the content of their messages, astute communicators also pay attention to the way in which their words are delivered.

NONVERBAL COMMUNICATION

Communication is not always verbal. Think about how a baby communicates his or her wants and needs. No words are spoken, and yet mom and dad know when the baby is hungry, when the baby is happy, when the diaper needs changing, and when the baby needs to be held. Each communication is different, and the parents learn quickly to distinguish the cries, squeaks, and giggles so that the baby's needs are met. Researchers estimate that nonverbal communication may account for more than 90% of the way messages are received.[8] The face alone is capable of expressing 250,000 messages.[9] ❺*Nonverbal communication includes body language, facial expressions, and even one's clothing choices.*[5,10,11]

Consider talking to pharmacists about a new approach to scheduling. One pharmacist looks at you directly and nods her head as you speak. The other crosses his arms, shifts from foot to foot, and looks around the room during the conversation. Neither individual uses words, but the first pharmacist conveys interest and openness, while the second signals disagreement or annoyance. Although interpreting body language is an imprecise art (e.g., folded arms may signal disagreement or it may be a reaction to a cold room), attention to people's posture, facial expressions, hand movements, sitting position, and eye movement and contact can provide clues about what they truly believe.[12,13]

Distance between communicating parties is another way people express nonverbal communication. For most people in western cultures like the United States, personal space falls between 18 inches and 4 feet. Unless two people have a close friendship or intimate relationship, getting closer than 18 inches may be perceived as rudeness or aggression.[11] A distance of more than 4 feet is equally awkward, as this space makes it difficult to have a private conversation and may make the other person uncomfortable.[11,14]

Facial expressions can encourage or discourage communication.[6] A smile is the most pleasant expression and can make difficult messages easier to hear. Eyes are another expressive attribute of the face. Steady eye contact is generally perceived as an expression of assertiveness as it communicates to the listener that you are in fact listening. Failing to maintain eye contact or shifting eyes from side to side may signal untrustworthiness. Some believe that looking down when answering a question can be a sign of lying. Caution is advised when interpreting the meaning of eye contact, however, as in some cultures, a direct gaze is disrespectful.[15,16]

The way one presents himself or herself is another form of nonverbal communication. An assertive walk; erect posture; good eye contact; a strong, firm handshake; neatness; and professional and well-pressed attire are all signals of personal and professional confidence.

REDUCING BARRIERS TO EFFECTIVE COMMUNICATION

A variety of factors can impede effective communication, including physical barriers, status differentials, time constraints, and word choices.[4-6]

Physical Barriers

One of the most common physical barriers to communication is distance between two parties. When a manager works in one location and an employee works in another, the lack of day-to-day interaction can result in inadequate or strained communication. Individuals within proximity to one another tend to engage in both formal and informal communication more frequently and find their interactions to be less strained than those who interact less often.[6] Regular communication can mitigate physical barriers. Phone calls, regular meetings, text or e-mail messages, webcams, and videoconferencing (e.g., **telepharmacy**) are all strategies to enhance communication when physical proximity is an issue.

◆ *Physical communication barriers can often be more symbolic than real.* Classic examples of this phenomenon are an office or a large desk that separates the manager from the employee. Pharmacist managers should be aware that entering an office may feel like an intrusion or that a large desk may make the employee feel less important—perceptions that may reduce their comfort in communicating. Keeping an office door open and meeting side by side at a table rather than across a desk can encourage better communication.

Status Differential Barriers

Communication often differs based on the direction messages are sent. Downward communication, in which a supervisor communicates with an employee, tends to command or instruct. Upward communication from an employee to a supervisor tends to inform, as employees are not typically expected to give directions to the people to whom they report.[17] Although downward and upward communication conventions are common, they do not lend themselves to effective organizational communication. Status differentials can impede effective communication when those with less status are discouraged from sharing concerns and those with more status are not open to hearing them.[6] Minimize status barriers by creating an environment in which all employees feel free to ask questions, and opinions are solicited and valued regardless of one's title or professional status. Such openness is especially critical in a pharmacy setting in which failure to raise objections or concerns could affect patient safety. For example, a pharmacist technician should feel comfortable telling a pharmacist when he or she believes a prescription may be filled incorrectly to prevent a medication error.

Time Barriers

Time barriers are common in pharmacies as they are often busy and high-stress environments, and pharmacist managers may be perceived as being too busy to talk. Given this, it is important for managers to talk with employees, even when they do not indicate an immediate need for conversation. Scheduling regular opportunities to talk with employees individually and collectively may seem time consuming but may actually save time and resources in the long run as valuable suggestions are provided and potential confusion is minimized.

Semantic Barriers

◆*Semantic barriers occur when people assign different meanings to words.* For example, a pharmacist may use the word "soon" to signify "in the next hour," while a technician may believe "soon" implies "within the week." We all tend to assume that because we know what we mean to say when we speak that everyone else will know as well. However, words are often assigned different meanings by different people.[12] Unless two people agree on the meaning assigned to those words, communication can be hampered. Words with ambiguous or vague meaning, such as "several," "few," "shortly," "soon," or "in the near future," should be avoided to minimize confusion and disappointment. An individual's background, occupation, or experience can affect verbal understanding as well. Literacy levels can also influence how people interpret and understand messages. When delivering a message to a group with variable literacy levels, communicating so that those with the least education can understand the message ensures that all employees have the opportunity to grasp the key points. For example, the phrase "providing even better customer service will help us increase sales" is more likely to be understood by all employees than "sustained increases in month-over-month profitability will require us to enhance the patient and customer value proposition." **Table 21-1** lists some factors that can lead to word disagreement:

- Consider the words "cut" and "heel." When hearing these words, a butcher may envision something very different than a healthcare professional.
- The acronym "GI" will be understood differently depending on context. Does it mean a group of veterans or gastrointestinal tract?
- Does "cheap" mean inexpensive or poor quality?

Cultural and Gender-Related Barriers

The United States is increasingly diverse,[6,18] and the ability to communicate effectively with people of varied backgrounds and experiences is essential for providing quality health care. Sensitivity to varied traditions (e.g., home remedies, use of

TABLE **21-1**	**Factors That May Lead to Word Disagreement**

- Age
- Context
- Connotation
- Culture or subculture
- Experience
- Gender
- Geographic origin
- National origin
- Occupation
- Slang
- Type or level of education

healers, religious beliefs) is critical to providing advice in a professional setting.[19] Appreciating cultural differences also supports effective management and ensures that all members of the organization feel respected and included. Culture can influence how people address one another (e.g., first names or Mr./Mrs./Dr.), how they handle conflict, and how they interpret nonverbal behavior, such as eye contact or hand gestures. For example, in the United States, the A-OK hand gesture means everything is fine, but in some cultures, the gesture is obscene.[16]

Gender-related communication styles can also contribute to cultural and semantic barriers. Linguist Deborah Tannen's research on communication styles has revealed that women and men often differ in their speaking characteristics and conversational rituals, which can result in significant misunderstandings. Through her field research, Tannen discovered that women are more likely than men to be indirect in their workplace conversations. For example, a female manager who asks,

"Can you have this ready by 5:00?" may actually mean "Please have this done by 5:00." Tannen also found that women sometimes ask questions rather than make demands to maintain relationships and to convey teamwork and mutual cooperation.[20]

A lack of directness is also observed in many nonwestern cultures, where the ability to sense another person's meaning and intentions is considered a sign of maturity. Indeed, in some cultures, direct demands may be considered infantile, rude, and unprofessional.[21,22] ❽ *Sensitivity to cultural and gender-related communication styles is an essential competency for members of the pharmacy profession.*

COMMUNICATION APPROACHES

Active Listening

Active listening, the act of hearing with thoughtful attention, is difficult for most people. While listening involves the same language skills as reading and writing, few people receive significant formal instruction about how to be a good listener.[23] Listening is also difficult because of the difference in the amount of material people can understand in a minute versus the amount of information that most people can speak in a minute. Most people speak at about 150 words per minute, yet the human mind can understand at a rate of approximately 400 words per minute.[8] This gap leaves time for our minds to wander and makes it difficult to stay focused on the speaker.

Active listening is affected by the four S's: speaker, setting, style, and subject.[24] Think of the active listener as the center of a circle surrounded by these four elements. Does the listener know the speaker? Does a relationship already exist? Is it positive or negative? What about the setting? Is it a noisy conference hall or a quiet room? Are there few people present or is there a crowd? If you are listening to a speech, is the speaker's style making appropriate use of technology? Does the slide presentation complement or overpower the speaker's message? And last, is the subject simple or complex? Is it something familiar to the audience, or is the material completely new? All of these factors affect recipients' ability to listen.

There are many benefits of active listening for the manager.[4,25] When managers listen carefully,

they learn from what they hear. The people to whom they are listening appreciate that they are paying attention to them and are usually willing to share even more information. When employees know that their manager is listening attentively, there is often increased cooperation, greater productivity, and better morale.

To improve listening, the pharmacist manager should remove any communication barriers and then focus on the conversation. Stop talking and do not interrupt. Discontinue all other tasks and look directly at the person. Listen for the message, considering both verbal and nonverbal communication. Then provide a response or feedback.[26] There are several techniques that a pharmacy manager can use to show the employee that he or she is listening:[4,25]

- Let the employee know you hear the message, both the emotion and content.
- Probe or ask questions to clarify the information presented.
- Advise or provide comments.
- Paraphrase or use your own words to describe what the person is saying.
- Reflect by providing an empathetic response.
- Use nonverbal communication such as head nodding.

Tailoring the Message to the Audience

When communicating with any audience, it is best to know as much as possible about them.[19] Messages should contain the appropriate language and content for the audience and be sensitive to cultural, generational, and gender differences. Simple language is generally most effective, and excessive jargon should be avoided.[12] Aligning messages with employee interests is critical as well.[25] For example, if the pharmacy is getting a new computer system and all employees are required to attend training, the message should be delivered in a way that is appealing to them. Simply telling employees that they are required to attend a computer training program may not be well received. A better approach would be to stress the ways in which the new system will streamline work.

Taking care to communicate in ways that recipients are most comfortable is important as well. If the person to whom you report appreciates concise executive summaries, providing long and detailed reports would be unwise. Likewise, communicating key information verbally to an employee who prefers written instructions may result in miscommunication and even serious errors.

Demonstrating Authenticity

The path of authenticity takes us inwards to our highest truth and qualities. The path of voice takes us back outwards into the world through our words and actions. Voicing—and putting into action—our highest truth and qualities is the greatest service we can offer others . . . and ourselves. Ordinary people can do extraordinary things when they find their authentic voice. Good organizations become great organizations. An authentic voice is an unstoppable force.[27]

—*Alexander Massey*

In addition to tailoring the message to interest the receiver, the pharmacy manager must be authentic. Massey's quote concisely expresses the importance of managers ensuring that their communications express clear, believable messages. For this to occur, the manager not only needs to be knowledgeable of the topic but must truly believe in the message. If your staff senses hesitancy or distrust in either the words that you choose or the characteristics of your voice when the message is delivered, then they will distrust the message too. This may result in resisting the adoption of an idea or complete lack of "buy-in" from the staff. Other common mistakes include making potentially unpopular announcements without laying appropriate groundwork, telling well-intentioned lies or partial truths, and overlooking the effect of power on relationships. Some communications will be controversial (e.g., "We are merging with another company."), and before making such announcements, rumors tend to produce tension or anxiety. If the manager paves the way for such announcements by doing some public relations work with individual employees beforehand, anxiety can be minimized. When faced with the prospect of delivering difficult news or being asked to comment on a confidential matter, it may be tempting to limit information or tell partial truths, but doing so will typically reduce employee trust in you. If you cannot comment on something, simply tell the employees that you are not free to comment at this time but will inform them as soon as possible about the subject.

Individuals in management positions sometimes fail to receive critical information from employees until it is too late to prevent or easily address a problem or a concern. Letting employees know that you want an honest assessment of all problems, even if the employee perceives the message to be "bad news,"[28] can encourage open and timely communication.

Active and Passive Voice

Active and passive voice should also be considered.[5] Active voice is when the subject is performing the action, and passive voice is when the subject is acted on. Consider the following statements:

Statement 1: "Everyone must read the policies and procedures."
Statement 2: "The policies and procedures should be read by everyone."

Statement 1 is active voice since the subject—"everyone"—is performing the action. *Statement 2* is passive voice as the subject is being acted on. Pharmacist managers should use the active voice when an action is required. Active voice is generally appropriate when writing letters, business proposals, policies and procedures, and other business correspondence.

Sometimes, however, the passive voice is a better option than the active voice. For example, the passive voice can be used when you do not want to assign blame, directly state who did something, or communicate bad news. For example, if a prescription error occurs, it is best not to associate a name with the prescription error or imply that someone may have contributed to the problem. Thus, it is better to say, "The wrong medication was pulled from the shelf today resulting in a prescription error" as opposed to "Our technician, Jeff, pulled the wrong medication from the shelf today." Using passive voice to say, "The customers are not being counseled" may be a better way to approach the pharmacists compared with "You pharmacists are not counseling patients." The passive voice is likely to be better received than blaming the pharmacists directly for not counseling adequately.

CHOOSING A MEDIUM

Each day, pharmacists and pharmacist managers are challenged to determine the best **medium** (i.e., channel through which messages pass) for communicating a message.[6] In some cases, a one-on-one exchange will be best. In others, a larger group meeting makes sense. Communication using memos, e-mails, or written reports are other options. Each of these approaches has inherently different communication challenges. One-on-one communication allows managers to observe the nonverbal messages of the other person, which is more difficult in a group setting. A one-on-one conversation makes it easier to tell whether the other person understands your message, but it is hard to be sure that the intended message reaches every participant in a larger group meeting. However, meetings consume valuable staff time, so unless discussion is required, updates and other informational items can be effectively conveyed through written communication.

One-on-one or small-group meetings are appropriate when delivering a message that may elicit a strong reaction or when discussion or input is needed. Communicating by phone can also yield feedback but does not offer the opportunity to evaluate nonverbal responses. Memos or messages are suitable when the information is straightforward, not subject to varied interpretation, or unlikely to provoke a strong reaction from the reader.[6]

Meetings

Employee or staff meetings are an effective way to communicate.[6,29] They are beneficial when trying to solicit ideas and solutions, when complex problems need to be addressed, new policies or procedures need to be explained, or technical or complex information must be conveyed. Employees often complain that meetings are a waste of time, are too long, are unorganized, or have no purpose. To avoid such criticism, pharmacist managers should hold meetings only when necessary, start and end on time, encourage appropriate discussion,

prepare an agenda that includes the responsible party, determine time limits for each item, and establish a protocol for ensuring that action items are appropriately assigned and completed.[12] **Table 21–2** provides an array of tips for holding an effective meeting. Routine staff meetings are often perceived by employees as a way for them to stay informed, so managers should take care to ensure they are consistently meaningful for those who attend.

Telephone

Several conversations occur by telephone.[29] When using this medium, pharmacist managers and pharmacists must pay attention to their tone of voice, as a receiver cannot see the sender and therefore will be listening to the words and the tone of voice to decipher the message.

Often pharmacists will find themselves communicating through voice mail, either leaving messages for others or receiving messages from others. Pharmacist managers and pharmacists who have voice mail should check their messages regularly and respond in a timely way. Failing to respond promptly communicates that you are not listening or not interested in their message. The following suggestions should be considered when leaving a message for someone:[6]

- Speak clearly and slowly.
- Identify yourself and leave a phone number. If possible, repeat your name and phone number.
- Keep the message to one or two issues.

Conference calls and teleconferences pose additional challenges. To get the most out of them, participants should know the audience and purpose and avoid multitasking (e.g., eating, typing, reading e-mail) in order to focus on the meeting.

Memos

A memo informs the reader about a certain issue or makes an announcement.[6,29] This medium may be used to persuade employees or to encourage or instruct them to complete some task or action. Once a manager decides to send a memo, the audience must be considered. Limiting distribution

TABLE **21–2**	**Holding an Effective Meeting**

1. Is the meeting necessary? Do not have a meeting if there is no real purpose for one or if the information you want shared can be transmitted by memo or e-mail.

2. Know the meeting's purpose. Are you trying to solve a problem, inform employees, or something else?

3. Determine meeting invitees. Invite people who will have an interest in or need to discuss the agenda items. Consider letting certain people leave the meeting when topics relevant to them have been covered.

4. Prepare an agenda and distribute before the meeting.

5. Select a time and place that is convenient for a majority of invitees. Often Friday afternoons, unless an urgent matter, is not an optimal time for a meeting.

6. Start and end the meeting on time.

7. Have someone take minutes or notes during the meeting. Distribute the minutes after the meeting.

8. Create a culture of respect and openness at the meetings so people will communicate honestly.

9. If new and potentially extraneous issues are raised, suggest that the new topic be considered in a future meeting to facilitate completion of the original agenda.

10. Assign responsibility for follow-up items and establish a time frame for completing tasks or reporting back.

Sources: Data from Adler RB, Elmhorst JM;[6] Griffin J;[12] Lesikar RV, Flatley ME.[29]

to those who need to receive the message and tailoring content to intended recipients is essential. Before writing the memo, determine answers to the following questions:

- What does the reader need to know?
- Why does the reader need to know it?
- How might the reader react to the information?

Most memos follow an established format. They typically begin with the names of those receiving the memo, the name of the sender, the date, and the subject. The subject should be specific to inform the reader of the memo's content. The body of the memo should contain the following components:

- Purpose: Why you are writing?
- Background: What context does the reader need to make sense of the message?
- Action: What action is required of the reader or should be expected from the sender and by when?
- Closing: A brief summary

E-mailing

E-mailing is a common method for managers and employees to communicate, and guidelines for sending memos apply to e-mail messages as well.

Organizational policies typically guide e-mail usage in the workplace, and it is important to remember that work accounts can often be viewed by the employer. Because e-mail can be forwarded easily, do not write anything in an e-mail that would cause embarrassment if forwarded to others.[6] ◆*E-mail is appropriate for the one-way dissemination of easy-to-understand messages.* Managers should be cautious when using e-mail to communicate complex concepts, deliver bad news, or communicate emotionally charged material—situations better suited to face-to-face or phone conversations.

Messages can seem abrupt or rude, even when the sender does not intend to convey a sharp tone. Using words like "please" and "thank-you" can soften messages and increase the recipient's receptivity to the message.[6,30] "Lock the back door before you leave today" may be interpreted as a command. Inserting the word "please" so the message reads, "Please lock the back door before you leave today" makes the message seem more

respectful and friendly. **Table 21–3** offers other suggestions for effective e-mail use.

SPECIAL SITUATIONS

As detailed in the following sections, some communication experiences require special care and attention.

Communicating with Angry or Upset Employees

The pharmacist manager should consider the following when dealing with an angry employee:

1. Listen well so that the employee feels heard.
2. Provide an empathetic response. Let the employee know that you understand how he or she feels. Express interest in hearing more about the problems or concerns.
3. Recognize the problem or issue. Paraphrase responses so the employee knows you are

TABLE **21–3**   E-mail Guidelines
1. Provide a subject line that alerts the reader to action required or purpose of the message.
2. Keep the message concise and limited to one topic.
3. Explain the reason for sending the e-mail in the first paragraph.
4. Employ a professional tone, and use proper spelling and correct grammar.
5. Use expressions such as "please" and "thank-you" to soften messages.
6. Do not use all capital letters because this may be interpreted as shouting.
7. Keep the message concise and include attachments only if essential.
8. Use bullets, lists, headings, and ample white space for easy reading and comprehension.
9. Avoid sending copies of e-mails to others unless the recipients truly need the information.
10. Do not forward other people's e-mail messages without their permission.
11. Include comprehensive contact information in your signature line (e.g., name, title, institution, e-mail address, phone number).

Sources: Data from Adler RB, Elmhorst JM;[6] Hogan RC.[30]

listening. Repeat back to ensure that you are hearing what is being said.

4. Respond to both the problem and the emotions, and work together to develop a solution. After agreeing on a course of action, ask the employee whether the solution has resolved his or her concerns.

Delivering Bad News

Pharmacist managers must deliver bad news from time to time. In these situations, the manager must be assertive and clear in delivering the message. Showing empathy when delivering the news is important. Consider the following:

Example A

Statement 1: "We are not providing staff pharmacists with annual bonuses this year."

Statement 2: "I know this is going to be disappointing, but staff pharmacists will not be receiving annual bonuses this year because of our company's financial situation. We hope compensation decisions made this year will position us for a better year next year."

Example B

Statement 1: "I cannot offer you a promotion."

Statement 2: "A promotion will not be possible this year given pending changes in our organizational structure. When the restructuring is complete, I will reconsider a new role for you. We value your contributions and are committed to your career growth."

The first statement in both examples is true but unlikely to be well received. The second statements are likely to be more effective as they show empathy and provide context for the news provided. ❿ *Employees are more likely to accept difficult news if they understand the rationale behind it.* When managers share more information, employees are more likely to perceive them as open, informative, and honest.

SUMMARY

The importance of effective patient communication in pharmacy settings has been well established. Pharmacy professionals interact with a variety of people in their roles in addition to patients, and these parties include other healthcare professionals, suppliers, employees, coworkers, other managers, corporate or institutional leaders, and the media. Being sensitive to the varied information needs of each population and working to build trust and rapport with each will position the pharmacist manager for professional success. Attention to the content of all messages and the way they are delivered is critical for pharmacists and pharmacist managers to communicate effectively.

References

1. 2007 National Health Quality Report, Agency for Health Research and Quality. 2007. Available at: http://www.ahrq.gov/qual/nhqr07.htm. Accessed July 28, 2008.

2. Employee Engagement. Gallup Institute Inc, 2008. Available at: http://www.gallup.com/consulting/52/Employee-Engagement.aspx. Accessed November 2, 2008.

3. Metropolitan Life Insurance Company. Study of employee benefits trends: findings from the National Survey of Employers and Employees. 2008. Available at: http://whymetlife.com/trends/downloads/MetLife_EBTS08.pdf. Accessed October 15, 2008.

4. Beardsley RS, Kimberlin CL, Tindall WN. *Communication Skills in Pharmacy Practice*. 5th ed. Baltimore, MD: Lippincott Williams and Wilkins; 2007.

5. Krizan A, Merrier P, Jones CL. *Business Communication*. 5th ed. Cincinnati, OH: South-Western Thomson Learning; 2002.

6. Adler RB, Elmhorst JM. *Communicating at Work: Principles and Practices for Business and the Professions*. 6th ed. Boston, MA: McGraw-Hill College; 1999.

7. Mehrabian A. *Silent Messages: Implicit Communication of Emotion and Attitudes*. 2nd ed. Belmont, CA: Wadsworth;1981.

8. Qubein NR. *How to Be a Great Communicator: In-Person, on Paper, and on the Podium*. New York, NY: John Wiley and Sons Inc; 1997.

9. Birdwhistell R. *Kinesics and Context*. Philadelphia, PA: University of Pennsylvania Press; 1970.

10. Wick, Jeannette Y. *Supervision: A Pharmacy Perspective*. Washington, DC: American Pharmacists Association; 2003.

11. McKay M, Davis M, Fanning P. *Messages: The Communication Skills Book*. 2nd ed. Oakland, CA: New Harbinger Publications Inc; 1995.

12. Griffin J. *How to Say It at Work: Putting Yourself Across with Power Words, Phrases, Body Language, and Communication Secrets*. New York, NY: Prentice Hall Press; 1998.

13. Bolton R. *People Skills: How to Assert Yourself, Listen to Others, and Resolve Conflicts*. New York, NY: Simon and Schuster; 1979.

14. Hall E. *The Hidden Dimension*. Garden City, NY: Doubleday, 1966.

15. Galanti GA. Caring for culturally diverse patients. *Home Home Health Care Consultant* 1999;6(1):33–34.

16. Moran RT, Harris PR, Moran SV. *Managing Cultural Differences: Global Leadership Strategies for the 21st Century*. 7th ed. Boston, MA: Butterworth-Heinemann; 2007.

17. Fisher D. *Communicating in Organizations*. St. Paul, MN: West Publishing Company; 1981.

18. US Department of Commerce. *Population Projections of the United States by Age, Sex, Race, and Hispanic Origin*: 1995–2050. Washington, DC: Bureau of the Census; 1996.

19. Chisholm MA. Viewpoints. Diversity: a missing link to professionalism. *Am J Pharm Educ* 2004;68(5): 1–3.

20. Tannen D. *Talking from 9 to 5*. New York, NY: William Morrow Co; 1994.

21. Clancy P. The acquisition of communicative style in Japanese. In: Schieffelin B, Ochs E, eds. *Language Acquisition and Socialization Across Cultures*. Cambridge: Cambridge University Press; 1986:213–150.

22. Lebra TS. *Japanese Patterns of Behavior*. Honolulu, HI: University of Hawaii Press; 1976.

23. Hyslop NB. Listening: are we teaching it, and if so, how? ERIC Digest 3, Eric ID ED295132; 1988–00–00. Available at: http://www.ericdigests.org/pre-928/listening.htm. Accessed September 19, 2008.

24. Study guides and strategies: active listening. Available at: http://www.studygs.net/listening.htm. Accessed July 20, 2008.

25. Locker KO, Kaczmarek SK. *Business Communication: Building Critical Skills*. New York, NY: McGraw-Hill Irwin; 2004.

26. Berger BA. *Communication Skills for Pharmacists*. Washington, DC: American Pharmacists Association; 2002.

27. Massey A. Authentic voice: The gift of authenticity. Available at: http://authenticvoice.blogspot.com/2008/02/does-authority-matter.html. Accessed August 14, 2008.

28. Robbins S. *Seven Communication Mistakes Managers Make*. Boston, MA: Harvard Business Publishing; 2009. Available at: http://blogs.harvardbusiness.org/hmu/2009/03/seven-communication-mistakes-m.php?cm_re=homepage-041409-_-body-left-r2-_-management. Accessed June 16, 2009.

29. Lesikar RV, Flatley ME. *Basic Business Communication: Skills for Empowering the Internet Generation*. 9th ed. New York, NY: McGraw-Hill Irwin; 2002.

30. Hogan RC. *Explicit Business Writing*. Normal, IL: BWC Publishing; 2005.

Case Scenarios

CASE ONE: Pharmacist Angelika Jameson manages a pharmacy department that includes two other pharmacists, two technicians, and a cashier. As a result of a compensation decision announced by the corporate office, she calls a meeting of all department employees to share the decision from headquarters. "The corporate office has announced changes to our usual compensation program. Salary increases will be smaller than usual, just 1.5%. Unlike in past years, the performance-based bonus program will be available only for salaried workers." The pharmacists are salaried employees, and the technicians and cashier are paid on an hourly basis. How could Jameson have communicated this message in a way that minimized anger or disappointment among those not eligible for salary increases?

CASE TWO: Since Sam Chang joined City Hospital as its pharmacy manager nine months ago, three pharmacists and two technicians have accepted outside offers with higher annual salaries. Suspecting that there was more than compensation at play, Chang asked human resources to conduct exit interviews with employees who had already left and those who were about to leave. The human resources manager reported receiving such comments as (1) "Sam reorganized everything and wanted it done his way"; (2) "I asked if I could attend the continuing education program at the school of pharmacy last month, but he never responded. I think he is just too busy"; (3) "He is never around—he is always meeting with the hospital CEO or someone in purchasing. He has no idea what is happening in this pharmacy"; and (4) "I have no idea what is going on. Sam does not tell us much. We get an occasional e-mail, usually just to tell us how he has changed some policy or procedure." Given this feedback, what communication strategies might Chang employ to become a better pharmacy manager?

CASE THREE: As the lead pharmacist at a retail pharmacy, you have been alerted that several medication errors have occurred in the past week. You want to inform the pharmacy employees that errors are occurring, ask where the potential problems in the system may be, and encourage them to be extra careful when filling prescriptions. You also want to remind them of the safety and double-check procedures that the pharmacy has implemented. What strategies should you employ to convey your concerns?

Additional
Resources
Available
Online!

Visit the Student Companion Web site at http://healthprofessions.jbpub.com/pharmacymanagement for interactive study tools and additional resources.

See www.rxugace.com to learn how you can obtain continuing pharmacy education for this content.

Chapter 22

NEGOTIATION TECHNIQUES

CANDACE W. BARNETT, PhD, RPh

LEARNING OBJECTIVES

After completing the chapter, the reader will be able to

1. List the steps of principled negotiation.
2. Describe active listening techniques used to keep the parties and problem separate in principled negotiation.
3. Discern the difference between assertive and aggressive negotiation positions and counterpositions.
4. Explain how to diffuse emotional outbursts during principled negotiation.
5. Identify underlying concerns in principled negotiation.
6. Recommend actions that can facilitate idea generation during joint solution finding.
7. Document the purpose of applying standards in principled negotiation.
8. Demonstrate basic protective skills that are used in countermanipulation during negotiation.
9. Detail the strategies successful negotiators use when preparing for principled negotiation.
10. Explain why positional bargaining typically results in poor outcomes.

KEY CONCEPTS

❶ Principled negotiation is assertive. It lies at the center point between the two extremes of passively surrendering your position and aggressively forcing your position.

❷ Negotiations often involve parties with whom you as the pharmacist manager want to continue a relationship. One goal of principled negotiation is to settle the situation in a way that maintains that relationship. To do this, we must uncouple the negotiating parties from the situation or problem being addressed.

❸ Use active listening in negotiation to avoid judging and to keep your focus on the position rather than the person.

❹ The most successful negotiations drill beneath the positions of each individual or organization (i.e., what they say they want) to identify deeper underlying concerns (i.e., what they really want).

❺ The goal of joint solution finding is to generate as many solutions as possible. One rule prevails during joint solution finding—no criticism of ideas.

❻ To arrive at a negotiated agreement, objective standards are applied to each potential solution and a decision is made to accept or reject.

❼ To arrive at a final solution, each party should compare the negotiated agreement to its fallback position. The agreement is accepted if it is superior to the fallback position. The agreement is rejected if it is inferior to the fallback position.

❽ One's negotiating leverage is directly correlated with the strength of his or her fallback position.

❾ At the conclusion of a principled negotiation, analyze what occurred. Reasons for success or failure should be noted. Analyze what strategies worked and what did not for both sides. This information can be applied to future negotiations.

❿ Positional bargaining is most frequently used to negotiate problems in which the parties have had no prior relationship and have no plans for a future relationship.

INTRODUCTION

The term **negotiation** usually conjures up images of union officials and employers arguing about pay and benefits for striking workers or heads of state discussing world peace. Most people are continually engaged in negotiations, albeit on a smaller scale, in their daily lives. For example, pharmacy students in a study group may negotiate a meeting time; new pharmacy graduates negotiate the price of their first home or car; friends negotiate how they will spend their leisure time together; and

parents negotiate with their children about curfews.

Principled negotiation, the approach on which this chapter is based, was developed by Fisher and Ury and is described in their book *Getting to Yes*.[1] This approach uses objective standards to address the concerns of the individuals or organizations involved to reach mutually acceptable solutions.

Pharmacists engage in negotiations of varying magnitudes on a daily basis. Consider the following examples from a myriad of pharmacy settings: An independent pharmacy owner negotiates for lower rent on the building the pharmacy occupies. The manager of a small pharmacy chain negotiates the rates and terms of its contract with a pharmacy benefits manager for providing prescription services. An employee pharmacist negotiates with the pharmacist manager regarding work schedule, break times, and technical and clerical support. A clinical pharmacist negotiates with members of the hospital medical staff to use a newly implemented diabetes service for their patients. A hospital pharmacy preceptor negotiates with the chief of medicine to permit pharmacy students completing advanced pharmacy practice experiences to participate on medical rounds. A hospital pharmacy director negotiates with the Pharmacy and Therapeutics Committee to add or remove a drug from the hospital's formulary.

It is important to recognize such opportunities for negotiation, and this chapter will help pharmacists and pharmacist managers address these opportunities using principled negotiation. Because this form of negotiation considers the concerns of all negotiating parties, using it will increase the chances for favorable outcomes and preserve relationships.[2]

PRINCIPLED NEGOTIATION

Negotiation style is closely related to communication behavior mode. Most people operate in one of three modes: (1) passive, (2) aggressive, or (3) assertive. Those who operate in a passive mode seek to avoid conflict at all costs. In negotiations, they adopt a soft style and tend to concede to the other side in favor of maintaining the relationship. As a result, they often leave negotiations feeling angry at themselves for not advancing their

position and resenting the other party for winning. Aggressive communicators focus on winning, despite the cost and adopt a hard style when negotiating. They stick to their position without wavering and, in doing so, often wind up damaging relationships with the other people involved.[3]
◆ Principled negotiation *is assertive. It lies at the center point between the two extremes of passively surrendering your position and aggressively forcing your position.* Giving and receiving respect is a fundamental tenet of assertive communication and of principled negotiation.[1,3]

Abraham Lincoln once wrote, "When I'm getting ready to reason with a man, I spend one-third of my time thinking about myself and what I am going to say—and two-thirds thinking about him and what he is going to say."[4] Lincoln's words indicate his appreciation that negotiation is a deliberate process that should only be entered into after significant mental preparation with most of that time focused on the other party. Principled negotiation consists of the following four sequential steps: (1) uncouple parties from the problem, (2) target underlying concerns, (3) develop joint solutions, and (4) apply objective standards.[1] These steps serve as a blueprint for negotiating any situation and are described in the following sections.

Step 1: Uncouple Parties from the Problem

❷*Negotiations often involve individuals with whom you as a pharmacist manager want to continue a relationship. One goal of principled negotiation is to settle the situation in a way that maintains that relationship. To do this, we must uncouple the negotiating parties from the situation or problem being addressed.*[1] Consider this example: The owner of an independent pharmacy recognizes that the pharmacy is not in compliance with the **Health Insurance Portability and Accountability Act** (HIPAA; for a comprehensive discussion of HIPAA, refer to Chapter 5, "Significant Laws Affecting Pharmacy Practice Management"). The owner asks an employee pharmacist to serve as HIPAA compliance officer for the pharmacy, but the employee pharmacist does not want to add this assignment to her long list of responsibilities.

It is human nature to take another's refusal of our requests and our counterpositions personally.

A common reaction is to respond with anger toward the person rather than the situation. You can help yourself keep the parties and problem separate by listening actively, framing negotiation positions and counterpositions assertively, and diffusing emotions.[1]

Use Active Listening

When we hear an opinion or position that is different from our own, we naturally tend to judge the messenger negatively. We make overt statements or implications that the other party should not feel the way he or she does. For example, consider the following statement made by the employee pharmacist to the owner regarding the HIPAA compliance request: "You're not being realistic." This statement judges the owner negatively. Equally negative is the owner's statement, "You're not being a team player." These judgmental statements can cause negotiations to veer off course. The individuals in this case are likely to feel personally attacked, and if they are not skilled at negotiation, they become defensive and respond with a personal attack. Worse yet, they may simply refuse to continue negotiating. ❸ *Use **active listening** in negotiation to avoid judging and to keep your focus on the position rather than the person.*[1]

Active listening means remaining nonjudgmental while you digest another's message or position and then responding in a way that conveys you have done that.[5] The active listening techniques known as summarizing and reflecting feelings will accomplish this.[6] When people present their negotiation positions, their message contains both facts and feelings. To use summarizing, mentally separate the facts of a person's negotiation position from any feelings that were presented. Take the facts and rephrase them using your own words. Invite the other party to correct your understanding.[6] For example, consider this summarizing statement made by the pharmacy owner regarding the HIPAA noncompliance issue: "So you're saying becoming our HIPAA compliance officer does not seem possible given your other responsibilities. Is that correct?" Reflecting feelings in negotiation involves identifying any feelings that accompanied a person's position and sending them back without agreeing or disagreeing.[6] Continuing with the HIPAA noncompliance issue, consider this reflecting statement made by the owner after identifying the employee pharmacist's feelings: "It sounds like you're feeling a little overwhelmed." The following statement by the owner combines summarizing and reflecting, "So adding HIPAA compliance officer to your current responsibilities seems overwhelming. Is that right?"

When the active listening techniques of summarizing and reflecting are used, the other person feels heard and is often willing to elaborate, opening the door for a discussion of how each party views the problem.[6] **Table 22–1** lists viewpoints that may be revealed through active listening by the employee pharmacist and the pharmacy owner when negotiating the HIPAA noncompliance issue.

Frame Assertive Negotiation Positions and Counterpositions

When stating your negotiation position, frame it in the three-part assertive message:

- Describe the situation or problem in terms of facts. Also, show your understanding for the other party's feelings. In other words, begin with active listening by summarizing and reflecting feelings.
- Tell the other party how you feel about the situation or how it affected you.
- State what you want or what you are willing to do or both.[7]

For example, after exploring the viewpoints associated with the HIPAA noncompliance issue (Table 22–1), the pharmacy owner states his negotiation position using the three-part assertive message as follows: (1) "HIPAA legislation mandates we designate a privacy officer, and I'd like it to be you. I know you're feeling hesitant about it because of the heavy workload you already have." (2) "Based on your past work record and the respect you receive from the other employees and patients, I feel you are the best choice." (3) "I'm willing to reassign some of your workload so that you can assume this responsibility."

Frame counterpositions using the two-part assertive response:

- Show you have listened by summarizing, reflecting feelings, or both.

- State your counterposition in terms of what you think, feel, or are willing to do.[8]

For example, in response to the pharmacy owner's negotiation position, the employee pharmacist uses the two-part assertive response as follows: (1) "I know we must comply with the law, and you'd like me to ensure that's done." (2) "I'm flattered you feel so confident in me, but I'm simply not interested in trading some of my present responsibilities for those of a HIPAA compliance officer. I think you should identify another employee for this responsibility."

Diffuse Emotions

Watch for the following subtle nonverbal indications of disagreement that may be displayed by the other party, such as rubbing behind or beside the ear, or rubbing the eye or across the back of the neck.[9] Emotions can run high in negotiations, so allow a party to express his or her feelings. Sometimes the expression of pent-up emotion is necessary before a person can move on to solution finding. Do not attempt to quiet the speaker or argue with the words. Instead, remain silent and nonverbally attend to the speaker through consistent eye contact and an interested, sincere facial expression. By remaining silent, you offer no new information to further stimulate the emotional outburst. Once expressed, with no additional fuel provided, the emotions diffuse.[10]

Step 2: Target Underlying Concerns

❹ *The most successful negotiations drill beneath the positions of each individual or organization (i.e., what they say they want) to identify deeper underlying concerns (i.e., what they really want).*[1] To know your own underlying concerns, engage in some self-inquiry before entering into negotiations. Reflect on the following questions:

- What outcomes do I want from this negotiation?
- Which of the outcomes are essential?
- Which are desirable but not essential?
- Can the outcomes be prioritized in some fashion?
- What are my reasons for desiring these outcomes?

TABLE **22–1**	**Negotiating Viewpoints Revealed Through Active Listening**

Owner's Viewpoint	Employee Pharmacist's Viewpoint
I went to my other pharmacist with the last two extra work assignments.	He always asks me to pitch in when there is extra work to be done.
She is definitely the most qualified of my employees to take on this important responsibility.	He's sparing the other pharmacist the work because they are golfing buddies.
She can't be that overworked. She's always out the door by 5 p.m. on the dot.	I already have so much to get done that I come in an hour before opening time every day, and I also work straight through my lunch break.
She seems to handle all her responsibilities with ease. I have never heard any complaints about her or seen any errors in her work.	My other work will suffer if I take on more responsibility.
I know plenty of pharmacy owners who pay their pharmacists less salary for more responsibilities than she has.	I have pharmacist friends who have less work to do than I do and get paid more.
She's my most assertive employee. She'll be able to speak up and correct any HIPAA violations.	He thinks I'm too passive to challenge him on this.
I don't micromanage my employees.	I doubt he knows how much I do. He never asks me how my work is going.

Note: HIPAA = Health Insurance Portability and Accountability Act.

- Are my motives in the best interest of the people and organization I represent?
- Are my motives self-serving?

Probing is essential to identify the other party's underlying concerns. Inquire about why the other party favors its position. You can also learn about underlying concerns by inquiring about why the party opposes your position.[1] Begin the inquiry with words other than "why," as many people become defensive when this word is used. Instead, begin your probes with phrases such as, "Tell me more . . . ," "For what reasons . . . , and "Help me understand . . . "[11]

Potential solutions should then target the underlying concerns.[1] For example, in the negotia-tion regarding the HIPAA noncompliance issue, probing reveals that the pharmacy owner's main concern is short term. He feels it is important to comply with HIPAA regulations immediately. The employee pharmacist's main concern is long term. She fears taking on additional work and a title that will prevent her from having the time later to implement her real interest, providing clinical services in the community setting. A workable solution would satisfy both concerns.

STEP 3: DEVELOP JOINT SOLUTIONS

With underlying concerns identified, both parties should together generate potential solutions and consider whether concerns are addressed. ❺ *The goal of joint solution finding is to generate as many solutions as possible. One rule prevails during joint solution finding—no criticism of ideas.*[1] Idea generation can be facilitated through the physical environment, the attitudes of the negotiating parties, detailed issue examination, and attention to **compromise** mode.

PHYSICAL ENVIRONMENT

The physical environment can aid idea generation. The negotiating parties should sit side by side as partners rather than across from one another as adversaries.[1] Potential solutions developed should be written on a flip chart or other medium that is in plain view of all parties. This aids in generating additional ideas and emphasizes the focus on joint idea generation. If possible, a neutral party should facilitate the session.[12]

NEGOTIATION ATTITUDES

Idea generation is a creative process. You can increase the number and variety of suggestions you offer by adopting attitudes often associated with creativity. These include optimism, neutrality, and perseverance.[13] Creative people are optimistic. They view problems as opportunities, not obstacles. They enjoy the challenge of problem solving. Creative people do not prejudge their own ideas, or those of others, as good or bad. A seemingly poor idea initially could evolve into a worthy solution as the creative process unfolds. The process of generating potential solutions can become slow and arduous. Creative people demonstrate perseverance at these times. They pose questions to get at who, what, where, when, and why. They ask hypothetical "what if" and "I wonder what" questions. They "compare and contrast" the situation under negotiation to past problems they have negotiated and resolved.[14]

DETAILED ISSUE EXAMINATION

One technique for increasing the number of ideas generated is to examine the issue under negotiation on four levels: (1) the problem, (2) the diagnosis, (3) strategies for curing, and (4) treatments. This examination is similar to models used in medicine for moving from problems to treatments. First, define the problem in terms of the symptoms and what is wrong. These symptoms may be based on objective facts, as well as subjective information about the problem, including perceptions and experiences. Next, diagnose the cause of the problem. Grouping related symptoms can help identify causes or barriers impeding solutions. Then, suggest strategies for curing the problem. At this point, the strategies should be broad and theoretical. From the general strategies, develop specific treatments, defined as ideas for specific steps that could be taken to solve the problem.[15] **Table 22–2** illustrates the examination of the negotiation issue, noncompliance with HIPAA, on these four levels.

In developing solutions, the parties should look for ways of satisfying the underlying concerns of each side. Some of these underlying concerns may be shared. If so, emphasizing them can ease the negotiation process. Sometimes several underlying concerns of one negotiating party directly oppose those of the other. A series of solutions that address all concerns for both parties should be generated. The parties can then combine solutions in a back-and-forth manner, making and receiving concessions, based on which solutions are priorities for each.[1]

COMPROMISE MODE

Compromise means making or receiving concessions. In negotiation, the process of achieving compromise is called the **give/get principle**. Negotiating parties operate in one of three compromise modes:

- The "give/get–give/get" mode is poised for success. Both parties are willing to give something upfront in exchange for getting what they desire.
- The "give/get–get/give" mode also has a fairly strong likelihood of success. Each party accepts the basic concept of giving to get something in return; however, one party will only give after getting. If this party stalls too long to maximize gain, the other party may withdraw its concessions and negotiations come to a standstill.
- The "get/give–get/give" mode is doomed for failure. Both parties are unwilling to give until they receive. If neither party changes mode, negotiations stop.[16]

TABLE **22–2**	**Examination of a Negotiation Issue on Four Levels**

"Problem"
- The pharmacy is not in compliance with HIPAA.
- No formal policies have been established regarding how private health information is used, disclosed, and requested.
- Wording of the Notice of Privacy Practices (NOPP) was borrowed from another store. It is not distributed with consistency to new patients, not posted, and no attempt is made to obtain the patient's acknowledgment that the NOPP was received.
- The pharmacy does not maintain business associate agreements.
- None of the employees have been HIPAA trained.
- There is no information firewall between the prescription department and other areas of the store.
- Patients have complained about breaches of their privacy when counseling in the store is not private and when information is revealed through the public address system.
- Patients have complained that too much information is revealed to relatives or friends picking up their prescriptions.

"Diagnosis"
- No one has been assigned responsibility for HIPAA compliance.

"Strategies for curing"
- Assign responsibility for HIPAA—i.e., designate a HIPAA compliance officer.

"Treatments"
- Assign HIPAA responsibility to the employee pharmacist involved in the negotiation.
- Assign HIPAA responsibility to the other full-time pharmacist.
- Adjust the workload of any full-time pharmacist assigned HIPAA responsibility.
- Implement a pay increase for any full-time pharmacist assigned HIPAA responsibility.
- Periodically rotate HIPAA responsibility among the pharmacists.
- Assign responsibility for short-term immediate HIPAA compliance to the employee pharmacist involved in the negotiation.
- Once compliance is achieved, shift responsibility for HIPAA compliance maintenance to another pharmacist.
- Hire a part-time pharmacist to assume HIPAA responsibility.
- Hire an additional technician to free up more time for the pharmacist(s) assuming responsibility for HIPAA compliance.
- Assign HIPAA responsibility to a technician.

Note: HIPAA = Health Insurance Portability and Accountability Act.

Step 4: Apply Standards

The final step in this blueprint for effective negotiation involves applying standards or principles, hence the term "principled negotiation." Two types of standards are applied sequentially. At first, objective standards are applied to reach a negotiated agreement or tentative solution. Then, personal standards are applied to reach a final solution.

Objective Standards

Objective standards are criteria that both negotiating parties agree on and in which they have confidence. The objective standards selected for use depend on the problem being negotiated. Examples of objective standards include fair market value, legal precedent, precedent based on past experiences, tradition, professional codes of ethics, workplace safety standards, patient care standards, moral codes, and equality. *❻To arrive at a negotiated agreement, objective standards are applied to each potential solution and a decision is made to accept or reject.*[17]

Several acceptable solutions may be combined and edited to best reflect underlying concerns. For example, in the negotiation of the HIPAA noncompliance issue, the following objective standards could be applied to the potential solutions developed: HIPAA legal requirements, personnel law, fair employment practices, and HIPAA compliance practices of similar independent pharmacies. The negotiated agreement combines several potential solutions and takes into account the owner's underlying concern regarding immediate compliance and the employee pharmacist's concern regarding time to implement clinical services. The negotiated agreement reached includes a reassignment of workload so that the employee pharmacist can bring the pharmacy into full HIPAA compliance in three months. The job and title of HIPAA compliance officer will then transfer to another employee who will maintain that compliance. The altered workload will remain in place so that the employee pharmacist can then pursue implementation of clinical services.

Personal Standards

Personal standards refer to each party's **best alternative to the negotiated agreement**—its fallback position.[1] This is the course of action a party would take if it were not pursuing negotiation.[1] For example, in the HIPAA noncompliance negotiation, the owner's fallback position is to assume the role of HIPAA compliance officer himself. The employee pharmacist's fallback position is to resign and work for another community pharmacy where she has a job offer in hand. *❼ To arrive at a final solution, each party should compare the negotiated agreement to its fallback position. The*

agreement is accepted if it is superior to the fallback position. The agreement is rejected if it is inferior to the fallback position. Two options can be followed: (1) the agreement can be renegotiated or (2) the parties can disband and pursue their fallback positions.[18,19]

❽ One's negotiating leverage is directly correlated with the strength of his or her fallback position. If your fallback position is strong, reveal it. The other person or entity will give more credence to your proposals for fear you will pursue your fallback position. A weak fallback position should not be divulged. Knowing your options are few, the other party is less likely to entertain your proposals.[18,19] In the case of the HIPAA noncompliance negotiation, the employee pharmacist has a strong fallback position. She is negotiating at a time when the number of available pharmacy positions greatly exceeds pharmacists. She also has another job offer in hand. If she leaves her present position, it could be difficult for the owner to fill the position. Given these facts, it is in her best interest to make her fallback position known. Conversely, the pharmacy owner's fallback position is weaker. Though he can assume the responsibilities of HIPAA compliance officer, he prefers not to do so.

FAILED NEGOTIATIONS

❾At the conclusion of a principled negotiation, analyze what occurred. Reasons for success or failure should be noted. Analyze what strategies worked and what did not for both sides. This information can be applied to future negotiations. Negotiations can fail for various reasons. Two of the most common are tough tactics and inadequate preparation.[16]

Tough Tactics

When one negotiating party attempts to manipulate the other, it leads to resistance.[16] Attempts at manipulation can be confronted through some basic verbal protective skills. The protective skills known as agreement, disagreement, inquiry, fogging, postponing, and broken record are important to master before entering negotiations.

Tough Tactic Response 1: Agreement

During negotiations, the person with whom you are negotiating may criticize you in an attempt at manipulation. If you feel the criticism or a portion of it is valid, simply agree with it, without offering any explanations or apologies.[3] For example, in the course of negotiating the HIPAA noncompliance issue, the employee pharmacist says to the owner, "You don't know how overworked I am because you're not here to observe it." In response, the owner states, "You're right, I have not been in the pharmacy much lately."

Tough Tactic Response 2: Disagreement

If you feel a criticism voiced during the negotiation is not legitimate, disagree with it without any apologies or excuses. Most important, do not retaliate by criticizing the other party.[20] For example, in negotiating the HIPAA noncompliance issue, the owner disagrees with the statement that he is not present in the pharmacy. The owner responds, "That's not correct. I am in the pharmacy daily."

Tough Tactic Response 3: Inquiry

When faced with an unexpected criticism voiced during negotiations, your curiosity may be peaked. If you would like the other party to elaborate, ask; however, inquire only if you are prepared to accept another criticism.[3] For example, in negotiating the HIPAA noncompliance issue, the owner would like more information regarding the employee pharmacist's perception that she is overworked. The owner responds, "Tell me more. How are you overworked?"

Tough Tactic Response 4: Fogging

Sometimes during negotiations, a criticism will be voiced, but you are unsure of its accuracy. Fogging involves agreeing to the chance that the criticism is correct because you are unsure.[3] For example, in negotiating the HIPAA noncompliance issue, the owner is unsure about the truth of the statement that the employee pharmacist is overworked. He uses fogging and responds by saying, "That may be true." As with agreement, disagreement, and inquiry, a fogging statement should be made without apologies or excuses, which can be used for further manipulation.

Tough Tactic Response 5: Postponing

The back and forth, give and take of negotiation should not be rushed. When it is, one party can feel manipulated. Negotiators should postpone providing a response when asked to accept a negotiation term about which they are unsure. After adequate thought, they should then return to the negotiation in a reasonable length of time.[20] For example, in negotiating the HIPAA noncompliance issue, the owner is unsure about permanently maintaining the employee pharmacist's altered workload. The owner postpones responding by saying, "I need some time to further evaluate this. Let's break now and resume our negotiations in 30 minutes." Postponing is also an effective technique to use when faced with an unexpected criticism. Take some time to evaluate the criticism and decide how best to respond.

Tough Tactic Response 6: Broken Record

When a negotiator is not interested in altering his or her position, the broken record response can be highly effective. This response involves restating your negotiation position without providing additional information that could be used in manipulation. The restatement often needs to occur several times, like a broken record, until the other person realizes that the position is not negotiable.[3] For example, in negotiating the HIPAA noncompliance issue, the employee pharmacist states her position: "I am not interested in being the permanent HIPAA compliance officer." After the owner's attempt to convince her otherwise, the employee pharmacist restates her position, "I realize having a permanent HIPAA compliance officer is important, but I'm not interested." The restatement continues several more times before the owner drops this negotiation term.

Inadequate Preparation

Successful negotiators study before engaging in principled negotiation. They define their goals and objectives, think about the outcome they want, and identify their underlying concerns. They determine what they are willing to concede to approximate the outcome they desire and know their fallback position. Successful negotiators

- Anticipate how the other person or organization views the issues and uses this information to plan how they will support their own position.

- Think about the personality characteristics of the other party to anticipate what communication techniques may be necessary.

POSITIONAL BARGAINING

Positional bargaining is a negotiation strategy whereby a party holds onto its position without regard for the other party or underlying concerns.[21] Positional bargaining is highly competitive and pits one party against the other in pursuit of winning. ⑩ *Positional bargaining is most frequently used to negotiate problems in which the parties have had no prior relationship and have no plans for a future relationship.* Thus, there is little worry about image or reputation.[22]

Pharmacists interact with the same coworkers, employees, managers, directors, patients, physicians, nurses and other healthcare professionals, wholesalers, bankers, etc., for years. Thus, for pharmacists, occasions for using positional bargaining are rare. One instance in which positional bargaining is frequently used is in the purchase or sale of a pharmacy, provided the former owner completely removes himself from any future association with the business.

Positional bargaining typically results in poor outcomes. Since the positions of the individuals involved are often diametrically opposed, this form of negotiation can quickly reach a **stalemate**, a situation in which neither side can prevail in a negotiation, and the parties disband.[23] If a final solution is reached through positional bargaining, it is usually a compromise where the difference is split and both sides feel dissatisfied.[2]

SUCCESSFUL OUTCOMES

The negotiated agreement reached by the pharmacist owner and employee pharmacist regarding HIPAA noncompliance proved successful. With her altered workload, the employee pharmacist brought the pharmacy into full HIPAA compliance in three months. She then shifted her focus from HIPAA compliance officer to clinical services provider and was able to implement clinical services and document improved patient outcomes and revenue. The title of HIPAA compliance officer and its associated responsibilities were transferred to the other full-time employee pharmacist. The additional revenue obtained from providing clinical services enabled the hiring of a part-time pharmacist to assist with all pharmacy services.

SUMMARY

Pharmacist managers and leaders must be successful negotiators, and this requires preparation, creativity, patience, active listening, and empathy. When demonstrated well, negotiation facilitates positive results. When exhibited poorly, trust can be damaged. This chapter advocates using principled negotiation, a four-step process that includes (1) uncoupling parties from the problem, (2) targeting underlying concerns, (3) developing joint solutions, and (4) applying objective standards. Principled negotiation is an effective approach for achieving desired results while maintaining vital relationships with healthcare professionals, colleagues, vendors, patients, and others.

References

1. Fisher R, Ury W, Patton B. *Getting to Yes: Negotiating Agreement Without Giving In*. 2nd ed. New York, NY: Penguin Books; 1991.

2. Spangler B. Integrative or interest-based bargaining. Available at: http://www.beyondintractability .org/essay/interest-baseed_bargaining/. Accessed September 7, 2008.

3. Smith MJ. *When I Say No I Feel Guilty*. New York, NY: Bantam Books; 1975.

4. Quote Cosmos. Quotes by Lincoln, Abraham. Available at: http://www.quotecosmos.com/quotes/ 38949/view. Accessed September 24, 2008.

5. Burley-Allen M. *Listening: The Forgotten Skill*. New York, NY: John Wiley & Sons Inc; 1982:2–3.

6. Wittmer J, Myrick RD. *Facilitative Teaching Theory and Practice*. Minneapolis, MN: Educational Media Corp; 1980:80–87.

7. Bolton R. *People Skills: How to Assert Yourself, Listen to Others, and Resolve Conflicts.* New York, NY: Simon & Schuster; 1986:141.

8. Hartley P. *Interpersonal Communication.* 2nd ed. New York, NY: Routledge; 1999:198.

9. Nierenberg GI, Calero HH. *How to Read a Person Like a Book.* New York, NY: Pocket Books Inc; 1973:74, 89–91.

10. Culp G, Smith A. *Managing People (Including Yourself) for Project Success.* New York, NY: John Wiley & Sons Inc; 1992:81–82.

11. Knapp H. *Therapeutic Communication: Developing Professional Skills.* Thousand Oaks, CA: Sage Publications Inc; 2007:119.

12. Cohen SP. Focusing on interests rather than positions conflict resolution key. Available at: http://www.pertinent.com/articles/negotiation/stevencohen.asp. Accessed September 7, 2008.

13. Rowse D. 9 attitudes of highly creative people. Available at: http://www.problogger.net/archives/2007/05/09/9-attitudes-of-highly-crreative-people/. Accessed September 16, 2008.

14. Force J. Creative questioning: the art of asking dumb questions. Available at: http://www.banffcentre.ca/departments/leadership/library/pdf/creative_questioning.pdf. Accessed September 16, 2008.

15. Alspaugh T. Human skills: negotiating for agreement. Available at: http://www.ics.uci.edu/~alspaugh/human/negotiating.html. Accessed September 17, 2008.

16. Maddux RB. *Successful Negotiation: Effective "Win-Win" Strategies and Tactics.* 3rd ed. Boston, MA: Course Technology Crisp; 1995:17.

17. Oregon Mediation Center Inc. Effective mediation resources: principled negotiation. Available at: http://www.internetmediator.com/medres/pg1028.cfm Accessed September 17, 2008.

18. Spangler B. Best alternative to a negotiated agreement (BATNA). Available at: http://www.beyondintractability.org/essay/batna/. Accessed September 20, 2008.

19. The Negotiation Experts. S-w-i-n-g your BATNA. Available at: http://www.negotiations.com/articles/best-alterntive/. Accessed September 20, 2008.

20. Nemire RE, Kier KL. *Pharmacy Clerkship Manual: A Survival Manual for Students.* New York, NY: McGraw-Hill; 2001:31.

21. Spangler B. Positional bargaining. Available at: http://www.beyondintractability.org/essay/positional_bargaining/. Accessed September 7, 2008.

22. MindEdge Inc. What is distributive negotiation? Available at: http://negotiation.atwork-network.com/. Accessed September 17, 2008.

23. Conflict Research Consortium, University of Colorado. International online training program on intractable conflict: Glossary. Available at: http://www.colorado.edu/conflict/peace/glossary.htm Accessed September 11, 2008.

Abbreviations

HIPAA: Health Insurance Portability and Accountability Act
NOPP: Notice of Privacy Practices

Case Scenarios

CASE ONE: You are the director of pharmacy in a small hospital. Discharge counseling in the hospital is currently provided by the nursing staff, an activity that you believe should be performed by pharmacists. You meet with the director of nursing to discuss this change. After exchange of pleasantries, you state, "I'd like to talk with you about my pharmacy staff assuming responsibility for discharge counseling." The director of nursing considers discharge counseling a nursing function and does not want her staff to relinquish this duty. Her eyes widen in response to your suggestion, and with an indignant voice she states, "But my nurses have always assumed responsibility for discharge counseling!" Describe actions you would take to uncouple the party

(continues)

from the problem and to target underlying concerns.

CASE TWO: You are a pharmacist in a combination pharmacy/grocery store. The automated blood pressure equipment is located in the grocery, rather than in the pharmacy. Although you use it frequently for your patients, its location is inconvenient. You feel it would be more appropriately placed in the pharmacy as it would be convenient for patients who forget their blood pressure and would minimize the time required for a pharmacist to accompany patients to the other side of the store. The grocery manager feels the equipment is appropriately placed near the low sodium products and health food in the grocery. He feels this strategic location boosts sales. You and the grocery manager pursue principled negotiation and reach the step where you develop joint solutions. To increase the number of ideas generated, analyze and describe the issue on four levels: (1) the problem, (2) the diagnosis, (3) strategies for curing, and (4) treatment.

Consider the perspectives of both the pharmacy manager and grocery manager in potential solutions.

CASE THREE: You are a pharmacy intern who has worked for the same pharmacist employer for two years. Your employer has never permitted you to counsel patients even though the law allows you to do so under the supervision of a pharmacist. You feel well prepared to engage in patient counseling and feel the time is right to approach your employer since she has recently been faced with an increase in requests for counseling from an influx of retirees into the community. During the negotiation, your employer tries some tough tactics, including trying to dissuade you, suggesting that you lack the education to be effective, and suggesting that you start working a very undesirable Saturday evening shift when the pharmacy is not as busy. What are some strategies you might use to achieve your desired results?

Additional Resources Available Online!

Visit the Student Companion Web site at http://healthprofessions.jbpub.com/pharmacymanagement for interactive study tools and additional resources.

See www.rxugace.com to learn how you can obtain continuing pharmacy education for this content.

CHAPTER 23

MANAGING CONFLICT AND BUILDING CONSENSUS

TARA L. JENKINS, PhD, RPh

LESA WAGGONER LAWRENCE, PhD, MBA

LEARNING OBJECTIVES

After completing this chapter, the reader will be able to

1. Define conflict and identify common causes of conflict.

2. Describe the positive aspects of conflict in an organizational setting.

3. Describe the pros and cons of various conflict management approaches.

4. Explain the importance of separating interests and positions in a conflict situation.

5. Identify prework to be done to prepare for a meeting to discuss conflicting needs or points of view.

6. Cite five steps of a collaborative conversation.

7. Explain the value of encouraging dissenting viewpoints within a workplace.

8. Describe strategies pharmacist managers can employ to bolster employees' ability to manage their own conflict situations.

KEY CONCEPTS

◆❶ Viewing conflict as an opportunity to understand and respond to the concerns of others, rather than a battle with winners and losers, can be helpful as this perspective makes it easier to pursue mutually beneficial agreements.

◆❷ Although managing conflict can be a difficult and sometimes uncomfortable process, there is nothing inherently negative about conflict.

◆❸ Individual perceptions, opinions, and life experiences can influence our interpretation of events and unexpectedly create conflicts. Perceptions are especially important to recognize and may be framed by many factors, including culture, race, and ethnicity; gender and sexuality; knowledge about the situation; and impressions of the person with whom the conflict is occurring.

◆❹ Personal awareness of one's typical approach to responding to and managing conflict can support effective resolution of conflict situations.

⑤ When all parties involved in a conflict believe there must be both a winner and a loser, a win/lose resolution is usually the outcome.

⑥ Collaboration, a problem-solving approach, is considered a win/win conflict resolution strategy.

⑦ Collaborative conflict resolution is not always easy; it takes time and effort from all involved parties and requires that participants be sensitive to the needs and feelings of others.

⑧ When assisting others through a problem-solving session, the facilitator should remind participants about the importance of separating interests from positions.

⑨ Although pharmacy managers are ultimately responsible for managing conflict within their organizations, the workplace will be more productive if employees are equipped to manage conflict without management intervention.

⑩ Organizations that acknowledge that conflict is normal, support dissenting points of view, and establish protocols for dealing with disagreement tend to achieve superior results compared with those that do not.

INTRODUCTION

When faced with personal or professional **conflict**, how do you respond? Do you view the situation as an opportunity to demonstrate your superior reasoning skills to defeat the other person? Do you get nervous about damaging a relationship? Are there times when you give in rather than debate options with someone else? Have you ever ignored conflict in the hope that the situation will eventually resolve itself? Do you see conflict as a nonthreatening opportunity to enhance your understanding of the other party's interests and motivations? All of these are common reactions to conflict. The more we understand our personal comfort with conflict and the way we

tend to react to it, the more successful we can become in achieving mutually agreeable results.

Poorly managed relationships between employees, other healthcare practitioners, and patients can negatively affect pharmacy operations and patient care; thus, effective conflict management skills are essential for pharmacist leaders, managers, and individual contributors in a pharmacy setting. This chapter will highlight techniques for managing typical conflict situations that arise in pharmacy practices and provide strategies for enhancing relationships, encouraging productive conversations, and supporting an effective and efficient workplace.

DEFINING CONFLICT

Traditional definitions of conflict are negative and may include language such as "any situation in which incompatible opinions, values, attitudes or intentions occur together."[1] Descriptions such as these can evoke visions of extreme workplace tension and battles with subsequent casualties. A less contentious view describes conflict as "disagreement through which the parties involved perceive a threat to their needs, interests or concerns."[2] ❶ *Viewing conflict as an opportunity to understand and respond to the concerns of others, rather than a battle with winners and losers, can be helpful as this perspective makes it easier to pursue mutually beneficial agreements.*

THE BENEFITS OF CONFLICT

❷*Although managing conflict can be a difficult and sometimes uncomfortable process, there is nothing inherently negative about conflict.* Many managers treat conflict as something that can be avoided by enhancing communication;[3,4] however, it can be beneficial to encourage people to express dissenting points of view. Disagreements about data or strategies can often be productive, as they force team members to analyze assumptions, a critical first step in developing more effective methods, services, and products.[5,6] Indeed, in some cases, failing to raise or consider objections can be dangerous. Take, for example, a hospital pharmacy technician whose morning routine includes labeling IV antibiotic bags. The technician has noticed that patients receiving the antibiotic Levaquin always have a single bag label printed. However, one morning he notices that a single patient has four labels for Levaquin 500-mg piggybacks. At this point, the technician can either choose to assume that the pharmacist most likely checked the medication dosage before entering it into the computer, or he can bring it to her attention, an action that may be construed as questioning her authority and reliability. In the interest of patient safety, the technician elects to talk to the pharmacist about the seeming dosage discrepancy. Working together, they realize that the night pharmacist had misread the order and entered it into the computer with the directions "Levaquin 500 mg IV QID (four times a day)" instead of entering it as "500 mg IV QD (once a day)" as had been ordered by the physician. In this instance, the technician's willingness to address his concerns with the pharmacist prevented a potential medication error. Situations like this occur often every day in pharmacy and clinical settings when people with less perceived status, such as paraprofessionals, demonstrate reluctance to challenge those with more perceived power. This points to the need to create a workplace culture in which all members feel free to express their opinions, knowing that their views will be considered thoughtfully and respectfully.

WHAT DRIVES CONFLICT?

Considering typical sources of conflict in a work setting can help managers and employees prepare for them. There are certain times when conflict is most likely to occur, and these may include periods in which workloads are heavier than normal, new members or a new manager is introduced into the work group, new work or procedures are required, a pharmacy is understaffed, noise levels are higher than normal, or patients, supervisors, or colleagues are more demanding than usual.[2] When pharmacy members are suffering personal stress or fatigue, the propensity for conflict can be especially high. Differences in personalities, communication styles, decision-making preferences, and work approaches can create tension and conflict as well. **Table 23–1** lists some common

TABLE **23–1**	**Factors That May Prompt Conflict Within a Pharmacy Setting**

- Heavier than normal workloads
- Being understaffed
- The introduction of new staff members
- Scheduling disagreements
- High noise levels
- Introduction of new protocols or procedures
- Inadequate understanding of job duties
- Impression that pharmacist makes the money but technician does the work
- After a medication error has occurred

factors that lead to conflict in organizations. Pharmacist managers should be sensitive to these situations and take steps to minimize unnecessary conflict whenever possible. Creating channels to express concerns and opinions, such as one-on-one conversations and regular staff meetings, can often encourage productive problem solving and minimize interpersonal conflict.

❸ *Individual perceptions, opinions, and life experiences can influence our interpretation of events and unexpectedly create conflicts. Perceptions are especially important to recognize and may be framed by many factors, including culture, race, and ethnicity; gender and sexuality; knowledge about the situation; and impressions of the person with whom the conflict is occurring.*[2] Harvard Negotiation Project members Douglas Stone, Bruce Patton, and Shelia Heen assert that, when conflict occurs, three issues are at play:

- *The "What Happened?" Conversation* is typically a disagreement about what happened or should have happened, and blame is often assigned.

- *The Feelings Conversation* is related to emotions inherent in the conflict, feelings that may include hurt and anger.
- *The Identity Conversation* is the internal conversation we have with ourselves about what a particular situation means to us personally. We may ask ourselves whether we are overreacting, behaving selfishly, or demonstrating incompetence.[7]

Understanding the many and often complex issues at play within each conflict situation can support swift resolution of disagreements or misunderstandings.

Our values and preferred modes of communication and decision making can also contribute to conflict. When individuals who value tradition are faced with changes that do not honor the past, conflict may emerge. When individuals who value innovation are criticized for boldness, tempers can flare. When individuals who have little patience for details are asked to comment on a technical and complex report, anger may surface. Likewise, when individuals who appreciate extensive background information and significant time for consideration before making a decision are provided with only sketchy details and a short time frame to decide on an approach, they may refuse to engage in conversation.[8] Understanding individual differences in terms of values, communication styles, and decision-making approaches, and aligning your approach with the preferences of other stakeholders, may minimize unnecessary and unproductive conflict. For example, if you know that a person typically needs several days to process information before making a decision, regularly provide adequate time before asking for feedback. If an individual values efficiency and cost savings, avoid framing decisions in terms of how they will contribute to workplace harmony, because this perspective will not be compelling. A great deal of potential conflict can be avoided by simply communicating with people in a way that they prefer to receive information.

RESPONSES TO CONFLICT

Just as individuals tend to instinctively communicate in a manner that feels comfortable to them, people usually have a default method for responding to conflict situations, and their approach is often linked to their personal level of assertiveness and cooperativeness.[9] ◆ *Personal awareness of one's typical approach to responding to and managing conflict can support effective resolution of conflict situations.*

Although there are several tools available to assess one's conflict resolution style, the Thomas-Kilmann Conflict Mode Instrument is one of the most popular and defines five conflict behaviors a person typically uses. These five conflict behaviors include:

- **Competing mode**: People in a competing mode manifest themselves as both assertive and uncooperative. They pursue a win-at-all-costs mentality when trying to achieve their goal, regardless of the effect on the other party and will use every tool available to achieve victory.
- **Accommodating mode**: This is the opposite of the competing mode. Individuals employing this mode are both unassertive and highly cooperative. They are prone to self-sacrifice and will often neglect their own needs in favor of the needs of others. Those who accommodate will often work to fulfill another's directives even if they do not agree with them or would rather not follow that particular course of action.
- **Avoiding mode**: These individuals are both unassertive and uncooperative. Avoiders do not pursue their own goals, nor do they pursue the goals of others. They simply do not deal with conflict. Avoiders will side step issues, put off a task that needs completing, or simply withdraw from a situation that may result in conflict.
- **Compromising mode**: Compromisers demonstrate moderate assertiveness and cooperativeness, and their goal is to find a common-ground solution that will satisfy all disagreeing parties. Compromisers tend to give up more ground than those who employ the competing mode because of their interest in preserving relationships with the other party.
- **Collaborating mode**: Collaborators are both assertive and cooperative. These individuals

attempt to find solutions that are mutually satisfying for all parties. This can often require more time investigating the true roots of a disagreement, but this approach allows the collaborator an opportunity to understand opposing points of view when trying to reach a consensus.[9]

People are capable of working within every conflict mode. However, as an individual becomes more adept at working within a specific conflict mode, he or she will begin to favor it over others. These conflict management strategies may be categorized as: win/lose, lose/lose, and win/win.[9] **Table 23–2** notes the pros and cons of each conflict management approach. ◆*When all parties involved in a conflict believe there must be both a winner and a loser, a win/lose resolution is usually the outcome.* Competing is considered a win/lose situation in which one person is perceived to be aggressive and uncooperative. People who use this strategy are concerned with controlling the behavior of their opponent, relying on a combination of threats and their own power to win a favorable outcome. Accommodating is a lose/win strategy, with one party acquiescing to the other despite his or her needs or interests. Avoidance is considered a lose/lose strategy, as failure to tackle the issue at hand tends to leave both parties' needs unmet. Compromise results in both parties sacrificing something they want. ◆ *Collaboration, a problem-solving approach, is considered a win/win resolution strategy*, as the process uncovers the needs and interests of each party and enables them to reach mutually acceptable agreements.

EMPLOYING A COLLABORATIVE APPROACH TO PROBLEM SOLVING

Resolving competing interests in the workplace can benefit significantly from advance preparation. Phil Harkins, the author of *Powerful Conversations*, provides a structure for holding conversations to work through conflict. Before holding a formal meeting to address concerns, Harkins recommends pre-work to include:

1. Analyzing your own interests and those of others.
2. Defining your desired outcome.
3. Considering natural points of agreement and intersection between your interest and others.
4. Listing factors that might derail the conversation and developing strategies to keep the conversation on track.
5. Paying attention to timing.[10]

TABLE **23–2** **An Analysis of Conflict Styles**	
Conflict Management Style	Result
Avoidance	Lose/Lose
Accommodation	Lose/Win
Compromise	Lose/Lose
Competing	Win/Lose
Collaboration	Win/Win

Source: Data from Thomas-Kilmann Conflict Mode instrument.[9]

Once planning and preparation are in place, the elements of a collaborative conversation should include the following five steps:[7,11]

1. *Identify the problem.* At this stage, participants must identify and define the problem. Equally important, those involved must also identify who "owns" the problem.
2. *Identify all possible solutions.* This is the time for brainstorming. All involved parties should come up with as many solutions to the identified problem as possible. This stage may take some time. There will be a variety of solutions advanced, but none should be criticized or discounted. However, participants are encouraged to improve on submitted ideas and even suggest ways in which these solutions can be combined. The goal of this brainstorming period is to create a relaxed atmosphere that ensures the free flow of ideas. Calmly and candidly expressing one's needs or interests can expedite problem resolution.[7] Examples might include, "I want a schedule that allows me to be home most evenings"; "I want to limit time with customers"; "We are hoping for a price that will enable us to be competitive with other pharmacies in town." There is nothing weak about expressing desires or concerns.
3. *Decide which solution is best.* Now that all ideas are on the table, revisit the problem and identify which solution is the best fit. Does this solution appeal to the parties involved?
4. *Determine how to implement the solution.* Once you have picked the solution that best fits your problem, devise a plan for implementing it.
5. *Assess the outcome of the solution.* Did the chosen solution result in a win/win outcome? Were all parties equally satisfied with the results of the solution? Was the problem preventable? If so, how?

❼ *Collaborative conflict resolution is not always easy, takes time and effort from all involved parties, and requires that participants be sensitive to the needs and feelings of others.* This approach is preferred by many because it focuses energy on attacking a problem instead of the individuals involved.

MANAGING CONFLICT WITHIN ORGANIZATIONS

Pharmacist managers are often called on to manage conflict within their organizations when employees or patients are unable or unwilling to resolve conflict themselves. In some cases, something that began as a simple misunderstanding may escalate into a team-dividing conflict. Levels of group conflict can take many forms, ranging from generalized complaints the warring sides have with one another to specific issues regarding specific employees.

In a team setting, a group session in which each individual is provided an opportunity to express his or her concerns can generate useful ideas. A neutral facilitator can often help. ❽ *When assisting others through a problem-solving session, the facilitator should remind participants about the importance of separating interests from positions.* What does it mean to separate an interest from a position? A position might be, "We need more staff," while an interest might be, "We want to ensure that we don't make errors as a result of time pressures." When interests are voiced, it is much easier to develop potential options to address them.

A facilitated process will be most productive if ground rules for communication are established (e.g., suggestions will not be judged or evaluated until all ideas are presented, there will be no interruptions); all participants are expected to voice their desired outcomes; and all parties are committed to resolving the issue under discussion.

The collaborative approach described earlier is effective for group conflict as well but may require extra steps. It is often helpful to:

1. Spend extra time assessing participant needs and concerns to understand fully the source of conflict and to minimize surprises during the facilitated session.
2. Use a "restating ground rule" to ensure that each party understands all perspectives. In this process, participants are asked to restate the previous person's viewpoint before presenting their own.
3. Seek common ground early to clarify areas of agreement that can be built on.

4. Allow various levels of negotiation. Cross-group discussion is important, but subgroup communication may also be productive.

5. Whenever possible, constitute subgroups with members who are not traditionally aligned. When existing coalitions are broken down, participants may more quickly move from adversarial to problem-solving behavior.

6. Be sensitive to group and individual dynamics, including the role of moderates and extremists. Ensure that all parties have an opportunity to express themselves and that no one individual or alliance dominates the conversation.

7. Be sensitive to your role as facilitator and ensure the appearance of neutrality.[2]

BUILDING CONFLICT COMPETENCE

❾ *Although pharmacist managers are ultimately responsible for managing conflict within their organizations, the workplace will be more productive if employees are equipped to manage conflict without management intervention.* Expecting employees to demonstrate conflict competence—the skills, knowledge, experience, and commitment required to manage conflict productively—is an essential foundation for building a productive workplace. In the event that group conflict occurs, pharmacist managers can employ a number of strategies to manage group conflict:

- Establish organizational protocols for managing conflict. In other words, agree as a group how conflicts will be managed.
- Equip employees with the tools and confidence to manage their own conflict.
- Screen for conflict competence during hiring and promotion processes.
- As a manager, refuse to hear arguments until the parties in conflict have exhausted their ability to reach consensus by themselves.
- Establish a conflict escalation protocol—require those who cannot reach agreement by themselves to jointly present their disagreement to management.
- Make the process of conflict resolution transparent—if your employees bring conflict to you, explain the factors that led to your even-

tual decision so that employees will understand the criteria for making decisions in the future.[11]

❿ *Organizations that acknowledge that conflict is normal, encourage dissenting points of view, and establish protocols for dealing with disagreement tend to achieve superior results compared with those that do not.*[5,11] Pharmacist managers can employ a number of techniques to encourage productive and respectful debate. First, cultivate a culture of openness in which dissenting opinions are solicited and valued. A manager can create such an environment by asking for advice and concerns before making decisions. The simple act of asking questions rather than expressing opinions can encourage employees to be better thinkers and provide previously unconsidered alternatives. Expecting staff to express their opinions and rewarding individuals for doing so will send a message about the importance of group input. Some managers hold meetings in which one person or group is designated as the devil's advocate and is expected to point out flaws or barriers to ideas and proposals. This can be an amusing and informative way to challenge ideas and approaches. Asking staff to provide a list of pros and cons for various options will stretch their analytical skills and signal that you want the good news and bad news about each approach. Most important, encouraging debate requires managers to be open to feedback even when the feedback about their own ideas or performance is not pleasant or comfortable to receive. Additional strategies are detailed in **Table 23–3**.

A great deal can be gained by a healthy discussion of opposing points of view. Innovative ideas may be introduced that reshape how a company does business, how patients can be protected, how positive intentions can be acknowledged and rewarded, and how people can become united while working toward a common goal.

SUMMARY

Well-managed conflict can lead to better ideas and enhanced approaches, while poorly managed conflict can lead to excessive turnover, disengage-

TABLE 23–3	Conflict-Diffusing Conversation Starters

Strategy	Conversation Points
Discuss Each Other's Perceptions	"What happened from your perspective?" "May I share how I see things?"
Acknowledge How You Might Have Contributed to the Conflict	"I assumed you knew that I wanted extra syringes ordered. I wasn't explicit about that, so I can understand why they weren't ordered."
Let People Talk	"I'm interested in your view of what happened." "Tell me more about that."
Consider Interest Rather Than Position	"Help me understand what you hope to achieve."
Collect Data to Understand the Perspective	"You say that you disagree with how I manage the pharmacy. Can you give me specific examples of things that need to be different?"
Establish Objective Standards for Making Decisions	"Let's agree to use regional salary data to determine a fair rate of pay for your new position."
Partner in Problem Solving	"Let's work together to propose some potential solutions." "Why don't we make a list of possible options and then review the pros and cons of each?"

ment, and compromised patient care. Pharmacist managers must work to ensure that their employees are able to work together productively and interact with patients and customers effectively. They can do this by creating a culture of respect, establishing standards of behaviors, creating opportunities to surface opposing points of view, and developing standard approaches to resolving conflict when employees cannot reach agreement themselves.

References

1. Hocker J, Wilmont W. *Interpersonal Conflict*. Dubuque, IO: William C. Brown Publishers; 1985.

2. Assumptions about conflict. University of Wisconsin–Madison Office of Quality Improvement and Office of Human Resource Development. Available at: http://www.ohrd.wisc.edu/onlinetraining/resolution/aboutwhatisit.htm#whatisconflict. Accessed February 27, 2009.

3. Kriesberg L. *The Sociology of Conflict*. Englewood Cliffs, NJ: Prentice-Hall; 1973.

4. March J, Simon H. *Organizations*. New York, NY: John Wiley & Sons; 1958.

5. Gary L. Bury your opinion, shortchange your team. *Harv Manage Update* May 2003:4–5.

6. Rogers Commission Report. Report of the Presidential Commission on the Space Shuttle Challenger Accident; 1986.

7. Stone D, Patton B, Heen S. *Difficult Conversations*. New York, NY: Penguin Books; 2000.

8. Keirsy, D. *Please Understand Me II*. Del Mar, CA: Prometheus Books; 1998.

9. Thomas-Kilmann Conflict Mode Instrument. Available at: http://www.kilmann.com/conflict.html. Accessed July 23, 2008.

10. Harkins P. *Powerful Conversations*. New York, NY: McGraw-Hill; 1999.

11. Weiss J, Hughes J. Want collaboration? Accept—and actively manage—conflict." *Harv Bus Rev* 2005;83(3): 92–101.

Case Scenarios

CASE ONE: You have been on the job as manager of a retail pharmacy for three months and find all of the members of your staff to be enormously agreeable. There are never any arguments and no one ever challenges your ideas about improving systems and protocols. While it is nice that everyone is so pleasant, you are frustrated by the lack of ideas emerging from your team. When you ask for feedback, the most common response is, "You're the boss, and we'll do whatever you think is best." After expressing your concern to a colleague, you learn that the previous pharmacy manager was known for blowing up at anyone who disagreed with his ideas. It appears that your staff developed "excessive pleasantness" as a career survival strategy. Recognizing that dissent and disagreement can be productive, how can you get your staff to express their ideas and concerns?

CASE TWO: Sarah Emory, a nurse manager from the general surgery unit at your hospital, has just called to lodge her second complaint about your procedures for delivering medication to the floor. Ms. Emory says a trained monkey could do a better job than you, and she believes you should be fired. How do you respond?

CASE THREE: Samir St. John has been a staff pharmacist longer than anyone else staffing the pharmacy. Given your policy of letting seniority dictate vacation schedules, you are consistently surprised that Samir tends to work most holidays, letting more junior pharmacists have this time off. Unfortunately, you and others tend to pay the price for Samir's "kindness." He is frequently petulant, and the day after major holidays he makes snide remarks, such as, "It must have been nice to spend time with your family while the rest of us were working." Given that Samir is the one influencing the schedule, how can you turn around his behavior?

CASE FOUR: After waiting three hours to see her doctor, Mrs. Ruiz has dropped her prescription off at the pharmacy to be filled. She does not feel well and is ready to go home. As the pharmacist on duty, you look at the prescription and realize it is not written correctly. You will need to call the doctor to get the problem corrected. Mrs. Ruiz becomes visibly agitated when you explain this to her, and Mrs. Ruiz begins to yell. "I hate this pharmacy," she says. "I always have a problem with you filling my prescription. If you know there is a problem with the prescription, why don't you just fill it right and let me go home? You are so incompetent!" How should you respond?

Additional Resources Available Online!

Visit the Student Companion Web site at http://healthprofessions.jbpub.com/pharmacymanagement for interactive study tools and additional resources.

See www.rxugace.com to learn how you can obtain continuing pharmacy education for this content.

CHAPTER 24

MANAGING YOUR TIME

RAFAEL SAENZ, PHARMD, MS

SCOTT M. MARK, PHARMD, MS, MED, MBA, FASHP, FACHE, FABC

ALLISON M. VAILLANCOURT, PHD, SPHR

LEARNING OBJECTIVES

After completing the chapter, the reader will be able to

1. Identify common barriers to effective time management.
2. Cite key areas of emphasis critical to managing time and level of effectiveness.
3. Explain the importance of establishing priorities.
4. Discern the value of developing and using a to-do list.
5. Document the value of using a schedule to work toward goals and important projects.
6. Establish an organizing system to manage paper and electronic documents.
7. Implement strategies for efficiently managing e-mail and voice mail messages.
8. Recommend tactics for keeping a meeting on track.
9. Recognize factors that lead to procrastination.
10. Describe why delegation is a critical time management strategy and how it can be used to decrease interruptions and achieve goals.

KEY CONCEPTS

❶ While everyone has 168 hours a week to work, sleep, and engage in other activities, those who manage their time effectively are best positioned to fulfill their responsibilities, accomplish key priorities, and achieve personal and professional goals.

❷ Time management challenges are typically a function of technical errors (e.g., disorganized work space, lack of planning time), external realities (e.g., new life events, working with disorganized people), and psychological obstacles (e.g., unclear priorities, fear of downtime).

❸ Effective pharmacist managers focus on accomplishing their priorities but appreciate the need to shift these priorities as new needs and opportunities arise. Defining what matters is a key step in managing one's time, and doing this requires determining which things will make you feel most successful.

❹ Given competing demands from patients, supervisors, employees, and others, pharmacist managers must learn to establish priorities.

❺ Good planning incorporates determining tasks that must be accomplished to reach goals and scheduling time required to complete them.

❻ Be strategic and selective as you create your to-do list. If a task is not essential or at least very important, it should not be added to your list.

❼ Scheduling is the process by which you look at available time and plan how you will use it to achieve the priorities or goals you have identified.

❽ Effective project managers break each project into its various elements, provide realistic time estimates for each required activity, and plug each step into their calendars over time.

❾ Effective managers set the tone for organized and efficient meetings by distributing a clear agenda, inviting the right people, and keeping the proceedings on schedule.

❿ Procrastination is a behavior that can be the result of several factors, including perfectionism, fear of failure, or even fear of success. Often, it is a function of having inadequate information or uncertainty about how best to proceed.

Case Study

Like he did every morning, Jake Wilson woke up at 5:45, met his running buddies at 6:05, and was on the train by 8:15 to reach the hospital by 9:00. Today was a big day that would begin with a meeting with the Joint Commission where he would present on medication safety goals and end by joining his tennis league for a few practice sets. After the meeting with the Joint Commission, Jake planned to complete six performance evaluations, speak to two infectious disease physicians about the new antibiotics stewardship program planned for implementation during the next week, review new formulary recommendations, attend a luncheon with the leadership team, check in with his pharmacy staff, and prepare a talk for next week's Rotary Club. As often the case with many managers, Jake, a dedicated employee who takes his work responsibilities seriously, actually accomplishes few of his daily goals. He felt particularly bad about missing the meeting with the infectious disease physicians because he was unable to prepare for it in time. He looked around his office, spied a stack of phone message slips and a screen full of e-mail messages and thought, "All I did today was put out fires. All I *ever* do is put out fires. How am I ever going to get to the things that matter?" As he packed up his things to leave, the director of nursing dropped by to ask Jake for his review of a grant submission proposal due in two days that would benefit the hospital, especially the pharmacy and nursing departments. "You said you would have your comments back a couple of days ago; we're running out of time," she said. "Sorry," Jake responded, "tonight's my tennis league and if I don't catch the 6:05 evening train, I'm doomed. I promise I will have it on your desk tomorrow morning. I promise."

INTRODUCTION

Getting everything done in a reasonable amount of time is a significant challenge for both pharmacists and pharmacist managers. ❶ *While everyone has 168 hours a week to work, sleep, and engage in other activities, those who manage their time effectively are best positioned to fulfill their responsibilities, accomplish key priorities, and achieve personal and professional goals.* Jake, the pharmacist manager, seems to be managing his exercising and socializing time very well as evidenced by his morning running routine and commitment to his tennis league; his life at work, however, is less successful. Jake should be commended for taking time to exercise and spend time with friends and should apply the same degree of focus on achieving more at work. Work–life balance is important, and pharmacists managers like Jake are not alone in their challenges to find such a balance. Given that it is difficult for professionals to completely "finish their work" at the end of the day, it is essential to establish priorities. This makes it easier to stop working at the end of the day and focus on other life interests and commitments. Effectively accomplishing pharmacist-related activities, including management goals, can be a huge and complex undertaking requiring constant balancing of tasks and priorities.

The nature of pharmacy work makes managing time especially difficult, as meeting basic patient needs and fulfilling management requirements can consume much of the workday and leave little time for other activities such as counseling patients and developing medication management plans.[1,2] Effectively managing time to be able to pursue meaningful activities requires an organized and disciplined approach. This chapter will discuss (1) barriers to effective time management, (2) how to determine key priorities, and (3) time management strategies for creating efficiencies and maximizing productivity.

BARRIERS TO EFFECTIVE TIME MANAGEMENT

❷ *Time management challenges are typically a function of technical errors (e.g., disorganized work space, lack of planning time), external realities (e.g., new life events, working with disorganized people), and psychological obstacles (e.g., unclear priorities, fear of downtime).*[3] Technical errors include such things as poor planning, continuing to use cumbersome ordering or inventory systems, or taking on tasks for which others are better suited. **Multitasking** is another technical error. Many people believe doing two or more things at once is a smart way to accomplish tasks, and they regularly read e-mails or check prescriptions while talking on the phone or scan reports while participating in meetings. While busy pharmacists may not be able to stop performing one function to accomplish another at all times (e.g., ceasing to fill a prescription while waiting on the phone for an insurance approval), use sound judgment when deciding when it is appropriate to multitask. Because the brain cannot focus completely on two things at once, multitasking tends to shortchange the effectiveness of each activity.[4] External realities can

also pose time management barriers. These can range from a health condition that limits your energy to an environment in which interruptions are constant (as is typical in a pharmacy setting).[3] The final and most complex barriers to time management are psychological obstacles. Psychological barriers can include fear of downtime, a belief that it is more important to care for others than it is to take care of ourselves, or even worries that adding structure to one's life will stifle creativity.[3]

ASSESSING YOUR CURRENT LEVEL OF EFFECTIVENESS

Root causes of one's time management issues must be uncovered before possible remedies can be considered, but uncovering these root causes can be challenging. As a first step toward gaining a better grasp of potential time management issues, Peggy Duncan, author of *The Time Management Jogger*, suggests spending a few days mapping the way time is used. She recommends recording how you spend each hour, whether the activity was planned or unplanned, who was involved, and the degree to which the activity is aligned with your goals.[5] Although it is relatively easy to document the amount of time spent on scheduled meetings and even unscheduled encounters, it is more difficult to quantify time required to attend to such things as staff conflict, staffing shortages, or inventory problems.[6] Furthermore, most pharmacists have responsibilities that depend on external forces (e.g., the number of prescriptions that need to be filled, unexpected health events of your patients that must be dealt with quickly), and this should be accounted for in the **activity log**. Despite expected and unexpected events, an activity log can uncover patterns of inefficient time usage and identify opportunities to increase focus and efficiency.

Compare Jake and his colleague, Maysoon Najeeb, a professional counterpart from a hospital in a nearby community. Their activity logs (**Table 24-1**) reveal that Jake moves from task to task, trying constantly to respond to the needs of others, being distracted by nonessential activities (for example, following internet links to new research studies), and failing to delegate tasks that could be done as well or better by others. For example, Jake should have arranged for the clinical coordinator,

TABLE 24-1	A Comparison of Two Hospital Pharmacy Managers' Daily Activities

	Jake Wilson		Maysoon Najeeb
5:45	Wakes up, has coffee, and puts on running clothes	**6:15**	Wakes up
6:05	Runs 5 miles with friends	**6:20**	Checks online news headlines, eats breakfast, showers, gets dressed, makes lunch
7:10	Showers, shaves, dresses, eats breakfast	**7:20**	Drives to pharmacy while listening to news on National Public Radio
7:50	Walks to train; rides train to hospital while reading a professional journal	**7:45**	Arrives at work. Reviews priorities for the day and notes that the cost reduction proposal is today's key priority
8:45	Checks in on pharmacy staff on the way to meet The Joint Commission Committee	**7:48**	Checks and responds to e-mails and then develops outline for cost reduction proposal
9:00	Meets with the Joint Commission Committee	**8:10**	Pharmacist in charge stops by with a question but agrees it can wait until scheduled 3:15 p.m. meeting
10:23	Tries unsuccessfully to find articles about antibiotic stewardship programs conducted at other facilities for 2:00 p.m. meeting with Infectious Diseases Department physicians	**8:12**	Completes cost reduction proposal outline and begins script
10:38	Reviews file with notes about Rotary Club speech, but is interrupted by business manager who wants Jake to edit a memo	**9:20**	Takes a 10-minute walk
10:49	Searches unsuccessfully for computer file that holds his presentation on trends in prescriptions costs	**9:30**	Meets with hospital chief financial officer concerning a possible grant proposal to implement clinical pharmacy services in the pediatrics clinic. Brings pediatric clinical specialist to meeting, as she will delegate the task of writing part of the proposal to this pharmacist
10:59	Takes call from shelf company interested in making a proposal for revamping the pharmacy layout	**9:50**	Develops slide content for proposal presentation

Jake Wilson		Maysoon Najeeb	
11:10	Reviews file to prepare for performance evaluations	**11:35**	Reviews and responds to e-mail and voice messages
11:23	Reads e-mails and writes responses to two inquiries	**12:00**	Has lunch with director of nursing
12:00	Meets leadership team for lunch	**1:15**	Returns to office to start working on grant proposal
1:25	Looks for clinical coordinator who has expertise on antibiotic stewardship programs but is unable to find her. Tries again to find journal articles about such programs	**3:15**	Has weekly meeting with pharmacist in charge
1:47	Takes call from nurse on 3 South who states patient in Room 311 has a rash on back and blames it on the sleeping medication that was administered last night	**3:45**	Reviews and lists priorities for the day ahead
2:00	Skips meeting with physicians from Infectious Diseases Department because he is not prepared for it	**4:00**	Attends continuing education program concerning medical management of asthma
2:05	Reads e-mail	**5:00**	Leaves to attend 6:00 spinning class with daughter
2:15	Receives a phone call from Infectious Diseases Department saying meeting has been delayed in anticipation of his arrival		
2:18	Returns to writing performance evaluations		
4:20	Checks stock market and news headlines		
4:05	Talks with his outstanding lead pharmacy technician who asks if he will serve as a reference for a job for which he has applied. Rather than ask what it would take to keep him, Jake says he would be happy to serve as a reference		
4:10	Gets bored with evaluations and moves to outline of Rotary Club speech		
5:30	Packs up to leave as director of nursing asks for grant		
6:30	Steps onto the tennis court		

who knows more about the antibiotic stewardship program, to meet with the infectious disease physicians; instead, he missed the meeting as a result of his last-minute efforts to prepare for it. Maysoon, however, spends more focused time on her key priorities, delegates tasks, and tends to consolidate tasks to be more efficient (e.g., spending quality time with her daughter while getting in some exercise at spinning classes).

MAXIMIZING PRODUCTIVITY

In the best of all possible worlds, we would have a well-ordered master list of all our life's priorities and conclude each day by making a prioritized list of key tasks for the day ahead designed to propel us toward our life goals. Then, after waking each morning, we would work through these priorities one by one. But, of course, that is not how life works. Phone calls interrupt our concentration, e-mail requests divert our attention, people drop in on us, bureaucratic processes impede our progress, and other people's emergencies become our own. Although time management discipline is an asset, flexibility with your time and the willingness to rearrange the order and value of established priorities to capitalize on new and unexpected opportunities are assets too. ❸ *Effective pharmacist managers focus on accomplishing their priorities but appreciate the need to shift theses priorities as new needs and opportunities arise.*

When it comes to managing both our time and our effectiveness, there are six key areas of emphasis:

- *Focus*: Establishing clear priorities aligned with personal and professional priorities; for example, allowing those with specialized training (e.g., board certification) to practice primarily in their specialty area.
- *Organization*: Minimizing clutter and ensuring that everything has a proper place and is easily accessible; for example, arranging all supplies for intravenous room and cart-fill area so they are in proximity to their respective work spaces.
- *Planning*: Taking the time to forecast needs, deciding which tasks are required to reach goals, and scheduling adequate time to com-

plete requirements; for example, determining how long it will take to run end-of-day prescription reports.
- *Systems*: Creating processes and using approaches that increase efficiency and minimize mistakes; for example, developing and implementing a protocol that prohibits pharmacists from being interrupted while checking medications before they are delivered to the floor.
- *Rituals*: Engaging in regular practices that maintain energy, purpose, and focus; for example, participating in monthly continuing education programs with the local pharmacy association.
- *Delegation*: Distributing work to those best suited to do it; for example, allowing the technician who has adequate knowledge and management skills to be in charge of technicians' work schedules.

Focusing on What Matters Most

❸ *Defining what matters is a key step in managing one's time, and doing this requires determining which things will make you feel most successful.* When you are clear about your personal and professional goals, making choices about how to organize and invest your time becomes easier.[7]

A classic experiment conducted in the late 1990s by researchers from Harvard University and the University of Illinois was designed to test people's ability to focus. In this experiment, which has since been replicated with audiences all over the United States, viewers were instructed to watch a video and count the number of times a basketball was passed among members of the same team. During the course of the videotaped game, a gorilla enters the screen, thumps his chest, and moves on. At the conclusion of the video, viewers are asked how many times the ball was passed and whether they noticed anything unusual. Most viewers were so focused on the counting exercise, they failed to notice the gorilla. When shown the tape again, many refused to believe it was the same footage.[8] Researchers call this "inattentional blindness," paying so much attention to one thing that you fail to notice other things.[9] While focus is a positive attribute, it is important to focus on the *right* things. When we are focused on things that do not matter, we tend to miss important opportunities. Therefore, before addressing *how* to get things done, it is essential to first determine *which* things are most important.

Stephen Covey, author of *The 7 Habits of Highly Effective People*, describes prioritization of one's work as evidence of the maturing of one's time management skills.[10] One transitions from making lists to identifying what is truly relevant work that must be done first. The reality is that time management becomes self-management.[11] ◆ *Given competing demands from patients, supervisors, employees, and others, pharmacist managers must learn to establish priorities.* Covey illustrates the importance of priorities by categorizing activities based on urgency and importance. He notes four types of activities: (1) important and urgent, (2) important but not urgent, (3) not important and urgent, and (4) not important and not urgent.[10] **Figure 24–1** provides examples of activities in each of Covey's quadrants. Covey suggests that the most enduring benefits come from focusing on important, but not urgent, activities, such as forging relationships with members of the pharmacy profession, reading a newly released journal article, and designing a quality improvement process. These activities are not urgent but can reduce time and create future opportunities.

While Covey stresses the importance of focusing on activities that are important but not urgent, he acknowledges that many activities that are both important and urgent require immediate attention. For example, addressing a medication error that resulted in a patient's severe bradycardia almost leading to cardiac arrest or investing time to determine what happened to the missing Diprivan and morphine would be important and urgent issues. Because these activities tend to feel like "firefighting" and divert time from other beneficial activities, effective time managers strive to minimize the emergence of these urgent activities by creating systems to prevent errors and to eliminate drug diversion. Additional efficiency strategies are described in Chapter 7 ("Pharmacy Operations: Workflow, Practice Activities, Medication Safety, Technology, and Quality").

Consider how our pharmacist manager Jake Wilson spends his time. While he clearly values fitness and the friends with whom he exercises, his work life seems to need more direction and focus. The good news is that he has made staying healthy and maintaining relationships with friends a priority, and his actions and commitments are aligned accordingly. Jake is also a committed professional. That his days are filled with work-related activity rather than personal pursuits suggests that his issues are a function of time management rather than a lack of professional commitment. In his book *Get Out of Your Own Way*, Robert Cooper reminds us that busyness does not translate into impact and that effort matters less than results. Says Cooper, "Trying harder is a prescription for dissatisfaction; it's trying differently that changes everything."[9] Jake needs to take stock of the way he spends his time and develop *new* methods to enable him to achieve his goals and objectives. Organizing, appropriately prioritizing, and delegating would likely be a wise investment of his time.

Getting Organized

Walk into some people's work spaces and you will see well-organized manuals, orderly files, and ample empty desk space. Visit others and you will observe numerous open journals, haphazardly placed files, sticky notes posted around the edge of the computer monitor, and several photos and items of memorabilia. Whereas "neat" people are often perceived to be more organized, they might not necessarily be so. Some people simply need the visual cues of files and reports to keep them on task, while others prefer to put items away until they are needed.[7] Regardless of whether you like your work space to appear pristine or "lived in," the key requirement is having enough space to work, determining a place for everything, and knowing where to find it when you need it. To be organized, your work space need not be paper free and your file cabinet need not be filled with color-coded file folders, but you do need some kind of system to ensure that you can find things when you need them.

The Power of Planning

Although organization is important, it does not lead to effectiveness without good planning. ❺ *Good planning incorporates determining tasks that must be accomplished to reach goals and*

FIGURE **24-1**   **Covey's Time Management Matrix.**

	URGENT	NOT URGENT
IMPORTANT	**I** • Providing medications to patients • Deadline-driven projects • Pressing problems (e.g., calling emergency meeting to discuss how to fix the main pharmacy computer system) • "Putting out some fires" • Results of broken processes or systems • New or emerging crises (e.g., addressing occurring medication errors)	**II** • Relationship building (especially with change agents, such as those who have vision, resources, and ability to implement e-prescribing) • Recognizing new opportunities (e.g., implementing new pharmacy clinical services that will facilitate organization's mission) • Planning (e.g., setting up classes to teach pharmacy personnel about the latest dispensing robotic system before implementation) • Preventing potential medication errors
NOT IMPORTANT	**III** • Interruptions (e.g., unexpected visitors, such as sales representatives) • Some e-mails and calls • Some meetings • Popular activities • Non-productive work • Work resulting from non-optimized processes or systems (e.g., writing medication profiles instead of having computer-generated profiles) • Activities of historical importance but still insignificant • Typically redundant work (e.g., in some cases, manually double checking medications instead of using technology, such as bar coding and cameras, to facilitate process)	**IV** • Trivial activities • Busy work (e.g., unnecessary paperwork) • Time wasters (e.g., meeting for the sake of meeting and void of purpose)

This figure displays examples of activities in each of Covey's time management quadrants: (I) Important–Urgent; (II) Important–Not Urgent; (III) Not Important–Urgent; and (IV) Not Important–Not Urgent.

Source: Adapted with permission from the Franklin Covey Co. From Covey SR. *The 7 Habits of Highly Effective People*. New York, NY: Simon & Schuster, Fireside Division; 1989:151.

scheduling the time required to complete them. A critical planning tool is a good to-do list that consolidates all tasks, responsibilities, and commitments into one record. Once items are listed, they can then be prioritized in order of importance. Although to-do lists are very simple, they are also extremely powerful, both for organizing yourself and for reducing stress.

Preparing a to-do list is as simple as writing down the tasks you need to complete. If the tasks are complex, they should be broken down into their component elements and listed individually.[12] Lists can be maintained on paper or on a computer or personal digital assistant (PDA). ❻ *Be strategic and selective as you create your to-do list. If a task is not essential or at least very important, it should not be added to your list.* The most productive people tend to maintain a master to-do list and then develop a daily to-do list at the conclusion of each workday to start the next day in the most productive manner. Taking 10 minutes to do this at the end of each day can help increase focus and reduce anxiety.[13,14]

Good scheduling practices are an important complement to a well-managed to-do list.[15] ❼ *Scheduling is the process by which you look at available time and plan how you will use it to achieve the priorities or goals you have identified.* By using a schedule properly, you can achieve the following:

- Understand what you can realistically achieve with your time.
- Plan to make the best use of the time available.
- Leave enough time for things you absolutely must do.
- Preserve contingency time to handle "the unexpected" and to take advantage of new opportunities that are aligned with your goals.
- Minimize stress by avoiding overcommitment to yourself and others.

For example, in Jake's case, he should have reviewed the time available in the days leading up to his meeting with the infectious disease physicians and scheduled time to prepare for the meeting.

As a manager, you may have someone who maintains your schedule for you or you may main-

tain it yourself. Regardless, there are many good scheduling tools, including electronic calendars, personal digital assistants, integrated software suites, and paper-based organizers. The scheduling tool that is best for you depends on your situation, the current structure of your job, your taste, and your budget.

Scheduling important goals is best done on a regular basis—for example, at the start of every week or month.[15] To ensure that there is a suitable amount of time devoted to priority items, you must schedule these first; otherwise, your calendar will fill up quickly with low-priority tasks. The following steps are designed to ensure that you have time for high-priority tasks, meetings, and projects:

- *Step 1*: Start by identifying the time you want to make available for specific goals. This will depend on the design of your job and your personal goals in life.
- *Step 2*: Schedule actions you absolutely must take to do a good job. These will often be the things against which you are evaluated. For example, if you manage people, scheduling ongoing, one-on-one meetings (e.g., every other Thursday at 2:00 p.m.) will ensure that you stay in touch with your employees and eliminate the constant need to schedule mutually agreeable meeting times. If you are expected to produce a monthly report, setting aside regular analysis and writing time each month will enable you to meet deadlines without sacrificing other obligations.
- *Step 3*: Review your to-do list, and schedule in high-priority, urgent activities, as well as the essential maintenance tasks that cannot be delegated or avoided.
- *Step 4*: Schedule appropriate contingency time. You will learn how much of this you need by experience, but most people need at least 20% of their time to be unscheduled to respond to unexpected matters.[3] Normally, the more unpredictable your job, the more contingency time you need. The reality of many pharmacists' work includes constant interruptions. For example, if you know that every morning you generally need to deal with staffing issues and residual problems left over

from the night shift, it makes sense to consider this when scheduling your morning. Obviously, you cannot tell when interruptions will occur. However, by leaving space in your schedule, you give yourself the flexibility to rearrange your schedule to react effectively to issues as they arise. Strategies such as leaving the first hour of the day unscheduled and building in 30-minutes to an hour between meetings can offer the buffer needed to respond to urgent or unplanned issues.

Project Planning

Large projects can present special scheduling challenges, as it is common to underestimate the length and complexity of a project and the time it will take to complete component parts. ◆ *Effective project managers break each project into its various elements, provide realistic time estimates for each required activity, and plug each step into their calendars over time.*[7] While significant time is required to develop a project plan, the exercise can save time in the long run and ensure that the project is done well and completed on time. For large projects extending over several months, constructing a Gantt chart, a graphical representation of the duration of tasks against the progression of time, may be helpful (refer to Chapter 14, "Pharmacy Business and Staff Planning").

Adopting Effective Systems

Effective managers employ a variety of time-saving systems to achieve goals and manage documents, meetings, mail, correspondence, and projects. The most common strategies include clustering tasks, developing intuitive filing systems, automating activities, using templates, reducing distractions, and minimizing time unnecessarily spent in meetings.

Clustering Tasks

Clustering tasks involves consolidating the time devoted to certain activities, such as paying bills, or taking and ordering pharmacy-related inventory (refer to Chapter 8, "Purchasing and Managing Inventory"). Because shifting back and forth between one activity and another can add as much as 25% to the time required to complete the primary task, clustering tasks can increase efficiency significantly.[4] Try making several phone calls in a row (e.g., such as returning voice messages), opening all of your mail at once, and reading and responding to e-mail only a few times a day.

Using Templates

Developing templates for responding to routine inquiries can save an enormous amount of time for you and your staff. In addition to document templates (e.g., fax cover sheets, insurance inquiry response letters, patient counseling leaflets, and prescription and medication direction labels), some managers find it helpful to develop boilerplate (standardized) phrases, sentences, and paragraphs that can be used in routine memos, letters, reports, employee evaluations, and e-mails. Such templates and boilerplate statements may be helpful to Jake as he prepares both employee performance evaluations and his Rotary Club talk.

Managing Documents

Managing paper tends to be a challenge for many people, and a working file system can help. A "to read" file can be used to hold articles and reports that you would like to read when you have time. A "pending" file can be used to hold items for which you are waiting on information or a decision or action from others. A set of 12 files labeled with each month of the year and a set of 31 files (representing each day in one month) labeled from 1 to 31 can be enormously helpful in managing mail and documents required for future meetings and obligations. The "1–31" files can be used to hold future meeting agendas, invitations, and other items that will be required throughout the month. The "January–December" files can be used to hold items that will be needed later in the year (e.g., a conference program, a reminder to complete your self-evaluation). Filing by topic is also helpful. For example, a file entitled "Antibiotic Stewardship" (that Jake needed; see Table 24–1) may include important documents pertaining to this program.

Rather than using a straight alphabetizing system to manage files, many people find it helpful to separate files by type and to color-code them. For example, green for active files (e.g., active committees or ongoing projects), yellow for historical files (e.g., audit reports), and purple for resource files (e.g., copies of journal articles or another person's presentation materials that might help you write a paper in the future). When several files are stacked on your desk, the color-coding system facilitates returning them to their proper place.

Managing Electronic Files

While many people struggle to keep documents organized, managing electronic files can present special challenges. How often have you heard someone complain that they cannot remember what they named an important document and do not even know what key words to use to search for it? Electronic files, like paper files, are best organized based on whether they are active files, historical files, or resource files. An electronic folder labeled "Presentations" can be used to hold multiple subfolders on topics ranging from "hypertension" to "anxiety disorders." A folder labeled "Committees" can hold subfolders ranging from "Pharmacy and Therapeutics Committee" to "Building Addition Task Force." Once you have established a workable filing system, use a consistent naming convention to locate documents in the future. For example, naming a patient satisfaction report produced February 5, 2010, "PatientSatisfactionReport_2010_02_05" and another produced February 6, 2011, "PatientSatisfactionReport_2011_02_06" will support your ability to locate both files and easily sort them by date created.

Managing E-mail

If appropriate, "read, respond, and delete" is a good routine when it comes to managing e-mail.[16] That said, messages should only be deleted in accordance with established protocols, as a great deal of pharmacy-related communication must be maintained for auditing and other purposes. The sheer volume of received mail can be daunting, and responding to messages and inquiries can easily consume several hours each day. While the desire to check each e-mail as it arrives can be enticing, clustering e-mail reading and responses tends to be a more effective time management strategy. There are a variety of other strategies to minimize time spent on e-mail. You may find it helpful to do the following:

- Turn off the message notification function.
- Create a to-do/high-priority file folder and a to-do/lower-priority file folder and move all e-mails that require action into them.[17]
- Create topic file folders (e.g., "Antibiotic Stewardship") and move appropriate e-mails into the file.
- Establish storage folders to minimize messages in your in-box.
- Put your requested action in the subject line.
- Unsubscribe from unnecessary distribution lists.
- Create filters that direct nonurgent messages to folders that can be opened later.
- Discourage your staff and colleagues from using the "reply all" function when doing so is unnecessary.
- Regularly purge unnecessary items from your storage folders.

Responding to Phone Messages

Responding to phone messages in a timely way demonstrates that you value and respect your callers, but responsiveness does not necessarily require lengthy and time-consuming phone exchanges. When your caller needs an answer rather than a conversation, consider ways to convey the information in a more efficient way. Be sure to keep the requirements of the Health Insurance Portability and Accountability Act (HIPAA) in mind (see Chapter 5, "Significant Laws Affecting Pharmacy Practice Management") when discussing patient-related issues. Always consider options for minimizing phone discussions because of the frequent time waste of tracking people down and the relative inefficiency of some, but not all, discussions. If your caller regularly uses e-mail or text messaging, responding using one of these means can be especially efficient. If voice mail options allow you to "reply to caller," press the appropriate button and do so. If it is possible and appropriate to leave a message with a front-desk person, you may wish to try that as well. Leaving a voice mail response during lunch hours or after traditional work hours, when your caller is unavailable, can enable you to convey important information without requiring a protracted conversation. When all else fails, leading with, "I'm on my way out to a meeting, but I wanted to give you a quick call to respond to your question," can limit potential engagement and lengthy conversation. There are times, of course, when only a conversation will suffice, so it is important to balance the desire for efficiency with the more important goals of effectiveness, customer service, and relationship management.

Managing People Who Consume Excessive Time

As a pharmacist manager, you will find that certain colleagues and employees consume a great deal of your time. Spending time with employees to help them develop project ideas, learn how to use new systems, or pursue career goals is a good investment of your time. However, some employees will demand your time for less beneficial activities. Some will want to update you on details you do not need to know, others will ask permission for things that do not require your attention, and a few will express concerns over issues that have long been decided and resolved. Responding fully to each interruption will demonstrate your commitment to supporting others but will also take away time that should be devoted to other tasks and responsibilities.[13] The following strategies will help you minimize the effect of these individuals on your day:

- If you absolutely have to protect a given time period, you may want to consider closing your door, assuming you have one. Closing your door does not mean that you are not accessible (provided that you do not do it all the time). People will generally respect a closed door and will defer less urgent issues to another time.[14]
- When someone interrupts you in your office, stand up to signal that the encounter should be brief. Likewise, when a conversation has outlived its usefulness, consider standing up. The other party will feel obliged to stand as well, and you can walk them to the door.[14]
- Set up regular meetings with employees and coworkers who demand much of your time. These employees often want to be heard or recognized for the activities they are working on, so give it to them, but on your terms. In this manner, the exchange is bound to a

certain allotted time and is not unpredictable, thus providing a built-in reason to end the exchange.[13]
- Teach employees to solve their own problems. When an employee brings an issue to you for resolution, consider asking, "What do you think we should do?" If extra information is required to make a decision, ask your employee to gather it.

Making Meetings Efficient

Effective managers always consider whether a meeting is necessary before arranging or attending one. Updates and information can often be shared through e-mail, memos, or casual conversations that will take far less time than scheduling and holding a meeting. When a meeting is required, however, organization and preparation are essential. ❾ *Effective managers set the tone for organized and efficient meetings by distributing a clear agenda, inviting the right people, and keeping the proceedings on schedule.*[18] Agendas should include a list of topics with the name of the presenter and a time limit for each item. If reading is required before the meeting, it should be sent well in advance to ensure that participants have time to review it.

Meetings should begin on time and end on time. If your organizational culture makes it acceptable to join or begin meetings late, you can set a different standard by starting all of your meetings on time. Closing, and perhaps even locking, a meeting door so that latecomers are obvious is typically an effective strategy for communicating that you are serious about start times. And just as you expect people to be respectful by arriving on time, you should be respectful by ending the meeting on time so that participants can attend to other matters.

Completing necessary discussions during the meeting time allotted may require using a "parking lot," or **bin list**, to identify critical topics that merit consideration in the future. Parking lot issues are temporary holding areas for ideas or suggestions that are not directly on-topic with the issue facing the group. The facilitator may maintain a separate, visible easel pad to capture these ideas. It conveys the message that the idea will not be discounted and could form the basis for a follow-up agenda or discussion point. By listing these issues (perhaps on a flip chart), participants feel heard, important issues are noted, and the meeting can stay on track. Managing people's concerns before a meeting is another way to keep gatherings on track. Speaking to especially vocal staff and colleagues to hear and understand their concerns before a meeting can minimize time spent on these issues in front of the larger group. The most effective managers turn meetings into short, productive sessions where discussions are focused, decisions are made quickly, and employees work collaboratively and collegially to solve problems.

Minimizing Procrastination

🔟 *Procrastination is a behavior that can be the result of several factors, including perfectionism, fear of failure, or even fear of success. Often, it is a function of having inadequate information or uncertainty about how best to proceed.* In some cases, people procrastinate because they simply dislike the task before them. To overcome procrastination, it is often helpful to ask yourself a series of questions:

* Why am I putting this off?
* What is worrying me?
* What are my instincts telling me?[3]
* Can I do part of the project?[3]
* Can I delegate this to someone else?
* If I dislike this task, can I combine it with something I enjoy (e.g., editing a report while enjoying lunch at a Thai restaurant)?[19]

Strategies that may reduce tendencies to procrastinate include breaking large tasks into smaller, more manageable components, limiting the time you will spend on a task, and working on those projects you most dislike or fear during the time of day you have the most energy.[18]

Establishing Essential Rituals

The most effective time managers tend to follow established patterns or rituals to achieve their goals. Examples of rituals include the following:

* *Planning for tomorrow today.* One of the most common and effective strategies is to determine the first and second priorities for the day ahead before leaving work each day.[4]

* *Tackling the top priority first.* Using the to-do list developed the day before, effective time managers start their workday by working on the day's most important priority.
* *Observing personal energy cycles.* Most managers function at their absolute best during certain hours of the day, whether early morning, just before lunch, or late afternoon when most others have left and there is less noise and distraction. Scheduling the most challenging tasks during the time when you have the most energy and focus is a good strategy for ensuring that tasks are completed.[20] To extend the number of high-energy hours each day, many people find it helpful to alternate tasks every 60–90 minutes (e.g., writing a report for an hour and then placing calls for 15 minutes before returning to the report). Others find it helpful to take a short break every 90 minutes or so to reduce fatigue.[4,21] Breaks need not be long and can involve changing your surroundings, doing some quick stretches, eating an apple, or listening to music you enjoy.[17] The key is to break your current pattern by doing something different and, preferably, something enjoyable.
* *Examining whether commitments are aligned with your personal and professional goals.* People tend to have the most energy for activities that are aligned with their interests and values.[4] If you are offered an opportunity to join an organization or work on a project that does not excite you, politely declining will save you both time and psychic energy.

Using Delegation to Your Advantage

The most effective managers delegate tasks better suited for others when possible and appropriate. In some cases, they delegate tasks they do not like to others. Managers should not delegate *all* tasks they find unpleasant, but if a task requires a particular skill, knowledge, or experience that a staff member possesses, delegation may be entirely appropriate.[22,23] For example, if you find it difficult to write comprehensive reports, you may be able to identify an employee who is able to craft compelling documents. Some employees would view this task as an exciting challenge, an opportunity to showcase their skills and creativity, and a reprieve from their normal duties. Time management authority Julie Morgenstern argues, "Delegating is not something you do to avoid your responsibilities; it's a technique you use to fulfill them."[3] Thus, Jake would have been wise to ask the clinical coordinator, who set up the antibiotic stewardship program and who is the local expert, to present at the meeting with the infectious diseases physicians, rather than trying to tackle it himself. A key to effective leadership and management is surrounding yourself with capable and effective people, such as Jake's clinical coordinator, who is known for her competence. In other words, Jake does not have to accomplish all goals on his own; in fact, most goals require the help of others (refer to Chapter 13, "Achieving Results Through Others and Strategic Planning"). Whether you consider yourself a manager, a leader, or an individual contributor, pharmacists must involve others to increase effectiveness. Involving the clin-ical coordinator certainly would have prevented Jake's frustration and embarrassment and would have saved him time. More important, involving the clinical coordinator early on would have provided her with a valuable professional opportunity and Jake with the chance to demonstrate the quality of his professional team.

SUMMARY

Time management is critical for pharmacists and pharmacist managers alike. This chapter discusses the importance of establishing priorities and reviews key elements of time management, such as overcoming procrastination, organizing work spaces, using to-do lists and electronic media, making meetings effective, and scheduling strategically. By applying these simple strategies, you will maximize your effectiveness, performance, and, ultimately, satisfaction with how you use your time.

References

1. Bell H, McElnay J, Hughes C. A self-reported work sampling study in community pharmacy practice. *Pharm World Sci* 1999;21(5):210–216.

2. Schommer J, Pedersen C, Gaither C, Doucette W, Kreling D, Mott D. Pharmacists' desired and actual times in work activities: evidence of gaps from the 2004 National Pharmacist Workforce Study. *J Am Pharm Assoc* 2006;46(3):340–347.

3. Morgenstern J. *Time Management from the Inside Out*. New York, NY: Henry Holt and Co; 2000.

4. Schwartz T, McCarthy C. Manage your energy, not your time. *Harv Bus Rev* 2007;85(10):63–73.

5. Duncan P. *The Time Management Jogger*. Salem, NH: GOAL/QPC; 2008.

6. Gaynor GH. *What Every New Manager Needs to Know: Making a Successful Transition to Management*. New York, NY: AMACOM; 2004.

7. Lehmkuhl D, Lamping DC. *Organizing for the Creative Person*. New York, NY: Crown Publishers Inc; 1993.

8. Simons D, Chabris C. Gorillas in our midst: sustained inattentional blindness for dynamic events. *Perception* 1999;28:1059–1074.

9. Cooper R. *Get Out of Your Own Way*. New York, NY: Crown Business; 2006.

10. Covey SR. *The 7 Habits of Highly Effective People*. 1st ed. New York, NY: Simon & Schuster, Fireside Division; 1989.

11. English L. The 7 habits of highly effective information professionals. Part 5: Plain English about information. *Information Management Magazine*. July 1, 2004. Available at: http://www.information-management.com/issues/20040701/1005673-1.html. Accessed January 15, 2009.

12. MindTools. To-do lists. Available at: http://www.mindtools.com/pages/article/newHTE_05.htm. Accessed February 20, 2009.

13. Stettner M. *Skills for New Managers*. New York, NY: McGraw-Hill; 2000.

14. Straub JT. *The Rookie Manager*. New York, NY: AMACOM; 2000.

15. Hill LA. *Becoming a Manager: How New Managers Master the Challenge of Leadership*. New York, NY: Penguin Books; 1992.

16. Nelson M. *Stop Clutter from Stealing Your Life*. Franklin Lakes, NJ: Career Press; 2008.

17. Leeds R. *One Year to an Organized Work Life*. Cambridge, MA: Da Capo Press; 2009.

18. Watkins M. *The First 90 Days*. Boston, MA: Harvard Business School Press; 2003.

19. Morgenstern J. *SHED Your Stuff, Change Your Life*. New York, NY: Fireside; 2008.

20. Finzel H. *The Top Ten Mistakes Leaders Make*. Trenton, NJ: Nexgen Press; 2000.

21. Rossi EL, Nimmons D. *The 20-Minute Break: Reduce Stress, Maximize Performance, and Improve Health and Emotional Well-Being Using the New Science of Ultradian Rhythms*. Los Angeles, CA: Jeremy P. Tarcher Inc; 1991.

22. *Coaching and Mentoring: How to Develop Top Talent and Achieve Stronger Performance*. Boston, MA: Harvard Business School Press; 2004.

23. Hunsaker PL, Alessandra AJ. *The Art of Managing People*. New York, NY: Simon and Schuster Inc; 1980.

Abbreviations

HIPAA: Health Insurance Portability and Accountability Act
PDA: personal digital assistant

Case Scenarios

CASE ONE: Miguel Aguilar is the pharmacist in charge at a local chain drug store. He often works 10–12 hour days and is in charge of four different technicians throughout the day in various shifts. He has a very busy store, and he barely has any time to eat lunch. Dr. Aguilar works six-day stretches and has recently been making easily avoidable mistakes in his work. While analyzing the way he spends his workdays recently, Dr. Aguilar found that he spends 50% of his time in crisis mode (calling insurance companies, settling irate customers, etc.), 30% in non-productive work (helping store customers find tissue paper, answering calls for the photo department, filling out paperwork for returns on non-medication items, etc.), and 20% in preventative work (e.g., breaking up arguments between technicians). When he does catch up on work, he often busies himself with smaller unnecessary tasks, such as filling the medication vial bins, cleaning the shelves, running miscellaneous reports, and restocking the small dispensing robot. He would enjoy having time to talk to his patients and helping them use their medications better. What are ways Dr. Aguilar could make better use of his time and avoid burnout?

CASE TWO: Jim Stevenson has recently been appointed as head pharmacist in a hospital clinical pharmacy service. Part of his new responsibilities includes running weekly meetings of all of the pharmacists in the program. These meetings are thinly attended because pharmacists complain that they are chaotic. The pharmacists who do attend typically jump from topic to topic, so following an established agenda is a challenge. How can Dr. Stevenson help make this meeting successful and productive while increasing voluntary participation?

CASE THREE: Clarisse Hill is a new pharmacy manager in a teaching hospital. Coming from a corporate pharmaceutical research environment, she assumed the hospital's academic commitment would enable her time to do research and write manuscripts. That has turned out not to be the case. Nine months into the job, Dr. Hill is overwhelmed by the constant demands on her time. Her typical day involves going back and forth between meetings, attempting to resolve office staffing issues, and dealing with interruptions from pharmacists, technicians, and other hospital personnel. The pharmacy is constantly running out of necessary medications and supplies, and she spends significant time each week making last-minute orders to meet patient needs.

(continues)

What are some strategies Dr. Hill might employ to be able to focus more time on her personal priorities and commitments?

CASE FOUR: Victoria Grey is a pharmacy manager within a large hospital in an urban area. Retaining hospital staff is a constant battle as there seems to be a tendency for people to "move across the street" for small increases in salary. While Ms. Grey's pharmacist team has been relatively stable, turnover among pharmacy technicians is getting harder to manage. She feels like she and the other members of the pharmacy are constantly hiring and training new people—activities that make it difficult to meet patient needs. During one of her quarterly check-in meetings with the director of pharmacy, she was shown the results of two years of pharmacy technician exit survey reviews. Comments included, "I was overwhelmed with work"; "Work was unfairly distributed"; "I never knew if I was doing a good job or not"; and "Any time I asked a question, the pharmacy manager made me feel guilty for wasting her time." The director of pharmacy said to Ms. Grey, "Victoria, you and I have talked about the importance of time management on several occasions, but it's clear that your inability to manage your time is costing us in terms of personnel. I really need you to turn this around." What does time management have to do with turnover, and what changes should be considered?

Additional Resources Available Online!

Visit the Student Companion Web site at http://healthprofessions.jbpub.com/pharmacymanagement for interactive study tools and additional resources.

See www.rxugace.com to learn how you can obtain continuing pharmacy education for this content.

CHAPTER 25

DEVELOPING PROFESSIONALISM

DANA LYNN PURKERSON HAMMER, PhD, MS, RPh

REBEKAH M. JACKOWSKI, PharmD

ROBERT S. BEARDSLEY, PhD, RPh

LEARNING OBJECTIVES

After completing the chapter, the reader will be able to

1. Define professionalism and describe the qualities that exemplify professionalism in pharmacy.
2. Discuss the professional socialization process.
3. Explain the association between professionalism and pharmacists' standards of conduct (the Oath of a Pharmacist and the Pharmacist Code of Ethics).
4. Discuss professionalism in the context of developing your personal brand.
5. Cite important features of professional interactions with patients.
6. Discuss actions to facilitate positive interactions with fellow professionals.
7. Identify strategies to cultivate professionalism in pharmacy practice.
8. Describe the importance of self-assessing professionalism on an ongoing basis.

KEY CONCEPTS

❶ Simply stated, professionalism refers to the standards, behaviors, and character of an individual engaged in tasks related to his or her work or profession. Professionals, particularly in healthcare professions, generally place the needs of others before their own. It is essential that student pharmacists learn what it means to act professionally, how to foster professionalism, and the importance of professionalism from the first day of pharmacy school and throughout their careers.

❷ Professional socialization literature suggests that the primary factors that influence professional attitudes and behaviors are (1) the values and behaviors that the individual brings into professional programs, (2) role models in professional and academic environments, and (3) the environments themselves.

❸ When pharmacists take the Oath of a Pharmacist, they are affirming that they will establish covenantal relationships with their patients to serve them to the best of their ability. In addition to the Oath of a Pharmacist, expected professional behavior is articulated in the Code of Ethics for Pharmacists in statements centered on professionalism.

④ Professionals should develop a set of strategies to prevent or remediate unprofessional behavior, including removing themselves (if possible) from the work environment for a few minutes to relax and calm down or offering a sincere apology for questionable behavior.

⑤ Perhaps the most central feature of the patient–pharmacist interaction, and thus the chief mechanism by which a pharmacist's professionalism is established, is communication. The way patients perceive their pharmacists' ability to communicate with them and other healthcare providers influences perceptions of professionalism.

⑥ Many pharmacists may have difficulty in dealing with coworkers, subordinates, or supervisors because they do not understand the social and professional characteristics of their practice environments.

⑦ Pharmacist managers directly affect the culture of professionalism in their practice sites by establishing positive work environments through policies and their interactions with staff and pharmacy patrons.

⑧ Students, pharmacists, and pharmacist managers and leaders should self-assess their professionalism and be aware of factors that can contribute both positively and negatively.

INTRODUCTION

A pharmacist makes an after-hours delivery to a homebound patient. A student pharmacist enthusiastically participates in a health fair at a homeless shelter. At a particular pharmacy, patients are asked to sign a waiver of counseling without a description of what they are signing. In class, there are episodes of student pharmacists bringing concealed notes to closed-book exams or participating in social networks on their laptops. Each of these scenarios is an example of **professionalism**

(the after-hours delivery, participation in a health fair) or lack thereof (unexplained waiver, concealed notes, social networking during class). Professionalism is not a concept that can simply be learned from a textbook or in the classroom. Ask any pharmacist to define professionalism, and you will get as many different answers as the number of pharmacists who are queried. In many ways, it is easier to define a lack of professionalism rather than define professionalism; however, a clear definition of professionalism is essential. Thus, in this chapter, the concept of professionalism is defined and elaborated on in relation to its development among student pharmacists, its intersection with **ethics**, and its importance in the creation of a **personal brand**. Further, the integral role of professionalism in the work of pharmacists and pharmacist leaders and managers is discussed, as well as how professionalism may be enhanced within pharmacy practice.

PROFESSIONALISM DEFINED

① *Simply stated, professionalism refers to the standards, behaviors, and character of an individual engaged in tasks related to his or her work or profession. Professionals, particularly in healthcare professions, generally place the needs of others before their own. It is essential that student pharmacists learn what it means to act professionally, how to foster professionalism, and the importance of professionalism from the first day of pharmacy school and throughout their careers.* Within pharmacy, the definitions of professionalism tend to come from position papers developed by various pharmacy associations, several of which are identified in **Table 25–1**.[1-5] Qualities noted as exemplifying professionalism include the following:

- *Altruism*: Serving the best interests of the patient, even above the needs of the pharmacist or the employer.
- *Accountability*: Honoring the oath you have taken to serve the patient and the public.
- *Excellence*: Ensuring that you are a lifelong learner to serve your patients in the best possible manner using the most up-to-date information.

TABLE **25–1**	**Pharmacy Association Position Papers on Professionalism**

- American Pharmacists Association Academy of Student Pharmacists (APhA-ASP) and the American Association of Colleges of Pharmacy Council of Deans' (AACP-COD) joint "White Paper on Pharmacy Student Professionalism"[1]
- AACP's Excellence Paper on "Student Professionalism"[2]
- American Society of Health-System Pharmacists' (ASHP) "Statement on Professionalism"[3]
- American College of Clinical Pharmacy's (ACCP) "White Paper on Development of Student Professionalism"[4]
- ACCP's Student Commentary on "Professionalism Tenets for Pharmacy Students"[5]

Sources: Data from APhA-ASP/AACP-COD Task Force on Professionalism;[1] Hammer DP, Berger BA, Beardsley RS, Easton MR;[2] American Society of Health-System Pharmacists;[3] Roth MT, Zlatic TD;[4] American College of Clinical Pharmacy.[5]

- *Duty/responsibility*: Serving the patient to meet his or her needs even when it is not convenient to you or your pharmacy.
- *Honor and integrity*. Being truthful and honest, ensuring that the patient is never compromised by a conflict of interest.
- *Respect for others*: Maintaining respect not only for your patient but also for your colleagues and other healthcare professionals with whom you may interact.[1,2]

Keep in mind that, as professionals, pharmacists have a certain responsibility to society, and it is crucial to maintain behaviors and attitudes worthy of the respect the public has for the pharmacy profession.

DEVELOPING PROFESSIONALISM AS A STUDENT PHARMACIST

The responsibility to act in a professional manner begins in pharmacy school. However, the process of **professional socialization** generally begins before pharmacy school entrance and is explained as "the process by which people selectively acquire the values and attitudes, the interests, skills and knowledge—in short, *the culture*—current in the groups of which they are, or seek to become, a member."[6] This socialization process begins the moment a student or potential student observes or interacts with pharmacists, evaluates what they do, or actively seeks information about the profession. Beliefs, attitudes, and behaviors begin to develop with regard to pharmacists' roles. ❷ *Professional socialization literature suggests that the primary factors that influence professional attitudes and behaviors are (1) the values and behaviors that the individual brings into professional programs, (2) role models in professional and academic environments, and (3) the environments themselves.*[7–12] Although professionalism can be considered a product of the professional socialization process, remember that an individual can be "negatively" socialized just as easily as he or she can be "positively" socialized. If an individual enters a program with values incompatible with those of the profession and the environment, has negative role models, and learns to practice in an unprofessional manner, it is highly probable that this person will neither develop nor exhibit a high level of professionalism until some of those factors are modified. The converse, of course, is also true.

Pharmacists can have a direct influence on the professional socialization and development of student pharmacists, particularly if they serve as **mentors**, role models, or practice experience supervisors (e.g., preceptors). During interactions with and observations of mentors, role models, and practice experience supervisors, student pharmacists may learn about and emulate those behaviors that convey professionalism, such as demonstrating respect toward colleagues or providing extra counseling time to patients when needed. The influence of others and environment and culture on one's professionalism applies not only to pharmacy students, but to pharmacists.

It is also worth noting those behaviors and actions that seem to lack professional conduct, as these situations may provide significant learning opportunities that facilitate professional development. For example, a student pharmacist is placed in a community pharmacy for an advanced pharmacy practice experience (APPE). It is a common policy in this pharmacy to have patients sign waivers of counseling without an accurate description of what they are actually signing. The student pharmacist believes this is unprofessional and is concerned about the level of care provided to patients. Rather than publicly expressing her concerns with limited knowledge of all the facts surrounding the policy, the student pharmacist seeks the advice of a pharmacy professor mentor who recommends that she schedule a meeting with her practice site supervisor. During this meeting, the student pharmacist gains a better understanding of the reasoning behind this policy, expresses concerns, and has a dialogue with her supervisor about potential ways to address concerns. Thus, the student pharmacist both learned to act in a professional manner (based on feedback from her mentor) and demonstrated professionalism (acting in the best interests of the pharmacy's patients).

Interactions and observations of peers, such as fellow student pharmacists, may also be instrumental in the development of professionalism. Student pharmacists may serve as positive role models for each other by seeking and obtaining leadership positions in student pharmacy organizations, volunteering at community health fairs, or simply demonstrating engagement and attention within the classroom setting (e.g., taking careful notes rather than text messaging during class time). A fallacy students sometimes operate under is that their classroom behavior and their actions as students do not reflect their professional conduct and demeanor. Yet, actions in and related to the classroom and the pharmacy education program—for example, timeliness, appropriate attire (when in doubt, err on the conservative side), a good attitude, and knowledge of pertinent policies/rules—are the foundation on which professionalism as a pharmacist is built. Moreover, such actions contribute to the first impressions pharmacists (professors, supervisors) and other healthcare providers (in practice experience settings) have of the student pharmacist. Similarly, student pharmacists need to consider what impressions are projected by their behavior in cyberspace and in public. Consider, would you have been comfortable showing your Facebook page to the pharmacy school admissions committee? What about the elderly woman who regularly visits your introductory pharmacy practice experience (IPPE) site? What do those photos and information say about you? One pharmacy school now includes a required workshop on appropriate cyberbehavior to make students more aware of these issues.[13] Consider also social habits that are in public view. For example, do you and your peers make it a habit to become inebriated or engage in rowdy behavior? We are continually being judged by others, and society expects certain behaviors from professionals. These impressions do not just reflect on you the individual but also your school, university, and the entire profession.

Examples of student professionalism include forming study groups to enhance learning (not only to pass the exam in the short term but to better care for patients in the long term), offering to tutor fellow students who are struggling in a course, or reporting violations of academic honesty, such as cheating or plagiarism. These examples can easily be transformed into actions that may be taken by a pharmacist in the course of acting as a professional—forming a wellness group for obese adolescents or offering medication therapy management to seniors who are struggling with their medication regimens. These examples also represent leadership opportunities. Thus, student pharmacists must recognize how their behaviors today may establish the paths they follow as they become practicing pharmacists, pharmacist managers, or leaders.

INTERSECTION OF ETHICS AND PROFESSIONALISM

After graduating from pharmacy school and entering the pharmacy practice environment, pharmacists are expected and mandated to engage in ethical conduct, defined as conduct based on moral principles which provide knowledge and insight regarding what we ought to do to attain the most of what is best in human life. Professionalism is a key component of successful and ethical patient care. Refer to Chapter 6 "Ethical Decision Making." Patients trust their pharmacists to provide the best care possible, without ulterior motives. ❸ *When pharmacists take the Oath of a Pharmacist, they are affirming that they will establish covenantal relationships with their patients to serve them to the best of their ability.*[14] This relationship between pharmacist and patient is described as a **fiduciary** relationship. Roth and Zlatic define a fiduciary relationship as a "faith bond" or one in which the patient has faith and trust in the pharmacist to make the best decision possible on behalf of the patient.[4] Remember that this relationship does not

begin the day an individual starts working as a pharmacist but much earlier. For example, as a student pharmacist participates in IPPE under the supervision of licensed pharmacists, he or she will begin to make decisions on behalf of patients, and patients will have certain expectations of the student pharmacist, placing their faith and trust in the student to make the best decisions for their care. ❸ *In addition to the Oath of a Pharmacist,*[14] *expected professional behavior is articulated in the Code of Ethics for Pharmacists in the professionalism-centered statements elaborated in* ***Table 25–2***.[15]

Another important aspect to consider in any discussion of ethics and professionalism is the "self-governing" nature of professions. Most professions are governed by boards of peers and community members, such as State Boards of Pharmacy, that determine regulations of how professionals should practice. They are also represented by professional associations that help to establish policy and influence decision makers. The ethical aspect of this self-governing nature of professions, particularly healthcare professions, is that it is necessary to identify and address unprofessional behavior of peers and employees, especially when such behavior could result in patient harm. This is difficult to do, whether as a student,

TABLE **25–2**	**Professionalism-Centered Statements in the Code of Ethics for Pharmacists**

- A pharmacist respects the covenantal relationship between the patient and pharmacist.
- A pharmacist promotes the good of every patient in a caring, compassionate, and confidential manner.
- A pharmacist respects the autonomy and dignity of each patient.
- A pharmacist acts with honesty and integrity in professional relationships.
- A pharmacist maintains professional competence.
- A pharmacist respects the values and abilities of colleagues and other health professionals.

Source: Data from Code of Ethics for Pharmacists.[15]

practitioner, manager, or leader, because of the collegial nature of student and professional networks. No one wants to be considered the "tattletale" who got someone else in trouble; nor do individuals want to put themselves at risk of retaliation or becoming unpopular. Our human nature and desire to avoid conflict usually prevent us from engaging in this process. However, it is incredibly important since not to do so would be unethical, would not be in our patients' best interests, and would possibly damage the reputation of the profession as a whole.

Opportunities to address unprofessional behavior throughout the professional continuum are numerous—everything from asking peers in class to cease unnecessary chatter to talking with a colleague about a potential addiction. Not only should pharmacist managers and leaders set and maintain standards of professionalism consistent with state and federal regulations and confront unprofessional and unethical behavior among employees, but these should be daily goals of all pharmacists. However, to reinforce the importance of ethical, professional practice, pharmacist managers and leaders may be required to take remedial actions, such as holding development workshops on professionalism and ethics, or suspending or terminating unprofessional employees. Further details regarding ethics may be found in Chapter 6, "Ethical Decision Making."

INCORPORATING PROFESSIONALISM INTO PERSONAL BRAND

As described previously, pharmacists and pharmacist managers and leaders are expected to adhere to many principles, and professionalism is a cord that runs through each of these principles. One cannot be an effective practitioner, manager, or leader without being viewed as a professional, garnering the respect and trust of others. The development of a personal brand that emphasizes professionalism is a crucial strategy in building credibility, authenticity, respect, and trust, not only among colleagues but also among patients (the concept of personal branding is further discussed

in Chapter 26, "Creating Your Personal Brand and Influencing Others").

The core of professionalism is truly caring about others and putting their needs above your own. For example, the pharmacist manager of an independent pharmacy reflects the qualities of professionalism by implementing free medication counseling and support programs for low-income patients, modeling respectful treatment of all patients, and funding training and development opportunities for his staff. As a result, his personal brand as a credible and dedicated professional is strengthened. Yet even the most professional individual can have a bad moment. An important and sometimes difficult aspect of professionalism to master is the ability to adhere to professional qualities and values in the face of stress, fatigue, personal attack (e.g., the disgruntled or dissatisfied patient or employee), or other challenging situations. However, inappropriate, thoughtless, or unprofessional behaviors and actions may easily derail efforts to establish an authentic, well-respected personal brand and dismantle an individual's professional reputation. In the case of the aforementioned pharmacist manager, one "off" day or lapse in judgment—such as yelling profane language at a pharmacy technician who was running a few minutes late because of bad weather—could jeopardize a carefully constructed "good" brand of professionalism. ❹ *Professionals should develop a set of strategies to prevent or remediate such moments, including removing themselves (if possible) from the work environment for a few minutes to relax and calm down or offering a sincere apology for questionable behavior.*

In every encounter, the other party (e.g., patient, coworker, employee, boss) will be developing opinions and judgments of your brand based on how you carry yourself, including appearance, body language, and tone, among other things. These opinions may encompass not only the role an individual is functioning within, such as pharmacist manager, but also the pharmacy setting and other employees. Therefore, in addition to developing a respected personal brand, pharmacists, pharmacist managers, and leaders must also carefully consider the development of the "brand" of the organization (e.g., pharmacy or other pharmacy-related work environment), including factors such as staff, physical location and appearance, services offered, etc. Keep in mind, perceptions of the organization's brand may affect perceptions of the professionalism of those employed by the pharmacy, as they are the representatives, or "human faces," of the pharmacy.

PROFESSIONAL INTERACTIONS

Having defined and described professionalism, including its role in ethical conduct and brand development, its tenets will now be applied to issues involving interactions with both patients and fellow healthcare professionals (peers, staff, superiors, and other providers) in various work environments.

Interactions with Patients

The primary action of the pharmacist as a professional—the pledge to serve patients in the best manner possible without prejudice—may result in certain expectations. These expectations may include, but are not limited to, the following actions, which are central to good patient care:

- A willingness to spend time answering patient questions.
- Providing counseling regarding disease state and medication therapy.
- Dispensing safe and effective medications.
- Assisting in identifying appropriate financial mechanisms to pay for needed medications.
- Practicing in a **culturally competent** manner, and treating patients with respect and consideration regardless of their gender, race, ethnicity, sexual orientation, or socioeconomic status.
- Refraining from any actions that may stigmatize the patient or compromise his or her dignity.
- Maintaining patient confidentiality.

Thus, every patient–pharmacist interaction is likely to be evaluated by patients based on their expectations regarding pharmacists and the pharmacy profession. Pharmacists will be assessed on their demeanor, ability to communicate, mood, appearance (most pharmacists would not come to

work dressed in clothing more appropriate for a night out on the town or in clothing with holes and tears), perceived competence, and services rendered; they may also be judged according to the work environment. Thus, it is important to promote a professional personal brand as well as the "brand" of the organization throughout these interactions. Refer to Chapter 26, "Creating Your Personal Brand and Influencing Others."

❺ *Perhaps the most central feature of the patient–pharmacist interaction, and thus the chief mechanism by which a pharmacist's professionalism is established, is communication. The way patients perceive their pharmacists' ability to communicate with them and other healthcare providers influences perceptions of professionalism.* Imagine a patient overhearing a pharmacist using foul language when conversing with a pharmacy technician or a pharmacist using highly scientific language in an abrupt manner when counseling a patient on his or her medication. These seemingly small incidences can have great consequences in the eyes of the patient and his or her judgment of a pharmacist as a professional. Remember, the work environment—the pharmacy—is often a public setting, and as such, suitable/appropriate language should be used with coworkers, subordinates, supervisors, and patients at all times. When providing information to patients, clear, easy-to-understand language, rather than technical terms or jargon, should be used; however, pharmacists must be cautious, as there is a fine line between presenting information in understandable terms and "dumbing things down"—an action patients may perceive as condescending.

Indirect actions can play an equally important role as direct interactions with patients in building up or tearing down a pharmacist's professional reputation. Many times, behind-the-scenes actions in a pharmacy are not known to a patient but are still serving the best interests of the patient. For example, when a patient presents a prescription that has potential for a harmful interaction with another medication he or she is taking, it is the pharmacist's responsibility to act with regard to that problem (e.g., contact the prescriber for a more appropriate medication or counsel the patient on how to minimize or avoid the interaction). The patient has placed his or her trust in the pharmacist to fill his or her prescription correctly and to ensure that the medication will not be harmful. Failure to act in the patient's interests, particularly when such actions are necessary to protect the patient from harm, is a failure in both professional duties and ethical obligations.

Interactions with Fellow Professionals

Most pharmacists do not actively plan to behave unprofessionally; they do not wake up and say, "I think I will be unprofessional today!" However, as mentioned previously, incidents happen due to unforeseen circumstances, stressors, etc. Unprofessional behaviors have many underlying causes, and it is important to determine what might promote these behaviors as a means of preventing them. This section of the chapter discusses some potential areas of concern that may affect interactions with fellow professionals.

❻ *Many pharmacists may have difficulty in dealing with coworkers, subordinates, or supervisors because they do not understand the social and professional characteristics of their practice environments.* Often, individuals act inappropriately because they do not realize that they must adjust their behavior based on the management hierarchy of the organization. For example, a staff pharmacist at an academic medical center tries to look impressive by taking a proposal directly to the chief executive officer (CEO) of the hospital rather than talking to the pharmacy director first. These errors may occur because pharmacists do not understand the management structure within their organization, the appropriate ways of "doing business," and the importance of these channels. Pharmacists and pharmacist managers and leaders must realize that they need to vary their approach based on the organization's nuances and protocols (both formal and informal). That is, a specific behavior might be judged to be appropriate on one level of the organization's hierarchy but unprofessional on another level. For example, you would approach a conversation with your manager or director regarding implementation of a new program differently than a discussion with a technician who is helping you prepare intravenous medications. You might call the technician by his or her first name, but you may not do the same

when interacting with your boss because doing so without his or her consent could be perceived as unprofessional.

Related to acting appropriately within the hierarchy of the organization, individuals may behave questionably or unprofessionally when they do not understand their role or status in the organization compared with the role or status of others. Most practice environments are complex organizations with a variety of people fulfilling various roles and responsibilities, and various levels of status typically exist based on role or title within the work environment. Moreover, each organization has a unique approach to determining how decisions are made, who has the authority to make certain decisions, and who is responsible for carrying out specific assignments. If pharmacists violate these predetermined codes of conduct or rules of operation for their particular roles, then their behaviors might be labeled as unprofessional. For example, as a manager within the pharmacy department, a more assertive, direct approach may be appropriate to use when giving instruction to technicians who are expecting you to set the tone for the pharmacy. However, this approach would not be suggested when advocating for new resources from the pharmacy director. Although a subordinate can still be assertive with a superior, this knowledge is tempered by the acknowledgment that judgment on issues such as resource allocation and program implementation may have to be deferred to the superior based on his or her status within the organization. Thus, it is critical for pharmacists and pharmacist managers and leaders to understand how to adjust their approaches based on the status and role function of the various parties involved. The following sections discuss some challenges to professionalism in interactions with peers, pharmacy support staff, supervisors, and other healthcare providers.

Peers

Professional peer relationships are typically more collegial because of similar roles and levels of power or authority within an organization. In other words, peers know what to expect from their interactions and can be more relaxed. However, professionalism issues may still arise within a designated peer group. For example, more experienced pharmacists might believe themselves to have increased status over other pharmacists, or graduates from a certain high-ranking college of pharmacy may perceive themselves as being better than graduates from other colleges. Thus, you may think you are in a peer relationship but perceived underlying differences in status and rank may exist, preventing a peer group from working together optimally in a professional manner. Such differences based on factors unrelated to work efforts and organizational structure may be unprofessional and immature, yet violations of informal peer group protocols may alienate the rest of the group. To promote professionalism within the organization, members of pharmacist peer groups, as well as pharmacist managers and leaders, must devise ways to change these inappropriate status differences and facilitate interactions based on mutual respect.

On a positive note, interactions with peers provide opportunities to receive feedback regarding how individual behavior is perceived. Candid conversations with colleagues could reveal specific behaviors, actions, or habits you are not aware of that may be viewed as unprofessional by others. Learning about "blind spots" is an essential component of enhancing professional development. Refer to Chapter 26, "Creating Your Personal Brand and Influencing Others". In addition, receiving feedback from peers about your behavior is probably less threatening than receiving comments from superiors or individuals whom you supervise.

Pharmacy Support Staff

Because of power differentials, professional relationships with pharmacy support staff are generally more difficult to balance than peer relationships. Individuals in positions of greater power and authority, such as pharmacist managers, need to be respectful of subordinates but must also be able to give instruction and direction when needed. To do otherwise would be unprofessional. You may want to be friends with staff members; however, caution and sound judgment should be employed to prevent friendship from interfering with making difficult but necessary decisions about workload and job responsibilities. Also, annual performance evaluations and management-related functions should not be compromised because of personal

relationships. In addition, staff may want to be friendlier than you deem appropriate, and you must be sensitive to staff members' expectations of their relationships with you. How you communicate expectations regarding relationships is critical—you should appear to appreciate and respect staff, while at the same time, maintaining appropriate boundaries and lines of authority. The key is to articulate your expectations and boundaries in an empathetic and sensitive manner. Refer to Chapter 21, "Communicating Effectively with Others."

The ability to interact professionally with support staff is often influenced by differing value systems—your own and those of various staff members. For example, staff members might approach work differently (a vocation to bring in income versus a career) or view work as a short-term option rather than a long-term commitment. In addition, they may act differently because of generational differences that have been discussed extensively in the literature.[16,17] Although it is beyond the scope of this chapter to discuss all the ramifications and strategies to deal with these generational and value system differences, it is imperative that pharmacists in management and leadership positions (whether formal or informal) recognize the existence of such differences and consider how they might affect interactions with subordinates on a professional level.

Superiors

Interactions with superiors will typically be more formal because of their status within the organization, and the evolution of this professional relationship is largely dictated by the actions of the superior. Some superiors choose to be informal and casual, while others feel more comfortable keeping things more formal—this decision may depend on the environment, culture, the policies of the organization, or the personality of the individual. The key to professional interaction in this case is to respect that your superior will set the tone for the relationship, just as you set the tone for relationships with your support staff. Attempts to wrest control or dictate the direction of the relationship may be perceived as unprofessional by your superior and may, in turn, compromise your position within the organization. Refer to Chapter 2, "Management Essentials for Pharmacists."

As a subordinate of your superior, sensitivity and professional decorum must be demonstrated in situations in which your direct supervisor interacts with his or her superior. For example, you are attending a reception within the institution and your pharmacy department director is speaking with the hospital's CEO. It would not be advisable to interrupt the conversation without acknowledgment. You also should refrain from bringing up departmental issues before the CEO that may reflect negatively on the department or may embarrass the director, even if discussing these issues might make you look good. Within the organization, acceptable channels of communication are typically established, and professionals should not circumvent one level to reach a higher level without just cause.

OTHER HEALTHCARE PROVIDERS

Many of the same rules discussed previously apply to acting professionally around other healthcare providers. That is, you must understand the structure of the organization in which you practice and the various roles and status differences that exist. While all healthcare providers make valuable contributions to patient care, they do not share equal status within the healthcare system.[18] In the typical U.S. healthcare institution, physicians are designated as team leaders and may be given higher status than other providers. Thus, when you interact with team leaders, you may have to defer to their decision making. Now, that does not mean that pharmacists should not express opinions or articulate their points of view. Pharmacists, pharmacist managers, and leaders must be assertive in advocating for their points of view without being aggressive, as aggression is typically considered an unprofessional behavior. At the same time, nonassertive approaches (such as not saying anything) are also not appropriate, as failure to act as an advocate for the patient's best interests would also be considered unprofessional. There is a delicate balance between assertiveness and passivity or agression.[19] Thus, pharmacists must learn to maintain this balance in their professional relationships with other healthcare team members.

Within the practice environment, a pharmacist must be sensitive to his or her role compared with the roles of other healthcare providers and adhere to the organization's rules and policies for that role. For example, some practice environments might not allow pharmacists to immunize patients even though state laws and regulations allow it. If you started a pharmacy department immunization program despite the institution's policy, you might be perceived as acting unprofessionally (acting outside the acceptable role definition for pharmacists). To change standard practices, pharmacists must recognize that role restrictions probably evolve from limited perceptions of administrators and other healthcare providers regarding pharmacists and the pharmacy profession. As representatives of the pharmacy profession, pharmacists must attempt to change misperceptions or biased perceptions of pharmacy by acting professionally, demonstrating knowledge and competence, and advocating assertively that pharmacists are capable of performing expanded patient care functions.

CULTIVATING PROFESSIONALISM IN PRACTICE AS A PHARMACIST MANAGER

❼ *Pharmacist managers directly affect the culture of professionalism in their practice sites by establishing positive work environments through policies and their interactions with staff and pharmacy patrons.* Granted, pharmacist managers will likely have to also abide by policies set forth by *their* superiors, but the nature of their role as managers allows these individuals influence over their practice settings and staff. The following sections describe how pharmacist managers help cultivate professionalism in the practice environment.

Staff

Probably the most important element in cultivating professionalism is the pharmacy staff. Do pharmacist managers and staff treat patrons of the pharmacy with courtesy and respect? Are they helpful and attentive? What kind of images do managers and staff project (think attire, conversations among staff, etc.)? These are important questions to consider when trying to improve the professional image of a practice setting.

Individuals employed by a pharmacy should not only have the appropriate training and credentials, but they should also conduct themselves in a professional manner and exhibit a strong work ethic. Pharmacy staff should be able to interact respectfully and politely with all whom they come into contact, either in person, on the phone, or through the internet. Consider that you and your staff have to communicate with a wide variety of audiences—patients, their families and caregivers, other healthcare providers, wholesalers and suppliers, insurance company representatives, etc. Many organizations have periodic "customer service" training programs for their employees, which help managers and staff members develop and maintain these skills; such programs are particularly useful for those employees who may not be "naturals" in customer service. Another useful mechanism for addressing possible deficits in customer service is to collect "patient/customer satisfaction" data through surveys, interviews, focus groups, or other methods. Reviewing that information might be insightful about service areas needing improvement as well as strengths to be maintained. More information about this can be found in Chapter 12 ("Achieving and Measuring Patient Satisfaction").

Practically, a pharmacist manager also needs to consider appropriate staff attire and other behaviors. What is the dress code at the practice site? Does it project an image of trust, competence, credibility, and respect? Professional attire does not necessarily mean wearing a long white lab coat with your hair kept short or pulled back, but it does mean considering those whom you serve and the services you provide. Many institutions and corporations already implement dress codes and other standards for personal appearance. If yours does not, then pharmacist managers should consider implementing appropriate standards for hygiene and appearance to engender credibility and trust among those being served.

Another issue to consider is the level of professionalism displayed during conversations among staff, particularly communications regarding patients, as such discussions must comply with the **Health Insurance Portability and Accountability Act** (HIPAA), which protects confidential patient information (HIPAA is further discussed in Chapter 5, "Significant Laws Affecting Pharmacy Practice Management"). Are staff conversations professional? If patrons overheard these conversations, would they have cause to be concerned that pharmacy staff were not focusing on their responsibilities? While camaraderie and collegiality are important for a positive work culture, pharmacist managers must ensure that communication among the pharmacy staff is task-focused and does not violate HIPAA standards of confidentiality or jeopardize the perceived professionalism of the pharmacy and its employees. In addition, the efforts of pharmacist managers to minimize social and inappropriate conversations may also prevent distractions that could lead to medication errors.

Pharmacist managers should ensure that staff members engage in roles and responsibilities appropriate for their training and talents. Certainly, there are rules that help guide the responsibilities and relationships of pharmacists versus technicians and other staff members, but good managers get to know their staff well enough to engage them in responsibilities that will maximize their potential, as well as benefit the pharmacy and its patrons. Establishing proper roles and responsibilities with staff is also necessary in promoting a safe, efficient workflow for pharmacy services. Setting role-appropriate goals with your staff and providing them with frequent objective feedback about their progress toward achieving those goals also enhances professionalism in the pharmacy.

Related to the behaviors of pharmacist managers and staff members are the behaviors of patients, providers, and others with whom managers and staff interact. It is much more difficult to maintain an attitude of service and professionalism when the person with whom you are communicating is not doing the same. Consider the common occurrence of patrons' irritation at the pharmacy staff because of insurance problems or the time taken to fill their prescriptions. Educate pharmacy patrons about what pharmacy staff members do to ensure safety and effectiveness of medications and services. An example of how a pharmacy helped educate its patients on the important functions of the pharmacy staff follows. It has several signs hanging in the pharmacy waiting area, which communicate some of the challenges that may be encountered. For example:

We know it may take us several minutes or longer to fill your prescription. Our primary concern is your health and safety. In the process of filling your prescription we make sure that the prescribed medication is appropriate for you, the dosage is correct, there are no interactions with other medications you are taking, and that you are not allergic to any components of the prescribed medication. In some instances, we may have to call your prescriber to clarify this information. We appreciate your patience.

That same pharmacy posted another sign about its interactive patient counseling practices so that patients know what to expect from pharmacists. Pharmacy staff noted that after these signs were placed in the waiting area, the behavior of many patients changed to be more accommodating and receptive of the pharmacy's services.

Services and Inventory

The types of services offered by a particular pharmacy can enhance or detract from its professional image. Does the community retail pharmacy offer services that extend beyond traditional dispensing, such as medication therapy management (MTM), health and wellness screenings, follow-up monitoring, etc.? If you are in an institutional setting, are there (1) regular interactions with prescribers; (2) patient education, monitoring, and follow-up; and (3) in-service education provided to other healthcare staff? Careful consideration of and planning for these types of services can improve professionalism in practice. However, degree of influence and power may limit a pharmacist manager's ability to offer services that facilitate and enhance a pharmacy's professional image. If this is a concern, the pharmacist manager should communicate with his or her supervisor to learn whether he or she is willing to entertain well-thought-out and detailed service/program proposals from the manager and pharmacy staff.

Related to services offered is the inventory carried by the pharmacy: Are products of high quality? In community and outpatient practices, do the retail products your pharmacy carries enhance patient health and wellness? What about products completely unrelated to health care, such as garden hoses, jewelry, and the like? Is there inventory that is actually detrimental to health and wellness, such as tobacco products? It is difficult to have control over nonpharmacy inventory if your practice is located in a grocery or mass merchandise–type store. If you are responsible or partially responsible for purchasing your pharmacy's inventory, do your homework—research quality-related information on products, and select those products meant to enhance health and wellness.

Physical Facilities

The general appearance of the pharmacy also adds to or detracts from its professional image. What does it say to those who enter an environment (pharmacy) if it is cluttered and disorganized, aisles are messy and cramped, and desired products are difficult to locate? The underlying message may be that the organization and its staff do not care to make the effort to be clean and organized. This feeling about the physical facilities of a pharmacy may permeate consciously or subconsciously into patients' and others' impressions about the practice—based on their poor impressions of the facility, they might believe that pharmacy staff do not care enough to provide high-quality services to patients and providers. In addition, the lack of cleanliness could lead to other problems, especially if compounding or other intensive product preparation is part of the services offered.

Other physical aspects of the pharmacy project an image, such as the pharmacy's or store's layout, waiting areas, counter height, and private consultation areas. Aisles should be clean and wide enough to navigate. If possible, given available space, there should be a comfortable waiting area for patients awaiting prescriptions. Some pharmacies provide educational handouts and health-related magazines to browse or show health-related videos or health cable channels on a continuously running small television in their waiting areas. For many years, retail pharmacy departments were located in the back of stores, elevated from the floor, and behind a thick counter with many shelves. In hospitals, pharmacies were often found in the basement with no windows. Although these designs may have provided some advantages (e.g., less high-profile areas), they presented significant disadvantages to patrons. Many community and outpatient pharmacies now have counters on the same level as patients to facilitate communication, as well as the opportunity to observe the care that is going into prescription preparation. For example, some retail pharmacies implemented what might be called the Subway (sandwich preparation) concept: the primary prescription-filling counter is at the same level as the patients and is protected by a layer of clear glass so that patients can see what activities go on "behind the counter." Hospital pharmacies may still maintain preparation and dispensing facilities in a basement, but many hospitals have decentralized or satellite pharmacies in various patient care areas throughout the hospital to better integrate pharmacists into patient care. Pharmacies that have remodeled to remove some of the traditional barriers must also make sure that patient confidentiality is maintained. Computer terminal screens with patient information should not be easily viewed, nor should individuals' prescriptions or other identifiable documents be in plain sight. Private areas in community and outpatient pharmacies for consultations and other services are also important. Most pharmacists are aware that it is not professional to consult with a patient on his or her medication when there is a line of patients standing directly behind him or her. A common solution is to have one or more private areas set up for patient consultation. The key to their successful use, however, is the ease of accessibility by patients and pharmacy staff, and how well they are integrated into the normal workflow of the drop-off, pick-up process. Some pharmacies not only have private or demarcated areas for patient consultation but also separate rooms for physical assessments and other more involved services, such as blood pressure monitoring or glucose and lipid testing. If necessary, a private area for counseling can be easily established by setting aside some patient-level counter space and installing a moderately soundproof divider. This arrangement can be practical and sends the message that the pharmacy cares about privacy.

ASSESSMENT OF ONE'S PROFESSIONALISM

It has been alluded throughout this chapter that one's professionalism and professional image are often assessed or judged by others, usually infor-mally. ❽ *Students, pharmacists, and pharmacist managers and leaders should also self-assess their professionalism and be aware of factors that can contribute both positively and negatively.* Ongoing reflection on one's behavior is an important component to professional development as it allows a better understanding of professional strengths to be built on and deficits to be redressed. There are self-evaluation instruments available that may help an individual determine personal views toward certain aspects of professionalism.[20,21] Whether an individual chooses to formally document professional development, such as what might be found in a portfolio, or to informally reflect on personal behavior, it is important to conduct a professionalism self-assessment as often as possible. Reflect periodically with a trusted colleague to make sure personal perceptions are accurate. This is important to note, as an individual's view of his or her own professional development and image may be disparate from those with whom he or she interacts. Refer to Chapter 26 ("Creating Your Personal Brand and Influencing Others").

The cycle of continuous professional development (CPD) process is being studied as an enhancement to usual licensure requirements (such as annually documenting a certain number of hours of continuing education credits) and may be a useful tool in self-assessment of professionalism.[22] The CPD process engages the practitioner to self-identify learning needs, set goals for how to meet those needs, and then assess whether the goals were met and how to proceed. CPD encourages the use of a professional portfolio to manage this process.

SUMMARY

Perhaps the most fundamental responsibility of pharmacists is to act in a professional and ethical manner. As students, pharmacists, and pharmacist managers and leaders, professionalism is a quality that others such as patients and fellow healthcare professionals will expect you to embody. Without professionalism, pharmacists are merely a cog in the wheel of health care, rather than trusted, compassionate healthcare providers. Student pharmacists, practitioners, leaders, and managers should make positive and continuous efforts to improve their professionalism. This chapter defines professionalism and discusses its development and self-assessment, its relationships with ethics and personal branding, its effect on patient and other professional interactions, and its cultivation in practice. Although there are oaths, codes, and laws that exist to suggest behaviors for pharma-

cists, ultimately it is the responsibility of the individual to determine the kind of professional he or she aspires to be and to take action to fulfill those aspirations. The success of the pharmacy profession depends on professionalism; thus, it is the responsibility of every pharmacist to continually develop professional qualities.

References

1. APhA-ASP/AACP-COD Task Force on Professionalism. White paper on pharmacy student professionalism. *J Am Pharm Assoc* 2000;40:96–102.

2. Hammer DP, Berger BA, Beardsley RS, Easton MR. Student professionalism. *Am J Pharm Educ* 2003:67. Article 96.

3. American Society of Health-System Pharmacists. ASHP statement on professionalism. *Am J Health Sys Pharm* 2008;65:172–174.

4. Roth MT, Zlatic TD. Development of student professionalism. ACCP white paper. *Pharmacotherapy* 2009; 29:749–756.

5. American College of Clinical Pharmacy. Professionalism tenets for pharmacy students. Student Commentary. *Pharmacotherapy* 2009;29(6):757–759.

6. Merton RK, Reader GG, Kendall PL. *The Student-Physician: Introductory Studies in the Sociology of Medical Education.* 1st ed. Cambridge, MA: Harvard University Press; 1957.

7. Sherlock BJ, Morris RT. The evolution of a professional: a paradigm. *Soc Inq* 1967;37:27–46.

8. Simpson IH. Patterns of socialization into professions: the case of student nurses. *Soc Inq* 1967;37:47–54.

9. Lacy WB. Interpersonal relationships as mediators of structural effects: college student socialization in a traditional and an experimental university environment. *Soc Educ* 1978;51:201–211.

10. Baszanger I. Professional socialization and social control: from medical students to general practitioners. *Soc Sci Med* 1985;20:133–143.

11. Fitzpatrick J, While AE, Roberts JD. Key influences on the professional socialisation and practice of students undertaking different preregistration nurse education programmes in the United Kingdom. *Int J Nurs Stud* 1996;33:506–518.

12. Yang TS, Fjortoft NF. Developing into a professional: students' perspectives. *Am J Pharm Educ* 1997(suppl); 61:83S.

13. Cain JJ. Pharmacy students' use of Facebook and attitudes toward its usage by authority figures. *AACP Annual Meeting* 2008;72(3). Abstract.

14. Oath of a Pharmacist. American Pharmacists Association. Available at: http://www.pharmacist.com/AM/AMTemplate.cfm?Section=Home2&TEMPLATE=/CM/HTMLDisplay.cfm&CONTENTID=18306. Accessed July 11, 2009.

15. Code of Ethics for Pharmacists. American Pharmacists Association. Available at: http://www.pharmacist.com/AM/Template.cfm?Section=Search1&template=/CM/HTMLDisplay.cfm&ContentID=2903. Accessed July 11, 2009.

16. Lancaster LC, Stillman D. *When Generations Collide.* New York, NY: HarperCollins; 2002.

17. Zemke R. *Generations at Work.* New York, NY: American Management Association; 2000.

18. Howard M, Trim. K. Collaboration between community pharmacists and family physicians. *J Am Med Assoc* 2003;43:566–572.

19. Kimberlin C. Assertiveness. In: Beardsley RS, Kimberlin CL, Tindall WN, eds. *Communication Skills in Pharmacy Practice.* Baltimore, MD: Lippincott Williams & Wilkins; 2007.

20. Chisholm MA, Cobb H, Duke L, McDuffie C, Kennedy WK. Development of an instrument to measure professionalism. *Am J Pharm Educ* 2006;70(4). Article 85.

21. Schack DW, Hepler CD. Modification of Hall's professionalism scale for use with pharmacists. *Am J Pharm Educ* 1979;43:98–104.

22. Rouse MJ. Continuing professional development in pharmacy. *Am J Health-Syst Pharm.* 2004;61:2069–2076.

Abbreviations

AACP:	American Association of Colleges of Pharmacy
AACP-COD:	American Association of Colleges of Pharmacy Council of Deans
ACCP:	American College of Clinical Pharmacy
APhA-ASP:	American Pharmacists Association Academy of Student Pharmacists
APPE:	advanced pharmacy practice experience
ASHP:	American Society of Health-System Pharmacists
CEO:	chief executive officer
CPD:	continuous professional development
HIPAA:	Health Insurance Portability and Accountability Act of 1996
IPPE:	introductory pharmacy practice experience
MTM:	medication therapy management

Case Scenarios

CASE ONE: You are the manager of a busy independent pharmacy. The pharmacy runs multiple patient care programs and has always been highly requested as a rotation site by students at the local college of pharmacy. The lead preceptor stops by to ask you to meet with the current rotation student. He does not have an interest in counseling patients, is constantly texting on his cell phone, and has been overheard asking what he is getting out of the rotation when he is "just working for free." The preceptor has talked to the student about the consequences to his grade based on his actions but is hoping you can have a conversation with the student about professionalism. What would you say?

CASE TWO: A patient has requested to speak to the manager of the pharmacy. She has already spoken with the staff pharmacist, but the patient is not happy with the explanation from the pharmacist regarding the cost of her medication. She wants to speak with you and wants to know why her medicine costs so much, especially since "all you have to do is count the tablets and put them in a bottle!" How do you respond?

CASE THREE: John Barton is a staff pharmacist in an outpatient clinic within a large hospital center. Margaret Evans, the pharmacy director for the clinic, overhears Dr. Barton respond with obvious annoyance to a patient, Jerome White, who expressed confusion about how to take his medication. Unfortunately, this is not the first time that Dr. Evans has observed Dr. Barton acting unprofessionally, and thus she asks him to step into her office to discuss things.

Dr. Barton enters the director's office and states, "Well Maggie, what is it this time?"

What would you say to Dr. Barton if you were Dr. Evans?

CASE FOUR: Albert Reynolds is a pharmacist at McGregor's Pharmacy and needs to discuss Mrs. Fieldings's prescription with Dr. Snyder, her internist. Mr. Reynolds calls Dr. Snyder's office and ends up speaking with Phyllis Rivers, the nurse/office manager for Dr. Snyder. The interaction is described below:

Pharmacist Reynolds: I need to speak with Dr. Snyder about Mrs. Fieldings's Lipitor prescription. Please have Dr. Snyder call me as soon as possible.

Nurse Rivers: It may be quicker if you tell me what the problem is.

Pharmacist Reynolds: I really need to speak with him directly.

(continues)

Nurse Rivers: He is really busy today, and I always talk to you pharmacists. That's just the way we do things here in the office. So, why don't you just tell me what the problem is.

What would you say in this situation if you were the pharmacist?

CASE FIVE: You are a pharmacist manager in a busy anticoagulation clinic with extensive pharmacy services, and today you are filling in for one of your staff pharmacists who is ill. A representative from a pharmaceutical company comes in to speak with you about a new anticoagulant therapy. You ask if you can make an appointment with her the following week when you are not working with patients. She is rather impatient and says that she only has time to talk with you today and that the information she has for you is critical for your patients. How do you handle this situation?

Additional Resources Available Online!

Visit the Student Companion Web site at http://healthprofessions.jbpub.com/pharmacymanagement for interactive study tools and additional resources.

See www.rxugace.com to learn how you can obtain continuing pharmacy education for this content.

CREATING YOUR PERSONAL BRAND AND INFLUENCING OTHERS

JOHN A. DALY, PhD

SHARON MURPHY ENRIGHT, MBA, RPh

LEARNING OBJECTIVES

After completing the chapter, the reader will be able to

1. Describe the concept of personal branding and its benefits for personal and career development.

2. Identify elements of personal brand credibility.

3. Evaluate strategies for changing or improving brand fit.

4. Cite two key principles of transforming personal brand.

5. Explain key elements critical to influencing.

6. Describe characteristics of compelling persuasive evidence/messages for influencing others.

7. Determine the importance of emotionally connecting to stakeholders as a powerful influencing tool.

8. Discuss four steps in presenting a persuasive argument to influence decision makers and other stakeholders.

KEY CONCEPTS

❶ Personal brands are the cumulative perceptions others have of individuals' traits, behaviors, and actions. These brands affect the success with which individuals are able to influence others.

❷ What you think of yourself is your internal brand. It is how you would describe yourself. How others see you is your external brand.

❸ Personal brand credibility is a function of others' perceptions of your competence, trustworthiness, passion, tenacity, and objectivity.

❹ To begin transforming your brand in a professional context, identify resources (knowledge, skills, etc.) most valued and needed by the organization, and develop those resources.

❺ Influence is the power to effect change, the capacity to shift other people's thinking or actions by means of discussion, example, or even by mere force of personality.

⑥ Influencing involves four critical elements: (1) establishing credibility, (2) framing goals to identify common ground, (3) reinforcing position with compelling and vivid evidence, and (4) connecting emotionally with the audience.

⑦ To influence effectively, you need to identify shared benefits, as well as connections between what you are proposing and what your audience needs or wants relative to your idea. In other words, you must find common ground with stakeholders (especially decision makers).

⑧ To present persuasively and with credibility, you should state your assumptions clearly and openly, expose any potential conflicts of interest, present all sides of the argument, and avoid the temptation to oversell weak arguments.

INTRODUCTION

Coca-Cola, McDonald's, Apple, Google, and Eli Lilly, among others, are powerful brand names. They reflect perceived quality and trust, are clearly recognized, and are generally preferred by consumers, often leading to greater economic value, higher prices, and greater market share than similar or competing products with weaker brand names. Like products and organizations, people also have **personal brands**. ① *Personal brands are the cumulative perceptions others have of individuals' traits, behaviors, and actions. These brands affect the success with which individuals are able to influence others.* Influence, defined as affecting the beliefs of others, is a basic part of our culture and economic life.[1] Pharmacists and pharmacist managers and leaders face a multitude of challenges related to their ability to influence in their professional lives. We commonly assume that responsibility for influencing others rests with a leader who is designated by **positional authority** (defined as authority based on position within an organization; refer to Chapter 2, "Management Essentials

for Pharmacists"); however, today's increasingly complex, often chaotic healthcare environment demands that every professional take a measure of leadership responsibility to advocate for ideas, manage demands, and optimize opportunities. This chapter discusses personal branding, explores topics associated with creating and building personal brand, and addresses the power of effective influence in pharmacy settings. Although this chapter focuses largely on personal brand and influence within a professional/organizational context, many of the topics addressed also apply to other aspects of your life, such as family and community involvement.

PERSONAL BRAND

In a 2007 article, Tom Peters, considered one of the most influential figures in modern business, opened discussion of personal branding with the quote: "It's a new brand world."[2] While your personal brand may not have the stature and familiarity of Merck's and Starbucks's instant recognition, you *do* have a brand. Whether you are considered to be the most dependable pharmacist in your organization or the friendliest member of your team when it comes to interacting with patients, your personal brand is simply this—the cluster of ideas and expectations that come into people's minds when they think of you. Personal brand communicates what you stand for, your beliefs, values, knowledge, and passions; it makes you unique, memorable, and hopefully a valued asset to your organization. It defines how people view and relate to you and frames their perceptions of your role and effectiveness. Brand is based on many aspects of your personal and professional lives—skills, experience, communication style, the way you dress, the car you drive, the people with whom you associate, and a host of other factors that communicate something about you. Whether you are seen as an innovator, a hard worker, a source of credible drug information, or someone who cannot be counted on to fulfill an obligation, a wide range of factors define your brand in both your personal and professional lives.

You can, to a great extent, create your brand. **Table 26–1** provides 10 suggestions for building

TABLE **26–1**	Ten Suggestions for Building a Better Personal Brand

- Become an expert source. For example, deliver a speech, write an article, or volunteer to make presentations on medication use in your community.

- Develop great written and verbal communication skills.

- Develop a 30-second "elevator speech"[a] to deliver a succinct description of what you do, what differentiates you from peers, and your value features.

- Build relationships, stay in touch, maintain regular communication, and consider participation in Web-based social networks. Ensure your Web-based social networking sites are free from questionable or possibly negative content, as current or future employers may check such sites and negative perceptions of your social networks may reflect poorly on you.

- Keep your boss as a valued ally to building your brand. Make him or her look good and speak kindly or not at all about everyone.

- Dress for the job you want, not the job you have, and be attentive to style patterns within your organizational culture.

- Know about people, their families, special interests, and issues that might be dominating their lives. Be helpful. Do a favor a day. Do one thing you are proud of every day.

- Be a class act, learning good business and social etiquette, cultivating skills of social conversation, and learning to be comfortable in any social situation.

- Give often and generously. Giving your time, talent, and money to professional organizations and charitable causes nurtures your brand, especially when it complements your brand strategy.

- Be kind, and think about how your words and actions may affect others.

[a]Elevator speech is defined as a brief (e.g., 30 seconds; 100–150 words) summary of a service, program, or good/product.

a better personal brand. Building and nurturing personal brand can have several benefits:[3]

- It increases your recognition, establishes expertise, and enhances your ability to influence—for example, the esteemed pharmacist who specializes in geriatrics and is often asked to give presentations on medication therapy management services for seniors to community pharmacies that are considering implementing such programs.

- It heightens professional visibility, thereby building perceptions of your capabilities, successes, and value as a resource in your field

of expertise. For example, pharmacists who are well known in their fields are often asked for their advice on therapeutic treatments, to participate in the development of practice guidelines, etc.

- It creates a compelling reason for others to want to associate with you or use your services and enhances expectations of performance capability. Your brand creates a personal "link," builds relationships, and attracts colleagues (or clients) you want to work with because you are sending a clear, consistent, and targeted message about what you stand for. For example, pharmacists who are respected in their practice settings often attract pharmacy students, residents, and others who want to work and learn from them.

To begin building your brand, conduct a personal assessment and define your unique characteristics. What accomplishments set you apart? What are your greatest strengths and weaknesses? What knowledge and skills distinguish you from colleagues? A strong brand is one that is distinctive from others. For example, if you received national or international recognition/awards for your pharmacy-related skills (e.g., winner of a clinical skills competition, recipient of a clinical practice award), then you have exemplified expertise in that area. Strong brands are also relevant to the needs of the organization—the skills and talents that make up your brand name are considered important and valuable by people in your work environment. Ideally, the skills and talents that make up your brand should also be perceived to be scarce within the organization, as scarcity increases value. Peters suggests applying a feature-benefit model that involves making a list of every feature (resource) you bring to the organization and assessing the unique and valued benefit of each resource to your organization, team, and client/customer.[2] Are you dependable? Do you complete work on time? Do your critical thinking skills allow you to anticipate problems and resolve them before they become crises (of course, some people have a brand as great crisis managers)? Are you accountable for your areas of responsibility and willing to take on new challenges, even without being asked? Are you a team player who works well with others? These are just a few of the questions that must be addressed as you work toward building an effective personal brand within the organization. If the answer to each is "yes," you are on your way to a good brand name. If you are distinctly better than others at these, then your professional brand is probably quite good.

Internal Versus External Brand

❷ *What you think of yourself is your **internal brand**. It is how you would describe yourself. How others see you is your **external brand**.*[4] **Brand clarity** compares your internal brand with your external brand (**Figure 26–1**). To get a sense of

brand clarity, write down five words that describe you, and then ask some colleagues to think of five words that come to mind when they think of you. How closely are the lists aligned? If the lists are similar, then you have a fairly clear perception of yourself and your brand, regardless of whether you like that brand. However, if you see yourself as an outgoing strategic thinker with an eye on future possibilities and others see you as more introspective and focused on day-to-day operations, you may need to work on reconciling your internal and external brands. **Figure 26–2** demonstrates brand clarity matches and gaps regarding the perception of intelligence, including blind spots (unrecognized weaknesses or limitations) and the self-deceptive façade that might exist if your perception of your brand is more fully defined than the way others see you. What matters is how others see you; therefore, the challenge you face is shaping others' perceptions of you. One of the most important aspects of others' perceptions of you is your perceived credibility.

Credibility of Personal Brand

❸ *Personal brand credibility is a function of others' perceptions of your competence, trustworthiness, passion, tenacity, and objectivity* (**Figure 26–3**). Competence is defined as being adequately qualified in knowledge, skills, and abilities. Credibility is built through consistent demonstration of competence over time—a process that may be accelerated by delivering more or performing better than people expect. As suggested by a former State Department negotiator, brand credibility requires never overpromising, or promising more than you know you are able to deliver.[5] Instead, your promises should be realistic about what you will deliver while striving to exceed expectations.

The second crucial aspect of brand credibility is perceived trustworthiness. If you are trusted, decision makers may be more receptive to your ideas and less critical of your work.[6] Trust involves four critical components: (1) consistency, (2) honesty, (3) benevolence, and (4) vulnerability (Figure 26–3). What shapes people's perception of others' *consistency*? Among other things are punctuality, follow-up (e.g., returning calls promptly, replying to e-mails, finishing what you start), keeping commitments (even the very small ones), and

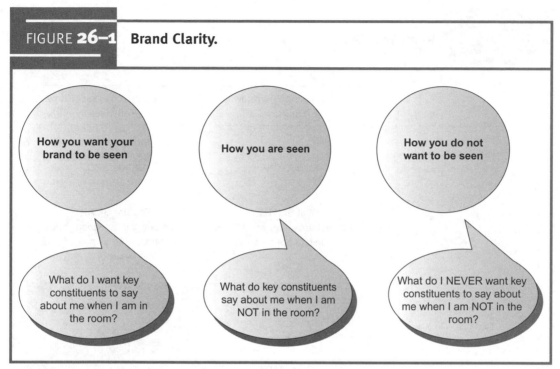

FIGURE **26–1** **Brand Clarity.**

This figure displays three key perspectives/questions to consider when comparing your internal and external brands.

demonstrating dependability on important issues (e.g., people who have a reputation for always changing their opinions on important issues diminish their perceived consistency). *Honesty* is the foundation of trust; if you are perceived to be dishonest, decision makers will discount or dismiss your input. Honesty will bolster your perceived trustworthiness and enhance your brand. *Benevolence* is the "good faith" dimension of trust—you are perceived to be a good person. You demonstrate a real interest in others, focus both on task and on non-task-related issues, are sensitive to territoriality ("turf"), and avoid contributing to divisiveness. For instance, if you are preparing a communication to be sent on a sensitive issue, such as a formulary approval for a costly new agent where there are polar opinions among Pharmacy and Therapeutics (P&T) Committee members, have colleagues review a draft in advance to make sure you are not misrepresenting any of the issues. Do

not appear manipulative; instead, be modest, act on principle, and take positions based on solid values, such as patient safety, practice excellence, performance improvement, business ethics, and sustainability. Demonstrating *vulnerability* is an important way to build trust. People with strong personal brands willingly disclose their shortcomings or mistakes. They are the first to announce errors and problems, and never cover up mistakes. What gets people in trouble is not their mistakes but rather their attempts to hide these mistakes.

In addition to demonstrating personal trustworthiness, people with strong personal brands surround themselves with people who are trusted. You are known by the company you keep; therefore, make sure your team is perceived as trustworthy, and seek out allies who add to your perceived honesty. One last thing: you and your team should be aware of your limitations—do not pretend to be something you are not. Your

FIGURE 26–2 **Know Your Brand.**

	The Brand You Know You Have	The Brand You Don't Know You Have
The Brand Others See in You	**MATCH** "I'm SMART." I think I am smart and others think I am smart.	**BLIND SPOT** "You are SMART." Others see you as smart, but you do not see this as part of your brand.
The Brand Others Don't See in You	**FAÇADE** "I'm SMART." I think I am smart, but others don't see me this way.	**IRRELEVANT**

This figure presents how you see yourself versus how others see you. For example, if you see yourself as being smart and that is how others view you, that is a match. However, if others do not see you as smart and you do, that is a façade (defined as an artificial or deceptive appearance). Also, if others view you as smart and you do not, that may be a blind spot (a subject in which one is ignorant or unable to view accurately and objectively) of yours.

personal brand is often enhanced by honesty—for instance, saying "no" to opportunities or assignments for which you lack the necessary skills or admitting unfamiliarity with things you do not understand. Also, when you make a mistake, apologize and try to learn from the mistake to prevent reoccurrence.

Other elements of credibility include passion, tenacity, and objectivity. *Passion* is demonstrated through enthusiasm for work, ideas, and the organization's mission and vision. *Tenacity* is defined by an individual's determination and willingness to continue working or advocating despite problems or challenges that may arise (Figure 26–3).

Passion and tenacity provide evidence of dedication and will likely result in decision makers taking your brand seriously. However, passion and tenacity for your work, proposal, ideas, etc., should be balanced by *objectivity*, which requires that individuals base judgments and decisions on sound evidence rather than on personal feelings or beliefs. Your credibility depends, in part, on your ability to make sure that people see you as an independent thinker. For example, as a leader you may be called on to take positions that reference a larger set of issues than just what might be in the best interest of your pharmacy.[7] In this case, arguing against what others might expect you to

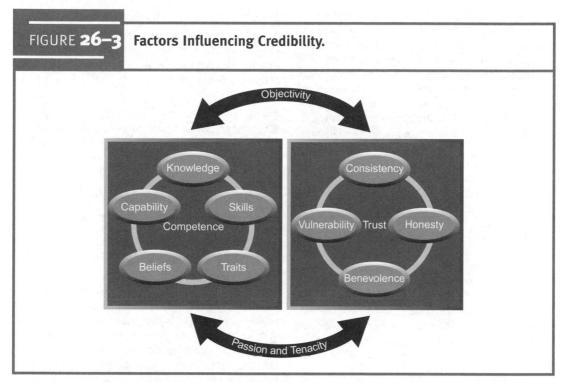

FIGURE **26–3** Factors Influencing Credibility.

Factors influencing credibility include objectivity, passion, tenacity, competence, and trust. Competency includes elements of one's skills, traits, beliefs, capability, and knowledge. Trust is comprised of many factors, such as consistency, honesty, benevolence, and vulnerability.

support (e.g., arguing for something that would be good for the entire organization despite how it might affect the pharmacy) may bolster the credibility of your brand.

Changing or Improving Brand Fit

As you build personal brand over time, you may find a disconnect or lack of fit between your brand and the duties, expectations, or goals of your current position/division within the organization. There are five strategies to change or improve brand "fit":

- *Leave the organization.* There is always an opportunity to create success in another organization where you better fit with the culture, goals, and aims of the organization. If the brand you want to emphasize is a clinical patient care role, and you are seen in your

organization as being tied to a distributive function with little or no direct patient care opportunity, you might want to consider moving to an organization with a different clinical service vision to rebrand yourself.

- *Move within the organization.* Internal transfers or assignments in other departments or locations can create the opportunity for a new or reconfigured brand. For example, one pharmacist who passionately focused on patient safety and performance improvement spent most of her time outside the central pharmacy role, winning fans among administrators, medical staff, and nursing with her observations of process and opportunities to do things differently. However, those activities did not win her positive brand recognition with other pharmacists in the central dispensing area and created staffing issues and communication breakdowns with department leadership. The brand she wanted to have and the brand others in the pharmacy had of her just did not match. Her subsequent move to the quality department enhanced her personal brand, permitted her to focus on the issues she was most concerned with and passionate about, and allowed her to become an advocate for critical medication use safety and delivery system issues that supported the pharmacy department in some of its larger goals.

- *Associate with different people.* Since you are known by the company you keep, if you want to change or bolster your brand name, you should try to discover people who have successfully developed positive brands and build relationships with them. Study what makes their communication strategies and behaviors effective, and emulate those that make sense to you. Volunteer for a multidisciplinary task force in your organization or community, engage and interact with well-respected leaders in your corporation, and seek mentors who have great reputations similar to how you would like to be seen.
- *Take advantage of opportunities presented when a new boss comes from outside the organization.* When someone is promoted into a leadership role from within the organization, he or she already "knows" people. Already established brand images seldom change. However, when a new leader comes from the outside, there are new opportunities to realign what you as an employee of the new leader stand for and how you (employee) are perceived. When an outsider is brought in as a new leader, each employee under this leader should quickly work to establish a positive reputation with this individual. New bosses want to have an effect quickly in organizations, and they often are looking for innovative ideas. Bring up your ideas, make sure they know and appreciate what you contribute, and be seen as a team player, not someone who is going to challenge everything.
- *Transform your brand.* Even in the same organization, with the same players and the same chain of command, it is possible to reinvent your brand. The question is, How?

TRANSFORMING YOUR BRAND

Transforming your brand involves two key principles: (1) the value of resources you offer your organization and (2) the scarcity of those resources (**Figure 26–4**).

Principle of Resources

❹ *To begin transforming your brand in a professional context, identify resources (knowledge, skills, etc.) most valued and needed by the organization, and develop those resources.* The more valuable the resources or assets you provide to your organization, the better your brand may be to that organization. Start by writing down five resources you offer your organization; for example, think about your knowledge (of clinical practice, special patient populations, **adherence** issues, etc.), experience, collaborative and technical skills, strategic vision, and leadership abilities. Then, ask yourself, how important are each of these resources to my organization? In bolstering your brand name, you should try to identify the resources that are particularly valued in your organization, and focus on developing and demonstrating (showcasing) these resources as you transform your brand. Some valued resources are not necessarily obvious but have an important place in organizational success, for instance:

- You may have excellent editing or writing skills that may be needed for items such as patient counseling materials, drug pipeline analysis, or grant proposal writing for educational or research grants.
- Your relationships with other healthcare professionals may provide you access to information, knowledge, and innovative ideas for planning a new pharmacy service.
- Your volunteer activity in a local nursing home may create a link for your employer to provide contract services.

Principle of Scarcity

In transforming personal brand, offering valuable resources is only the first step. The resources that matter most are those that are both valuable and *scarce* within your organization. In a U.S. pharmaceutical firm, speaking English is a valuable but not

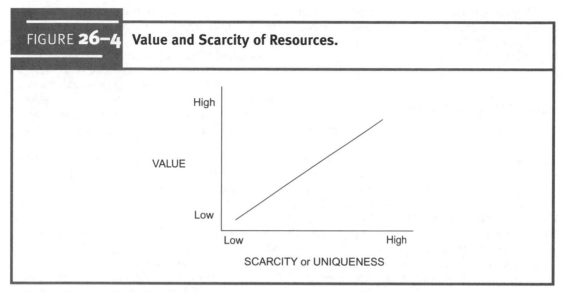

FIGURE **26–4** **Value and Scarcity of Resources.**

To transform your brand, identify and focus on those resources you possess that are highly valuable and scarce within your organization. As the value and scarcity of the resources you offer an organization increase, the greater your competitive advantage becomes and the more likely your brand transformation will be successful.

scarce resource, while speaking another language that is often needed for translation may be both valuable and scarce. For example, a pharmacist manager who is able to speak Spanish and facilitate the provision of culturally sensitive care may be a valuable and scarce resource in urban retail pharmacies serving a large Hispanic population. Gold, emeralds, fine art, Wii technology, and Kindles have taken on an exclusivity that are associated with episodic scarcity or rising value due to limited supply. Years ago at the University of Virginia, some old dorms with tiny rooms and no bathrooms were particularly out of favor with students. In a miraculous transformation of brand, the university reframed the exclusivity (i.e., scarcity) of these dorms by "selecting" the most outstanding senior leaders and offering them the "opportunity" to compete for the prestigious honor of living "On the Lawn"—these very same dorms. Because so few selected individuals could be accommodated, living "On the Lawn" became a prized honor.

Reinventing Your Brand

Although it is possible to transform or reinvent your brand, it may not be easy to do so. Any attempt to transform your brand needs to be thoughtful and both personally and professionally sound. Personal goals and aspirations should be kept in perspective within the larger picture of professional issues and organizational aims. Any brand transformation needs to be authentic and reflect who and what you truly are, or your efforts will appear self-serving and transparent.

Brand Importance Revisited

A great brand is important not only for success in an organization but also because it is difficult to successfully propose an idea that does not match your brand. If you are not viewed as a successful change agent, proposing a major change initiative will probably not be taken seriously by decision makers. Being a pharmacist allows you to raise certain issues such as pharmacokinetics and therapeutic effect of various agents and product safety and efficacy that cannot be raised by people without a pharmacy degree and experience. The remainder of this chapter focuses on *influence*; however, remember that your ability to get people to change and adopt your ideas is directly tied to your brand name. People accept ideas from those they respect. If you are not seen as credible, if your brand name does not match what you are proposing, you are likely to get little or no traction in influencing others.

INFLUENCING OTHERS

Personal branding creates a platform from which to influence issues, ideas, proposals, or positions. Influencing involves recognizing a need, championing a position, overcoming resistance, building affinity for an idea as it moves through the decision process, and leaving relationships stronger for the interaction. ❺ *Influence is the power to effect change, the capacity to shift other people's thinking or actions by means of discussion, example, or even by mere force of personality.* An individual's ability to influence others may be subtle, such as offering a suggestion or opinion during an informal conversation that results in significant change, or it may require a more active approach, such as the use of explicit **persuasion** to advocate for an idea or a proposal. Many people do not think of themselves as influencers and often do not consciously work to develop influence skills or recognize the personal responsibility of being a change agent in virtually every aspect of their lives.

Influencing is widely perceived as a skill reserved for selling products and making deals and is frequently presumed to be a form of manipulation.[8] In reality, effective influence is a process and skill set that supports learning, exploring issues and options, and, at its best, generates thoughtful dialogue. It virtually always involves compromise, so effective influencers are open-minded, active listeners, willing to adjust their own position. The most successful influencers "pre-sell" their ideas—even before formal meetings happen, every major decision maker has already given their informal approval. Successful pharmacist leaders who are interested in expanding retail operations within an integrated delivery network should not just write a proposal and send it off to decision makers. Rather, they should carefully build a case of support for the need and the financial effect by considering all alternatives and their pros and cons; assuming the proposal involves pharmacy services and direct patient care issues, this may include looking at space availability and competition for that space, and evaluating the **return on investment** (ROI; profit or some other value earned by an investment) and **opportunity loss** (value or benefit lost if a particular alternative is not chosen) effect, as well as the effect on patient access to care. They seek to understand who the **stakeholders** are in the idea and where they stand in support or opposition and work to strengthen the stand of supporters and shift the thinking of detractors. Before the proposal is finalized, the pharmacist leader understands where everyone stands on the decision, has lined up allies for support, and has effectively "pre-sold" the opportunity and its features and benefits, effectively minimizing the potential for a negative decision. **Table 26–2** provides tips on tools to increase your ability to apply the psychology of influence.[9,10]

❻ *Influence involves four critical elements (discussed in the following sections): (1) establishing credibility, (2) framing goals to identify common ground, (3) reinforcing position with compelling and vivid evidence, and (4) connecting emotionally with the audience.*

Establishing Credibility as an Influencer

Credibility, in addition to playing an important role in building personal brand, is also a foundational requirement for effective influence[8] and largely depends on your perceived expertise and the strength of relationships you have with those you are trying to persuade. Expertise is determined by knowledge, skills, and the ability to apply them, and more important, the capacity to display sound judgment and a proven track record. Being well informed and associated with prior successes enhances credibility. For example, those pharmacists who own multiple stores started out small and, based on the success of one store, were able to use their experience and assets to build other stores. Credibility is also built on relationships developed over time, demonstrated through the ability to listen to the perspectives of others and be seen as fair and balanced in evaluating each individual's position to reach a shared position of agreement. Strong **emotional intelligence** (defined as the ability of a person to perceive, assimilate, understand, and manage their own

TABLE **26–2**	**Psychological Tools for Influence**

Tool	Description	Example
The Contrast Principle	The way we compare things that are presented to us in sequence may influence our perception of those items presented later in the sequence.	Following a myocardial infarction, it is recommended that patients begin aspirin therapy to prevent recurrence of cardiac events. The benefits of taking aspirin therapy for those with no contraindications outweigh the risk and adverse sequelae of a second myocardial infarction
The Rule of Reciprocation	We should repay, in kind, what is given to us; this is a powerful rule with social roots that often produces a "yes" response on issues/requests that may have been otherwise refused were it not for this sense of indebtedness.	A community pharmacy has a large number of senior patrons who pay for medication therapy management services. To repay the patronage and support of their consumer base, the community pharmacy's staff pharmacists provide free health screening fairs and medication question-and-answer sessions at the local senior center once a month.
Consistency with Prior Commitments	Once we have made a choice, there is internal and external pressure to be consistent with that choice through subsequent decisions and behaviors to continue justifying the earlier choice or act. Facilitating another individual to make some commitment, no matter how small, is the first step for subsequent automatic actions for consistency with the first commitment. Even harmless concessions to small points begin the initial commitment process. An even more powerful force is commitment documented in writing; there is something about the act of writing out the agreement that makes it more compelling.	A pharmacist manager in a large urban medical center is asked to take part in a pilot study of best practice guidelines for a particular medication regimen. The guidelines are implemented in one clinic within the medical center. The successful results of the pilot study are used to encourage the pharmacist manager to implement the guidelines on a full-scale basis across the medical center (i.e., in inpatient units and within numerous outpatient clinics).

Sources: Data from Cialdini RB;[9] Gladwell MB.[10]

emotions), fairness, honesty, and consistency are vital behaviors that contribute to credibility. Remember, credibility lives in the minds of others, rather than in objective credentials and skills, hence it is fragile and can be fleeting. A single misstep, miscalculation, or foolish mistake can tarnish or destroy it.

Knowing how you are perceived in terms of credibility demands an honest self-assessment of where you stand on expertise and relationships. This self-assessment includes answering a few simple questions:[8]

- How do others perceive my knowledge and skills related to the issue I am trying to influence?
- Do I have a track record in this area that others know and respect?
- Do those I am hoping to influence see me as helpful, trustworthy, and supportive?
- Will they see me as in sync with them emotionally, intellectually, and politically on issues like this one?

As with any other self-assessment, you need to test and validate your perspectives by getting feedback from others who may provide you with valued insights into perceived strengths and weaknesses related to your credibility on the issue you are trying to influence.[8] The results of your self-assessment should represent opportunities to build strengths and address gaps in expertise and relationships. Building expertise may require you to learn through educational programs, self-study, or conversations with other experts. Consider establishing a partnership with colleagues who have higher levels of expertise, factoring in their expertise to enhance your own. Use research, seminal articles from the literature, independent reports, and expert presentations to enhance your understanding and as persuasive evidence of the wisdom of your ideas. If your gaps involve relationships, reach out to individuals you plan to persuade in face-to-face meetings, not to "make your case" but to gather a range of perspectives on the issue, to understand individual positions, to get a sense of what motivates or drives each individual, and to find out their concerns or fears. Finally, use existing relationships to initiate and build new

ones; for example, ask colleagues to make introductions or to coordinate meetings.

Find Common Ground

❼ *To influence effectively, you need to identify shared benefits, as well as connections between what you are proposing and what your audience needs or wants relative to your idea. In other words, you must find common ground with stakeholders (especially decision makers).* Effective influence involves creating or framing a compelling message that highlights meaningful advantages for decision makers. If people think you are gaining while they are losing, they are not going to be open to your proposal. The best influencers show decision makers how their proposals provide decision makers with some benefits (e.g., profitability, better recruiting) and eliminate some problems (e.g., reduce medication errors). Effective influencers use observation, conversation, dialogue, questioning, and **active listening** to fine-tune their proposals to ensure that they are addressing what matters to decision makers.

Building Compelling Evidence

With credibility and a common frame of reference for the issues established, an influential message is built around compelling and vivid evidence. Compelling evidence has a number of characteristics:[5]

- It must be seen as *relevant* to stakeholders (e.g., decision makers). If you spend your time pitching a proposal for **Six Sigma** (which is discussed further in Chapter 7, "Pharmacy Operations: Workflow, Practice Activities, Medication Safety, Technology, and Quality," and is defined as a set of quality improvement practices to improve processes, eliminate defects, and produce high output) by referencing quality initiatives completed in industries other than pharmacy or health care, decision makers for a medical center might not "get it" as much as using evidence drawn from a healthcare industry.
- It must be *believable*. If you offer plausible statistics and examples, you will get more traction for your ideas (e.g., we can reach

more than 50% of our rural population if we use a certain type of technology).

- It must be *new*. When you provide decision makers with data they have seen before, they are not going to recognize any additional value in your ideas. A meta-analysis that has been presented at meetings for the past three years is less powerful than a new one.
- It must be supported with multiple sources of *unbiased evidence*. If you have only one study to support your argument, you will be less successful than if you have multiple studies. Equally important, where does the evidence come from? A study suggesting the efficacy of a drug produced by investigators working for the company that created and marketed the drug may be perceived as less credible than one completed by independent researchers.

Too often, when people want to propose something their tendency is to gather hard numbers and immediately write a summary memo or to put together a PowerPoint presentation describing their proposal/idea/goal and its potential effect. Although data and statistics may present a compelling concept, many people cannot draw the full meaning and effect from numbers alone. Wise influencers start by considering the common ground they share with decision makers and other stakeholders and then craft striking messages using vivid and memorable language, analogies, metaphors, and stories to create a vision of what might be and what will happen if the idea is not adopted (people often fear missing out on something more than they are excited about potential benefits). Analogies and metaphors are powerful tools for influence. Used well, analogies and metaphors provoke your audience to think in new ways, question the obvious, and put themselves in the mind-set of "the other side": patients, vendors, the community, health plans, etc. Health care is filled with good examples of this—think of things like the "house" people work in (pharmacy), how we may be "bleeding" cash, how some studies seem "fishy," etc.

Storytelling is also a powerful tool for influence. Effective stories are *vivid*. When we attempt to be concise in our presentations, we often lose the richness that typically triggers emotion, excite-

ment, and willingness to take a chance on a new idea. Good stories are told with vivid details. They clearly convey cause and effect and create touching emotion in listeners and a memorable flow of ideas. Influential stories are also believable. In general, people are skeptical when someone is trying to convince them to change. Stories, amazingly, mitigate this natural mistrust, pulling listeners into the story line, and creating a vivid image with a scenario that allows people to suspend preconceptions and make sense of an idea. A well-told story is more memorable than mere words and transports people away from the role of cynical, critical listener, engaging them instead as participants in the message. The more vibrant and compelling the story, the more listeners are invested in the message. In a great story, listeners are drawn into identifying with characters, which in turn, allows them to imagine that *this* could happen to them.[11,12] At their best, stories provoke emotions—listeners empathize with the characters or message and connect the dots to their own life, directly stimulating their imagination and creating vicarious experience that becomes both intellectual and emotional reality. This emotional connection motivates individual stakeholders to take action.

One additional bit of advice: keep the narrative rich with detail, and spin your tale with craft and care. See **Appendix A** as it demonstrates several powerful stories that have been used to effectively influence listeners to stop, listen, think, and take action to change behavior.[13,14] Describe the harsh (or inspirational) realities, but be sure to provide concrete and detailed plans for change to provide hope. Done well, a story brilliantly answers the questions any decision maker has about a new idea: "Is it worth it?" and "Can we do it?"

Connect Emotionally

Our discussion about stories points out that most decisions—even the most basic business decisions—have a measure of emotion attached to them. Knowing this, effective influencers create emotional connections, beyond the use of narrative, in two ways. First, they demonstrate their own passion and emotional commitment to the position they advocate. Passion is seductive—it is hard to turn down people who truly believe in what they are advocating. Second, they effectively read the audience for just the right emotional tone and substance to be persuasive. Keeping a pulse on the likely emotional responses of key individuals, testing possible reactions in advance, and gathering information about the way decision makers typically react to new ideas aid influencers in sculpting their messages in ways that appeal to the audience. Keep in mind that people who are strongly involved in an issue may process persuasive messages very differently than those who are uninvolved in the topic. Involved people want good data, logical arguments, and understandable messages. Their less involved counterparts are persuaded by the credibility of the influencer, the number of points he or she makes, and the length of the proposal. If you are attempting to influence an investigational review board (IRB) decision regarding the viability of a new study proposal, physician specialists and researchers are likely to respond to very different information than the administrators responsible for research financials or the vice president for community relations, but all need to be effectively influenced by the data you provide.

One way to connect emotionally is to personalize your message: put a face on it. A health system in the Midwest, firmly believing that a culture of safety was essential but elusive, charged administrative staff to find out facts and details about patients who died, sentinel events, adverse events, medication errors, and wrong-site surgeries. At a retreat meeting, each told painful stories about these incidents and the effect on the patient, the family, and the healthcare providers involved. The result: a dramatic top-to-bottom refocusing of the vision, mission, goals, and daily practices in the organization, as well as a commitment to building and sustaining a culture of medical treatment efficacy and safety for all patients. Patient safety was no longer an abstract concept.

Presenting Persuasively

Persuasive presentation requires careful planning, including consideration of your audience and stakeholders (particularly, the decision makers) and how best to package your message **Table 26–3** provides a list of questions that may be useful in your presentation preparations.[13] ◆ *To present persuasively and with credibility, you should state your assumptions clearly and openly, expose any potential conflicts of interest, present all sides of the argument, and avoid the temptation to oversell weak arguments.* Presenting your persuasive

---

TABLE **26–3**	**Questions to Guide Preparation of Persuasive Presentations**

- What is your elevator (30-second) message for the idea?
- Who are the stakeholders and decision makers, and what role does each play?
- What is your role in the encounter with a decision maker or other stakeholders?
- What is the basis of your credibility (brand) for each decision maker or other stakeholders?
- How do individual stakeholders prefer to receive information and what form of evidence do they find most persuasive?
- What commitments can you request?
- How can you leave the relationships stronger than they are currently?

Source: Data from Schell RG, Moussa M.[13]

argument to influence decision makers involves four steps:[13]

- *Statement of the problem.* This is basically an answer to the "so what" question: why is this important, and to whom. Be specific and present vivid examples of why the situation requires change.
- *Background on causes and related factors.* Why do we have this problem? What caused it? Explaining in rich detail contributing factors and exploring causes of problems in an open dialogue can point to solutions.
- *Recommendations for solutions.* Here you get the opportunity to make your persuasive argument, show how it will solve the problem, and demonstrate the practical aspects of executing your idea. According to the **primacy and recency effects** (people remember best what comes first and last in an event, presentation, etc.), make your best points early and summarize briefly in your close. Be direct and memorable, and use concise and high-level statements, but bring all the data to back up every point you make.
- *Overview of available options and analysis of why your solution is optimal.* This is often the greatest challenge—establishing evidence that your plan or solution will work and is superior to alternatives. Assumptions, pilot tests, market analysis, probability, statistics, and intuition based on experience all have a place in your persuasive message, along with data and hard informational findings. Use examples liberally, share your personal and collegial experience to support the idea, use personal testimony from credible sources wherever available, and test the credibility of evidence with others before you present it.

Sometimes, when presenting persuasively to a nonexpert audience, you need to find a "hook" to get the listeners to accept your solution and to gain their agreement and support. Human consequence is just such a "hook." An example involved the thousands of consumer suits against Merck, alleging life-threatening heart attacks and death as a result of using Vioxx. At the first trial, conducted in Texas, Merck put on a lengthy and powerful scientific argument citing drug studies, including their methodology, purpose, and statistically sound results, as well as the dramatic sales figures for this widely used product. The plaintiff's lawyer told a short, simple story of innocence, trust, suffering, and loss. The jury found for the plaintiff, demonstrating that 100 words may have more influence than thousands. In subsequent trials, Merck explicated the human side of its story first to increase its influence with juries: Merck emphasized that patients died from a bad heart, not bad medicine, and provided a shorter and simpler version of the science. Their success rate rose considerably as a result.[13]

SUMMARY

Building a strong personal brand is a powerful strategy that will help pharmacists and pharmacist managers and leaders gain recognition and distinguish themselves in the profession. A well-respected personal brand creates the foundation for being influential when advocating important issues, changes, proposals, and programs. As a successful influencer, you will add to your personal and professional satisfaction, success, and legacy, not to mention the betterment of your organization, patients, and the world.

References

1. Zimbardo P, Leippe M. The psychology of attitude change and social influence. New York, NY: McGraw Hill; 1999.
2. Peters T. The brand called you. Fast Company. December 2007. Available at: http://www.fastcompany.com/magazine/10/brandyou.html. Accessed February 18, 2009.
3. Winder D. What personal branding can do for you and your business. Available at: http://www.i-define.co.uk. Accessed February 18, 2009.

4. Pavlina S. Personal branding. Available at: http://www.stevepavlina.com/blog/2008/02/personal-branding/. Accessed February 18, 2009.

5. Washingtonian. March 2001, p. 76.

6. Szulanski G. The process of knowledge transfer: a diachronic analysis of stickiness. *Organ Behav Hum Decis Processes* 2000;82:9–27.

7. Benoit W, Kennedy K. On reluctant testimony. *Commun Q* 1999;47:376–387.

8. Conger JA. The necessary art of persuasion. *Harv Bus Rev* 1998;76(3):84–95.

9. Cialdini RB. *Influence: The Psychology of Persuasion*. New York, NY: William Morrow & Co; 1993.

10. Gladwell MB. *Blink: The Power of Thinking Without Thinking*. Boston, MA: Little, Brown and Co; 2005.

11. Fryer B. Storytelling that moves people. *Harv Bus Rev* 2003;81(6):51–55.

12. Patterson K, Grenny J, Maxfield D, McMillan R, Switzler A. *Influencer: The Power to Change Anything*. New York, NY: McGraw-Hill; 2008.

13. Schell RG, Moussa M. *The Art of Woo: Using Strategic Persuasion to Sell Your Ideas*. New York, NY: Penguin Group; 2007.

14. Berwick DM. *Escape Fire*. San Francisco, CA: Jossey Bass; 2004.

Abbreviations

IHI: Institute for Healthcare Improvement
IRB: investigational review board
P&T: pharmacy and therapeutics
ROI: return on investment

Case Scenarios

CASE ONE: Jose Diaz has been working in the Excelsior Health System Pharmacy for the past three years since graduating from pharmacy school. He is the pharmacy's best (and only) sterile compounding specialist. During each of his last few appraisals, he has reminded Marie Rodriguez, the head of the pharmacy, that he is valuable because of his special skills, and this has led to consistent raises. Last month, Dr. Diaz completed his MBA. Now he wants to move up into a management position. When he started hinting to Dr. Rodriguez and others that he now has business knowledge that he would like to use, he did not get much traction. In fact, Dr. Rodriguez said to Dr. Diaz, "You're so valuable at what you do. What would we ever do if you weren't our sterile compounding pharmacist?" How is Dr. Diaz's brand associated with his current situation, and what are some possible options for him to accomplish his goal of moving into a management position?

CASE TWO: "It was horrible," Sarah Johnson told Jeff Parker. "I went into that meeting sure that the committee would love the proposal. But as soon as I got started with my slide presentation, people kept interrupting me with questions. They just did not want to listen. Now I look stupid, and when my supervisor hears about how it went, any chance of getting that promotion is gone."

Two hours before, Dr. Johnson was at lunch thinking about how she was going to persuade the medication error committee to launch a new initiative intended to increase medication error reporting. Clearly, reducing errors was important. Anyone could see how establishing benchmarks on current appropriate practices was valuable. To her, it was a no-brainer. She had spent the last day working up some slides describing what she wanted to accomplish. When she entered the meeting, she was surprised by some of the people who attended. She had not expected so many people. She did not know some of them, and when people started

(continues)

quizzing her, some of the questions surprised her. What things could Dr. Johnson have done to prepare better for this meeting?

CASE THREE: Alecia Jones began working for SuperMedx as a student. Her strong clinical skills, work ethic, and good relationships with her peers led to an offer for a position after graduation. The patient base for the pharmacy includes a large—and growing—number of diabetics, their conditions often coupled with multiple other chronic illnesses. Dr. Jones is also diabetic and has a strong desire—a passion—to help others facing the challenges of this complex disease, its symptoms, and adverse sequelae. As a "patient" serving patients, her attention to patient counseling is more acute, as she is aware that patient counseling in the community setting, while mandated, is typically completed for only half of all patients. The SuperMedx environment does not support counseling because the goal is to fill prescriptions in a speedy manner. More prescriptions, more revenue, and financial rewards are associated with prescription processing. Dr. Jones would like to propose a program for addressing the opportunity to comply with the legal counseling requirement and to meet the increasingly important quality-based outcome indicators as regulatory accreditation moves into community practice. What can she do to influence SuperMedx to improve patient counseling?

CASE FOUR: Tim Porter's practice for the past six years has been in an extremely innovative independent community pharmacy. He is familiar with the patients he sees and their general health status. He is concerned because Mrs. Hoffman has recently been inconsistent with her medication refills for her multiple chronic illnesses. Knowing the importance of adherence, Dr. Porter is challenged to find a way to frame the issue persuasively in talking with Mrs. Hoffman about this apparent lack of adherence. As he thinks about it, Mrs. Hoffman's behavior may be tied to any number of things. Maybe she does not see him as a partner in her health care or maybe he has not been persuasive enough. He starts to reflect and generate ideas. What can Dr. Porter do to improve Mrs. Hoffman's adherence?

APPENDIX A	**Examples of Compelling Evidence Presentations**

- At a large academic medical center, the classic hygiene issue of hand washing best practice plagued infection control teams facing significantly higher instances of hospital-acquired infections. Each physician was convinced that someone else was responsible; therefore, administrators were faced with the challenging task of changing behavior that involved deeply ingrained habits. They tried both data-driven messages and inspirational messages, but nothing worked. Inspired to try something visual and unique, the administrator responsible for infection control surprised the senior medical staff during a luncheon by providing a set of lab trays to record the bacterial cultures on their hands. Full-color graphic images of those colonies were turned into screen savers on every computer in the hospital, and compliance with hand washing increased by nearly 100% (and was maintained).

(continues)

- The launch of the Medicare Part D prescription drug benefit was a sentinel event in health care. From the outset, health plans recognized the wisdom and business necessity of moving market share from brand to generic products. Savvy pharmacists in these plans also recognized the need to persuade patients that this shift was in their best interests. In a series of targeted communications, a plan in the Southwest established the credibility of its pharmacy professionals, referencing their history and experience in managed care, as well as their understanding and expertise relative to the Part D benefit. They went on to establish the common ground for the plan and the beneficiary: keep out-of-pocket costs low to delay reaching the dreaded "donut hole" (i.e., the gap between periods of coverage). They further agreed to suspend copays for generic products, which served to increase their credibility and trustworthiness in the eyes of the beneficiary. They presented evidence regarding the quality of generic products and the relative cost differences and clearly pointed out that the switch to generics would not compromise therapeutic integrity. Finally, they personalized the message for each beneficiary, laying out estimated annual costs for that person for generic and brand products, graphically displaying the real dollar effect that the decision to choose generic products would have over a year's time. Generic usage exceeded 75% in year 1 of the program, 10–20% higher than other plans, with a net benefit of millions of dollars to the plan and substantially lower out-of-pocket costs for the beneficiary.

- Establishing a point of reference to make a connection between seemingly disparate situations may set off mental light bulbs of acceptance in delivering a persuasive message. Donald Berwick, President of the Institute for Healthcare Improvement (IHI), is a pediatrician who has become the voice for quality in American health care. Each year at the IHI's National Quality Forum, his keynote address weaves a story that is compelling, vivid, and memorable in persuading health professionals that they can do more to improve the quality and safety of the care they provide. He effectively makes the case for high-reliability organizations (organizations that effectively avoid serious detrimental incidents in environments, where such incidents might be expected because of increased risk factors) by telling the story of the Mann Gulch wildfire where smoke jumpers faced a small manageable fire that quickly turned into something much more dangerous. A few courageous and inventive firefighters radically changed the popular wisdom and rules of how forest fires should be fought using "escape fires," setting a fire to create a burned out area to slow the main fire's development. He weaves the theme of this counterintuitive strategy and the principles of high-reliability organizations vividly and poignantly to discuss the need for a healthcare "escape fire" strategy to overcome fundamental flaws in the care we provide to patients in every part of our system. The story makes the message so much more memorable because of the vivid images created by the stories.

Sources: Data from Fryer B;[11] Schell RG, Moussa M;[13] Berwick DM.[14]

Additional Resources Available Online!

Visit the Student Companion Web site at http://healthprofessions.jbpub.com/pharmacymanagement for interactive study tools and additional resources.

See www.rxugace.com to learn how you can obtain continuing pharmacy education for this content.

CHAPTER 27

PERSONAL FINANCE

KEITH NICOLAS HERIST, PharmD, CPA

MARIE A. CHISHOLM-BURNS, PharmD, MPH, FCCP, FASHP

LEARNING OBJECTIVES

After completing the chapter, the reader will be able to

1. Discuss the signs of poor financial management.
2. Describe the importance of setting financial priorities and goals
3. Explain the difference between simple and compound interest.
4. Discern the importance of future and present value in various investment alternatives.
5. Differentiate the risks and benefits of various investment vehicles.
6. Discuss the importance of liquid assets in an investment portfolio.
7. Describe the effects of dollar cost averaging and portfolio diversification.
8. Evaluate the effects of taxation on wages and interest income.
9. Define adjusted gross income and its impact on federal income tax.
10. Recognize the importance of investing in tax-deferred investment tools, such as 401(k), 401(a), 403(b), IRAs, SEP, and 457 and 529 plans.

KEY CONCEPTS

❶ Budgeting facilitates financial discipline. A well-designed budget is not restrictive but allows for the opportunity to track finances, optimize outcomes, and achieve goals. Although everyone's budget is different, gen-erally one rule is consistent: expenses should not exceed income.

❷ Individuals should develop a financial plan early in their careers.

❸ Creditworthiness is the lender's assessment of the borrower's ability to repay the debt incurred. Much of an individual's perceived creditworthiness is based on his or her FICO score.

4 A dollar today is worth more than a dollar in the future, as the dollar today can earn interest up until the time the future dollar is received.

5 Interest is the most common way to quantify the time value of money concept and represents an expressed charge for the use of money.

6 The present value (PV) of a future amount to be received by an investor is the equivalent value, in today's dollars, of the single payment or stream of payments, to be received in the future after considering the effect of the rate of interest (or return on investment), referred to as the discount rate.

7 Risk is defined as the chance that the actual return on an investment will be different from the expected return. Risk is quantifiable and includes the possibility of losing or not gaining in value during a stated period.

8 Maintaining an appropriate level of liquid assets is crucial when developing an investment portfolio.

9 The purpose of dollar cost averaging is to minimize the effects of market fluctuations over time.

10 Portfolio diversification is simply investing in a variety of options and classes (stocks, bonds, etc.) to spread the risk inherent to any one investment item.

INTRODUCTION

Encounters with personal finances occur long before entering the workforce and continue throughout life, as pharmacists are faced with many challenges regarding spending, investing, and allocating personal resources. Many financial decisions must be made during one's life and career. Preparation and information allow you to optimize and protect your resources. This chapter addresses the importance of financial discipline, including minimizing bad debt and optimizing

wealth. Specifically, this chapter discusses some basic concepts and tools that facilitate financial decision making, including, but not limited to, budgeting, setting financial goals, and understanding some basic investing and income tax strategies.

BUDGETING AND SETTING FINANCIAL PRIORITIES

During 2005–2008, more than 4.5 million bankruptcy filings occurred.[1] Coupled with economic uncertainty, this has prompted individuals to emphasize not only how they *invest* their money but also how they *spend* their money. No doubt, it is easy to get in financial trouble. Spending too much without having adequate resources to cover expenses can lead to financial difficulties. A common mistake people make is purchasing items without considering their purpose, need, and future consequence. See **Table 27–1** for some of the typical ways individuals get in financial trouble[2] and **Table 27–2** for signs that indicate financial trouble.[3]

Budgeting, defined as developing a detailed plan for expenses/expenditures, can be used as a tool to help you realize where you spend your money and set priorities on spending and wealth building. **1** *Budgeting facilitates financial discipline. A well-designed budget is not restrictive but allows for the opportunity to track finances, optimize outcomes, and achieve goals. Although everyone's budget is different, generally one rule is consistent: expenses should not exceed income.*[4] **Figure 27–1** is an example of a budget worksheet.[5] **Table 27–3** provides strategies to help you comply with your budget.[4]

Financial success is due to a combination of factors, including but not limited to discipline, knowledge, skills, determination, and luck, as well as the following practices of many of America's first generation millionaires:[6,7]

- Focus on accumulating wealth rather than spending money.
- Borrow money only when necessary to achieve a goal rather than to make standard purchases.

TABLE **27–1**	**Common Ways to Get in Financial Trouble**

- Borrowing needlessly to maintain a lifestyle beyond your means
- Depending on credit cards for most purchases without having the funding to pay the monthly credit card balance
- Refinancing and using loans to pay off other loans
- Ignoring warning signs of financial problems, such as overdrafts, constant late payments, and only paying minimum payments on loans and credit card balances

Source: Data from MoneyMatters101.com.[2]

TABLE **27–2**	**Signs That You Could Be in Financial Trouble**

- Having an inadequate emergency fund or little in savings
- Constantly depending on friends or family members to bail you out on monthly bills
- Putting off saving for retirement
- Being turned down for a loan or credit card
- Using short-term or payday loans on a regular basis
- Financing a vehicle for more than 5 years
- Using credit to pay for basic needs because you don't have cash available
- Making only minimum payments on your credit cards
- Using a credit card to make minimum balance payments on your other credit cards
- Having a large number of credit cards
- Lacking articulated monetary goals or no plan to reach them

Source: Data from Generation X Finance.[3]

- Pursue educational opportunities.
- Maintain balance between career and personal life.
- Recognize that hard work and self-discipline increase the probability of success.

Not all of us will become millionaires; however, these practices are useful in achieving any level of financial success. Setting financial goals and, in turn, exercising discipline and making sound financial decisions provide the foundation for accumulating wealth.

Setting Financial Goals

Short of inheriting wealth or winning a big lottery, accumulating wealth is a lifelong process, and significant attention must be given to planning for the future and accumulating enough wealth for a

---

FIGURE **27–1**   **Budget Worksheet Template.**

Budget Worksheet

Monthly Income. Enter your gross and net (after taxes) income from all sources. For income received infrequently, such as bonuses for tax returns, calculate the annual income, then divide by 12 to find the monthly amount.

Source	Gross	Net
Job		
Spouse's job		
Part-time job		
Rental/room & board received		
Commissions/bonuses		
Tax refunds		
Investment income		
Government benefits		
Unemployment insurance		
Child support/alimony		
Support from family/friends		
Other		
TOTAL		

Monthly Expenses. Since many expenses are variable, such as utilities and groceries, it is important to average these expenses. Other expenses are periodic (such as insurance or vehicle registration). Again, calculate the annual amount and divide by 12.

Category	Expense	Average per Month	Goal per Month
HOUSING	Rent/mortgage		
	2nd mortgage/equity line		
	Homeowner's/renter's insurance		
	Condo fees/HOA dues		
	Home maintenance		
	Gas/electric		
	Water/sewer/garbage		
	Telephone		
FOOD	Groceries/household items		
	At work/school		
INSURANCE (Exclude payroll-deducted amounts)	Health/dental/vision		
	Life/disability		
MEDICAL CARE (Exclude payroll-deducted amounts)	Doctor/chiropractor		
	Optometrist/lenses		
	Dentist/orthodontist		
	Prescriptions		
TRANSPORTATION (Exclude payroll-deducted amounts)	Car payment #1		
	Car payment #2		
	Auto insurance		
	Registration		
	Gasoline/oil		
	Maintenance/repairs		
	Public transportation/tolls/parking		
CHILD CARE (Exclude payroll-deducted amounts)	Daycare		
	Child support/alimony		
SAVINGS	Emergency		
	Goals		
INCOME TAXES	Prior year		
	Estimated tax payments (self-employed)		
UNSECURED DEBT	Loan payment		
	Credit card #1		
	Credit card #2		
	Credit card #3		
	Credit card #4		

(continues)

FIGURE **27–1** (continued)

Category	Expense	Average per Month	Goal per Month
PERSONAL	Beauty/barber		
	Clothing/jewelry		
	Cosmetics/manicure		
ENTERTAINMENT	Cable/satellite		
	Movies/concerts/theater		
	Books/magazines		
	CD/tapes/videos/DVD		
	Dining out		
	Sports/hobbies		
	Vacation/travel		
MISCELLANEOUS	Banking fees		
	Laundry		
	Union dues		
	Internt service		
	Pet care		
	Gifts for holidays/birthdays		
	Cell phone/pager		
	Postage		
	Cigarettes/alcohol		
	Contributions to church/charity		
	Other		
	Other		
	Other		
	Other		
	Other		
	Other		
	Other		
	Other		
TOTALS (include totals from previous page)			

Bottom Line. Once you have determined the total of your take-home pay and expenses you are ready to determine your bottom line. Subtract the total of all expenses including debt payments from your net income. If the result is a positive number, you can add the extra money to your savings to reach your goals sooner. If your expenses exceed your income, you'll need to make some adjustments to bring your finances back into balance.

Total Monthly Income (Net)	Total Expenses	Balance
	−	=

Source: Courtesy of BALANCE.

TABLE 27–3	Strategies for Complying with Your Budget

- Avoid temptation areas! If you always spend too much at certain places, do not go to those stores (or limit visits).

- Stick to a list. Knowing what you need before you go will help avoid "impulse" purchases.

- Reward your efforts with an occasional, yet affordable, reward.

- Get a budget buddy who is onboard with your budgeting goals. When you want to splurge, call your buddy for moral support.

- Charge purchases only when you can afford to repay the balance in full by the due date.

- Use debit cards. They provide much of the consumer protection and convenience of a credit card without a bill at the end of the month, and because of the detailed statements you receive, you can track spending easier than with cash.

- Ask some hard questions about each potential purchase: Is it a want (nonessential) or a need (essential)? Recognizing the difference between the two can help you avoid unnecessary spending and impulse shopping.

- Remind yourself often of your long-term goals. By sacrificing those things you do not really need today, you can attain your more meaningful financial objectives in the future.

Source: Data from BalanceTrack. Money matters. Available at: http://www.balancetrack.org/moneymanagement/index.html. Accessed March 27, 1009.

comfortable retirement. ❷ *Whatever dreams and financial goals are desired, individuals should develop a financial plan early in their careers.* As part of the planning process, an assessment of one's current situation, coupled with a realistic evaluation of future potential, is important. Knowing where you are financially and where you want to be form the basis of a financial plan. If wealth building is important, then one's standard of living will have to be accommodated. For example, a more modest home may enable one to save a larger proportion of income for other significant items, including saving for retirement. Although financial plans can be specific and short term, broader, more long-term financial goals can include the following:

- Saving for your "emergency reserve fund"
- Paying off debts, including college loans
- Saving for retirement

- Saving for a downpayment on a house
- Saving for a child's college education

Individuals will likely set different financial goals at different points, or stages, in their lives (for example, entering a new profession or starting a family). Whether you are a pharmacist preparing for the birth of your first child or saving for retirement, the most critical behavior for achieving financial success is to be disciplined when it comes to implementing your plan. The most important rule for the success of any individual's savings plan is to always make payments to yourself first. Treat yourself as your major creditor, or someone to whom a debt is owed, and make regular payments to yourself. One method to easily develop this habit is to establish a regular (e.g., monthly) automatic transfer from your checking account into a savings account, beginning with your very first paycheck. An emergency reserve fund will quickly build, which should only be used in emergencies, such as a period of unemployment lasting for a couple of months. An emergency reserve fund is usually defined as three to six months of living expenses and can be used to pay ongoing expenses, such as mortgage or rent, utilities, and food. Once this account has reached its target goal, continuing the process of regular saving becomes routine and almost effortless.

Another critical financial goal should be establishing a high credit rating, or score. An individual's credit score affects his or her ability to receive loans and negotiate lower **interest rates** when purchasing important items, such as a home (mortgage) or automobile. Credit scores may be negatively affected by risky financial behaviors, such as defaulting on loans.

Credit Score

Credit is the contract created by a borrower and a lender, whereby the borrower receives a benefit (cash loan, automobile, credit card) and agrees to repay the lender at a future date. Included in the agreement is an interest rate, which depends on the risk of the borrower, as assessed by the lender. Therefore, lower interest rates are extended to borrowers associated with less risk. Just as a high interest rate is desired when making investments, the lowest interest rate is sought when an individual is seeking to borrow. ❸ *Creditworthiness is the lender's assessment of the borrower's ability to repay the debt incurred. Much of an individual's perceived creditworthiness is based on his or her FICO score.* Currently, the FICO score is used by lenders to rate the potential risk of borrowers. FICO scores range from 300 to 850, and higher FICO scores are deemed to be better credit risks and earn lower interest rates.[8] A FICO is based on five elements: (1) types of credit in use (10%), (2) payment history (35%), (3) length of credit history (15%), (4) amounts owed (30%), and (5) new credit (10%).[9] By establishing appropriate amounts of credit and making regular, on-time payments, a high FICO score can be achieved and maintained, resulting in the best interest rates when borrowing in the future.

In addition to a FICO score, a credit report is maintained on all borrowers. An individual's credit report will contain identifying information, places

of employment, addresses, all consumer credit for the past 7 years, and payment history and other various public records. Equifax, Experian, and TransUnion are credit-reporting agencies. The government also allows everyone to get a free credit report annually by visiting https://www .annualcreditreport.com/. As identity theft is a threat to every credit consumer, regular monitoring of one's own credit report with all three credit agencies is a good idea.

Credit cards offer consumers great convenience and, when appropriately used, can be an integral part of a financial plan. In today's economy, a variety of credit cards are available; remembering some basic tips will allow you to use them effectively. When choosing a credit card, the card with the lowest interest rate and lowest fees is usually best. Some cards offer rewards, such as airline miles or rebates, but annual fees usually accompany these benefits. Credit cards offering frequent flier miles may not meet one's needs if traveling is not important. Because credit card interest is not tax deductible, carrying balances and incurring monthly interest charges can be costly. Credit cards can be used for daily purchases and are a great convenience; however, carefully manage charges and pay them off at the end of every month. Using credit cards this way will build the rewards offered with each card, as well as your credit report and FICO score. In the event you are unable to pay your balance in full each month, paying your minimum balance on time is critical. Failure to do so will typically result in a late fee, may result in a higher interest rate, will lower your FICO score, and may even affect the interest rates on your other credit cards.

BASICS OF INVESTING

To implement any financial plan, knowledge of the fundamental basics of finance is essential. Since building wealth is the accumulation of money or other assets, it is important to understand some key points when dealing with money. In all investments, the date of receipt of money is critical in determining how much growth there will be, and contributions may be made on a one-time basis (lump sum) or on a regular basis (series of payments). Knowing how to effectively grow money will be the key to implementing the financial plan you create.

Time Value of Money

◆ *A dollar today is worth more than a dollar in the future, as the dollar today can earn interest until the time the future dollar is received.*[10] To explain further, receiving a fixed amount sooner rather than later (for example, you are offered $100,000 today versus 1 year from today) is advantageous because you can invest this amount immediately and begin earning interest (for example, $200 per month). Using the example, by the time you reach the 1-year mark, you will have accumulated $2,400 of interest, bringing your total amount to $102,400—in contrast to the $100,000 you would have if you had chosen to receive the amount at the later date. The amount of interest earned during the period between the "sooner" date and the "later" date is known as the **time value of money**.

INTEREST

◆ *Interest is the most common way to quantify the time value of money concept and represents an expressed charge for the use of money.* Interest rates are usually expressed as an annual percentage rate, which is applied to the principal, or amount borrowed, to determine the **interest expense**. The **prime rate** is the gold standard for the financial industry; commercial lending institutions use it to set rates for their customers. Loans are stated agreements between two parties. The lender, or creditor, is the holder of the assets and agrees to lend an amount to the other party, the borrower, to use over a specified period and at a stated interest rate. Accordingly, the borrower agrees to repay the lender either in a single payment or with a series of payments over the life of the loan. Payments consist of a portion of the original principal (the amount invested) and interest expense, which represents the total amount of interest charged on the principal amount outstanding, or owed, during a certain time. In addition to borrowers and lenders, the term investor is used when the primary motivation for agreeing to part with assets for another's use is the return on investment or income (i.e., interest) to be received.

Simple and Compound Interest

Simple interest is defined as interest computed on the principal and does not include more than one period. Simple interest is calculated with the following formula:

$$FV = P\,(1 + r)$$

where FV = future value of original principal; P = principal amount invested; and r = interest rate. For example, assume a bank pays 10% a year on invested funds. Using this formula, investing $1,000 for a year would earn interest of $100; therefore, FV = $1,100.

The compound interest principal takes simple interest a step further and applies it to interest over more than one period. When calculating compound interest, interest is earned during the first period exactly as the simple interest calculation. During the second (and future periods), the interest rate is applied to both the original principal and the interest earned in the first period (and subsequent periods). Extending the previous example to a 2-year period with compound interest, the interest earned for the second year would be $110, calculated as the 10% interest rate on $1,100 (original principal of $1,000 plus the $100 interest from the first year). Compound interest is calculated using the following formula:

$$FV = P\,(1 + r/n)^{nt}$$

where FV = future value of original principal; P = principal amount invested; r = interest rate; n = number of periods; and t = number of times per year interest is compounded. Thus, the future value of the account for the second year, including interest and principal is

$$FV = \$1{,}000\,(1 + 0.10/1)^{(2)(1)}; \text{ thus } FV = \$1{,}210$$

The effects of earning compound interest, also known as compounding, are significant compared with simple interest earnings. Compound interest calculations rely on accrued interest, which is interest earned and due to the investor but not actually paid to the investor. Instead, the amount of interest earned in the previous period, the accrued interest, is included in the principal balance in the interest calculation for the next period. **Table 27–4** shows the effects of simple

TABLE 27-4 Comparison of the Effects of Simple and Compound Interest

Time Period in Years	Simple Interest Calculation				Compound Interest Calculation			
	Principal Balance Earning Interest	Interest Rate	Interest Earned for the Period	Ending Principal Balance with Interest	Principal Balance Earning Interest	Interest Rate	Interest Earned for the Period	Ending Principal Balance with Interest
1	$1,000.00	8%	$80	$1,080.00	$1,000.00	8%	$80	$1,080.00
2	$1,000.00	8%	$80	$1,160.00	$1,080.00	8%	$86.40	$1,166.40
3	$1,000.00	8%	$80	$1,240.00	$1,166.40	8%	$93.31	$1,259.71
4	$1,000.00	8%	$80	$1,320.00	$1,259.71	8%	$100.78	$1,360.49
5	$1,000.00	8%	$80	$1,400.00	$1,360.49	8%	$108.84	$1,469.33
6	$1,000.00	8%	$80	$1,480.00	$1,469.33	8%	$117.54	$1,586.87
7	$1,000.00	8%	$80	$1,560.00	$1,586.87	8%	$126.95	$1,713.82
8	$1,000.00	8%	$80	$1,640.00	$1,713.82	8%	$137.11	$1,850.93
9	$1,000.00	8%	$80	$1,720.00	$1,850.93	8%	$148.07	$1,999.00
10	$1,000.00	8%	$80	$1,800.00	$1,999.00	8%	$159.92	$2,158.92

Note: In the simple interest calculation, P, or the principal amount invested, remains constant regardless of the interest earned. In the compound interest calculation, the interest earned in each period is added to the principal amount from the prior period, and interest is calculated on both principal plus the interest earned from prior periods. The effects of compounding can be seen in just a few years. This interest rate of 8% is for the purpose of this example and does not necessarily represent current interest rates.

interest and compound interest on the future value of an investment.

Although interest is expressed in annual terms, compounding can use any time period. As a rule, the greater the number of time periods, the greater the effect compounding has on the principal balance. As shown in **Table 27–5**, although the effects of daily compounding (final principal balance of $618.31) may seem small compared with the annual compound interest calculation for a 1-year period ($600.00), the true power of compound interest becomes apparent when both the principal balance continues to increase from regular contributions (e.g., monthly) over a lifetime of savings. **Table 27–6** shows the cumulative effects of a systematic savings plan of $500 per month over 40 years, at interest rates of 6% and 8% (please note that these banking interest rates of 6% and 8% are for the purpose of this example and do not necessarily represent current interest rates). The power of compound interest can be seen by analyzing the results, and the greatest growth is seen in the final 10 years of investing. To understand the effect of time, assume the monthly contributions were stopped after the first 10 years. If no additional contributions are made to the savings account, the 10-year ending principal

balance with interest of $82,849 will grow to $498,964 (after 30 more years) at an annual interest rate of 6%. In comparison, if $500 monthly contributions remained constant and continued to earn 6% interest compounded monthly, the final amount at 40 years will be $1,001,224. The $502,260 difference is more than double, although the actual amount of the $500 monthly contributions during those 30 years was only $180,000 ($240,000 – $60,000).

The other major contributor to the power of compounding is the interest rate. Again in Table 27–6, the effect of earning 8% on a $500 monthly savings plan for 40 years results in a balance of $1,757,641, approximately 75% higher than the same savings plan that earned 6%. It takes only a 2% increase in the interest rate to generate the higher accumulated investment balance seen in this example. The final point regarding the power of compounding is seen in Table 27–6 by analyzing the significance of the last 10 years of savings. By saving for another 10 years, or 25% of the average 40 years of working time for most pharmacists, the final accumulated balances increase over 100% at both interest rates. For example, Year 30 ending principal with interest of 8% is $750,648 compared with Year 40 (10 years later) ending principal with

TABLE **27–5**	Effects of Length of Time Periods on Compound Interest				
Period	Number of Periods	Interest Rate	Beginning Principal	Interest Earned in One Year	Final Principal Balance
Annually	1	6%	$10,000.00	$600.00	$10,600.00
Semiannually	2	6%	$10,000.00	$609.00	$10,609.00
Quarterly	4	6%	$10,000.00	$613.64	$10,613.64
Monthly	12	6%	$10,000.00	$616.78	$10,616.78
Weekly	52	6%	$10,000.00	$618.00	$10,618.00
Daily	365	6%	$10,000.00	$618.31	$10,618.31

Note: The table shows the effects of compounding after one year. Beginning principal is $10,000 with an interest rate of 6%. The effects of compounding interest are shown for the different time periods indicated. This interest rate of 6% is for the purpose of this example and does not necessarily represent current interest rates.

TABLE **27–6**   Interest Rate Comparison in Compound Interest and Number of Periods

Time Period in Years	Original Principal Invested	Interest Rate	Interest Earned for the Period	Ending Principal Balance with Interest	Interest Rate	Interest Earned for the Period	Ending Principal Balance with Interest
10	$60,000	6%	$22,849	$82,849	8%	$32,583	$92,583
20	$120,000	6%	$89,827	$232,676	8%	$144,391	$296,974
30	$180,000	6%	$212,593	$505,269	8%	$393,674	$750,648
40	$240,000	6%	$435,955	$1,001,224	8%	$946,993	$1,757,641

Note: The table reflects the cumulative growth of a monthly savings amount of $500 over 10-year periods, at interest rates of 6% and 8%, compounded monthly. The effect of time is seen prominently in the final 10 years of investing. The affect of a higher interest rate also has the greatest effect in the final 10 years. The figures expressed in this table ignore the influence of inflation and income taxes.

interest at $1,757,641. What does this mean to the new graduate? In this example, by delaying a simple monthly payment of $500 with your very first paycheck for 10 years, the monthly amount needed to catch up would be nearly $1,200 monthly for the next 30 years. Clearly, when developing and implementing a financial plan, starting as soon as possible is beneficial, as the factor of time is an extremely important concept as it relates to finances.

The effects of time, interest rates, and compounding can also be seen in reverse, in the case of a home mortgage or automobile loan. Refer to **Table 27–7** as an example of how much a $40,000 automobile can cost if you borrow $40,000 from a bank at 10% interest for either a 3- or 6-year loan. In this example, note that the total principal paid in both loans is $40,000, although the 6-year loan has total interest of $6,889.76 more than the 3-year loan—a high price to pay for a $549.66 lower monthly payment of $741.03. Purchasing a car that fits into your budget is a much better option than extending the life of the loan to reduce the monthly payment. Regarding home mortgages, most homes are acquired through a mortgage, which is typically a 15- or 30-year loan that a future home owner (borrower) obtains from a bank and repays in monthly payments. Each monthly payment includes a principal reduction and an interest expense amount. **Table 27–8** is an amortization table and demonstrates the effects of the monthly payment reducing the mortgage. As demonstrated in the amortization, even after 20 years (Payment 240) the principal ($493.50) still represents less than 50% of the monthly payment amount of $1,048.82. Over the life of this mortgage, interest expense totals $227,576 in addition to the $150,000 in principal reduction. Given the time value of money concept, it is intuitive that a 15-year fixed mortgage would result in a smaller interest expense over the life of the loan. A 15-year mortgage at the same interest rate results in $100,293 in interest expense, a savings of $127,283. The monthly payment on a 15-year mortgage on a $150,000 loan at 7.5% interest would be $1,391 compared with $1,049 for a 30-year fixed mortgage. Many homebuyers may opt for a 30-year fixed mortgage to avoid the higher monthly payment difference between the 15- and 30-year mortgage. By making mortgage payments in biweekly installments, a 30-year mortgage payoff can be shortened by seven years,[11] thus demonstrating that the time value of money and the power of compounding can provide great rewards when used effectively.

A variety of mortgage options (in addition to fixed rate/fixed term) are available, and many buyers can be overwhelmed. One popular mort-

TABLE 27–7	Total Cost of Borrowing for Automobile Loans	
Assumptions: $40,000 borrowed at 10%		
Length of Loan	3 years	6 years
Monthly Payment Amount	$1,290.69	$741.03
Total Principal Paid	$40,000	$40,000
Total Interest Paid	$6,464.74	$13,354.50
Total of All Payments	$46,464.74	$53,354,50

Note: The total principal paid in both loans is $40,000, although the 6-year loan has total interest of $6,889.76 more than that of the 3-year loan—a high price to pay for a $549.66 lower monthly payment of $741.03. Purchasing a car that fits into your budget is a much better option than extending the life of the loan to reduce the monthly payment.

TABLE **27–8**   **Typical Mortgage Amortization Schedule**

Mortgage Amount: $150,000.00

Mortgage Term: 30 years

Interest Rate: 7.5%

Payment Number	Principal Balance	Payment Amount	Principal Amount	New Balance
1	$150,000.00	$1,048.82	$111.32	$149,888.68
60	$142,086.93	$1,048.82	$160.78	$141,926.15
120	$130,426.14	$1,048.82	$233.66	$130,192.48
240	$88,851.22	$1,048.82	$493.50	$88,357.72
359 (next to last)	$2,078.14	$1,048.82	$1,035.83	$1,042.30

This amortization schedule represents a 30-year, fixed interest rate of 7.5%, and details how the payment represents both principal and interest. The amount of interest associated with each payment can be calculated by subtracting the principal amount from the payment amount.

gage is the 1-year adjustable rate mortgage, or ARM. This type of mortgage often has a term of 30 years; however, the interest rate can change periodically as indicated in the loan agreement. The purpose of these loans is to provide potential home owners with a lower monthly payment to establish themselves with home ownership. Then, the mortgage payment increases over time. As other mortgage products are developed, potential buyers must remember the basics of borrowing: Greater benefit is seen with higher principal payments over a shorter time period at the lowest rate available. Buyers must read all loan documents carefully and ask questions to understand the effect of the decisions they are making.

Current and Future Value of Money

The actual passage of time is not necessary to determine what the maturity value of an investment will be on the maturity date. Given an accurate earning rate, estimates can be made to help predict the value of an investment over time by using the concept of future value (FV). Future value is simply the amount of money a principal amount invested today will grow to be at some future, or maturity, date. The time value of money concept implies that the future value will be greater than the current value because of the interest rate, which is always a positive percentage. The difference between the current value and the future value depends on two factors: (1) number of time periods involved and (2) **rate of return**. Future value is an important tool when evaluating different investment alternatives. With careful analysis, the effect of different return rates, timing of cash flows (contributions), and investment periods can be seen in the cumulative growth of each investment alternative.

Investments are often quoted in terms of the **maturity value**, the investment value at the end of all the stated time periods. In these instances, the **present value** (PV) concept provides essential information for an evaluation of the investment. ❻ *The present value of a future amount to be received by an investor is the equivalent value, in today's dollars, of the single payment or stream of* *payments, to be received in the future after considering the effect of the interest (or return on investment), referred to as the **discount rate**.* In other words, the discount rate is the interest rate that an investment earns for the investor and can be evaluated against other investment options. A stream of fixed payments over a fixed number of years at a specified discount rate is an annuity.

The future value and present value concepts can be readily understood in the example of a lottery. Many state lottery jackpots are structured as annuities in which the jackpot is paid to the winner for a stated amount per year for a stated number of years (for example, 30 years). The future value of that annuity is the jackpot. The winner can also choose the "cash option," or lump-sum payment, which is the present value of that annuity. By using present value formulas, the discount rate can be determined. With the cash option, the present value of each individual payment for each of the next 30 years is determined at an assumed discount rate and totaled. For example, a $10,000,000 jackpot paid out over 30 years would have a cash option, or present value, of $1,313,671 at a 7% discount rate. This information is valuable to the winner because if other available investment options are earning 8%, the prudent choice would be to take the lottery winnings as the cash option and invest it in the alternative earning 8%. Over the 30 years, the investor would be earning 1% higher interest than if the annual payment from the lottery system had been chosen. By taking the $10,000,000 over 30 years instead of the cash option lump-sum of $1,313,671 and investing the proceeds in a vehicle earning an average 8%, the winner may actually experience a great loss in **opportunity cost** over the 30 years.

Risk

A major determinant of rate is the level of risk involved in the transaction. ❼ *Risk is defined as the chance that the actual return on an investment (discussed further in the following section) will be different from the expected return. Risk is quantifiable and includes the possibility of losing or not gaining in value during a stated period.* Another important consideration in determining investment options is inflation risk. Inflation is the general rise in prices of goods and services over time and is expressed

as a percentage, called **inflation rate**. Therefore, investors need to earn an interest rate higher than the inflation rate to have real growth of their money. Failure to earn a rate of return in excess of the inflation rate results in a decrease in one's actual purchasing power; in other words, the dollar today will buy less tomorrow than it will today. Alternatively, in periods of deflation, an investor may enjoy an increase in the purchasing power of the dollar. **Risk tolerance** is the degree of risk, or potential loss, an individual investor can accept in any investment. The rate of return will be higher on an investment that has more volatility than others. Younger investors usually tolerate a higher degree of risk than older investors, as younger investors generally have many more years to recoup losses on risky investments than older investors. Risk calculators, available free on the internet, can help one assess comfort level with risk. Major classifications for investors relating to the level of risk are aggressive, moderate, and conservative.

Major Investment Classes

Investors have many investment options, and each option has inherent risks and associated return rates. Many commonly known types of investments are **certificates of deposit**, **mutual funds**, **money market funds**, real estate, **stocks**, and **bonds**. When deciding among these options, consider short-term and long-term goals within one's financial plan. The balance between having enough cash for current needs and saving for the future can be complex, and **liquidity** helps meet this need.

A liquid asset is an investment that can be converted into cash with relative ease and without a loss in value. ❽ *Maintaining an appropriate level of liquid assets is crucial when developing an investment portfolio.* Liquid investments are cash, checking accounts, savings accounts, and money market funds. Less liquid investments would be items such as a car, home, stocks, and bonds because their market value fluctuates over time, making their cash value uncertain. In addition, a longer time period may be required to convert these items into cash. For example, owning a home is a common investment but is not as liquid as money market funds. In the event of an emergency, money market funds can be quickly redeemed into cash; however, selling a home and receiving the cash proceeds may take significantly more time (e.g., several months).

CASH AND CASH EQUIVALENTS

Cash is the most liquid investment of all. Interest is earned on cash accounts; however, since there is little risk in the loss of value of cash, the rate of return is usually quite low. Any investment portfolio, or collection of investments, should include cash and cash equivalents. Cash equivalents are short-term investments that are convertible to a known cash amount or are sufficiently close to their maturity date, such that their market value is not sensitive to fluctuation in interest rates.

STOCKS

Investments are commonly made in stocks of many companies. A stock is a certificate that represents the shareholder's ownership in a corporation and gives one the privilege to have a vote in matters of corporate operations. Typically, investors have an electronic account that represents their shares, and the actual paper certificate is seldom received. The marketplace determines the value of a stock and may fluctuate daily and vary widely. Market fluctuations are a result of many factors, both national and international, and therefore investing in stocks has more risk than more liquid investments. Gains or losses are incurred depending on the price received when the stock is sold compared with the price of the stock when it was purchased. Stocks do not pay a stated interest rate; instead, their value stems from market fluctuations that it is hoped will increase over time. However, some stocks do pay **dividends**, defined as the portion of a corporation's earnings paid to stockholders. Dividends can be thought of as interest payments, but there is no legal requirement for a company to declare and ultimately pay dividends.

The two major classes of stocks are common and preferred. One advantage of common stock is that it comes with owner voting rights, usually one vote per share, within the corporation (preferred stocks do not come with voting rights). In addition, common stock can appreciate or depreciate in its market value, resulting in profits or a loss to the

shareholder when the common stock is sold. Finally, common stock is eligible to receive dividends whenever authorized by the corporation. Preferred stocks usually guarantee a regular dividend payment and do not fluctuate with the overall stock market as do common stocks. Instead, their value will fluctuate with interest rates due to the guaranteed dividend payment. Preferred stock prices usually decline when interest rates rise and vice versa.

Individual corporate stocks are also classified in different ways, according to the earning and appreciation potential of the various corporations. Growth stocks include companies that focus on increasing revenues and earnings, whereas income stocks are those companies that emphasize providing steady dividends to their shareholders. Value stocks include those companies that may be undervalued by the markets, and although these stocks are riskier, they also have a potential for greater return. Another classification of corporate stocks is based on the market capitalization of the company, which refers to the current market value of a company. The current market value is calculated as the market price per share multiplied by the number of outstanding shares of stock (stock owned and held by investors). When using this classification scheme, companies are divided into small cap, mid cap, or large cap, based on current ranges. Large-cap companies tend to be less risky, given that they typically distribute dividends and have a strong history of earnings (defined as large accumulated retained earnings or invested capital [thus the term large-cap] on their balance sheets). In contrast, small-cap companies, though they have a greater potential for growth than large cap, tend to be riskier, as they usually do not distribute consistent dividends and have relatively small retained earnings and higher liabilities on their balance sheets.

BONDS

In contrast to stocks, bonds are issued and sold by a company for raising capital and have no ownership rights like stocks. Bonds are usually issued in $1,000 increments and are redeemed at par, or face value, at maturity. During the life of the bond, interest is paid at the stated rate within the bond. Bonds are traded on the bond market, with their value adjusted to market price with a discount or premium. Market price, or value, is based on investor perceptions of the company's ability to pay the debt and current interest rates, especially in relation to the interest rate specified in the bond. Since bonds do not represent an ownership right, or equity, as in the case of stocks, market fluctuations on bond prices are less than that of stocks and therefore bonds are considered less risky than stocks. Premium bonds sell at a price higher than their face value, while discounted bonds sell at a price less than their face value. Stocks and bonds should be considered as less liquid investments than cash or cash equivalents because of market fluctuations and the corresponding risk. Therefore, investors should minimize the risk of market fluctuations by planning to own these investments for a minimum of five years.

Investment Strategies to Reduce Risk

All financial plans will consist of some combination of investments, and there are several strategies that can help maximize the growth of principal. Investors must balance the effects of overall market volatility (risk) and interest rates with their personal risk tolerance. Two widely used methods to help minimize risk include **dollar cost averaging** and portfolio diversification.

Dollar Cost Averaging

9 *The purpose of dollar cost averaging is to minimize the effects of market fluctuations over time.* By investing systematically at regular intervals, without regard to the current market price, investments may not always be purchased at the lowest price or highest price. Given the discussion of market fluctuations and the corresponding effects on the prices of stocks and bonds, one might wonder just when is the right time to invest. Obviously, when market conditions are such that prices are down, we may be inclined to purchase more shares of stocks or bonds. For example, let's envision Pfizer stock trading at $14.50 per share on the day one wishes to invest $1,000, and one could possibly buy, at most, approximately 69 shares (not including **trade cost**). On the following day, news of a patent extension for one of Pfizer's drugs is received positively in the market, and the price of Pfizer stock rises to $25.00 per share overnight.

Now the $1,000 investment will only yield, at most, 40 shares of Pfizer stock (not including trade cost)—almost 45% fewer shares than the day before. To minimize the effect of market fluctuations, dollar cost averaging is a good practice to implement. Dollar cost averaging is the process of investing a fixed dollar amount on a regular basis, thus consistently purchasing more shares when the stock is down and less when up. As shown in Table 27–6, investing $500 monthly for 40 years can yield a very large balance.

Portfolio Diversification

Another way to reduce the total risk of an individual's investments is through portfolio diversification. **10** *Portfolio diversification is simply investing in a variety of options and classes (stocks, bonds, etc.) to spread the risk inherent in any one investment item.* Since risk is the uncertainty that you may not earn your expected rate of return, diversification allows several expected rates of returns on various portions of the total portfolio. Asset allocation, or choosing investment vehicles whose investment returns do not move together in response to a certain market event or condition, aids investors in achieving diversification of their investments. Asset allocation can be achieved in several ways. Selecting an appropriate balance between liquid and nonliquid investments is a start. Also important is selection of several different categories of investments within individual classes, such as municipal or corporate bonds within a bond portfolio. Municipal bonds are issued by state and local governments and may offer the investor a level of security in the ability of repayment over a corporate bond. Often municipal bonds are issued at rates earning less than corporate bonds, but the interest earned is exempt from federal, state, and local income taxes, which effectively increases the final yield to the investor. Corporate bonds, as a rule, offer higher interest rates but are secured only by the financial strength of the issuing corporation. Interest earned from corporate bonds income is taxable at the federal, state, and local levels unless otherwise noted. Mutual funds offer immediate portfolio diversity, given their structure of investing in many different options (thereby mitigating risk through their diversification), and are a great alternative to an individual investor's buying a variety of individual stocks. Further diversification may be obtained by investing in a variety of mutual funds. Diversification can also be obtained by dividing companies into their market sector, or core business activity, and choosing a variety of companies (small cap, mid cap, or large cap) in which to invest. For example, a sample portfolio invested 70% in stocks (equal holdings of two pharmaceutical companies) and 30% in corporate bonds (one large high-tech corporation) could be quickly diversified by changing stock holdings to 60% (several diverse companies), increasing liquidity by having a 10% cash balance and having a balance of 30% equally divided between a corporate and a municipal bond fund. Decreasing the percentage held in stocks and increasing the position in bonds and cash can also make the portfolio less aggressive, thus decreasing risk.

DEFINING AND CALCULATING NET WORTH

A personal financial statement can be developed and is similar to a business's financial statement, as discussed in Chapter 10 ("Cents and Sensibility: Understanding the Numbers"). Personal financial statements can take many forms. While a business uses the term "retained earnings," individuals simply refer to the difference between assets and liabilities as net worth.

INCOME TAX BASICS

Taxation on an individual's income can occur at many levels: federal, state, county, and city. Although taxation is complex, this section will provide the most elemental information to increase awareness about the effects taxes have on one's financial plan and various investment options. Reference will be made only to federal taxation, but recognize that state and other taxes influence your finances.

The Internal Revenue Service (IRS) taxes all income for individuals, the majority of whom use Form 1040.[12] Income reflects the collective benefit of wages from your job, interest and gains from investing activities, rents, and any other form of earnings for a specific period of time. Income is different from principal wealth, which is the aggregate dollar value of all assets as of a specific date. When income is referred to for income tax purposes, the word "income" is not used alone; it is used with total income, adjusted gross income (AGI), and taxable income. Total income is simply the total of all sources of income, such as income derived from working (wages), interest income, and dividends. Adjusted gross income is defined by taking total income and subtracting certain items, such as moving expenses and student loan interest, which may or may not be applicable to all individuals (reasoning for excluding these items from total income is beyond the scope of this chapter). Taxable income is defined as adjusted gross income less **itemized deductions** or the **standard deduction**, less allowable personal exemption amounts. A personal exemption, defined by the IRS, is an amount excluded from taxable income and given to any taxpayer who cannot be claimed as a dependent by another taxpayer. Tax is determined on taxable income and is the amount due to the IRS. Tax liability is the remaining amount of tax due to the IRS after any credits and advance payments, such as **withholding tax** or estimated tax payments made by the taxpayer during the taxable year. Withholding tax is taken from each paycheck the taxpayer receives during the year and represents a prepayment of that individual's tax. The withholding tax provides the government with cash during the year, rather than waiting until the end of the year when taxes are generally filed. Many taxpayers are happy to receive a tax refund on their tax return and proudly state that they paid no federal income taxes. In actuality, the taxpayer's prepayments through withholding were greater than the total tax liability, which therefore generated the tax refund. However, when the taxpayer's withholding taxes (prepayments) are less than the tax liability, additional payments are required by the taxpayer.

A **tax deduction** is an amount paid by an individual that may be subtracted from AGI and is otherwise taxable or amounts not subject to taxation when declared as a deduction. A tax credit is a reduction of tax owed by a taxpayer. Therefore, a tax credit is much more valuable than a deduction because a credit is a dollar-for-dollar reduction in tax, compared with a deduction that only reduces your taxable income. Because deductions only reduce taxable income, the benefit is only the **marginal tax rate** multiplied by the amount of the deduction. The marginal tax rate refers to the highest rate of tax applied to an individual's income. Items that are deemed a deduction from income are often called deductible, and the benefit of the corresponding savings at the taxpayer's marginal tax rate is implied.

The IRS has established two types of deductions: standard deduction and itemized deductions. A standard is a base amount not subjected to income tax. Blind taxpayers and those age 65 years or older have slightly higher standard deductions. Taxpayers who may be claimed as dependents on another taxpayer's return may have reduced standard deductions. For example, standard deduction amounts for 2010 were $5,700 for single taxpayers and $11,400 for married taxpayers. Itemized deductions are certain personal expenditures allowed by the tax code as deductions from AGI and include home mortgage interest, charitable contributions, and real property (defined as land and buildings) taxes. When preparing an individual's federal income tax return, if the taxpayer's itemized deductions exceed the standard deduction allowed, the higher amount of deductions is subtracted from AGI.

A personal exemption is an amount excluded from taxable income and given to any taxpayer who cannot be claimed as a dependent by another taxpayer. In other words, the personal exemption is for yourself and your spouse if you are married. A dependent exemption, also defined by the IRS, is an individual who qualifies to be claimed as a dependent exemption on another person's tax return, usually by receiving over one-half of their support for the year. Examples of dependent exemptions are your children and elderly parents whom you may support. In addition, a child tax credit for each qualifying child is also available to qualified taxpayers. The tax effect of exemptions can be substantial.

The IRS has separate taxation rules for individuals, businesses, charities (not for profit), and government entities; this chapter focuses only on taxation of individuals. The IRS uses a graduated tax table, which means different tax rates are applied to different amounts of income. In addition, there are five filing statuses (single, married

filing jointly, married filing separately, head of household, qualifying widower), each with a different tax rate. The term "effective tax rate" is the net rate a taxpayer pays on taxable income. The effective tax rate is calculated by dividing the total income tax paid by the taxable income. Many people prefer this calculation as it indicates overall the individual's taxation, not only the marginal effects, from year to year.

The Social Security Administration also collects taxes as a percentage of payroll taxes through the **Federal Insurance Contributions Act (FICA)** to pay its current beneficiaries, or people who have retired from active work and earned the right to benefits under Social Security laws. Social Security benefits are a "pay as you go" plan, meaning current workers support current retirees. An individual employee's Social Security benefits are determined by the employee's work history and federal law. As of 2010, the FICA tax percentage was 6.2% of gross wages up to $106,800 for each individual. In addition, as of 2010, there was a Medicare Hospital Insurance Program tax of 1.45% of wages without a taxable maximum. These taxes are deducted from an individual employee's pay.

PAYCHECK STUBS, W-2 FORMS, AND INCOME TAX FORMS

A variety of items can affect one's earnings, and the term "take-home pay" is often used to refer to the actual amount an individual receives after FICA, insurance, withholding, and other deductions are taken. **Table 27–9** illustrates a typical pay stub, indicating gross pay and itemized deductions that correspond to the discussions in this chapter. As can be seen, the take-home pay of $59,723.80 is only 63.6% of gross pay. The deductions, some of which are matched by the employer, represent federal and state withholding tax, FICA, employer-provided health insurance premiums, and 457 and 403(b) contributions. A W-2 form illustrates the net effect of pretax items and is a detailed statement, issued by an employer, of an employee's total federal and state wages and withholding and FICA taxes (**Figure 27–2**). In Box 1, wages are $84,884.00, $9,016.00 less than the total wages of $93,900 shown on the sample pay stub in Table 27–9. The difference is the pretax

TABLE 27-9   Sample Pay Stub

Employee Name	Employee Number	Federal Exemptions	State Exemptions	Period End
Jon Doe	••-••-••	S 05	S01	12/31/09

Your Total Salary and Benefits	Current Pay Period	Year to Date
Your Gross Compensation (before deductions)	$7,825.00	$93,900.00
Employer Contributions to Your Benefits (See details below)	$1,543.16	$18,402.02
Total Salary and Employer Contributions	**$9,368.16**	**$112,302.02**

Description	Current	YTD
Gross Pay	$7,825.00	$93,900.00
Deductions (Details Below)	$2,866.86	$34,176.20
Net Take-Home Pay	**$4,958.14**	**$59,723.80**

Itemized Taxes, Deductions, and Contributions

Description	Employee Deductions		Employer Contributions	
	Current	YTD	Current	YTD
Federal Withholding	$1,006.50	$12,022.58		
State Withholding	$296.75	$3,565.20		
FICA	$598.61	$7,183.35	$598.61	$7,183.35
Health Insurance	$208.75	$2,389.07	$306.81	$3,567.79
457	$391.25	$4,695.00	$637.74	$7,652.88
403(b)	$365.00	$4,321.00		
Total	**$2,866.86**	**$34,176.20**	**$1,543.16**	**$18,404.02**

Note: FICA = Federal Insurance Contributions Act; YTD = year to date.

items noted on the pay stub: 457 contributions of $4,695.00 and 403(b) contributions of $4,321.00.

STUDENT LOAN REPAYMENTS

As many pharmacists have student loans, the IRS currently (at the time of this publication) allows a deduction for interest paid on a student loan during the year and includes interest on both required and voluntary student loan payments.[12]

Make payments on student loans according to the schedule defined by the lender. Student loans are generally not dischargeable through bankruptcy. Student loans may be turned over to a

FIGURE 27–2 **Sample W-2 Form.**

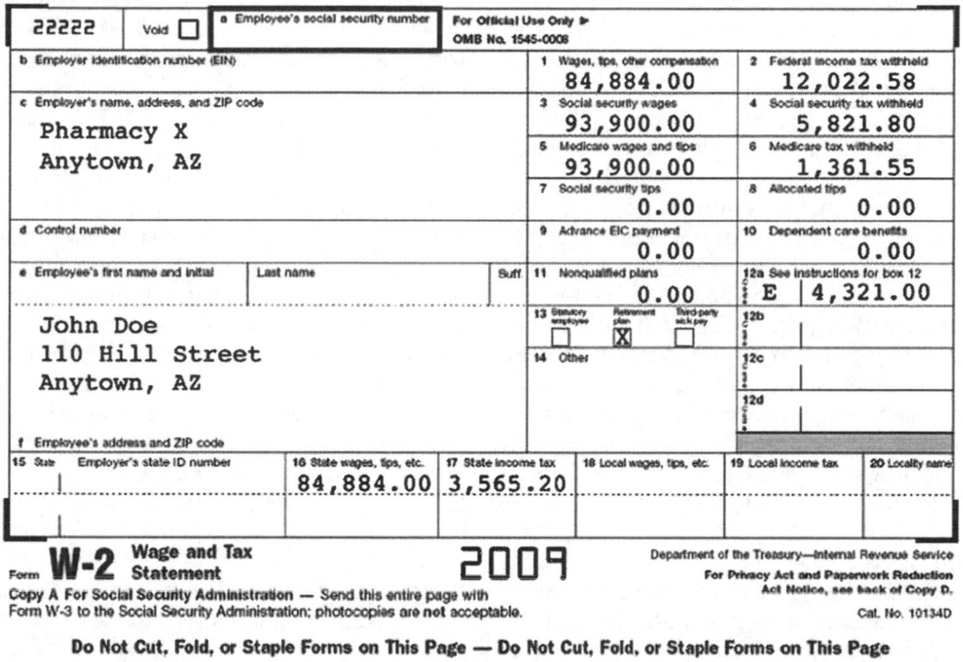

22222 Void ☐ a Employee's social security number For Official Use Only ▶ OMB No. 1545-0008

b Employer identification number (EIN)	1 Wages, tips, other compensation 84,884.00	2 Federal income tax withheld 12,022.58
c Employer's name, address, and ZIP code Pharmacy X Anytown, AZ	3 Social security wages 93,900.00	4 Social security tax withheld 5,821.80
	5 Medicare wages and tips 93,900.00	6 Medicare tax withheld 1,361.55
	7 Social security tips 0.00	8 Allocated tips 0.00
d Control number	9 Advance EIC payment 0.00	10 Dependent care benefits 0.00
e Employee's first name and initial / Last name / Suff.	11 Nonqualified plans 0.00	12a See instructions for box 12 E 4,321.00
John Doe 110 Hill Street Anytown, AZ	13 Statutory employee ☐ Retirement plan ☒ Third-party sick pay ☐	12b
	14 Other	12c
f Employee's address and ZIP code		12d

15 State Employer's state ID number	16 State wages, tips, etc.	17 State income tax	18 Local wages, tips, etc.	19 Local income tax	20 Locality name
	84,884.00	3,565.20			

Form **W-2** Wage and Tax Statement 2009

Department of the Treasury—Internal Revenue Service

Copy A For Social Security Administration — Send this entire page with Form W-3 to the Social Security Administration; photocopies are not acceptable.

For Privacy Act and Paperwork Reduction Act Notice, see back of Copy D.

Cat. No. 10134D

Do Not Cut, Fold, or Staple Forms on This Page — Do Not Cut, Fold, or Staple Forms on This Page

collection agency for nonpayment, and the loan holders are liable for the costs associated with collecting on loans, including court costs and attorney fees. Also, for those who default on student loans, wages may be garnished (withheld by the employer), federal and state income tax refunds may be intercepted, and loan defaults will appear on your credit report and adversely affect your FICO score.

RETIREMENT

As most pharmacists will work for organizations that offer retirement plans, it is beneficial to understand the importance of retirement benefits and vehicles used to save for retirement. Without a doubt, saving for retirement is a critical component of any savings plan. Years ago, companies often provided pension plans for their employees. Pension plans continued to pay retirees a percentage of their prior annual earnings based on a variety of factors, most notably the length of employment with the company. As the workforce became more mobile, lengthy employment with one employer was (and still is) less common. In response to these events, individual retirement accounts (IRAs) were developed.

A traditional IRA is owned and managed by the employee, relieving the employer of the burden and cost of administering a pension plan.[12] A traditional IRA generally allows for contributions up to a certain amount (for example, in 2010, the maximum was $5,000 for individuals under 50 years of age and $6,000 for those 50 and older) to be deductible in determining AGI, and therefore not subject to income taxes and resulting in savings determined by the taxpayer's marginal tax rate. For a single taxpayer in the 28% marginal tax bracket, a $1,400 savings is generated on the $5,000 annual contribution (28% of $5,000 is $1,400). The net effect, and attractiveness of an IRA, is that a $5,000 principal balance is accumulating for use at retirement, but only $3,600 was needed to actually fund the IRA contribution due to the tax effect of $1,400. Traditional IRA earnings grow tax deferred, meaning the interest earned each year is not included in total income for the taxpayer. Instead, withdrawals from the IRA account at retirement are taxed 100% as income; however, because the taxpayer is retired, the anticipated income is lower, and if that is the case, he or she is in a lower tax bracket, which helps offset the effects of taxation. The deductibility of the annual contributions and the deferment of taxes on earnings until withdrawal result in the traditional IRA's effectiveness as a retirement plan.

A Roth IRA differs from the traditional IRA in that contributions are not deductible for income tax purposes; however, the earnings do accumulate free of taxation in the same manner.[12] Another major difference from the traditional IRA is there is no federal income tax when withdrawals from the account are made at retirement. Roth IRAs are popular because tax-free earnings and withdrawals represent a significant **after-tax** savings to the investor. There are AGI limits for participation in a Roth IRA (as well as traditional IRAs); for example, in 2010, this limit was an AGI greater than $105,000 for a single taxpayer ($167,000 for married filing jointly).

Some employers may also offer a simplified employee pension (SEP) plan. A SEP IRA allows employees to make **pretax** contributions toward their own retirement similar to an IRA and is less complex than establishing a pension plan.[12] As with both the traditional and Roth IRAs, the pretax treatment of contributions and the tax-deferred growth of earnings are attractive features of these retirement investments.

Many of today's corporate employers offer 401(k) plans, which are retirement plans that allow employees to make pretax contributions of a portion of their wages to the plan that is then

invested.[12] These contributions are not subject to federal or state income taxes, which result in savings based on the marginal tax rate of the employee. For example, if you earn $120,000 per year and contribute 10% of it toward a 401(k) retirement savings account, then your current taxable income is lowered to 90% of $120,000, which is $108,000. Also, many companies match a portion of the employee's contributions, and this greatly affects the growth of the account. In a 401(k) retirement plan, earnings on all contributions accumulate tax free until withdrawal. Individuals should always try to contribute the full portion of their earnings that is eligible for the match from their employer because this amount represents a very significant initial investment return. For example, a home health company offers a 401(k) plan, which has a dollar for dollar employer match of up to 6% of an employee's annual wages. Assuming annual wages of $100,000 and if the employee contributes $6,000, the total employer contribution would be $6,000. If the employee only contributed 4% ($4,000), he would forfeit $2,000 of the maximum match from his employer. Additional investments should be made as practical and within limitations, as all contributions are pretax and result in the savings from the marginal tax rate of the employee. As stated previously, portfolio diversification is essential, even within a 401(k) plan portfolio. Employees of many universities, government agencies, and not-for-profit companies may qualify to contribute to 401(a), 403(b), and 457 plans. These plans operate similarly to 401(k) plans and allow an employee's wages to be deferred from income taxes. The major difference between 403(b) plans and 401(k) plans is that 403(b) plans can only be offered by nonprofit institutions while 401(k) plans are offered by for-profit institutions.

When saving for retirement, the essentials of investing remain the same. An investment that is made with pretax or deductible contributions is usually preferred because investors receives an immediate return at their marginal tax rate. This immediate return adds to the total rate of return on the investment as a whole. Investments that grow tax deferred are advantageous, as earnings are not subject to annual taxation, allowing more principal and interest to accumulate with the power of compound interest. In addition, these concepts apply to posttax savings, such as with your emergency fund and other savings. While the immediate return of the marginal tax rate may not be gained, the growth of principal over time, without the income tax effect on earnings each year, yields great rewards.

COLLEGE EDUCATION SAVINGS PLANS

Whether it is saving for your children's education or for significant others, establishing a savings plan for college should be considered. The U.S. government enacted tax legislation in Section 529[12] of the Internal Revenue Code, which authorizes college savings plans, also known as 529 plans. While contributions are not tax deductible, the earnings do accumulate tax free and withdrawals, when used to fund the named beneficiary's college education expenses, are also tax free.[13] As 529 plans are designed and administered by each state, tax treatment at the state level of contributions and withdrawals can vary widely between states. In addition, states may treat resident and nonresident plan members differently.[14] Given the complexity of these plans, professional advice should be considered before investing in any 529 plan or a **prepaid tuition plan**.

PROTECTING ASSETS

Once a financial plan is under way, results can be seen almost immediately. One final element of a financial plan is essential and that is insurance. Most are probably already familiar with the concept of insurance, or the right to compensation for a future loss in exchange for a periodic payment (premium), from car insurance or professional liability insurance. Insurance offers protection to individuals, or the insured, in many ways. Health insurance helps to pay for both wellness exams and medical treatment. Most employers provide health insurance and share the payment of health insurance premiums with the employee. Professional liability insurance protects one from judgments if a serious mistake, causing injury or harm to another, occurs during the normal course of work as a pharmacist. Property insurance can protect physical assets, such as homes and their contents, cars, boats, and similar valuable items. As one approaches retirement, long-term care insurance is available to cover the cost of nursing home care. Many long-term care policies also offer care in the event of a debilitating accident or injury.

Life insurance protects dependents in the event of your death. During your career, your need for life insurance will vary depending on whether your spouse or partner is employed, whether you have children, and other personal needs. Most employers offer some life insurance as a benefit of employment. In the unlikely event of a serious accident or illness, you may be unable to work. Disability insurance, both short term (less than 6 months) and long term (greater than 6 months), can provide for a continuation of a percentage (usually 60%) of earnings to help meet living needs. Individuals with substantial savings (e.g., 12 months or more of living expenses) may choose not to purchase short-term disability. The full spectrum of insurance products should be addressed in any financial plan.

FINANCIAL PLANNER

Given the myriad insurance and investment options and their associated risks, many individuals seek professional advice to help them in their financial planning. There are a number of well-qualified financial planners, stockbrokers, and bankers who can offer advice and financial investment products and services. However, commissions on the sale of financial products often determine the salaries of these professionals. Often, the products offering the highest commission to the broker or banker may be investments offered by their employer and may bias their advice to their clients. To obtain more independent advice, the services of a certified financial planner (CFP) can be engaged. A CFP assists individuals with planning to obtain a client's long- and short-term financial goals. Many services may be paid for on either a fee-for-service basis or simply a flat fee, rather than on commissions of the products they sell. **Table 27-10** reflects the basic questions investors should ask when choosing a financial planner.[15] Investors should have an element of trust with their financial advisor and should never

TABLE 27–10	Ten Questions to Ask When Choosing a Financial Planner

- What experience do you have?
- What are your qualifications?
- What services do you offer?
- What is your approach to financial planning?
- Will you be the only person working with me?
- How will I pay for your services?
- How much do you typically charge?
- Could anyone besides me benefit from your recommendations?
- Have you ever been publicly disciplined for any unlawful or unethical actions in your professional career?
- Can I have it in writing?

Source: Data from Certified Financial Planners Board of Standards Inc.[15]

feel pressured into investing in something they do not fully understand.

SUMMARY

All pharmacists and pharmacy students should be interested in their personal finances and financial status. This chapter briefly reviews important concepts concerning personal finance, including budgeting, setting financial goals, and FICO scores. Value money by being conscious of your spending habits and by developing healthy financial behaviors. The time value of money is the foundation of any financial plan. Understanding the effects of risk and inflation, as well as your personal FICO score, are also important in optimizing financial success. It is important to be proactive and involved in your financial planning and realize that a financial plan should be an evolving process that uses personal strategies to facilitate creating wealth.

References

1. American Bankruptcy Institute. Annual business and non-business filings by year (1980–2008). Available at: http://www.abiworld.org/AM/AMTemplate.cfm?Section=Home&CONTENTID=56822&TEMPLATE=/CM/ContentDisplay.cfm. Accessed March 27, 2009.

2. MoneyMatters101.com. How we get in financial trouble. Available at: http://www.moneymatters101.com/financialhealth/trouble.asp. Accessed March 27, 2009.

3. Generation X Finance. 24 signs that you could be in financial trouble. Available at: http://genxfinance.com/2007/03/06/24-signs-that-you-could-be-in-financial-trouble/. Accessed March 27, 2009.

4. BALANCE. Money matters. Website withheld at request of BALANCE.

5. BALANCE. Budget worksheet. Website withheld at request of BALANCE.

6. New York Life. Who wants to be a millionaire? Available at: http://www.newyorklife.com/cda/0,3254,11024,00.html. Accessed November 24, 2008.

7. Stanley TJ, Danko WD. *The Millionaire Next Door*. Atlanta, GA: Longstreet Press; 1996.

8. myFICO®, a division of FairIsaac. The score that matters. Available at: http://www.myfico.com/Default.aspx?semengine=google&semcampaign=S-Brands_MyFICO&semadgroup=S-. Accessed February 17, 2009.

9. *Wall Street Journal*—Eastern Edition. The anatomy of a credit score. *Wall Street Journal* December 31, 2008, B2.

10. Davies Glyn. *A History of Money from Ancient Times to the Present Day*. 3rd ed. Cardiff: University of Wales Press; 2002.

11. Florida Mortgage Corporation. Bi-weekly mortgage. Available at: http://www.floridamortgagecorp.com/biweeklyarm.html. Accessed February 17, 2009.

12. Internal Revenue Service, United States Department of Treasury. Available at: http://www.irs.gov/individuals/index.html. Accessed February 17, 2009.

13. Garver R. The 529 evolution. *Bank Investment Consult* 2008;16(9):37–39.

14. U.S. Securities and Exchange Commission. An introduction to 529 plans. Available at: http://www.sec.gov/investor/pubs/intro529.htm. Accessed February 10, 2009.

15. Certified Financial Planners Board of Standards Inc. Questions to ask when choosing a financial planner. Available at: http://www.cfp.net/. Accessed January 14, 2009.

Abbreviations

AGI:	adjusted gross income
ARM:	adjustable rate mortgage
CFP:	certified financial planner
FICA:	Federal Insurance Contributions Act
FV:	future value
HELOC:	home equity line of credit
IRA:	individual retirement account
IRS:	Internal Revenue Service
n:	number of periods
P:	principal amount invested
PV:	present value
r:	interest rate
SEP:	simplified employee pension
t:	number of times per year interest is compounded

Case Scenarios

CASE ONE: Kristin and Tyler Williams have been married for four years, having met in pharmacy school during their second year. They are both community pharmacists, and each earns approximately $120,000 annually, although they work for different national chains. They were fortunate to receive the down payment for their home as a wedding gift from Tyler's parents. Delighted to get such a great "head start" on their financial plan, they went ahead and decorated their house in a very elegant manner, using six credit cards, which are currently at the credit limits; however, all minimum payments are made on time each month. They contribute 2% each to their 401(k) plans. Kristin's employer matches employee contributions up to 5%, while Tyler's employer matches up to 6%. The entire 401(k) investments are currently in cash equivalents and could meet

(continues)

their monthly needs for almost nine months. Kristin surprised Tyler with a new car for his birthday last month, which was financed at a rate of 4% for seven years. Their home mortgage is an ARM, and the rate has recently risen 3%, raising their monthly mortgage payment by $535. Kristin has always managed the household finances and is concerned about the effect the extra amount will have on their cash flow, especially since she has been using a new credit card for dry cleaning, groceries, and dining out since the new car payments have been added to the monthly budget. What are some of the warning signs indicating that Kristin and Tyler may need to make some changes in the management of their finances?

CASE TWO: It has been five years since your graduation. You are still single, own your home (which has an existing mortgage), and have a great full-time job earning $135,000 annually. Despite diligent loan repayments, you still have $50,000 in school loans that have been consolidated at 6.25%, resulting in student loan interest of $3,200 for the year. Your mortgage company has offered you a home equity line of credit (HELOC) with enough availability to pay off all your student loan balances. The HELOC interest rate is 7.5% and is tax deductible. Assume your federal marginal income tax rate is 28% and AGI is $120,000. What are the major factors to consider in determining whether to borrow $50,000 on the HELOC to pay off all of your student loan debt?

CASE THREE: At the 10-year homecoming football game at your alma mater, one of your former classmates, Missy Dean, confides her financial history in you. She has noticed that you seem to be very successful based on the car you drive and the neighborhood in which you live. Missy, 34 years old, is recently divorced with two children (ages 4 and 6) and is beginning to discover that her financial situation is not very sound. During her marriage, she trusted her husband completely and allowed him to handle all financial matters. You are not sure that you can help but want to try. Missy has a good job and earns just over $125,000 annually. While she has a home, her monthly mortgage payment of $2,178.98 is two months behind. There are three credit cards, with balances of almost $30,000 at an average of 15%. Only minimum payments have been made in the past, but now they are also several months late. Missy checked her FICO score and it is in the low 600s. Although she buys a daily latte for $3 and a gourmet sandwich for $7, she does not have any emergency savings, nor does she participate in her company's 401(k) plan (which matches up to 4% if the employee contributes 8%). The children's 529 college education savings plans are currently being funded with $500 each month for each child. What are some important considerations for Missy?

Additional Resources Available Online!

Visit the Student Companion Web site at http://healthprofessions.jbpub.com/pharmacymanagement for interactive study tools and additional resources.

See www.rxugace.com to learn how you can obtain continuing pharmacy education for this content.

Glossary

Accommodating mode: A conflict response in which the person responds in an unassertive but cooperating manner.

Accountability: Responsibility to someone or organization for some activity.

Accounts payable: Accounts of companies that must be paid for goods and services received.

Accounts receivable: Current asset representing future payment of services performed or merchandise sold on credit.

Active listening: The act of hearing with thoughtful attention in which the listener seeks to confirm the meaning of the speaker's message; remaining nonjudgmental while digesting another person's message or position and then responding in a way that conveys you have listened.

Activity log: A record of all activities performed and events attended over the course of a day or time period.

Adherence: Correspondence between an individual's behavior regarding a medical treatment regimen and the agreed-on recommendations of a healthcare professional.

Adulterate: To make impure by adding ingredients that are inferior, improper, or unnecessary.

Advertising: A process that announces a position vacancy to those who are in the market for employment; the placement of announcements and persuasive messages in the media and venues with public exposure.

Affirmative defense: A defense that is raised after admitting the allegations in the complaint are true. Notwithstanding the truth of the allegations, the defendant may raise, as a defense, new information that would absolve it of liability.

After-tax: An amount (usually income) after taxes have been subtracted.

Americans with Disabilities Act Amendments Act of 2008: An amendment to the Americans with Disabilities Act of 1990 that provides greater protections to people with disabilities.

Apothecary: Pharmacy that maintains a prescription department and perhaps some durable medical equipment or nonprescription products, but little or no other merchandise.

Applied ethics: The attempt to implement general norms and theories for particular problems and contexts.

Asset: Items owned by an individual or a company, which have exchange or commercial value. These may consist of specific property or claims against others, in contrast to obligations due others.

At will employment: Describes an employment relationship in which either party to the relationship may terminate it without liability. The employer is free to terminate the individual's employment "for good cause or no cause at all"; however, it may not terminate an employee if doing so violates public policy or law. Similarly, the employee may terminate the relationship without liability and without notice.

Automated/automatic teller machine (ATM): A mechanical device that allows an individual to conduct unassisted business transactions (obtain cash) using a personal coded card.

Automation: Any technology, machine, or device linked to a control system, such as computers to control machinery and processes; may reduce manpower requirements to perform the same process.

Autonomy: At a minimum, the self-rule that is free both from controlling interference by others and from limitations, such as inadequate understanding, that prevents meaningful choice.

Average manufacturer's price (AMP): The average price paid by wholesalers to manufacturers for drugs distributed through retail pharmacies, or by retail pharmacies that buy directly from manufacturers after deducting all discounts. The Centers for Medicare and Medicaid Services uses AMP to calculate a unit rebate amount for each covered outpatient drug and provides the unit rebate amounts to the states. The states determine the total rebates that participating manufacturers owe by multiplying the unit rebate amount by the number of units of the drug dispensed to Medicaid beneficiaries.

Average wholesale price (AWP): A suggested list price for products purchased from wholesalers by pharmacies (both retail and nonretail). This list price is publicly available in industry compendia, including First DataBank's *Annual Directory of Pharmaceuticals* (*Blue Book*) and National Drug Data Files, Medi-Spans' *Price Alert* and Master Drug Data Base, and Thomson Reuter/Micromedex *Red Book*. The AWP has become an important prescription drug pricing benchmark for payers throughout the healthcare industry. Payments are typically based on AWP minus some percentage. Despite its name, AWP does not accurately reflect actual market prices for drugs. As noted, it is a price derived from self-reported manufacturer data for both brand and generic drugs and does not account for the deep discounts available to various purchasers.

Avoiding mode: A conflict response in which the person responds in an unassertive and uncooperative manner. This is simply avoiding the conflict.

Balance sheet: A statement that itemizes total assets and total liabilities of a given company to portray its net worth at a given moment in time. The amounts stated on a balance sheet are typically the historic cost of items and not current values.

Bar-coding systems: These systems electronically compare a patient's identity and medical information (e.g., in an electronic medication order) against a bar-coded medication, alerting the healthcare professional (e.g., nurse) of the potential for a medication administration error.

Base pay: Regular and expected wages and salary provided to an employee.

Behavioral interview: An interview approach that asks candidates to describe how they behaved in a past situation, on the assumption that past behavior is the best predictor of future performance.

Benchmarking: Practice of comparing and analyzing performance or position with established standards or with the performance of others.

Beneficence: The moral obligation to act for the benefit of others.

Best alternative to the negotiated agreement: The course of action a negotiating party would take if it were not pursuing negotiation.

Bin list: Temporary holding areas for ideas or suggestions that are not directly on-topic with the issue facing the group.

Bioethics: The branch of ethics that investigates issues related to medical and biological practice.

Bond: A long-term debt instrument expressed at par, or face, value often issued in $1,000 increments at a fixed interest rate; the purpose is to raise capital by the issuer, with a guarantee to repay principal and interest.

Boundaryless organization: An organizational structure that attempts to flatten hierarchical relationships, create teams, and extend spans of control.

Brainstorming: A technique designed to generate a large number of ideas to solve a problem.

Brand: The perception that comes to mind when people think of an individual, business, program, and organization.

Brand clarity: Compares how you want (and do not want) your brand to be seen with how you are actually seen by others, identifying blind spots and self-deceptive perceptions where internal and external brands do not correspond.

Branding: Developing an image for a company, product, or service.

Brand name: A drug that is protected by a patent and can only be produced or sold by the company holding that patent.

Break-even analysis: The point where total revenue (TR) received equals the total costs (TC) associated with the sale of services or product; TR = TC.

Breakthrough innovation: An innovation that results in disruption or discontinuation of the current market environment through development of a new product, business model, or service.

Budgeting: Documenting intended expenditures over a specified period (normally one year) along with proposals for generating revenues to meet them.

Business plan: A formal document containing background information about the intended business and key business members, as well as detailing business goals, supporting beliefs concerning attaining goals, and describing plans for achieving these goals. Business plans are decision-making tools and, if done correctly, will provide data so you can objectively decide the challenge level of achieving goals while assessing and balancing your risk tolerance.

Buying group: Cooperative used by smaller organizations, such as independent pharmacies, to improve buying power by purchasing larger quantities as a combined entity. (Group purchasing organizations, or GPOs, are a form of buying group used more often by larger organizations, such as hospitals.)

Capital budget: Estimated expenditures for capital items in a given fiscal period. Capital items are fixed assets, including buildings and equipment, the cost of which is typically written off over a number of fiscal periods. The capital budget consists of the expenditures made within a fiscal year comparable to the related operating budgets.

Care-based ethics: Respects individual uniqueness, human relationships, and the interrelatedness and interdependence of individuals, systems, and society.

Career map: A detailed outline describing the desired future direction of an individual's career.

Case study question: An interview question designed to understand how a candidate solves problems or makes decisions.

Cash: Money, in the form of notes and coins, used as payment for goods and services at the time of purchase.

Cash equivalents: Short-term investment assets that are convertible to a known cash amount or are sufficiently close to their maturity date (usually within 90 days) that market value is not sensitive to fluctuation in interest rate.

Centers for Medicare and Medicaid Services: A federal agency within the United States Department of Health and Human Services (DHHS) that administers the Medicare program and works in partnership with state governments to administer Medicaid, the State Children's Health Insurance Program (SCHIP), and health insurance portability (HIPAA) standards.

Certificate of deposit (CD): Evidence of a deposit, written by a bank or other financial institution, with the issuer's guarantee to repay the deposit, plus earnings, for a specified period at a specified interest rate.

Channel: A medium used to transmit information.

Coaching: Providing support, direction, and advice to an individual or group; helping employees recognize ways in which they can improve their performance.

Collaborating mode: A conflict response in which the person responds in an assertive and cooperative manner. This is also known as problem solving.

Collaborative Drug Therapy Management Agreements: The practice in which prescribers authorize pharmacists to engage in specific activities, such as initiating, adjusting, or evaluating drug therapy.

Collaborative Practice Agreements: A voluntary agreement between one or more prescribers (generally physicians but in some states includes nurse practitioners) and pharmacists establishing cooperative practice procedures under defined conditions or limitations that authorize pharmacists to engage in specified activities, including adjusting and initiating drug therapy. Typically, it is a voluntary written agreement in which prescribers (usually physicians) authorize a pharmacist to perform certain activities of patient care under their authority.

Common law: As distinguished from enactments of legislatures, common law evolves through decisions of courts, applying statutory and other principles of law.

Compensation philosophy: A statement that describes the principles that drive compensation allocation decisions.

Compensatory time: Paid time off from a job that is offered in lieu of cash for overtime.

Competency: A knowledge, skill, or attitude that enables one to perform effectively the activities of a given occupation or function to the standards expected in employment.

Competency development: Employee growth and acquisition of knowledge, a skill, or ability required to properly perform in the position.

Competing mode: A conflict response in which the person responds in an assertive but uncooperative manner.

Competitive advantage: The position an organization occupies against rivals, typically emphasizing the delivery of products or services that have a unique mix of value for consumers.

Competitive analysis: Analysis that identifies competitors and evaluates their strengths and weaknesses relative to those of your own service or product.

Competitive edge: Holding a clear advantage over competing organizations within a market.

Compressed workweek: A schedule that allows employees to shorten their workweek by one or more days by working longer days for a shorter period of time—for example, 40 hours in four days (4/40) or 80 hours in nine days (9/80).

Compromise: Making or receiving concessions.

Compromising mode: A conflict response in which the person responds in an unassertive but cooperative manner.

Conflict: A situation where incompatible opinions, values, attitudes, or intentions occur together.

Consumer price index for all urban consumers (also called the *cost-of-living index*): An inflation index that is published monthly and measures the change in prices of goods and services, including housing, electricity, food, and transportation. It measures consumers' payments for day-to-day goods.

Contextual advertising: An approach that uses key words on a Web page or search engine that triggers a pop-up advertisement on a related topic. For example, typing "arthritis" into a search engine results in a variety of advertisements for such things as glucosamine and local pain specialists.

Continuous quality improvement: An approach to quality management that brings together established quality assurance methods by emphasizing the organization and systems and focusing on the process rather than on the individual.

Control chart: A type of run chart consisting of a line graph displaying observed performance data in a time sequence. It is used to determine whether a process is in a state of statistical control and visually displays upper and lower control limits.

Controllable expenses: Expenses that can be restrained or controlled by management. Certain costs of doing business can be delayed, postponed, or spread out over a longer period of time (e.g., hiring additional personnel, travel and entertainment, marketing expenses).

Controlled Substances Act: Federal law that restricts the prescription and dispensing of drugs considered dangerous, particularly those that are psychoactive (e.g., narcotics); delineates five categories, or schedules, of restricted drugs.

Copayment: A fixed dollar amount per prescription or other unit of medical service utilization (e.g., a physician's office visit) that an insured person is expected to pay when using medical services.

Cost avoidance: Benefits realized by avoiding a relatively certain future expenditure, although the projected expenditure has not been budgeted or obligated.

Cost–benefit analysis (CBA): One type of formal, comprehensive economic evaluation that compares the costs and monetary outcomes associated with a new technology versus those costs and monetary outcomes associated with an alternative technology. A CBA may synonymously appear as a net present value (NPV) financial analysis if the outcome involves monetary outcomes associated with a business entity.

Cost-effective: Providing sufficient return (generally, financial) given costs or money spent to provide a good or service.

Cost of goods sold (COGS): The cost to the pharmacy of the goods that composed the inventory and were sold to patients; usually reported as an annual figure.

Cost-of-living allowance: An increase in salary or wages that is typically tied to changes in the consumer price index.

Cost sharing: A contribution to the costs of health care, or a portion of healthcare costs paid by the patient.

Covered entity: A person or organization that provides health care or possesses healthcare records.

Creative destruction: The process of implementing entrepreneurial approaches of replacing or improving products, processes, or services.

Creditors: Individuals or companies entitled to receive payments from a business entity.

Criminal background check: A preemployment screening approach in which a job candidate grants permission to the hiring organization to verify the accuracy of information provided on a résumé or job application. Information that may be a part of this screening include state and federal records, criminal records, education, social security number validity, driver's license history, civil court records, past employment, references, professional license/registration in all states, and credit reports.

Criterion contamination: The extent of factors outside one's control that can influence performance or the ability to achieve goals.

Criterion deficiency: Failure of standards to represent and illustrate the entire range of one's responsibilities.

Critical incident: Unusual event denoting superior or inferior performance.

Cultural competence: The ability to interact effectively with people of different cultures.

Cultural variables: Factors that collectively form a distinguishing system of shared meaning that sets the organization apart from others.

Data processing: The process of inputting, storing, organizing, transforming, and extracting meaningful information from data.

Deflation: A contraction of economic activity resulting in a decrease in prices.

Delegate: To designate responsibility over people, assignments, or outcomes to another.

Deontology: A theory concerned with which actions are judged right or wrong based on inherent right-making characteristics, or principles, rather than on their consequences.

Diagonal selection: A process by which participants are chosen from across the organization and at various levels to evaluate candidates for employment.

Diffusion: A process in which an innovation is communicated over time among members of a social system.

Direct cost: That component of cost that is directly expended in producing a product or service for sale and is included in the calculation of cost of goods sold (i.e., labor and inventory, which can be traced to a given cost object in an economically feasible manner). The opposite of indirect cost.

Direct-to-consumer advertising: Healthcare advertising targeted specifically to the patient.

Discount rate: Interest rate used in determining the present value for future cash flows.

Discretionary effort: Opportunities for employees to perform in a manner that furthers their organization's interests beyond what is required to accomplish their job responsibilities.

Distributive justice: Fair, equitable, and appropriate distribution determined by justified norms that structure the terms of social cooperation.

Diversity: In an employment context, refers to the employment of a broad mix of people that reflect the general demographic characteristics of an organization's community, customer base, and profession.

Dividends: Corporate payments to shareholders representing a return of corporate earnings.

Dollar cost averaging: Systematic investing of regular amounts at time intervals without regard to the current purchase price to minimize the effects of market fluctuations over time.

Drug samples: Unit of a drug that is not intended to be sold and is intended to promote the sale of a drug.

Drug utilization review committee: A committee whose purpose is to improve the quality of pharmaceutical care by ensuring that prescriptions are appropriate, medically necessary, and that they are not likely to cause adverse drug effects; the Omnibus Reconciliation Act of 1990 mandated that each state establish a drug utilization review (DUR) program by January 1, 1993, for Medicaid beneficiaries. Since that time, many private insurers have followed suit and established DUR programs for their organizations as well.

Due diligence: That level of care that an employer takes to ensure that a prospective employee meets the minimum qualifications, including that the employee possesses that level of character and professionalism to perform the job.

Durable medical equipment: Medical devices (such as wheelchairs, crutches, hospital beds, etc.) to be used in the home by sick or injured patients; usually prescribed by a healthcare practitioner. These are "durable" because they are meant for more than a single use.

Early adopter: A consumer who is one of the first to develop/implement or adopt an innovation soon after its introduction into the market.

Economic order quantity: Optimum number of units per order.

Emotional intelligence: The ability of a person to perceive, assimilate, understand, and manage his or her own emotions.

Employee engagement: The extent to which employees commit to something or someone in their organization, how hard they work, and how long they stay because of that commitment.

Employee retention: An organization's ability to keep employees.

Employee turnover rate: The percentage of employees who leave an organization each year divided by the total number of employees.

Employee value proposition: What an employer offers its employees in return for their effort and commitment.

Empower: To give power or authority to others through trust and confidence.

Encryption software: Systems that electronically store and transmit information and translate it into incomprehensible code, making the information meaningless to unauthorized individuals.

Entrepreneur: Traditionally, those who organize, manage, and assume the risk of a business. More contemporarily, emphasizing the role of innovation.

Entrepreneurial perspective: The comprehensive mix of attributes, characteristics, and behaviors that define an individual's entrepreneurial potential.

Entrust: To charge or invest with a trust or responsibility for an action or outcome.

E-prescribing: Allows prescribers to electronically send a prescription directly to a pharmacy from the point-of-care, and it is believed to be an important element in improving the quality of patient care and reducing medication errors.

Essential function: The tasks and responsibilities fundamental to doing a particular job.

Ethical dilemma: Choosing between two or more equally unappealing or compelling alternatives.

Ethics: A branch of philosophy that focuses on the systematic inquiry into that nature of morality and right and wrong actions; a disciplined study devoted to the rational analysis and justification of moral principles that provides knowledge and insight regarding what we ought to do to attain the most of what is best in human life.

Evaluation: Assessment of performance, work progress, or results, usually against standardized expectations or metrics.

Executive coaching: Objective feedback related to one's leadership style and communication provided by an individual outside the organization.

Exempt employees: Employees who, because of the type of duties performed, level of decision-making authority, or method of compensation, are not required to be paid overtime pay.

Expenses: Outflows of company assets used to generate sales.

External brand: How others see and define your brand.

External stakeholders: People or entities outside the organization who patronize, seek assistance from, or have a vested interest in the organization.

Failure mode and effects analysis: An analysis of potential failure modes within a system for classification by severity of the effect of failures on the system.

Fair Labor Standards Act: An act that establishes minimum wage, overtime pay, recordkeeping, and youth employment standards affecting employees in the private sector and in federal, state, and local governments.

Fair market value: The price at which a willing seller will sell and a willing buyer will buy when neither is under obligation to sell or buy.

Federal Insurance Contributions Act (FICA): The U.S. law requiring U.S. employers to match the amount of Social Security tax deducted from an employee's paycheck.

Federal upper limit: The maximum amount for which state Medicaid programs may receive federal matching funds as reimbursement for some outpatient multisource prescription drugs.

Feedback: Evaluative information provided to individuals regarding their proposals, performance, and achievements; sharing observations, concerns, and suggestions between individuals with an intention of improving both personal and organizational performance.

Fidelity: The obligation to act in good faith to keep promises, maintain relationships, and discharge fiduciary responsibilities. A fiduciary relationship is based on trust and confidence that commitments made between parties will be honored.

Fiduciary: A relationship based on trust and confidence; when someone acts in the best interests of another party based on faith, trust, and confidence.

Financial Accounting Standards Board: The private sector organization in the United States that establishes standards for financial accounting and reporting.

Financial statements: Written reports that describe the financial health of a company in quantitative terms; includes four basic statements: (1) the balance sheet, (2) the income statement, (3) the statement of owner's equity, and (4) the statement of cash flows. Usually are completed on an annual basis for external users, and on an interim basis for internal users.

Firewall: An assemblage of security features, using both hardware and software, which prevents unauthorized access to a network of computer systems.

Fishbone diagram (also known as the *Ishikawa diagram*): A cause-and-effect diagram that visually displays in a fishbone shape the many potential causes for a specific problem or effect.

Fixed costs: Costs that are incurred regardless of the volume of the service.

Flat organization (also known as a *horizontal organization*): An organizational structure with few or no levels of intervening management between staff and managers.

Focus group: Small group selected from a wider population for its members' opinions about a specific topic.

Food and Drug Administration: An agency within the U.S. Department of Health and Human Services responsible for the safety and efficacy of drugs (both human and veterinary), biological products, medical devices, cosmetics, food supply, and radiation-emitting products.

Formal leader: Individuals who are granted formal power by a higher organizational authority; formal power is often the result of a position held within the organization or a specific assigned role affecting key outcomes.

Formulary: A listing of drug products approved for use by an entity.

Full-time equivalents: A way to normalize personnel numbers and measure workers' involvement. An FTE of 1.0 means that the person is equivalent to a full-time worker, while an FTE of 0.5 means that the person is a half-time worker.

Gantt chart: A bar chart that illustrates the start and finish dates of the goals of a project.

Gender identity: A personal conception of oneself as male or female.

Generally accepted accounting principles (GAAP): An established set of accepted accounting principles, standards, and procedures.

Generic: Less expensive drugs that are considered bioequivalent to brand-name products; not protected by patent.

Give/get principle: The process of achieving compromise in negotiation.

Gross margin: The difference between total sales or revenue minus cost of goods sold; it is used to pay expenses and can be expressed in dollars or as percentage of total sales. It indicates whether the average markup on goods and services is sufficient to cover expenses and produce a profit. The gross margin should remain stable over time, and fluctuations indicate changes in productivity.

Hard skill training: The skills and knowledge that have to be acquired to operate equipment, technology, and processes for an organization.

Hardware: The equipment that is needed to perform data processing functions.

Headhunters: Third-party recruiters often retained when normal recruitment efforts have not proved successful.

Health Belief Model: A behavioral model that describes the likelihood that a person will change behavior based on perception of disease, real and perceived barriers, and patient education.

Healthcare Effectiveness Data and Information Set: A tool available from the National Quality Measures Clearinghouse to measure performance in aspects of health care and service.

Health Insurance Portability and Accountability Act (HIPAA): Enacted by the U.S. Congress in 1996. Title I of HIPAA protects health insurance coverage for workers and their families when they change or lose their jobs. Title II of HIPAA (known as the administrative simplification provisions) requires the establishment of national standards for electronic healthcare transactions and national identifiers for providers, health insurance plans, and employers to protect patient privacy and confidentiality.

Health maintenance organization (HMO): A type of managed care that provides members with comprehensive health care using a "capitated" system of financing (i.e., care provided to each member of the plan for a fixed amount; members who go outside of the HMO network to receive care will probably pay all or most of the cost of that care out of their own pocket). If the HMO is efficient and keeps its members healthy, it will make a profit.

Hierarchical organization: An organizational structure in which every entity in the organization, with few exceptions, is subordinate to at least one other entity; most large companies have hierarchical organizations.

Histogram: Graphical display of tabulated frequencies within categories that are shown as bars.

Horizontal financial analysis: Compares the financial results of one company's ratios to the ratios of other similar companies, as well as to standard average industrial ratios and internal industrial deviation of these ratios.

Hostile work environment: A workplace characterized by harassment; intimidation based on unlawful discrimination on the basis of race, religion, sex, national origin, age, disability, veteran status, and, in some jurisdictions, sexual orientation, gender identity, political affiliation, marital status, or other protected class.

Human capital: An organization's employees.

Human capital management: Ensuring that employees have the information and necessary tools or resources to do their jobs effectively and efficiently.

Human dignity: From the Latin *dignus* meaning worthiness or honor.

Human resource variables: Factors that directly involve employee selection, development, and evaluation.

Image advertising: Advertising designed to highlight the employer as a great place to work with the hopes that candidates will be predisposed to openings at that employer in the future.

Incidence: The number of new occurrences of an event (such as a disease state) in a specified period.

Incidental disclosures: Unintentional release of protected health information that may be overheard or viewed in the provision of otherwise permitted disclosures; for example, if a patient counseling session is overheard by a patient other than the one for which it was directed. The provider should take measures to reduce the chance of these occurrences, but it is accepted that they may be unavoidable in some situations.

Income statement: Statement that subtracts expenses incurred from revenues generated within an entity to yield a net income or loss over a designated period; also includes any gains or losses during this period.

Income tax expense: A tax owed on earnings or profit generated from employment or business operations, or capital.

Incremental innovation: Improvements made to existing products, processes, or services that do not typically create radical disruptions in market environments or organizations.

Independent contractor: A person who is hired to do work for an entity but who is not an employee or agent of that agency.

Indirect cost: That component of cost that is indirectly expended in producing a product or providing a service for sale (cannot be traced to a given cost object in an economically feasible manner) and is excluded in the calculation of cost of goods sold (i.e., rent, utilities, equipment maintenance). The opposite of direct cost.

Inflation: An increase in the general price level of goods and services resulting in a decrease in the purchasing power of common currency.

Inflation rate: The rate of increase in the general price level of goods and services resulting in a decrease in the purchasing power of common currency.

Informal leader: Individuals who create and articulate compelling visions of the future to achieve success but do so without the power and authority granted to formal leaders.

Informational interview questions: Contains fact-based questions used to gather or clarify pertinent information necessary to evaluate candidates.

Innovation: A specific type of change wherein new ideas may lead either to radical break-throughs that completely transform environments or to incremental improvements in existing products, processes, or services. Overall, innovation describes the process of translating knowledge into economic growth and social well-being. It encompasses a series of scientific, technological, organizational, financial, or commercial activities.

Institute of Medicine: One of the United States' National Academies; it is a not-for-profit, non-governmental organization. Its mission is to serve as advisor to the nation to improve health.

Integrated marketing communication: A planning process designed to ensure that all brand contacts received by a customer or potential customer are consistent over time.

Interest expense: Cost of borrowing funds in a designated period. It is shown as a financial expense item within the income statement.

Interest rate: The rate charged for the use of money and usually expressed as a percentage of the principal amount.

Internal brand: Self-perception of traits, behaviors, and actions that make you uniquely memorable to others.

Internal rate of return: The rate of return on investment that would make the current value of an investment's future cash flow plus the end market value of the investment equal to the present market value of the investment.

Internal stakeholders: Those people within the organization who interact with or need the services of the pharmacy.

Intrapreneur: A person within a larger organization who uses entrepreneurial skills to develop a new service, program, or process for use within that organization.

Inventory carrying cost: Sometimes referred to as "holding costs"; reflects the cost of holding, or carrying, the product in inventory; includes costs of capital investment, storage, and risk.

Inventory turnover rate: The rate at which supply of an item is completely exhausted and replaced.

Itemized deductions: Various personal expenses defined by the Internal Revenue Service as deductible in calculating taxable income. The most common deductions are medical expenses, mortgage interest, charitable contributions, and state income taxes.

Job analysis: The process of collecting information about the duties, responsibilities, necessary skills, outcomes, and work environment of a particular job.

Job description: Document that lists a position's duties, responsibilities, and requirements.

Job sharing: Two people sharing one job, typically working different days or hours of the week.

The Joint Commission: An independent, not-for-profit organization that accredits and certifies more than 15,000 healthcare organizations and programs in the United States. Its mission is to continuously improve the safety and quality of care provided to the public through the provision of healthcare accreditation and related services that support performance improvement in healthcare organizations.

Just cause: Legally acceptable or sufficient reason on which to take employment action, such as dismissal, suspension without pay, or other disciplinary action based on an employee's conduct.

Justice: The ethical principle that focuses on the fair distribution of benefits and burdens.

Justification: To show to be just, right, or in accord with reason; the "why" of ethics.

Just-in-time purchasing: Orders are placed at the precise point in time when the sales will just deplete all inventory on hand.

Leadership: An act or instance of leading, guiding, or providing direction. Also an act of creating inspiration and sharing a vision.

Learning organization: An organizational structure that attempts to develop a continuous ability to adapt and change.

Liabilities: Creditor's claims on an organization's assets; involves an expected payment of assets, products, or services that a company is obligated to make because of past transactions or events.

Likert scale: A response format in which a respondent is asked to indicate level of agreement or disagreement (though wording may be modified) with a particular statement. For example, 1 = strongly disagree, 2 = disagree, 3 = neither agree nor disagree, 4 = agree, and 5 = strongly agree.

Line of sight: Visibility between an employee's responsibilities, work direction, and achievement and the organization's mission, vision, strategic goals, and objectives.

Liquidated damages: A specific amount of money or form of recovery set forth in an agreement, which will apply in the event of a breach of the agreement. To be distinguished from damages that cannot be quantified at the time an agreement is made.

Liquidity: Ability of an asset to be quickly converted to cash.

Locus of control: The extent to which individuals believe circumstances are within their direct control (i.e., internal locus of control) or beyond (i.e., external locus of control). Individuals with a high internal locus of control believe that events result primarily from their own behaviors and actions, whereas those with a high external locus of control believe that powerful others, fate, or chance primarily determine events.

Management: The guidance and control of action required to execute a program.

Management by objectives: Rates performance on the basis of employee goal achievement set by mutual agreement between manager and employee.

Managing up: The process of working with one's boss to achieve good outcomes for self, the boss, and the organization; may be thought of as "managing the boss."

Marginal tax rate: The highest rate of income tax applied to an individual's earnings.

Market analysis: A systematic investigation or assessment used to inform a business about the needs and interests of a particular target audience. A large number of market analysis techniques are related to sales or need forecasting.

Marketing: The activity, set of institutions, and processes for creating, communicating, delivering, and exchanging offerings that have value for customers, clients, partners, and society at large.

Marketing mix: How an organization will position its products and services and the approach for allocating resources.

Marketing strategy: The plan an organization uses to define and achieve its marketing objectives.

Market niche: A well-defined segment of a population that needs or desires specialized goods or services.

Market position: Ranking of an organization relative to its competitors.

Market research: An assessment used to investigate a product's or service's potential in a given population or area.

Market segment: A group of individuals or organizations that have similar needs and characteristics.

Market share: The portion of the total available market that is served by an organization; also, the percentage of sales of a good or service that may be attributed to an organization.

Matrix organization: An organizational structure in which employees with similar skills are pooled for work assignments.

Maturity value: The amount to be received at the time a security is redeemed at its maturity. Often, maturity value equals par value (as in bonds).

Maximum allowable cost: The maximum amount per unit of medication that third-party payers will pay pharmacies for multisource drugs (i.e., brand and generic drugs with the same active ingredients, dosage form, and strength).

Medicaid: A joint federal–state program that provides health coverage for low-income families and individuals; primarily managed by the states.

Medicare: A federally funded health insurance program for individuals who are 65 years of age and older, have disabilities, or have end-stage renal disease.

Medicare Advantage plans: An option provided by Medicare for enrollees who choose to receive healthcare services from a private managed care organization (e.g., a health maintenance organization or a preferred provider organization) rather than through the original Medicare Part A (hospitalization insurance) and Part B (medical insurance).

Medicare Part B: Supplemental medical insurance for Medicare-eligible recipients that currently pays for services from physicians, nurse practitioners, physician assistants, and others.

Medicare Part D: The outpatient prescription drug benefit for Medicare beneficiaries.

Medication error: A preventable event that may cause or result in inappropriate medication use leading to patient harm.

Medication order: A prescriber's (e.g., physician's, nurse practitioner's) order for the preparation and administration of a medication for a patient. The term "medication order" is used mostly in institutional environments, whereas the term "prescription" is used in outpatient or community environments.

Medium: A channel through which a message moves.

Mentor: A wise and trusted counselor or teacher. The term *mentor* originated from Homer's *The Odyssey* in which Ulysses entrusted the education of his son to the servant, Mentor.

Mentoring: Professional guidance offered by a more senior person to a less experienced individual; considered a leading method through which adults acquire new knowledge or skills.

Merit increases: Additions to pay based on performance.

Metric: A measure used to quantify or to indicate level of performance of some action or task.

Misbranding: An imitation product or one offered for sale under the distinctive name of another article; labeling or packaging of a product so that the public will be misled or misinformed about the contents of the product.

Mission statement: A description of the purpose of the organization.

Money market fund: A fund investing in short-term investments, such as certificates of deposit and treasury bills.

Monitoring: Ongoing oversight or supervision to ensure that the work process remains on course and on schedule toward achieving results.

Mortgage payable: Legal loan agreement that gives a lender the right to be paid from cash proceeds from the sale of a borrower's assets identified in the mortgage.

Motivation: The reason or reasons for engaging in a particular behavior; that which gives purpose and direction to behavior.

Multitasking: Working on more than one task at the same time.

Multi-tool performance communication and development program: A performance management approach that allows for nonuniformity in the use of multiple performance appraisal, communication, and development forms and tools.

Mutual fund: A fund using investors' collective investments to invest in stocks, bonds, and other investments designed to reduce overall risk. Individual investors in the fund own shares, which represent ownership of the entire fund. The fund is managed by a professional money manager.

National Quality Measures Clearinghouse: A database and Web site for information on specific evidence-based healthcare quality measures and measure sets. Its mission is to provide an accessible mechanism for obtaining detailed information on quality measures, and it promotes widespread access to these quality measures. The URL is http://www.qualitymeasures .ahrq.gov/about/about.aspx.

Needs assessment: Collection of data to assess the need for a particular service or product within a defined population or community

Negotiation: The process of dealing or bargaining with another or others to achieve a goal, reach an agreement, and/or resolve a dispute.

Net present value: Current value of an investment's future cash flow, not including the initial investment.

Noncompete clauses: A written term in an employment agreement that requires a former employee to do or to refrain from doing certain things—for example, from opening up a competing business after termination of employment with the present employer for a specific time period within a specific geographic area. These clauses are more typical in industries with limited clientele or specialized knowledge, where competition is fierce and customer goodwill can be usurped.

Nonexempt employees: Employees who, because of the type of duties performed, level of decision-making authority, or method of compensation, are subject to all Fair Labor Standards Act provisions that require overtime pay when they are asked to work more than 40 hours during a workweek.

Nonmaleficence: Asserts an obligation not to inflict harm on others.

Nonroutine disclosures: A HIPAA term that refers to disclosures not required in the provision of healthcare services; would include release of information for research purposes or disclosure of prescribing or dispensing monitoring.

Nonverbal communication: Movements or sounds that communicate messages without words.

Ombudsman: An organizational employee who investigates the complaints of other employees and mediates solutions.

Open communication: Communication based on trust and respect in which there is a free exchange of information.

Operating budget: An itemized listing of all estimated revenue that a given company anticipates receiving, along with a listing of estimated costs and expenses that will be incurred during a given period, usually one business cycle or year.

Opportunity cost: The cost to a company or individual of the path not taken, calculated by measuring the projected return of the chosen option compared with the anticipated return of the highest yielding alternative investment.

Opportunity loss: The value or benefit lost if a certain alternative is not chosen.

Organizational chart: Illustrates formal lines of authority as well as relationships between positions within the organization.

Organizational ethics: Examination of ethical questions focused on the conduct of an organization as a whole, including the role of mission, core institutional values in the activity of the organization, and the relation of these standards to the judgments and actions of the individuals playing specific roles within the organization.

Organizational culture: The personality of the organization. Culture consists of assumptions, values, norms, and tangible signs (artifacts) of organization members and their behaviors.

Orientation: A program that helps a newly hired employee become familiar with the new position and the organization.

Owner's equity: Owner's claim on the remaining interest in the assets of a company after deducting liabilities; also known as net assets, equity, net worth, and stockholder's and shareholder's equity.

Pareto chart: A bar chart in which plotted values are arranged in descending order and the graph is accompanied by a line graph that shows the cumulative totals of each category. It is developed to clearly illustrate the top 80%.

Pareto's law: For many situations/events, approximately 80% of the effects may result from 20% of the causes.

Participative management: A form of management wherein employees are afforded a strong role in decision making.

Patient-centered care: Sharing the management of a medical condition between a patient and his or her healthcare team; considers patients' cultural traditions, personal preferences and values, family situations, and lifestyles.

Patient satisfaction: Degree to which a consumer perceives a healthcare good or service (or delivery of said good or service) to be valuable, beneficial, useful, appropriate, and effective.

Performance evaluation: A summary of employee performance, achievement, and development needs.

Performance management: A process of assessing progress toward achieving predetermined goals.

Performance S.C.O.R.E.: An acronym identifying management's successful application of performance management techniques—**s**trategic, **c**ommunicative, **o**pportunity, **r**ecognition, and **e**ngagement.

Performance standard: A measure, quality, or expectation related to how and what an employee achieves in the performance of his or her job.

Permitted disclosures: Ability to share protected health information among healthcare professionals and their patients in the provision of services.

Perquisites (also known as *perks*): Fringe benefits, such as health insurance, vacation time, relocation packages, professional education dollars, 401(k) plans, bonus plans, and other factors that entice employees to join and stay with an organization.

Personal brand: Cumulative perceptions others have of your traits, behaviors, and actions, reflecting your beliefs, values, passions, and knowledge, making you uniquely memorable.

Personal selling: A face-to-face approach designed to encourage the purchase of a product or service.

Persuasion: A process and skill set to explore issues and options intended to influence the thinking and actions of others, involving establishing credibility, framing goals to identify common ground, providing supportive evidence, and connecting emotionally with the audience.

Pharmaceutical care: The responsible provision of drug therapy for achieving desired outcomes that (1) cure a disease, (2) eliminate or reduce a patient's symptomatology, (3) arrest or slow a disease process, or (4) prevent a disease or symptomatology.

Pharmacy benefit manager (PBM): Entity that manages and administers prescription drug benefits (programs) for insurers. PBMs are responsible for establishing benefit structure and design; maintaining a network of retail pharmacy providers; claims processing and adjudication; and establishing policies and programs to monitor and control drug use, such as formulary development and management, drug therapy interchange programs, drug utilization review activities, disease management initiatives, and mail service programs.

Pharmacy informatics: The use of technology within healthcare systems and settings to access, store, analyze, and disseminate medication-related data and information to optimize patient care, safety, and outcomes.

Phased retirement: Agreements that gradually allow employees to reduce their percentage of effort to transition into retirement.

Plaintiff: A party who initiates a lawsuit in court alleging to have been aggrieved by the actions of another (a defendant).

Plan-do-study-act cycle: This continuous quality improvement model provides a framework for improving a process or system. It can be used to guide the entire improvement project or to develop specific projects once target improvement areas have been identified. It consists of four major parts: (1) plan (identify an opportunity for improvement and plan a change); (2) do (implement the change on a small scale [pilot]); (3) study (collect data on the change and compare to the baseline, study the effect of these changes on the pilot, and [if applicable] show the effects of multiple changes on a process over time); and (4) act (if the change was successful, implement it on a wider scale and continuously assess results; if the change does not work or meet goal, begin the cycle again).

Pneumatic tube systems: Systems in which cylindrical containers are propelled by compressed air or by vacuum through a network of tubes; used for transporting medications throughout a facility such as a hospital.

Polypharmacy: The prescription of numerous medications to or use of numerous medications by a patient.

Positional authority: Formal authority granted to an individual based on his or her position within an organization.

Positional bargaining: A negotiation strategy whereby a party holds onto its position without regard for the other party or underlying concerns.

Position announcements: Detailed information about a particular position opening and the organization in which it exists.

Prepaid tuition plan: A college tuition savings account that allows parents/guardians the opportunity to pay the cost of their child's college tuition in today's dollars, even though their child might not attend college for several years. This type of plan allows parents/guardians to "lock-in" the cost of college tuition for their child by buying tuition units at an institution now, thereby paying no additional tuition when their child attends that institution, even if tuition rates have increased in the intervening years.

Prescription: A prescriber's (e.g., physician's, nurse practitioner's) order for the preparation and administration of a medication or device for a patient. Prescriptions are usually designated with an "R" or "Rx," which stands for the word "recipe," which means "to take" in Latin.

Prescription Drug Marketing Act: Includes the prohibition of reimportation of prescription drugs that have been manufactured in the United States, restrictions regarding the distribution of drug samples, and bans on the resale of drugs by hospitals and other entities.

Present value: The value of a payment or stream of payments to be received in the future, discounted at a specific interest or discount rate in order to recognize the time value of money.

Pretax: The amount before taxes have been deducted.

Prevalence: The total number of cases of an event (such as a disease state) at a specific time.

Primacy and recency effect: Remembering best what comes first and last.

Primary research: Original research conducted for answering the question at hand.

Prime rate: The interest rate that banks charge to their most creditworthy customers. The prime rate affects other rates, such as the federal funds rate and credit card and home mortgage interest rates.

Principled negotiation: A deliberate negotiation process aimed at reaching mutually acceptable solutions based on the concerns of the parties involved and objective standards.

Principlism: Also known as the four principles approach to biomedical ethics: (1) respect for autonomy, (2) nonmaleficence, (3) beneficence, and (4) justice.

Prior authorization: Obtaining advanced approval from a third-party payer for prescription medications and other health-related items so that the provider can receive payment for the item.

Privacy notice: A detailed document that explains how patient medical information is protected or might be disclosed by a providing entity. It is a HIPPA requirement that these policies be disclosed to and acknowledged by the patient.

Procrastination: Putting off, delaying, or deferring an action to a later time.

Procurement cost: The cost associated with the act of purchasing; includes personnel time required for placing the order, checking the order, stocking, paying the invoice, and other purchasing-related paperwork.

Product cost plus fee payment method: A formula used to determine the amount that third-party payers will pay pharmacies for covered prescriptions. The formula is specified in the contract between the payer and the pharmacy. Payers will pay an amount equal to the product cost allowance plus a dispensing fee minus the patient cost share.

Professionalism: The standards, behaviors, and character of an individual engaged in tasks related to his or her work or profession; it encompasses values and behaviors of altruism, accountability, excellence, duty, responsibility, honor, integrity, respect for others, and other honorable traits.

Professional socialization: The process by which people acquire the current values, attitudes, interests, skills, and knowledge in the group to which they belong or seek to become a member.

Profit margin: The percentage of sales that remain as profits after all expenses have been paid.

Pro forma statement: A hypothetical financial statement, which includes assets and liabilities (or revenues and expenses), that projects future financial situations or developments.

Promotion: Various communication techniques, such as advertising, personal selling, sales promotion, and public relations/product publicity.

Protected classes: Categories that are defined by federal, state, or local law, including gender, race, ethnicity, religion, national origin, disability, marital or veteran status, sexual orientation, political affiliation, or genetic predisposition. It is illegal to discriminate against individuals based on their membership in these classes.

Protected health information: Any form of data identified with a particular patient that might be received or created by a covered entity; includes prescription files or patient profiles maintained by a pharmacy, as well as electronic data that might be shared with third parties, payers, physician offices, billing records, conversations with the patient or others about the patient's health care.

Psychosocial: Relates to both psychological and social aspects of well-being.

Quality assurance: Systematic process of evaluating a product or service in which actual processes and outcomes are compared with predefined criteria or requirements to ensure quality.

Quality control: Processes implemented to ensure products or services are designed that meet or exceed requirements.

Quality improvement: Systematic process of enhancing a service or product.

Quid pro quo sexual harassment: According to the Equal Employment Opportunity Commission, this occurs when a job benefit is directly tied to an employee submitting to unwanted sexual advances. Submission to the conduct is made either explicitly or implicitly a term of an individual's employment. Such harassment can only occur when the individual seeking the sexual favor is in a position of power over the other individual. *See* 29 CFR § 1604.11(a)(2).

Rate of return: The gain (or loss) of an investment over a specific period, including all interest income and capital gains, quoted as a percentage. The rate of return, adjusted for the effects of inflation, results in the real rate of return.

Ratio analysis: The concept of conversion of financial numbers for a company into ratios. This then allows comparison of one company to another. Since ratios evaluate relationships within a company, a company of one size can be directly compared to a second company (or a collection of companies), which may be larger or smaller, or even in a different business. A method of comparison not dependent on the relative size of either company; provides a broader basis of comparison than of the numbers themselves.

Reasonable accommodation: A modification of a job to allow an otherwise qualified person to perform the job.

Rebate: The discount received by a pharmacy benefit manager (PBM) from a pharmaceutical manufacturer for placing a drug on a PBM's formulary or giving it a preferred status designation. Rebates can be based on a flat percentage of any market share or dispensing achieved by the PBM or based on achieving a specific percentage of market share.

Reconciliation: Adjusting the difference between two items (e.g., balances, amounts, statements, or accounts) so that the amounts agree. Reasons for the differences should be explained and accounted for.

Recruitment: The active process that seeks to cultivate applicants from the universe of possibly qualified applicants, whether or not they are actively on the market for an opportunity at a particular point in time.

Relationship marketing: A marketing approach that focuses on developing long-term and mutually beneficial relationships with both patients and business and clinical partners.

Reliability: The same data are collected across multiple measurements of the same construct; the degree to which procedures yield comparable data (results) over time and across measures.

Restrictive covenant: A written term in an employment agreement that requires a former employee to do or to refrain from doing certain things—for example, from opening up a competing business after termination of employment with the present employer for a specific time period within a specific geographic area. These clauses are more typical in industries with limited clientele or specialized knowledge, where competition is fierce and customer goodwill can be usurped.

Retail: Selling goods directly to consumers; generally in small quantities for personal possession and not for the purpose of resale.

Retained earnings: Business profits that have not been distributed to owners as of the balance sheet closing date. The earnings have been "retained" for use in the business. "Retained earnings" is listed as an account in the equity section of the balance sheet.

Retention bonus: An incentive such as cash, a car, or travel designed to encourage an employee to remain with an employer.

Retrospective, fee-for-service payment: A payment process in which third-party payers pay a specified amount for a prescription or service unit to pharmacies after the prescription or service has been provided to the patient.

Return on investment (ROI): The profit or some other value earned by an investment.

Revenue: Gross increase in equity from a company's business activities that result in income; also called sales.

Revenue projection: A forecast of the gross increase in equity from a company's business activities that earn income.

Risk aversion: A predominant attitude of individuals wherein risk is generally avoided unless adequate compensation is offered.

Risk tolerance: The extent to which an investor will accept risk in the pursuit of a reward. The greater an investor's tolerance, the more risk he or she will accept to reach the goal, and the more willing he or she will be to invest in higher-risk assets with correspondingly higher returns.

Root cause analysis: A systematic evaluation and problem-solving method to identify the root causes (or initiating causes) of problems. By directing corrective action against the "root causes," it is believed the probability of problem recurrence will be reduced.

Run chart: A line graph that displays observed performance data in a time sequence.

Safety stock: Additional quantity of a product that is kept on hand as a buffer to enable response to an unanticipated demand; provides "safety" from an out-of-stock occurrence.

Scatterplots: A graph of plotted points that shows the relationship between two sets of data.

Secondary research: Research that has already been conducted for another purpose and is usually publicly available.

Self-enhancement bias: A psychological condition in which an individual grows convinced that he or she is the only one who can produce the necessary level of acceptable work.

Sensitivity analysis: A type of analysis that examines how projected performance may vary based on changes in assumptions upon which performance projections are determined.

Sexual harassment: Unwelcome sexual conduct that is a term or condition of employment. Such harassment may either be in the form of quid pro quo or hostile environment.

Shareholders: Owners of a corporation or business entity; also called stockholders.

Shelf sweeper: Independent contractor service for on-site returns without a centralized processing facility; usually fee based.

Shrinkage: A loss of inventory due to theft, inventory counting errors, accounting errors, loss, damage, or deterioration of products. This represents the difference between shelf count and the count according to accounting records.

Situational interview: Contains questions that ask the candidate how he or she might respond to a hypothetical scenario.

Six Sigma / Six Sigma Quality: A set of practices designed to improve processes, eliminate defects or errors, and reduce process variation through sustained quality improvements. Six Sigma is derived from a field of statistics known as process capability studies. Many industries use Six Sigma applications as a set of practices designed to improve processes, eliminate defects, and produce a high proportion of output within specification. Processes that operate with Six Sigma quality over the short term are assumed to produce long-term defect levels below 3.4 defects per million opportunities. Six Sigma's implicit goal is to improve all processes to that level of quality or better.

Skills inventory: A listing of abilities, qualification, and competencies usually created through an evaluative process.

Slack resources: Those resources that are either in abundance within an organization or are allocated specifically for innovative activities.

Smart pumps: Infusion pumps that use technology (specifically, software that monitors recommended medication parameters) to promote patient safety and reduce errors in intravenous medication administration.

SOAP method: A method of documenting a patient interaction: (1) Subjective: documentation of the subjective reporting from the patient interaction. (2) Objective: documentation of the objective measures, physical exam, or tests performed with the patient encounter. (3) Assessment: documentation of the provider's assessment of current patient issues associated with the patient encounter. (4) Plan: documentation of the actions initiated by the provider to resolve the patient's healthcare issues or problems.

Social capital: The productive potential resulting from strong relationships (including networking), goodwill, trust, and cooperation.

Social intelligence: The ability to understand and manage human interactions and relations.

Soft skill training: The practical skills or knowledge that relate to competencies associated with a position.

Software: Computer programs, procedures, and documentation that perform operational and application tasks.

Sole proprietorship: A type of business in which, for tax and liability purposes, the owner and the company are considered a single entity.

Sourcing: The identification and uncovering of potential candidates through proactive or reactive advertising and recruiting techniques.

Stakeholder: Anyone who has an interest in or may be affected by a company, product, or service, which can include the public, company shareholders, employees, company management, or anyone else who under any particular circumstances may have an interest in or may be affected by the company or its products or services.

Stalemate: A situation in which neither side prevails.

Standard deduction: An amount determined by federal law that reduces income of taxpayers who do not itemize allowable deductions on their tax returns.

Start-up costs: The costs or expenses involved in setting up a business.

Statement of cash flows: Financial statement that itemizes cash inflows (receipts) and cash outflows (payments) during an accounting period; usually listed by operating, investing, and financing activities.

Statement of owner's equity: Financial statement that lists all initial and closing balances of each major equity account and reconciles all changes in those accounts over an accounting period.

Statutes of frauds: A legal requirement that certain types of contracts be evidenced by in writing for example, a contract that cannot be completed within one year; a contract for the transfer of land; contracts for the sale of goods over a certain dollar amount; contracts in which an individual acts as a guarantor of the debts of another. These statutes differ from one state to another.

Step therapy: A prescription cost control mechanism in which the most cost-effective drug is used first followed by more costly alternative drug options.

Stock: A share of the ownership of a company.

Stock depth: The point at which you may be reasonably certain that the item will be available when needed.

Stockholders: Owners of a corporation or business entity; also called shareholders.

Stock keeping unit (SKU): The unique product identifier (number, alphanumeric, or bar code) assigned to a specific item held in stock.

Strategic planning: The process whereby a blueprint is developed for defining an organization's strategy (direction) and achieving its desired goal; included in the blueprint are a description of the organization's mission, vision, and values; an analysis of the organization's current situation; an action plan detailing objectives and tactics or strategies for achieving those objectives, including decisions on allocating resources to pursue strategies; and a system for monitoring and evaluating the implementation of the plan.

Strategic positioning: Performing different activities from competitors or performing similar activities in different ways.

Strategic relevance: Extent to which performance standards relate to the strategic goals and objectives of the organization.

Strategy: A pattern or plan that integrates an organization's major goals, policies, and action sequences into a cohesive whole.

Stretch assignments: Challenging assignments that provide opportunities to learn new things.

Structural variables: Factors involving the organization as a set of functional parts that can be arranged to achieve better performance (e.g., teams, mergers, acquisitions, consolidations).

Succession planning: Identifying, developing, and tracking key employees for senior- and executive-level opportunities.

Supply chain management: Management of the interrelated businesses involved in the production of a product or service.

SWOT analysis: An analysis of the strengths, weaknesses, opportunities, and threats for a service, product, or organization that may impact the work process and achievement of desired results.

Target market: The clientele whom your organization seeks to serve.

Tax deduction: An item or expense subtracted from adjusted gross income to decrease the amount of income subject to tax, thereby reducing tax liability.

Telecommuting: A work arrangement in which an employee works from home and stays connected to colleagues through various technologies.

Telemedicine: The use of telecommunication technology to provide medical information to patients at a distance.

Telepharmacy: The use of telecommunication, information technology, and communication technology to provide and support pharmacy services when distance separates the participants.

Third-party payments: A payment for a beneficiary's medical services or medications made by a public or private organization (Medicare, Medicaid, or a private health insurance plan). These organizations underwrite coverage for their beneficiary's healthcare expenses; the beneficiary usually pays a premium for the coverage.

Threat: A perceived danger to the solvency of a business (may be specific to a particular good or service offered by the business or may pertain to the business as a whole).

360-degree assessment: A feedback tool that collects and synthesizes performance perspectives from peers, colleagues, direct reports, customers, and others with whom an employee works.

Time period principle: The concept that an organization's activities can be divided into specific time periods (i.e., months, quarters, or years).

Time value of money: The notion that a dollar today is worth more than a dollar in the future, as the dollar received today may earn interest until the date the future dollar is received.

Tort: A civil wrong, other than a breach of contract, for which a court may provide a remedy in the form of damages.

Trade cost: Expenses associated with the purchase and sale of shares of stocks and other investments.

Transformation: The change process.

Turnover: The ratio of employees who leave an employer during a time period to the number of employees at the beginning of the time period.

United States Pharmacopeia: An official public standards-setting authority for all prescription and over-the-counter medicines and other healthcare products manufactured or sold in the United States.

Utilitarianism: The view that an action is deemed morally acceptable because it produces the greatest balance of good over evil, taking into account all individuals affected.

Validity: A measure or instrument that reflects the construct it purports to measure.

Values: The organization's central priorities.

Variable costs: Costs directly related to the service volume that increase as the service volume increases. An example is prescription vials. The total cost of vials increase as the number of prescriptions dispensed increases.

Variable pay programs: Compensation tied to the accomplishment of goals or organizational performance that is not added to base pay.

Venture capital: Monetary resources provided by investors or private equity firms particularly to early-stage projects or companies that often involve high-risk or high-earning potential.

Verbal communication: The process of sending messages using words, including speaking and writing.

Vertical financial analysis: The process of comparing the financial ratios of a single company over time, relating current results to historical performance as well as future performance.

Videoconferencing: A type of telecommunication that allows individuals at two or more locations to interact in real time using video and audio technology.

Virtue: A morally valuable trait of character.

Vision/vision statement: An articulation of future goals or desired long-term achievements; a description of the organization's desired future direction.

Web banners: Horizontal strips that appear on the top of a Web page related to the content of the page.

Wholesale acquisition cost (WAC): The manufacturers' published catalog (list) price for sale of a drug (brand name or generic) to wholesalers and distributors before any rebates, discounts, allowances or other price concessions have been applied by the manufacturer. In practice, wholesalers do not pay WAC for drugs; instead, they pay some lesser amount. WAC may be used as a basis or index for determining contract prices between wholesalers and retail pharmacies.

Wholesaler: Intermediary purchasing products from manufacturers or other wholesalers with the intent to sell these products to retailers or other wholesalers.

Willingness to pay analysis: Assessment of the maximum amount a customer is willing to pay for a product or service.

Withholding tax: Amounts withheld from individuals' wages on their behalf and remitted directly to the government to account for individuals' tax liability on their compensation.

Word-of-mouth promotion: A process by which one person shares product- or service related information with another.

Yield ratio: Details the relative success of that particular sourcing activity as compared with other activities. It contains a number of components, including how much it cost to advertise or recruit applicants, the number of applicants generated by the source, and a comparison of the percentage of interview and job offers accepted by source.

Zero-based budget: A budget that starts from zero at each budget cycle. All prior years' expenses are not considered when developing budget levels for the future period. All expenses within the budget must be evaluated as being necessary, thus "zero base."

INDEX